Making the Most of College

SPENCER A. RATHUS
St. John's University

LOIS FICHNER-RATHUS
Trenton State College

PRENTICE HALL, Englewood Cliffs, New Jersey 07632

Library of Congress Cataloging-in-Publication Data

Rathus, Spencer A.
    Making the most of college / Spencer A. Rathus, Lois Fichner-Rathus.
        p. cm.
    ISBN 0-13-142076-3
    1. College student orientation. 2. Study, Method of. 3. College students—Miscellanea. I. Fichner-Rathus, Lois, 1953– II. Title.
LB2343.3.R38   1991
378.1'98—dc20   90–33968
                                                                      CIP

*For Allyn, Class of 2000,
and Jordan, Class of 2002*

Editorial/production supervision: Jan Stephan
Interior design: Lisa Domínguez
Cover design: Lisa Domínguez
Cover Art: William Whitehurst/The Stock Market
Prepress buyer: Herb Klein
Manufacturing buyer: Dave Dickey
Photo Editor: Lorinda Morris-Nantz
Photo Research: Ilene Cherna

Acknowledgments appear on page 385, which constitutes an extension of the copyright page.

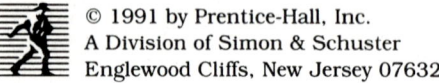 © 1991 by Prentice-Hall, Inc.
A Division of Simon & Schuster
Englewood Cliffs, New Jersey 07632

All rights reserved. No part of this book may be reproduced, in any form or by any means, without permission in writing from the publisher.

Printed in the United States of America
10 9 8 7 6 5 4 3 2 1

ISBN 0-13-142076-3

Prentice-Hall International (UK) Limited, *London*
Prentice-Hall of Australia Pty. Limited, *Sydney*
Prentice-Hall Canada Inc., *Toronto*
Prentice-Hall Hispanoamericana, S.A., *Mexico*
Prentice-Hall of India Private Limited, *New Delhi*
Prentice-Hall of Japan, Inc., *Tokyo*
Simon & Schuster Asia Pte. Ltd., *Singapore*
Editora Prentice-Hall do Brasil, Ltda., *Rio de Janeiro*

Contents

Preface   vii

1 MAKING THE TRANSITION TO COLLEGE LIFE   2

A Personal Confession   4
What Lies Ahead   6
- Who's in Charge Here?   7
- The Expectancy for Success Scale   16

Basic Equipment   18
Summing Up   22

2 MAKING USE OF CAMPUS AND COMMUNITY RESOURCES   24

Using Campus Resources   26
- Survey of Political and Social Attitudes   33

Using Community Resources   41
- Selecting a Day-Care Center   42
- What Do You When . . . ?   46

Summing Up   48

3 MANAGING TIME   50

How to Manage Time   52
- Finding Out How You Spend Your Time   53

How to Set Up a Schedule: General Advice   54
How to Set Up a Schedule: The Specifics   60
How to Handle Distractions   62
How to Move Ahead When You're Stuck: Ways of Accomplishing Something When You Can't Do Anything   65
Summing Up   68

4 MANAGING MONEY   72

What College Costs   72
Where the Money Comes From   72
How to Make a Budget   74
Money-Management Issues: From Checking Accounts to Insurance   79
How to Practice Self-Control in Spending   83
Sources of Financial Aid   88
- Questions to Consider Before You Commit Yourself to a Loan   90
- One Hundred Free (or Almost Free) Turn-Ons   95

Summing Up   98
Budget Worksheet and Expense Records   100

5 ATTENDING CLASSES, TAKING NOTES, AND STUDYING   102

Attending Classes   104

Reasons for Not Paying Attention in Class   106

Changing Attitudes That Encourage You to Cut Classes and Allow Your Attention to Wander   108

Taking Notes   110
Studying   116
Summing Up   124

6 WRITING PAPERS   126

Writing: Not for College Only   128
Kinds of Writing   129

Rules for Good Writing   130

The Freshman Composition Course   130
Critical Thinking   132
General Guidelines for Good Writing   132
Specific Guidelines for Writing Papers   138

Overcoming a Writing Block   145

Summing Up   154

7 TAKING TESTS   156

General Advice   159
What to Bring   161
How to Handle Multiple-Choice Questions   162
How to Handle True–False Questions   165
How to Handle Short-Answer Sentence-Completion Questions   167
How to Handle Matching Questions   168
How to Handle Essay Questions   170
How to Handle Test Anxiety   174

The Suinn Test Anxiety Behavior Scale   177

Replacing Self-Defeating Thoughts with Rational Alternatives   179

Summing Up   184

8 MANAGING STRESS   186

Stress   188
Effects of Stress   191

Going Through Changes: The Social Readjustment Rating Scale   192

Are You a Type A Student?   195

Coping with a Suicide Threat: Ten Things to Do When You Fear That Nothing Can Be Done   198

Ways of Managing Stress   199
Poor Ways of Reacting to Stress   199
Better Ways of Reacting to Stress   201
Summing Up   210

9 DEVELOPING RELATIONSHIPS AND DEALING WITH LONELINESS   212

Friendship   214
Fraternities and Sororities: "The Greeks versus the Geeks?"   216
Love   219
Attraction   220

The Love Scale   221

What Do You Look at First?   223

Stages in Relationships   226

How to Improve Date-Seeking Skills   228

Loneliness   233

The UCLA Loneliness Scale   234

Summing Up   236

10 RESOLVING SOCIAL CONFLICTS   238

How to Handle Conflicts in Relationships   240

Ideas About Relationships   241

Enhancing Communication Skills   244

The Rathus Assertiveness Schedule   252

Prejudice   257

Sex Differences: Vive la Différence or Vive la Similarité?   259

How to Handle Prejudice   262

Summing Up   262

11 STAYING (AND BECOMING) PHYSICALLY FIT   266

Nutrition   268

How to Handle an Invitation
to Eat   276

How to Handle Anorexia
Nervosa   278

Exercise: Not for Athletes Only   278

How to Get Started Exercising   282

Sleep   283
If You Get Sick . . .   287

Encouraging a Student to Go for Medical
Advice   290

Summing Up   291

12 LIVING WITH SEX   292

Collegiate Sexual Behavior in Perspective:
  A Tale of Three Generations   294
Patterns of Sexual Behavior   296

Attitudes That Contribute to
Rape   301

Sexually Transmitted Diseases   303

Making Sex Safe(r) in the Age of
AIDS   310

Birth Control   311
Sexual Decision Making   316
Summing Up   319

13 HANDLING DRUGS   320

What Is Substance Abuse?   322
How Do Students Get Involved
  with Drugs?   323

Alcohol   324

Reasons for Drinking   328

How to Cope with the Urge to
Drink   330

Cigarettes   331

Methods for Quitting and Cutting Down
on Smoking   333

Steroids and Growth Hormone   336
Marijuana   337
Cocaine   339
Amphetamines   341
Opiates and Opioids   341
Tranquilizers   342
LSD: "Lucy in the Sky
  with Diamonds"   343
Summing Up   344

14 MAKING THE TRANSITION FROM COLLEGE TO THE CAREER WORLD   346

How to Make Career Decisions   348
How to Find a Job   356
How to Write a Résumé   357
How to Handle a Job Interview   362

Coping with a Job Interview   364

Summing Up   367
Education and Work Experience
  Worksheets   368

Notes   370
Acknowledgments   385
Index   386

Preface

College for many is the opportunity of a lifetime. This book is intended to help students make the most of that opportunity.

The central purpose of college is to foster the intellectual development of students. Our years of teaching experience, however, have given us to believe that the central purpose of the college student—whether residential, commuting, or returning—often becomes coping with the myriad academic, personal, and social challenges posed by college life. The concerns of students range from the sublime to the mundane—although not usually the ridiculous. On a theoretical level, students may be concerned with questions such as "What is the mind?", "What is knowledge?", and "What is the true nature of the universe?" On a practical level, they may be equally concerned with questions such as "Where will I find a parking space?", "How can I fit in a part-time job?", and "What do I do for a date?"

As a primary, research-based textbook for the college-orientation or college-success course, *Making the Most of College* is intended to help students cope with all of these challenges. In doing so, the book addresses five broad areas:

1. Orientation to the college and local community,
2. Management of time and money,
3. The academic side of college life,
4. The personal and social sides of college life, and
5. Making the transition to the career world.

Orientation to the College and Local Community

Chapters 1 and 2 help orient students to college and the community. Chapter 1 assists students to form accurate expectations about college; to recognize, for example, that college professors are not carbon copies of high school teachers. It discusses some of the equipment that facilitates performance in college, from dictionaries to computers. All students, moreover, need to identify and learn how to use the resources on their campuses, and residential students need to locate the services that are available in their communities. So Chapter 2 tours facilities ranging from the campus library to health-care services, day-care centers, and environmental groups.

Management of Time and Money

Chapters 3 and 4 help students learn how to manage their time and money. Some college students are just beginning to learn how to manage money, and some literally do not know where next year's tuition will come from. Residential students may be faced with changes in eating and sleeping habits, and with new responsibilities, such as underwear that must be washed and toothpaste that must be replenished. Some new residential students find that they miss classes because no one gets them out of bed in the morning. Most students complain that there are not enough hours in the day for them to meet all their obligations and still find the time to breathe. Commuting students may face special problems in buying and maintaining cars and finding strategic times of day when the freeways are not extended parking lots. Returning students must often juggle the demands of family and college life—a difficult balancing act, indeed. Returning students often miss classes or are late in completing assignments because the children are ill or the babysitter had to study for a test. Chapter 3 will help students fit classes, studying, meals, family life, a social life, work, extracurricular activities, recreational activities, and sleep into their schedules. Chapter 4 will help them find and manage money.

The Academic Side of College Life

Chapters 5, 6, and 7 will help students manage the academic

side of college life—attending classes, taking notes, studying, writing papers, and taking tests. Academically, many students find college far tougher than high school. In some colleges, the scramble for grades can be crushing; students may feel that their admission to graduate school or success in finding a lucrative job hinges on their performance on every quiz, test, and term paper. Poor grades may not only signify a waste of time and hard-earned money; they may also contribute to a collapsing self-identity and feelings of guilt and shame. So a major part of this text is devoted to imparting skills that will help students learn the subject matter in their courses and perform well on tests.

The Personal and Social Sides of College Life

Chapters 8 through 13 offer advice on ways of meeting the personal and social challenges of college life. College life can be stressful, and Chapter 8 enumerates many strategies for managing stress. Social relationships are also an integral feature of college life. Residential students may have to adjust to living with a roommate from across the country—or the world. For single students who have not developed social skills, a swarming campus of 20,000 students may only render feelings of loneliness more poignant. So Chapters 9 and 10 are devoted to helping students form and maintain sustaining relationships. Chapter 11 advises students on many health matters, including how to initiate and maintain healthful lifelong dietary habits and exercise programs. College life brings many students new freedom, but freedom is a double-edged sword that carries the burden of personal responsibility. Chapter 12 provides students with the information they need about sexual behavior to make mature sexual decisions and to protect themselves from unwanted pregnancies and sexually transmitted diseases. Whether we like it or not, drugs ranging from the old campus standby—alcohol—to cigarettes, marijuana, cocaine, and steroids are readily available on most of our campuses. Chapter 13 therefore contains information about the uses and hazards of a variety of substances, information that students can use to make mature decisions.

Making the Transition to the Career World

Whereas Chapter 1 helps students make the transition to college life, Chapter 14—the final chapter—is designed to help students make the transition from college to the career world. Many students begin to make this transition early through their selection of a major field. Chapter 14 is replete with practical information on choosing a field that is compatible with one's interests and abilities, finding a job, writing a résumé, even handling a job interview.

All in all, we confess that this book will not provide answers to the questions "What is the mind?", "What is knowledge?", and "What is the true nature of the universe?" However, this book will help students manage the academic, personal, and social aspects of college life so that they have the time and energy to muse upon these questions for themselves.

FEATURES OF THE TEXT

Several features throughout the text stimulate student interest and promote learning. These include:

"Truth or Fiction?" Items   Each chapter begins with "Truth or Fiction?" items. The items stimulate reader interest, sometimes by challenging common sense or folklore. A "Truth or Fiction Revisited" insert is placed at the point in the text where each "Truth or Fiction?" item is discussed. These inserts afford readers the opportunity to check their presumptions against the facts.

Questionnaires   Numerous questionnaires are found throughout the text. These questionnaires afford students insight into their personalities, behavior patterns, and attitudes as they bear on their adjustment to college life.

"What Do You Do Now?" Sections   "What Do You Do Now?" sections place students in demanding and sometimes perplexing situations, and challenge them to indicate how they would handle them. Then we suggest possibilities with which readers can compare their own solutions. These interactive features afford students the opportunity to test their own coping skills. Then they receive feedback that helps them assess the appropriateness of their ideas.

"In Your Own Write" Features   The "In Your Own Write" features are journal entries that give students an opportunity to organize and express their thoughts and experiences on issues raised in the chapters. During a time in which "Writing Across the Curriculum" is being emphasized in American colleges and universities, these features give students practice in expressing ideas through the written word. They also serve as a springboard for class discussion and involve students personally in the subject matter of the chapters.

"Summing Up" Features   Each chapter ends with a list of ten questions that summarize the material. This feature encourages students to reflect on what they have read and discussed in a nonacademic, personalized way. The feature will promote retention by rendering the material more relevant to students' lives.

Lists of Detailed Instructions   Lists of instructions offer detailed advice for handling various matters. Chapter 7, for example, includes lists of things to bring to a test and of hints for taking multiple-choice tests. Chapter 12, similarly, offers a detailed list of strategies for averting sexually transmitted diseases.

Extracts from Literature and the Popular Culture

Numerous excerpts from sources as wide ranging as Plato, Samuel Johnson, Shakespeare, Mark Twain, Michael Jackson, and Mae West demonstrate the enduring intellectual and entertainment value of adages and aphorisms and offer wisdom in their own right.

Writing Style The writing style of the textbook is "user-friendly" in tone, personalized. It speaks directly to the student, using the first person, contractions, and humor, where appropriate. As a result, we hope that students will find the book useful and engaging. We want them to perceive the book as part of the solution to the challenges they are facing, not as part of the problem.

SUPPLEMENTARY MATERIALS

Making the Most of College is accompanied by an extensive array of supplementary items designed to facilitate learning, teaching, and assessment of student progress.

Student Journal One contemporary trend in education is the encouragement of students to maintain journals. Journals allow students to record their experiences, organize their intellectual and emotional responses to their experiences, and express their views through writing.

Foremost among the supplementary materials, then, is the *Student Journal*, which was written by the authors of the textbook itself. The journal accompanies the textbook at no extra charge and provides students with an opportunity to respond to the concepts and strategies that are advanced in the textbook. It is not just a series of blank pages. It contains exercises that encourage students to reflect upon the issues raised in the textbook and to "make them their own." Exercises in the journal are numbered according to the chapters to which they refer. Pages are perforated and there are places for students to write in their names and the date, so that students can hand in journal pages as written assignments.

Annotated Instructor's Edition This informative Annotated Instructor's Edition is designed specifically for the first-time instructor of the college orientation course, although experienced instructors will find it a useful reference as well. It consists of the entire student text with marginal annotations providing a wealth of ideas for classroom preparation. There are five types of annotations printed in red ink in the margins: Learning Objectives at the beginning of each chapter; Background Information, which includes references to suggested readings; Discussion Suggestions; Class Activities; and cross-references to topics contained in the *Student Journal*.

Test Item File This booklet contains 500 questions comprised of multiple choice, fill-in the blank, true/false, short answer, and essay questions which can be used as a basis for examinations and quizzes. This test bank is also available in a computerized format for the IBM. This program, the *Prentice Hall Testmanager*, allows you to add, delete, and edit questions within the file in order to create customized tests.

Prentice Hall Critical Thinking Audio Study Cassette This 60-minute cassette helps students develop their critical thinking skills. The first part, which runs approximately 50 minutes, demonstrates how asking the right questions leads to better critical reading and thinking skills. The second section consists of helpful tips on how to study, how to take effective notes, and how to become a more active learner. These tapes are available free in quantities of up to 10 upon adoption.

In addition to these supplements, videotapes are available free to qualified adopters of *Making the Most of College*. These videos deal with such topics as substance abuse, stress, fitness and exercise, and study skills. Please ask your Prentice Hall Sales Representative for details.

ACKNOWLEDGMENTS

A textbook, unlike a poem, is something of a collaborative project. We are deeply indebted to those who helped us hone our subject matter and transform it into a bound book.

First, we thank our professional colleagues, who reviewed our manuscript at various stages in its development: Georgia A. Newman, Polk Community College; Curtis Beckman, DeVry Institute; Margaret Anne Langer, University of the Pacific; Wendy Leeds-Hurwitz, University of Wisconsin, Parkside; David Moore, Metropolitan State College; Maralyn W. Mason, Camden County College; Phyllis N. Weatherly, Southern College of Technology; Joyce E. Rogers, MTI Business College; Allen Carter, College of DuPage; and Thomas Sheeran, Niagara University.

We are also indebted to the publishing professionals at Prentice Hall. Philip Miller, Editor-in-Chief, Humanities, is responsible for the enthusiastic investment that Prentice Hall made in our book. Fran Falk, Phil's Editorial Assistant, cheerfully carried out day-to-day tasks too numerous to mention. Jan Stephan, the Production Editor, provided the skills that transformed our typed pages into a bound textbook. Lisa Domínguez, Designer, and Florence Silverman, Design Director, are responsible for much of the physical appeal of the work you are now holding in your hands. Lorinda Nantz-Morris, Photo Editor, and Ilene Cherna, Photo Researcher, compiled the choice collection of photographs that illustrate the text. Ann Knitel, Supplements Editor, Humanities, organized and developed the fine array of supplements that complement the text.

Finally, we thank our children who, by sacrificing a bit of parenting today, made it possible for us to help serve *in loco parentis* for many thousands of college students for years to come.

Spencer A. Rathus
Lois Fichner-Rathus

Making the Most of College

1

Making the Transition to College Life

 **TRUTH OR FICTION?**

_____ Many straight-A high school students become "C" college students, even though they continue to work as hard and perform as well.

_____ In college, resident and academic advisors make certain that you adhere to curfews and get your work done.

_____ Most beginning college students believe that they can get by academically in college without missing out on interesting social activities.

_____ College teaching is superior to high school teaching.

_____ College professors try to motivate their students.

_____ The primary purpose of college is to help you get a good job.

_____ Some colleges require students to purchase personal computers.

Beginning is what this book is about. Beginning college, beginning adulthood, beginning again. Beginnings are exhilarating. They offer the opportunity for boundless success. And for failure.

We wrote this book to help you take full advantage of the promise of college. This book can help you whether you're the first one in your family to go to college or the well-to-do offspring of a family in which six generations have trodden the ivy halls ahead of you. It can help you whether you're fresh out of high school or returning to college after rearing a family. This book can help you whether you're a conscientious student or your report card has seen better days.

This book can help you

Fit classes, studying, meals, family life, a social life, work, extracurricular activities, recreational activities, and sleep into your schedule.

Find and manage money.

Get the most out of your classes.

Study and remember what you've heard and read.

Improve your grades on tests and papers.

Make and keep friends.

Handle the conflicting needs of family and college life.

Initiate and maintain healthful lifelong exercise programs and dietary habits.

Cope with the pressures of sex.

Handle the issue of drugs.

This book can also help you if you're not sure about where you're headed after you graduate—or how to get there.

Although college promises to enhance your skills and sophistication, doing well in college requires some skills and sophistication at the outset. Study skills and sophistication in the form of "test-wiseness" are basic to success. Knowledge of ways of handling stress, getting along with instructors and peers, and coping with distractions also has its place.

In this chapter we'll discuss what lies ahead in college and some of the basic equipment you'll need. First, however, your first author shares some of his early college experiences with you.

A PERSONAL CONFESSION

My own experience highlights some of the things that can happen when a naive teenager goes off to college. Whether you are at a 2-year school, a 4-year school, or a university, knowledge of my experiences may be of use to you.

When I went off to college some years ago—how many is my business—my classmates and I attended an orientation session in a grand auditorium. We were heartily welcomed by a progression of campus dignitaries. Then the dean of students made an ominous speech, which, I suppose, was intended to arouse us to do our best. He told us that we "A students" had better get used to C's because we were no longer at the top of the class, as we had been in high school. A grade of C defined "average" work at college. The average first-year student at this college had gotten an A− to B+ average in high school, so that student was probably now headed for a C average.

TRUTH OR FICTION *Revisited*

It is true that "straight-A" high schoolers sometimes become "C" college students, even though they continue to perform as well. One reason is that college competition is tougher.

The dean noted that our health, like our grades, might also decline over the next four years. Studying through the night; loading up on fast foods, candy bars, and Cokes; and the stress of striving for A's weren't likely to make us models for workout tapes.

Then he said, "Look at the person to your left. Now your right. Now look at yourself—yes, at yourself. One of the three of you will not make it through." I had no idea it would be me.

I had breezed through high school. I had assumed that I would breeze through college. Not so. I had little idea of what I was doing. My official major was "Undesignated," and it is hard to stay motivated when you're heading for an "undesignated" career. I was in an alien town. I was also a bit shy, so friends didn't come easily. The competition for grades was cut-throat. Although I continued to suppose that somewhere in my head there dwelled a brain, I didn't apply it very well.

Completing assignments and studying were hit-or-miss for me. Papers abruptly came due and I had little time to compose them. Sometimes I hadn't even selected a topic by the due date. Tests, too, were suddenly upon me. With the distractions of dating, bridge (the card game), science-fiction novels, TV, writing letters, and calling home (collect, of course)—somehow I wasn't prepared.

When it finally dawned on me that there might be a problem, I didn't know whom to talk to about it. I didn't even know that people *spoke* to other people about problems. I wasn't being tough or blindly self-assured. I was just plain ignorant.

I didn't flunk out. I edged out, slipped out, drifted out. It was a piecemeal and painful process. It took me six years to receive my bachelor's degree—from another college. (Your second author wants it understood that she received her B.A. in three years and doesn't understand the first author at all.)

The school referred to in the personal confession is a residential 4-year college. Some of you are commuting. If so, you may be able to rely on the emotional support you receive from family ties when you experience

> Chiefly the mould of a man's fortune is in his own hands.
>
> FRANCIS BACON

 ## IN YOUR OWN WRITE

Now that you've read the confession, write in your own words some of the concerns you have about the college years that lie ahead.

_____
_____
_____
_____
_____
_____
_____

Making the Transition to College Life 5

> They always say that time changes things, but you actually have to change them yourself.
>
> ANDY WARHOL

stress and personal doubts. On the other hand, consider the experiences of Roberto, who commuted to North Lake College, a community college in Irving, Texas.

> I was one of the stars in high school and the first one [in the family] who went to college. My family looked at the textbooks I brought home and shook their heads in wonder. My mother hugged me all the time, but my father sort of looked at me—not knowing what to make of it all. I didn't know what I wanted to do [that first year], and I started getting some bad grades. But I had to hide it at home. I was the savior, you see, and [my younger brothers and sisters] were going to follow me. I had to keep my happy face even though I was struggling. I found myself spending more time away from home, and I felt [alienated] from school and my family. Fortunately I could talk to my psychology professor and he was a big help to me.

Returning to school while raising a family—or after raising a family—can be yet more difficult. And today about 6 million college students are age 23 or above.[1] Parents who attend college are likely to be pulled in many directions at once. The need to prepare dinner for a family may conflict with the need to spend time in the library or to write a paper. (The "Just-Say-No" motto applies to parents attending college as well as to substance-abuse campaigns.)

People who return to college after raising a family are likely to fear that their academic skills have gotten rusty. Fortunately, you don't forget how to write, even if you do not recall the names of all the parts of speech. And if some skills in, say, math have gotten rusty, the high levels of motivation mature students bring to their work usually more than compensate. Older students who attend college usually know exactly why they're there, which gives them an advantage over many younger students.

There's no doubt about it. College makes major demands on students and differs from high school in important ways. The chief message of this book is that it is up to you to take charge of your own college experience, even if you do not feel perfectly prepared for what lies ahead. It is up to you to find out what lies ahead. It is up to you to make decisions and not just fall into things. The nearby questionnaire will afford you some insight as to whether or not you are a take-charge type of person. Don't take the results of this questionnaire, or any other questionnaire in this book, as carved in stone. If you are not now a take-charge kind of person, why not resolve to become one? You'll also fare better in college if you adjust your expectations to mesh with the realities that lie ahead. Some of those are discussed in the next section.

> Men at some time are masters of their fates:
> The fault, dear Brutus, is not in our stars,
> But in ourselves, that we are underlings.
>
> SHAKESPEARE,
> *Julius Caesar*

WHAT LIES AHEAD

Perhaps the greatest difference between high school and college life is the freedom. Many of the requirements and constraints of the high school years draw to an end. Freedom is a heady elixir. In college you have the freedom to make something wonderful of your life, and the freedom to make a mess of it.

Freedom

Consider one of the ways in which Lisa, a first-year student at the University of Michigan, reacted to her new-found freedom:

> I'd gone to church every Sunday as long as I could remember, unless I was sick or there was an emergency. When I got to school and the

❓ QUESTIONNAIRE
Who's in Charge Here?

One of the reasons that one of us had so much trouble as an undergraduate was failure to take charge of his college career. He let life take charge of him. Rather than establishing clear goals and making a plan as to what he had to do to meet those goals, he drifted along from day to day—cutting classes, getting poor grades, trying not to think about the future.

What about you? Do you believe that you are in charge of your own life—that you are the master of your fate? Or do you believe that most of what happens to you is a matter of chance or luck—that your fate lies in your "stars"?

To learn more about whether you see yourself as in charge, take the following questionnaire. For each item, place a checkmark in the Yes or the No column. When you have finished, turn to the answer key at the end of the chapter.

		Yes	No
1.	Do you believe that most problems will solve themselves if you just don't fool with them?	___	___
2.	Do you believe that you can stop yourself from catching a cold?	___	___
3.	Are some people just born lucky?	___	___
4.	Most of the time do you feel that getting good grades means a great deal to you?	___	___
5.	Are you often blamed for things that just aren't your fault?	___	___
6.	Do you believe that if somebody studies hard enough he or she can pass any subject?	___	___
7.	Do you feel that most of the time it doesn't pay to try hard because things never turn out right anyway?	___	___
8.	Do you feel that if things start out well in the morning, it's going to be a good day no matter what you do?	___	___
9.	Do you feel that most of the time parents listen to what their children have to say?	___	___
10.	Do you believe that wishing can make good things happen?	___	___
11.	When you get punished, does it usually seem it's for no good reason at all?	___	___
12.	Most of the time, do you find it hard to change a friend's opinion?	___	___
13.	Do you think cheering more than luck helps a team win?	___	___
14.	Did you feel that it was nearly impossible for you to change your parents' minds about anything?	___	___
15.	Do you believe that parents should allow children to make most of their own decisions?	___	___
16.	Do you feel that when you do something wrong, there's very little you can do to make it right?	___	___
17.	Do you believe that most people are just born good at sports?	___	___
18.	Are most other people your age stronger than you are?	___	___
19.	Do you feel that one of the best ways to handle most problems is just not to think about them?	___	___
20.	Do you feel that you have a lot of choice in deciding who your friends are?	___	___
21.	If you find a four-leaf clover, do you believe that it might bring you good luck?	___	___
22.	Did you often feel that whether or not you did your homework had much to do with what kind of grades you got?	___	___

23. Do you feel that when a person your age is angry with you, there's little you can do to stop him or her? _____ _____
24. Have you ever had a good-luck charm? _____ _____
25. Do you believe that whether or not people like you depends on how you act? _____ _____
26. Did your parents usually help you if you asked them to? _____ _____
27. Have you ever felt that when people were angry with you, it was usually for no reason at all? _____ _____
28. Most of the time, do you feel that you can change what might happen tomorrow by what you do today? _____ _____
29. Do you believe that when bad things are going to happen, they are just going to happen no matter what you try to do to stop them? _____ _____
30. Do you think that people can get their own way if they just keep trying? _____ _____
31. Most of the time, do you find it useless to try to get your own way at home? _____ _____
32. Do you feel that when good things happen, they happen because of hard work? _____ _____
33. Do you feel that when somebody your age wants to be your enemy, there's little you can do to change matters? _____ _____
34. Do you feel that it's easy to get friends to do what you want them to do? _____ _____
35. Do you usually feel that you have little to say about what you get to eat at home? _____ _____
36. Do you feel that when someone doesn't like you, there's little you can do about it? _____ _____
37. Did you usually feel it was almost useless to try in school because most other children were just plain smarter than you were? _____ _____
38. Are you the kind of person who believes that planning ahead makes things turn out better? _____ _____
39. Most of the time, do you feel that you have little to say about what your family decides to do? _____ _____
40. Do you think it's better to be smart than to be lucky? _____ _____

Source: Nowicki and Strickland (1973).

> I was brought up to believe that the only thing worth doing was to add to the sum of accurate information in the world.
>
> MARGARET MEAD

> The apple cannot be stuck back on the Tree of Knowledge; once we begin to see, we are doomed and challenged to seek the strength to see more, not less.
>
> ARTHUR MILLER

first Sunday came, I stayed home, to prove to myself that I could. I didn't feel guilty, but maybe like I'd missed something. The next Sunday I went, because I wanted to, not because I had to. Since then I've gone about as often as not, and I've also stopped by the chapel during the week now and then, which I'd never done before. I'm the one going, and I'm going because I want to, not because I have to, and that makes the difference.

If you go away to college, whether or not you attend church or synagogue is just one of the decisions you will make for yourself. No one will yell at you to get up in the morning. No one will make you attend classes. No one will nag you to wash your clothes. No one will demand that you come to the table at dinnertime.

If you live in a dormitory, you may also find freedoms that you did not have at home. Not too many years ago, dormitory advisors and personnel acted *in loco parentis*—which is a Latin phrase meaning "in the place of a parent." Through the early 1960s, they kept track of your coming and going and set curfews. Today the picture is mixed. On most campuses, you can pretty much come and go as you please. This freedom is an outgrowth of the social protest movement of the 1960s and 1970s, which was largely

Years ago, dormitory advisors and personnel acted *in loco parentis*. They kept track of your coming and going and set curfews. Today on most campuses, you can pretty much come and go as you please, and most dormitories house both men and women.

spearheaded by students. Moreover, most of today's dormitories house both men and women, and there are few, if any, restrictions on visiting. In fact, constraints on visiting often go unenforced on the campuses that still have them.[2] Some colleges, on the other hand, are returning to the role of acting as parents away from home. There are several reasons for this. One is the conservative trends of the 1980s, which have to some degree countered the movements of the preceding two decades. Another is the advent of AIDS, a sexually transmitted disease that we'll discuss at length in Chapter 12.

Most students living away at college are likely to find, however, that they are, by and large, their own bosses.

> You are free and that is why you are lost.
>
> FRANZ KAFKA
>
> Liberty means responsibility. That is why most men dread it.
>
> GEORGE BERNARD SHAW

TRUTH OR FICTION *Revisited*

In most colleges, resident and academic advisors do *not* make certain that you stick to the straight and narrow. It is usually up to you to take charge of your personal and academic life.

If you are commuting to college, you may feel that you want more freedoms than you had in high school because college seems to be more a part of the adult world. If so, you may undergo the stress of trying to redefine your relationship with your family at the same time you are adjusting to the academic demands of college. Perhaps some of the suggestions on handling social conflicts found in Chapter 10 will be of help to you.

In one sense, the freedom of college life is illusory. We are all bound by the realities of the world outside. In college, as in the other arenas of adult life, our behavior has consequences. If you are living away from home,

Making the Transition to College Life

your parents may not be looking over your shoulder. If you don't get yourself to classes and complete your assignments, however, you may not last for long. If you don't wash your clothes, you may find the students in the seats around you clearing out. There may be no curfews or restrictions at the dormitory, but unless you define some restrictions for yourself, your social life may disrupt your academic life. The bottom line is this: If you don't take charge of yourself, it may be that your grades and perhaps your health will suffer for it.

IN YOUR OWN WRITE

Now that we have explored some of the freedoms that students find at college, discuss some of the opportunities and pitfalls that you think are offered by the freedom of college life.

_____
_____
_____
_____
_____
_____
_____

Students beginning college are only partly aware of the limitations on their freedom. In a survey run by the Carnegie Foundation for the Advancement of Teaching,[3] college-bound seniors revealed their expectations about college life by responding to statements like those shown in Table 1.1.

TABLE 1.1. Anticipations of College-Bound High School Students.

STATEMENT	PERCENT AGREEING	PERCENT DISAGREEING
Doing really well in college means you miss out on a lot of interesting social activities.	15	85
Most college students party every weekend.	51	49
Half the fun of going to college is making new friends.	92	8
The quality of teaching in college is usually no better than in high school.	17	83
College students have to study almost twice as hard as twelfth-grade students.	82	18

The Work Load

The expectations found by the Carnegie Foundation show some interesting discrepancies. Students at the beginning of their college careers recognize, correctly, that college students usually work harder ("study almost twice as hard") as high school seniors. But they seem to assume that it is possible to work harder without making any social sacrifices! Eighty-five percent do not recognize that academic success can require such sacrifices (that "you miss out on a lot of interesting social activities").

> Now, *here*, you see, it takes all the running you can do, to keep in the same place. If you want to get somewhere else, you must run at least twice as fast as that!
>
> LEWIS CARROLL,
> *Through the Looking-Glass*

TRUTH OR FICTION *Revisited*

Most beginning college students do not appear to realize that doing well in college requires some social sacrifices.

Moreover, about half the students believe that "most college students party every weekend"! Students cannot spend every weekend partying if they are carrying full academic loads—especially not if they are also working part or full time or are involved in extracurricular activities such as athletics.

Quality, Not Just Quantity Then, too, what is considered excellent, A-quality work in high school may be deemed only above average or even just average in college. In our own experience, we found out that the competition can be much tougher in college. College students almost invariably make up a more academically elite group than high school students. High schools teach nearly all of the teenagers who live within their districts. Some of them drop out without receiving their diplomas. Some barely scrape by. Others do very well, some in vocational programs, others in college-oriented programs. Universities and 4-year colleges usually tap successful, academically oriented high school students. Community colleges usually admit all high-school graduates from their counties, but students who elect to go to these colleges are more academically oriented than those who call it quits after high school—even if they have their minds on occupations that are accessible with an associate degree rather than on continuing for a bachelor's degree. So college students are by and large more capable and motivated than the average high school student.

Also, professors in many colleges tend to take basic reading, writing, and computational skills for granted. Your college may have first-year students take placement tests in these skills and then require students who have not reached certain levels to take basic skills courses for zero credits or perhaps one credit. If you wind up in such a course, choose a positive attitude. The alternative would be to muddle by (or worse, to fail to muddle by) in more advanced courses. Attaining these skills is an investment in life, not just in college. After all, you'll need them in the "real" world after college as well as in other courses. So count yourself lucky to be in a class where you can acknowledge your deficits to a sympathetic instructor and get to work on them with other students who are in the same boat.

In high school, many students earn A's and B's by completing reading assignments and using proper punctuation and grammar in papers. Depending on the nature of the assignment, in college you may not be able to get a B or an A unless you also show some clever insights and some original thinking. In college, that is, you may not be able to get by just on the basics or on effort. You may also be required to produce work of higher quality. Many professors, moreover, demand that you show *critical thinking* in your class discussions and in your written work.

Critical Thinking

Most of us grow up taking certain things for granted. For example, we may tend to assume that government and religious leaders tell us "the truth." We may tend to believe that things advertised on television or in newspapers can't be bad for us. We may assume that "health foods" are healthful and that people with experience—especially celebrities—know what's best. After all, if Bill Cosby advertises Jello™, can Jello™ be bad?

Most colleges today encourage something called critical thinking. Critical thinking has many meanings. For one thing, it means having a skeptical attitude—not simply believing something because it's in print or because

> What is easy is seldom excellent.
> SAMUEL JOHNSON

> The object of education is to prepare the young to educate themselves throughout their lives.
>
> My idea of education is to unsettle the minds of the young and inflame their intellects.
> ROBERT M. HUTCHINS

Making the Transition to College Life

it was said by an authority figure or a celebrity. On another level, critical thinking means the process of thoughtfully analyzing and probing the arguments and claims of other people. It means examining the premises or assumptions behind these arguments and then scrutinizing the logic with which they are developed.

Let us intentionally use a controversial topic as an example: Suppose that your class is discussing the issue of whether or not women should have the right to have an abortion. Consider some of the ideas that are usually employed in these discussions and how they might be approached in terms of critical thinking:

1. *Abortion is (or is not) the taking of a human life.* A critical examination of either pole of this argument requires defining terms. What do the words *human* and *life* mean? In thinking about this issue critically, one can enumerate and, perhaps, challenge the ways in which we determine what is or is not *human*. Is a developing embryo or fetus *human*? At what point? (When it is a single cell? When the major body organ systems have been formed? When the heart begins to beat? When the fetus is capable of "independent life"? What is meant by *independent* life?) What criteria, or standards, do we use to make the judgment that an embryo or fetus is a human life?

2. *A fetus is (or is not) a person.* One legal issue is that only *persons* are protected by the U.S. Constitution. The Constitution does not guarantee rights to lower animals, plant life, or inanimate objects. So a critical examination of this idea might involve deciding—presumably in legal terms—what is or is not a person. It's not enough to raise your voice and insist, "Of course a fetus is (or is not) a person!" Be prepared to define your terms, recognize your assumptions, and support them logically.

3. *A developing embryo or fetus experiences (or does not experience) pain when it is aborted.* One question concerning this issue is, "What is pain?" How can we know whether another organism or person experiences pain? What are the rules of evidence involved?

Like most other people, we have some opinions about abortion, but there is no reason to go into them here. We raise the question only to illustrate how critical thinking can be used in examining debatable issues.

Encouragement of critical thinking in students is one of the goals of most colleges and universities. Colleges nurture academic freedom, so few professors require students to share and express the professors' own beliefs. By and large, professors are more concerned that students learn to question and critically examine the arguments of others, including some of their own beliefs or values. This does not mean that professors insist that you change your beliefs, either. It does mean, however, that professors will usually ask you to *support* the views you express in class or in your writing. If your premises are shaky, or if your arguments are illogical, professors may ask other students to join in the discussion (to challenge you) or may personally point out the fallacies in your arguments. Most professors want you to learn to recognize the premises of your arguments, to examine whether you really accept these premises, and to understand whether or not you draw logical conclusions. Put it this way: *Professors don't tell you what to think; they try to teach you how to think.* On the other hand, if you intend to disagree with your professors in class, you should be prepared to offer a strong argument in support of your ideas. Arguing just for the sake of arguing usually does not promote a critical examination of ideas. Many professors interpret it as rudeness.

In the Carnegie Foundation survey,[4] 81 percent of the college-bound high school seniors agreed with the statement

Being in college helps to clarify one's values and beliefs.

> A great many people think they are thinking when they are merely rearranging their prejudices.
>
> WILLIAM JAMES

> Men become civilized, not in proportion to their willingness to believe, but in proportion to their readiness to doubt.
>
> H. L. MENCKEN

> I respect faith, but doubt is what gets you an education.
>
> WILSON MIZNER

12   Chapter 1

College emphasis on critical thinking is one reason why such clarification occurs.

Friends

Yes, as beginning college students expect, "Half the fun of college is making new friends." Whether you attend the community college a few miles from home or a college thousands of miles from home, you'll meet at least some people from other places and other walks of life. (Among these are your professors.) They will challenge some of your more dearly held values and beliefs. This is one reason that college is referred to as a "broadening" experience. Other students may inspire you to new insights. Some of them will befriend you, and you may, indeed, make some friendships that will last a lifetime. Friends help make college worthwhile. Friends can also distract you from your work, so it is wise to select friends who share your work ethic and help you study rather than hinder you.

In Chapter 9, we shall explore some ways of developing relationships and overcoming the problem of loneliness. In Chapters 3 and 10, we shall consider ways of preventing friends from interfering with studying and methods of dealing with social conflicts.

> Skepticism is the first step on the road to philosophy.
> DENIS DIDEROT

High School versus College Teachers

A major *mis*perception of beginning college students is that college teaching is superior to high school teaching. Not necessarily. Consider these differences between high school and college instructors.

College Professors May Not See Themselves Primarily as Teachers College professors are usually quite knowledgeable. Many of them have earned advanced or professional degrees or certificates in their fields. At a community college, you may be taught dental hygiene or nursing by practicing dental hygienists and nurses. Many of the professors at 4-year colleges

Most students will come away from college with special memories of professors who were experts in their fields, who were great communicators, who cracked jokes, or who took a warm interest in them. However, many college professors do not believe that professors should have to motivate or entertain students.

Making the Transition to College Life 13

and universities are nationally renowned. Some professors, in fact, see themselves primarily as professional practitioners (e.g., dental hygienists or nurses), scientists, writers, or critics, and only incidentally as teachers.

Moreover, teachers who know a great deal about a subject do *not* necessarily do a better job of teaching it. Research suggests that presenting material in a clear, organized fashion is nearly as important as expert knowledge.[5] College professors, it happens, do not usually receive formal training in teaching methods. High school teachers, by contrast, take courses in how to present their subject matter and are then supervised as student teachers.

Students at 4-year colleges and universities sometimes sign up for courses because the professor is famous. Then, when they show up, they find that discussion sections (also called "recitation sections") are taught by graduate students who are serving as teaching assistants, or TA's. First-year students may also find themselves in large sections of 150 or 1,000 students, or in courses that are taught completely by TA's. All in all, in college the responsibility for learning is placed much more directly on the student's shoulders.

TRUTH OR FICTION *Revisited*

It turns out that college teaching is *not* invariably superior to high school teaching. In college the responsibility for learning is more likely to be placed on the student's shoulders.

If you want more personal contact, either to get help or to discuss issues that weren't raised in class, remember that professors and TA's are available during office hours. Go see them and tell them what you need.

College Professors Do Not Necessarily Try to Motivate Students   Motivating students is usually part of the job of teaching in high school. Most students have had high school teachers who told jokes or fascinating personal tales to involve them in their subjects. Most of us will also come away from college with special memories of professors who were experts in their fields, who were great communicators, who cracked jokes, or who took a warm interest in us. However, many college professors believe that college students should come to the classroom motivated to learn. They do not believe that professors should have to entertain students.

TRUTH OR FICTION *Revisited*

Although many college professors are enjoyable in their presentations, many of them do *not* see motivating students as part of their jobs.

If you are taking a vocational sequence in dental hygiene at a community college, your professors have a right to assume that you signed up because you *want* to become a dental hygienist. And if you want to be a dental hygienist, you should find the subject matter interesting. The professor shouldn't have to crack jokes and find other ways of entertaining you. Similarly, if you're taking freshman composition at a university, your professors will usually assume that you're there because you want to be in college, even if writing isn't your favorite subject. Again, they tend to assume that you are motivated from within.

College Professors Usually Do Not Spoon-Feed or Coddle Students Most high school teachers carefully outline ("spoon-feed") all the material that students must know and go over it several times. In college you will find a great deal of variety in teaching methods.

Many college professors expect you to get through the texts and readings pretty much on your own. They reserve class time for critical discussions of controversial points. Many college professors present the material once and then expect to move on.

When high school teachers assign papers, they usually tell you precisely what they want. They may even have due dates for topic selection, outlines, and first and final drafts. When college professors assign papers, they may give you a style sheet but otherwise leave you on your own. Some professors urge you to ask questions in class and then patiently respond to every one—in more than one way, if asked to do so. But other college instructors consider step-by-step outlining of what you need to know and what you need to do to be "coddling." In sum, most students who in high school were directed by others find that they must learn to take charge of their academic progress and direct themselves.

It is up to you to ask questions about the subject matter and about professors' expectations. Stop by to see the professor or TA during office hours if you want extra clarification. If you want further help, check into the tutoring programs available at your college. (See the "Tutoring" section in Chapter 2.)

Although the chief responsibility for learning in college is placed on the student's shoulders, we have some good news for students who want close, nurturing teacher-student relationships: Most professors enjoy students and want to be helpful. You are likely to find that most instructors are happy to see you in their offices and discuss their subjects with you. From the student's perspective, informal contacts with instructors can enrich their college experience beyond the classroom.

The Core Curriculum: Why Must You Take Courses You Don't Like?

Most community colleges, 4-year colleges, and universities have some kind of core curriculum. This consists of some group of courses that all students are required to take, even if the courses bear no obvious relationship to the student's ultimate occupational goals. Core courses reflect the fact that many educators believe that the primary purpose of an undergraduate edu-

> Histories make men wise; poets, witty; the mathematics, subtle; natural philosophy, deep; moral, grave; logic and rhetoric, able to contend.
>
> FRANCIS BACON

Most professors are happy to see students in their offices and discuss their subjects with them. Informal contacts with instructors can enrich students' college experience beyond the classroom.

cation is not to get you a job upon graduation, but to make you an educated person. To accomplish this goal, most colleges require you to complete courses drawn from the arts and the sciences—regardless of your major field, regardless of your personal likes and dislikes. This is another reason that college is said to be a broadening experience.

In most colleges today, there is also general agreement that students should be exposed to "great" books. On the other hand, a debate is raging over just which great books should be the ones. There is widespread agreement[6] that being educated means being exposed to English composition, the arts, to the history of civilization, to math and the natural sciences, to the behavioral and social sciences, and to the thinking of philosophers and theologians. As noted in the section on critical thinking, most educators do not tell you *what* to think. Nevertheless, they believe that you cannot make intelligent choices without being exposed to a basic core of knowledge.

Educators also believe that the *educated* physician is superior to the merely *skilled* physician; that an educated businessperson is superior to just a skilled businessperson. Note Norman Cousins' remarks in the *Saturday Review*:

> The doctor who knows only disease is at a disadvantage alongside the doctor who knows at least as much about people as he does about

QUESTIONNAIRE
The Expectancy for Success Scale

College life is filled with opportunities and obstacles. What do you do when you are faced with an arduous challenge? Do you rise to meet it, or do you back off?

Psychologists note that there is a relationship between our belief in ourselves and the way we tackle challenges. For example, when we believe that we can achieve great things through our own efforts, we tend to marshal our resources and apply ourselves. When we expect our efforts to pay off, we are more likely to persist.[8]

The following scale* will show you whether you believe that your undertakings are likely to be successful. Compare your expectations for success with those of other undergraduates by filling out the questionnaire and turning to the scoring key at the end of the chapter.

Directions: Indicate the degree to which each item applies to you by circling the appropriate number, according to this key:

    1 = highly improbable
    2 = improbable
    3 = equally improbable and probable; not sure
    4 = probable
    5 = highly probable

In the future I expect that I will:

1. Find that people don't seem to understand what I'm trying to say.   1 2 3 4 5
2. Be discouraged about my ability to gain the respect of others.   1 2 3 4 5
3. Be a good parent.   1 2 3 4 5
4. Be unable to accomplish my goals.   1 2 3 4 5
5. Have a stressful marital relationship.   1 2 3 4 5
6. Deal poorly with emergency situations.   1 2 3 4 5
7. Find that my efforts to change situations I don't like are ineffective.   1 2 3 4 5

pathological organisms. The lawyer who argues in court from a narrow legal base is no match for the lawyer who can connect legal precedents to historical experience and who employs wide-ranging intellectual resources. The business executive whose competence in general management is bolstered by an artistic ability to deal with people is of prime value to his company. For the technologist, the engineering of consent can be just as important as the engineering of moving parts.[7]

TRUTH OR FICTION *Revisited*

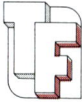

Although college helps students attain good jobs, most educators see the primary purpose of college as educating students—showing them how to engage in critical thinking and exposing them to the arts and sciences.

So it will be helpful if you open up your mind and are willing to modify your attitudes. You will need some other things as well—which is the subject of the next section.

8.	Not be very good at learning new skills.	1 2 3 4 5
9.	Carry through my responsibilities successfully.	1 2 3 4 5
10.	Discover that the good in life outweighs the bad.	1 2 3 4 5
11.	Handle unexpected problems successfully.	1 2 3 4 5
12.	Get the promotions I deserve.	1 2 3 4 5
13.	Succeed in the projects I undertake.	1 2 3 4 5
14.	Not make any significant contributions to society.	1 2 3 4 5
15.	Discover that my life is not getting much better.	1 2 3 4 5
16.	Be listened to when I speak.	1 2 3 4 5
17.	Discover that my plans don't work out too well.	1 2 3 4 5
18.	Find that no matter how hard I try, things just don't turn out the way I would like.	1 2 3 4 5
19.	Handle myself well in whatever situation I'm in.	1 2 3 4 5
20.	Be able to solve my own problems.	1 2 3 4 5
21.	Succeed at most things I try.	1 2 3 4 5
22.	Be successful in my endeavors in the long run.	1 2 3 4 5
23.	Be very successful in working out my personal life.	1 2 3 4 5
24.	Experience many failures in my life.	1 2 3 4 5
25.	Make a good first impression on people I meet for the first time.	1 2 3 4 5
26.	Attain the career goals I have set for myself.	1 2 3 4 5
27.	Have difficulty dealing with my superiors.	1 2 3 4 5
28.	Have problems working with others.	1 2 3 4 5
29.	Be a good judge of what it takes to get ahead.	1 2 3 4 5
30.	Achieve recognition in my profession.	1 2 3 4 5

BASIC EQUIPMENT

Along with accurate expectations, you also need a certain amount of physical equipment to get by in college. Of course there are the mundane things—socks, toothpaste, an alarm clock, underwear, running shoes, shampoo, aspirin, dental floss, soap, hangers, towels—that you probably already have. You may also already have some of the academically oriented items, such as a dictionary, calculator, or computer. Ironically, if you're going to be selecting these items now, you may be better off. You can find out whether instructors or students who have majored in your field for a while have some recommendations.

Let's go into some of this equipment a bit more deeply.

Calculator

Calculators are essential for the majority of science and business students. Your professors want you to be able to figure out what formulas and processes are necessary to solve problems, but they are usually willing to let you use a calculator to crunch the numbers.

You can get a reasonably good, general-purpose calculator for $10–$20. Science and business students can find high-quality, specialized calculators for under $100. A good business calculator, for example, allows you to calculate mortgage payments, to find the future value of a single deposit or of a series of equal deposits, and to estimate a bond's yield-to-maturity.

You can catch the professor as the course gets underway and ask what kind of calculator he or she recommends and whether or not you can bring it to tests. Other students, especially students who have already taken the courses, are also excellent guides.

Dictionary

You must have one dictionary, perhaps two. Buy the college version of *Webster's Dictionary* or an equivalent. You'll find a pile of them in the reference section of your local bookstore or at the college bookstore. They should cost less than $20.

You can't make a mistake if you buy standards like *Webster's New Collegiate Dictionary*, *Webster's New World Dictionary*, the *American Heritage Dictionary*, or *The Random House College Dictionary*. You can ask your freshman composition instructor if he or she has a preference. Also ask instructors if you can bring a small pocket dictionary to class so that you can check your spelling on essays.

Higher education, like other areas of life, is best navigated with the right equipment. Sometimes students find the selection task simplified by recommendations from instructors or students who have majored in the same field.

Encyclopedia

The college library has several encyclopedias that are available for use at no cost. A brief desk encyclopedia like the *Concise Columbia Encyclopedia* (published by the Columbia University Press), on the other hand, is both portable and affordable. With such a reference work in your room, you don't have to run off to the library to look up every little thing. That will save time and steps. If you decide to purchase a concise encyclopedia, don't pay more than $40.

Handbook of English Usage

A handbook of English usage will help you check for agreement between nouns and verbs, use parallel structure, check the difference between *lie* and *lay*,* and so on.

Your freshman composition instructor may assign or recommend a specific handbook. If not, these handbooks are classics: *The Elements of Style*, written by William Strunk and E. B. White, and published by Macmillan;† and *Manual for Writers of Term Papers, Theses and Dissertations*, written by Kate L. Turabian, and published by The University of Chicago Press. On the other hand, nearly all major publishing companies have handbooks of usage. These works are usually in stock at local bookstores and in college bookstores. If not, they can be ordered through any bookstore.

> I have laboured to refine our language to grammatical purity, and to clear it from colloquial barbarisms, licentious idioms, and irregular combinations.
>
> SAMUEL JOHNSON,
> *The Rambler*

Personal Computer

Computers make more of an impact on our lives every year. Not only are they indispensable tools in science and business. They also help run our automobiles and microwave ovens. In a few years, every home may have a central computer command system. Almost every college student is now required to have some familiarity with computers. Has a personal computer become as indispensable for today's college students as typewriters were for their parents?

It's a close call. A few schools, like Philadelphia's Drexel University, have required first-year students to purchase computers. For most students, however, computer equipment is optional.

Students seem to find two major uses for personal computers: word processing and use of workbook-like study diskettes.‡ You will probably not bring a personal computer to science and business tests—although computers are becoming so miniaturized that we may soon find them no more space-consuming than calculators. Nor will you use a computer for most homework assignments in science and business. For science and business problems, you'll need a calculator that you can hold in the palm of your hand. When science and business courses require computer applications, you'll usually be directed to the college or department computer facilities. You may not be able to use your own computer for these applications, even if you have one.

So what about word processing and those study diskettes? Word processing has many advantages over handwriting and typing, and these are enumerated in Chapter 6. Study diskettes are really the equivalent of study guides or workbooks. They may be helpful, but they're not sufficient reason to buy a computer. Word processing is the primary reason for most students.

So how much does it all cost? You can buy inexpensive word-processing

---

* Also see the section on correcting common writing errors in Chapter 6 of this book.

† But we have to admit that we experienced "sticker shock" when we saw the price of this thin paperback on a recent visit to a bookstore.

‡ These are usually optional purchases for courses and are available in the college bookstore. We're not convinced that they have reached a point where they're superior to the regular, paperback student study guides.

machines (they're electronic typewriters with small built-in memories, or "pea brains") that cost $600 or less. But all they do is process words—and not all that well. You can also spend thousands upon thousands for equipment that will store the works of Shakespeare, Webster's dictionary, your papers; rummage through it all to find the parts you want in a couple of seconds; and print it all so beautifully that it looks as though it were professionally typeset. The basic equipment described below, however, will cost you about $1,000–$1,500, if brand new. *Used computer equipment is usually nearly as good as new and often half the price or less.* This is the type of equipment you'll need:

An IBM, an IBM-compatible clone (Compaq, NEC, Epson, etc.), an Apple, or another machine with the equivalent of at least an 8088 processor. IBM imitations, or clones, are about as good as IBM models and usually cost less. *Any computer that comes on when you plug it in and switch it on will probably give you several years of trouble-free service.** The computer must have twelve *function keys* so that you can use popular programs. The size of the processor determines how many pieces of information the computer can process simultaneously. For word processing and study diskettes, an 8088 processor is enough. An 80286 or still more powerful processor will cost more and doesn't make a noticeable difference unless you're doing some real number crunching, as with a spreadsheet program.

At least 512K (kilobytes) of memory (called *random access memory*, or *RAM*). You need 512K of memory† for a sophisticated word-processing program like WordPerfect. You really don't need more.

Two floppy disk drives of at least 360K each, OR

One floppy disk drive of at least 360K and a fixed drive of at least 10 megabytes. You want to be able to load your basic software (operating system and word-processing program) by means of one drive and your data files (the papers and letters you are working on or have written) on another. If you can load your operating system and word-processing program from a fixed drive, you'll save time and effort every time you boot up your equipment.

A monochromatic monitor (that is, a one-color video screen on which you see what you're typing). In addition to black and white, there are monochromatic amber screens, green-on-black screens, blue-on-blue screens, and so on. See what looks good to you. (Color monitors are prettier but usually cost $150–$600 more. Unless money is no object, get a monochromatic monitor.)

A letter-quality or near-letter-quality printer. *Letter-quality* means sharp enough to use for an important business letter.

A disk operating system (e.g., MS-DOS, IBM-DOS, Unix). This *software* tells your computer (*hardware*) what to do. You need it to use word-processing programs, study diskettes, and so on. With some equipment, an operating system and even a word-processing program are built in to memory (RAM). In such cases, not only do you save the costs of this software, but you may be able to get by on a single 360K floppy disk drive. *On the other hand, built-in word-processing programs are likely to have minimal capacities. Don't expect them to include spell-check or thesaurus functions. You gets what you pays for.*

Word-processing software. Ask friends and instructors for recommendations. At a minimum, you want your word-processing program to be able to move around blocks (that is, rearrange paragraphs) and to merge programs (combine two separate documents into one). If it can also automatically renumber all your footnotes when you insert a new footnote at the beginning or in the middle, great!

* This is not a guarantee. It's an observation.
† If you're a business student, you may want to check that the hardware you buy is powerful enough to run spreadsheets and similar applications.

As with a typewriter, you're going to have to buy paper and ribbons (or wells of ink). If two systems look about the same to you, ask how much the paper and ribbons (or ink) cost for each. It might make the difference. Also make certain (by asking the dealer, or by buying everything in one place) that all this equipment is compatible. In other words, the hardware has to be able to accept the software; you have to be able to attach the monitor and printer to the computer *and* get them to work. Here are some hints for locating a used computer to purchase:

1. Check bulletin boards for used computers and consider buying them if they check out okay at the computer center or a local computer store. A salesperson or computer center employee may be happy to check out the system for a fee.
2. You may also be able to get good new equipment at a discount through the college computer center, especially if personal computers are required at your campus. For example, faculty and students at several colleges get special deals from IBM. It's worth a phone call to the computer center to find out. Many colleges also allow you to finance your purchase over your college career.

TRUTH OR FICTION *Revisited*

Yes, some colleges do require students to buy personal computers. A computer might be a good investment for you whether or not one is required.

Thesaurus

You must have a thesaurus. As with a handbook of usage and a dictionary, you can seek recommendations from your freshman composition instructor. On the other hand, *Roget's International Thesaurus*, published by Harper and Row, is a standard.

Thesauruses allow you to find words related in meaning to a target word by looking up the target word. You can use thesauruses to (1) find the exact word you need, (2) show variety in the vocabulary you use in a paper, and (3) build your vocabulary. Many word-processing programs have built-in thesauruses. We placed our cursor (the marker that tells you where you are on the screen) on the word *variety* in the sentence before last, and pressed the key marked "Thesaurus." This is what came up on our screen:

1. A. assortment
   B. collection
   C. conglomeration
   D. multiplicity
2. E. class
   F. kind
   G. species
   H. type
3. I. dissimilarity
   J. diversity
   K. heterogeneity

   *Antonym**
4. L. similarity

   *Antonyms are opposite in meaning to the word being looked up (from the Greek *anti*, meaning "opposite," and *onyma*, meaning "name"). Synonyms are equivalent in meaning (from the Greek *syn*, meaning "with").

So if we had used the word *variety* repeatedly on this page, we could have selected, say, *diversity*. Consider Shakespeare's line from *Antony and Cleopatra:* "Age cannot wither her, nor custom stale her infinite variety." With a little help from your thesaurus, the line could be changed to:

"Maturity cannot wilt her, nor familiarity spoil her boundless diversity,"

or to

"Development cannot shrivel her, nor habit wilt her limitless assortment."

Imagine what Shakespeare could have done with a thesaurus. We rest our case.

In this chapter, we have discussed some of the basic equipment you'll need to get by in college. In the next chapter, we explore the resources you will find on campus and in the community surrounding the college.

SUMMING UP

1. Can you think of at least two reasons why some straight-A high school students find themselves struggling in college?
2. What are some of the special concerns of commuting students?
3. What are some of the special concerns of students who return to school after starting or rearing families?
4. In what ways is your college experience likely to offer you more freedom than you found in high school?
5. How does the work load at your college differ from the work load in high school?
6. What is critical thinking? Can you apply critical thinking to any of the beliefs that you have held dear?
7. In what ways do the professors at your college seem to differ from your high school teachers?
8. Does your college require that most students take a common core of courses? If so, what are these courses? Do these courses make sense to you? Why or why not?
9. Do you expect to succeed in college? What is the connection between your expectations of success and your tendency to persist at difficult tasks?
10. How can each of the following tools help you reach your potential in college? Calculator? Dictionary? Encyclopedia? Handbook of English usage? Personal computer? Thesaurus?

Answer Key for the "Who's in Charge Here?" Questionnaire

Place a checkmark to the right of each item in the key when your answer agrees with the answer that is shown. Add the checkmarks to determine your total score.

1. Yes ___	11. Yes ___	21. Yes ___	31. Yes ___
2. No ___	12. Yes ___	22. No ___	32. No ___
3. Yes ___	13. No ___	23. Yes ___	33. Yes ___
4. No ___	14. Yes ___	24. Yes ___	34. No ___
5. Yes ___	15. No ___	25. No ___	35. Yes ___
6. No ___	16. Yes ___	26. No ___	36. Yes ___
7. Yes ___	17. Yes ___	27. Yes ___	37. Yes ___
8. Yes ___	18. Yes ___	28. No ___	38. No ___
9. No ___	19. Yes ___	29. Yes ___	39. Yes ___
10. Yes ___	20. No ___	30. No ___	40. No ___

Interpreting Your Score

Low Scorers (0–8). Nearly one student in three receives a score of 0 to 8. These students largely see themselves as responsible for the rewards they obtain or do not obtain in life.

Average Scorers (9–16). Most students receive from 9 to 16 points. These students view themselves as partially in control of their lives. Perhaps they view themselves as in control academically but not socially, or vice versa.

High Scorers (17–40). Nearly 15 percent of students receive scores of 17 or higher. These students view life largely as a game of chance. They see success as a matter of luck or a product of the kindness of others.

Scoring Key for the "Expectancy-for-Success Scale"

To calculate your total score for the expectancy-for-success scale, first reverse the scores for the following items: 1, 2, 4, 6, 7, 8, 14, 15, 17, 18, 24, 27, and 28. In other words, change a 1 to a 5; a 2 to a 4; leave a 3 as is; change a 4 to a 2; and a 5 to a 1. Now add up the scores.

The higher your score, the greater your expectancy for success in the future—and, presumably, the more motivated you will be to accept and meet challenges.

Fibel and Hale[9] administered their test to psychology students. Women's scores ranged from 65 to 143. Men's scores ranged from 81 to 138. The average score for both sexes was 112 (112.32 for women and 112.15 for men).

2

Making Use of Campus and Community Resources

 **TRUTH OR FICTION?**

_____ Commuting students frequently feel isolated from campus life.

_____ "Computer literacy" is a fundamental feature of education in the 1990s.

_____ Whether you're at a rural community college or a great university in a major metropolitan area, libraries are the great equalizers in college education.

_____ Test-preparation guides are not really of any help in getting ready for the Medical College Admissions Test or the Law School Aptitude Test.

_____ You can call the campus security office for an escort if you're afraid to walk alone across a section of campus at night.

_____ The majority of college students would support stronger environmental legislation, even at the expense of economic growth.

_____ Most communities have hotlines you can call when in a crisis.

Many college campuses are worlds unto themselves. You can do anything on them from checking into a hospital to buying fashionable clothing to seeing the latest films. You can even catch a class or two. Other campuses offer somewhat less. In this chapter, we explore the kinds of resources you'll find on campus and in the surrounding community.

USING CAMPUS RESOURCES

Resources such as the following will help you optimize your experiences on your campus. The list is intended both for students living away from home and for commuters. It is also intended to be of use to students who are returning to school while rearing families, or afterward. Returning students usually live in the community, have families of their own, and commute. Consider the following passage from a student newspaper, which highlights some of the differences between returning students (referred to as *commuters*) and students who live on campus:

> Commuters talk about their kids. Dorm students talk about how much beer they drank the night before. Commuters dress as if they were going to the office. A dorm student's wardrobe consists of bluejeans, sweatpants and T-shirts. Commuter students have trouble finding a parking space every morning. Dorm students have trouble finding matching socks. When a class is over, dorm students attend club meetings, act as campus hosts and hostesses, make posters for special events, play intramural sports and pursue a variety of other activities. Commuters go home. . . .[1]

TRUTH OR FICTION *Revisited*

Commuters are often isolated from campus life—whether they are 18, 28, or older. The following list will help commuters and students who live on campus make better use of campus resources.

Academic Services

Academic services range from photocopying to libraries to tutoring. Some of these services are essential to accomplishing anything at all; others just make life a little easier.

Copying Services   Photocopying machines are usually found in the library, in student centers, and at other strategic locations around campus. Be prepared to spend an exorbitant amount—a dime or so a page—for mediocre-quality copies. You must use the copying machines in the library if you want duplicates of reserve materials, but you don't have to use them for other documents. You may be able to find a cheaper copy service in the community and get better-quality copies to boot. Do some comparison shopping.

IN YOUR OWN WRITE

Our next topic is the computer center. Before getting to it, however, jot down some of your feelings about or experiences with computers. For example, do you find computers to be convenient? Confusing? Easy to use? Intimidating?

___

Computer Centers   Computer centers frequently contain mainframes and microcomputers. A mainframe is a powerful computer that may be used ("accessed") simultaneously by students at different terminals. Microcomputers are also referred to as personal computers, and each one is used by one student. In addition to the computer center, various schools and departments are likely to have their own computer setups. For example, computers with synthesizers may be available through the music department. Professional equipment can sound like a personal orchestra. Computers with advanced graphic capabilities may be available through departments of art, architecture, and design. Consider this description of what takes place in Professor Harry Holland's fine-arts classroom at Yardley University:

> [The] classroom is free of oil and turpentine smells; no easels stand under the muted lighting, no dropcloths beneath the students' feet. Instead, the aspiring artists sit in a semicircle and stare at computer screens. One student touches a metal stylus to a pressure-sensitive electronic pad; as she does so, the colors displayed in the lower third of the screen mix to her specifications. She can choose from 256 colors in this computerized palette created by her professor and blend them with the others in hundreds of subtle combinations. When the shade satisfies her, she uses the stylus to transfer it to the abstract drawing waiting farther up on her screen. . . . [Holland] considers the computer just another artist's tool, a technological paintbrush that expands [the] creative possibilities.[2]

Science departments often have computers that allow students to solve problems, calculate results of experiments, simulate experiments, and so on.

College computer centers will also inform you as to what special deals may be available for purchasing your own computer equipment. If you cannot purchase word-processing equipment, the college computer center may be able to provide access to everything you need—at least during certain hours. Ask.

Computer centers usually offer workshops that teach students how to work a computer's basic operating systems (e.g., MS-DOS, Unix, IBM-

DOS), use word-processing systems (e.g., WordPerfect, Wordstar, Microsoft Word, Pro Write), use a spreadsheet (primarily for business students), use BASIC (an easy-to-learn computer language that allows you to write and run programs of your own), use some computer graphics, and so on.

The acquisition of computer literacy—that is, familiarity with the applications of the computer and facility with some basic computer techniques—is a fundamental feature of education in the 1990s. Even if computer work is not required in your first-year courses, stop by the computer center and find out what it might have to offer you.

TRUTH OR FICTION *Revisited*

"Computer literacy" is a fundamental feature of education in the 1990s. The computer is here to stay, and educated people must be aware of its applications.

IN YOUR OWN WRITE

Next we'll be talking about libraries. Before we do, however, here's an opportunity to put into words your own thoughts and feelings about libraries and librarians:

_____
_____
_____
_____
_____
_____
_____
_____

> There is no book so bad but something valuable may be derived from it.
> — PLINY THE ELDER

Libraries The word *library* derives from the Latin *liber*, meaning "book." The word *liberty*, which means "freedom," has the same origin. Keep that in mind if you find yourself stuck working away in the library now and then during the wee hours. The knowledge available in the library means freedom from the slavery of ignorance.

Many colleges have a main library and a number of smaller, specialized libraries that may be located in academic departments. Libraries are good for many things: finding dates, writing letters, and watching people, to name a few. Oh yes, they also have carrels (individual study booths or stations), tables and chairs, armchairs, books, professional journals, magazines, newspapers, records (written and the kinds that make music), slides, filmstrips, works of art, microfiche (pronounced "MY-crow-feesh"—small sheets of microfilm on which many pages of newspapers and other sources of information can be found), dictionaries, encyclopedias, telephone directories, zip code directories, electronic information (you pull it up on a video monitor), and librarians. If the book you need is not owned by your library, librarians may be able to order it through an interlibrary loan. Computer searches can locate everything you want to know on a topic, and more, by looking up a few key words.

Humankind has accumulated countless billions of bits of information over the millennia. Your most personal computer—your brain—can store some of it. That, according to Samuel Johnson, is one kind of knowledge. With the possible exception of your authors, however, there's much too much for any one person to know. So knowing where you can *find* information about things is as vital as having it in mind. This is the other kind of knowledge Johnson was writing about. So one aspect of becoming an educated person is to learn how to search for information. And that information is either in your library or accessible through your library.

The Great Equalizer In the Old West, the six-gun was referred to as "the equalizer." That is, a weak person with a six-gun was as powerful as a strong person with a six-gun.

In education, libraries are the great equalizers. Whether you're at California State University at Los Angeles, Duke University, Miami-Dade Junior College, Loyola, Montclair State College, or Ohio State University, the information available in or through the library is pretty much the same. The writings of Ralph Waldo Emerson, Jane Austen, Malcolm X, and Sigmund Freud are identical in the libraries at Connecticut's Manchester Community College and at New Mexico State University. The articles in *The New York Times* and *Journal of Consulting and Clinical Psychology* are the same whether you pick them up at the University of Nebraska or Holy Cross. You can avail yourself of the greatest literature and the latest information through the library at nearly any college. It's largely up to you.

> Knowledge is of two kinds. We know a subject ourselves, or we know where we can find information upon it.
>
> SAMUEL JOHNSON
>
> There are two kinds of books: those that no one reads and those that no one ought to read.
>
> H. L. MENCKEN

TRUTH OR FICTION *Revisited*

Libraries are great equalizers in college education. Shakespeare did not write a separate set of plays for each college library.

On Librarians Let us put in a word for that most misunderstood of professionals: the librarian. Librarians are not simply directed by their genes to

Libraries are the great equalizers. The writings of Ralph Waldo Emerson, Jane Austen, Malcolm X, and Sigmund Freud are identical at major universities, community colleges, and vocational-technical schools. Students can avail themselves of the greatest literature and the latest information through the library at nearly any school.

Making Use of Campus and Community Resources

cast warning glances over bifocals and "shush" students. Librarians are highly trained information scientists who classify, store, and retrieve knowledge. *When in doubt, ask a librarian.* Librarians are pleased to provide maps of their libraries, lists of resources, and directions for using equipment.

Now, let us walk you through a number of features of libraries.

The Card Catalogue The card catalogue is where to begin most types of research. Materials are arranged according to author, title, and subject. When you look up information, use the name of the subject, the first word of the title of the work,* or the last name of the author. After each group of subject cards, you may find a *see also* card. *See also* cards refer you to information on related subjects.

Every library book is assigned a unique number—referred to as a *call number*—that indicates its placement on the shelves. Two systems for assigning call numbers and placing books are used in this country: the Dewey Decimal System, in which call numbers begin with numbers; and the Library of Congress system, in which call numbers begin with letters.

The Dewey Decimal System arranges books according to the following scheme:

> Books are not absolutely dead things, but do contain a potency of life in them to be as active as that soul was whose progeny they are; nay they do preserve as in a vial the . . . living intellect that bred them. . . . A good book is the precious lifeblood of a master spirit, embalmed and treasured up on purpose to a life beyond life.
>
> JOHN MILTON,
> *Areopagitica*

000	General works—books about books, magazines, newspapers	500	Natural sciences—biology, chemistry, physics
100	Philosophy and psychology	600	Applied arts and sciences—agriculture, business, engineering, medicine
200	Religion		
300	Social sciences—economics, sociology	700	Arts and recreation
		800	Literature—plays, poetry, speeches
400	Language—dictionaries, grammar, linguistics	900	History—biography, geography, travel

The categories are subdivided, as in the following examples from the 600s:

610 Medicine
620 Engineering
630 Agriculture

The Library of Congress system organizes information according to the letters of the alphabet, which allows for 26 rather than 10 major categories. The major categories are as follow:

A	General works	M	Music
B	Religion and philosophy	N	Fine arts
C	History and related sciences (genealogy, numismatics)	P	Language and literature
		Q	Natural sciences (including mathematics)
D	World and old world history		
E-F	American history	S	Agriculture
G	Geography and anthropology	T	Technology (engineering, manufacturing)
H	Social sciences		
J	Political science	U	Military science
K	Law	V	Naval science
L	Education	X	Bibliography and library science

*Disregard articles, however: *a, an, the.*

Open and Closed Stack Systems Libraries have either "open stack" or "closed stack" systems. If the stacks are open, you search for the book yourself. Open stacks allow you to peruse neighboring books, which are usually on the same or related topics. If the stacks are closed, you must write the call number on a slip of paper and hand it to a clerk, who then gets the book for you. But you can't look through the shelves by yourself (yuck).

Reference Materials Libraries have reference sections with books that offer answers to specific questions, such as, "Who was Polonius?" "What are the average daytime and nighttime temperatures in San Diego and El Paso during the month of February?" "What is the zip code of Glendale, California?" "What do the computer terms *RAM* and *megabyte* mean?"* and "Where does this Shakespearean quote come from: 'Age cannot wither her, nor custom stale her infinite variety' "?†

Reference books include

almanacs
atlases
biographical materials
dictionaries (many varieties)
directories
encyclopedias
handbooks
manuals
thesauruses
yearbooks

Reference materials cannot be taken out of the library. A reference librarian can help you find what you're looking for.

In addition to general dictionaries, like *Webster's*, you'll find specialized legal and medical dictionaries, foreign-language dictionaries, and dictionaries of quotations. The last permit you to find adages and quotes from literature by looking up a key word in the string of words. In our *Oxford Dictionary of Quotations*, the line from Shakespeare's *Antony and Cleopatra* was indexed according to each of the italicized words: "*Age* cannot *wither* her, nor *custom stale* her *infinite variety*." So you can usually retrieve quotes if you recall just one part of them.

Biographical information is found in *Webster's Biographical Dictionary*, *Who's Who* volumes, and related references.

Periodicals Periodicals are works such as newspapers, magazines, scholarly journals, and annual editions, that are issued at regular intervals. They usually contain the latest information. If you want to know what's happening *now* with the greenhouse effect or in Afghanistan politics, check out the articles in a periodical. Use a book on the subject for background, not for the latest scoop.

**RAM stands for "random access memory." Information "in" RAM can be processed by the computer. A *megabyte* is a million bits of information (mega = million, and byte = piece of information). Similarly, a *kilobyte* is a thousand pieces of information.
† Act II, scene ii, *Anthony and Cleopatra*. Have another few lines:
Age cannot wither her, nor custom stale
Her infinite variety; other women cloy
The appetites they feed, but she makes hungry
Where most she satisfies; . . .
Put another way: You don't check your watch when you're with Cleopatra.

Periodicals are frequently collected and bound into yearly volumes that are placed in the stacks. Current issues, however, are usually displayed separately. A number of indexes or guides will help you locate articles in periodicals in the same way that the card catalogue helps you find books. These include:

Reader's Guide to Periodical Literature (More than 160 popular magazines—no technical journals)

Access: The Supplementary Index to Periodicals (Includes additional popular magazines, such as *Glamour, Playboy,* and the most widely read periodical of all—*TV Guide*)

Applied Science and Technology Index

Art Index

Business Periodicals Index

*Chemical Abstracts**

Child Development Abstracts and Bibliography

Consumer's Index to Product Evaluation and Information Sources (Want to know which cars have the best repair records? Check it out.)

Education Abstracts

Education Index

Humanities Index

Monthly Index of the U.S. Government Printing Office (largest publisher in the world!)

New York Times Index (Articles from the newspaper)

Psychological Abstracts

Public Affairs Information Service Bulletin

Reserve Materials Professors frequently place various materials (e.g., books, periodicals, and photocopies of articles) on reserve for their students. Reserved materials may have to remain in the library or can be checked out only for short periods of time.

If you don't find what you're looking for in the college library, check out the library or libraries in the community surrounding the college.

Registrar The registrar's office is usually in the main administration building. It maintains records, sends transcripts, and handles grade changes. Call them to find out how to add or drop courses, how to change majors, or how to transfer credits.

Tutoring Tutoring can usually be arranged through academic departments or through special tutoring centers. The best way to make use of tutoring services is to arrange for a series of regularly scheduled appointments concerning difficult subjects. If you're having occasional problems in a course, it might be more efficient—and preferred by tutoring center personnel—for you to see the professor during office hours.

Ask your composition instructor where you can go to get help with the mechanics (punctuation, spelling, grammar, etc.) of your papers. Proofreading is sometimes available at no expense. But note that directors of tutoring offices sometimes complain that too many students like to drop papers off for proofreading and corrections before they hand them in, but not to work with tutors throughout the course of writing assignments.

* An abstract is a summary, or condensed version, of an article. Abstracts are intended to give you the information you need to determine whether or not it is worthwhile to locate and read the full-length article. Many researchers take the shortcut of citing abstracts in their papers rather than reading the articles. Abstracts, however, are incomplete and occasionally misleading.

Sometimes you will also find members of the community advertising their availability as tutors in the college newspaper. That's our next topic—college information services.

College Information Resources

Writers once began their essays with an *apologia*—an apology for presuming to intrude upon the leisure time of the gentle reader. Let us begin this section with an apology to librarians, who label their field *information science*. We discussed libraries as academic services. In this section, let us consider the sort of information you would put into the "What's happening?" category.

Campus Life Office Campus life offices are full of experts on what's happening. These offices also go by the monikers of Division of Student Life or Office of the Dean of Student Affairs, and they are usually located in the student center. Campus life offices can provide information about student organizations—such as fraternities, sororities, service clubs, veteran's organizations, religious groups, sports clubs, environmental groups, political groups, and student government.

Becoming involved in political and social issues is part of campus life. The nearby questionnaire on political and social attitudes will offer you some information as to where you stand on certain issues in relation to your peers.

Questionnaire
Survey of Political and Social Attitudes

Once on campus, many students become involved in political, social, and religious activities involving a wide variety of issues. Campus life offices list organizations ranging from gay and lesbian student groups to Young Americans for Freedom, Save the Whales, the Maranathas, Hillel, and the Newman Club.

Indicate your own attitudes on the following political and social issues by checking the Yes column if you agree with the statement and the No column if you disagree. Then refer to the key at the end of the chapter to compare your responses to a national survey of undergraduates.

		Yes	No
1.	More effort should be made to improve relations between the United States and the Soviet Union.	___	___
2.	Nuclear disarmament should be given high priority by our government.	___	___
3.	A woman should have the freedom to choose whether or not to have an abortion.	___	___
4.	I would support stronger environmental legislation even at the expense of economic growth.	___	___
5.	Laws should be enacted to control handguns.	___	___
6.	The United States is spending too much on national defense.	___	___
7.	Current unrest in Central America is caused by internal poverty and injustice rather than external political interaction.	___	___
8.	Our leaders are doing all they can to prevent nuclear war.	___	___
9.	Capital punishment should be abolished.	___	___

Catalogue The college catalogue has a useful campus map and lists campus offices and facilities. It lists these facilities' locations and telephone numbers. Use the catalogue to fill in some answers to the "What-Do-You-Do-Now?" exercise at the end of the chapter. Catalogues also inform you as to what courses are required for each major and list the order in which they are usually taken. (Don't sign up for a course unless you've taken the prerequisites! They may let you in, and then you're in trouble!) Many catalogues also contain interesting information about the faculty members—their ranks and department positions, where they got their degrees, when they got them, and how long they've been on campus.

College Newspaper Student organizations publish campus newspapers that are filled with articles on campus personages, campus activities, and campus political issues. These newspapers also contain advertisements by people who type papers and doctoral dissertations; advertisements by theaters and pizza restaurants (who deliver!); help-wanted ads (especially for part-time workers); rides available and riders who're looking for rides home, to resort areas, and so on; special vacation travel packages (spring vacation in Fort Lauderdale or the Bahamas, anyone?); and enjoyable personal ads. Check out the newspaper to find out what's hot and what's not.

Course List Prior to each term, a list of courses is printed up showing who is teaching what and when. These handouts usually also contain a few blank schedule sheets that are intended to help you create a reasonable schedule through trial and error. We usually underwent many trials in creating our schedules and also made countless errors.

You'll notice that some courses are scheduled to be taught by "Staff." Professor Staff is well versed in all the arts and sciences and is as accomplished a teacher as Anonymous is as an author. (Contact the department office for the most up-to-date information on who is teaching.)

Student organizations at some colleges also publish evaluations of the professors, which cover items like knowledge of subject matter, organization of lessons, openness to expression of student points of view, and fairness as a grader. Although we support freedom of speech and freedom of the press, few publications make us shudder as much.

Housing Office Housing offices usually help students find dormitory space and also list apartments and houses for rent in the community. To get their property listed in the housing office, landlords usually have to show that the property is sanitary, safe (that is, that it is unlikely to fall down or burn down while you're living there), and competitively priced. Because the housing office does some screening, you may be better off going through that office than through the local paper.

Since you are taking this course, you have probably already made housing arrangements for the current academic year. Here are some hints for the next few years:

1. Ask if you can rent for the academic year only. You may have to pay for the summer, especially if you want to stay for more than one year.
2. If you're going in with roommates and must sign a lease, see if you can have each roommate sign a separate lease with the landlord. In that way, you're not responsible for paying full rent if your roommate moves out in the middle of the term.
3. If you have to sign a lease as a group, have all roommates agree before signing that they have to pay rent until they're replaced if they leave.
4. To avert resentments, the roommate with the biggest bedroom (or the best view) should probably pay a bit more than an even share.

Equality is wonderful, but as George Orwell noted in *Animal Farm,* some folks have a "more equal" share than others.

5. A final word: Look as early as you can. The best places are snapped up quickly.

Preprofessional Advisors Colleges assign departments or individuals to serve as preprofessional advisors. Preprofessional advisors can inform you as to what courses you need to take to get into postgraduate programs in, say, law, medicine, or business. If you are at a 2-year school, you may want to know what courses you should take in order to transfer into a preprofessional program at a 4-year school later on. If you want to explore the possibility of majoring in, or pursuing graduate study in, an academic discipline such as mathematics, history, or psychology, ask the department chairperson or a department professor for information.

Also check the college bookstore for books on preparing for various professions and for the entrance examinations for graduate school (such as the Graduate Record Exam) and professional schools (for example, the Medical College Admissions Test or the Law School Aptitude Test). It is never too early to become aware of the types of subjects covered on these examinations.

Do test-preparation books do any good? Of course! At the very least, they alert you to the formats of the tests, the areas you need to study, and the pressures you're likely to encounter during the tests. Practice tests also make the real thing seem very familiar by the time you take it. And the competition (your fellow students who want admission) will be availing themselves of these sources of information. Even if the test-preparation guides do not provide you with the answers to specific questions, they help you become more "test-wise" by suggesting broad strategies for approaching the tests. And, like chicken soup, they usually don't hurt (except for causing a slight pinching sensation in the pocketbook).

TRUTH OR FICTION *Revisited*

Test-preparation guides are of decided help in preparing for entrance exams for graduate schools (e.g., the Graduate Record Exam) and professional schools (e.g., the Medical College Admissions Test or the Law School Aptitude Test).

And do test-preparation *courses* do any good? Pretend that we repeated the last six lines of the preceding paragraph.

Professors! Many students overlook one of the most obvious sources of information on campus—their professors. Professors are good for more than teaching. (Ask their spouses.)* For example, try asking your freshman composition instructor if word processing is for you. Ask your music teacher for information about community cultural events. Drop by the office (during office hours) and involve your professors in conversation. Some professors are willing to talk only about matters related to their courses, but others are more than happy to share their knowledge and opinions with you on subjects ranging from real estate to what is reality. Informal contacts with professors can be as educational as—or more educational than—what you learn in the classroom.

Student Handbook Student handbooks are sources of many kinds of information. They usually inform you of college policies about absences, "incom-

---

* On second thought, don't.

Making Use of Campus and Community Resources 35

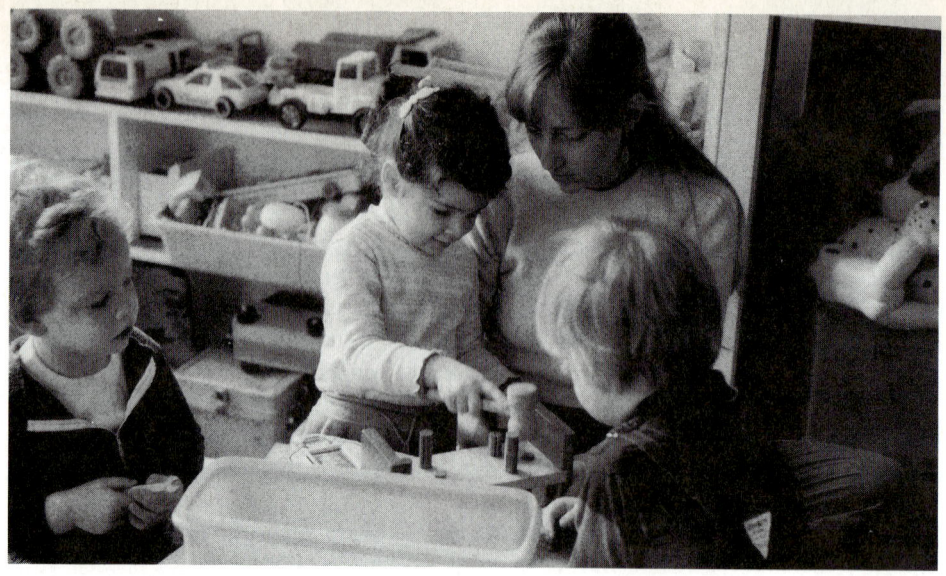

Child-care facilities are available on many campuses for student and faculty use.

pletes," registration, and dormitory rules and regulations. Leaf through one.

Professional Services

Professional services include child-care facilities, counselors and psychologists, financial aid specialists, health professionals, lawyers, and job-placement personnel. These are by and large the professional supports that do not teach but make it possible for you to stay in college and help you plan what you'll be doing after college.

Child Care Child-care facilities are available on many campuses for student and faculty use. Since campus child-care centers usually double as educational facilities for students who plan to work with children, the cost is usually minimal. The centers are usually staffed by one or two experienced, professional child-care workers and any number of education, home economics, family studies, or child psychology students who are in internships, work-study programs, and the like.

These centers are usually set up for regular daytime care that is scheduled in advance. If you need child care for an evening class or while you are carrying out episodic chores, however, you can try dropping by and asking the students working at the centers whether or not they can watch your child (on their own time) to meet your special needs. Or put a notice up on some bulletin boards, especially the boards in the education and psychology departments.

Counseling and Testing Centers (Dean's Offices or Psychological Services) Counseling and testing centers usually offer academic and personal counseling at little or no cost. When personal problems are too deep or persistent for the center to handle, students are referred to appropriate community agencies. Counseling center services tend to include the following:

1. *Psychological Testing and Counseling* Personal, confidential testing and counseling may be conducted on an individual or group basis. The purpose is to evaluate and help students resolve problems that interfere with academic functioning. Sessions may focus on ways of coping with anxiety or depression, resolving personal conflicts, or improving relationships with family members or friends.

2. *Career Testing and Counseling* Tests such as the Strong/Campbell Interest Inventory and the Kuder scales are available to help students identify career interests. Other tests are available to assess aptitudes (specific abilities) and general intelligence. Counseling helps students fit their personal qualities to the requirements of various occupations.
3. *Workshops* Counseling and testing centers tend to offer workshops on a wide range of topics. Coping with test anxiety and overcoming shyness (e.g., by assertiveness training) are always hot topics on campus.
4. *Hotlines* Phone numbers are made available for students who are in crisis (or whose friends are in crisis). Call them if you learn that someone is considering suicide or has overdosed on a drug.
5. *Training Programs* Counseling centers frequently serve as on-campus training sites for graduate psychology and counseling students. Undergraduates who are interested in helping other students may receive training in peer counseling.

Financial Aid Office Financial aid offices have information about scholarships, work-study programs, and other ways of financing your education. Minority students may also check for Educational Opportunity funds or offices. (There's more—much more—on finding money in Chapter 4.)

Health Services Colleges vary a great deal in the health services they offer. Some community colleges, attended mainly by commuters, have little more than a nurse's office. The assumption is that since you're living at home, you can continue to rely on the community health services you have been using all along. Many residential colleges and universities have comprehensive health centers or health clinics, however. Such centers are usually staffed by full-time nurses and part-time physicians and offer services such as the following:

1. Diagnosis and treatment of minor health problems at little or no cost
2. Inpatient care (that is, sleeping in)
3. Birth-control information and services
4. Information about sexually transmitted diseases, including counseling, pamphlets, and more detailed written materials
5. Referral to area clinics and hospitals for diagnosis and treatment of medical problems they are not equipped to handle

Campus health centers are usually staffed by full-time nurses and part-time physicians and offer services such as diagnosis and treatment of minor health problems, inpatient care, birth-control information and services, information about sexually transmitted diseases, and referral to area clinics and hospitals for diagnosis and treatment of medical problems they are not equipped to handle.

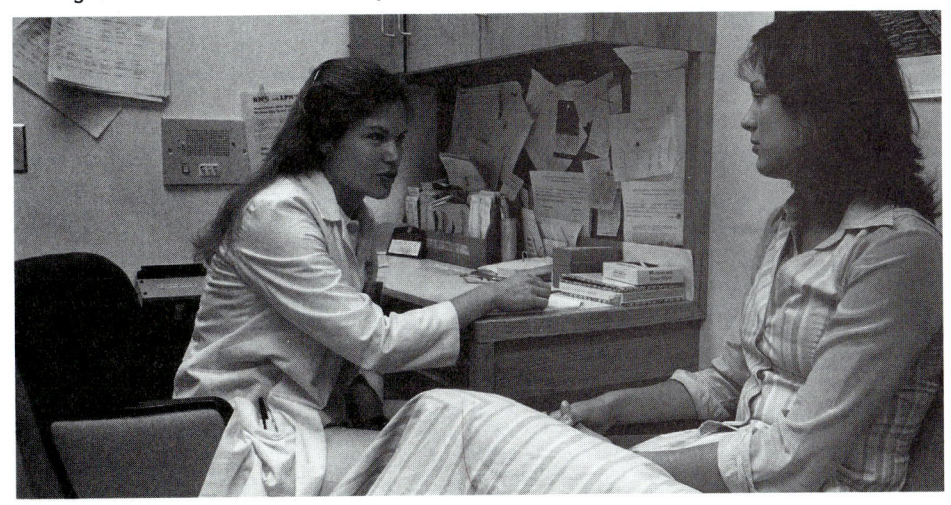

If your health concern doesn't seem to fit into any of these categories, you can drop by the health center anyway and find out what you can do about it.

Legal Services Many colleges have legal offices in which students can receive legal advice at little or no cost. Colleges that do not have attorneys on campus may refer students to local attorneys and absorb the cost of at least the initial consultation. Call the campus switchboard for information, check at the campus life office, or check with the office of the dean for student affairs. (Or call home!)

Placement Offices Placement means job placement. Career services or placement offices usually offer services such as the following:

1. Career counseling (check also with the counseling and testing center)
2. Advice about cooperative education—such as working one semester, attending school the next
3. A career library—job descriptions; salaries; traits and skills of those who succeed
4. Advice concerning preparation for graduate and professional schools
5. Placement counseling—how to find a part-time job or, upon graduation, an initial professional position
6. Notices of available part- and full-time jobs
7. On-campus interview programs and recruitment—such as scheduling interviews with representatives of businesses, government agencies, and the armed services
8. Notifying potential employers of your availability
9. Continuing placement services for alumni
10. Collecting and sending letters of reference from professors and others
11. Career-development workshops on topics such as organizing a job search, résumé writing, techniques of interviewing for a job

Let us give you a little sales pitch before leaving this section. If you feel strongly drawn to the types of people who staff the professional support offices and centers found in colleges, you may want to consider a career in one of those offices yourself. Some people—like your authors—were, in effect, never able to leave college and are much happier for it!

Recreational and Cultural Services

There is also variety in the recreational and cultural services offered by colleges. Many residential colleges offer an array of activities that can occupy you all day long. Some community colleges also offer most of the following kinds of activities.

Athletic Facilities (Not for Jocks Only!) Campuses may have athletic facilities such as aquatic centers (swimming pools), basketball courts, fitness centers (with exercise cycles, weight-training equipment, etc.), golf (if there's no course on campus, ask about student access to community facilities), lockers, gymnasiums, playing fields (e.g., baseball, field hockey, football, lacrosse, soccer), racquetball courts, saunas, showers, tennis courts, and tracks (outdoor and indoor). Roads that circle the periphery of campuses or campus lakes make excellent courses for jogging and long-distance running. These facilities are usually intended to promote leisure-oriented recreational activities (individual and group) as well as intercollegiate competition.

Many colleges have excellent art galleries, with both permanent collections and visiting exhibitions.

Ninety-three percent of students do not participate in intercollegiate athletics, and 70 percent do not participate in intramural sports.[3] If you're among these majorities, you can still use campus facilities to promote cardiovascular fitness, control weight, and unwind from academic stress (see Chapter 11). You may have to schedule ahead (sign up) to use facilities like racquetball courts and tennis courts. You may also be able to join aerobics classes or athletic workshops you'll see advertised from time to time. Why not use the college years to explore various physical activities and develop some exercise habits and skills that might serve you for a lifetime?

Campus Centers Campus Centers (also called *student centers*) contain facilities such as dining halls, bookstores (try to find out what books your professors are assigning and pick them up *before* the rush that occurs once classes begin!), study lounges, recreation areas (with billiards, video games, etc.). Other facilities sometimes found include branches of local banks, post offices, hair cutters (unisex), bulletin boards (check them out!) and service clubs.

Cultural Facilities Many campuses offer a surprisingly diversified array of cultural facilities and events. A few colleges and universities have remarkable museums, which, sad to say, are sometimes visited more extensively by local residents and tourists than students. Many colleges have excellent art galleries, with both permanent collections (which spend too much time locked away in storage) and visiting exhibitions. If you're an art student, ask the gallery director what's in the permanent collection and whether you can arrange to have a look. There are usually unexpected treasures in the storage bins.

Most colleges and universities also put on plays, bring in musical artists and films, and arrange for speakers to visit. Most events are scheduled well ahead of time, and you can usually pick up calendars for them.

Music Practice Rooms Music practice rooms are usually available for nonmusic students as well as music students. Stop by the music department and ask how to go about scheduling. Also ask which piano you can use, and when.

Religious Services

Residential colleges and universities have facilities that enable students to practice their religions and obtain advice from pastoral counselors.

Chapels These are serene spots on campus that are usually staffed by religious personnel with special interest and experience in helping college students. Go there to meditate, to try to put your values in order, or to talk things over with a chaplain. Many alumni return to their college chapels to get married.

Religious Organizations Most campuses have religious organizations that arrange for social and religious activities for students of various denominations. The Ecumenical Campus Ministries are sponsored by mainstream Protestant denominations. The Newman Club serves Catholic students, and Hillel House serves Jewish students. Evangelical groups like the Campus Crusade, the Maranathas, and the Navigators are also found on many campuses.

IN YOUR OWN WRITE

Next we'll be talking about campus security personnel. Before doing so, however, why not list some of the circumstances in which you think you would call on campus security.

_____
_____
_____
_____
_____
_____
_____

Security (Campus Police)

Security personnel patrol the campus, on the lookout for people who do not belong. They police parking lots so that there will be room for people who have a right to use them. In emergencies (e.g., fire, accident), they help maintain order and seek outside help (firefighters, paramedics, ambulances, community police), as needed. In addition to the usual functions, call campus security if

> You've locked your keys inside your car.
> You're afraid to walk across a dark parking lot at night.
> Someone's threatening suicide and you don't know what else to do.

TRUTH OR FICTION *Revisited*

On most campuses you can call the campus security office for an escort if you're afraid to walk alone across a section of campus at night.

USING COMMUNITY RESOURCES

Whether you attend college in Greenville, North Carolina, or Boston, Massachusetts, one of the more stimulating aspects of going away to college is learning about the resources in the community surrounding the college. In Greenville, home of East Carolina State University, the campus may have more facilities of interest than the town. In Boston, the opposite would hold true. But in each case, the campus and community resources complement each other, allowing students to enjoy well-rounded academic, social, and cultural lives. In each case, you—the student—have some exciting hunting cut out for you.

IN YOUR OWN WRITE

Before reading about the kinds of resources you will find in the community around your college, write about some of your initial impressions of that community. For example, is it a large city or a small town? Does it seem intimidating? Inconsequential? What kind of impacts do the college and community seem to have on one another?

_____
_____
_____
_____
_____
_____
_____
_____
_____

As you explore your community, be on the lookout for resources such as the following.

Community Service Agencies

Community agencies offer services that help people, including students, get through the day. These range from day-care centers and family agencies to the protective services provided by firefighters and police officers.

Day-Care Centers Caregivers at day-care centers watch children during working hours. Their days usually begin early enough for parents to commute (7:30 A.M., or so) and run late enough for parents to return from work (6:30 P.M. or so).

Family Agencies and Guidance Centers These centers provide counseling for parents and children undergoing adjustment problems. Some agencies are affiliated with religious denominations (e.g., Jewish Family Services). Others receive support from the city, county, or state.

Family-Planning Clinics Family-planning clinics offer birth-control information and devices, frequently at low cost. They usually also offer screening for gynecological problems. Try looking up *Planned Parenthood*. (Many

WHAT DO YOU DO NOW?
Selecting a Day-Care Center

More students than ever before are returning to college after starting families, and in many cases, they are finding that reliable day care is a ponderous chore. In one survey, 56 percent of parents reported having difficulty in arranging for high-quality day care; 54 percent complained that the costs of day care were excessive; and 51 percent had problems with the location and hours of their day-care centers.[4] Some parents are so burdened by the task of finding caretakers for their children that they quit or contemplate quitting college.

Choosing a day-care center can be overwhelming. Licensing standards for day-care centers vary from place to place, so a license may not guarantee adequate care. To help make a successful choice, parents can consider factors like the following:

1. Is the center licensed? By whom? What standards must be met to acquire a license in your locale?
2. What is the ratio of children to caregivers? Everything else being equal, caregivers can do a better job when there are fewer children in their charge.
3. What are the qualifications of the center's caregivers? Day-care workers are often poorly paid, and financial frustrations lead many of the best to look for other kinds of work.[5] Children fare better when their caregivers have specific training in child development.[6] Years of experience and academic degrees are less crucial.
4. How safe is the environment? Do swings and toys appear to be in good condition? Are dangerous objects out of reach? Would strangers have a difficult time breaking in?
5. What is served for meals and snacks? Is it appetizing and nutritious? Will *your child* eat it?
6. Which workers would be responsible for your child? What are their backgrounds? How do they relate to children? Why not watch them at work for a while?
7. What toys, games, books, and other educational materials are provided?
8. What facilities are available to foster your child's physical development? How well supervised are the children when they use tricycles and swings?
9. Are the center's hours convenient for your schedule?
10. Is the center's location convenient?
11. Are you comfortable with the center's overall "feel"?
12. Can you afford it?

There is much to weigh. Perhaps no day-care center will score 100 on every consideration, but some are more critical than others. This list should help students center on their chief concerns.

---

campus health centers offer similar services at no charge.) Check your college catalogue or ask a sophomore.

Fire Stations It's good to know where they are, especially if you live off campus. Write down the phone number. If you live on campus, however, you'll probably use the alarm in the dormitory or call the campus security office in case of fire.

Hotlines Hotlines offer counseling for people involved in crises concerning child abuse, drugs, rape, suicide, and so on. Call if a friend or roommate is going through a crisis. You don't have to be the victim to make good use of a hotline.

TRUTH OR FICTION Revisited

Most communities do have hotlines. They are staffed by personnel who are trained to help callers deal with various kinds of crises.

Humane Societies   Humane societies such as the ASPCA offer advice about stray or injured animals. They're also good places to find a healthy, inexpensive pet. (Some dogs "adopt" dormitories or campus centers. An animal with a collar is rarely a stray, however, even if it spends more time around your dormitory than on its home ground.)

Legal Aid Society   Legal aid societies offer low-cost legal advice for poor people and students. (Some colleges have legal counseling available at little or no cost right on campus.)

Police   Know where the police are and how to reach them in a hurry, especially if you live off campus. If you live on campus, however, call the campus security office about your police-related concerns. Campus security will call in the local police, if appropriate.

Community Information Resources

Communities, like campuses, have many ways of informing residents about activities, dangers, sales, and so on. One is the local radio station. Others include the chamber of commerce and local newspapers.

Chamber of Commerce   Chambers of commerce are not just for businesspeople. They offer information about points of interest, such as cultural facilities, zoos, public transportation (they can tell you how to get schedules!) and the like.

Newspapers   In addition to keeping you up on current events, local newspapers carry listings for theaters, advertisements for restaurants, information about local sporting events, advertisements by people who will babysit or type papers, and help-wanted advertisements. Watch for new exhibitions at art galleries and museums, concerts in the parks, plays put on by local theater groups, and the like.

Environmental Organizations

All people have needs that must be met if they are to remain physically and psychologically healthy. Environmental conditions such as temperature and population density affect their abilities to meet their needs. Since the 1960s, however, we have grown increasingly aware of the ways in which people also influence the environment. We have pushed back the forests and we have driven many species to extinction. In the second half of the century, our impact has mushroomed, as attested to by the debates over the greenhouse effect, the diminution of the ozone layer, oil spills, and acid rain. Most people also have an aesthetic interest in the environment and appreciate the remaining bastions of wilderness. As student activists have been asserting, protecting the environment is tantamount to protecting ourselves—for it is within the environment that humankind will continue to flourish or eventually fade away.

Students and environmental causes have been going together something like lovers and marriage. Seventy-six percent of college students would support strong environmental controls, even if it meant economic sacrifice.[7]

> I think having land and not ruining it is the most beautiful art that anybody could ever want to own.
>
> ANDY WARHOL

Students and environmental causes go together like lovers and marriage. Environmental organizations have chapters either on campus or within easy reach of most campuses.

TRUTH OR FICTION Revisited

The *great* majority of college students (three out of four) support stronger environmental legislation, even if it means slowing down economic growth.

Greenpeace, the Sierra Club, the Wilderness Society, and similar organizations may have local chapters. Check the phone book, the campus life office, or, if you are a residential student, call chapters in your home town or city for information. In addition to serving their stated environmental functions, these organizations are excellent places to meet other people who are committed to making the world a safer, cleaner place.

Health Facilities

Your college will have some health facilities, and health personnel can direct you to community health services, as needed. But here are some things to check out now.

Community Mental Health Center

> Canst thou not minister to a mind diseas'd,
> Pluck out from the memory a rooted sorrow,
> Raze out the written troubles of the brain,
> And with some sweet oblivious antidote
> Cleanse the stuff'd bosom of that perilous stuff
> Which weighs upon the heart?
>
> SHAKESPEARE, *Macbeth*

In these lines, Macbeth asks whether a physician can help his troubled wife, Lady Macbeth, who is suffering from emotional rather than physical problems. Community mental health centers (CMHCs) offer diagnosis and treatment of emotional problems and psychological disorders. Individual and group therapy are usually available. If your campus does not offer personal counseling, don't be surprised to find several students in CMHC groups. Fees are on sliding scales—you pay what you can afford. If you can't pay at all, you won't have to.

Dentists If you are a residential student, you can have your routine cleanings and checkups taken care of at home during vacations. However, it's a good idea to have a couple of local dentists recommended to you in case of a toothache, a chipped tooth, and the like.

Emergency Rooms General hospitals have emergency rooms where you can show up (or bring a friend) without appointment 24 hours a day in case of injury or sudden illness. It helps to be prepared to list your allergies (or those of your friend) and to be able to produce a card that indicates what medical coverage you have. In fact, many people complain that emergency rooms have refused to treat them because they could not produce evidence of coverage! So we recommend that you carry a medical coverage identification card (or student identification card if that will gain admission to campus facilities) at all times!

Unless your own campus has a 24-hour emergency medical facility, you should know where the nearest off-campus emergency room is. Also know the campus security or campus police telephone number; they can usually get you to the emergency room.

Public Transportation

Buses, subways, trams, and the like usually offer low-cost transportation in and around town. In Chapter 4, we'll talk about whether or not it is a good idea to have a car. In some states, such as California, people say that you cannot survive without a car. In many locales, a car is more optional. Your ultimate decision should be based, in part, on knowledge of the public transportation that is available in your college community.

Social and Religious Organizations

College communities also offer a variety of social and religious organizations, such as places of worship and "Y's."

Churches and Synagogues Churches and synagogues offer cultural and social programs as well as places of worship. Churches and synagogues will also direct you to community organizations for people of various ethnic backgrounds.

YMCA, YWCA, YMHA These are the acronyms for Young Men's Christian Association, Young Women's Christian Association, and Young Men's Hebrew Association. These organizations usually have excellent exercise facilities, including pools, exercise cycles, weight training, and the like. Classes are usually available in dancing, exercise and sports, and arts and crafts. The "Y's" are open to everyone—not just to people who share the religious orientation in the title. The same goes for gender; men are usually welcome at women's organizations, and vice versa. So find the area facility that has the services you want and feel free to attend, regardless of your religious preference or gender.

"Y" not fill in the following "What-Do-You-Do-Now?" exercise? It's a way of applying what we have discussed in this chapter to the resources of your own college and the surrounding community. It'll help you find the best of the best and cope with the worst of the worst. Then, in good time, turn to the next chapter, whose timely topic is . . . time.

WHAT DO YOU DO NOW?
What Do You When . . . ?

Now that we've considered the resources you'll find on campus and in the community, let's plan what to do in various situations. This is an open-book (and "open-town") exercise. Check your college catalogue for answers. Look through the student handbook. Check the local phone book, especially the Yellow Pages. Call the information operator. Go for a walk in town.

In many cases, there is more than one right answer. For example, if you want to explore whether to get a typewriter or personal computer, you could check at the computer center, with a writing or math instructor (or both), with the college tutorial service, with students who have typewriters and computers, with a student computer club or organization, even with a local computer store. Each source will provide you with a different perspective. By being persistent, you can soon gather enough information to make a reasonable decision.

Problem	Name of Appropriate Campus or Community Facility or Resource	Phone Number (if Applicable)
1. What can you do if you're not sure where your career interests and aptitudes lie?		
2. What can you do when you've locked yourself out of your dorm room?		
3. How can you find help in proofreading a term paper?		
4. What can you do when you feel that you've "lost it"— that you're short tempered with everybody and don't know what you're doing anymore?		
5. How can you get information about a part-time job?		
6. What do you do when you need a copy of your transcript sent out?		
7. What can you do if you want to learn how to do word processing?		
8. How can you find out how you can participate in school government?		
9. How can you find a ride home?		
10. How can you get information about "safe sex"?		
11. What do you do when you're afraid you may be failing a course and want to find out what you can do about it?		

12. What can you do when everything seems to have lost its meaning?

13. What do you do if you have a toothache?

(Would calling home help?)

14. What do you do if you have an unbelievably humongous toothache?

15. What do you do if you are undergoing withdrawal from pizza but your car broke down?

16. What can you do if you believe that an employer or campus official is discriminating against you because of your gender or race?

17. What do you do if you have test anxiety?

(And read Chapter 7.)

18. What do you do if you're wondering whether the library carries a particular journal?

19. Where do you go if you need to get slacks or a skirt dry cleaned?

20. What can you do if your car's battery suffers from cardiac arrest?

21. What's a good place to get breakfast on a Saturday or Sunday morning?

22. What's a good place to go for a snack and coffee at two o'clock in the morning?

23. Whom do you call when your roommate trips, hits her head, and falls unconscious?

24. What can you do if you need a book that's not carried by the college library?

25. What do you do when you need some new underwear?

(Must you *really* call home and have it sent by express mail?)

26. What do you do when you need legal advice?

Making Use of Campus and Community Resources   47

27. What do you do when you want to locate local art galleries and find out what's on exhibit?

28. What do you do when you need a new pair of jeans? (If you need new *genes*, you've come to the wrong book.)

29. How can you get information on the requirements for medical school?

30. What do you do if you want information about how to prepare for the Law School Aptitude Test?

31. How can you get a map of town and a bus schedule?

32. Whom do you call if your car skids in town and smashes into a parked car? (No one is hurt.)

33. Whom do you call if your car skids on the highway and smashes into another car, hurting the driver?

(Dial 911? Dial *0* for operator?)

34. What can you do if you're wondering whether or not you have contracted AIDS?

(And read Chapter 12.) National AIDS Hotline: 1-800-342-2437

35. What do you do if you want information about cocaine?

(And read Chapter 13.) National Cocaine Hotline: 1-800-COCAINE

SUMMING UP

1. What kinds of academic and professional services are offered on your campus? How can you find out what's available?
2. Can you use your college computer center for word processing? Can you get instruction on using computers?
3. Is your college library organized according to the Dewey Decimal System or the Library of Congress system? Can students make use of interlibrary loans? How do you carry out a computer search at your library?
4. Is there a tutorial service at your college? How can you arrange to make use of it?
5. How can you make use of your college's counseling and testing center? (What does the center have for *you*?) The college health services? The placement office?
6. What athletic and recreational facilities are available on campus? How can you arrange to use them?

7. How do you call campus security? The fire department? Police? An ambulance?
8. How can you find out what's going on in the community outside your college?
9. Where is the nearest emergency room? What information must you bring in order to get treated there?
10. Are there any campus or community social or political groups that hold an appeal for you? How can you find out?

Questionnaire Key: Percentage of Students Agreeing with Statements Expressive of Political and Social Attitudes

According to the Carnegie Foundation's National Survey of Undergraduates,[8] the following percentages of students agreed with each statement in the questionnaire:

Statement	Percent Agreeing
1. More effort should be made to improve relations between the United States and the Soviet Union.	93
2. Nuclear disarmament should be given high priority by our government.	76
3. A woman should have the freedom to choose whether or not to have an abortion.	76
4. I would support stronger environmental legislation even at the expense of economic growth.	76
5. Laws should be enacted to control the use of handguns.	72
6. The United States is spending too much money on national defense.	57
7. Current unrest in Central America is caused by internal poverty and injustice rather than external political interaction.	54
8. Our leaders are doing all they can to prevent nuclear war.	52
9. Capital punishment should be abolished.	24

QUEENSBOROUGH COMMUNITY COLLEGE

PERFORMING ARTS
BOX OFFICE 631-6311

PURLIE VICTORIOUS	FEB 8-25
ROSIES CAFE	MAR 3
BAO DAO OF TAIWAN	18
THE QUEENS SYMPHONIC BAND	24
BALLET LOS ANGELES	31
PETER RABBIT	APR 1
QCC ORCHESTRA	21
	28&29
KISMET	MAY 5
QCC CHORUS	11 12
QCC DANCE WORKSHOP	

3

Managing Time

TRUTH OR FICTION?

_____ Half of all college students spend two hours a week *or less* studying in the library.

_____ One third of all college students spend at least seven hours a week watching TV.

_____ Some students study most effectively in the morning, others in the afternoon.

_____ You forget about half of what you learn within half an hour.

_____ All work and no play make Jack and Jill dull students.

_____ You must adhere to all scheduled study periods, or else your self-discipline will fall apart.

_____ Saying "no" or "later" are great ways of managing time.

_____ It's better not to complete an assignment at all than to give it less than your best effort.

Remember," wrote Benjamin Franklin in *Advice to a Young Tradesman*, "that time is money."

Time is more than money. Time is your most valuable commodity. The time that passes from minute to minute, from day to day, from year to year . . . all of it is precious. "Dost thou love life?" asked Franklin in *Poor Richard's Almanac*. "Then do not squander time, for that's the stuff life is made of."

College life brings freedom, as noted in Chapter 1. Freedom, of course, is a double-edged sword. Your can use your freedom to spend time wisely or to squander time. Unless you manage time wisely, freedom may be nothing more than chaos. So it's time to get on with ways of managing time effectively. We expect that you will find this chapter timely.

HOW TO MANAGE TIME

> Time flies.
>
> Popular saying

> My object all sublime
> I shall achieve in time—
>
> SIR WILLIAM GILBERT,
> *The Mikado*

We are not born knowing how to manage time. We learn how to manage time. Learning how to manage time—and ourselves—is one of the unstated tasks of college life. Unstated, but vital.

Managing time means making a reasonable schedule and then sticking to it, except for . . . the legitimate exceptions. What are legitimate exceptions? Some are obvious, like getting sick or getting so wrapped up in library work that you get to dinner late. We can't list all the legitimate exceptions that will occur, but you'll know them when you see them. Watching *Police Academy 15* for the tenth time is not one of them.

IN YOUR OWN WRITE

Before proceeding, note some of the ways in which you squander time. Be honest. You don't make the most of every moment, do you?

_____
_____
_____
_____
_____
_____
_____

> No time like the present.
>
> MARY DE LA RIVIERE MANLEY,
> *The Lost Lover*

Now let's check your notes about squandering time against the facts. Fill out the following What-Do-You-Do-Now? exercise on "Finding Out How You Spend Your Time." Maybe you'll discover that you were too hard on yourself—that you don't waste as much time as you think. Perhaps you will find that you weren't hard enough on yourself. After we have seen how you actually spend your time, we'll go through the basics of making up a schedule.

WHAT DO YOU DO NOW?
Finding Out How You Spend Your Time

The goal of this chapter is to teach you how to spend your time more efficiently. Psychologists have found that when you're trying to help people change their behavior for the better, the best place for them to start is to find out exactly what they're doing now. Making a record of what you do is called recording a *baseline.* As a matter of fact, in one study, psychologists increased the amount of time students spent studying merely by having the students keep a record of where and when they studied![1]

Why does playing detective with yourself have such a remarkable effect? For one thing, if you find that you're squandering your time, coming face to face with the fact may help motivate you to do something about it. For another, the baseline record may suggest ways of marshaling your time. For example, the discovery that you spend 12 hours a week napping and another 12 watching television suggests a couple of "activities" that could be cut down. Then, too, the baseline makes you generally more aware of time. As a result, time becomes less likely to slip through your fingers.

You can create a record of your baseline by using the time chart in Figure 3.1 on page 55. The last months of high school or the first weeks of college are an ideal time to do so. Enter the hours spent in classes, at meals, studying, sleeping, socializing, musing, fantasizing, napping, watching TV, lying by the pool—all of it.

Now do some adding. How much time did you spend:

    In classes? _____
    Studying? _____
    At work? _____
    On chores (family, personal?) _____
    Preparing and eating meals? _____
    Sleeping? _____
    Socializing (friends, family)? _____
    In religious activity? _____
    Watching TV? _____
    Reading for pleasure? _____
    On athletics or exercise? _____
    On other leisure activities? _____
    On transportation (e.g., commuting)? _____
    Other? (_____) _____
    Other? (_____) _____
                               _____
    TOTAL _____

Now total the hours. There are 168 hours in a week, so if your total exceeds 168, you've overestimated here and there. On the other hand, if your total is less than 168, you've "lost" some time.

We're not going to be your judges. (In college, you're your own boss.) But we'll give you some information. (Sneaky?) In Chapter 11, you'll see that normal, healthy students can get by on about six hours of sleep a night, although they prefer to get eight or so. With naps, do you average ten or eleven hours of sleep a day? Are you squandering time?

Now check Table 3.1. It shows how much time a national sample of college students reports devoting to certain activities. How do your estimates compare? If, for example, you spent 11 or more hours watching television, you belong to the top 14 percent of students. We offer our congratulations or our commiserations—whichever you believe are in order.

TABLE 3.1. Number of Hours College Students Spend Each Week in Selected Activities (in percentages).

ACTIVITY	NONE	1–2	3–4	5–6	7–8	9–10	11 OR MORE
Talking informally to other students	3	19	16	13	9	9	31
Watching television	13	22	18	14	11	8	14
Leisure reading	23	35	17	11	6	4	4
Talking to faculty members	26	56	11	4	1	1	1
Studying in the library	27	24	14	9	5	6	15
Attending campus cultural events	46	36	11	4	1	1	1
Participating in organized student activities (other than athletics)	50	26	10	6	3	2	3
Participating in intramural sports	70	16	8	3	1	1	1
Participating in intercollegiate athletics	93	1	*	*	*	1	4

Note: According to the Carnegie Foundation national survey of undergraduates. Reported in Boyer, E. L. (1987). *College: The undergraduate experience in America.* Perennial Library: New York, p. 181.
* Less than one percent

TRUTH OR FICTION *Revisited*

Sad to say, half of all college students spend two hours a week *or less* studying in the library.

Yes, one third of all college students do spend at least seven hours a week watching TV. But we're sure that 90 percent of it is educational television....

So are you spending your time wisely or are you squandering time? How much time slips through your fingers? Are you willing to do something about it? If the answer is yes, keep reading. If not, well, why waste the time?

HOW TO SET UP A SCHEDULE: GENERAL ADVICE

Construct a Clear and Reasonable Schedule

You should be able to live with and feel good about your schedule. Give yourself some time for socializing or just for relaxing in a pretty part of campus.

Pick the Right Times of Day

Schedule classes for the time of day when you are most alert. Our bodies have certain built-in rhythms.[2] There are times during the day when functions like attentiveness are at their peak. Some of us ("morning people") are more productive and animated in the morning; others are at their best in the afternoons. Put your classes, especially your toughest classes, in the slots when you're at your sharpest.

I wake up every morning. I open my eyes and think: here we go again.

ANDY WARHOL

Gather ye rosebuds while ye may,
Old Time is still a-flying:
And this same flower that smiles to-day,
To-morrow will be dying.

ROBERT HERRICK,
"To Virgins, to Make Much of Time"

FIGURE 3.1. A Time Chart for Making a Baseline Record of the Ways in Which You Use Your Time.

Days / Time	Monday	Tuesday	Wednesday	Thursday	Friday	Saturday	Sunday
7:00							
8:00							
9:00							
10:00							
11:00							
12:00							
1:00							
2:00							
3:00							
4:00							
5:00							
6:00							
7:00							
8:00							
9:00							
10:00							
11:00							

Managing Time

TRUTH OR FICTION *Revisited*

Some students do study most effectively in the morning, and others are more efficient in the afternoon. We all have internal rhythms, and we may be at our peaks at different times of the day.

Schedule Enough Time for Studying

One common rule of thumb is that you should study for two hours for every hour of class. That approach works better for some subjects than for others. For example, in an art studio course, you may get all of your work done during class. In a course on the nineteenth-century English novel, you may need to read for five hours for every hour spent in class.

The flip side of this advice should be obvious enough: *Don't schedule several courses with heavy reading loads for the same term!* Not unless you're into masochism.

Schedule Time Between Classes

If possible, schedule some time between classes. This will allow you to preview the text and your notes before classes (10–15 minutes) and review your notes after classes (15–20 minutes). Research on memory shows that we forget about *half* of what we have learned *within a half hour*.[3] By studying course notes right after class, we strengthen our learning and remember more. If we wait until a few days before the exam to pull out our notes, we are trying to rebuild a crumbling edifice.

Schedule classes for the time of day when you are most alert. Our bodies have built-in rhythms. Some of us ("morning people") are more productive and animated in the morning; others are at their best in the afternoons. Put your toughest classes in the slots when you're at your sharpest.

TRUTH OR FICTION *Revisited*

Yes, you do forget about half of what you learn within half an hour. This is why it is worthwhile to review what you have learned soon afterward.

Plan Ahead!

Allow yourself enough time to prepare for examinations. Plan to have assignments completed a day or two ahead of their due dates, so that you have room in your schedule in case a problem causes you to fall behind.

Be Specific

Break big tasks like "work on paper" into concrete, reachable goals. "Work on term paper" doesn't tell you where to begin. Instead, you might break the task down into bits and pieces that you work on, say, twice a week. If you check Chapter 6, you will see that the first few scheduled slots could say something like "Select topic for paper," "Delimit topic," "Check library card catalogue for references." Slots scheduled later on could specify "Outline the paper," "Write an introduction, based on the outline," "Work on the body of the paper," and so forth. You could also specify slots for revising, proofreading, and producing the final draft.

Schedule Time for Mundane Chores

Give yourself time to take care of your personal responsibilities. Cleaning and doing laundry take time, so budget time for them in your schedule.

56 Chapter 3

Be Strategic

Study your difficult subjects during times of day when you are alert and when you are least likely to be disturbed or interrupted.

Give Yourself Some Variety

Yes, variety does appear to add some spice to life. We become more alert and motivated when we are presented with novel stimulation or a change of pace. Apply these maxims to your schedule as follows: Don't study physics all day Monday, literature all day Tuesday, and psychology all day Wednesday. Study each one for a while every day so as to avoid boredom and maintain a lively interest in the subject matter.

Save the Best for Last

Consider scheduling your most enjoyable work last. This will give you something to look forward to.

> The great source of pleasure is variety.
> — SAMUEL JOHNSON

IN YOUR OWN WRITE

Before proceeding, answer this question as best you can: How long can you study? What is your attention span? Use the following lines to explain what happens—how you feel and what you do—when you press beyond this time period.

_____
_____
_____
_____
_____
_____
_____
_____

Be Aware of Your Limits

The "In Your Own Write" exercise highlights the fact that we all have different attention spans. Some of us can work for two hours or more without looking up. Others cannot last for more than 15 minutes without needing a break of some kind. After years of high school, you must have a reasonably accurate impression of the extent of your own attention span.

Try not to be unrealistic by scheduling too many hours of studying in a row. For most students, we would not recommend more than three hours of studying without a break. Also, during those three hours, you will probably profit from a number of brief breaks. We recommend taking a 10-minute break each hour. Get up and stretch. Get a sip of water.

If you've been realistic and you've decided that you probably can't keep your nose to the grindstone as long as you need to in college, don't throw up your hands in despair. Many students have been able to gradually lengthen their study periods by adding a few minutes each day. Intersperse those brief breaks and tell yourself what a wonderful job you're doing!

> I have, all my life long, been lying till noon; yet I tell all young men, and tell them with great sincerity, that nobody who does not rise early will ever do any good.
> — SAMUEL JOHNSON

> Variety's the very spice of life
> That gives it all its flavour.
> — WILLIAM COWPER, *The Task*

"All work and no play" makes for a miserable and unproductive college career. Reserve slots for recreational activities, and don't study right through them.

"The Play's the Thing"

Remember that "all work and no play" makes for a miserable and unproductive college career. People who manage to fit some fun into their work tend to be more motivated and creative and more capable of meeting the challenges that lie ahead.[4] Reserve slots for recreational activities. Make sure that you don't study right through them! (Make an occasional exception when you're onto something great, but then reward yourself by having some extra fun later on.)

TRUTH OR FICTION *Revisited*

All study with no breaks is enough to dull and discourage most Jacks and Jills. Breaks should be scheduled every hour. Free time and recreational activities also need to be built into students' schedules.

Pat Yourself on the Back

Reward yourself for achieving your study goals on schedule. For some free goodies, check the Pleasant Events List in Chapter 4.

Be Flexible

Allow yourself some flexibility. After all, your schedule is intended to serve you, not to rule you. You may not be able to change the times that classes meet, but you may (occasionally!) find it worthwhile to cut a class because you're finally making excellent progress on a term paper that's been aging you prematurely. If you've got a part-time job, you have to show up regularly or else you may get fired. But you may be able to postpone a study session to a free period if you have the chance to spend some time with the man or woman of your dreams. It might also make sense to put off the laundry during finals week. Use your judgment and make sure that you're not using "flexibility" as an excuse for indefinitely postponing some of the less pleasant tasks on your schedule.

TRUTH OR FICTION *Revisited*

Actually, rather than stubbornly adhering to a schedule, it helps to be flexible. By being flexible, we take advantage of opportunities that arise and cope with unforeseen problems. The trick is to understand the difference between flexibility and neglect.

> Had we but world enough, and time, . . .
>
> ANDREW MARVELL, "To His Coy Mistress"
>
> So many women, so little time.
>
> Attributed to actor JOHN BARRYMORE, also to TED DANSON, in the film *Three Men and a Baby*

Set Down Priorities and Long-Term Assignments

List your top priorities and your long-term assignments at the top of each week's schedule. The priorities are the least flexible items. If you must do some switching around, these are the things you'll make up fast.

Check syllabi or class notes for long-term dates when papers are due and tests will be given. Note important long-term dates on a monthly calendar, like the one in Figure 3.2. Transfer some of the long-term dates from the calendar to your weekly schedule (Fig. 3.3 on page 61). Having your long-term assignments in front of you prevents you from forgetting about them and encourages you to do something about them on a weekly basis.

Carry Your Schedule with You

Put your schedule in a notebook that you can carry along. A schedule is like a wristwatch: It does no good to have either of them waiting for you in the room.

Scan Your Schedule

Briefly scan your schedule from time to time even when there's nothing that has to be done. These glances will help you track your priorities and keep long-term assignments in mind.

FIGURE 3.2. Monthly Calendar. Students can note important long-term dates on a monthly calendar and transfer them to their weekly schedules.

OCTOBER

Sunday	Monday	Tuesday	Wednesday	Thursday	Friday	Saturday
	1 Math quiz	2	3	4 Complete term paper outline	5 Psychology quiz	6
7	8 Spanish quiz	9 Fresh comp paper due	10 Chris's birthday	11	12	13 Home game
14	15	16	17	18 Complete term paper draft	19 Pick up J. (4:15 pm)	20
21	22 Midterms: Spanish + Math	23 Fresh comp paper due	24 Psychology midterm	25	26	27 Home game
28	29	30	31			

Managing Time

> "The time has come," the Walrus said,
> "To talk of many things:
> Of shoes—and ships—and sealing wax—
> Of cabbages—and kings—
> And why the sea is boiling hot—
> And whether pigs have wings."
>
> LEWIS CARROLL,
> *Through the Looking-Glass*

HOW TO SET UP A SCHEDULE: THE SPECIFICS

1. Map out a schedule like the one in Figure 3.3. Notice that the days of the week go across the top row, and the hours of the day go down the left column. Start with the hour you get up in the "Time" column. Give yourself enough hours to reach bedtime.

2. Fill in the hours you are in class. If you are piecing together a trial schedule for an upcoming term, try to leave some time between classes to review what you have learned and to preview the material that will be discussed in the next class.

3. Enter all other fixed activities, such as part-time work, dropping off or picking up the kids, meals,* athletic practices, athletic events, and appointments.

4. Enter mealtimes. Be realistic: If your stomach starts grumbling or you get the "shakes" at 11:30 A.M., don't write in lunch at 1:00 P.M. Or at least pencil in an earlier snack (preferably nutritious!†).

5. Put in the times when you plan to get to sleep. Don't be a hero and try to limit yourself to four hours of sleep a night. If you believe that you need more than nine hours, why not talk things over at the college health center?

6. Enter study periods.

7. List the week's priorities in the box at the upper left. Priorities include upcoming exams, important assignments that have to be completed in the near term, and appointments, such as dental cleanings.

8. Note long-term assignments in the box at the upper right. These are things like term papers and big tests that lie a few weeks ahead. The idea is to include some time to work on them each week.

9. Consider allowing yourself a bit of time—perhaps a half hour or so—to unwind before getting to bed. Some students find that there's no point to hopping into the sack with theorems on the brain.

10. Try to allow yourself at least a little free time every day. Don't book yourself solid for many days in a row. You'll find yourself wasting time on the lighter days and dreading the heavier days. Moreover, if a problem prevents you from meeting your work goals on the heavy days, you'll have a hard time playing catch-up.

11. Check items off as you complete them. If an unexpected problem or chore prevents you from studying or carrying out an assignment, pencil time in for it later in the week.

* If they're fixed, that is. If mealtimes are flexible for you, let them go for a while.
† Look, someone's got to act *in loco parentis*, so it might as well be us. Check for dietary hints in Chapter 11.

After keeping a record of how you actually spend time for several weeks, evaluate your use of time and then work up a realistic schedule that will help you accomplish the many things you have to do.

FIGURE 3.3. Trial Schedule.

Priorities for the Week		
Course	*Task*	*Due*

Long-Term Assignments		
Course	*Assignment*	*Due*

Days / Time	**Monday**	**Tuesday**	**Wednesday**	**Thursday**	**Friday**	**Saturday**	**Sunday**
7:00							
8:00							
9:00							
10:00							
11:00							
12:00							
1:00							
2:00							
3:00							
4:00							
5:00							
6:00							
7:00							
8:00							
9:00							
10:00							
11:00							

Sample Schedule

Now that you've considered guidelines for filling out a schedule and have made a schedule for yourself, let's consider the schedule Bernie devised, as shown in Figure 3.4. It has some strengths and some weaknesses.

Write down some of the strengths and weaknesses you find in Bernie's schedule in the spaces provided. Then check some of our thoughts in the key at the end of the chapter.

Strengths of Bernie's Schedule	Weaknesses of Bernie's Schedule

HOW TO HANDLE DISTRACTIONS

The Scottish poet Robert Burns wrote, "The best planned schedules of mice and college students go oft awry."* Despite the creation of a logical schedule and the best of intentions, things have a way of intruding when we are trying to complete assignments and study. First, indicate the types of things you do to prevent people from distracting you from your work. Then check the suggestions offered below.

IN YOUR OWN WRITE

What types of things do you do to prevent friends and other people from distracting you from studying? What works best for you?

---

* All right! We confess that Burns actually wrote
"The best laid schemes o'mice an' men
  Gang aft a-gley."

62 Chapter 3

Figure 3.4. Bernie's Schedule. What strengths do you see in this schedule? What weaknesses?

Time \ Days	Monday	Tuesday	Wednesday	Thursday	Friday	Saturday	Sunday
7:00	Get up and get ready	Get up	Get up and get ready	Get up	Get up and get ready	Get up and get ready	Get up and get ready
8:00	Child Development	Exercise	Child Development	Exercise	Child Development	Study	Study
9:00	Review Break Preview	Freshman Composition	Review Break Preview	Freshman Composition	Review Break Preview	Exercise	Exercise
10:00	College Math		College Math		College Math		
11:00	Spanish	Term Paper	Spanish	Term Paper	Spanish	Free	Free
12:00	Chemistry		Chemistry	Chemistry			Watch Bears vs. Cowboys football game on TV
1:00		Study		Lab	Study	attend football game	
2:00	Study		Study	Chores: Shopping + Laundry, etc.			
3:00					Dentist		Watch Jets vs. Raiders football game on TV
4:00				Free			
5:00							
6:00	Job	Job	Job	Job			Free
7:00					Free (Social Activity)	Free (Social Activity)	
8:00	Free						Study
9:00	Watch 49ers vs. Dolphins football game	Study	Study	Study			
10:00							
11:00		Sleep	Sleep	Sleep			Sleep

Managing Time 63

Placing a "Do Not Disturb!" sign on your door helps discourage people who would otherwise distract you from getting your work done.

Make Arrangements with Roommates

Make arrangements as to what times of the day will be quiet study periods. Use some of the methods described in Chapter 10 to resolve conflicts. For example, negotiate differences, or make exchanges. Try, "I'll stay out of the room from 3:00 to 6:00 on Monday afternoons, if you'll honor a quiet study period from 7:00 to 10:00 on Mondays, Tuesdays, and Thursdays."

If you live at home, try asking your family for quiet time in the house. Tell them specifically what hours you want for yourself. Help give them the resources they need to give you this time. Prepare meals in advance, have frozen pizzas available, or send everybody (but you!) to the fast-food restaurant. If your family knows exactly what you need, they may surprise you by cooperating.

If your family insists upon intruding, you might say something like, "Tell me your preference. Do you want me home for dinner or do you want me to stay on campus? If you want me home, you've got to pretend that I'm not here after dinner till 8:00. I'll put you to bed at eight, but you've got to get ready for bed yourself or else have your father help you. What'll it be?"

Keep the TV Off!

You may think that you can watch TV and work at the same time, but unless you're just treating the TV like background noise (that is, not really watching it), you're fooling yourself. Some students find that they can work with soft music in the background. Perhaps, perhaps not. If you suspect that music may be interfering with your ability to concentrate, you're probably right. Turn it off.

Handle Internal Distractions

If you're hungry, get a small, preferably nutritious, snack.* If you're uncomfortable, move to another spot. If some important ideas come to you, jot them down so that you can think about them later, during the first free time period that comes along. Then let them go.

Place a *Do Not Disturb!* Sign on Your Door

You'd be surprised. Lots of people really honor these signs. Of course, someone occasionally barges in and says, "Did you put up the sign now or leave it up from before?" or, "Listen, I'll only take a minute of your time."

My advice is to be assertive and . . .

Just Say No

Say, "I'm in the middle of something and can't get distracted. You'll have to stop back later." It's better to give a specific time than to say "later," because people are more likely to follow concrete suggestions and instructions.

If you have a hard time saying no, consider why. Is it because you're terribly afraid the intruder won't approve of your saying no or won't like you anymore? Psychologist Albert Ellis[5] notes that many of us hold the mistaken belief that we cannot survive unless other people approve of us all the time. And this belief makes us just plain miserable! *You don't need everybody's approval all the time!* You can be polite, but firm, with intrud-

---

* Too many students go through bag after bag of potato chips or half a jar of peanuts while they're working. If this sounds like you, read the section on eating a nutritious diet in Chapter 11.

ers. You can also offer a *brief* explanation ("I'm in the middle of something important.") If the intruder gets miffed, tell yourself that the problem lies with him or her, not with you. People who care about you want you to do well and respect your right to study without intrusion. If the intruder has no concern for your welfare, why should you worry about his or her approval?

Believe that you are a valuable person and that your time is important. *Believe* that people who are worthwhile will respect your rights. Work on saying no. Practice doesn't always make perfect, but most of the time it helps. And if you have tried and tried and you really can't say no,* study someplace where intruders won't find you.

TRUTH OR FICTION *Revisited*

Saying "No" and "Later" help students cope with people who distract them from their work and waste their time.

Control Phone Calls

You know not to make telephone calls when you're studying, but how do you handle incoming calls? After all, the person on the phone couldn't read the Do Not Disturb sign on the door and didn't know that this time is important to you. And of course you don't want to be rude. So it's not your fault if you get trapped in conversation, right? Wrong. You chose to have a telephone, so it's up to you to handle it.

One way to handle phone calls is to tell the truth. Say, "I really wish I could talk now, but I'm in the middle of _____ (you fill it in)." If the person says, "Really, this'll only take a minute," you can say, "I really can't interrupt what I'm doing right now; I'll call you back later." If you repeat the last sentence three or four times, the message will get through. If the caller then says, "Wow, you're in a mood, aren't you?" don't take up the challenge or you'll never get back to work. You can say something like, "Call me back after 8:00 or I'll call you." Then hang up.

If you really have trouble with phone calls while you're studying, unplug the contraption until you're finished, or study in the library or a study lounge.

Students are sometimes at their most inventive in the way they handle obtrusive callers. One student remarked, "The greatest invention in the world is my answering machine. I listen to who's calling and call back later unless it's an emergency. If I want to talk to the person, I break in and say, 'Hi! I just got in! Wait until the recording goes off and then we'll talk.'"

Another student noted, "I just say, 'Oops, So-and-So's calling me—gotta run! I'll talk to you later.'"

A third student occasionally solves the problem by saying, "Hello, hello! Listen, something happened and I can't hear you. If you can still hear me, call me back later. I'm going out now."

HOW TO MOVE AHEAD WHEN YOU'RE STUCK: WAYS OF ACCOMPLISHING SOMETHING WHEN YOU CAN'T DO ANYTHING

Sometimes you get to your study place and have all your equipment set up, and then you get stuck. You try to force yourself to do something, but

---
* Oh, come on! Sure, you can. Try it. Really, it won't hurt. Well, not too much.

> Don't put off till tomorrow what can be put off till day-after-tomorrow just as well.
>
> MARK TWAIN

nothing seems to work. Following are some ideas for getting past these blocks.

Do Something—Anything

If you can't force yourself to read the chapter, try skimming the table of contents, the preface, the index, or even the bibliography or references. Try leafing through the pages, dwelling on anything that catches your eye. If you can't force yourself to write the paper, jot down the random ideas about the topic that are swimming in your head. Or jot down a list of things to do for the paper. Or even switch to another subject; be flexible and switch slots on your schedule for the week.

Doing something accomplishes these goals:

1. You feel that you have accomplished something and haven't wasted all your time.
2. Sometimes doing something leads to doing more. When something catches your eye in the middle of the assigned chapter, or in another chapter, you may start reading around it and spend your time in a very worthwhile way.
3. You cut the big job down in size, even if just a little.

Look for Interference

Are you being distracted by thinking about your big date, or about what you need to do for another course? Get out your schedule and look for the next free period. Write in, "Worry about date!" or "Do a, b, and c for math class." Of course, if you have a real inspiration for math, consider making a switch. Get to work on math and change the next scheduled period for working on math to the course you let go.

IN YOUR OWN WRITE

Before going on to the next section, make a list of your reasons or motives for being on college. What is your most important reason for attending college?

_____
_____
_____
_____
_____
_____
_____
_____
_____
_____

Review Reasons for Being in College

Write down a list of reasons for being in college. Keep the list with you. When you can't get to work, review the reasons. They'll remind you that you're not being "victimized" by college. Even if the workload sometimes gets you down, there's a method to the madness. That is, your college education will help you meet your life goals. So reviewing your reasons for attending college will help motivate you.

Some students have told us that they've tried this method but haven't been able to come up with the list. Most of the time, they were not giving the list their full attention or were feeling sort of down about things in general at the time. But a couple of students had never really examined whether or not college was right for them. We don't recommend going into a week-long mental retreat to examine this question in the middle of a busy term, but you can always deal with it when the term is over.

Remind Yourself That the Assignment Is Time-Limited

Look at your schedule and note that you'll be finished working on this course in, say, 35 minutes. Then you don't have to deal with it again for, say, two days. Moreover, if courses in this field really turn you off, you don't have to take too many more of them. (To meet most core requirements, you don't have to take more than two courses in any particular area.)

Try to keep an open mind, too. It may be that you'll come across something in this subject that you really enjoy. If not this week, perhaps next week or next month.

Compromise

If you have 40 minutes left to go on the subject, study hard for 20 and then quit. Twenty may not be as much as 40, but it's a lot more than none! You can occasionally compromise on the quality rather than the quantity of your work. Read an annoying novel less closely, or skimp on writing parts of the body of a paper rather than not doing them at all. To make this kind of concession, perfectionistic students will have to live with the notion that some of their work can be less than exemplary.

TRUTH OR FICTION *Revisited*

Sometimes it is better to do less-than-perfect work rather than to let an assignment go completely. You accomplish something, or you hand something in. The trick is not to let slipshod work become a habit.

Don't Catastrophize!

Failure to study during this time block, this day, does not mean that you're a terrible student and that it's only a matter of time until you drop out or flunk out of college. All of us have periods when we just can't get anything done. Don't blow things out of proportion so that you believe that you'll be doomed to more of the same every time you sit down to work.

Learning to live within your means doesn't have to be a catastrophe, either. That's the topic of the next chapter—handling money. But before we get into that extravagant subject, let's do some summing up.

SUMMING UP

1. How do *you* waste time?
2. How can you find out how you spend your time?
3. What is your attention span for studying various courses, writing papers, and so on?
4. What problems did you encounter in creating your own schedule? Did you need to make any changes in your trial schedule to get it to work right for you?
5. Are you flexible in adhering to your schedule? Do you think of your schedule as being carved in stone? Is your attitude toward your schedule somewhere in between these extremes?
6. In what ways can you reward yourself for sticking to your schedule?
7. What types of problems do you encounter when you try to stick to your schedule?
8. What are your reasons for attending college? Does reflecting on them help motivate you?
9. How do you handle people who interrupt you when you're trying to study? What else can you do?
10. What things can you do in each of your courses to accomplish something when it seems impossible to keep your nose to the grindstone?

Strengths and Weaknesses in Bernie's Schedule

Let's start with the positive. Bernie's strong points include these:

1. Regular hours for getting up and getting to bed. Bernie seems to be following the adage "Early to bed, early to rise, makes a [student] healthy, wealthy, and wise."
2. Regular exercise hours. Bernie's apparently going to keep in shape, and he's given himself four well-distributed slots a week for doing so.
3. Bernie is a "morning person," and he's got his classes scheduled for the time of day when he's at his best.
4. Bernie also has regular, early hours scheduled for work on his term paper.
5. Bernie has allowed an hour between his child development and math classes for reviewing child development notes, taking a brief break, and previewing the math that will be covered.

Now, for the schedule's flaws:

1. Bernie has forgotten to enter his meals. For example, won't eating dinner come out of Bernie's time before he goes off to his part-time job?
2. Bernie allowed himself no time for winding down before sleep. Is he really going to go straight from studying to sleep, or is he likely to quit studying early or else get less sleep?
3. Tuesdays and Wednesdays are back-to-back horrors! Wouldn't Bernie be better off giving himself more breaks on those days?
4. Did Bernie allow himself enough time to get to and back from the dentist? What about waiting time?

5. Bernie seems to be addicted to football—whether on campus or on television. If he could let even one of the Sunday games go, he could get quite a bit more work done. That, in turn, could lighten his load on Tuesdays and Wednesdays.
6. Math, Spanish, and chemistry all in a row are likely to be too much on Mondays and Wednesdays. It would have been better to schedule Spanish for the afternoon.
7. Couldn't Bernie use a bit of a break between work and studying on Tuesdays, Wednesdays, and Thursdays?

You wouldn't give yourself these scheduling headaches, would you?

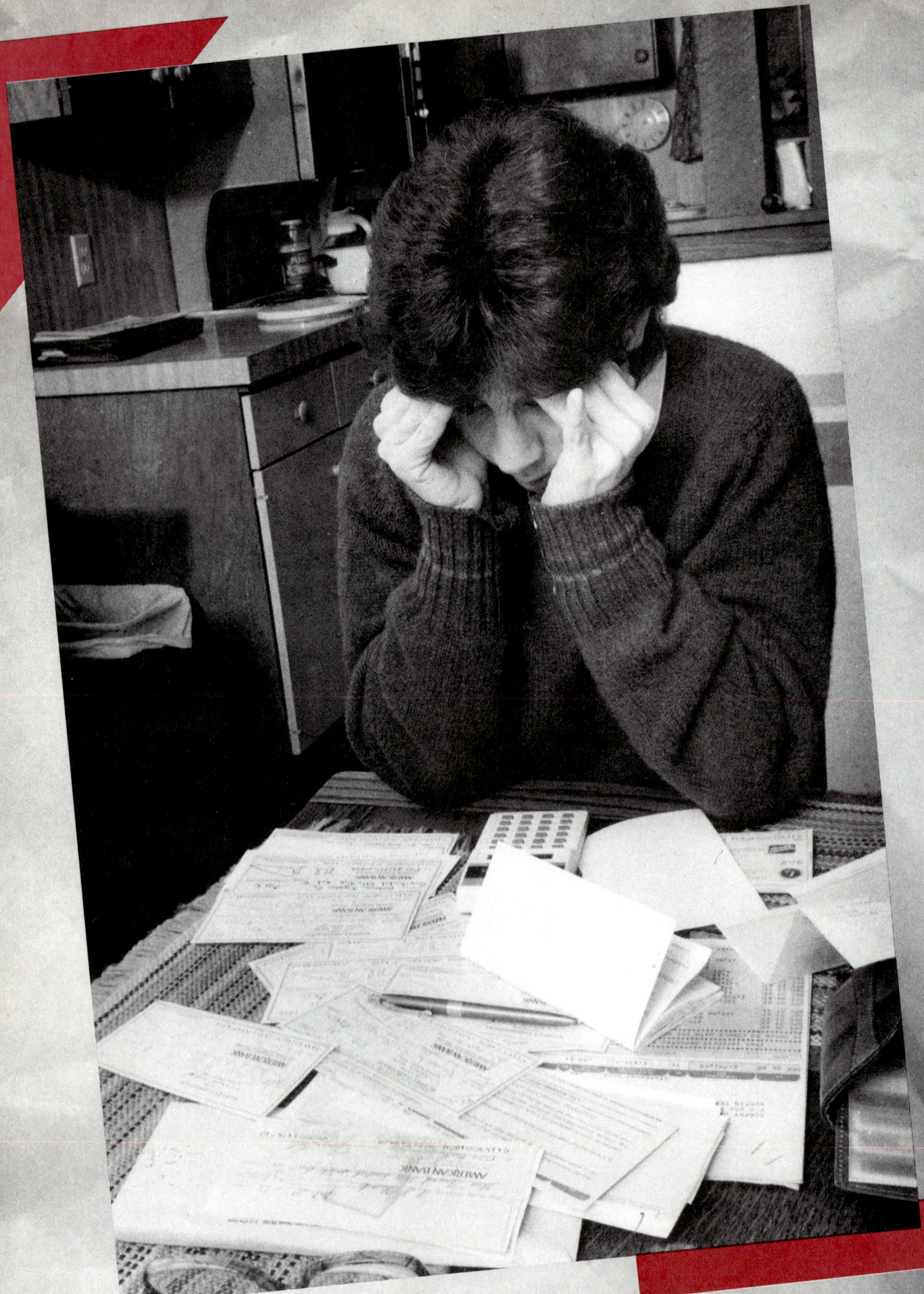

4

Managing Money

TRUTH OR FICTION?

____ Parents pay completely for the educations of the majority of college students.

____ The majority of college students work part time during the school year.

____ Students can get credit cards, even if they're unemployed.

____ Students who receive good grades may receive discounts on their automobile insurance.

____ Interest on college loans is tax deductible.

____ You can join the Reserve Officers' Training Corps as a sophomore or a junior.

____ Some schools arrange for you to work your way through college by alternating terms of full-time work with terms of full-time academic study.

____ (Many of) the best things in life are free.

In, out. In, out. Do you think we're talking about breathing? We could be, but we meant to refer to another of life's basic rhythms—the flow and ebb of money. For many students, and for many graduates, the pattern is more like out, out, in, out, in, out, out, out. The purpose of this chapter is to help you find ways of keeping that rhythm in balance—that is, to manage money. More is at stake here than getting through college. For richer or poorer, you're going to be managing, or mismanaging, money for the rest of your life. So it may be helpful to work on developing some good money-management habits now.

First we talk about the costs of college. Then we'll cover the basics of money management, including budgeting. Then we'll go over some sources of financial aid. You're here, so you've obviously made financial arrangements for the current academic term or year. Needs can change, however, so the sources of aid we discuss may be of help to you in the future.

WHAT COLLEGE COSTS

One of the axioms of life is that what goes up must come down. This principle has little bearing on college expenses, however; they seem to move in one direction only: up. The cost of college consists of tuition and fees, room and board, books and supplies, transportation, and personal expenses. To add it up right, you also have to figure in what you could have earned if you had been working full time instead of being in school.

So is college worth it? Sure. By attending college, you become an educated person and feel better about yourself. College graduates also earn 33 to 40 percent more in their lifetimes than high school graduates. For graduates who go on to professional schools, the earning differentials are still greater.

That doesn't mean that college is easy to afford. For most of us, college is the second largest financial investment we'll ever make—right behind buying a house. For parents who try to support more than one child in college, the costs can be absolutely staggering.

> The love of money is the root of all evil.
> *Philippians* vi. 10

> Lack of money is the root of all evil.
> GEORGE BERNARD SHAW

WHERE THE MONEY COMES FROM

If college is so expensive, how do students manage? Most students manage by piecing together the money they need from a variety of sources, as shown in Table 4.1.

Although parents contribute to the expenses of the great majority of college students, parents do not fully cover most of their children's costs.

TRUTH OR FICTION *Revisited*

Actually, parents cover only 40 percent of the costs of the average college student.

> If you think education is expensive, try ignorance.
> DEREK BOK

The only other financial resources that reach double digits for the average student are summer employment (11 percent) and Guaranteed Student Loans (10 percent). Half (51 percent) of students work during the summer, but summer earnings account for little more than 10 percent of the costs of college. One student in four (26 percent) uses other savings, but these meet only 6 percent of the costs. One student in four also has a Guaranteed Student Loan, but, as noted, this resource provides only 10 percent of

TABLE 4.1. Financial Resources Per College Student.

RESOURCES	PERCENTAGE OF STUDENTS HAVING RESOURCE	PERCENTAGE OF COSTS ATTAINED FROM EACH RESOURCE
Parental assistance	72	40
Savings from summer employment	51	11
Part-time employment	31	5
Other savings	26	6
Guaranteed (Stafford) Student Loan	25	10
College grant or scholarship	17	7
Pell Grant Program*	16	4
State grant or scholarship	13	3
College work-study program	9	2
Other sources	—	12

Note: Based on data from Astin, A. W., et al. (1986). *The American freshman: National norms for fall, 1986.* Los Angeles: American Council on Education and University of California at Los Angeles.
* A federal, needs-based student aid program.

the needed finances. Four out of 10 students work either part time (31 percent) or in work-study programs (9 percent) during the academic year, but their earnings make only small inroads against their costs.

TRUTH OR FICTION Revisited

The majority of students do *not* work part-time during the school year. Slightly more than half work during the summers, however.

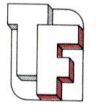

One reason for the relatively small impact of part-time wages is the number of hours worked. As noted in Table 4.2, about half (49 percent) of the full-time undergraduates who hold jobs put in 15 hours or less per

Fifty-one percent of students work during the summer. Unfortunately, summer earnings cover little more than ten percent of the costs of college.

> A billion here, a billion there—pretty soon it adds up to real money.
>
> SENATOR EVERETT DIRKSEN on the national debt

> A fool and his money are soon parted.
>
> Erroneous adaptation of a passage from the Letters of WILLIAM SHENSTONE

Managing Money

TABLE 4.2. Hours Spent Working by Employed Undergraduates in a Normal Week.

STATUS OF STUDENT	10 HOURS OR LESS	11–15 HOURS	16–20 HOURS	21–35 HOURS	36 HOURS OR MORE
Full-time undergraduate	29	20	22	21	8
Part-time undergraduate	2	4	10	14	70

Note: Based on data from the Carnegie Foundation national survey of undergraduates. Reported in Boyer, E. L. (1987). *College: The undergraduate experience in America.* Perennial Library: New York, p. 180.

week. For many students, squeezing in more hours would make a huge dent in the time available for studying and just plain living. There's no point to working part time if doing so kills your grade point average! A second reason for the small impact of part-time wages is the hourly wage itself. Most students who work part time provide unskilled labor, and they may make little more than the minimum wage.

In sum, students draw on many resources to attend college. At least for the majority of students, no single resource does it all. And millions of students would not be able to attend college without receiving some kind of financial aid.

Now that we've seen how students bring in money to finance their educations, let's see what we can do to exercise control over its outflow. But first make note of some of your feelings about college costs.

> Few of us can stand prosperity. Another man's, I mean.
>
> —MARK TWAIN

IN YOUR OWN WRITE

What are your feelings about the costs of college? What kinds of sacrifices will you and your family have to make to see you through? Does it all seem worth it to you? Why or why not?

_____
_____
_____
_____
_____
_____
_____

HOW TO MAKE A BUDGET

> When it is a question of money, everybody is said to be of the same religion.
>
> —VOLTAIRE

The first step in managing spending is to make a budget. A budget is a plan or schedule for adjusting your expenses so that they fit your income.

In Chapter 3, we showed you how making a schedule of your time helps you find out what you're doing with your time and suggests ways of finding better uses for your time. A budget is a schedule for money. It helps you understand where your money is coming from and where it's going. By raising your awareness of the ins and outs of your money, you can become a better money manager.

We suggest using three kinds of charts to track money:

1. A yearly budget to help you keep the big picture in mind
2. A monthly budget that allots money for specific kinds of expenses
3. A record of actual expenses.

Yearly Budget

This is the big picture—your overall estimate of your income and expenses for a year of college. You'll derive your monthly budget from the information included here. Much of the information you'll fill in here is exact, such as your tuition, your scholarships, and, if you're living on campus, the cost of room and board. Some information is estimated, such as what you'll bring in from your part-time job and the amounts you'll spend for personal expenses and entertainment. You'll find an extra budget worksheet at the end of the chapter. Make as many copies as you need.

> Always live within your income, even if you have to borrow money to do so.
> — JOSH BILLINGS

What comes in: *Income*

From family _____
Summer employment _____
Part-time job _____
College work-study program _____
Perkins Loan _____
Guaranteed Student Loan _____
Pell Grant _____
State grant or scholarship _____
College grant or scholarship _____
Savings _____
Other sources:
  1. _____ _____
  2. _____ _____
  3. _____
               TOTAL INCOME _____

What goes out: *Expenses*

Tuition _____
Fees (Registration fees; check catalogue) _____
Fees (Lab fees, tutoring, late registration) _____
Books and supplies (Estimate from catallgue) _____
Housing _____
Utilities (if not included as part of housing) _____
Furniture _____
Food
  Meal ticket _____
  Other meals not on ticket _____
  Snacks _____
Clothing _____
Athletic equipment (other than clothing) _____
Personal expenses (laundry, toothpaste, sanitary _____
    supplies)
Medical
  Health insurance or fee _____
  Medicines _____
  Other _____

Transportation _____
Auto insurance _____
Auto maintenance & repairs _____
Entertainment
    Fraternity/sorority dues _____
    Electronic (CDs, tapes, stereo, TV, etc.) _____
    Eating out _____
    Dating _____
Telephone _____
Other expenses
    1. _____ _____
    2. _____ _____
    3. _____ _____
Emergency fund (at least $100) _____
                   TOTAL EXPENSES _____

> I hate money, but it soothes my nerves.
>
> JOE LOUIS

After filling in the worksheet, subtract your total expenses from your total income. You should wind up with a plus sign—that is, you should have something left over. If you wind up with a minus sign, you're not alone. You and the federal government are both running deficits. The federal government has a slight advantage, however; it can print money. You can't. If you're running a deficit, you have some choices:

1. You can try to increase your anticipated income.
2. You can try to cut your anticipated spending.
3. You can run out before the end of the year.
4. You can pretend that the problem doesn't exist and try not to think about it. Like Scarlet O'Hara in *Gone with the Wind*, you can think about it "tomorrow."

> When I was young I used to think that money was the most important thing in life; now that I am old, I know it is.
>
> OSCAR WILDE

We hope that you will reject the third and fourth options. You're likely to just dig yourself in deeper.* If you cannot think of a way to increase your income, try to cut down. Tracking your expenses and following some of the tips in the section on self-control should cut the job down to size.

Assuming that you at least break even, it's time to work on the monthly budget.

Monthly Budget

A monthly budget is particularly useful for students who live off campus. Rents and mortgage payments are made on a monthly basis. The bills for fuel, electricity, the telephone, and the charge cards come in each month.

You can arrive at a monthly budget by doing the following steps.

STEP	EXAMPLE
1. Write down your total anticipated income for the year. In your estimate, include the savings from the previous summer's work; don't borrow against the following summer.	Your total anticipated income (including parental help, summer work, part-time work, and financial aid) is $21,150.00.

---

*Yes, this should be "more deeply," not "deeper." We're using the colloquialism for emphasis. See Chapter 6, in which we give ourselves permission to do so.

STEP	EXAMPLE
2. Deduct all one-shot expenses. These include tuition and fees (registration fees), insurance premiums (unless you pay them out monthly), textbooks (which are purchased at the beginning of the term), on-campus housing fees (unless these are paid out monthly), transportation (if you go back and forth between campus and home only once a term), and meal tickets.	Deduct the following: Tuition and fees: $12,400.00 Insurance: 300.00 Textbooks: 350.00 Room and board (meal ticket: 19 meals per week) 4,500.00 Transportation 900.00
3. Total the one-shot expenses.	Total: $18,450.00
4. Subtract the total expenses in item 3 from your total estimated income.	$21,150.00 − 18,450.00 = $2,700.00
5. Take the amount that's left and divide it by the number of months you will be at school. The result is the amount of money you have to spend each month for *everything else*—from meals not covered on the meal plan to clothes to entertainment.	$2,700.00/9 = $300.00
6. Allot a reasonable amount of money for each remaining category of expense.	Snacks: $30.00 Eight meals off campus: 32.00 Clothing: 45.00 Personal expenses: 60.00 Auto maintenance: 120.00 Entertainment: 60.00 Telephone: 25.00
7. Create a category for putting away monthly savings, no matter how small. This category will encourage you to remain within your spending limits.	Savings: 10.00
8. Total your estimated monthly expenses. If they don't fit your monthly allowance, do some pruning.	Your estimated total outflow, including savings, is $382.00—or $82.00 over budget! What are you going to downscale or give up?

Managing Money 77

STEP	EXAMPLE
9. Be reasonably flexible. It will take you a while to learn what electricity, the phone, snacks, and dating cost you. But remain within your total monthly allotment. If you go over budget in one category, make it up spending less in another category. If you don't, you'll be running a deficit. You might as well be in Congress.	You run for Congress. (Just kidding—wait until after you graduate.)

Expense Record

> When a fellow says, "It ain't the money, but the principle of the thing," it's the money.
>
> ELBERT HUBBARD

The budget is useful in theory. An expense record allows you to determine whether or not you are sticking to the budget. An expense record includes the following elements:

Date on which an expense was made

What the expense was for

The amount

Many different kinds of charts can be used for recording expenses. The trick is to use a chart that tells you what you need to know—fast. Here's a simple chart of expenses:

Expense Record, Month of _____—Simple

Date	Item	Amount	Date	Item	Amount	Date	Item	Amount

As we said, this record is simple. You begin at the beginning of the month and record through the end of the month. Then you add it all up. It'll do the job of telling you how much you spent, but it won't telegraph *where* the money went very well.

The next chart, which is more detailed, does a better job of showing you where your money goes. David filled in six categories of expenses, from housing to transportation, and left one column for items that didn't fit anywhere else ("Other").

Setting up a detailed chart takes a bit of work. Set up your categories in a way that makes the most sense for you. If you're living on campus, for example, you may choose not to include housing, since housing belongs

Expense Record, Month of _____ —Detailed

Date	Housing & utilities	Food— meals, snacks	Books and supplies	Personal supplies	Entertainment	Transportation	Other	Running Total
3/01	Rent							325.00
3/01		Snack						.75
3/02					Film			4.00
3/02		Snack						1.25
3/03	Elec.							32.47
3/03						Buses		3.00
Etc.								

to the one-shot expense category. Not including housing gives you another column to play with on the grid. It may take some trial and error for you to fill in the categories on the grid so that it works well for you.

With a detailed chart, you waste some space and some paper. Of the several columns that allow you to list items, you'll be using only one for each expense. The tradeoff is that with a detailed chart, you can readily see where your money goes.

We've put a few sheets of the detailed kind of chart at the end of the chapter. Fill them out in a way that makes the most sense for you. Duplicate as many copies as you need.

Now let's turn to some practical financial issues, like checking accounts and credit cards.

MONEY-MANAGEMENT ISSUES: FROM CHECKING ACCOUNTS TO INSURANCE

> Beware of little expenses: A small leak will sink a great ship.
> BENJAMIN FRANKLIN

> If you have to ask how much it costs, you can't afford it.
> J. PIERPOINT MORGAN

Should you open a checking account at school? Dare you have a credit card? Should you get a telephone? A car? What about insurance? These are some of the practical money matters that affect college students.

Checking Accounts

There are pluses and minuses to students having checking accounts. First, the pluses. Checking accounts are convenient. They help students establish a credit profile. They also provide a written record of expenses, which aids in money management. Many students open checking accounts at banks near their schools because some local merchants balk at taking out-of-town checks and because they can deposit their paychecks in them. On the other hand, if students are going to make their lives in their home towns, it may make sense to establish accounts there. It's also easier for parents to make deposits at home.

> The two most beautiful words in the English language are "check enclosed."
>
> DOROTHY PARKER

Now, the negatives. Checking fees can be expensive. There is usually a monthly fee and a fee per check. Sometimes these fees are waived if you maintain a minimum balance. It is easier to buy big-ticket items by check, so money can slip through your fingers more readily if you have an account.

If you are going to have a checking account, comparison shop for fees and interest. Often you do much better in a savings account. In either case, arrange for a cash card so that you have access to emergency funds 24 hours a day, if possible.

Credit Cards

Students can get credit. Visa and Mastercard offer cards with credit limits of about $600.00. Even prestigious American Express will issue credit cards to students with some verifiable income (even if only an allowance from parents) and no negative credit history.

TRUTH OR FICTION *Revisited*

Unemployed students can obtain credit cards so long as they have a verifiable income and no negative credit history.

The issue is whether or not it is *wise* for students to have credit cards.

It is advantageous to have a credit card if you want to prepay for airline reservations or rent a car. (Your parents can put these charges on their cards, however.) Moreover, many stores use a credit card as identification for accepting a check. Credit card companies also issue monthly statements that help you keep track of purchases.

The main danger is that you can have the feeling that you're spending "plastic," not money. You may be tempted to buy big-ticket items now rather than wait until you've saved enough. It is easy to dip into next year's finances if you ignore the devastating effects of compound interest. That tiny-sounding 1 1/2 percent a month interest charge is actually 18 percent a year. After a month goes by, you're also paying interest *on interest!* You can avert this particular problem by using the American Express card, which requires full payment upon billing.

You'll soon learn whether or not you can trust yourself in using credit cards. If you have any doubts, shred the monsters.

Credit cards are useful for prepaying airline fares or renting cars, providing a source of identification for accepting a check, or keeping track of purchases through monthly statements. The main danger is the feeling that one is spending "plastic," not money, so that people spend more than they otherwise would.

Telephones

Many college-age people seem to have telephones permanently attached to their ears. Is it a good idea for students to have phones in their rooms or apartments, or is a telephonectomy in order?

When students attend college away from home, homesickness and friends at other schools can lead to sky-high long-distance bills. If you live on campus and use the dorm phones, your long-distance bills will be curbed by the need to keep those quarters flowing (unless you're charging the call or calling collect). Having other people stamping their feet nearby while they're waiting to use the phone is also an excellent money-management device! We're not so concerned with the amount of time you spend on the phone in local calls. If you weren't doing that, you'd probably be using the same amount of time to socialize. But, as noted in Chapter 3, the trick is to control those incoming calls so that they don't bite into the time you set aside for studying.

If you live off campus, we strongly recommend a phone. You can get sick and find it easier to phone the health center (or home) than to drag yourself out. You also want to be able to put in a call to the police or fire departments when problems arise. In addition, you make it easier for people to get in touch with you when they are in need.

IN YOUR OWN WRITE

Do you need a car? Do you *really* need a car? Why or why not?

_____
_____
_____
_____
_____
_____
_____
_____

Cars

Cars play an almost mystical role in American life. Many people equate automobiles with their sense of personal freedom. In some locations, cars are a necessity, especially for commuting students. Many Californians, in fact, find that it is nearly impossible to survive without a car. If a car is optional in your situation, however, seriously examine whether the "freedom" you desire will be affordable and whether it will make it more difficult for you to practice the self-discipline required to succeed in college. Cars are distractions. It can be too easy to hop into the car and go for a ride when you find yourself annoyed by a reading assignment or a paper that has to get written. Because cars are so diverting, some colleges restrict first-year students from having them on campus.

Should students have cars? In some locations, like California, cars are a necessity, especially for commuting students. If a car is optional for you, however, consider whether the "freedom" you desire will be affordable and whether it will serve as a distraction from studying.

Managing Money 81

Commuters aren't the only people who need cars. If you're going to be driving to campus from a rural apartment or house, or if you're going to be going long distances at odd hours for a part-time job, you may need a car. Cars are also helpful at getting groceries from stores into apartments. But if you live on campus or in town near the campus, you can probably get around mostly on foot or by bicycle. Colleges with spread-out campuses frequently run shuttle buses from dorms to classrooms. Some colleges even run free shuttles between campus and town. Cars also have a way of creating more problems than they solve. For example, cars need parking spaces—which can be at a premium. Although faculty and staff may be able to park near classrooms and other campus facilities, students are frequently consigned to lots in Outer Mongolia.

If you are going to have a car, two of the most costly expenses will be for the car itself and for insurance. When choosing the car, weigh the relative merits of buying new or fancy "wheels" as opposed to a reliable used car that will get you from place to place. Many students go into major debt over their automobile purchases. They wind up holding jobs just to make their monthly payments. Jobs, of course, take time away from the books. If a job is enabling you to make tuition payments and meet your living expenses, it is probably laudable and necessary. If, however, a job serves the sole purpose of enabling you to make the payments on a sexy car, as opposed to a car that's just transportation, you may want to reconsider your priorities.

Now, a few words about insurance: *High-risk pools do not have piranha fish; they have insurance agents!* The merciless ripping away at your purse is about the same for the fish and the agents, however. College-age students, especially males, usually pay exorbitant insurance premiums.

Cars also require gasoline, tuneups, oil changes, registration fees, and, all too often, costly repairs. And, depending on your school situation, you may also run into parking fees and parking tickets!

Note that your parents may be able to receive discounts on their automobile insurance if you have gone off to college. Their rates may be reduced as much as 10 to 33 percent! (Perhaps your parents will be able to funnel some of the savings into your education.) Also note that you may be able to get insurance discounts for good grades. The idea behind such discounts is that good students spend more time hitting the books than other cars. If your insurance company does not offer such discounts, perhaps another one will.

TRUTH OR FICTION *Revisited*

Good grades do earn many students discounts on their automobile insurance. Apparently the grades attest to their sense of responsibility. (Remember to check with the insurance company!)

Health Insurance

Adequate health insurance is a must. Without it, you're playing Russian roulette with your financial well-being as well as your physical health. Parents' employment-related health plans usually cover children until the age of 18 or 19, but they may be extended for college students, even through the ages of 23 to 25. Most colleges sponsor student-health programs. See how far the benefits extend. Find out whether or not health benefits are included in overall college fees. If not, find out whether you can pay an additional fee to use campus health facilities. Also see whether benefits extend to off-campus hospital stays, surgery, laboratory tests, and the like. Many colleges offer supplemental health insurance for hospital care and medical services not routinely available on campus. One day in a hospital—uncovered—usually costs more than a year's worth of supplemental insurance.

Most college students are young and healthy, but students get sick. Students get injured. Trying to save money by foregoing health insurance is a bad bet.

Renter's Insurance

What if there's a fire in your dorm room or apartment? What if someone walks off with your stereo and your personal computer? Are you covered? Many residential students are covered by their family's homeowner coverage. Homeowner insurance policies may cover students' property that is stolen from a dormitory or an off-campus apartment—as long as the student is still a permanent resident of the family household. Students who live in apartments near campus year round normally do not qualify.

Student's coverage is usually limited to 10 percent of the coverage for home contents. Contents coverage is normally half the house coverage. If the house is covered for $180,000, the contents are probably covered for $90,000. Coverage for students' property in a dormitory or an apartment near the school is then $9,000. A deductible amount is also subtracted from the value of the loss to determine the payout. So if the $500 stereo is stolen and the deductible is $250, the payout is $250.

When the homeowner policy does not cover students living away at college, this coverage is often available for additional premiums. Policies that cover movable items are called "floaters," and they can be bought to protect specific big-ticket items like computers and stereos. Students who are not permanent residents of the family household can take out their own renters' policies to cover personal property, medical payments, and liability.

Unfortunately, you can't take out insurance to protect yourself against a spending spree. For that, you need to practice some self-control. The following section has suggestions for how to handle the feeling that you've got to buy that special _____ (you fill it in) *now*.

HOW TO PRACTICE SELF-CONTROL IN SPENDING

Does it seem that mysterious forces are at work to prevent you from living within your means? After all, how can you be expected to hold down spending when that sweater finally goes on sale? And it's not your fault that the pizza place raised its prices, is it? Or that tuition was raised again? And how can you go on living in your apartment without giving it a couple of coats of paint? And don't you want to see *Rocky 17* and *Jaws 42*, in which the shark takes bites out of your wallet?

Yes, life is filled with temptations. So what is there to do? Actually, quite a lot. Here are some ideas.

Avoid Temptations

Are your legs in danger from money burning a hole in your pocket? One way to control spending is to avoid obvious sources of temptation. Students who go window shopping often wind up with more than windows. If you can't browse in the bookstore without picking up sweatshirts for all your relatives, stay out of the bookstore. If you can't walk through the mall without checking out all the clothing sales, don't walk through the mall.

One way to control spending is to avoid obvious sources of temptation. Students who go window shopping often wind up with more than windows.

> Part of the loot went for gambling, part for horses, and part for women. The rest I spent foolishly.
>
> Actor GEORGE RAFT, explaining how he squandered $10 million throughout his career

> Resolve not to be poor: whatever you have, spend less. Poverty is a great enemy to human happiness; it certainly destroys liberty, and it makes some virtues impracticable and others extremely difficult.
>
> SAMUEL JOHNSON

A list of places that vacuum the money from your wallet may help you develop strategies for avoidance:

In Your Own Write

Note some of the places where you get (your budget) into trouble.

1. _____
2. _____
3. _____
4. _____

> I couldn't help it. I can resist everything except temptation.
>
> Oscar Wilde, *Lady Windermere's Fan*

It also helps to make a list of items you need before you go shopping, and then to stick to it. Try to walk through stores as if you had blinders on. In Chapter 11 you'll see that you should avoid pretty packages at the supermarket, because fattening things come in them.* Expensive things do, too. Shop owners put hot items on display up front in stores. In racks or on the counter near the cashier lurk small items intended to lure you into impulse buying. Beware!

A Sale! sign will only *mark down* your resistance, *discount* your intelligence, and lead to a *reduction* of your *special* savings. You'll wind up disgusted with yourself, into the *bargain*. Fire Sale! only means that your savings will be *burned up* twice as fast. The best sale is the one that doesn't take place.

Consider the line from Shakespeare's *Othello:* "Who steals my purse steals trash." It may have been spoken by someone who attended too many sales.†

Place Yourself in Settings in Which There's Little to Spend On

> 'Tis one thing to be tempted, Escalus, Another thing to fall.
>
> Shakespeare, *Measure for Measure*, II, i.

Sound impossible? How about the library? You wanted to spend some time there, anyhow, and there's little to spend on in the library except for the vending and copying machines. What about the gym? You wanted to do something to get in shape, anyhow, and there's little to spend on at the gym except for those vending machines. All right, you may need some workout clothes for the gym, but you don't really have to buy the most fashionable sweats, do you?

---

* Ironically, "Chapter 11" also refers to laws concerning bankruptcy.

† Actually, the line is used to make the point that one's reputation is more important than money:

> Who steals my purse steals trash; 'tis something, nothing;
> 'twas mine, 'tis his, and has been slave to thousands;
> But he that filches from me my good name
> Robs me of that which not enriches him
> And makes me poor indeed.
>
> *Othello*, III, iii

IN YOUR OWN WRITE

Note here some free or really cheap places you can go to or use.

1. _____
2. _____
3. _____
4. _____
5. _____

Leave Your "Spending Equipment" at Home

Your impulse buying is curbed when you leave your checkbook in the drawer, shred your credit cards, and carry only a couple of dollars with you.

Make Spending Complicated

Is it too easy for you to pull out the checkbook from the drawer? Why not put the checkbook, the credit cards, and the big bills in a locked box? Put the box on the top shelf in the back of the closet. Put the key in the drawer of the desk. When you feel the urge to make a big purchase, you've got to get out the key, move the chair, reach for the box, and so on. All that time you can be asking yourself, "Do I really want to do this?"

> Lead me not into temptation; I can find the way myself.
>
> RITA MAE BROWN

IN YOUR OWN WRITE

Jot down some ridiculous but reasonable places where you can stash your checkbook, cash, and credit cards.

1. _____
2. _____
3. _____

Count to 10 (Days)

You have probably heard the old saw that you should count to 10 when you get angry. By doing so, you give yourself time to cool off and avoid doing something you'll regret. When you feel the urge to buy new outerwear,

Managing Money 85

> If you get things when you really want them, you go crazy. Everything becomes distorted when something you really want is sitting in your lap.
>
> ANDY WARHOL

sports gear, or whatever, first count to 10—10 days, that is, for a really big-ticket item. Make yourself wait a day for every 10 dollars. If at the end of five days, you still believe that you really can't do without the $50 athletic equipment, perhaps you can't.

Do Something Else

When you feel like spending the cash in your pocket on something that you can live without, why not go to the bank and deposit it instead? You can't deposit and spend money at the same time. Yes, we know that you can write a check on the account after you've made the deposit, but you're putting your checkbook in that locked box on the top shelf, aren't you? So you'll have time to think it over.

Spark Motivation by Considering Your Reasons for Not Going over Your Budget

Write down a list of reasons for holding onto your money. Perhaps you don't want to have to take out a college loan. Or perhaps you are in serious danger of running out before the end of the term! When you are tempted to spend, read through the list first.

IN YOUR OWN WRITE

Write down some of your reasons for not spending money and going over budget. The following are some samples:

Because I don't know where tuition for next year is coming from.
Because I'm only halfway into the semester and I've already spent 65 percent of my food budget.

1. _____
2. _____
3. _____
4. _____
5. _____

> Virtue is insufficient temptation.
>
> GEORGE BERNARD SHAW

> A penny saved is a penny earned.
>
> BENJAMIN FRANKLIN

Reward Yourself for Not Spending Money

Reward yourself when you avoid spending, but not by buying yourself something! Instead, pick out one of the free (or at least inexpensive) enjoyable activities from the list of 101 turn-ons that you will find on the following pages, or put a dollar *away* toward a necessary big-ticket item.

Save Money

We suggested that you set aside something every month, even if it's only a few pennies. In this way you will get into the habit of winding up with small surpluses instead of deficits. You can also save toward costly items such as a spring vacation and athletic equipment.

Review reasons for setting money aside on a regular basis.

IN YOUR OWN WRITE

Compile a list of reasons for saving money here. The following are some samples:

> *To pay for a membership at the "Y" so I can use the pool and go to aerobics classes.*
> *To take a trip to visit Les.*
> *To create an emergency fund.*

1. _____

2. _____

3. _____

4. _____

5. _____

HOW TO OBTAIN (MORE) FINANCIAL AID

Let us assume that you have established a reasonable budget. You may still discover that you need more money. Students' financial needs change for many reasons. For one thing, some items may cost more than anticipated.

Financial aid comes from many government and private sources, including self-help. Your college Financial Aid Office can help put together a financial aid package that meets your needs.

> Put money in thy purse.
> SHAKESPEARE, *Othello*, I, iii

Managing Money 87

For another, your family situation may change. Your family's income might undergo a dramatic decline because of illness or economic conditions. Or you may now be attending a 2-year school and realize that you're going to need to make financial arrangements for completing four undergraduate years. Or you may be thinking about graduate or professional school, but you have only enough resources to get your bachelor's degree.

Although you have apparently made financial arrangements for the current academic term or year, you may have a number of concerns about financing the remainder of your education. So the following sections review some of the basics about attaining financial aid.

Financial aid comes from many government and private sources, including self-help. Your college financial aid office can help put together a financial aid package that meets your needs.

Showing Need

To be eligible for most kinds of financial aid, you must show financial need. If you applied for financial aid when you were in high school, you probably filled out the Financial Aid Form (FAF), printed by the College Scholarship Service (Box CN 6341, Princeton, NJ 08541), or the Family Financial Statement (FFS), published by the ACT Student Assistance Program (2201 North Dodge Street, P.O. Box 1000, Iowa City, IA 52243).

You may have discovered that the College Scholarship Service and the ACT Student Assistance Program expect families to make serious sacrifices to send their children to college—the equivalent of taking out mortgages and sizable automobile loans. If, now that you are at college, you believe they have completely overestimated your family's ability to pay, drop by the financial aid office and explain why.

Most students receive aid from a number of sources. A financial aid package usually includes:

> What's great about this country is that America started the tradition where the richest consumers buy essentially the same thing as the poorest. You can be watching TV and see Coca-Cola, and you can know that the President drinks Coke, Liz Taylor drinks Coke, and just think, you can drink Coke, too.
>
> ANDY WARHOL

1. *Grants and Scholarships* These kinds of aid are gifts. You need not repay them or work to collect them. Grants are typically awarded because of need. Scholarships are usually awarded on the basis of academic achievement as well as need, although some scholarships are awarded for academic excellence alone.
2. *Educational Loans* Educational loans are often subsidized or guaranteed by the federal or state government or by the college. They carry low interest rates and usually do not have to be repaid until you have graduated or left college or are taking less than a full-time load.
3. *Student Employment* The federal college work-study program is an example of student employment or work aid. Students must usually work 10 to 15 hours a week to earn this kind of aid.

Let's go through the sources of these kinds of aid. Fortunately, there are many of them.

SOURCES OF FINANCIAL AID

There are federal, state, college, and private sources of financial aid that are available to first-year and more advanced students as well as to high school seniors. We will try to describe these sources in sufficient detail to make you aware of them, but you can get complete descriptions of the programs and learn about your eligibility for them at your campus financial aid office.

Federal Sources

In recent years, federal aid programs have not kept pace with college costs. There has also been a shift of emphasis from grants and scholarships to loans. These changes reflect political conflict over the role of the federal government in education and efforts to cope with the increasing federal budget deficit. Still, a great deal of money is available. *The Student Guide*, a free government publication, fully describes the first five of the following programs. Check the list of bibliographic resources.

Pell Grant Program This is the largest need-based aid program. The amount awarded depends on the student's need and the costs of his or her college.

Supplemental Educational Opportunity Grant Program This is a campus-based program. This means that the college determines who receives the grants, although the money comes from the federal government. It is also based on need.

College Work-Study Program Work-study programs are campus-based, and eligibility is based on need. Students are paid at least the minimum wage and work 10 to 15 hours a week, on the average. Most jobs are on campus, and students often work in the dining halls or libraries. They may also work as office secretaries, groundskeepers, peer counselors, or assistants to faculty. Now and then, jobs are arranged off campus. *Scout around campus and try requesting a job that is consistent with your academic or career interests.*

Perkins Loan Program Perkins loans are campus-based and available to graduate as well as undergraduate students. They carry low interest rates (currently 5 percent), and payment is deferred until nine months after graduation, although additional delays are available for military or some other kinds of service (e.g., the Peace Corps). Perkins loans are paid back over a 10-year period.

Guaranteed Student Loan (GSL) Program With the GSL—also known as the Stafford Student Loan—you borrow money from a private lender (for example, a bank, credit union, or savings and loan association) or your college. In some states, a public agency acts as a lender, too. Interest rates are lower than those for most commercial loans, but not as low as those in the Perkins Loan Program. Repayment is deferred until graduation. Further deferment is possible for military or similar service or for graduate school. Most states guarantee these loans. If your state doesn't, the federal government will; then they're called Federally Insured Student Loans.

You can borrow larger amounts through the GSL than the Perkins program, but, if possible, stick to the Perkins. You're charged an origination fee of 5 percent on the GSL. In other words, if you borrow $4,000 a year, you get only $3,800, but you have to pay back the full amount. In addition, your guaranty agency may lop off another 3 percent as an insurance premium. Ouch.

Parent Loans for Undergraduate Students (PLUS) This federally subsidized program makes loans to parents. The interest rate "floats" and is indexed to Treasury Bills, which most of the time means that they will be less costly than other loans.

> Neither a borrower, nor a lender be;
> For loan oft loses both itself and friend,
> And borrowing dulls the edge of husbandry,* . . .
>
> Polonius's advice to his son Laertes, in *Hamlet*, I, iii.

*Careful management; thrift.

Managing Money 89

Whereas payments on student loans are deferred until after graduation (or after the student drops out of school), payments on PLUS loans begin within 60 days after borrowing and must be repaid within 10 years. Check with local banks to find out whether or not they participate in the program. Interest on PLUS loans and other college loans is not tax deductible.

TRUTH OR FICTION *Revisited*

Interest on college loans is *not* tax deductible.

QUESTIONNAIRE
Questions to Consider Before You Commit Yourself to a Loan

Taking out a loan is a huge responsibility. In a sense, you're taking out a mortgage on your future. Before you commit yourself to any loan, government subsidized or commercial, it is a good idea to weigh the answers to the following questions:

1. What is the interest rate? (Financial advisers suggest that you comparison shop between loans by using the simple interest rate.)
2. When do you have to start to repay the loan? (Under what circumstances can repayment be deferred?)
3. How much will the monthly payments be? What is the term of the loan (that is, how long will you have to repay it)?
4. Are there hidden or extra charges for taking the loan? (Is there an origination fee? How much? An insurance premium? How much?)
5. Can the lender cancel the loan? Under what circumstances?
6. Do you have to be notified before the loan is terminated?
7. Can you cancel the loan before the end of the contracted period? How much notice do you have to give? Is there a prepayment penalty? What is it?
8. Is there a balloon clause? (That is, do you have to make one big payment at the end? If so, you may need to refinance at that time, and for less favorable conditions.)
9. Can your wages be assigned or garnisheed in case of default?
10. Are you really comfortable with this loan? Can you pay it back without breaking your back?

90   Chapter 4

Parents, therefore, may want to consider the alternatives of home-equity loans or refinancing their homes. Mortgage interest is deductible and the period of repayment may be more favorable.

Supplemental Loans for Students (SLS) SLS loans are like PLUS loans, but they are taken out by the student rather than the parent. SLS loans are available to self-supporting undergraduates and to students in graduate and professional schools.

Reserve Officers' Training Corps (ROTC) ROTC scholarships are competitive and are available to high school seniors. To qualify, you have to meet academic and physical standards and agree to enter the military as a commissioned officer upon graduation. You'll serve for a minimum of four years' active duty and two years' reserve duty.

For high school seniors, the payoff is solid: four-year ROTC scholarships typically cover tuition, fees, and books, *and* provide a stipend of $100 a month. At a private college or university, that's a package worth $40,000 to $60,000!

But here's the good news for students who weren't thinking about the ROTC during their senior years in high school! In some cases, you can join as a sophomore or even as a junior. Entry requirements and obligations differ from those for students on four-year scholarships.

TRUTH OR FICTION *Revisited*

In some cases, you can join the Reserve Officers' Training Corps as a sophomore or a junior.

If you're thinking about going the ROTC route, contact the units at your college, or write:

Air Force ROTC Four-Year Scholarship Branch
Maxwell Air Force Base
Maxwell, AL 36112

Army ROTC Scholarship Program
Fort Monroe, VA 23651

Navy-Marine Corps NROTC Scholarship Program
P.O. Box 3060
Hyattsville, MD 20784
(Phone: 1-800-NAV-ROTC)

In addition to the ROTC, there are financial aid programs available to students who pledge to fulfill a term of military service upon graduation. Funds are available under the new GI bill that pay for college courses while on active duty or allow service people to accumulate benefits for use after discharge. Check with the financial aid office.

State Sources

All states have grant or scholarship programs for legal residents. Most programs are based on need, but some awards are available purely because of academic excellence. Some states limit their awards to colleges and universities within the state. A few have reciprocal arrangements with nearby states.

Most state colleges and universities charge out-of-state residents higher tuition. Sometimes you can become eligible for lower tuition in your upper-class years by assuming legal residency when you go off to college. Check with your college or university about residency requirements.

College Sources

College and university scholarships and grants are usually awarded to students who show a combination of need and academic promise. Once the college kicks in, you might find that it costs little or nothing more to attend a private college than a public institution. Private colleges usually offer more aid than public colleges[2]—at least to students who show need. It may be easier for a college to offer you a "tuition remission"—that is, to let you sit in class for free—than to actually hand out cash. Ask about a tuition remission if you're in need and you've proved yourself academically. You may be a better candidate for a tuition remission in your second, third, or fourth years than you were as a high school senior.

Occasionally, wealthy alumni leave endowments that make funds available to students entering their fields of interest, and not all of these are based on financial need. So check them out if you're changing your major field. Your college catalogue and financial aid office should have a list.

Colleges also put students to work through offices other than the college work-study program. These jobs are intended to get things done on campus as well as to help students. So they are more likely to be based on your skills than on your need. Positions as resident advisers (RA's) and laboratory assistants usually fall into this category. So check out these positions once you have gotten some basic courses under your belt.

Almost any college will provide you with a short-term or emergency loan to bridge a gap in your finances.

Cooperative Education   Cooperative education programs alternate terms of full-time employment with terms of full-time study. At Boston's Northeastern University, the largest of the "co-op" schools, undergraduates graduate in five rather than four years. Their undergraduate programs are almost completely paid for by their employment, however.

TRUTH OR FICTION *Revisited*

Some schools do arrange for you to work your way through college by alternating terms of full-time work with terms of full-time academic study. This practice is referred to as cooperative education.

Co-op programs offer more than a way of working your way through college. They offer valuable experience and meaningful job references. This is because colleges develop work sites in industry and government that teach students skills and provide them with experience in their chosen fields. As a result, students are much more marketable upon graduation. Students also have the opportunity to test whether or not their expectations about their fields fit the realities.

Cooperative education is offered by 1,000 colleges and universities and 50,000 companies. The 200,000 co-op students in the nation average $7,000 a year. Yes, you can transfer into a co-op program!

A free directory of colleges offering co-op education is available from

National Commission for Cooperative Education
P.O. Box 775
Dept. RD
Boston, MA 02115

Private Sources

There's less money available from private sources than from the government or from one's college. On the other hand, these sources can spell the difference between staying or not staying in college. If you're in need, leave no stone unturned.

Many private sources have restrictive and detailed eligibility requirements. For example, you might have to be a New Jersey resident of Polish origin—and show that you're in dire financial straits! It's not unusual for private sources to make awards on the basis of

- academic performance
- religious affiliation
- racial or ethnic heritage
- proposed major field
- proposed career
- parents' employment
- parents' union membership
- parents' membership in a fraternal or civic organization
- your special abilities, interests, hobbies, and *need.*

The financial aid office may keep track of some of these sources. Also check with your church or synagogue, local civic and fraternal groups, even veterans' posts. A few hundred here, a few hundred there—it all adds up. Be on the alert.

The following "In Your Own Write" worksheet may be of help.

IN YOUR OWN WRITE

Note here some local groups you may be able to contact in the search for additional scholarships and grant money.

Church and Religious Groups

1. _____
2. _____
3. _____
4. _____
5. _____

Managing Money 93

Civic and Fraternal Organizations

1. _____

2. _____

3. _____

Bibliographic Sources

That's where the money is.

> Notorious criminal WILLIE SUTTON's answer to the question, "Why do you rob banks?"

The sources listed in Table 4.3 do not give you money. Instead, they tell you—in Willie Sutton's words—"where the money is."

Now that we have come to the end of our list of financial resources, let's turn to some of the things you can do with or without cash.

TABLE 4.3. Bibliographic Resources for Financial Aid.

SOURCE	COMMENTS
Annual Register of Grant Support, Wilmette, IL: National Register Publishing Company.	Updated annually. Too expensive to buy. Check with your guidance counselor or library.
The College Blue Book: Scholarships, Fellowships, Grants, and Loans. New York: Macmillan.	Too expensive to buy. Covers undergraduate, graduate, and professional programs.
Financial Aid to Education. New Haven, CT: Knights of Columbus.	A freebie. Financial aid for children of members of the Knights of Columbus.
Keeslar, O. *Financial Aids for Higher Education.* Dubuque, IA: Wm. C. Brown.	Expensive. Updated biennially. Focuses on students entering as college first-year students.
Lesko, M. *Getting Yours: The Complete Guide to Government Money.* New York: Penguin Books.	Affordable. Lists federal government programs—scholarships, grants, and fellowships (for graduate students).
Need a Lift? Indianapolis: The American Legion.	Updated annually. $1, prepaid. Lists sources of aid, emphasizing opportunities for veterans, dependents, and children.
Renz, L. *Foundation Grants to Individuals.* New York: Foundation Center.	Expensive. Focuses on monies offered by U.S. foundations and companies.
Student Aid Annual. Moravia, NY: Chronicle Guidance Publications, Inc.	Expensive. Lists government and private sources of financial aid for undergraduate and graduate students.
The Student Guide: Five Federal Aid Programs. Washington, DC: U.S. Government Printing Office. Catalogue number 511T.	This is another freebie, updated annually. Write: Consumer Information Center, Pueblo, CO 81009.
Betterton, D. M. *How the Military Will Help You Pay for College.* Princeton, NJ: Peterson's Guides.	Inexpensive, comprehensive guide to programs offered to service personnel, students who enter college directly from high school, ROTC programs, the service academies, and more.
Higher Education Opportunities for Minorities and Women. Washington, DC: U.S. Government Printing Office. Stock number 065-000-00252-3.	Inexpensive. Organized by fields of study. For minorities and women.
Bureau of Indian Affairs Higher Education Grants. Washington, DC: Bureau of Indian Affairs.	Free. You must be at least one-fourth Native American (including Alaskan) to qualify for the sources of aid listed here.
Schlachter, G. A. *Directory of Financial Aids for Minorities* and *Directory of Financial Aids for Women.* Redwood City, CA: Reference Service Press.	Both volumes are expensive and kept up to date. Check with your guidance counselor, your college financial aid office, and your library. (Arrange for an interlibrary loan, if possible.)

WHAT DO YOU DO NOW?
One Hundred Free (or Almost Free) Turn-Ons

Working out, loving, reading, collecting, redecorating—different people enjoy different things. Here is a list of 100 free, or nearly free, activities that you can schedule in your free time or use to reward yourself for meeting study goals.[3]

TRUTH OR FICTION *Revisited*

Sure, many wonderful things in life are free, or at least relatively low in cost. Participate in some of them and your life may be immeasurably enriched.

You can use the following list to help get in touch with what turns you on by rating the activities according to the scale given below.

As you go through the list, some favorite, inexpensive activities that are not mentioned here are bound to pop into mind. There is some space at the end of the list for you to write them in.

3 = Fantastic!
2 = Very pleasant
1 = Pleasant
0 = Yuck (not pleasant)

_____ 1. Being in the country
_____ 2. Wearing old clothes
_____ 3. Wearing new clothes
_____ 4. Talking about sports
_____ 5. Meeting someone new
_____ 6. Writing a letter-to-the-editor about a pet peeve
_____ 7. Playing baseball, softball, football, or basketball
_____ 8. Going to an on-campus aerobics class
_____ 9. Starting a game of tic-tac-toe with a stranger
_____ 10. Being at the beach
_____ 11. Doing artwork (painting, sculpture, drawing, moviemaking, etc.)
_____ 12. Rock climbing or mountaineering
_____ 13. Reading the Scriptures
_____ 14. Rearranging or redecorating your room
_____ 15. Playing video games (one owned by you or a friend—the slots at video arcades devour quarters like peanuts)
_____ 16. Going to a free intramural or intercollegiate sports event
_____ 17. Shooting a few baskets
_____ 18. Weaving a few baskets
_____ 19. Reading stories, novels, poems, plays, magazines, newspapers
_____ 20. Going to a free lecture or talk
_____ 21. Creating or arranging songs or music
_____ 22. Boating (don't get a yacht; some campuses make small boats available for student rental at nominal charges)
_____ 23. Restoring or repairing furniture (doesn't your Salvation Army chipped-and-frail need some loving attention?)
_____ 24. Watching television or listening to the radio
_____ 25. Camping

_____ 26. Working in politics
_____ 27. Working on machines (cars, bikes, radios, television sets)
_____ 28. Playing cards or board games (don't get addicted!)
_____ 29. Doing puzzles or math games
_____ 30. Having lunch with classmates or friends
_____ 31. Playing tennis (you really don't need the most expensive racket and balls)
_____ 32. Woodworking, carpentry (can you sell something you make?)
_____ 33. Writing stories, novels, poems, plays, articles (can you sell articles to student or local newspapers?)
_____ 34. Being with animals
_____ 35. Exploring (hiking away from known routes, spelunking, etc.)
_____ 36. Singing (if you're like your first author, you need to find a spot where you won't offend anyone)
_____ 37. Going to a party
_____ 38. Going to church functions
_____ 39. Playing a musical instrument
_____ 40. Snow skiing, ice skating
_____ 41. Acting (you don't have to pay to get in the play)
_____ 42. Being in the city, downtown
_____ 43. Taking a long, hot bath (unless you pay for your own hot water)
_____ 44. Playing pool or billiards (available at the student center?)
_____ 45. Using a microcomputer
_____ 46. Watching wild animals (not your roommates)
_____ 47. Gardening, landscaping
_____ 48. Sitting with your eyes closed for five minutes
_____ 49. Dancing
_____ 50. Sitting or lying in the sun
_____ 51. Just sitting and thinking
_____ 52. Going to a fair or zoo
_____ 53. Talking (arguing?) about philosophy or religion
_____ 54. Giving a friend a massage or back rub
_____ 55. Getting a massage or a back rub
_____ 56. Dating, courting
_____ 57. Having friends come to visit
_____ 58. Going out to visit friends
_____ 59. Giving gifts of no monetary value
_____ 60. Listening to sounds of nature (not your roommates)
_____ 61. Photography (will the photography club equipment save you money? Can you sell photos to school or local newspapers?)
_____ 62. Checking through your stamp, coin, or rock collection
_____ 63. Skipping stones across the surface of the lake
_____ 64. Eating good (nutritious and tasty, not costly) meals
_____ 65. Working on your health (changing your diet, having a checkup at the student health center)

_____ 66. Fishing (can you reel in an inexpensive meal?)
_____ 67. Looking at the stars or the moon
_____ 68. Horseback riding
_____ 69. Protesting social, political, or environmental conditions
_____ 70. Going to the movies (on campus? in the library?)
_____ 71. Cooking meals
_____ 72. Washing your hair
_____ 73. Putting on some cologne or perfume (don't buy some especially for this occasion!)
_____ 74. Getting up early in the morning (really—watch the sun rise)
_____ 75. Keeping a diary and making entries
_____ 76. Meditating
_____ 77. Practicing yoga
_____ 78. Doing heavy outdoor work
_____ 79. Being in a body-awareness, encounter, or "rap" group
_____ 80. Swimming
_____ 81. Running, jogging
_____ 82. Walking barefoot
_____ 83. Playing frisbee or catch
_____ 84. Doing housework or laundry, cleaning things (honest, for some people it makes a nice break)
_____ 85. Listening to music
_____ 86. Knitting, crocheting
_____ 87. Being with someone you love
_____ 88. Going to the library (yes, we're serious)
_____ 89. Preparing a new or special dish (not one with expensive ingredients)
_____ 90. Watching people
_____ 91. Bicycling
_____ 92. Writing letters, cards, or notes
_____ 93. Talking about politics or public affairs
_____ 94. Watching attractive women or men
_____ 95. Caring for houseplants (root a cutting for a friend)
_____ 96. Having coffee, tea, or Coke, etc., with friends
_____ 97. Beachcombing
_____ 98. Going to thrift shops, garage sales, etc.
_____ 99. Surfing, diving
_____ 100. Attending the opera, ballet, or a play (special student rates?)
_____ 101. _____
_____ 102. _____
_____ 103. _____
_____ 104. _____
_____ 105. _____

How nice to end the chapter with a list of turn-ons!

Managing Money

SUMMING UP

1. How do students generally finance their college educations? Do your own financial arrangements fit the typical picture?
2. How is a budget akin to a time schedule? What are the steps in making out a budget?
3. Do you keep an expense record? Why or why not?
4. What are the pros and cons of your keeping a checking account? Of using credit cards?
5. Do you have a telephone? Should you?
6. Do you need a car? What financial sacrifices does having a car entail?
7. Do you have adequate health coverage? How can you find out? What does adequate coverage cost?
8. What temptations make it difficult for you to remain within your budget?
9. What are some ways in which you can fight the temptation to squander money?
10. Do you think that you will need more financial aid as you further your educations? What sources of aid are available to you?

Budget Worksheet—Yearly Version

What Comes in: *Income*

From family _____
Summer employment _____
Part-time job _____
College work-study program _____
Perkins Loan _____
Guaranteed Student Loan _____
Pell Grant _____
State grant or scholarship _____
College grant or scholarship _____
Savings _____
Other sources:
   1. _____ _____
   2. _____ _____
   3. _____ _____
                                TOTAL INCOME _____

What Goes out: *Expenses*

Tuition _____
Fees (Registration fees; check catalogue) _____
Fees (Lab fees, tutoring, late registration) _____
Books and supplies (Estimate from catalogue) _____
Housing _____
Utilities (if not included as part of housing) _____
Furniture _____

Food
    Meal ticket   _____
    Other meals not on ticket   _____
    Snacks   _____

Clothing   _____

Athletic equipment (other than clothing)   _____

Personal expenses (laundry, toothpaste, sanitary
      supplies)   _____

Medical
    Health insurance or fee   _____
    Medicines   _____
    Other   _____

Transportation   _____

Auto insurance   _____

Auto maintenance & repairs   _____

Entertainment
    Fraternity/sorority dues   _____
    Electronic (CDs, tapes, stereo, TV, etc.)   _____
    Eating out   _____
    Dating   _____

Telephone   _____

Other expenses
    1. _____   _____
    2. _____   _____
    3. _____   _____

Emergency fund (at least $100)   _____

                         TOTAL EXPENSES   _____

                          Total Income: _____
                      – Total Expenses: _____
                                                           _____

                          Surplus/Deficit: _____

Expense Record, Month of _____

Date									Running Total

Expense Record, Month of _____

Date									Running Total

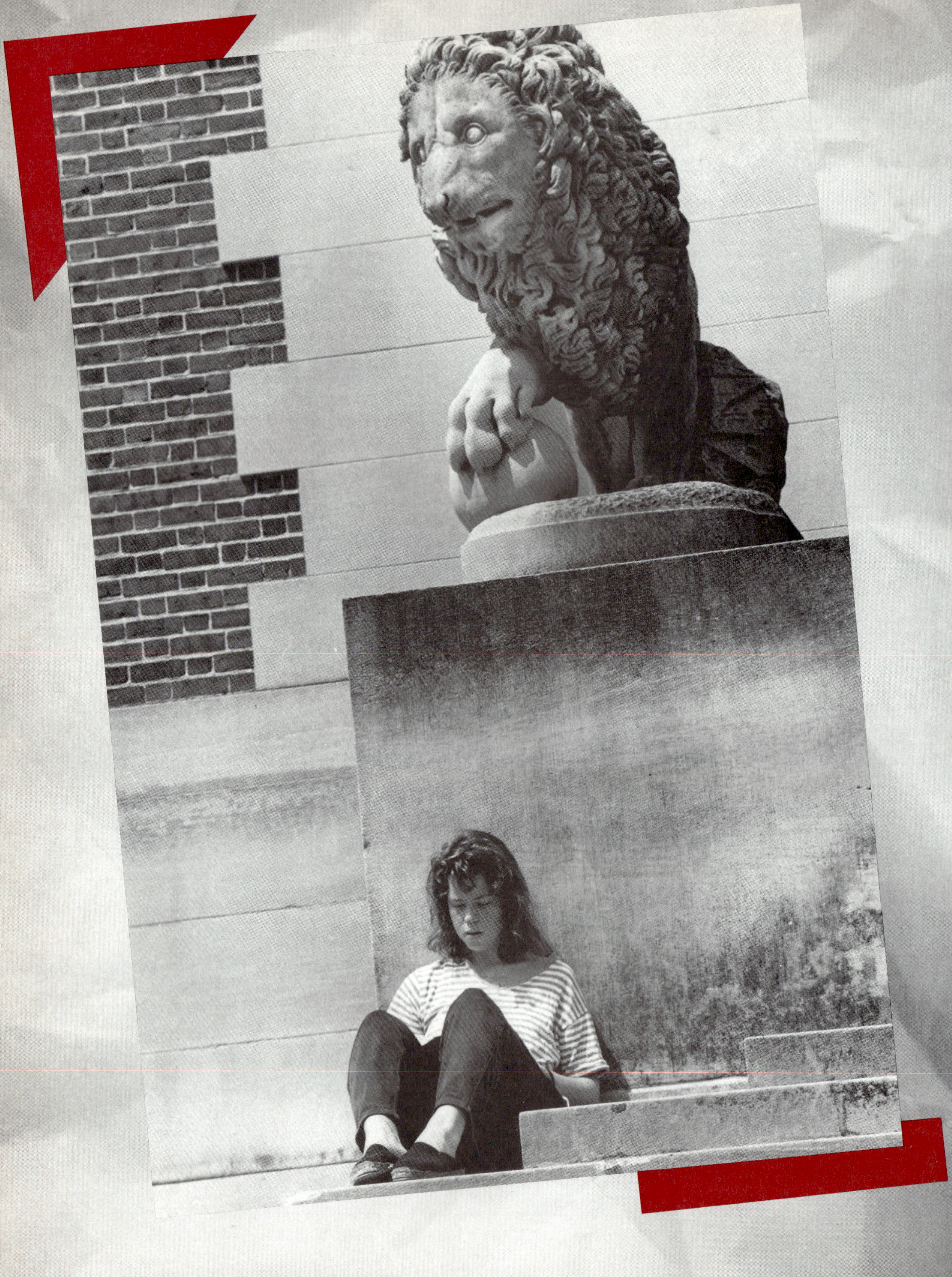

5

Attending Classes, Taking Notes, and Studying

TRUTH OR FICTION?

_____ It doesn't matter whether you attend classes when professors allow you to cut and you keep up on your assignments.

_____ You really can't be expected to pay attention in class when the professor is a bore.

_____ You really can't be expected to pay attention in class when you have to study for a test in another course.

_____ Students are evaluated only on the basis of test performance, not the amount of effort they put into their courses.

_____ The best way to learn subject matter is to go over it again, again, and again.

_____ Your job as a student is to sit back and try to absorb the information dispensed by your instructors and textbooks.

_____ You should postpone all pleasures until the term draws to an end.

It is true, as you say, that Harvard has become a storehouse of knowledge. But I scarcely deserve credit for that. It is simply that the freshmen bring so much and the seniors take away so little.

CHARLES W. ELIOT, President, Harvard University, 1869–1909

Eliot's remarks are tongue-in-cheek, of course, but they point to the main purpose of this chapter—to help you "take away" a great deal of knowledge from your college experience.

In this chapter, we consider ways of taking charge of attending classes, taking notes, and studying. We take notes from our classes and our reading assignments. We study from our books and our notes. To take notes from lectures, you must *pay attention* to them, and that is where we begin.

ATTENDING CLASSES

"Attending classes" has two meanings: getting yourself there and paying attention.

Getting There

Many professors do not take attendance. They allow students to decide whether or not to attend class. Why? Sometimes it's college or university policy. Some professors don't believe in coercing students to come to class. They would rather relate to students who want to be there than to a captive audience. And many professors are committed to the idea that college students are adults who must be free to make choices—including the choice of whether or not to attend classes.

What if your college or your professor has a voluntary attendance policy? Should you bother to attend classes? After all, you have the textbook, and the class is given at 8:00 A.M. You even have friends who let you copy their notes, so why bother to attend classes? There are many reasons:

> Studies serve for delight, for ornament, and for ability.
>
> FRANCIS BACON

1. You're paying for them. Even if you're on a scholarship or your family is footing the bill, you're paying for classes by spending years of your life in college. Time is your most precious asset.

2. Much of what you learn in college stems from personal interaction with professors, not textbooks. Professors not only know about subjects; they represent their disciplines. That is, your chemistry teacher is a chemist as well as a teacher. You have the opportunity to get to know someone who is devoted to chemistry and may help advance the field. As a rule, we should enjoy relating to people who are successful in our chosen fields (see Chapter 14). In other words, if you don't enjoy relating to chemists, you may not be suited for a career in chemistry.

3. You give your professors a chance to get to know you, which can influence them to think positively about you. *Trap:* If you're going to snooze or chat with neighbors in class, you may be better advised not to attend. The professor will probably develop a negative attitude toward you if you show up to write letters and do your nails rather than learn.

4. Professors tend to highlight the key terms and concepts. They often explain essential terms and give examples. If you don't catch on at first, you have the opportunity to ask questions—something you can't do with a textbook or with a friend's notes.

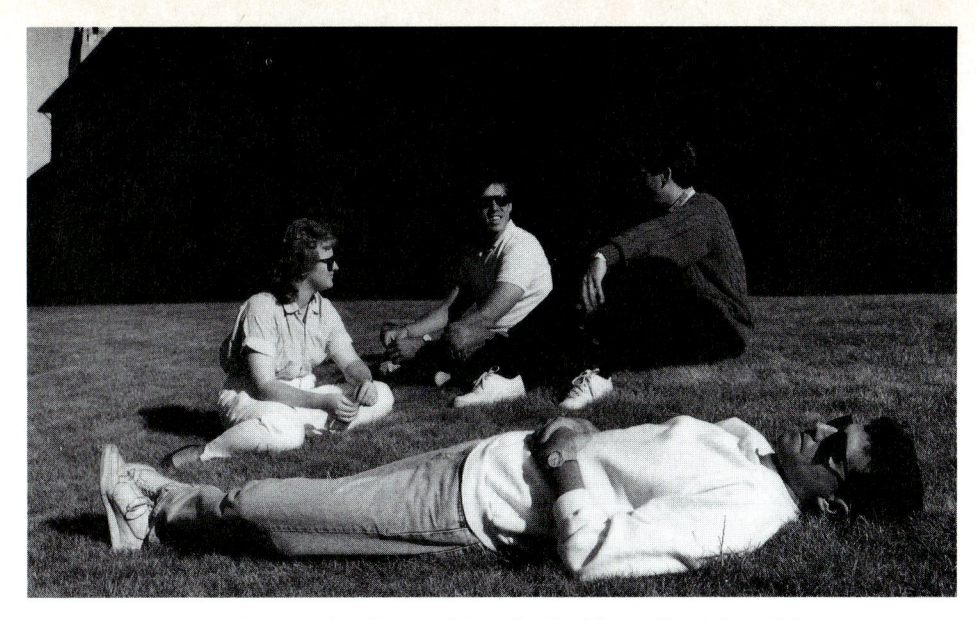

When professors have voluntary attendance policies, why should you attend classes? For many reasons: for example, you're paying for them, and much of what you learn in college stems from personal interaction with professors, not textbooks.

5. Attending classes gives you an opportunity to get inside your professors' minds to figure out what they consider most important. This helps on tests and perhaps helps you understand the subject matter better. Look for cues (and clues) such as the professor's saying, "The major reason that . . . ," "The important thing to know about this is that . . . ," "My view is that . . . ."
6. Attending classes is an efficient use of time. It might take you two or three times as long to learn the same amount of subject matter from the textbook or from a friend's notes. Even then, you won't be sure about what your professor considers important. *By investing time in class, you may wind up saving time.*

TRUTH OR FICTION *Revisited*

It does matter whether or not you attend classes. Classes encourage you to relate to your professors and provide you with many types of useful information.

Focusing Your Attention

So you've decided to come to class. (Pat on the back.) What do you do now? You *pay attention.* Paying attention in class or in the lecture hall is not like paying attention elsewhere. When we listen to our friends at lunch, we're often thinking more about the food or watching the leaves turning and falling outside the cafeteria window. When we listen to our families at home, sometimes we're filtering their words through the blabber of the television set. But if we give our professors only part of our attention, if we allow ourselves to drift, we may be squandering time and losing the chance to gather information that can help us "ace" the course.

The point is that listening in class should be goal-oriented and purposeful, not passive. Even though your professor may be doing most or all of the talking, you can be an alert, dynamic seeker and integrator of information.

What *can* you do to focus your attention on the lecture? You can do many things:

QUESTIONNAIRE
Reasons for Not Paying Attention in Class

Over the years, we have collected reasons students have given us for not paying attention in class. For a while we were going to donate them to a museum of excuses, but we thought better of it and saved them for this questionnaire.

In completing this questionnaire, consider each of the following reasons. Write a checkmark if you have ever used the reason, or a similar reason, for not paying attention. Then there's room for you to add reasons you've used that aren't on the list. When you are finished, see the following "What Do You Do Now?" exercise.

1. An important practice session is coming up for the big game. _____
2. I drank too much beer last night. _____
3. I'm way ahead in this course. _____
4. I'm way behind in this course. _____
5. The trees outside the window are really gorgeous this time of year. _____
6. I really don't want to be in college. _____
7. I have to write that letter to _____. _____
8. I'm wiped out from that all-nighter. _____
9. I'm never going to use the subject matter in this course anyhow. _____
10. I got an F on the last test, so what's the point? _____
11. I got an A on the last test, so what's the point? _____
12. My girlfriend (boyfriend) is angry with me. _____
13. Everything's going great with my girlfriend (boyfriend). _____
14. I hurt my knee during the track meet. _____
15. The carburetor has to be fixed. _____
16. I'm starved! _____
17. I'm stuffed! _____
18. I didn't get the part-time job at the hamburger place. _____
19. The professor is a bore. _____
20. I don't know what the professor's talking about. _____
21. I know what the professor's talking about. _____
22. I didn't read the chapter in time for class. _____
23. I'm sitting all the way in the back of the room. _____
24. I have to study for a test in another course. _____
25. I have to listen to the nerd sitting next to me who wants to tell me about the weekend. _____
26. It's 8:00 in the morning! _____
27. It's just before lunch (dinner) and I'm starved! _____

Now it's your turn. Add your own reasons here. Then go on to the following "What Do You Do Now?" exercise.

28. _____
29. _____
30. _____

Chapter 5

Attending class is of little value unless you pay attention. Do you find excuses for failing to pay attention in class?

Head Off Attitude Problems First, head off possible attitude problems with courses you may not particularly like. Rather than thinking, "Ugh, I hate this course," think something like, "I may not be crazy about this course, but the subject matter is part of my general education." Also remind yourself that the grade for the course is important. Connect it to your eventual goal of landing a good job or getting into graduate school, both of which can be highly competitive. Moreover, your attitude about the course may change as you find out more about it.

You can work toward changing your attitudes about the course by relating the subject matter to your own life. Doesn't the discussion of social stratification in sociology relate to your own family's background? Doesn't the discussion of compound interest in math relate to your own eventual retirement funds? Doesn't the discussion of neurotransmitters in biology relate to your own changes in mood? Later we shall see that relating material to things you already know not only motivates you, but also helps you remember it.

TRUTH OR FICTION *Revisited*

Yes, you *can* be expected to pay attention in class when the professor is a bore! Your intent is to gather whatever information you can from the lectures.

And yes, you *can* be expected to pay attention in class when a test in another course is coming up. Try planning ahead so that you have completed your studying for the test before attending class in another course. It is easy to find excuses for not paying attention, but not paying attention winds up hurting *you*.

Sit Front and Center! Second, sit front and center (and hope everyone else in the class isn't following the same advice!). In this location, the professor's voice will be loudest. Audiovisual displays will be clearest. You will have the opportunity to make eye contact with the professor. Nodding off, writing a letter to a friend, and talking to the person sitting next to you are also most likely to be noticed by the professor when you sit up front, so you're less likely to fall into these traps.

Attending Classes, Taking Notes, and Studying

What Do You Do Now?
Changing Attitudes That Encourage You to Cut Classes and Allow Your Attention to Wander

Now you have identified some reasons for not paying attention in your classes. The following exercise will help you to challenge them and see if they're accurate or if they're simply excuses for sloughing off.

Let's say that you find yourself thinking, *I don't know what the professor's talking about,* and so you drift off in class. Here we have a self-defeating way of responding that can pervade every area of life—not just college. Rather than evading the classroom challenge, you can take charge of the situation—and your life—by thinking: "What can I do so that I will know what the professor is talking about? How can I better prepare myself for class? I'm letting events control me rather than taking charge of things myself."

A couple of additional examples of self-defeating attitudes and suggested alternatives follow. Then there's some space for you to list excuses and attitudes that have been getting in your way and alternatives that you come up with.

Excuses and Attitudes That Encourage You to Cut Classes and Allow Your Attention to Wander	Alternative Attitudes That Encourage You to Make Optimal Use of Classes
"This professor is a bore."	"So if I wanted entertainment, I should have stayed home watching soap operas and listening to the stereo all day. The issue is whether I can gather information from class that will help me get good grades and get on with my life."
"I have no idea what's going on in this class. So why bother?"	"So it's time to make a decision rather than just let things happen to me. I have to figure out what the problem is. Maybe I should get some tutoring or work harder. I've got to make concrete plans to do better."

Now write in the attitudes that are causing you problems, and suggest some alternatives:

IN YOUR OWN WRITE

What if you enroll in a course with a friend who wants to sit in the back of the class to doze off or chat, but you would rather sit front and center? How might you handle this conflict?

Preview Lecture Material Third, preview the material to be discussed in the class. Check the syllabus or course outline to see what topic or topics will be covered. Or ask your professor what will be covered next time at the end of the class.

Leafing through the pages of a "whodunit" to identify the killer is a guaranteed way to destroy the impact of a mystery novel, but it can help you learn class and textbook material. Many textbooks have devices that can help you survey the material—such as chapter outlines, section heads, and chapter summaries. In a literary work, it makes sense to begin at the beginning and read page by page. But with textbooks, it is usually more effective first to examine the chapter outlines, skim the minor heads not covered in the outlines, and read the summaries. Familiarity with the skeletons or advance organizers of the chapters provide you with frameworks for mastering the meat of the chapters.[1]

If you don't have time to read the whole chapter before class, at least check the chapter outline (or table of contents for the chapter) or read the chapter summary. Thus you will enter the class with the bare bones of the material in mind and be prepared to flesh it out.

Pick Out Key Terms and Concepts Fourth, pay particular attention to new vocabulary in the text. If you check the meanings of these terms before class, you will follow class discussion better. Even if the professor carefully defines new terms, the professor's efforts will allow you to check the accuracy of your definitions and will reinforce your memory. If the professor uses a new term without explaining it, ask for a definition. If necessary, ask the professor to provide some examples of usage of the term. *Don't worry about looking ignorant. You are in college to learn.* Moreover, if you didn't understand the term, other students might not have grasped it either.

Review Fifth, reread or at least skim the notes from the previous lecture before class. They will fine-tune your expectations for the lecture and set the lecture within your growing understanding of the subject.

Participating

It may not be possible to have discussions in large lecture halls, but it is valuable to participate in them in regular classroom meetings or in discussion sections. Discussion sections—also referred to as recitation sections—frequently accompany large lecture sections. The professor may lecture 120 or 1,000 students in lectures that are held once or twice weekly. But students may then discuss the material and take tests in small groups that are led by teaching assistants (TA's). TA's are usually graduate students who are earning their way through their programs by assisting in classes or laboratories.

There are excellent reasons for participating in discussion groups, even if you're not graded on class participation:

1. Knowledge that you will be participating encourages you to preview the material and to take notes.
2. Participating helps you organize the subject matter in your mind as well as in your notes.
3. Participating provides you with practice in speaking before groups of peers (fellow students) and supervisors (in this case, professors or TA's). You develop skills that will help you in the "real world"—for example, in business meetings—after college.
4. Participating underscores your presence to the professor or TA. As noted earlier, this is a double-edged sword. When you make your presence known, you want to do so in an appropriate, helpful fashion. Most professors and TA's may grade you on the basis of assignments and tests, and not on the basis of whether or not they like you. But if you have a borderline grade, it doesn't hurt to have professors or TA's develop positive attitudes toward you. Both in academia and in the workplace, your performance may be evaluated on the basis of the general impression you make and the amount of effort you put in, as well as on your test scores (or on your job performance).[2]

TRUTH OR FICTION *Revisited*

Students are frequently evaluated on the basis of effort and the general impression they make, as well as on their test performances.

Now that you see the wisdom of participating in class, check out the do's and don'ts in Table 5.1.

TAKING NOTES

Taking notes is an annoyance. It's easier to file your nails or to look through the photos in you wallet while the professor is lecturing. It's easier just to read a textbook or a work of literature than to stop to jot things down. So why bother? There are several reasons:

1. Taking notes is part of active listening and helps you focus your attention. It's difficult to take notes and write a letter home at the same time. So taking notes helps keep you focused on what's important.
2. Notes help you remember the content of lectures and of texts. Most students retain very little of the information that is dispensed during lectures or gleaned from a first reading of a chapter in a textbook. Noting the central ideas and important pieces of information helps

TABLE 5.1. Somes Do's and Don'ts of Class Participation.

DO	DON'T
Come with good questions that you want answered. *Ask them.* If you are shy and uncomfortable in group discussions, ask something early—break the ice.	Argue for the sake of arguing. Aim, instead, for honest expression of ideas.
Answer questions on topics about which you are knowledgeable.	Show off. If you know more than most other students, you can afford to express yourself diplomatically and intermittently. Your expertise will show without your making a point of it.
Share information when appropriate. Be concrete: Provide dates, statistics, and names. (There is no harm in checking through your notes to do so.)	Monopolize discussion. Give others a chance. The point of group discussions is to afford everyone an opportunity to participate.
Show how to solve problems.	Go on and on with personal stories. Your personal life may be more interesting to you than to others. Ask yourself whether you're really making a contribution or talking to hear yourself talk.
Point out, diplomatically, the errors of others. Do so in a helpful way. Otherwise you seem nasty and picky.	
Share your opinions. In math and chemistry there is frequently (but not always!) one correct answer to a problem and, sometimes, one proper way to arrive at that answer. But in literature, philosophy, and behavioral and social sciences, it is usually appropriate to share opinions as to what a passage or a behavior pattern means.	Interrupt. Wait until others have finished what they have to say or until the instructor cuts them off.
	Chat with a neighbor, or hum, or tap your foot while another person is talking.
	Accept remarks that you believe are wrong, prejudiced, or foolish. Wait for an opportunity and voice your opinions.
Listen to others when they speak. Give them eye contact and, perhaps, nod your head when you agree with them. It is the decent thing to do and will also be appreciated by your instructor.	

you remember them. You can also return to your notes to check your memory or to freshen it.

3. Notes help you stay in tune with the instructor—to pick out and record the main points of lectures and of chapters. When you're taking notes, you tend to listen or read carefully for the main points so that you're recording key ideas, not every word that is uttered or written.

Taking notes helps you focus on what is important. It helps you to remember the content of lectures and texts, and to pick out and record the main points.

4. Taking notes helps you understand the lecturer's or author's plan. Lecturers tend to organize their subjects according to a plan. For example, they may describe experiments and then indicate what is to be learned from them. They may list or enumerate items, such as the causes of the Civil War or reasons that people acting as groups make riskier decisions than they would make as individuals. They may state general principles, then provide examples; or they may present historic events in sequence, pausing to describe major personalities. As time passes, you begin to organize your notes according to the professor's plan. Note taking becomes efficient and you learn what is important to the professor, enabling you to "psych out" or anticipate test questions.

5. Taking notes heightens your awareness of key terms and concepts. Professors frequently point out new terms and concepts in classes. They write them on the blackboard. They may underline them.

6. Notes become a record of the course. You can use them as a basis for advanced courses in the same field or, in the case of class notes, to ferret out what your professor considers most important for tests. If the professor says you're not responsible for certain subject matter on October 18, then tests you on it on November 9, you can show him or her your notes after the test. (Do so privately, so that the professor will not be embarrassed before a group.)

7. You can study notes as well as the textbook before exams. If you find out that your professor tests you only or mostly on material covered in class, you can pay special attention to class notes.

8. Taking notes puts you in charge of your learning. Yes, your professor is dispensing the subject matter. However, *you* are recording what *you* determine to be the main points and key ideas. Yes, your textbook is the source of information. However, *you* are jotting down the important points and main ideas in a way that is helpful to you.

How to Take Notes

So there are many good reasons for taking notes. The following are some suggestions about how to take them.

Use Proper Equipment Use the right equipment in class and while reading. *Equipment* means writing instruments and your notebook.

Pencils are useful because you can erase and rewrite. It may be helpful in class to jot down key terms in pencil when you're uncertain of the spelling. Then you can rewrite them in ink once you've checked. Pens create a permanent record. We suggest using pens with black and dark blue ink because they are easy to read and can be readily duplicated by copying machines. You may also want to use a yellow felt-tip highlighter to signify main ideas or key terms.

Exception! We suggest blue and black ink to students who aren't committed to another color. If you've successfully taken notes in green ink throughout your high school years and you're attached to green ink, feel free to continue. If you've successfully highlighted by underlining or using an orange highlighter for four years, feel free to continue. Why upset the applecart?

Use a loose-leaf notebook of standard dimensions—preferably 8 1/2 by 11 inches. Loose-leaf notebooks have the advantages of allowing you to add and reorganize pages. For example, if you discover in October that your notes from September show a misunderstanding of the main ideas of the course, you can revise the earlier notes by replacing a page or two. When noteworthy thoughts come to you, you can jot them down without worrying about where they fit. When the professor takes things out of sequence, you can backfill.

You can use one or several loose-leaf notebooks. You can tab one notebook with sections for a single course: sections for lecture notes, laboratory notes, key terms, and creative thoughts that come to you. Or you can tab one notebook with sections that correspond to courses.

Jot Down Key Phrases and Words Do not attempt to write down every word that comes out of the instructor's mouth! Even if you succeed, you will have to reread every word of the lecture in order to ferret out the main points. Try to note the main ideas in class.

Phrase Questions About the Material "Question" your reading assignments. That is, *generate questions* about the subject matter. Generating questions about textbook material has been shown to promote retention.[3]

Phrase questions for each head in the chapter. Write them down in a notebook. Some questions can also be based on material within sections. For courses in which the textbooks do not have helpful major and minor heads, get into the material page by page and phrase questions as you proceed. You will develop questioning skills with practice, and your questions will help you perceive the underlying structure of each chapter.

Many students find it helpful to set up pages in their notes in two columns. They record questions in the left-hand column and answers in the right-hand column. When you skim a chapter before class, you can write down questions about it in the left-hand column and then answer them with class notes. In this way, you make note taking active and purposeful: You attend class *to answer the questions you have posed.*

One way of phrasing questions is to turn the heads within chapters into questions. Consider a chapter from a biology textbook, "DNA and Genetic Information." The heads within the chapter go like this:

Evidence That DNA Is the Genetic Material
    Bacterial Transformation
    Bacteriophages
    The Quantity of DNA in Cells
    Base Content of DNA
The Structure of DNA
DNA Replication
    Proteins of DNA Replication
    DNA Repair
Mutations

Note the use of indentation to reveal the organization of the chapter. The major heads give the major ideas. The minor heads provide supportive information and are indented. Here is one way in which these heads might be rephrased as questions on the basis of skimming the material in the chapter. Note that we show the questions and answers as you might set them up in your notebook. There is space between questions for filling in longer answers:

QUESTIONS   ANSWERS

I. What evidence is there that
   DNA is the genetic material?

| QUESTIONS | ANSWERS |

A. How does research in bacterial transformation provide evidence that DNA is the genetic material?

B. How does research with bacteriophages provide evidence that DNA is the genetic material?

C. How does the quantity of DNA in cells provide evidence that DNA is the genetic material?

D. How does the base content of DNA provide evidence that DNA is the genetic material?

II. What is the structure of DNA like?

III. How is DNA replicated (duplicated?)

A. What proteins are involved in the replication of DNA?

114 Chapter 5

QUESTIONS	ANSWERS
B. How does DNA repair itself?	_____
	_____
	_____
	_____
	_____
	_____
IV. What are mutations? What causes them?	_____
	_____
	_____
	_____
	_____
	_____

Note that we looked up the term *replication* and wrote a synonym (duplication) in the question we phrased. We also lettered and numbered the heads to reveal their organization. Major heads are usually given Roman numerals and the next level of head is usually assigned capital letters. If you use three or four levels of heads, you can also use Arabic numerals and lower-case letters, as follows:

I. Major head
   A. Second-level head
   B. Second-level head
      1. Third-level head
         a. Fourth-level head
         b. Fourth-level head
      2. Third-level head

IN YOUR OWN WRITE

In this exercise, let's consider the chapter on socialization from a widely used introductory sociology textbook. The major and minor heads are written as follows:

      "Nature" and "Nurture"
      Effects of Childhood Isolation
          "Feral" Children
          Children Reared in Isolation
          Institutionalized Children
          Monkeys Reared in Isolation
      The Emergence of the Self
          Cooley: The Looking-Glass Self
          Mead: Role-Taking
      Learning to Think
      Learning to Feel
      Agents of Socialization
          The Family
          The School
          The Peer Group
          The Mass Media

Let's work together to phrase questions based on this outline. We'll write in a few. Why don't you fill in the rest? Note that all we need for now is the questions. In a real class, you'd also leave room for the answers.

I. What are the influences of "nature" and "nurture" on socialization?
II. _____
    A. _____
    B. What happens to children who are reared in isolation?
    C. _____
    D. _____
III. What is the self? How does it emerge?
    A. _____
    B. What is George Herbert Mead's view of the emergence of the self?
IV. _____
V. _____
VI. What are the agents of socialization?
    A. _____
    B. _____
    C. How do peers influence the process of socialization?
    D. _____

Note Key Terms It is helpful to keep a list of key terms in your notes. These terms are frequently **boldfaced** or *italicized* in textbooks. Professors tend to highlight them in lectures. If you are in a large lecture hall in which student participation is not encouraged, you can jot down terms you do not understand (leaving proper spelling for later), and check them out in the glossary, the dictionary, or with your professor or a TA after class. If you're in a small class, it's reasonable to interrupt and ask for an explanation of the term or a couple of examples of usage. One of the traps students fall into is that they cut some classes or fail to preview the class material. As a result, they are reluctant to ask questions for fear of sounding "out of it."

STUDYING

You may think of studying as something that is done after classes and after reading, primarily in preparation for tests. Actually, *Webster's New World Dictionary* defines studying as applying oneself attentively to try to learn or understand. Studying includes reading, reviewing, listening, even thinking about subject matter. Studying is an active process, an effort to learn and understand.

And so it happens that our discussions of attending classes and taking notes were all about studying. But in this section we're going to acquaint you with the so-called PQ4R study method and give you some additional hints.

PQ4R: Preview, Question, Read, Reflect, Recite, and Review

PQ4R stands for *Preview, Question, Read, Reflect, Recite, and Review*, a method that is based on the work of educational psychologist Francis P. Robinson.[4] PQ4R has helped many students raise their grades.[5]

By reflecting on your reading, you may embed the subject matter so firmly in your memory that you retain it on the basis of one or just a few reviews. Memorization may otherwise require many repetitions.

Previewing and Questioning

We have already discussed the values of previewing material and phrasing questions about it. Previewing fine-tunes your expectations. It helps set up mental compartments into which you fit the material. Phrasing questions about the material makes learning an active process. You attend class or read the text *in order to answer questions* you have phrased.

Reading

Once you have phrased questions, read the material so that you can answer them. The sense of purpose this method engenders will help you focus on the key points of the subject matter. As you respond to each question, jot down some key words in your notebook that will telegraph the answer to you later when you recite and review.

If the reading assignment is fine literature, feel free to read it through first so that you can appreciate its poetic aspects. But when rereading it, use PQ4R to tease out the key information you will need when you are trying to recall the material.

Reflecting

Reflecting on the material is extremely important. It takes time to sit back and relate what you have been reading to your own life, but it's a worthwhile investment. *Through effective reflection, you may embed the material so firmly in your memory that you retain it on the basis of one or just a few reviews. Memorization may otherwise require many repetitions.*

Relating the New to the Old We normally expand our knowledge base by relating new items to things we already know.[6] Children learn that a cello is similar to a violin, only larger. They learn that a bass fiddle is also similar to a violin, but larger yet. We can reflect on information about whales by relating whales to other mammals. Then we will better remember that whales are warm-blooded, breathe air rather than water, bear their young live (rather than lay eggs), and nurse their young. Similarly, we better learn information about porpoises and dolphins if we reflect on them as small whales—not as intelligent, friendly fish.

> Every man who knows how to read has it in his power to magnify himself, to multiply the ways in which he exists, to make his life full, significant and interesting.
>
> ALDOUS HUXLEY

> Read not to contradict and confute, nor to believe and take for granted, nor to find talk and discourse, but to weigh and consider.
>
> FRANCIS BACON

> People in general do not willingly read, if they can have anything else to amuse them.
>
> SAMUEL JOHNSON

Attending Classes, Taking Notes, and Studying

Relating New Information to Old Rules Sometimes reflecting on information means applying rules. For example, you can recall the spelling of *retrieve* by retrieving the rule "*i* before *e* except after *c*." There are exceptions to rules: A moment's reflection will reveal that *weird* doesn't follow the spelling rule because it's a "weird" word.

Relating New Information to Events in Our Personal Lives The media (and sometimes our personal lives) are replete with stories about people whose behavior is deviant or abnormal. To help learn about the mental disorders outlined in psychology textbooks, think of media portrayals of characters who had the problem. Or perhaps a friend or family member has one of the problems mentioned. Consider how the behavior patterns displayed by these people are consistent (or inconsistent) with the descriptions given in the text and by your professor. You will learn the subject matter more effectively and become a critic of media depictions of psychological problems.

Using Mnemonic Devices Mnemonic (pronounced *NEH-mon-ick*) devices, broadly speaking, refer to any system for remembering information. But we are usually referring to devices that combine chunks of information into a format like an acronym, jingle, or phrase. Acronyms are words that are made up from the first letters of the series of words they represent. The acronym *laser* stands for *light amplification by stimulated emission of radiation. NATO* stands for *North Atlantic Treaty Organization.*

Consider some more examples: Recalling the phrase "Every Good Boy Does Fine" has helped many people remember the musical keys E, G, B, D, F. In neurology, the acronym *SAME* serves as a mnemonic device for distinguishing between afferent and efferent neurons. (*Sensory* information is brought in by means of *afferent* neurons, and commands for *motor* activity are issued to muscles by means of *efferent*.) Biology and psychology students use the acronym *Roy G. Biv* to remember the colors of the rainbow (red, orange, etc.), even though your backward authors chose to use the "word" *vibgyor* many years back.

Acronyms have found applications in many disciplines. Consider geography. The acronym *HOMES* stands for the Great Lakes: *H*uron, *O*ntario, *M*ichigan, *E*rie, and *S*uperior. In astronomy, the phrase "*M*ercury's *v*ery *e*ager *m*other *j*ust *s*erved *u*s *n*ine *p*otatoes" helps students recall the order of the planets Mercury, Venus, Earth, Mars, Jupiter, Saturn, Uranus, Neptune, and Pluto.

What about biology? You can remember that Dromedary camels have one hump, while Bactrian camels have two by turning the letters *D* and *B* on their sides.

And how can you math students ever be expected to remember the reciprocal of pi (that is, 1 divided by 3.14)? Simple: Just remember the question "Can I remember the reciprocal?" and count the number of letters in each word. The reciprocal of pi, it turns out, is 0.318310. (Remember the last two digits as 10, not 1–0.)

TRUTH OR FICTION *Revisited*

It is *not* always true that the best way to learn is to go over the subject matter repeatedly. Sometimes it's more efficient to meaningfully relate the material to other aspects of your life, to find acronyms, and so forth.

Some other widely used mnemonic devices can be found in Table 5.2.

TABLE 5.2. Some Mnemonic Devices.

MNEMONIC DEVICE	ENCODED INFORMATION
Washington and Jefferson Made Many a Joke; Van Buren Had to Put the Frying Pan Back. Lincoln Just Gasped, "Heaven Guard America." Cleveland Had Coats Made Ready-to-Wear Home. Coolidge Hurried Right to Every Kitchen Jar Nook. Ford Cut Right Brow.	Presidents of the United States: Washington, Adams, Jefferson, Madison, Monroe, Adams, Jackson Van Buren, Harrison, Tyler, Polk, Taylor, Fillmore, Pierce, Buchanan Lincoln, Johnson, Grant, Hayes, Garfield, Arthur Cleveland, Harrison, Cleveland, McKinley, Roosevelt, Taft, Wilson, Harding Coolidge, Hoover, Roosevelt, Truman, Eisenhower, Kennedy, Johnson, Nixon Ford, Carter, Reagan, Bush.
Poor Queen Victoria Eats Crow at Christmas.	The seven hills of Rome: Palatine, Quirinal, Viminal, Esquiline, Capitoline, Aventine, Caelian.
A True Conservative Can Not GOVern Virtuously; They Do Not Themselves Hate Avarice Altogether.	The Roman emperors: Augustus, Tiberius, Caligula, Claudius, Nero, Galba, Otho, Vitellius (the last three in the same year), Vespasian, Titus, Domitian, Nerva, Trajan, Hadrian, Antoninus Pius, Aurelius.
No Plan Like Yours to Study History Wisely.	The royal houses of England: Norman, Plantagenet, Lancaster, York, Tudor, Stuart, Hanover, Windsor.
X shall stand for playmates Ten. V for Five stalwart men. I for One, D for Five. M for a Thousand soldiers true. And L for Fifty, I'll tell you.	The value of the Roman numerals. "D for Five" means D = 500.
Mary Eats Peanut Butter.	The first four hydrocarbons of the Alkane class: Methane, Ethane, Propane, and Butane, in ascending order of the number of carbon atoms in their chains.
These Ten Valuable Amino Acids Have Long Preserved Life in Man.	Ten vital amino acids: Threonine, Tryptophan, Valine, Arginine, Histidine, Lysine, Phenylalanine, Leucine, Isoleucine, Methionine.
All Hairy Men Will Buy Razors.	Constituents of soil: Air, Humus, Mineral salts, Water, Bacteria, Rock particles.
Soak Her Toe.	Translates into SOHCAHTOA, or: Sine = Opposite/Hypotenuse Cosine = Adjacent/Hypotenuse Tangent = Opposite/Adjacent
Krakatoa Positively Casts off Fumes; Generally Sulfurous Vapors.	Biological classifications in descending order: Kingdom, Phylum, Class, Order, Family, Genus, Species, Variety.
On Old Olympia's Towering Tops, a Finn and a German Vault and Hop.	The twelve pairs of cranial nerves: Olfactory, Optic, Oculomotor, Trochlear, Trigeminal, Abducens, Facial, Auditory, Glossopharyngeal, Vagus, Accessory, Hypoglossal.
Never Lower Tillie's Pants; Mother Might Come Home.	The eight bones of the wrist: Navicular, Lunate, Triangular, Pisiform, Multangular greater, Multangular lesser, Capitate, Hamate.
Camels Often Sit Down Carefully. Perhaps Their Joints Creak. Persistent Early Oiling Might Prevent Permanent Rheumatism.	The geological time periods: Cambrian, Ordovician, Silurian, Devonian, Carboniferous, Permian, Triassic, Jurassic, Cretaceous, Paleocene, Eocene, Oligocene, Miocene, Pliocene, Pleistocene, Recent.
Lazy French Tarts Sit Naked In Anticipation.	The nerves that pass through the superior orbital fissure of the skull: Lachrymal, Frontal, Trochlear, Superior, Nasal, Inferior, Abducent.

Using Mediation Mediation is a kind of mnemonic device in which you form associations: You link two items with a third that ties them together. Using mediation to link foreign vocabulary words to their English equivalents makes them easier to recall.[7] For example, the *peso*, pronounced *pay-so*, is a unit of Mexican money. Form a link to English by finding a part of the foreign word (in this case, the *pe-* [pronounced *pay*] in *peso*) and constructing a phrase like, "One pays with money." The next time you hear or read the word *peso*, you associate it with the phrase "One pays with money" and reconstruct the translation, "a unit of money."

Mediation helps build English vocabulary also. *Entomology*, for example, means the study of insects. *Ent* is close in sound to *ant*, so one can think "entomology—ant—insect—study of insects."

In the example of retrieving the spelling of *retrieve*, the rule "*I* before *e* except after *c*" mediated the sound of the word and its proper spelling.

By the way, we used the term *mnemonic device*, which means a technique or system for improving the memory. How can you remember how to spell the word *mnemonic*? We always say to our classes, "Be willing to grant *amnesty* to those who can't." Then we write "aMNesty" on the blackboard, capitalizing the *MN*.

Forming Unusual, Exaggerated Associations Certain information seems to stick with us permanently, perhaps because it is unusual and particularly meaningful. For example, most of us will never forget where we were and what we were doing when we learned of the explosion of the space shuttle *Challenger* in January, 1986. Many of us who are middle aged will always remember where we were and what we were doing when President Kennedy was assassinated. Similarly, we tend to remember details of the events surrounding the losses of close relatives. Psychologists refer to such memories as "flashbulb memories" because of the detail with which they imprint our surroundings.

Flashbulb memories apparently become firmly embedded for two reasons.[8] One is that they are unusual; they stand out. The second is that we tend to reflect on them extensively. They are laden with meaning for us and have an impact on important areas of our lives.

We can transform some of the subject matter in our courses into "flashbulb memories" by forming unusual, exaggerated associations.

Your first author used a combination of mediation and formation of unusual associations to help him remember foreign vocabulary words in high school and college. For example, the Spanish verb *trabajar* means "to work," in the sense of harassing, laboring, straining. Although *-jar* is pronounced "har," he nevertheless formed a mental image of a "trial by jars" when he laid eyes on the word. He saw himself running the gauntlet with strange enemies pouring jars down upon him until he was so laden that he could barely move. "Now," he thought, "that trial by jars was really *work*!" Trabajar—trial by jars—work.

And now we pause for a commercial for learning word origins—or *etymology*. Checking the origins of foreign words, such as *trabajar*, opens fascinating worlds of information. *Trabajar* derives from the Latin *tripalium*, which was an instrument for torture composed of three (*tri-*) stakes. (*Palium*—impale?) We suppose you could conjure up some unusual imagery based on the word's root, but note also that the English word *travail*, meaning very hard toil or labor, stems from the same root. And the French verb for "to work" happens to be *travailler*. Convenient?

In going from one language to another, there are often consonant and vowel shifts that can help us decode the foreign words. For example, the Spanish *b* often "translates" into the English *v*, as in *trabajar–travail*. The German *b* also often translates into the English *v*, and the German *t* into the English *d*. For example, the German *taub* translates into the English *dove*. Any guesses as to what the German word for "drive" might be? Is that question giving you a *Teufel* of a time?

By the way, the word *mnemonic* is derived from Mnemosyne, the Greek goddess of memory. Her name is pronounced *Nee-MOS-uh-nee*. How can you remember the pronunciation? How about thinking of the goddess getting down on her two knees (*nee-nee*) to worship?

Commercial over. Now return to Spanish for a moment so your first author can share another bit of mediation he used. *Mujer* (pronounced *moo-hair* [almost]), is the Spanish word for "woman." Women have mo' hair than he does. And so this bit of mediation was helpful to him: Woman—mo' hair—mujer. This would no longer work, because now nearly all men also have more hair than he does, but the association was so outlandish that it has stuck with him. (Your second author is contemplating a divorce—which would break her outlandish association with the first author.)

And how can we remember that *etymology* refers to word *origins*? How about this: Word origins go back through *time*. We could also spell time as *tym*. So: "etymology—tym—time—origins go back through time—word origins."

So there are many ways to reflect upon the material you are studying. Broadly speaking, when we reflect on material we *relate* it to other things. This may mean relating it to personal experiences. It may mean categorization or classification, as in classifying whales as mammals. It may mean constructing bizarre, unusual associations. It may mean using mnemonic devices such as acronyms and mediation.

Does it seem that there is a game-playing aspect to reflection? Does it seem that reflection can sometimes make learning enjoyable? True, it can, and perhaps this is not too great a price to pay.

Reciting

Once you have read a section and jotted down the key words to the answer, recite each answer aloud, if possible. Doing so may depend on where you are, who's around, and your level of concern over how you think they'll react to you. Reciting answers aloud helps us to remember them in various ways. For one thing, we repeat our study of the material, and repetition fosters retention. For another, we produce the concepts and ideas we have taken in. By so doing, we associate them with spoken words and gestures. Recitation also provides feedback on the helpfulness of the key words we have chosen.

Some educators recommend writing a summary of the material as a way of organizing thoughts and fostering retention.[9] Writing a summary may also translate into helping you write essay questions on a test. If you have organized most of your notebook into sections with two columns, you may want to leave blocks of room for summaries. Many students profit from summarizing each class, which often represents a major section in a chapter of the textbook. Others summarize chapters in their textbooks.

Reviewing

One way to foster retention is to relate subject matter to things you already know. Another is to repeat or review it according to a reasonably regular schedule, such as once weekly.

To effectively review material, you need to establish goals and plan ahead to meet them. Assess the amount of material you must master by the next exam or by the end of the term and relate it to your rate of learning. Consider these questions:

How long does it take you to learn the material in a chapter or in a book?

How many hours do you spend studying each day?

How much material is there?

When is the next quiz or exam?

Does everything add up right?

Will you make it?

It may be that you will not be able to determine the answers until you have gotten into the book for a week or two. But once you have, be honest with yourself about the mathematics of how you are doing. Be willing to revise your initial estimates.

Once you have determined the amount of study time you will need, try to space it out fairly evenly. For most of us, spaced or distributed learning is more efficient than massed learning or cramming.

Maintenance Rehearsal Psychologists and educators refer to such review as *maintenance rehearsal*, or rote repetition. Actors learn their roles by means of rehearsal. Students learn much of their subject matter by means of review. Memory traces of much subject matter decay with the passage of time, and when you review, you relearn this material. Relearning material regularly is much easier than initial learning, and there may come a time when you accurately anticipate every word in the pages of your notebooks.

Maintenance rehearsal may seem a mechanical way for a capable and inventive college student to learn material, but remember that this is how you learned the alphabet and how to count! There is no logical reason that the written letter A should evoke the sound of the spoken A; you learned this association by repetition or maintenance rehearsal. There is no logical reason that the numerical symbols should be spoken in the order "One, two, three," and so on. We learn the alphabet and number sequences by repetition, by rote, by drill and practice. We write spelling words over and over to remember them. Athletes and gymnasts repeat movements to facilitate their bodies' skill memories. Review helps you get formulas down pat. When formulas are memorized, you can use your time and your creative energies pondering when to apply them, not trying to recall them. When the wide receiver in football has his moves down pat, he can focus on field condition and the location of defenders. He doesn't have to focus his efforts on recalling the basic patterns.

Flash Cards Many college students find it helpful to use flash cards. For example, in learning the vocabulary of a foreign language, you might write the foreign word (e.g., *trabajar*) on one side of the card and the English equivalent ("to work") on the other. Then you can go to and fro, sometimes trying to remember the English word when you see the foreign word, and vice versa. You check the accuracy of your response by looking at the back side of the card. Art history students frequently sketch works on one side of a flash card and the name of the work and the artist, the date, and the period on the other.

Question and Answer If you have organized your notes according to questions and answers, you can review the material as follows: Conceal the answer column and go through the questions as though they were a test. Recite the answers and check them against the key words in the answer column. Reread the textbook or other sources when you do not know an answer. If you find that you do not know a large number of answers, it could be that you haven't phrased the questions in a way that is helpful to you, or that you have not reviewed your notes often enough. Or perhaps you did not read the material closely enough at the outset.

Find a place for studying that will help you, not hinder you. An ideal location is comfortable and free from distractions.

TRUTH OR FICTION *Revisited*

Your job as a student is definitely *not* to sit back and try to absorb the information that is dispensed. Your job is to take active control of your coursework by previewing it, phrasing questions, relating it to other areas of life, and so on.

Overlearning When you have reviewed the subject matter without making any errors, you have learned it very well indeed. But if you have time, you can go one step further and *overlearn* it. That is, review it again. Overlearning buttresses retention and gives you more confidence during tests.

Now that we have previewed, questioned, read, reflected, recited, and reviewed the PQ4R method, let us now consider two other issues in studying: coping with distractions and rewarding ourselves for being good. (We are, aren't we?)

Finding an Ideal Place for Studying

It's helpful to be front and center not only in class, but also when you are studying. By that we mean find a place for studying that will help you, not hinder you. An ideal location is both comfortable and free from distractions. It should be comfortable, because you need to spend a good deal of time there. It should be free from distractions, because environmental stimuli vie for our attention. To better understand how distractions work, consider the case of Maria:

> All through high school, Maria withdrew to her bedroom to study—the one room where she had complete privacy—and studied in her bed. She assumed that it would be easy to do the same thing in college. But in college she has two roommates, and they very often want to chat while Maria is hitting the books. Or if they're not talking together, one of them may be on the phone. Or if no one's on the phone, someone is likely to come knocking at the door. Maria has put a sign up on the door that says "No knocking between 7:00 and 10:00 P.M.—This means you!" Nevertheless, someone's always coming by and saying, "Oh, but I wanted to see if Nicky or Pam was in. I didn't mean to disturb you."

Attending Classes, Taking Notes, and Studying

Pam, it happens, likes to study with the stereo on—soft, but on, nevertheless. Nicky eats in bed—incessantly. While Maria is trying to concentrate on the books, she's assailed by the chomping of potato chips or pretzels.

Finally, Maria gets disgusted and gets up to go for a brief walk to clear her head. She passes the lounge and is intrigued by glimpses of a new hit series. A friend calls her over to pass the time. Before she knows it, it's 8:30 and she hasn't really begun to get to work.

Avoid Maria's pitfalls by letting your place for studying—your room, a spot in the library, a study lounge (not the one with the TV set!) tucked away in the dorm—come to mean studying to you. Let the environment work for you, not against you. Do nothing but study there. Don't leaf through magazines. Don't socialize. Don't snack.

Using Self-Reward

After all these *don'ts*, let us remind you of a *do* from Chapter 3: After you have studied for, say, 50 minutes, reward yourself with a 10-minute break. Also reward yourself for meeting daily study goals. Rewards highlight the fact that you've done something worthwhile, and they inspire repetition of desirable behavior. You don't have to be a martyr to be a good student. You needn't postpone all pleasures until the term draws to an end. Some students can delay gratification indefinitely, but that isn't necessary. And students who are not used to nonstop studying may be asking too much of themselves.

When you have met your study goals for the day, you may want to choose one or two activities from the list of turn-ons in Chapter 4 (pp. 95–97) to reward yourself the next day or on the weekend. Go ahead. Have some fun. You deserve it.

TRUTH OR FICTION *Revisited*

Trying to postpone all pleasures until the term has ended is self-defeating for most students. However, it is helpful to make rewards contingent upon completion of study goals.

SUMMING UP

1. What is meant by taking an active approach to studying? Are you an active student or a passive student? Are you active in some classes and passive in others?
2. What motivates you to attend (or not to attend) classes?
3. Do you find your attention wandering when you attend classes? What can you do about it?
4. What are the benefits of participating in class? Do other students do things that annoy you when they participate in class? Are you a good classroom citizen?
5. What system do you use for taking notes in class? Can you think of any ways of making note taking in class more efficient and useful?
6. Do you take notes on your reading? Do you use a system for doing so? How can you make notes on reading more useful?
7. What is the PQ4R method for studying?

8. What strategies do you use for memorizing formulas in mathematics, vocabulary in foreign languages, historical facts? Can you think of ways of improving your memory?
9. Where do you do most of your studying? Have you selected a good place for studying? Why or why not?
10. Do you just study through from beginning to end, or do you give yourself breaks? Do you reward yourself for meeting study goals, or do you just take good work for granted?

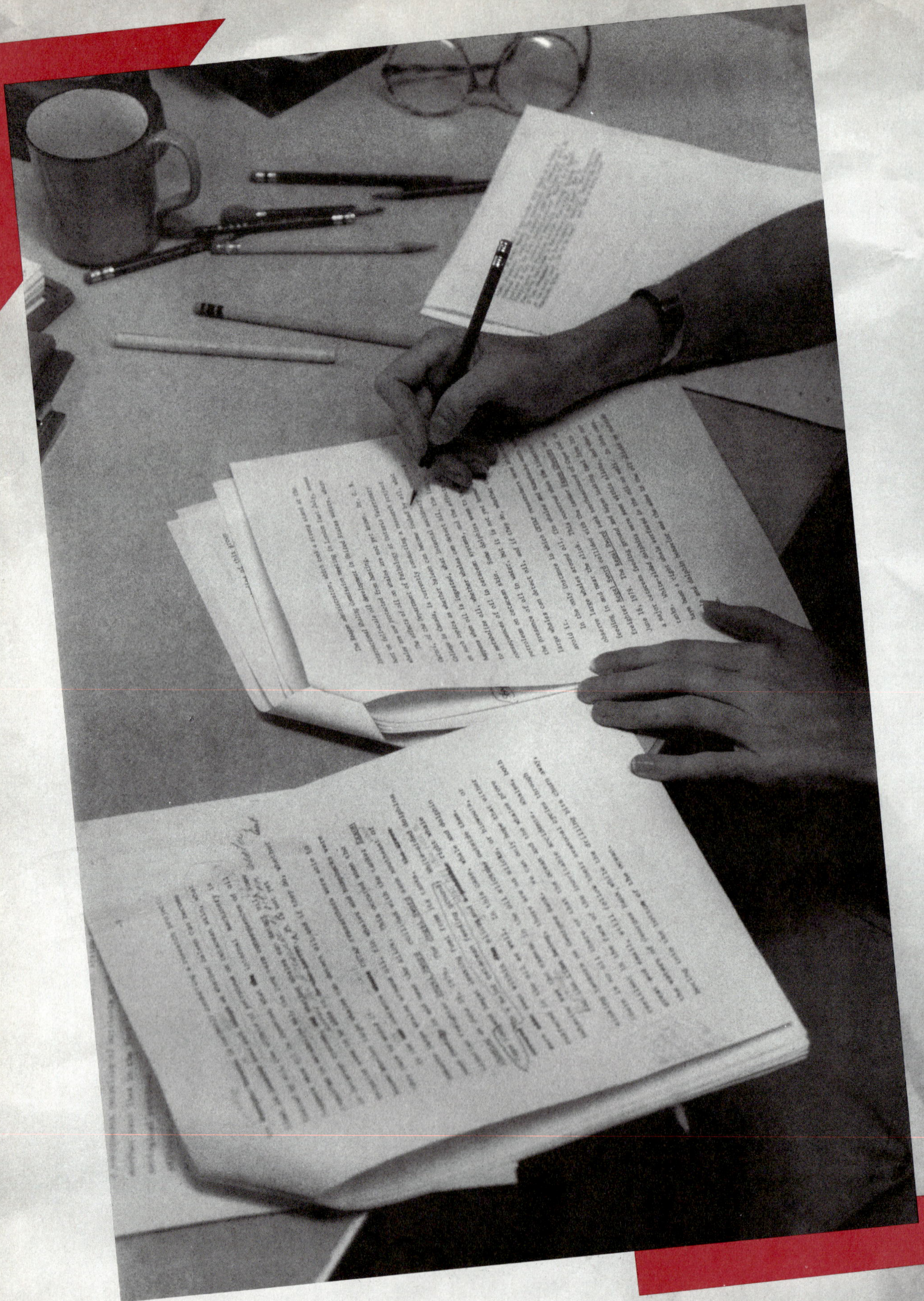

6

Writing Papers

TRUTH OR FICTION?

_____ You really don't have to be able to write very well in the real world. Writing papers is just one price you have to pay to get the college degree.

_____ Freshman composition focuses on the basics: grammar and punctuation.

_____ You cannot learn how to write—either you have it or you don't.

_____ You usually get better grades by using large vocabulary words.

_____ It's more difficult to write a long paper than a short paper.

_____ Professors cannot tell whether or not you are using your own words in your papers.

_____ Using another person's words is not plagiarizing as long as you credit the source.

_____ To write successfully, you must wait for inspiration to strike.

_____ Good writing requires poetic touches.

It seems fitting to begin this chapter on writing with an "In Your Own Write" feature:

IN YOUR OWN WRITE

What are your own feelings about writing? Do you find writing enjoyable or tedious? Why or why not?

_____
_____
_____
_____
_____
_____
_____
_____

WRITING: NOT FOR COLLEGE ONLY

Throughout high school and college, many students have the feeling that compositions and papers are part of the price they have to pay to get a diploma and, eventually, a decent job. But they do not see writing as something valuable in itself. In the United States, as a matter of fact, many students think of reading and writing as "feminine" activities—activities that are more right and proper for women than for men.[1] And some believe that it is "masculine" to paint important ideas in broad swaths, but "feminine" to attend to such niceties as spelling and punctuation. These stereotypes are biased and harmful, especially to students who use them to justify a dislike of writing or an unwillingness to look up the proper spelling of words.

The fact is that writing is essential, not only in college but also in most professional careers. Business executives need to be able to communicate their ideas through writing. Marketing plans, advertising copy, and proposals for new products must all be fleshed out in words and sentences. Very few lawyers put on courtroom shows like the fabled Perry Mason; most lawyers spend far more time writing contracts and persuasive letters. Technicians, engineers, and scientists have to be able to write precise reports. Think of all the writing that goes into directions for using a stove or a VCR. Consider the detailed writing that is found in armed forces weapons manuals. Engineers and scientists also write technical articles for journals; they review the research in their fields and report on their own experiments. They have to be able to write clearly enough so that other people can follow their directions and arrive at the same results accurately and safely. Doctors, psychologists, counselors, nurses, and dental hygienists must be able to write up reports describing the problems and progress of their patients and clients. Managers of fast-food restaurants write evaluations of employees. Everyone writes business letters of one kind or another—or is inconvenienced if he or she cannot.

So writing skills are not for college only. Writing skills are not just the province of English teachers, poets, novelists, and journalists. They are for everyone who is receiving an education and contemplating a career.

> Books are the carriers of civilization.
>
> BARBARA TUCHMAN

TRUTH OR FICTION *Revisited*

You *do* need to be able to write well in the real world—if, for you, the "real world" means a profession or a white-collar occupation.

Many college students fear writing assignments. Often they have not been given enough training in high school to make them feel comfortable. Most college instructors of writing see their job as enhancing their students' creativity, critical thinking, and explanatory powers, but not teaching students basic sentence structure and punctuation. Professors in other disciplines often rely completely on short-answer tests to arrive at grades, protesting that their job is to teach their subject, not to suffer through their students' incoherent essays and papers. High school English teachers sometimes complain that basic skills were not taught in the elementary schools. Elementary school teachers, in turn, often criticize children's home environments for not helping incubate basic writing skills. In short, writing skills are valued in college and are essential afterward, but they are taught only by a minority of instructors in a few disciplines.

> No man but a blockhead ever wrote except for money.
>
> SAMUEL JOHNSON

> Writing is an exploration. You start from nothing and learn as you go.
>
> E. L. DOCTOROW

KINDS OF WRITING

There are many kinds of writing. Writing can be broken down into fiction (imaginary happenings, such as short stories, plays, and novels) and nonfiction (such as directions for assembling machines, essays, theme papers, and term papers). The writing of fiction is usually taught in creative writing courses, although fiction is sometimes assigned in freshman composition classes. Students need not be good at writing fiction to get by in college—unless they're making up excuses as to why they are late with their assignments! By and large, however, college students are required to show or develop some skill at writing nonfiction.

The kinds of nonfiction required of college students are mostly essay answers on tests, theme papers, and term papers. Chapter 7 offers advice on writing essays for tests. In this chapter, we focus on theme papers and term papers. A theme is a relatively short paper and is the most common type of paper assigned in courses like freshman composition. There are different kinds of themes, including argumentative, descriptive, and expository. The aim of the argumentative theme is to persuade the reader to adopt a certain point of view. Papers intended to convince the reader that Lady Macbeth was motivated by infertility or that the greenhouse effect will eventually cause persistent droughts in the midwestern breadbasket are argumentative. A descriptive theme paints in words persons, places, or ideas. The infamous "What I Did on My Summer Vacation" theme is basically descriptive. If you have poetic urges, it is usually best to give vent to them in descriptive themes. Expository themes are explanatory in nature. They are concrete and logically developed. Expository themes apply to the instructions in your cookbook for concocting guacamole and to laboratory reports. Laboratory reports are required in many science courses. Each discipline (biology, physics, psychology, etc.) has its own way of doing things, its own traditions, but they also have some things in common: Explanations are kept as brief and precise as possible. Usually, you explain what you

> I love being a writer. What I can't stand is the paperwork.
>
> PETER DE VRIES

set out to do, why you set out to do it, what you actually did, what you found out, and, sometimes, the implications of what you discovered. Keep this in mind: In science, the goal is to write the report like a cookbook, so that anybody could follow the record of what you did and achieve the same results. In descriptive writing, you want to render even ordinary events so poetically that no one else could possibly mimic your style. Well, at least that's a nice goal.

Term papers differ from theme papers in a number of ways. One is length. The paper is called a term paper because it is supposed to take a good part of the term to write it, or because it is intended to reflect what you have learned during the term. Also, term papers usually require references to books and articles on their subjects. That means that research is also required. If the research base of your term paper is to be solid, it could take you longer to do the research, including taking notes, than to write the paper itself.

> Writing is the only thing that, when I do it, I don't feel I should be doing something else.
>
> GLORIA STEINEM

Eighty-five percent of colleges require at least one course in English composition that focuses on writing skills.[2] The course may be called Freshman Composition, Introduction to College Writing, College English, or simply English 101. We'll talk about that course in a minute, but first we'll have a look at the following questionnaire on rules for good writing.

QUESTIONNAIRE
Rules for Good Writing

Although you may be new to college, you probably gained an understanding of several rules for good writing during your elementary and high school years. Following are a number of rules you may have come across. Indicate whether you believe that each of them is true or false by checking True or False. We shall refer to each rule as the chapter progresses. There is also an answer key at the end of the chapter.

We'll give you one hint: Not all of these rules are true.

		True	False
1.	You should not start a sentence with the word *I* or write in the first person.	___	___
2.	You should not write about yourself.	___	___
3.	You should not begin a sentence with a conjunction such as *and* or *but*.	___	___
4.	You should not begin a sentence with a conjunctive adverb such as *however* or *nevertheless*.	___	___
5.	You should not use slang or regional words in formal writing.	___	___
6.	You should not use curse words in formal writing.	___	___
7.	You should not use exclamation points.	___	___
8.	You should not use incomplete sentences (sentence fragments).	___	___
9.	You should always plan your outline before you start writing the paper itself.	___	___
10.	You should wait for inspiration rather than try to force writing.	___	___

THE FRESHMAN COMPOSITION COURSE

We have some good news and some bad news about freshman composition. First, the good news: Many freshman composition instructors are more likely to focus on what you say and how you say it than on the fine points

Freshman Composition is primarily intended to help you write clear, interesting essays. Some Freshman Composition instructors also ask students to try their hands at poems or short stories, but theme papers—especially argumentative themes—tend to be the meat of the course.

of grammar and punctuation. Now, the bad news: Many freshman composition instructors are more likely to focus on what you say and how you say it than on the fine points of grammar and punctuation.

Sound ironic? Perhaps.* The point is that in freshman composition, you may be free to concentrate on creating and expressing ideas through writing. However, if you haven't learned how to string words into sentences (grammar) and how to use punctuation by the time you arrive at college, you may have to develop these skills on your own or take a preliminary basic skills course. Freshman composition instructors talk about emphasizing the origin, critical examination, and expression of ideas. Nevertheless, your grades will probably suffer if you repeatedly write run-on sentences and misspell words. Some instructors may take the "mechanics" for granted, even if the student finds the mechanics to be a ponderous chore.

> Slang is a language that rolls up its sleeves, spits on its hands and goes to work.
>
> CARL SANDBURG

TRUTH OR FICTION *Revisited*

Freshman composition usually focuses on more advanced issues than grammar and punctuation. However, if you have not mastered these mechanics, it would be helpful to do so early in your college career.

What can you do if you're troubled by the mechanics? First of all, don't use this difficulty as an excuse to avoid writing. Instead, write as much as you can. Visit the college learning center, where tutoring can be arranged for you. Ask your instructor to explain some fine points during office hours. Get an English-usage handbook that explains grammar and other points of usage. Also have a friend—or a tutor at the learning center—read the paper as it is being developed. If you do not understand why your usage is in error, ask. If you do not understand the explanation, say so and ask that it be put into terms you can understand. Ask for several

*Note two sentence fragments in a row.

examples of the correct usage; you can learn to understand a principle of grammar *inductively* (by generalizing from examples) as well as *deductively* (through theoretical explanation). Learning inductively—from examples—is not a bad way to do it; that, in fact, is how children learn to speak the language used in the home.[3]

Freshman composition is primarily intended to help you write clear, interesting essays. Some freshman composition instructors also ask students to try their hands at poems or short stories, but theme papers—especially argumentative themes—tend to be the meat of the course. When you learn how to write better theme papers, you also tend to write better answers to essay questions on exams, better term papers, business reports, memos, even letters.

TRUTH OR FICTION *Revisited*

You can learn a great deal about writing in college, and some of the learning involves training in critical thinking rather than writing *per se*.

CRITICAL THINKING

> Most people would sooner die than think; in fact, they do so.
>
> BERTRAND RUSSELL

Writing and thinking tend to go hand in hand. For this reason, freshman composition instructors and other instructors usually aim to help their students engage in critical thinking. As noted in Chapter 1, critical thinking involves analyzing arguments that you read and hear about, examining the premises or assumptions of the writers or speakers, and then scrutinizing their logic.

Professors may write comments like "This assumption seems arbitrary" or "This idea does not follow" on papers to point out fallacies in thinking. When you see such comments, do not assume that professors disagree with your conclusions or are prejudiced against your arguments. Remember that most professors do not tell you *what* to think. Instead, they see their roles as trying to teach you *how* to think. So be open to recognizing the assumptions or premises of your arguments. Are your premises supported by the facts? Are they self-evident? (Really?) Also ask yourself whether your arguments are logical. Do they truly follow from your premises, or could other conclusions have been drawn as well? When in doubt, *list* the premises of your paper on the left side of a piece of scrap paper. List your paper's conclusions on the right side. Draw arrows from the premises to the conclusions, and write question marks above the arrows, like this:

$$\text{Premise} \overset{?}{\rightarrow} \text{Conclusion}$$

Ask yourself how you arrived at each conclusion from each premise. Is your argument tight? If you're too close to your paper to arrive at an unbiased answer, ask your professor or a friend for an opinion. (The right time to do this is before you hand your paper in!)

GENERAL GUIDELINES FOR GOOD WRITING

Just as no two people are exactly alike (even identical twins have their own private thoughts), no two people write exactly alike. Good writing takes many forms. Some people use slang very well, whereas others fare better when taking a more formal approach. Some writers show strong organizational skills, whereas others have a fine poetic touch and the ability to create vivid images through words. Yet, there are a number of general guidelines that hold true for most of us most of the time.

Complete the Assignment

It may not matter how your intelligence and sophistication shine through or how your prose sparkles if you do not follow instructions and carry out the assignment. Make sure that you understand the instructions. If your professor asks for a reaction paper to an essay, make sure that you understand what the professor means by *reaction paper.* Don't hesitate to ask in class; if you are unclear about how to complete the assignment, other students may be also. If, however, you are concerned that you might take up too much class time, or if you want still more information than can be covered in class, see your instructor during office hours. If general discussion of the requirements does not create a clear picture for you, ask for examples. You can also ask the instructor to show you one or more models (pieces of writing) that fulfill the assignment.

Write for Your Audience

If you are writing a children's story, keep the vocabulary simple and the sentences short. If you are writing an argumentative theme to persuade prochoice people that abortion is morally wrong, don't begin with, "Abortion is murder and people who support abortion are murderers." All you will accomplish is to alienate your audience. Instead, write something like, "Abortion is a complex and troubling issue to most of us, and people on all sides of the issue share deep, sincere convictions." In this way, you recognize your audience's earnestness and get them involved. You can make your points later.

The book you are holding in your hands is intended to help college students make the transition to college life. We wrote it in a "user-friendly" manner—speaking directly to students in everyday language; we use the first person, contractions, and so on. Our purpose is to make readers feel comfortable with the book—to be part of the solution, not part of the problem.

> I can't write without a reader. It's precisely like a kiss—you can't do it alone.
> JOHN CHEEVER

Write Clearly and Simply

Most good writing is reasonably easy to read. Don't have the idea that intelligent writing has to be hard to follow, like a Henry James novel or a Shakespearean play. Unless your assignment is to write a Victorian novel or an Elizabethan play, don't try to manufacture an intricate style or several layers of meaning.

Here are some examples of writing that are awful because they lack clarity and simplicity. We also note changes that make them clearer, simpler, and at least a bit better.

Just Plain Awful	Better
Prevaricators often arrive at the point where the recipients of their fabrications no longer place credence in their utterances.	People lose their trust in liars.
As the sun set glowingly in the distant mountains, she cast about for direction and thought, "Whither shall I meander at this time?"	It was getting dark. "Where do I go now?" she wondered.

Writing Papers 133

> Failure is the condiment that gives success its flavor.
>
> TRUMAN CAPOTE

Just Plain Awful	Better
Scientists have run multiple complex experiments in the Canadian wilderness, ascertaining whether acid rain has effects that are irreversible and, if so, how rapidly they occur.	Scientists have run experiments in Canada to determine the effects of acid rain.
In your writing, it is a good idea to keep your sentences as simple as you can reasonably do.	Keep sentences simple.
There are many different views and controversies surrounding the right and proper economic roles of capital gains taxes. Are capital gains taxes meant primarily as methods of revenue enhancement or as inducers of long-term investment?	There is debate about whether capital gains taxes are primarily sources of revenue or incentives for long-term investment.

TRUTH OR FICTION Revisited

You get good grades by using the right word, not big words. Keep your writing as clear and simple as possible.

Be Willing to Make Mistakes

At the end of the movie *Some Like It Hot*, a female impersonator who is being romanced by Joe E. Brown tries to explain why Brown should forget about him. But Joe E. Brown accepts every flaw. In exasperation, the impersonator yanks off his wig and confesses, "I'm a man." Brown, nonplussed, retorts, "Nobody's perfect."

Nor is any college student or any other person a perfect writer. Everyone makes mistakes. If you didn't make mistakes, you wouldn't need an education, would you?

Learn from your errors. When some aspect of your writing is marked as poor, or wrong, make sure that you understand why. If you do not, you may repeat the mistake.

134   Chapter 6

The point is to learn from your errors. When some aspect of your writing is marked as poor, or wrong, make sure that you understand why. If you do not, you may repeat the mistake.

Now and then, your instructor may label your usage as incorrect, although you believe that you are correct. For example, your instructor may be from the old school and insist that you not use the word *I* in your papers, or that you never begin a sentence with a conjunction (e.g., *and* or *but*). You may disagree, and, in fact, you would find some support from many instructors. In such a case, our advice is not to blow the disagreement out of proportion. If you generally get along with the instructor and find his or her other suggestions useful, why heighten conflict? Follow the instructor's wishes for the remainder of the term and then reassert your preferences in other classes. On the other hand, if the instructor is generally cramping your style, it may be wise to switch to another section of the course.

Keep a Notebook

Creative writers, journalism students, and English majors are encouraged to keep notebooks to jot down important thoughts as they occur. Sometimes they record the events of nature—the heavy sky that threatens to burst into a storm or the suspended animation of a frozen January hillside.

Creative writers, journalism students, and English majors keep notebooks to jot down their thoughts. They make a record of nature or note shards of nearby conversation.

IN YOUR OWN WRITE

Look out a nearby window or step outside. Try to capture features of your environment, including weather conditions, in no more than two to three sentences.

___

Sometimes writers jot down shards of conversation they overhear in the lounge or the cafeteria. At other times, they write questions about current events or their own feelings about the issues of the day, about articles and books, even about films and TV shows. They may even write parts of letters. Then, during spare moments, they may come back to these pieces and see what other ideas they engender, perhaps beginning to flesh some of them out.

Keeping a notebook or a journal is also an excellent practice for those of us who would not necessarily call ourselves writers. They are fun and sometimes a little embarrassing to peruse in later years, and they serve immediate purposes as well. First, they get us into the habit of expressing our ideas by means of the written word. When we put our ideas into writing, we not only filter them through the sieve of grammar. We also examine our ideas for completeness and form, and, sometimes, we give form to the shapeless.

Our notebooks may also record the germs of various papers that we may eventually develop and hand in for college courses. A random comment on "The Cosby Show" can give birth to a paper titled "The Portrayal of Fathers in Situation Comedies: 1950–1990." Comments on a criminal trial in which the defendant claimed to be not guilty of the charges by reason of insanity may eventually yield a paper titled "U.S. Public Reaction to the Insanity Plea."

> Keep a diary and one day it'll keep you.
> MAE WEST

Determine Length Intelligently: How Long Should a Paper Be?

Voltaire, the eighteenth-century French man of letters, once apologized to a friend for writing such a long letter. He had not had the time, he noted, to write a brief letter.

TRUTH OR FICTION *Revisited*

It can actually be more difficult to write a short paper than a long paper, because you have less space in which to express your ideas.

> The most valuable of all talents is that of never using two words when one will do.
> THOMAS JEFFERSON

Then there is the legend of the philosophy professor who assigned a term paper. The topic was "Why?" Most students, it is told, pondered the matter deeply and investigated numerous avenues of response. One clever student, however, received an A by writing a two-word term paper: "Why not?"

Students are perpetually concerned about how long a paper should be. The correct answer is simple in principle, but it still leaves many students dissatisfied. Generally speaking, the right number of words is the minimal number it takes to do the job. Put another way: Everything else being equal, a briefer paper is better than a longer paper.

If you're not sure how long a paper should be, ask the professor or check out previous papers that earned high grades. If the professor is not specific about numbers of words or pages, perhaps he or she can give you an impression of how long it should take to write the paper. Is it a paper that you ought to be able to write in one afternoon or evening? Perhaps that would be two to five pages long (typed, double-spaced). Is it a term paper that requires a few days of library work and a few more days of writing? If so, 20 to 30 typewritten, double-spaced pages (including footnotes and bibliography) might be in order.

Avoid Plagiarism

> I found your essay to be good and original. However, the part that was original was not good and the part that was good was not original.
> SAMUEL JOHNSON

Plagiarism derives from the Latin *plagiarius,* which roughly translates as "kidnapper" in English. Plagiarism is literary theft—the stealing of another person's ideas or words and passing them off as your own.

Let's be honest. Some students intentionally steal the work of others. They pass off a paper that was written by a fraternity brother eight years ago as their own, or they copy passages of book verbatim. We have even known architecture students to steal designs from magazines. Other students plagiarize inadvertently, however. The penalties for plagiarism can be severe. Failing the paper is a minimal penalty; plagiarizers can also fail the course. Now and then, students are pressured to withdraw from college as a result of plagiarism. Stiff penalties seem appropriate for purposeful plagiarism. It is a pity to suffer them, however, for accidental plagiarism.

Professors may not be able to determine whether students have adapted or copied the papers of other students. It is relatively easy, however, for professors to discern passages that have been taken whole from books or articles. The passage may show a level of literary sophistication that exceeds that of the great majority of students. There may be a cogent recounting of facts that could be created only by an expert in the field. There may also be obvious inconsistencies in the paper: The student's own writing may struggle for clarity, while pilfered passages shine through.

TRUTH OR FICTION *Revisited*

Professors can frequently tell whether or not you are using your own words, especially when you use the words of excellent writers or experts in a field.

By using the following guidelines, you can avoid the pitfalls and penalties of plagiarism.

1. When you mention other people's ideas or theories, attribute the ideas to their proper source. Write, for example,

   > Although chimpanzees and gorillas have learned to use American Sign Language to make requests, Herbert Terrace* argues that apes have not mastered even the basics of grammar.

2. When you use other people's words, either place them in quotation marks or indent the material. Let length be your guide. When a passage runs from a few words to about four lines, use quotation marks. If a passage runs to five or more lines, indent the material similarly to the way we indented the preceding material about apes and sign language.* Place your footnote, however, at the end of the quoted material. Whether you use quotation marks or indent, note the source of the material, including the page or pages on which it is found.

TRUTH OR FICTION *Revisited*

Using another person's words *can* be plagiarizing, even when you credit the source. You must also use quotation marks or indent to show that you have used the writer's words as well as his or her ideas.

3. You can usually use a brief string (say two or three words) of your source's writing without using quotation marks. But use quotation marks if one of the words is a technical term or shows a fine literary turn of phrase—something you would not have arrived at on your own.

   *Here you footnote the source according to your professor's instructions or style sheet. You usually include the name of the author or authors, the title of the work, and other information as specified. For books, you also usually include the name of the publisher and the city and date of publication. For magazine and journal articles, you also usually include the name of the magazine or journal, the volume number, the issue number, and the page numbers.
   *Your professor's guidelines may differ somewhat, so it's a good idea to check. For example, some professors prefer that indented citations be single-spaced, whereas others insist that an entire paper be double-spaced.

Writing Papers

4. Hold on to the outline (if you used one) and the working drafts of your paper. If you are falsely accused of plagiarism, you can trace the development of your ideas and your phrasing.

SPECIFIC GUIDELINES FOR WRITING PAPERS

So much for generalizations.* Let us now consider specific guidelines for writing papers—from choosing the topic to proofreading the final draft.

Pick a Topic

Sometimes professors assign concrete topics, such as a reaction to a piece of writing. Or they provide a list of concrete topics, from which the student must choose. Sometimes professors purposefully leave topics wide open. Professors may also assign a paper on some aspect of a topic, which tends to leave the decision pretty much to the student.

There are no hard-and-fast rules to picking a topic. By and large, however, writers—including college students—tend to be at their best on subjects with which they are familiar. Let us consider some motives for picking topics and ways to make them manageable.

> You say there is nothing to write about. Then write to me that there is nothing to write about.
> PLINY THE YOUNGER

Write About Things You Know About The first novels of writers tend to be autobiographic. This is true, in part, because writers seek ways of expressing their own ideas and making sense out of their own experiences. It is also true because it is helpful to write about things you know about. When you write about things you know about, you can devote more of your energies to the writing itself and relatively less to research. Also, we tend to think more deeply and critically about things with which we are familiar. Everything else being equal, essays about the familiar may impress the instructor as more sophisticated than essays about unfamiliar topics.

> There are no dull subjects. There are only dull writers.
> H. L. MENCKEN

Write About Things That Interest You Another motive for writing is to help you learn and organize your thoughts about an interesting topic. Let's return to the abortion issue. You may have strong ideas about abortion but little or no knowledge of the legal issues involved or the history of prolife and prochoice movements. Thus, you could focus on historic and legal issues as a way of expanding your knowledge of the subject.

> I should not talk so much about myself if there were anybody else whom I knew as well.
> HENRY DAVID THOREAU

Or consider environmental issues such as acid rain or the greenhouse effect. You may have heard that Earth is undergoing a warming trend (greenhouse effect) because of certain emissions, but you may have little or no idea about what emissions are. So you could write a paper on the greenhouse effect as a way of becoming familiar with the atmospheric effects of various chemicals, the sources of these chemicals, and scientific and political efforts to control their emission.

What if the instructor provides a list of topics and none of them interests you? For example, what if you must write a paper on some aspect of the greenhouse effect, but you have little interest in environmental and political issues? Perhaps you are interested in business and finance, in which case you could focus your paper on the potential costs of using fuels with fewer harmful emissions to utilities and smokestack industries. Or perhaps you are interested in poetry, in which case you could report on poems about the greenhouse effect. (Yes, they exist.)

---

*Another sentence fragment. Fragments can be properly used for emphasis, or as a device for grabbing the reader's attention. Deviations from standard usage, such as sentence fragments, should normally be used sparingly. An obvious exception would be the recording of local language usage, as found, for example, in Mark Twain's marvelous depiction of Nineteenth Century speech in sections of the Midwest and Far West.

Delimit the Topic There is usually no magical fit between a topic and, say, a theme paper of 1,500 words or a term paper of 25 typewritten pages. By and large, you must make the topic fit. Believe it or not, it may be easier to blow up, or expand, an apparently small topic to term-paper size than to cut a broad topic down to size. What if you are interested in the stock market? There are many stock markets around the world. All of these stock markets are influenced by social, political, technological, and psychological events; they influence all these events in turn. Moreover, all these stock markets have histories that are open to various interpretations. It requires some work to cut the topic "the stock market" down to manageable size. On the other hand, it is easy to write a term paper titled "The Development of the Financial Times Stock Exchange (Footsie) Index" (the London equivalent of the New York Dow Jones index), or "Evidence Against a Wave-Theory Approach to Stock Market Index Behavior."

What if you are interested in art? Conceivably you could attempt a theoretical paper on what art is, but first you should take out an insurance policy that protects you from sheer exhaustion. As a first step, it would be wise to choose between a paper on art techniques (art fundamentals) or on the history of some aspect of art (perhaps an art movement, perhaps an artist). A historical paper on art techniques might be called something like "Development of Serigraphy" (silk-screen printing). Or you could write a paper on art fundamentals called "A Comparison of Oil and Acrylic Painting." Such a paper might examine the relative ease of working in these media and the quality of the outcomes. Rather than writing a paper called "History of Western Art," we would recommend focusing on, say, "The New York School in the 1950s" or "Postmodern Architecture of the 1980s." In either case, you could select a handful of renowned artists (or architects), recount criticisms of some of their works, include illustrations, and look for threads that seem to tie them into a movement.

An advantage to writing about a narrow topic is that your knowledge of the topic may soon surpass that of your instructor. Therefore, your paper may not be closely scrutinized on every detail. On the other hand, narrow topics usually require deep research and great focus on detail. For this reason, the issues you deal with in narrow topics may be hardest to research and to understand.

Write a Thesis Statement

If you are writing an argumentative theme paper, it is helpful to clarify your purpose through a thesis statement. A thesis is a proposition that is maintained or defended in an argument. Once you have narrowed your topic, try to express the thesis of your paper as briefly as possible—in a single sentence, if you can. You don't have to include the thesis statement in your paper. Instead, you can pin it up on the wall and use it as a guide in writing. A thesis statement helps keep you from straying; it channels your arguments and evidence toward a goal.

If you are writing about abortion, for example, your thesis statement could be "Abortion is the taking of a human life," or "The individual woman has a right to exercise control over the events occurring inside her body." Your paper "Postmodern Architecture of the 1980s" could be mainly descriptive or expository. On the other hand, you could express a thesis such as "Postmodern architecture is the humanization of technology."

Don't Wait for Inspiration—Get Going!

The idea of getting going is not elementary or silly, even if it sounds so. Many students bog down soon after they select a topic. (So do many professional writers!)

> Here lies the sense of literary creation: to portray ordinary objects as they will be reflected in kindly mirrors of future times.
>
> VLADIMIR NABOKOV

> "Where shall I begin, please your Majesty?" he asked.
> "Begin at the beginning," the King said, gravely, "and go on till you come to the end: then stop."
>
> LEWIS CARROLL,
> *Alice in Wonderland*

> The idea is to get the pencil moving quickly.
>
> BERNARD MALAMUD

> The art of writing is that art of applying the seat of the pants to the seat of the chair.
>
> MARY HEATON VORSE

Getting going can mean going to the library and beginning to research the topic. Getting going can mean making an outline. Getting going can mean following inspiration and jotting down the beginning of the paper, the conclusion,* or some of the ideas that you will probably use in the body of the paper. You can write down ideas on index cards or on loose-leaf pages that you reorder later on. If you are using a word processor—or, more likely, a personal computer with a word-processing program—you can save random thoughts in separate files and integrate them later. You can also save them in the same file and then move them around as blocks of text later on.

The point is this: You've got to get going somewhere and at some time. If you have no plan at all, spend a few minutes to formulate a plan. If you have a plan and some useful thoughts come to you, feel free to stray from the plan and jot these thoughts down. It is easier to return to a plan than to reconstruct moments of inspiration!

TRUTH OR FICTION *Revisited*

Successful writing does *not* require inspiration. One can do excellent work by following a plan (e.g., an outline) and writing clearly and simply.

> I just sit at a typewriter and curse a bit.
>
> P. G. WODEHOUSE

For most of us, writing, like invention, is 10 percent inspiration and 90 percent perspiration. You cannot force inspiration. You can only set the stage for inspiration by delving into your topic—perhaps by formulating a plan (e.g., beginning with library work), perhaps by writing an outline, perhaps by talking with other people about the topic. Then, when inspiration strikes, jot it down. Keep this in mind, too: A good paper does not have to be inspired. A good paper can address the topic in a coherent, useful way without bursts of genius, without poetry.

TRUTH OR FICTION *Revisited*

Good writing does *not* require poetic touches. Good writing is writing that gets the job done, and most "jobs" are not to write poetry.

Make an Outline

With nearly any kind of writing, it is helpful to make an outline. Short stories and novels profit from outlines of their plots and characters. Essays, even brief essays of the sort you may write on a test,† profit from a listing of the issues to be raised or topics to be covered. With term papers, most students find it essential not only to list the topics that are to be covered, but also to sketch out how they will be covered.

As noted in Chapter 5, outlines usually take the following form:

I. Major head
   A. Second-level head
   B. Second-level head
      1. Third-level head
         a. Fourth-level head
         b. Fourth-level head
      2. Third-level head

---

*That's right! There's nothing wrong with writing down the conclusion of a paper, or the tentative conclusion of a paper, at the beginning. Just don't leave it there when you hand the paper in!

†See Chapter 7 for advice on writing essay questions.

Papers have beginnings (introductions), middles (bodies), and ends (conclusions). In writing theme papers and term papers, students can use a major head for the paper's introduction, one or more major heads for the body of the paper, and another major head for the conclusion. Let us assume that you are taking a health course, a child development course, or a biology course, and that you are writing a paper on ways of coping with infertility. Your outline might look something like this:

Paper title: "Ways of Coping with Infertility"

Partial Outline
  I. Introduction
     A. Attention getter (Kirsten's story)
     B. Extent of the problem
     C. What I will do in this paper
 II. Sources of infertility
     A. Problems that affect the male
        1. Low sperm count
        2. Difficulty depositing sperm
        3. Infectious diseases
        4. Trauma or injury
     B. Problems that affect the female
        1. Lack of ovulation
           a. Hormonal irregularities
           b. Malnutrition
           c. Stress
        2. Infections
        3. Endometriosis
           a. Special problems of "yuppies"
        4. Obstructions or malfunctions of the reproductive tract
III. Methods for Overcoming Infertility
     A. Methods for overcoming male fertility problems
        1. Methods for overcoming low sperm count
           a. Artificial insemination
        2. Methods for overcoming difficulty depositing sperm
        3. Methods for overcoming infectious diseases
        4. Methods for overcoming trauma or injury

Outlines are helpful with nearly any kind of writing. Fictional writing profits from outlines of plots and characters. Essays profit from a list of issues to be raised or topics to be covered.

Writing Papers   141

    B. Methods for overcoming female fertility problems
        1. Methods for overcoming lack of ovulation
        2. Methods for overcoming infections
        3. Methods for overcoming endometriosis
        4. Methods for overcoming obstructions or malformations
            a. In vitro fertilization
            b. Donor IVF
            c. Embryonic transfer
            d. Surrogate motherhood
IV. Psychological Issues
V. Financial Issues
VI. Legal/Moral Issues
VII. Conclusions
    A. Brief review (summary)
    B. Conclusions (points to be made)
    C. Future questions or directions

Compose a Draft

A draft is a rough or preliminary sketch of a piece of writing. One way to write a draft of a theme paper or term paper is to flesh out an outline of the paper. Another is to start writing the sections you know most about, or have the strongest feelings about, and then assemble them like a puzzle. Still another is to just start writing, without even a mental outline, and somehow to arrive at what seems to be a completed work.

Let us assume that you are using an outline and consider how you might flesh it out, section by section.

Introduction to the Paper The introduction has a number of functions, including arousal of reader interest, presentation of a number of the issues involved, and an explanation of what you will cover. You may want to include your thesis statement somewhere in the introduction (i.e., "It will be shown that . . ."), but it is not necessary. In the paper on fertility problems, readers' interest is to be aroused by an *anecdote* recounting the anguish encountered by a woman (Kirsten) who suffered from blocked fallopian tubes (an obstruction of the reproductive tract). If you're going to wax poetic in a paper, the beginning is as good a place as any. Here are just a handful of the ways in which writers grab the reader's interest:

1. Using an anecdote (as with the plight of Kirsten).
2. Using an interesting piece of information from within the paper (e.g., "One American couple in six cannot conceive a child.")
3. Coupling a fact with irony (e.g., "Despite the concern of environmentalists that we are witnessing a population explosion, one American couple in six cannot conceive a child." Or, 'In an era when we are inundated with news about the high incidence of teenage pregnancy, one American couple in six cannot conceive a child.")
4. Using a quote from literature (e.g., "In Genesis 3:16, it is written, 'In sorrow thou shalt bring forth children.' Sad to say, it is the sorrow of one American couple in six that they shall *not* be able to bring forth children." This example combines a Biblical quote, irony, and a play on words—that is, the double use of the word *sorrow* and pointing out that so many parents will *not* bear ["bring forth"] children.).
5. Using a rhetorical question ("Did you know that one American couple in six cannot conceive a child?" Or, "Did you know that many couples who delay marriage and childbearing in an effort to establish careers are playing Russian roulette with fertility?"). A so-called rhetorical question is not really meant to be answered, but is intended as an attention-grabbing way of leading into a topic.

If you can't annoy somebody, there's little point in writing.

KINGSLEY AMIS

The lovely woman-child Kaa was mercilessly chained to the cruel post of the warrior-chief Beast, with his barbarian tribe now stacking wood at her nubile feet, when the strong clear voice of the poetic and heroic Handsomas roared, "Flick your Bic, crisp that chick and you'll feel my steel through your last meal."

STEVE GARMAN (winning entry in contest for the worst opening sentence of a novel, *New York Times*, May 13, 1984.)

You can also leave the writing of the important beginning lines of the paper until the end, when you have a greater grasp of the subject and are more acquainted with the issues involved. Of course, you are free to jot down notes about possible beginnings as you work on other parts of the paper—whenever inspiration strikes.

Then the introduction explains the issues (e.g., the extent of fertility problems) and indicates how the paper will approach the topic. In this case, the writer can explain that the paper will discuss kinds of problems, their sources, possible solutions, and the psychological (legal, religious, etc.) issues raised by the problems and various ways of overcoming them.

Body of the Paper The body of the paper is the meat of the paper. If you are criticizing a work of literature, a film, or an art exhibit, this is where you list the strengths and weaknesses of the work and support your views. If you are writing an argumentative theme, this is where you state your premises and explain your logic. If you are reviewing research, this is where you explain who did what, when, and how. If your paper explains a number of processes (e.g., methods for overcoming infertility), this is where you get down to their nuts and bolts.

In the body of the paper, you paint in the details. If you are writing a theme paper, in section II (according to your outline), you may describe endometriosis in a sentence or two and then mention that women with endometriosis frequently find it difficult to become pregnant. If you are writing a term paper on the subject, you may spend more time describing endometriosis and then explore various theories as to how endometriosis impairs fertility. Similarly, in section VI of a theme paper, you may briefly state that surrogate mothers are the actual biological mothers of the children who are born to them and that courts are in conflict as to whether biological mothers can sign away their rights to their children. If you are writing a term paper on infertility, you may want to explore religious opinions on surrogate motherhood and other issues and also devote a page or two to the psychological and legal ramifications of the celebrated Mary Beth Whitehead case.

Sometimes it seems that subject matter must be organized in a certain way. At other times, organization may appear more flexible. In the paper on infertility, the body began with a section on sources of infertility. Then there was a section on methods of overcoming infertility, followed by sections on psychological and related issues. The body of the paper could also have been organized according to kinds of problems. Section II could have been labeled "Problems That Affect the Male." Subsection 1 of section II could still have discussed low sperm count. Sections within subsection 1, however, could have discussed (a) sources of low sperm count, (b) methods of overcoming low sperm count, and (c) psychological and (d) other issues involved in handling the problem in the prescribed ways. Section III could then have discussed problems that affect the female.

Conclusion of the Paper The conclusion of a paper is a section that contains more than conclusions. Like the introduction, the conclusion has a number of functions.

In the paper on infertility, the last part of your introduction tells readers where they're going. In this example, the first part of the conclusion tells readers where they've been. The first part of the concluding section is an excellent place for summarizing or briefly reviewing the information presented in the body. In summarizing the body, you are not simply adding words—that is, "padding" to meet a length requirement. You are reminding the reader of the major points as a way of leading up to your judgments, inferences, or opinions.

Then you may arrive at the conclusions themselves. Your conclusions put everything together. They explain what it all means. One conclusion of the infertility paper could be that science is continually finding innovative ways of overcoming fertility problems. Another conclusion could be that these innovations have created new ethical and religious issues. You could also take a personal ethical or religious stance on one or more matters—assuming that you have laid the groundwork in the body of the paper. Still another conclusion could be that certain aspects of modern life (e.g., toxins, delay of childbearing) contribute to infertility.

Ideally, the conclusion section ends with a bang. The beginning of a paper may attempt to grab the reader's interest, and the ending sometimes also aims to achieve an impact. You can refer to future directions—perhaps the possibility that someday it may be possible to create a child by processing nearly any cell from the father and any cell from the mother. You can go for shock value with the notion that the parents could conceivably be of the same sex, or that there might be only one parent (as in cloning). You can return to Kirsten's suffering and suggest that would-be parents will no longer have to undergo her travails. You can speculate on how reproductive technology may have a wide impact on social, religious, and political institutions. In a more matter-of-fact mode, you can suggest new avenues of research. But you can also use humor, irony, or rhetorical questions—the same devices that draw readers into papers.

The first few lines of the paper make your first impression. The last few lines make your final impression. These are the places where you want to make the greatest impact. If there are sentences you are going to work, work, and rework, let them be the first and last few sentences of the paper.

Revise the Paper

Wolfgang Amadeus Mozart is the great musician who bridged the Baroque and Romantic movements. His musical compositions are distinctive not only for their majesty, but also because they were composed practically without revision. It is as though his original conception of his music was complete and flawless. He is a rarity in the world of music.

It is also rare in the world of writing that our original ideas are complete and flawless. There are many false starts, many bad passages. Good writing usually requires revision, sometimes many revisions, even when the writer is experienced. Revision is a natural part of the writing process. Frequently, revision spells the difference between a paper that deserves an F and one that earns an A.

On the other hand, papers should not be revised just for the sake of revision. Now and then we may produce a first draft that we cannot improve. When this occurs, an old saying applies: "If it ain't broke [sic], don't try to fix it."*

There are revisions, and then there are revisions. Rarely is every sentence or even every section of a paper revised. Sometimes we revise papers in order to fine-tune our prose, to improve our sentence structure, to reconsider our choice of words. This type of revising is referred to as *editing*. Editing involves scrutinizing the paper word by word and changing anything that looks wrong, weak, or inappropriate. Editing extends to replacing words, sentences, and paragraphs with improved versions.

Sometimes we revise in order to reshape our ideas so that they fit together more coherently. At other times, we revise to fill gaps. At still other times, we labor to perfect our beginnings and endings.

> Writers have two main problems. One is writer's block, when words won't come at all, and the other's logorrhea, when words come so fast that they hardly get into the wastebasket in time.
> CECILIA BARTHOLOMEW

> Everything goes by the board: honor, pride, decency . . . to get the book written.
> WILLIAM FAULKNER

> It's none of their business that you have to learn how to write. Let them think you were born that way.
> ERNEST HEMINGWAY

> I can't write five words but that I change seven.
> DOROTHY PARKER

---

* *Sic* is Latin, meaning "thus" or "so." When placed in brackets, it means that text has been reproduced precisely, even though it may contain errors. "Ain't broke" is the way in which this adage is frequently expressed.

WHAT DO YOU DO NOW?
Overcoming a Writing Block

Ah, that blank sheet of paper! The possibilities are endless, so why can't you get something down?

All writers, not just college students, find themselves staring at that empty page now and then, wondering what they should do now. Everyone must occasionally cope with what writers refer to as "blocks."

Imagine that you have picked a topic and have gotten going on your paper, but now you have hit a wall. You have been staring at the page for half an hour, and nothing is coming to mind. What do you do now? There are no certain answers, but here are a number of suggestions that have been used successfully by other students.

1. *Brainstorming.* In brainstorming, you do not try to narrow in on a single way to solve a problem. Instead, you generate as many kinds of approaches as possible. Set a time limit for your brainstorming. Then sit back and allow any relevant ideas to pop into mind, even outlandish ideas. Or ask roommates and friends for their ideas—even silly ones. During the session, just record ideas; don't judge them. When the session is finished, consider each idea and test those that seem most likely to be of help.

2. *Take a break.* Have a snack, call a friend, take a shower, get on the rowing machine. Then get back to work. You may find that your ideas have incubated while you were taking your break. Incubators warm chicken eggs so that they will hatch. In solving problems—including writing problems—incubation involves standing back from the problem for a while as we seem to continue to work on it at some level.[4] Later on, a solution may appear to us as in a flash.

3. *Work on another assignment.* Instead of continuing to frustrate yourself, complete another assignment. Then return to the paper refreshed.

4. *Force yourself to write.* Make yourself write on the subject for a specific amount of time—say, for 20 minutes. Try to develop the arguments in the paper. Then critically examine what you have written.

5. *Switch tools.* If you've been processing words on a personal computer, try a typewriter for a while. Or use longhand.

6. *Skip to another section.* Work on another section of the paper. Type up the bibliography, for instance. (It's amazing how reviewing sources helps generate ideas!) Or work on your "dynamite" opening paragraph.

7. *Let the paper go for a few days.* This alternative may help when a short break is ineffective and you still have plenty of time to complete the paper.

8. *Check with the instructor.* He or she may have some excellent advice for resuming the paper. Some instructors do not mind offering detailed suggestions.

9. *Copy and go!* Copy the last sentence or paragraph you wrote and just go with it! Or sketch four or five different directions you can take.

10. *Accept reality?* Sometimes you can't go on because your ideas are truly at a dead end. If the block persists, consider tossing out what you have written and starting from scratch. Perhaps you should change topics. If you have already written 20 pages or checked 50 sources, however, you may find it worthwhile to explore switching topics with your instructor before chucking it into the circular file (that is, the wastebasket).

Writing Papers

Sometimes our efforts fall short of our standards and the best course is to throw work into the wastebasket—painful as it may be. An important difference between artists and hacks is that the former are more willing to toss their failures onto the scrap heap.

> Writers take words seriously—perhaps the last professional class that does.
>
> JOHN UPDIKE

How much revision is enough? That depends on you as a writer, on the piece that you are writing, and on the expectations of your instructors. As you move more deeply into your college career, you will gain a more accurate impression of how much revision your work usually requires to satisfy your professors—and yourself.

Here are some specific suggestions for revising your papers:

1. *Create distance between you and your work.* Sometimes you need a bit of distance between yourself and your work to recognize weaknesses and errors. One good way to create this distance is to let time pass between drafts—at least a day. In this way, you may be able to look at certain passages or ideas from a new perspective. Of course, you cannot use this method if you don't begin a term paper until a few days before it is due! Another method is to have a trusted friend, family member, or tutor at the college learning center look over the paper. Then you must try to listen to suggestions with an unbiased ear.

2. *Check the draft against the outline.* Are there obvious omissions? Have you strayed from the topic?

3. *Place earlier drafts beside you as you write.* Start writing from scratch, but follow the earlier versions as you proceed. Use segments of earlier versions that seem right. Omit sections that are weak or incorrect.

4. *Set aside earlier drafts and sketch a new version.* Then compare the sketch with earlier drafts, and incorporate the strengths of each version.

5. *Read the draft aloud.* When we listen to ourselves, we sometimes gain a new perspective on what we are saying—or not saying. This is another way to create a bit of distance between our writing and ourselves. You can also try reading the paper aloud to a friend.

6. *Try a new direction.* If something isn't working, consider taking a different approach. It is not unusual, for example, to change a thesis statement after completing a draft of a paper. Or you could find that you need to check out a different kind of research.

7. *Drop passages that simply aren't working.* This may be the hardest piece of advice to follow. It is painful to throw a piece of work into

> Read over your compositions and, when you meet a passage which you think is particularly fine, throw it out.
>
> SAMUEL JOHNSON

the wastebasket, especially if we have devoted hours to it. Yet, not every effort is of high quality. *One of the important differences between artists and hacks is that the former are more willing to acknowledge their failures and to toss them onto the scrap heap.*

8. *Ask the instructor for advice.* Drop by during office hours and share some of your concerns with the instructor. You help organize your own thoughts and show respect for the instructor's time when you preplan your questions and make them fairly concrete. Don't say, "I think something's wrong with my paper, but I don't know what." Say, instead, "My thesis was A, but the research seems to be showing B. Should I modify the thesis? Have I hit the right research?" By asking the instructor for advice, you do not appear weak and dependent. Instead, you appear sincere and interested in self-improvement. This is precisely the attitude that your instructor respects.

Using a Word Processor   Professor Jacqueline Berke at Drew University notes that because of word processing,

> "[Our] understanding of the way people write—the stages—the process—has changed. The phase of writing that is actually most important is revision. Yet how much time does the poor student give to revision?" She remembers a comment from a student's journal: "The computer makes revision a playground instead of a punishment."[5]

Word-processing has several advantages, including the ability to edit a manuscript indefinitely without having erasures, arrows, and chicken scrawls between the lines. Many word-processing programs will automatically renumber footnotes when a new one is inserted, check your spelling, and provide a thesaurus.

Writing Papers   147

A good word-processing program can help you in many ways:

1. The single greatest advantage to word processing is that you can edit a manuscript indefinitely without having erasures, arrows, and scrawls between the lines. With every change, the material on the screen is brand new. The actual mechanics of making changes are relatively effortless and do not compromise your wish to achieve perfection.
2. You can save each draft of a paper for future reference. For example, in the paper on infertility, the outline could be saved as

    INFERT.OUT

    The first draft could be saved as:

    INFERT.D1

    Subsequent drafts can be numbered accordingly. Students should always make and keep copies of the papers they submit. When you use word processing, you save your papers electronically on fixed disks or floppy disks. Each copy of the paper is an original (called a "hard copy" or a "display copy"), and you can generate as many original copies as you like.
3. In case the question arises as to whether your paper is original, or written by you, copies of each working draft can be produced in evidence.
4. You can save related thoughts or abstracts of research studies in separate files and integrate them later on.
5. Many word-processing programs automatically renumber all footnotes or endnotes when you insert a new entry.
6. Many word-processing programs check the spelling for you. Such programs catch the following errors:

    I shall show that Woody Allen's recent <u>tradegies</u> are less <u>successfull</u> than his early comedies as works of art.

    However, programs that check spelling do not catch errors such as the following:

    I shall show <u>than</u> Woody Allen's recent tragedies <u>art</u> less <u>successfully that</u> his early comedies as <u>words on</u> art.

7. Many word-processing programs have thesauruses that allow you to search for better wording conveniently.

Proofread the Paper

> A man occupied with public or other important business cannot, and need not, attend to spelling.
>
> Napoleon Bonaparte

> I know not, madam, that you have a right, upon moral principles, to make your readers suffer so much.
>
> Samuel Johnson, *letter to Mrs. Sheridan,*
> *after publication of her novel in 1763*

Napoleon was probably powerful enough, of course, that few would have brought misspellings to his attention. Most of us do not have the prerogatives of Napoleon. Proofreading is intended to catch the kinds of errors that make many professors groan and, in Johnson's words, "suffer so much." Proofreading is a form of editing directed at catching errors in spelling, usage, and punctuation, instead of enhancing the substance of the paper. Proofreading is not generally a creative process; it is more mechanical. On the other hand, if in proofreading you discover that a word does not accurately express your intended meaning, a bit of creativity might be needed in order to replace it or recast the sentence.

Importance of Proofreading For a largely mechanical process, proofreading is extremely important. For example, poor spelling and sentence structure suggest ignorance. Whether or not the instructor states that attention will be paid to spelling and so forth, you may still be judged by the mechanics. That is, an instructor who believes that you cannot spell may also believe that you cannot write a good paper.

When a paper has mechanical errors, the message to the instructor is very clear: You don't care enough to proofread the paper yourself or to have it proofread by someone who knows the mechanics.

Many campuses have tutorial centers at which you can have your papers proofread without charge. You may have a variety of reasons for not using the tutorial service: unwillingness to have your work scrutinized by someone else (but your instructor will scrutinize it, anyway); lack of time or inconvenient location (which is more inconvenient in the long run: writing the paper in time to have it proofread, or receiving a poorer grade than necessary?); or simply not caring. Whatever your reason, your instructor will interpret the flaws as signs of (1) lack of knowledge and (2) not caring—leading to lack of effort. Lack of knowledge and lack of effort are the two major reasons for poor grades on papers.

On the other hand, don't expect a proofreader to catch every error. Most tutors, for example, point out errors but do not make corrections themselves. Moreover, having a tutor check your paper does *not* remove your responsibility for catching and correcting errors. Nor does it guarantee that all errors have been highlighted. So don't blame your tutor for your own errors. The best way to work with a tutor is to have him or her read over your paper and make suggestions at various stages of the paper's development. You should also be striving to learn rules for proper usage—not just to catch the errors in a single paper.

Tips for Proofreading The following guidelines will help you proofread successfully:

1. When proofreading, read your paper letter by letter, word by word, phrase by phrase, punctuation mark by punctuation mark. (Some English professors recommend starting at the end of your paper and reading it backwards sentence by sentence as a way of catching small errors.) Don't focus on issues such as poetic value and persuasiveness of arguments. Pay attention to the littlest things. Are you using slang words to add color and help make your arguments, or are you just careless?

2. Check as to whether your tenses are consistent. Are you saying "Hamilton *noted* (past tense) that . . ." in one place and "Hamilton *argues* . . . (present tense)" in another?

3. Check whether subjects and verbs are in agreement. *Everyone* is a singular pronoun. Did you write "Everyone in *their* (plural) right mind . . ." when you should have written "Everyone in his or her right mind . . ."?

4. Check that sentences are, in fact, sentences, not fragments and not run-ons. If you're using sentence fragments here and there, be certain that they help highlight your points (e.g., "Not likely!") and do not reflect carelessness. Use fragments purposefully, not by accident.

5. Have a trusted friend proofread your papers in exchange for your proofreading the friend's. A page may look correct to you because you are used to looking at it. Errors might leap off the page upon perusal by someone else, however.
6. When in doubt, use a dictionary.
7. Check that your footnotes and bibliography contain the information required by your professor and are in the specified format.
8. Make certain that you have credited your sources so that you are not suspected or accused of plagiarism.
9. At the risk of being boring, we repeat: If the learning center at your college offers a proofreading service, use it.

Proofread to Correct Common Writing Errors Also proofread to correct common errors. Consider this piece of romantic dialogue:

"I love you alot," said Marsha, "accept when your mean to me."

"Just among you and I," John responded, "I'm alright when I'm laying down. You should of known that standing up gives me a headache. Anyways, I didn't no that I had that affect on you."

All right, we confess: No student of ours ever wrote anything this awful. We had to piece together multiple errors to arrive at this gem.

The purpose of Table 6.1 is to alert you to a number of errors that are commonly made by students—and occasionally by college professors. Look for them as you proofread your paper. The table could have been endless; however, we chose to focus on some of the errors that are most likely to make instructors think that students might be better off working in a car wash than attending college.

TABLE 6.1. Common Errors in English Usage and How to Correct Them.

SOURCE OF CONFUSION	CLARIFICATION
Confusing *accept* and *except*	*Accept* is a verb meaning "to receive favorably" or "to approve," as in "accepting someone's point of view." *Except* can be a verb, meaning "to leave out," or a preposition meaning "leaving out," as in, "They invited everyone *except* me."
Confusing *advice* and *advise*	*Advice* is a noun, something that is given, as in "This is my advice to you." *Advise* is a verb, meaning "to counsel" or "to give advice," as in "I advise you to be cautious."
Confusing *affect* and *effect*	Most of the time, *affect* is a verb meaning "to stir or move the emotions" or "to influence." Consider this example: "I was affected by the movie." Most of the time, *effect* is a noun meaning "something brought about by a cause," as in the phrase "cause and effect." Consider this example: "The movie had an enormous effect on me." *Affect* is also used as a noun, but usually only by mental-health workers. In that case, it is pronounced AF-fect and means "an emotion or emotional response." *Effect* is also occasionally used as a verb, meaning "to bring about or produce a result," as in "to effect change."
Confusing *affective* and *effective*	*Affective* is a word usually used only by psychologists or mental-health workers, meaning "of feelings" or "of emotions." Students are far more likely to used the word *effective*, meaning "having an effect" or "producing results." Consider this example: "Lisa made an effective speech."
Confusing *all right* and *alright*	Use *all right*. *Alright* is technically incorrect, and the Third College (1988) Edition of *Webster's New World Dictionary* (Simon & Schuster) lists "alright" as a variant spelling of "all right," whose usage is disputed. If your instructor marks "all right" wrong (which sometimes happens!), see him or her during office hours, pull out your dictionary, and be a hero. Be nice, not snide!

150   Chapter 6

TABLE 6.1 *continued*

SOURCE OF CONFUSION	CLARIFICATION
Confusing *allot*, *alot*, and *a lot*	Use *a lot* if you mean "many, plenty" or "a great deal." *Allot* (with two *l*'s) is a verb meaning "to apportion" or "to distribute." There "ain't" no such word as *alot*.
Confusing *all ready* and *already*	*All ready* means "Everyone" or "everything" is "ready," as in "We are all ready to get into the car," or "Dinner is all ready." *Already* means "done previously," as in "I wrote the paper already," or "The paper is already finished." *Already* can also be used at the end of a phrase to express impatience, as in "Stop it already!"
Confusing *allude*, *elude*, and *illude*	*Allude* means "to refer," as in "I alluded to Hemingway's *The Sun Also Rises* in my paper." *Elude* means "to avoid" or "to escape," as in, "He eluded the enemy." There is no such word as *illude*.
Confusing *allusion* and *illusion*	An *allusion* is a reference, as in "I made an allusion to Hemingway's *The Sun Also Rises*. An *illusion* is "a false idea or conception," or "a misleading appearance." Consider this example: "He used clothing to create the illusion that he was quite slender."
Confusing *all together* and *altogether*	*All together* means "all in the same place" or "all at once," as in, "Let's try singing that song again, all together this time." *Altogether* means "completely," as in "I'm altogether disgusted with the way you did that."
Confusing *among* and *between*	*Among* is used when there are three or more people or objects. *Between* is usually used when there are two people or objects. "We had $10 between us" and "Between you and me" is correct when two people are involved. "They distributed the money among us" is correct when three or more people have received the money.
Confusing *as* and *like*	As a preposition, *like* means "similar to" or "resembling," as in "The clouds look *like* cotton candy," or "This problem wasn't *like* the other problems." *As* usually means "to the same degree" ("The missile flew straight *as* a bullet") or "at the same time" ("He read *as* he watched TV").
Confusing *backward* and *backwards*	Use either one! They mean the same thing and are both acceptable.
Confusing *cite*, *sight*, and *site*	*Cite* is a verb usually meaning "to quote" or "to refer to," as in, "She *cited* the views of many experts in her argument." *Sight* is eyesight, or vision. A *site* is a piece of land, as in a "construction *site*," or the place where something happens, as in "the *site* of a battle."
Confusing *data* and *datum*	*Data* is a plural noun, and *datum* is singular. A *datum* is a single piece of information, whereas the "*data* obtained in a study" usually refers to the entire mass of information assembled.
Confusing *etc.* and *et al.*	*Etc.* is the abbreviation of *et cetera* and means "and so forth." For example, "The company ran over budget on salaries, paper clips, coffee cups, etc." *Et al.* is the abbreviation of *et alia*, meaning "and others." For most students, use of *et al.* is limited to lists of authors, as in, "In the study by Saeed et al., it was found that . . ." Note that *al* is followed by a period, whereas *et* is not.
Confusing *farther* and *further*	Today these words appear to be interchangeable, each one meaning "more distant or remote" or "additionally." *Farther* used to be limited in meaning to "more distant," however, as in, "They ran farther," and *further* used to be limited to "additionally," as in "They further investigated the issue." You will probably look more sophisticated if you stick to the older usage. You can pull out your dictionary if your instructor takes issue with your usage.
Confusing *flammable* and *inflammable*	Despite the fact that the prefix *in-* usually means "not," both words have the same meaning: "capable of catching on fire."
Confusing *have* and *of*	The confusion here usually occurs in contractions, such as *should've* or *could've*. When you can also use the verb *have*, use *'ve*, not the preposition *of*. Never write *could of, should of, would of*.
Confusing *I* and *me*	*I* is the subject of a verb, as in "*I* am going" or "She and *I* are going." *Me* is the object of a preposition, as in "Give it to her and (to) *me*," or the object of a verb, as in "Don't discourage John and *me*." Write "He and *I* gave books to charity," but write, "They threw the books at Jack and *me*"—which, of course, we hope never happens.

TABLE 6.1 *continued*

SOURCE OF CONFUSION	CLARIFICATION
Confusing *irregardless* and *regardless*	When in doubt, use *regardless*. *Irregardless* is nonstandard and technically incorrect, although it can be used humorously, as in, "*Irregardless*, as they say in Brooklyn, . . ." (Just kidding, Brooklynites.)
Confusing *lie* and *lay*	This is where you make your mark! The verb *lie* means "recline," as in "*Lie* down" or "We have to *lie* low for a while." (*Lie* also means "to tell a lie.") The verb *lay* means "put or place down" and always takes a direct object, as in "*Lay* the book (direct object) on the table."

The tenses of *lie* are as follows:

Present tense:	*Lie*, as in "I need to *lie* down," or "We intend to *lie* in wait right here."
Past tense:	*Lay*, as in "Earlier this morning I *lay* down for a while," or "This is where they *lay* in wait the other day."
Past participle:	*Lain*, as in, "By the time dinner was ready, he had already *lain* down for a nap," or "They had *lain* in wait for six hours when the sun set."

The tenses of *lay* are as follows:

Present tense:	*Lay*, as in "*Lay* down your weapons (objects)," or "Please *lay* the groundwork (object) for the meeting."
Past tense:	*Laid*, as in "They *laid* down their weapons," or "He *laid* the groundwork for the meeting."
Past participle:	*Laid*, as in "They had already *laid* down their weapons," or "By the time the speaker was ready, the master of ceremonies had *laid* the groundwork."

Never, never (never) write or say "Lay down." Always use "Lie down."

Confusing *leave* and *let*	*Leave* can mean "to go away"; "to cause to stay," as in "*Leave* some food"; and "to bequeath," as in "*leaving* money to one's children or charity." *Let* usually means "to allow," as in "*Let* me go" or "*Let* it be."
Confusing *lend* and *loan*	*Lend* is a verb and *lent* is the past tense, as in "She *lent* me some money yesterday." *Loan* is preferably used as a noun, as in "She gave me a small *loan*." There is no such word as *loaned*.
Confusing *loose* and *lose*	*Loose* is an adjective, meaning the opposite of tight, as in "The knot came *loose*." *Lose* (pronounced *looz*) is the verb meaning "to misplace."
Confusing *media* and *medium*	The noun *medium* is singular; *media* is plural. Television is a medium. Television, cinema, and photography are media.
Confusing *ones* and *one's*	*Ones* is a plural noun, as in "This column contains four ones." *One's* is possessive, as in "It is good to do one's own work." *One's* is also the contraction of *one is*.
Confusing *phenomena* and *phenomenon*	*Phenomena* is the plural form of *phenomenon*.
Confusing *principal* and *principle*	A *principal* is an important or central person, as in a "school's principal" or "a principal (person) in a business transaction." A *principle* is a guiding rule, such as the "principle" of the Golden Rule.
Confusing *set* and *sit*	To *set* is "to arrange or put in place." Set takes a direct object, as in "*Set* the table (object)" or "*Set* the carton (object) down on the floor." To *sit* is "to be seated" or "to remain in place." Sit does not take a direct object, as in "Please *sit* down" or "The vase *sits* on the mantel."
Confusing *shall* and *will*	These auxiliary verbs are used to show future tense ("They *will* be ready tomorrow") or to express determination or obligation ("You *shall* do what I tell you to do!").

We recommend the formal approach of showing the future tense as follows:

I shall go tomorrow
You will go tomorrow
He/she/it will go tomorrow
We shall go tomorrow
You (plural) will go tomorrow
They will go tomorrow

TABLE 6.1 *continued*

SOURCE OF CONFUSION	CLARIFICATION
	We recommend showing determination or obligation as follows: I will get this done You shall get this done He/she/it shall get this done We will get this done You (plural) shall get this done They shall get this done Your instructor may have other ideas. Why not stop by during office hours and ask about them?
Confusing *stationary* and *stationery*	*Stationary* means "still" or "in one place," as in "A mountain is a stationary object." *Stationery* is what you write on—paper.
Confusing *taught* and *taut*	*Taught* is the past tense of *teach*. *Taut* means "tight," as in "The rope is taut."
Confusing *their*, *there*, and *they're*	*Their* is possessive, as in "They met *their* obligations." *There* shows location, as in "here and *there*." *They're* is the contraction of "they are."
Confusing *to*, *too*, and *two*	*To* is the preposition that shows location or destination, as in "Give the book *to* her" or "Go *to* school." *Too* is the adverb meaning "also," as in "I want to go, *too*," or "extremely," as in "That's *too* much!" *Two* is the number.
Confusing *toward* and *towards*	These prepositions have the same meaning and are both considered correct. We recommend using *toward* unless you are quoting someone's speech, in which case you would record what the person said or what you think the person would have said.
Confusing *use* and *utilize*	There is a slight difference in meaning between these words; to *utilize* is "to put to practical or profitable use." *Utilize* can make it seem that you're trying too hard, and you can't make a mistake if you stick to *use*. In short, use *use*.
Confusing *who* and *whom*	*Who* (or *whoever*) serves as the subject of a verb, as in "*Who* did this?" *Whom* (or *whomever*) serves as the object of a preposition, as in "To (preposition) *whom* did you lend my car?" or as the object of a verb, as in "Choose (verb) *whomever* you prefer."
Confusing *whose* and *who's*	*Whose* is possessive, as in "*Whose* paper is this? It has no name!" *Who's* is the contraction of "who has" or "who is," as in the bear's lament, "*Who's* been sleeping in my bed?"
Confusing *your* and *you're*	*Your* is possessive, as in "This is *your* book." *You're* is the contraction of "you are," as in "I assume that *you're* going."

Produce the Final Copy

If you were applying for a job as a management trainee at a bank, you probably wouldn't show up in unwashed jeans and a T-shirt. You would want to make a good first impression, to look like a serious contender for the position, to put your best foot forward. First impressions count with papers, too. You want your paper to look like a serious contender for an A.

The following are some guidelines for producing and packaging the final copy:

1. Consider buying a plastic or paper binder for your paper. Use a binder that's serious and professional looking, not frivolous. Stiff brown paper and clear plastic are superior, for example, to lavender-tinted plastic.
2. Follow the specified format exactly. For example, if your professor specifies margins of a certain width, stick to them like glue.
3. If your professor does not specify a format, ask about his or her preferences. If you make this request during office hours rather than in

Writing Papers 153

class, you may become privy to some information that most of the class is unaware of.* This may sound like an unfair way to gain an advantage, but college is competitive.

4. Include a cover page (unless instructed *not* to do so) with the following information:

   Title of paper
   Your name
   Course title
   Instructor's name
   Date

5. *SPELL THE PROFESSOR'S NAME CORRECTLY.* You can find the proper spelling in the syllabus, college catalogue, or—usually—on the door of the professor's office.

6. Learn the professor's preferred title (e.g., Ms., Dr.) and use it on the title page. A professor who has labored for many years to earn a doctorate may be justifiedly annoyed if you do not write "Dr." on the title page.

7. If the paper is a term paper, include a table of contents.

8. Use good-quality white paper. Do not use lined paper, onion-skin paper, or the cheapest quality ditto paper.

9. Type your paper, double-spaced. (No excuses!)

10. Back in the days of the Model-T, it used to be said, "Make my car any color as long as it's black." Similarly, use any color of ink as long as it's black.

11. Make sure the ribbon is new or nearly new.

12. Try to use a standard pica or elite typeface, either 10 or 12 characters to the inch. If you're going to be creative, do so in your formation of ideas and in your masterly usage of the English language—not in your typeface. If you're using word processing and a printer, choose a letter-quality (or near-letter-quality) printer, not a dot matrix printer with annoyingly large dots.

13. Use margins of about an inch all around. Wider margins make a paper look skimpy. Narrower margins make a paper look cramped and hard to read. If you're using computer paper, carefully tear off the edges that contain the guiding holes.

14. Keep a copy of the paper. Professors may decide to hold on to some papers, and now and then a paper gets lost.

We hope that this chapter has been clear and simple, that you have not been offended by our departures from formal usage, and that our attempts at humor have met with more chuckles than groans. Now get out there and write those papers!

SUMMING UP

1. What roles is writing likely to play in the careers you are contemplating? Does good writing provide people in these careers with any advantages?

2. What kinds of reading and writing—fiction or nonfiction—are of most interest to you? On what topics or assignments do you write most effectively?

3. What are the goals and purposes of your freshman writing course? Is the classroom emphasis on basic English usage, or is skillful usage generally assumed?

*Yes, we ended this sentence with a preposition. So sue us.

4. What are your greatest problems or shortcomings in writing? What can you do to surmount them?
5. Why is it important for you to be willing to make mistakes in your writing?
6. How can you determine how long your papers should be?
7. What can you do to avoid plagiarism?
8. What are some of the ways in which you can select topics for papers?
9. How can you get going on a paper when you're not sure what you should do first?
10. What kinds of editing should you do on papers before you hand them in? What other editing strategies can you use to make your papers more forceful and mechanically correct?

Key to "Rules for Good Writing" Questionnaire

We gave you the hint that not all of the rules presented were true. Actually, none of them is true. No rule need guide your writing all of the time. On the other hand, departures from formal usage should be intentional, not accidental. It may be that anything goes in writing, as long as there is a rationale for it. When in doubt, however, adhere to formal usage.

Most abstract artists can represent reality precisely and beautifully, when they choose to do so. Similarly, it is important for writing students to be able to recognize and produce formal usage, whether or not it serves their purposes in a given paper.

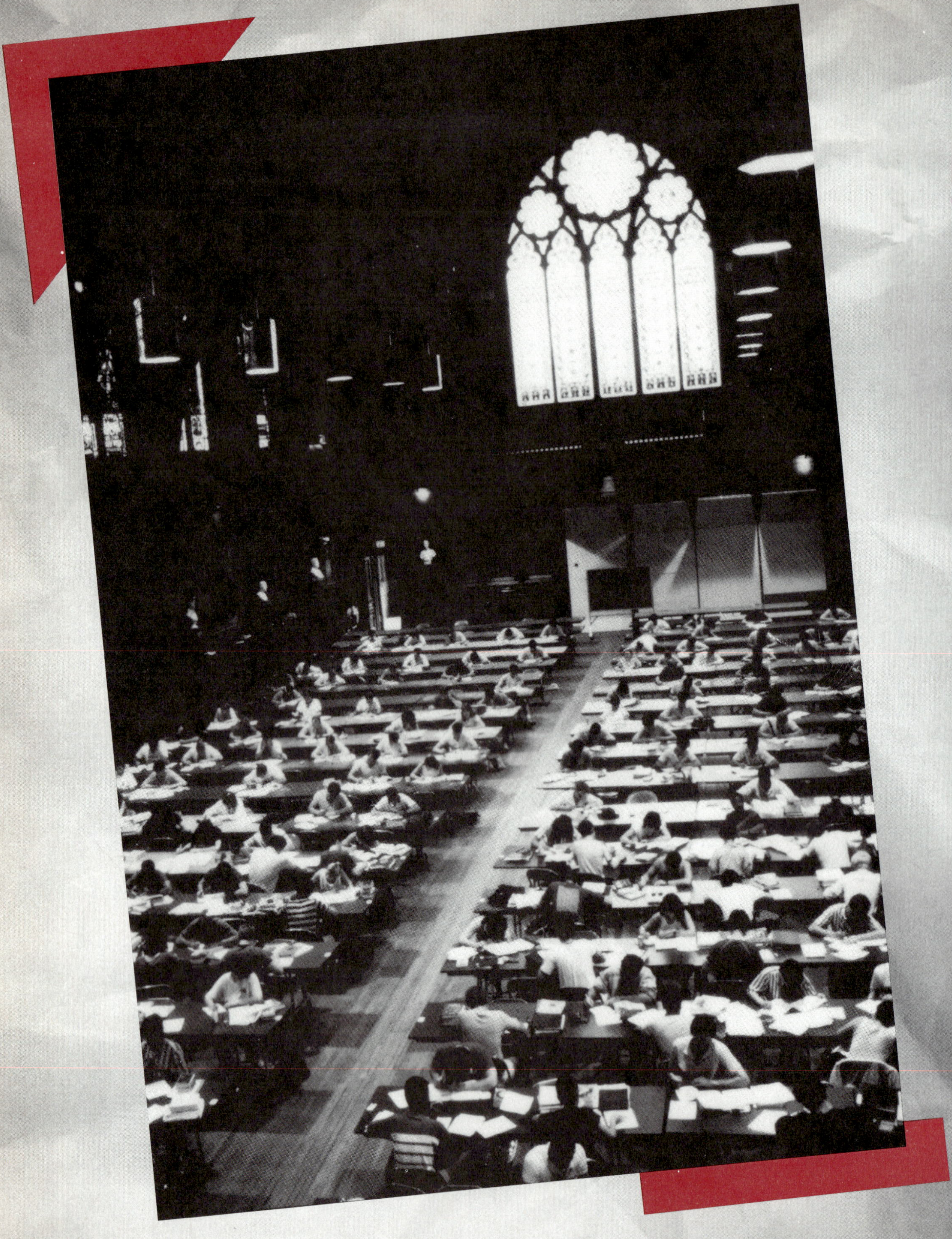

7

Taking Tests

TRUTH OR FICTION?

____ Some students know the subject matter, but when they take a test they get stuck with the answers "on the tips of their tongues."

____ It is a good idea to ask your professors what they consider important to know for the test.

____ One of the best ways to study for a test is to review old tests made up by the professor.

____ Professors don't mind students' asking them for pens and pencils during tests.

____ You should never guess on multiple-choice tests.

____ You should always guess on multiple-choice tests.

____ Neatness really isn't very important on essay questions.

____ We contribute to our own feelings of test anxiety with self-defeating thoughts.

____ You can cope with feelings of test anxiety by focusing on your breathing.

This chapter begins with a test question. Circle the number that best completes the following statement:

Tests are

1. opportunities for me to show how smart I am.
2. opportunities for me to show how obtuse I am.
3. ordeals that raise the hair on the backs of my arms.
4. a standard ingredient of college life.
5. five feet of heaven in a ponytail.
6. all of the above.
7. some of the above.
8. none of the above.

Most students would characterize tests as 7, "some of the above." At the risk of dating ourselves, choice 5 actually parrots the definition of love from a popular song of the 1950s. Some students, of course, simply view tests as a normal part of college life (4), and a few look forward to them as opportunities to demonstrate their academic superiority. Unfortunately, many respond to tests with a great deal of fear of the sort that literally raises the hair on their arms and causes them to break out in sweat. Tests for them are the banes of college life.

IN YOUR OWN WRITE

How do you feel about tests? Are they generally a source of stress for you or an opportunity to show what you know? Do you feel that your test grades reflect your knowledge of your courses?

_____
_____
_____
_____
_____
_____
_____

Many students say, "I know all this stuff, but I just can't do well on tests." We're sympathetic to students who feel this way, but sometimes they are incorrect in their assumptions. When you feel that you know something but can't quite get to it—when it seems to be on the tip of your tongue—it might also be because you didn't learn it well enough in the first place.[1] We're not being moralistic; we're only pointing out that many students who have trouble on tests don't know the subject matter well enough. Or they don't know it as well as they think they know it. For them, much of the cure lies in developing better study habits, as outlined in Chapter 5.

TRUTH OR FICTION *Revisited*

Students who know the subject matter well are actually unlikely to get stuck with the answers on the tips of their tongues.

This chapter focuses on handling tests. First, we offer some general advice. Then we outline some strategies for handling various kinds of tests, from multiple-choice tests through essay tests. Finally, we describe some of the causes of test anxiety and ways of handling them.

GENERAL ADVICE

The single most important piece of advice we can give you about tests is this: You are *not* a victim. You are *not* a lamb being led to the slaughter. You are in college because you believe that college can do something for you. Tests are a part of college life. Taking charge of your own life includes taking charge of tests.

It may seem to you that your professors are in control. They determine the kinds of tests they will use, and they schedule them. True enough. But don't minimize the impact of all the things you can do:

1. Determine where and when the next test will be held and what material will be covered. The course syllabus frequently offers some information, so check there first. But the syllabus may only offer dates and not indicate what you need to know.
2. If you and other students must take another test on the same day, ask if your professor would mind moving the test back a class.
3. Ask what types of questions will appear on the test. This question is most important before the first test, when you don't know what to expect. There are different strategies for answering short-answer and essay questions, and it helps to know what's coming.
4. Ask your instructor what will be most important for you to know, and check with students who have already taken the course to determine the sources of test questions—chapters in the text, lecture notes, student study guides, old exams, and so on. Old tests are valuable

It is appropriate to ask your professor what types of questions will appear on a forthcoming test and what will be most important for you to know.

Taking Tests 159

sources of information. They show the type of question that the professor likes to ask on a topic, and professors often repeat questions, even when they are making them up for each test. (There are just so many ways to phrase questions on a topic!) Fraternities and sororities frequently file old tests. If these tests are not available to you, go to the instructor and say, "Several students in the class are studying your old tests in the fraternity and sorority test files. Would you allow me to look over some of your old examinations so that I'm not at a disadvantage?" Fair is fair.

TRUTH OR FICTION *Revisited*

It is an *excellent* idea to ask your professors what they consider important to know for the test.

Yes, one of the best ways to study for a test *is* to review old tests made up by the professor.

---

5. "Psych out" tests by generating possible test questions from the reading assignments and your notes. If you're going to have multiple-choice questions, ask yourself what kinds of distractors (e.g., things that are only partly true) the professor might use. If you're going to have essay questions, check the guiding words in Table 7.1 on page 170 to anticipate the questions that will be asked.

6. Plan study periods during which you will generate questions from lecture notes, old exams, the student study guide, and so on.

7. Plan for weekly study periods during which you will compose and take practice tests. During these practice tests, define the key terms. Explain how they relate to one another. Outline the answers to practice essay questions, setting down key words in your outlines.

8. Take the practice quizzes and tests in the student study guide. Many instructors reinforce use of the study guide by adopting some exam questions from them. The authors of the study guide also try to provide questions that cover the main points of each topic.

9. Arrange study groups in which students share possible test questions and quiz one another. Answering essay questions verbally is excellent preparation for writing them. This type of group also offers social stimulation (which is an incentive for being there) and social support. But beware: When study groups seem in danger of degenerating into bull sessions or Let's-go-out-for-pizza-now-that-we've-studied-for-15-minutes groups, bow out and prepare for tests on your own.

10. Keep a diary or log in which you record your progress, including when, where, and how long you study, and how well you perform on practice tests. A diary motivates you to perform more consistently and helps point out your weak spots. It helps you keep in touch with whether or not you are achieving what you think you are achieving.

11. Write your name on the test! Yes, this means *you*.

12. Become "test-wise"! Know what to bring! Read the directions! Know how to be a good guesser on multiple-choice questions! Know how to make a good impression on essay questions, even when you're not sure of the material! Many instructors and students believe that there is something underhanded about being test-wise. They argue that if you study hard and learn the material, you shouldn't have to worry about other ways of making a good impression or about "tricks." They are not necessarily wrong. However, test-wiseness also helps you optimize the presentation of what you know. And there's something else: If you're not test-wise, you can bet that other students in the class will be. And when grades depend on your performance relative to theirs, why be at a disadvantage? Again: Fair is fair.

Which brings us to our next point—what to bring to a test.

WHAT TO BRING

One of the most concise ways of informing your instructor that you're not a serious student is to ask to borrow a pencil or a pen during a test. This is the message you communicate: "I'm not prepared. I don't take this seriously. I'm in college because somebody put me here, not because I have concrete goals and want to be here."

TRUTH OR FICTION *Revisited*

Most professors *do* mind students' asking them for pens and pencils during tests. Being unprepared suggests that you are not a serious student.

So: Be prepared, whether or not you're a Boy Scout. Here are the types of things to bring to quizzes and tests:

Sharpened pencils. The old standard number 2 pencils are ideal for electronic scoring methods.

Pens. Pens should be blue or black because these colors are legible and create the impression that you are a serious student. Green is also possible because it's bright and doesn't look frivolous. Red and orange do look frivolous. Professors also like to use red and orange to grade papers and make comments, so they're out.

Paper. You should always have $8\frac{1}{2}$-by-11-inch loose-leaf paper available, if only as scrap paper. Some professors or institutions provide "blue books" for examinations; others require that you purchase them in the bookstore and bring them to essay examinations. Even when they are provided in class, it can be helpful to bring along a couple of extra blue books.

A watch. You want to keep track of time, and there may not be a strategically placed clock in the testing room.

Bring the right equipment to a test. Depending on the course, your professor may permit you to bring a dictionary or a calculator.

A dictionary. Ask the professor whether you can use a pocket dictionary so that you can check your spelling (and be sure that you're using the right word) on essay questions. Simply asking the question will show that you are a serious student and make a positive impression. Professors in advanced foreign language courses will sometimes allow you to use foreign language–English dictionaries in writing essays. This is especially so when they are focusing on your knowledge of the literature of the language and your compositional abilities, rather than on your memorization of vocabulary.

Calculators and pocket computers. These may be allowed for math, science, and business tests, especially when the important issue is whether you know how to approach a problem, not how to do the calculations. Check with the instructor.

Formulas. You may ask whether or not you can bring a list of formulas for math, science, and business tests. Some instructors believe that it is more important to know when and how to use a formula than to memorize it. If your instructor is one of them, you can focus your studying on applying formulas in practice problems, not on memorization.

Paper clips or a small stapler. They will save you from dog-earing papers together or having sheets get lost. In the event that you run out of time, you can attach worksheets (e.g., computations or outlines of essays) to your test in an effort to attain partial credit.

Handkerchiefs, tissues, and so on. Try to anticipate your personal needs so that you don't have to bother the professor or your neighbors or leave the room during the test.

Now that you've filled your suitcases with the proper items, let's focus on handling test items themselves.

IN YOUR OWN WRITE

How do you feel about multiple-choice tests? Do you prefer them to essay tests? Do you feel that you do better on essay questions that cover the same material?

_____
_____
_____
_____
_____
_____
_____
_____

HOW TO HANDLE MULTIPLE-CHOICE QUESTIONS

Multiple-choice tests are extremely popular. They are used in standardized tests such as the Scholastic Aptitude Tests (SAT) and the Graduate Record Examination (GRE), and in classroom quizzes and examinations. Educators use them because:

1. They compel the student to focus in on the one correct answer (and to reject incorrect answers).
2. Grading is completely objective and fair. (You cannot get a better grade on a multiple-choice test because the instructor likes you or because you have neat handwriting.)
3. Multiple-choice tests can be graded rapidly and mechanically. Thus they allow for the rapid grading of dozens, hundreds, or even thousands of examinations.

Some students think that instructors like multiple-choice tests because they can be graded more rapidly than essays. This is only partly true. Although multiple-choice tests can be graded quickly, they take more time to compose.

Regardless of your feelings about multiple-choice questions, you are going to see many (many!) of them. Here are a couple of examples:

1. A negative reinforcer
    a. increases the frequency of behavior when it is applied.
    b. decreases the frequency of behavior when it is applied.
    c. increases the frequency of behavior when it is removed.
    d. decreases the frequency of behavior when it is removed.
2. Which of the following allows fluid inside the cochlea (the inner ear) to move back and forth?
    a. The tympanic membrane.
    b. The round window.
    c. The oval window.
    d. The stapes.

The item about negative reinforcement has a sentence-completion format. It consists of (1) a stem, (2) a statement that correctly completes the stem (choice c), and (3) a number of misleading statements (a, b, and d) that are referred to as *distractors*. "Easy" multiple-choice questions often have distractors that seem obviously incorrect, even outrageous. Multiple-choice questions are frequently made difficult by plausible distractors. These items are difficult in that the distractors are phrased as plausibly as the correct answer.

The item about the ear has a question-and-answer format. It consists of (1) a question, (2) a statement that correctly answers the question (b), and, again, (3) distractors. These are the main types of multiple-choice formats. Here are some things you can do to maximize your potential to do well on them:

1. Bear in mind that you are usually looking for the answer that *best* answers the question or completes the stem. Perhaps no answer is perfect.
2. Try to complete the stem or answer the question before you look at the choices. When you see the stem "A negative reinforcer," turn it into a question: "What is a negative reinforcer?" If you arrive at the definition, "a stimulus that increases the frequency of behavior when it is removed," you will then be able to select the correct choice with ease.
3. Place a mark next to questions that strike you as difficult and return to them later. Don't let a tough question consume half the time allotted for the test. In addition to devouring time, difficult questions can sap your morale and make it harder for you to concentrate on other questions.
4. Be suspicious if the right answer "pops out" at you, especially when it's choice (a). "Trick" questions frequently have partially correct an-

swers as early distractors. Consider every possible answer, especially when the last choice may read "All of the above."

Consider this question about meditation:

Benson found that people who meditate twice daily
a. show lower blood pressure.
b. show normalized blood pressure.
c. produce more frequent delta waves.
d. show higher respiration rates.

For those familiar with meditation, choice (a) pops out as correct because meditation can lower your blood pressure—*if you have high blood pressure*. However, Benson also found that meditation tends to raise the blood pressure of people with low blood pressure. So choice (a) is only *sometimes* correct. However, meditation does tend to *normalize* the blood pressure, as in choice (b). Which brings us to the next suggestion . . .

5. Eliminate distractors that are incorrect. Read all answers and, if you have enough time, find a reason for eliminating each and every distractor. Can you explain to yourself why each distractor is wrong as well as why the answer you are selecting is right? A knowledgeable student who had checked out choice (b) in the meditation question would not have been able to eliminate it and would thus have probably chosen it over choice (a).

Consider the multiple-choice example on negative reinforcers. You should be able to eliminate choices (b) and (d) on the basis that *all* reinforcers, positive and negative, *increase* the frequency of behavior. You should be able to eliminate choice (a) on the basis that it defines a positive reinforcer, not a negative reinforcer.

6. Follow directions! Sometimes you are told to darken a space indicating your chosen answer with a number 2 pencil on an answer sheet. Darken it completely and use the right pencil, or else the grading machine may not credit your answers. Or you may be told, "*Circle* the letter [or number] that indicates your choice." If you underline the letter or number instead, you may lose credit. If you are told to circle the *letter* that indicates the correct choice, do *not* circle the entire statement or answer!

7. Look out for qualifying terms such as *all, completely, never, always,* and *only*. Because these qualifiers severely limit the applicability of the stem or question, they frequently indicate incorrect answers. On the other hand, more moderate qualifiers such as *usually, sometimes, frequently, probably,* and *often* tend to indicate correct choices.

8. Check that the statement you are choosing to complete the stem makes grammatical sense. That is, the stem plus the correct choice should read as a sentence. If it doesn't, check whether the other possibilities read as sentences. If you are convinced that your choice is correct, but it doesn't make a complete sentence when tacked on to the stem, ask the instructor about it. He or she may say, "Don't worry about the grammar in that one," which is a clear hint that your tentative choice is correct. If he or she says, "The correct answer makes sense," or "There's enough information in the question to make the right choice," take it as a hint that another choice is correct.

9. When you see two answers that are opposite in meaning, there's a good chance that one of them is the correct answer.

10. Keep in mind that all parts of the right choice will be (or should be) correct. Consider the question on negative reinforcers again. The correct choice indicates that negative reinforcers *increase* the frequency of behavior when they are *removed*. The second part of distractor (a) is incorrect, and the first part of distractor (d) is incorrect.

11. Change answers when you realize that you have made a mistake or you find a choice that looks more correct. It's only a myth that you

should go with your first hunch and never change an answer on a multiple-choice test.
12. Guess when the odds of gaining points outweigh the odds of losing points. Here are some guidelines that are really nothing more than common sense:
   A. If the instructor says that guessing will be penalized, ask how or how much. (Do so privately if the instructor's attitude suggests that making this request in front of the class would be viewed as flippant.) You need to know what the penalty is so that you can make an intelligent decision as to whether you ought to guess when you're not sure of the answer.
   B. Always guess when there's no penalty for wrong answers.
   C. If the penalty for wrong answers is subtraction of full credit, you probably shouldn't guess unless you've got the answer narrowed down to two choices and one of them looks a bit better than the other. That's because you will be correct more than half of the time in this way.
   D. If you lose a quarter credit or half a credit for wrong answers, you should probably guess, even when you've only been able to eliminate one distractor, or when two or three choices look equally good to you (e.g., avoid choice [a], pick the longest or most complete answer, and go with it).
   E. If full credit is subtracted for wrong answers and you have no idea which is the correct answer, don't guess.
   F. If the instructor's formula for subtracting points for wrong answers is so complicated that you can't weigh the odds, guess only when you've eliminated all but two choices and have a vague idea as to which of the remaining two looks better.

TRUTH OR FICTION *Revisited*

It turns out that you should guess on multiple-choice tests when the penalty for wrong answers does not outweigh the benefits of guessing. Most of the time, guessing helps more than it hurts.

13. When guessing, consider that with most instructors the first choice is least likely to be correct. This is especially true when choices such as "All of the above" and "None of the above" are included. Many instructors believe that you should have to read through or eliminate at least one distractor before reaching the correct answer. So they limit the number of items that are correctly answered with the first choice.
14. When guessing, keep in mind that answers with more words tend to be correct. Correct answers may require more qualifiers or more complete detail than incorrect responses.
15. If two of the answers look very much alike, one of them is probably the right answer. (The trouble with the sample question on negative reinforcers is that all four statements look alike.) Perhaps one answer will contain the word *macroeconomics* and another the word *microeconomics.* Or if the answers are mathematical quantities, perhaps they will differ only in sign, or they will be very close in magnitude.

HOW TO HANDLE TRUE–FALSE QUESTIONS

True–false questions can be tricky, at times. After all, assuming that half are true and half are false, you would earn a grade of 50 percent merely by guessing. And so instructors sometimes use items that are apparently true but turn out to be false upon close inspection.

The following suggestions will help you maximize your performance on true–false items:

1. For the item to be true, every part of it must be true. If one part of the item is false, then the entire item is false. Consider the following statement derived from our sample multiple-choice questions:

   T F 1. A negative reinforcer increases the frequency of behavior when it is applied.

   The first part of the statement is true; that is, negative reinforcers do increase the frequency of behavior. However, they do so when they are removed, not when they are applied. Since the second part of the item is false, the entire item is false.

2. Watch out for qualifiers such as *all*, *always*, *never*, *sometimes*, *often*, *usually*, and *generally*. Items that use absolutes such as *all*, *always*, or *never* are usually false. But items that use moderating qualifiers such as *generally* tend to be correct more often than not. Consider the following items:

   T F 1. Most kinds of human cells normally have 46 chromosomes.
   T F 2. Some human cells have 46 chromosomes.
   T F 3. All human cells have 46 chromosomes.
   T F 4. Human cells have 46 chromosomes.

   The fact is that the normal complement of chromosomes in human cells—other than sperm cells and egg cells (ova)—is 46. But in a number of chromosomal abnormalities, individuals may have 45 or 47 chromosomes in most of their cells. So item 1, with its two moderating qualifiers (*most* and *normally*) is true. Item 2, with the qualifier *some*, is also true. But item 3 has an absolute qualifier (*all*) and is false. Item 4 has no written qualifier, but the qualifier *all* is *implied*. Therefore, item 4 is also false.

3. As a general (not absolute!) rule, items that provide more information and are longer tend to be true. *But* check each part of the item to make sure that none is false.

4. Watch out for negatives. Negating words such as *no*, *not*, and *never* can confuse the issue, especially if there is double negation. Consider these items:

   T F 1. Some human cells have 46 chromosomes.
   T F 2. Human cells never have 46 chromosomes.
   T F 3. It is never the case that human cells fail to have 46 chromosomes.

   The first item is a repeat and is included for comparative purposes. The second item has a negative absolute qualifier (*never*) and, of course, is false. Item 3 is a student's nightmare. Take a moment to decode it. *Fail to* is a negative, along with *never*. Although most *never* statements are false, the double negative makes the statement positive in this case. With a statement worded like this, it might be appropriate to raise your hand or walk up to the professor and say something like, "I'm confused about the way this item is written. Could you explain it to me?" You might also want to mark it and come back later if you

---

In order for a true-false item to be true, every part of it must be true. If one part of the item is false, then the entire item is false.

> Toots Shor's restaurant is so crowded nobody goes there anymore.
>
> YOGI BERRA

> It ain't over till it's over.
>
> YOGI BERRA

have time. If there's no time and no major penalty for wrong answers, you could just assume that the double negative neutralizes the *never* and mark it as true.

HOW TO HANDLE SHORT-ANSWER/ SENTENCE-COMPLETION QUESTIONS

These items ask for a brief response to a question or present a sentence with a blank space that needs to be filled in.

Short-Answer Questions

Here are sample short-answer questions:

1. What are negative reinforcers?
2. What is the stapes?
3. Where is the stapes?
4. How many chromosomes are found in most kinds of normal human cells?

Such items usually ask for definitions, amounts, locations, or brief descriptions. An ideal response is a brief sentence, such as "Negative reinforcers are stimuli that increase the frequency of behavior when they are removed." Try to hit key words in your answers, such as *stimuli, increase* or *decrease, frequency, behavior,* and *apply* or *remove.*

If there's no time for sentences, use phrases that contain the essential information, as in "Stimuli that increase the frequency of behavior when removed." With item 2, the ideal response is, "The stapes is a bone that looks like a stirrup and conducts vibrations produced by sound waves in the middle ear." *Use all the detail you are sure of and time allows.* With little time and incomplete knowledge, you might be able to get away with "A bone in the ear," or "in the middle ear." *There is no harm in showing the professor a couple of items you have completed and asking if they offer enough detail or if more is desired.* Answers of various detail are also possible for item 3. You might get partial credit for "The ear," and full credit for "The middle ear." A demanding professor might require you to say, "A bone in the middle ear that lies between the incus (another bone in the middle ear) and the oval window (which conducts vibrations into the inner ear)." After a while, you will get to know what your professor wants, but again, during early questions you can ask whether you've used enough detail. For item 4, a complete and correct answer is "46." If there is enough time, you could write the sentence, "Forty-six chromosomes are found in most kinds of normal human cells." *The professor may award you a mental "A for effort" that translates into giving you full credit for another item in which you could have included more detail.*

Sentence-Completion Questions (Fill-in-the-Blanks)

Sentence-completion items tend to be phrased as follows:

1. _____ reinforcers are stimuli that increase the frequency of behavior when they are removed.
2. Negative reinforcers are stimuli that _____ the frequency of behavior when they are removed.

Taking Tests 167

3. Negative reinforcers are stimuli that increase the frequency of behavior when they are _____.
4. The stapes is a bone in the _____ ear.
5. The stapes is a bone in the middle ear that lies between the incus and the _____ window.
6. Most kinds of normal human cells contain _____ chromosomes.
7. Most kinds of normal human cells contain 46 _____s.
8. Persons with Down's syndrome have _____ chromosomes in most of their cells.
9. Persons with _____ syndrome have 47 chromosomes in most of their cells.

As short-answer questions, sentence-completion items frequently check whether you are capable of making precise definitions. On the other hand, sometimes there is more than one correct answer.

Notice that items 1–3 involve the same sentence, but each seeks a different piece of information. (No, you would never see an array like this on an actual test! But sometimes the answer to one question is accidentally provided in information given in another part of the test.) Item 1 requires the word *negative*, but you could get item 2 correct by using *heighten* rather than *increase*, and item 3 correct by writing in *taken away* rather than *removed*.

Consider item 4. What if you cannot recall whether the stapes is a part of the outer, middle, or inner ear? The answers *human* and *normal* might also be acceptable, even if they are not what the professor was looking for. *When you don't know the answer the instructor is seeking, try to write in a correct alternative.* You may get partial or full credit.

Items 6 and 7 are included to illustrate types of sentence-completion items that call for quantities.

Item 8 requires the number *47*, although you could hope for partial credit with *extra*, if you can't recall the proper number. There are actually a number of syndromes that fit the bill in item 9. For example, *Klinefelter's syndrome* and *XYY syndrome* also work. In an item like this, put in some syndrome when you're not sure of the answer, unless there's a heavy penalty for wrong answers. You could also try the word *several* as an answer, but you should avoid it unless you know that your professor has a sense of humor.

Additional Hints for Sentence-Completion Items In answering sentence-completion items, also note that:

1. Your answers should make grammatical sense. For example, the answer to item 6 could not be *one*.
2. If the article *a* is used before the blank space, the answer probably begins with a consonant.
3. If the article *an* is used, the answer probably begins with a vowel. (One of us is tricky and always writes *a(n)*.)
4. Some answers call for more than one word, but remember that the answers should fit grammatically.

HOW TO HANDLE MATCHING QUESTIONS

In matching questions, you associate items from one list with items from another. For example, you may be asked to associate names of artists with the periods in which they worked. You may be asked to associate historic events with dates, or foreign words with their English equivalents. Consider the following matching exercise, which uses information of the kind presented in Chapter 13.

Directions: In the column to the left are the names of a number of drugs. In the column to the right are a number of facts about drugs. Match the fact with the drug by writing the letter of the fact in the space next to the drug.

_____ 1. Benzedrine
_____ 2. Lysergic acid (LSD)
_____ 3. Cocaine
_____ 4. Demerol
_____ 5. Methadone
_____ 6. Ritalin
_____ 7. Valium
_____ 8. Alcohol
_____ 9. Marijuana
_____ 10. Morphine
_____ 11. Heroin
_____ 12. Secobarbital

A. Used to treat hyperactivity in children
B. Used to treat addiction to heroin
C. Most widely prescribed tranquilizer
D. An amphetamine
E. Named after the Greek god of dreams
F. Most widely used drug on campus
G. A hallucinogenic associated with flashbacks
H. A barbiturate
I. An opium derivative used widely as an analgesic today
J. Contains THC
K. "Crack" is derived from this
L. Once used to "cure" addiction to morphine

Let's note a few things about the directions and the questions. First of all, the directions are not very well written, which happens often enough. The essential task is to place the correct letter from the right-hand column in a blank space to the left of the appropriate drug. Note also that the drug facts are a grammatical nightmare: Some items begin with the present or past tense of a verb, others with an article (*a* or *an*). This is an inconsistency you must live with.

In the sample questions, we have provided an equal number of drugs and facts about drugs (12 in each column). And so you might assume that each letter (or drug fact) is used once. *But you should ask whether items can be used more than once. Raise your hand or approach the desk.*

If items can be used only once, handle the questions as follows: Look at item 1. Scan choices A through L quickly and write in the answer if you know it "cold." The answer is D. If you think you recognize the answer, try it out in a sentence: "Benzedrine is classified as an amphetamine." If the sentence sounds right to you, write the D next to the 1 *in pencil*, and draw a line through the entire choice *D. An amphetamine*—in pencil!— in the right-hand column. Check item 2 and repeat the procedure, skipping choice D (which has a line through it). Mark the items you're unsure of and complete the list.

Now you may be left with a couple of blank spaces and a couple of possible choices (phrases without lines drawn through them). Guess by writing in the unchosen answers in the blank spaces, but leave question marks in pencil next to your guesses.

If answers can be used more than once, put a checkmark next to items you have already used rather than draw a line through them. Other than this, follow the outlined method.

If time permits, go back over the items next to which you have written question marks. See if an answer you've used elsewhere (one with a line drawn through it) seems correct. If it does, reconsider whether your first use of that answer was right.

Let us give you an example of how to find an error in a matching exercise. When you have finished the list, you find that you have a question mark next to _____ 8. *Alcohol*, and that you have not used answer *J—Contains THC*. You know that alcohol does not contain THC, and so you must have made an error somewhere else. But what contains THC? Try to use *Contains THC* in a sentence. You may come up with "THC stands for, um, tetrahydrocannabinol, which is the active ingredient in . . . marijuana!" So you check the answer you had used for item _____ 9. *Marijuana*. Lo and behold! You had written D in the blank space next to the number 9, signifying "Most widely used drug on campus." Now you remember that alcohol is actually the most widely used drug! You had been thinking of the most widely used *illegal* drug.

Hint: When two answers seem to fit one item (e.g., when *F. Most widely used drug on campus* and *J. Contains THC* both seem to fit *Marijuana*) write *F or J?* in pencil next to marijuana. Then, when you see that you have no answer for *Alcohol*, ask yourself whether F or J might fit the bill.

After making your corrections, erase your pencil answers, if there is time, and write the correct answers in black or blue ink.

HOW TO HANDLE ESSAY QUESTIONS

Essay questions require you to produce written responses to questions. Essays can vary in length from a few sentences to several paragraphs. You

TABLE 7.1. Sample Essay Questions and Guiding Words **(Boldface)**

SAMPLE ESSAY QUESTION	DEFINITION OF GUIDING WORD
Analyze Canadian research concerning the effects of acid rain on the ecological systems of freshwater lakes.	To analyze is to separate into parts to find out their nature, function, interrelationship; to examine in detail.
Compare the political systems of the United States and the United Kingdom.	To compare is to examine two or more things to observe or discover their similarities and differences. However, *compare* focuses on similarities, whereas *contrast* focuses on differences.
Contrast the behavioral and psychodynamic approaches to the explanation of phobias.	To contrast is to examine two or more things to point out the differences, to set off one against the other.
Criticize Mark Twain's "The Mysterious Stranger" in terms of philosophical implications and stylistic features.	To criticize is to analyze and judge as a critic. In many cases, the term *criticize* implies finding fault; however, literary and artistic criticism are specific processes that may lead to praise as well as disapproval.
Define the terms incus, stapes, and malleus.	To define a term is to explain its meaning. More generally, to define is to trace the outlines of a topic, to determine or state its exact extent and nature.
Describe various corporate responses to social demands.	To describe objects or events is to give detailed accounts of them, to create pictures of them in words.
Discuss the ethical issues involved in allowing terminal patients to use experimental drugs.	To discuss is to consider and weigh the pros and cons of a topic.
Enumerate the lobes of the cerebral cortex.	To enumerate is to name one by one, as in a list.
Evaluate the argument that one must "carry the history of art" in one's mind in order to be an effective, creative artist.	To evaluate is to judge or determine the quality or worth of an argument, concept, theory, approach, etc.
Explain how businesses carry out marketing research.	To explain is to make clear or understandable; to give the meaning of; to give the reasons for. In the example, the goal is to make marketing-research methods clear and understandable.

may be asked to define 10 terms in an essay quiz that lasts half an hour, in which case you can devote only three minutes and two sentences or so to each question. Or you may be given three hours to complete one or two essay questions on a final examination.

The first step in writing an essay is making certain that you understand the question. We cannot estimate the number of times we've written these comments on students' essays: "Strays from the question!", "Nicely written, but misses the point," "A commendable job in many ways, but you didn't answer the question." So read the directions very, very carefully. Otherwise, you risk receiving no credit for your work, regardless of the amount of time you spend on the question, and regardless of your neatness and your general worth as a human being. In reading the question, look for guiding or key words that should guide your answers.

Guiding Words

Table 7.1 lists many of the formats used in essay questions. The guiding words are **boldfaced.** These are the words that should direct your answer. If you fail to follow them, you can get yourself into trouble.

Outlining

Before you start writing the essay, invest a few moments making a quick outline on a piece of scrap paper or, if scrap paper is not allowed, in the margin of the test paper. The outline will help you organize your thoughts

SAMPLE ESSAY QUESTION	DEFINITION OF GUIDING WORD
Identify the nations that are considered part of the "Third World."	To identify (these nations) is to show those that belong to the category (Third World).
Illustrate the usage of the technique of "positive visualization" in enhancing athletic performance.	To illustrate is to make clear or plain, usually by offering examples and comparisons.
Interpret Marx's statement, "Religion is the opium of the people."	To interpret is to explain the meaning of, to translate into terms that explain meaning.
Justify the use of nonmilitary foreign aid to Communist nations.	To justify is to show to be correct, to be consistent with logic and reason.
List the divisions of the nervous system.	To set forth a series of items or names in order. (To enumerate.)
Outline the causes of the Civil War.	To outline is to set forth the main points or ideas, usually in somewhat abbreviated form. However, the term does not usually mean that you should write an actual outline with Roman numerals, etc., as in your notes (see Chapter 5).
Prove that the universe is composed of that which is *X* and that which is *not X*.	To prove is to demonstrate as true, to establish as factual. Different academic disciplines have different rules of "proof." For example, in philosophy and mathematics, many proofs rest on deductive logic. In natural sciences, proof frequently rests on experimentation.
State the reasons for the separation of powers in the U.S. Constitution.	To state is to explain precisely, to express specifically.
Support the view that animal research is necessary for the advancement of medical science.	To support is to uphold, to show to be true, to help prove. (You are sometimes asked to support statements with which you strongly disagree. Follow the instructions as an exercise to show that you can do it and earn a good grade. You can write an "addendum," if you have time, explaining your personal disagreement. Or you can discuss it with the instructor after the test.)
Trace the evolution of the horse.	To trace is to follow the development or history of; to outline a process.

Before you start writing the answer to an essay question, invest a few moments to make an outline on a piece of scrap paper or in the margin of the test paper. The outline will help you organize your thoughts and make sure that you touch upon the main points of your answer.

and help make sure that you touch upon the main points of your answer, rather than getting wrapped up in a detail. Don't worry about the niceties of Roman numerals. Sketch the main points, where you will start and end, and jot down key words that represent ideas that you will elaborate. If you don't have enough time to finish the essay, attach your outline to show the instructor where you were heading. It may help your grade (and it certainly won't hurt).

Introductory and Summarizing Statements

There are different points of view as to whether you should include elaborate introductions and summaries or just get to the business of the essay. The argument against excessive language is that instructors haven't time for it and they resent it. The argument for introductions and summary statements is that they establish where you're going and where you've been.

Let us take a middle road by recommending a brief introduction and a brief conclusion or summary statement. Consider the essay question, "Support the view that animal research is necessary for the advancement of medical science." You can begin with two sentences that show your grasp of the issue and define your direction:

> In recent years great controversy has emerged concerning the use of animals in medical research. In this essay I will support that view that animal research is an essential aspect of the advancement of medical knowledge.

Notice what you've accomplished: You have stated the contemporary controversy and you have specified the direction you will take. Paraphrasing the essay question demonstrates comprehension of it. You also make a good first impression, and first impressions count.

Similarly, at the end you can briefly state, "In this essay I have shown that . . ."

Getting There "Firstest with the Mostest"

After your introduction, express your strongest ideas first. (Try to adjust your outline to enable you to do this.) When you lead with the things you know the most about, you build your powerful first impression. It is easy for graders to become fatigued when they must pore over dozens or hundreds of essays, so hit them first with your most powerful weapons. If they are satisfied that you are in control of the essay, they may skim the remainder.

Determining Length

How long should your essay be? How many words should it have? We usually advise, "Don't count words; answer the question." But there are some rules of thumb that you can consider.

For example, if you know the topic cold and you write flawlessly, be as brief as you feel you can afford to be. Graders appreciate brevity when it is right on the mark. Otherwise, they may construe it as laziness.

If you have many questions and little time, each essay will have to be brief. If you have two or three questions and three hours, it may be that you should fill three blue books.

In all cases, *make sure you answer the question.*

Dotting the *i*'s and Crossing the *t*'s

Students wonder and often ask whether spelling and neatness count. The answer is simple: Spelling and neatness always count, even when the instructor states (and *believes*) that they do not. Keep in mind that essay questions are graded more subjectively than short-answer items, even when instructors try to be objective. In other words, the general impression you make on the instructor counts. When you use a legible pen, use decent handwriting (or print, if necessary!), attend to sentence structure, and watch your spelling, you create a document that is more enjoyable to read—and more likely to earn a good grade.

TRUTH OR FICTION *Revisited*

Yes, neatness counts! So does spelling.

When students ask your first author about spelling and neatness, he tells them "Pretend that this is the real world—that you're an employee, I'm your supervisor, and that your salaries, raises, and even keeping your jobs depend on the quality of the work you hand in."

There is a relationship between the amount of time you have and the finished quality of your essay. If there's time to spare, handing in sloppy work becomes less excusable.

There is also a relationship between the resources you have available and the quality of the work you hand in. If the essay is an open-book essay, you should get all your facts right. If you are permitted to use a dictionary, there should be no misspelled words.

What Do You Do When You Don't Know What to Do?

Sometimes you're faced with an essay question that you just cannot answer. The question may direct you to criticize or evaluate a novel or a philosophical theory, and you may just not be familiar enough with the material to follow the directions.

What do you do? That depends.

One thing to consider is the number of questions on the test. If there are many questions and relatively little time, it may be worthwhile to skip the question, or to write, "I did not have time to answer this one." (Don't use this excuse and then leave the room early!) Your instructor may appreciate the fact that you did not attempt to "bull" your way through the question.

But if there are few questions and a great deal of time, you are better off answering the question as best you can. Use a brief introduction as we have suggested. State that you will answer the question. Write an outline of what you know about the subject matter on a piece of scrap paper. Select the items from the outline that come closest to answering the question. Then write about them as neatly as you can. Perhaps the guiding word directs you to *criticize* or *evaluate* the material, and you are not prepared to do so. Nevertheless, you may be able to define or describe the material, to outline it, or to trace its development. Do it, using as much factual information as you can. For example, even if you are not sure how to criticize a certain aspect of *Macbeth*, you can sketch the outline of the plot and enumerate some of the conflicts in the play. Perhaps you can even venture an interpretation of Lady Macbeth's motivation, or recollect an important passage (e.g., "Canst thou not minister to a mind diseas'd, . . . ") and comment on it. Your goal in such an approach is to show that you have done your homework—or at least part of it—and that you are somewhat familiar with the material. Perhaps you will be granted partial credit for your efforts. And again, neatness and spelling count!

IN YOUR OWN WRITE

Now we'll talk about test anxiety. Before doing so, however, describe how you feel when you're taking an important test. What thoughts do you have? What do you sense happening within your body?

_____
_____
_____
_____
_____
_____

> If you can keep your head when all about you are losing theirs, perhaps you haven't grasped the situation.
> — JEAN KERR

HOW TO HANDLE TEST ANXIETY

Can tests really raise the hair on the backs of your arms? Sometime they can. Hair "standing on end" is one of the physical signs of anxiety.

What types of things do you hear students say when they have test anxiety? Here's a sampling:

"I just know I'm going to flunk."

"I study as hard as I can and I get everything memorized, but when I get in there, my mind just goes blank."

How do you know when you're test-anxious? Some of the physical aspects of anxiety are rapid heart beat, rapid breathing, heavy sweating, "butterflies in the stomach," muscle tension, and dryness in the mouth.

"What's wrong with me? I know everything, but I just can't take tests."
"With the way I do on tests like the GRE, I'll never get into graduate school."

Test anxiety is a frustrating problem. When we study assiduously, test anxiety seems an especially cruel handicap.

What Is Test Anxiety?

In terms of thoughts and feelings, anxiety consists of feelings of dread and foreboding. Anxious students feel that awful things will happen, even if they can't enumerate them. On a physical level, anxiety involves overactivity of the parts of the nervous system that control the heart rate, respiration rate (breathing), and some other functions. The physical aspects of anxiety include rapid heartbeat (you may feel that your heart is pounding), rapid breathing, sweating (very heavy at times!), butterflies in the stomach, muscle tension, dryness in the mouth, and other equally bothersome signs.[2]

Understand this: Anxiety is *not* always bad. It is normal to feel anxious when an important test, job interview, or even a big date is drawing near. Anxiety shows that we understand the magnitude of the occasion and that we are aware that failure can be harmful. Test anxiety is a kind of *performance anxiety*. During tests, at interviews, and on dates we can become anxious about how well we are performing.

Why Do Students Encounter Test Anxiety?

Although you may think you *always* had test anxiety, you were not born with it. Test anxiety reflects self-defeating thoughts before and during tests, including disparaging self-evaluations. High-test-anxious students report more negative thoughts and are more self-critical than other students, *even when they are performing just as well.*[3]

TRUTH OR FICTION *Revisited*

We do tend to create or compound feelings of test anxiety with our self-defeating thoughts.

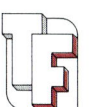

Taking Tests 175

The kinds of thoughts we're talking about are listed in Table 7.2. Many of these thoughts tend to blow things out of proportion. Moreover, test-anxious students allow these thoughts and their self-criticisms to *distract* them from focusing on their tests.[4]

What to Do

Now that you know what test anxiety is, and have some basis for assessing your own level of test anxiety, we are going to describe a number of ways of handling test anxiety. These include being well prepared, changing the ways you talk to yourself about tests, and directly changing the ways your body feels about tests.

Being Well Prepared

A simple, obvious, and effective way of cutting into test anxiety is to be well prepared. Actors who repeatedly rehearse their roles may still be a bit anxious when they get on stage, but at least they don't have to worry that they will forget their lines. Professors who carefully outline their lectures may still experience some anxiety, especially when they meet a new class, but at least they are assured that they will disseminate the subject matter in a coherent way.

Similarly, students who follow the suggestions for studying outlined in Chapter 5—particularly students who regularly review the subject matter—can be confident that they will be able to summon up most of what they have learned, even if they are somewhat anxious. This kind of confidence helps you place normal amounts of anxiety in perspective. And even if

TABLE 7.2. Percentage of Positive and Negative Thoughts for University Students with Different Levels of Test Anxiety.

	TYPE OF THOUGHT	LOW TEST ANXIETY PERCENTAGE	HIGH TEST ANXIETY PERCENTAGE
POSITIVE THOUGHTS	"I'm doing just fine on the test." "Everything will be all right."	71	43
	"My mind is clear." "I can concentrate."	49	26
	"I'm in control." "I can handle my reactions."	46	23
NEGATIVE THOUGHTS	"I wish I could get out of here! I wish the test were over!"	46	65
	"This test is really hard."	45	64
	"I'm not going to have enough time to finish."	23	49
	"I worked so hard to prepare for this test, and it won't be shown by my grade."	16	44
	"This question is impossible. I'm stuck. How will I be able to get on with other questions?"	13	34
	"My mind is a blank!" "I can't think straight."	11	31
	"I'm going to do poorly on this test."	11	28
	"It's going to be awful if I fail or do poorly!"	11	45

Test-anxious students report fewer positive thoughts and more negative thoughts during tests.

QUESTIONNAIRE
The Suinn Test Anxiety Behavior Scale

What about you? Do you view tests as opportunities to display your knowledge, or do you get yourself bent out of shape with self-criticism and expectations of doom? How does your test anxiety stack up next to that of other students? To get an idea, take the Suinn Test Anxiety Behavior Scale (STABS). Then compare your answers to other students' by checking the key at the end of the chapter.

Questionnaire items portray experiences that cause some students anxiety. For each item, place a checkmark in the column that shows how much it upsets you.

	Not at all	A little	A fair amount	Much	Very much
1. Rereading the answers I gave on the test before turning it in.	___	___	___	___	___
2. Sitting down to study before a regularly scheduled class.	___	___	___	___	___
3. Turning in my completed test paper.	___	___	___	___	___
4. Hearing the announcement of a coming test.	___	___	___	___	___
5. Having a test returned.	___	___	___	___	___
6. Reading the first question on a final exam.	___	___	___	___	___
7. Being in class waiting for my corrected test to be returned.	___	___	___	___	___
8. Seeing a test question and not being sure of the answer.	___	___	___	___	___
9. Studying for a test the night before.	___	___	___	___	___
10. Waiting to enter the room where a test is to be given.	___	___	___	___	___
11. Waiting for a test to be handed out.	___	___	___	___	___
12. Waiting for the day my corrected test will be returned.	___	___	___	___	___
13. Discussing with the instructor an answer I believed to be right but which was marked wrong.	___	___	___	___	___
14. Seeing my standing on the exam relative to other people's standing.	___	___	___	___	___
15. Waiting to see my letter grade on the test.	___	___	___	___	___
16. Studying for a quiz.	___	___	___	___	___
17. Studying for a midterm.	___	___	___	___	___
18. Studying for a final.	___	___	___	___	___
19. Discussing my approaching test with friends a few weeks before the test is due.	___	___	___	___	___
20. After the test, listening to the answers my friends selected.	___	___	___	___	___

you tend to have more "butterflies" or sweat more heavily than your neighbors, at least you can think, "Yes, but I'll get through the test and do okay."

Regular review also helps you avoid cramming. Learning takes time, and distributed review sessions are more effective than pulling an all-nighter. Cramming is desirable only when compared to the perils of knowing nothing at all about a subject.

This is the point: *You can start coping with test anxiety right at the beginning of the course by planning regular study habits and sticking to them.*

Overlearning Let us also reinforce the value of overlearning. Overlearning means continuing to review the subject matter *even when you can recite it flawlessly.* Overlearning accomplishes two very helpful things:

1. Overlearning leads to longer retention of material. That is, you will probably retain material longer if you overlearn it.
2. Overlearning builds confidence. You realize, "Hey, I know this stuff! I *really* know it." Believe it—there's no better feeling than that when you're walking into a test!

Now let's talk about some ways of directly handling the thoughts and physical reactions that contribute to test anxiety.

Cognitive Restructuring

What if you are reasonably well prepared for tests but make yourself uptight with the kinds of thoughts listed in Table 7.2? Test anxiety often reflects catastrophic, irrational thoughts that distract students from the tasks on the test itself. So one way of coping with test anxiety is to challenge these thoughts and return your attention to the test.[5] College students on several campuses have reduced test anxiety and improved their test grades through such a method—cognitive (mental) restructuring.

In one study,[6] for example, students selected anxiety-evoking items from the Suinn Test Anxiety Behavior Scale (STABS). They sat back and imagined themselves in these situations. They examined the thoughts that popped into their minds, pinpointing their irrational, self-defeating thoughts. Then they changed, or restructured, their responses to these situations by constructing alternative, rational thoughts.

For example, one student found himself thinking, "I'm going to fail this test, and then everyone's going to think I'm stupid." He restructured these catastrophizing thoughts as follows: "Chances are I probably won't fail. And even if I do, people probably won't think I'm stupid. And even if they do, that doesn't mean I *am* stupid."[7]

Some of the situations outlined in the STABS may apply to you. Jot down the ones that do. Take a few minutes and jot down other situations related to tests that get you worked up. Write down five of them in the left-hand column below:

Test-related situations in which I feel anxious | Irrational, catastrophizing thoughts that pop into mind

1. _____   _____
   _____   _____
   _____   _____

2. _____   _____
   _____   _____
   _____   _____

3. _____   _____
   _____   _____
   _____   _____

4. _____   _____
   _____   _____
   _____   _____

5. _____   _____
   _____   _____
   _____   _____
   _____

Now sit back and relax. Picture yourself in each situation. After a while, write down the distressing thoughts that come to mind in the column labeled "Irrational, catastrophizing thoughts that pop into mind."

Examine each thought. Make a judgment: Is it logical and factual, or is it unfounded? Does it blow things out of proportion? Produce incompatible reasonable alternatives for each irrational thought that is irrational, as suggested in Table 7.3 on page 180. We've left some space at the end of the table for you to write in some of your own self-defeating thoughts and then construct rational alternatives.

Anxiety has physical as well as mental aspects. Cognitive restructuring aims to change the mental contributors to test anxiety. But you can also deal directly with the physical aspects of anxiety. Let us look at two ways of quelling them: muscle relaxation and diaphragmatic breathing.

Muscle Relaxation

One of the chief physical aspects of anxiety is muscle tension. So measures that relax muscles can also lower anxiety. One popular method of relaxing muscles is progressive relaxation.[8]

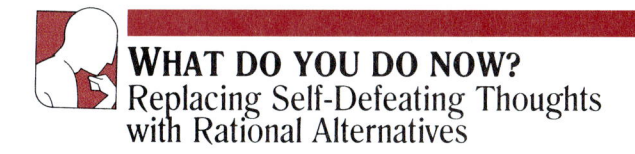

WHAT DO YOU DO NOW?
Replacing Self-Defeating Thoughts with Rational Alternatives

Now that we have discussed the method of cognitive restructuring, how can you employ it to challenge and change the self-defeating thoughts that contribute to your own test anxiety?

We recommend using four steps to restructure your own thoughts about taking tests:

1. Pinpoint the irrational thoughts, especially the catastrophizing thoughts that tend to blow things out of proportion.

2. Construct more rational, alternative thoughts—thoughts that are incompatible with the "downers."

3. Imagine yourself in the testing situation and practice thinking the rational alternatives you have constructed.

4. Reward yourself for thinking the productive thoughts rather than making yourself a basket case. For example, say to yourself, for example, "That's much better; now I can get back to the test," or, "See, I don't have to be victimized by self-defeating thoughts. I can take charge of my thoughts." After the test, think something like, "I did it! The test is finished and I feel much better than I felt before. I didn't let self-defeating thoughts distract me, and I may have gotten a better grade as well."

TABLE 7.3. Rational Alternatives to Irrational Cognitions Concerning Test Taking.

IRRATIONAL, CATASTROPHIZING THOUGHTS	INCOMPATIBLE, RATIONAL ALTERNATIVES
"I'm the only one who's going so bananas over this thing."	"Nonsense, lots of people have test anxiety. Just don't let it take your mind off the test itself."
"I'm running out of time!"	"Time is passing, but just take it item by item and answer what you can. Getting bent out of shape won't help."
"This is impossible! Are all the questions going to be this bad?"	"Just take it question by question. They're all different. Don't assume the worst."
"I just can't remember a thing!"	"Just slow down and remember what you can. Take a few moments and some things will come back to you. If not, go on to the next question."
"Everyone else is smarter than I am!"	"Probably not, but maybe they're not distracting themselves from the test by catastrophizing. Just do the best you can and take it easy. Breathe easy, in and out."
"I've got to get out of here! I can't take it anymore!"	"Even if I feel that I need to leave now and then, I don't have to act on it. Just focus on the questions, one by one."
"I just can't do well on tests."	"That's only true if you believe it's true. Back to the items, one by one."
"There are a million questions left!"	"Quite a few, but not a million. Just take them one by one and answer as many as you can. Focus on each question as it comes, not on the number of questions."
"Everyone else is leaving. They're all finished before me."	"Fast work is no guarantee of good work. Even if most of them do well, it doesn't have to mean that you *won't* do well. Take all the time you need. Back to the questions, one by one."
"If I flunk, everything is ruined!"	"You won't be happy if you fail, but it won't be the end of the world either. Just take it question by question and don't let worrying distract you. Breathe easy, in and out."

Add some of your own self-defeating thoughts here:

1. _____
_____
_____

2. _____
_____
_____

3. _____
_____
_____

Write rational alternatives for these thoughts in this column:

_____
_____
_____

_____
_____
_____

_____
_____
_____

To restructure irrational ideas that contribute to test anxiety, construct reasonable alternatives and rehearse them. Don't blow things out of proportion and allow yourself to be distracted from the test.

In progressive relaxation, you purposefully tense then relax a group of muscles. The tension–relaxation sequence fosters awareness of muscle tensions and helps you differentiate between feelings of tension and relaxation. The method is *progressive* in that you move, or progress, from one muscle group to another.

Before relaxing, create a favorable setting. Settle back on a recliner, couch, or a bed with a pillow. Select a place and time when you're unlikely to be disturbed. Make the room warm and comfortable. Dim sources of light. Loosen tight clothing.

Use the instructions below.* Tighten muscles about two-thirds as hard as you could if you were trying your hardest. If you sense that a muscle could have a spasm, you are tightening too much. After tensing, let go of tensions completely.

You can memorize instructions (small variations from the text won't do any harm), tape record them, or have a friend read them aloud.

After you have repeated tensing and relaxing a few times, you can shift to relaxing muscles only.

Relaxation of Arms (time: 4–5 minutes) Settle back as comfortably as you can. Let yourself relax to the best of your ability. . . . Now, as you relax like that, clench your right fist, just clench your fist tighter and tighter, and study the tension as you do so. Keep it clenched and feel the tension in your right fist, hand, forearm . . . and now relax. Let the fingers of your right hand become loose, and observe the contrast in your feelings. . . . Now, let yourself go and try to become more relaxed all over. . . . Once more, clench your right fist really tight . . . hold it, and notice the tension again. . . . Now let go, relax; your fingers straighten out, and you notice the difference once more. . . . Now repeat that with your left fist. Clench your left fist while the rest of your body relaxes; clench that fist tighter and feel the tension . . . and now relax. Again enjoy the contrast. . . . Repeat that once more, clench the left fist, tight and tense. . . . Now do the opposite of tension—relax and feel the difference. Continue relaxing like that for a while. . . . Clench both fists tighter and together, both fists tense, forearms tense, study the sensations . . . and relax; straighten out your fingers and feel that relaxation. Continue relaxing your hands and forearms more and more. . . . Now bend your elbows and tense your biceps, tense them harder and study the tension feelings . . . all right, straighten out your arms, let them relax and feel that difference again. Let the relaxation develop. . . . Once more, tense your biceps; hold the tension and observe it carefully. . . . Straighten the arms and relax; relax to the best of your ability. . . . Each time, pay close attention to your feelings when you tense up and when you relax. Now straighten your arms, straighten them so that you feel most tension in the triceps muscles along the back of your arms; stretch your arms and feel that tension . . . . And now relax. Get your arms back into a comfortable position. Let the relaxation proceed on its own. The arms should feel comfortably heavy as you allow them to relax. . . . Straighten the arms once more so that you feel the tension in the triceps muscles; straighten them. Feel that tension . . . and relax. Now let's concentrate on pure relaxation in the arms without any tension. Get your arms comfortable and let them relax further and further. Continue relaxing your arms even further. Even when your arms seem fully relaxed, try to go that extra bit further; try to achieve deeper and deeper levels of relaxation.

Relaxation of Facial Area with Neck, Shoulders and Upper Back (time: 4–5 minutes) Let all your muscles go loose and heavy. Just settle back quietly and comfortably. Wrinkle up your forehead now; wrinkle it tighter. . . . And now stop wrinkling your forehead, relax and smooth it out. Picture the entire forehead and scalp becoming smoother as the relaxation increases. . . . Now frown and crease your brows and study the tension. . . . Let go of the tension again. Smooth out the forehead once more. . . . Now close your eyes tighter and tighter . . . feel the tension . . . and relax your eyes. Keep your eyes closed, gently, comfortably, and notice the relaxation. . . . Now clench your jaws, bite your teeth together; study the tension throughout the jaws. . . . Relax your jaws now. Let your lips part slightly. . . . Appreciate the relaxation. . . . Now press your tongue hard against the roof of your mouth. Look for the tension . . . . All right, let your tongue return to a comfortable and relaxed position. . . . Now purse your lips, press your lips together tighter and tighter. . . . Relax the lips. Note the contrast between tension and relaxation. Feel the relaxation all over your face, all over your forehead and scalp, eyes, jaws, lips, tongue, and throat. The relaxation progresses further and further. . . . Now attend to your neck muscles. Press your head back as far as it can go and feel the tension in the neck; roll it to the right and feel the tension shift; now roll it to the left. Straighten your head and bring it forward, press your chin against your chest. Let your head return to a comfortable position, and study the relaxation. Let the relaxation develop. . . . Shrug your shoulders, right up. Hold the tension. . . . Drop your shoulders and feel the relaxation. Neck and shoulders relaxed . . . . Shrug your shoulders again and move them around. Bring your shoulders up and forward and back. Feel the tension in your shoulders and in your upper back. . . . Drop your shoulders once more and relax. Let the relaxation spread deep into the shoulders, right into your back muscles; relax your neck and throat, and your jaws and other facial areas as the pure relaxation takes over and grows deeper . . . deeper . . . ever deeper.

Relaxation of Chest, Stomach and Lower Back (time: 4–5 minutes) Relax your entire body to the best of your ability. Feel that comfortable heaviness that accompanies relaxation. Breathe easily and freely in and out. Notice how the relaxation increases as you exhale . . . as you breathe out just feel that relaxation. . . . Now breathe right in and fill your lungs; inhale deeply and hold your breath. Study the tension. . . . Now exhale, let the walls of your chest grow loose and push the air out automatically. Continue relaxing and breathe freely and gently. Feel the relaxation and enjoy it. . . . With the rest of your body as relaxed as possible, fill your lungs again. Breathe in deeply and hold it again. . . . That's fine, breathe out and appreciate the relief. Just breathe normally. Continue relaxing your chest and let the relaxation spread to your back, shoulders, neck and arms. Merely let go . . . and enjoy the relaxation. Now let's pay attention to your abdominal muscles, your stomach area. Tighten your stomach muscles, make your abdomen hard. Notice the tension. . . . And relax. Let the muscles loosen and notice the contrast. . . . Once more, press and tighten your stomach muscles. Hold the tension and study it. . . . And relax. Notice the general well-being that comes with relaxing your stomach. . . . Now draw your stomach in, pull the muscles right in and feel the tension this way . . . . Now relax again. Let your stomach out. Continue breathing normally and easily and feel the gentle massaging action all over your chest and stomach. . . . Now pull your stomach in again and hold the tension. . . . Now push out and tense like that; hold the tension . . . once more pull in and feel the tension . . . now relax your stomach fully. Let the tension dissolve as the relaxation grows deeper. Each time you breathe out, notice the rhythmic relaxation both in your lungs and in your stomach. Notice thereby how your chest and your stomach relax more and more. . . . Try and let go of contractions anywhere in your body. . . . Now direct your attention to your lower back. Arch up your back, make your lower back quite hollow, and feel the tension along your spine . . . and settle down comfortably again relaxing the lower back. . . . Just arch your back up and feel the tensions as you do so. Try to keep the rest of your body as relaxed as possible. Try to localize the tension throughout your lower back area. . . . Relax once more, relaxing further and further. Relax your lower back, relax your upper back, spread the relaxation to your stomach, chest, shoulders, arms and facial area. These parts relax further and further and further and ever deeper.

Relaxation of Hips, Thighs and Calves Followed by Complete Body Relaxation (time: 4–5 minutes) Let go of all tensions and relax. . . . Now flex your buttocks and thighs. Flex your thighs by pressing down your heels. . . . Relax and note the difference. . . . Straighten your knees and flex your thigh muscles again. Hold the tension . . . . Relax your hips and thighs. Allow the relaxation to proceed on its own. . . . Press your feet and toes downwards, away from your face, so that your calf muscles become tense. Study that tension. . . . Relax your feet and calves. . . . This time, bend your feet towards your face so that you feel tension along your shins. Bring your toes right up. . . . Relax again. Keep relaxing for a while . . . . Now let yourself relax further all over. Relax your feet, ankles, calves and shins, knees, thighs, buttocks and hips. Feel the heaviness of your lower body as you relax still further. . . . Now spread the relaxation to your stomach, waist, lower back. Let go more and more. Feel the relaxation all over. Let it proceed to your upper back, chest, shoulders and arms and right to the tips of your fingers. Keep relaxing more and more deeply. Make sure that no tension has crept into your throat; relax your neck and your jaws and all your facial muscles. Keep relaxing your whole body like that for a while. Let yourself relax.

Now you can become twice as relaxed as you are merely by taking in a really deep breath and slowly exhaling. With your eyes closed so that you become less aware of objects and movements around you and thus prevent any surface tensions from developing, breathe in deeply and feel yourself becoming heavier. Take a long, deep breath and let it out very slowly . . . . Feel how heavy and relaxed you have become.

In a state of perfect relaxation you should feel unwilling to move a single muscle in your body. Think about the effort that would be required to raise your right arm. As you *think* about raising your right arm, see if you can notice any tensions that might have crept into your shoulder and your arm . . . . Now you decide not to lift the arm but to continue relaxing. Observe the relief and the disappearance of the tension. . . .

Just carry on relaxing like that. When you wish to get up, count backwards from four to one. You should then feel fine and refreshed, wide awake and calm.

Letting Go Only After you have practiced alternate tensing and letting go a few times, try relaxing just by letting go. Focus on the muscles in your arms; allow them to relax. Keep letting go. Allow feelings of relaxation to develop. Repeat for the facial area, neck, shoulders and upper back; chest, stomach and lower back; hips, thighs, and calves. You can "skim" some areas. Allow relaxation from one area to flow into another. Play with the instructions to meet your own needs.

Once you have acquired relaxation skills, call on them as needed. If you find yourself tensing up during an exam, for example, allow feelings of relaxation to flow in to, say, your forehead, your arms, and the hand holding the pen. Note whether you've tightened up in the shoulders and the back of your neck. If you have, take a moment to breathe in, tell yourself to relax, and let your breath out.[9] Picture these parts of your body becoming relaxed—then return to the test.

Diaphragmatic Breathing

Diaphragmatic breathing tends to turn down feelings of anxiety by slowing down your breathing and, perhaps, by activating parts of the nervous system that counter anxiety.[10]

TRUTH OR FICTION *Revisited*

You really can cope with feelings of test anxiety by focusing on your breathing.

To practice diaphragmatic breathing, sit back in a recliner or lie on your back. Place your hands on your stomach lightly. Breathe in such a way that you watch your stomach rise as you inhale and go down as you exhale. In this way you breath through the diaphragm. These suggestions will also help you maintain calm, regular breathing:

1. Breathe only through your nose.
2. Take equal amounts of time to breathe in and out.
3. Inhale and exhale continuously and leisurely. For example, count "one thousand one, one thousand two, one thousand three," and so on, as you inhale and exhale.
4. To breathe diaphragmatically while sitting in a chair, monitor your chest with a hand to help you deter it from rising and falling. Monitor your abdomen with the other hand to check that it's rising and falling.

When your breathing is calm and regular, return to the test.

A final word of advice: When a test is over, *let it be over.* Check answers to help you master key material, if you like, but not just to see how many items you got wrong. Go out and do something enjoyable. Pick something from the 100 free (and nearly free) items listed at the end of Chapter 4. You've earned it!

SUMMING UP

1. How do you feel about tests? Do your test performances usually reflect your knowledge of the subjects?
2. How can you find out or make educated guesses about what will be covered on tests?
3. Are you "test-wise"? For example, do you know when to guess on short-answer questions?
4. How can you tell which answers are likely to be right and wrong when you don't know the answers to multiple-choice, true–false, or matching items?
5. What types of things can you do when you don't know the answer to an essay question?
6. How can you make a solid first impression in your answers to essay questions?
7. Are you test-anxious? How test-anxious are you as compared to other college students?
8. What does the chapter suggest is the single, best way to handle test anxiety?
9. How can you use the method of cognitive restructuring to reduce test anxiety?
10. What kinds of things can you do to reduce the physical aspects of test anxiety?

Scoring Key for the "Suinn Test Anxiety Behavior Scale (STABS)"

To figure out your STABS score, assign the following points to your responses:

Not at all = 1
A little = 2
A fair amount = 3
Much = 4
Very much = 5

Now add up the numbers.

The following norms were attained with Northeastern University students. There were no sex differences. Interpret percentile scores as follows: If your raw STABS score was 68, your level of test anxiety is about equal to that of about 95 percent of your peers—that is, other college students. If your raw STABS score was 39, your level of test anxiety approximates that of 20 to 25 percent of your peers.

Raw Stabs Score	Percentile
68	95
61	80
57	75
52	60
49	50
45	35
41	25
38	20
32	10

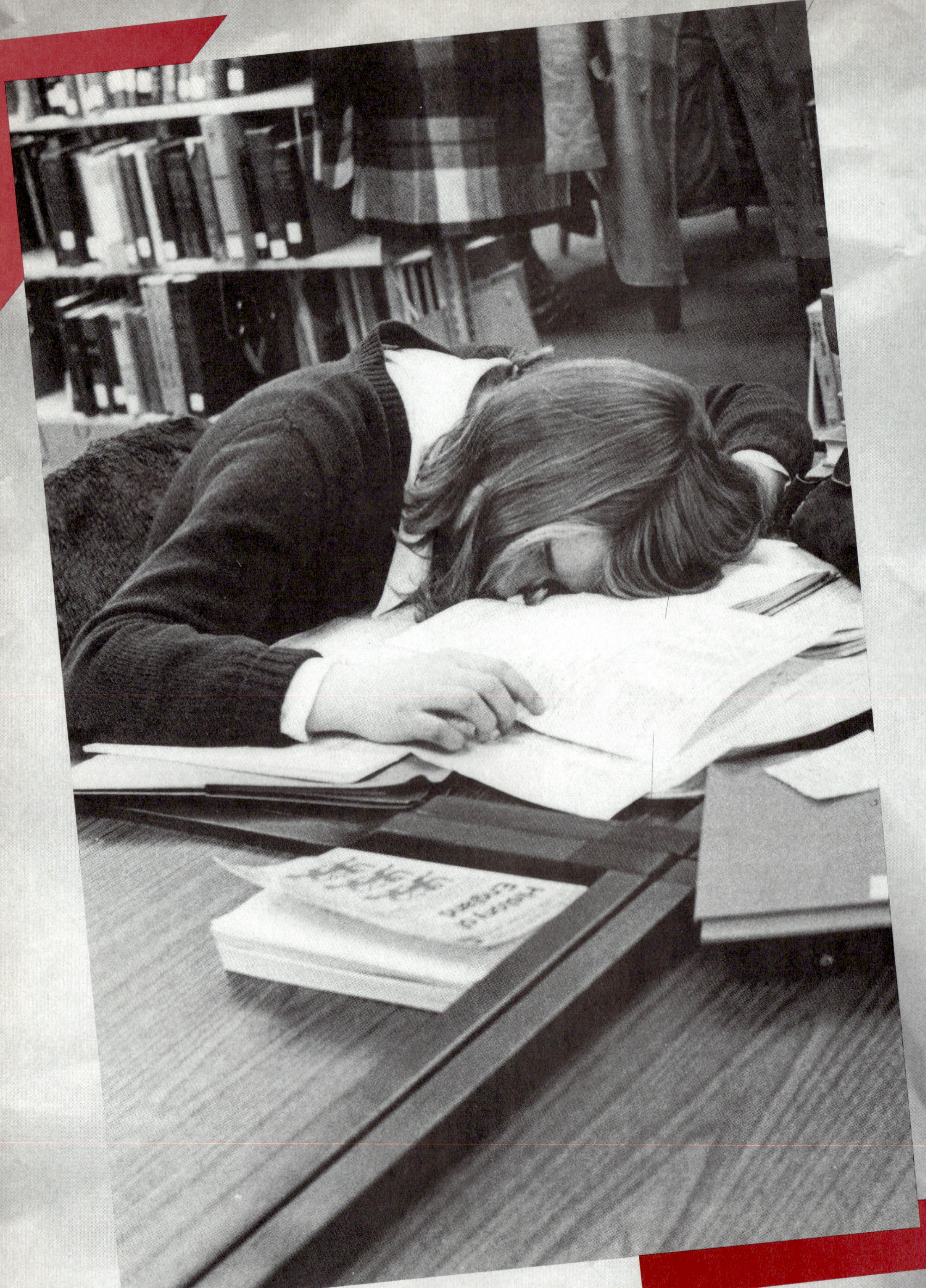

8

Managing Stress

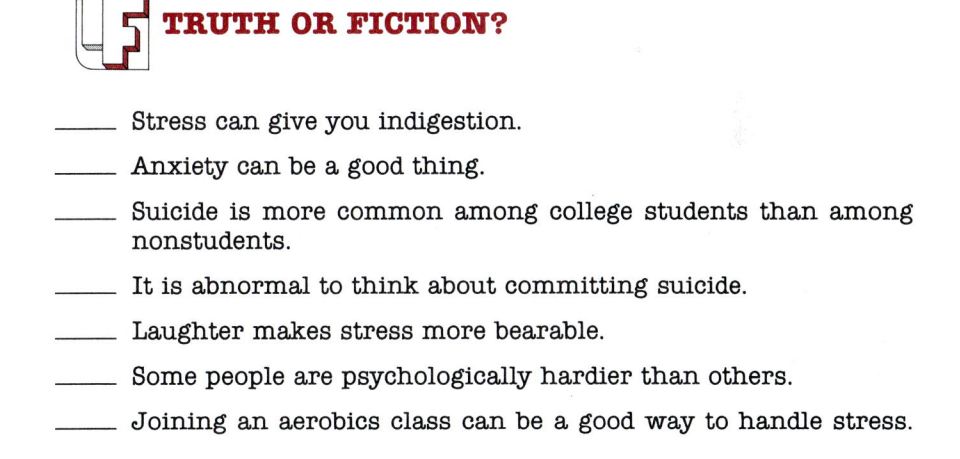

TRUTH OR FICTION?

____ Stress can give you indigestion.

____ Anxiety can be a good thing.

____ Suicide is more common among college students than among nonstudents.

____ It is abnormal to think about committing suicide.

____ Laughter makes stress more bearable.

____ Some people are psychologically hardier than others.

____ Joining an aerobics class can be a good way to handle stress.

College is for many the chance of a lifetime. College is a ticket of admission to an education and a career. But college can also be one of the most stressful experiences of a lifetime. There are so many changes. Overnight, new students—especially those who attend college away from home—are plucked from the familiar. They are faced with changes in eating and sleeping habits, new acquaintances, and, often, greater academic demands. For those who are socially uncertain, a swarming campus of 20,000 students may only render feelings of loneliness more poignant.

New social pressures may heighten conflict over sexual behavior. Some collegians undergo a gradual process of experimentation. A few are thrown into a swinging whirlpool in which casual sex is the norm and the key to peer approval.

New independence means new responsibilities. Residential students have a myriad of personal chores—underwear that must be washed, toiletries that must be replenished. Many students must begin to learn to manage money. The scramble for grades can be crushing, and grades mean graduate school or jobs. Poor grades not only signify squandering hard-earned money but also a collapsing self-identity and feelings of guilt and shame.

In this chapter, we consider the sources of stress that affect collegians and explore ways of managing them. But first, take a moment to consider stress in your own "write."

IN YOUR OWN WRITE

What kinds of stressors assaulted you when you first came on campus? How are you coping with them?

_____
_____
_____
_____
_____
_____
_____
_____

STRESS

Actually, some stress is good for us. It keeps us alert and occupied.[1] But potent or sustained stress can overwhelm our ability to adjust and impair our psychological and physical well being.[2] Some of the stressors encountered by college students are daily hassles, life changes, frustration, conflict, and Type A behavior.

Daily Hassles

Daily hassles are regular aggravations and annoyances.[3] High numbers of daily hassles are strongly linked to illness among college students and other people.[4] College students encounter hassles like the following:[5]

1. *Household hassles.* Having to cook meals; having to buy food and toilet articles; having to do the laundry; having to do minor repairs.
2. *Time-pressure hassles.* Having to read too many books; having to study for too many quizzes and tests; having to write too many papers; having to hold a part-time job along with a full-time class schedule. For commuting students, wasting time in traffic.
3. *Course-related hassles.* Concern about whether you're taking courses that will help you in a career or help you get into graduate school; concern that you don't like some of your courses; concern about the difficulty of some of your courses; concern about your schedule (e.g., early-morning or late-afternoon classes, Saturday classes).
4. *Social-relationship hassles.* Concern about making new friends; concern about finding dates; concern about getting along with roommates; concern about being away from people you love. For commuting students: concern about redefining one's relationship with one's family. For returning students: concern about balancing academic and family responsibilities.
5. *Health hassles.* Not getting enough sleep; having to pretty much take care of yourself when you get the flu; for sexually active students: concern about sexually transmitted diseases and the side effects of methods of birth control; concern about drinking or smoking.
6. *Inner-concern hassles.* Having to balance the need for independence with the need to be at least partly dependent on parents; having to balance personal values with peer pressures; worry about grades and what average or poor grades mean about you as a person.
7. *Environmental hassles.* Being shoehorned with two roommates into a room that was designed for one; concern about walking on campus after dark; traffic noise that interferes with sleeping or concentrating on assignments; a roommate's or neighbor's stereo (prolonged exposure to loud noises can impair our hearing, elevate our blood pressure, and hinder learning[6]); winters that are too cold; coping with a roommate who smokes.
8. *Financial-responsibility hassles.* Concern about covering tuition, room, and board; concern about getting enough money to dress like other students; concern about maintaining a car; concern about getting a part-time job; concern about getting or keeping a scholarship.

> [People] always have some problem, even if it's only that the toilet doesn't flush.
> ANDY WARHOL

> The trouble with the rat race is that even if you win, you're still a rat.
> LILY TOMLIN

In addition to carrying out academic tasks, students face many "hassles," such as doing the laundry and trying to carry out a part-time job.

9. *Work hassles.* Holding a part-time job that is meaningless or boring; concern about not getting along with your supervisor or co-workers; concern about co-workers who think your job should go to local people and not to college students; concern about whether or not you will get part-time or summer work.
10. *Future-security hassles.* Concern about paying off a huge loan; concern about whether you'll graduate and get a good job or get into graduate school.

Life Changes

Changes require adjustment, even if they are pleasant changes. Many college students undergo enormous numbers of life changes, whether they are resident students, commuters, or returning students. Life changes differ from daily hassles in that hassles are negative, whereas some life changes, like outstanding achievements and vacations, are positive and desirable. Also, daily hassles occur regularly, whereas life changes are irregular, like changes in living conditions or financial circumstances. But like daily hassles, high numbers of life changes (even positive ones) can dampen our moods and give rise to illness, accidents, even poor grades.[7]

How many life changes have you encountered during the past year? If you're like other beginning college students, there may have been a lot of them. The Social Readjustment Rating Scale on pages 192–193 will help you compare the number of changes you've experienced to those encountered by other students.

Frustration

We feel frustration when we are prevented from obtaining our goals. Consider just a few of the frustrations that beset college students. One student may want to play on the football or basketball team but be too lightweight or too short. Another may be denied a part-time job in the community because of ethnic background or favoritism.

College students may also be frustrated by heavy study schedules that prevent them from socializing. Or they may have to wait for hours in registration lines. We may also contribute to our own frustrations if our goals are unrealistic. For example, if we can't survive without the approval of our peers or our families, we will frustrate ourselves by failing to follow our own bents. If we insist that every assignment and quiz receive an A+, we will probably fall short and feel as though we have failed.

Tolerance for Frustration Completing college and getting ahead in the business world are gradual processes that require us to endure frustration and delay gratification. So we need some of what psychologists refer to as *tolerance for frustration.* Students who have faced and surmounted moderate levels of frustration have more tolerance for frustration than students who have either never experienced it or have been beaten down by it. We are also better able to endure frustration when we are committed to what we are doing.

Conflict

How many times do students feel "damned if they do and damned if they don't"? How often have you regretted that you could not be in two places, or do two things, at the same time? Have you ever wanted to see a film but had to turn in an assignment the next day? Have you wanted to get to sleep but had to study for a test? These are examples of *conflict*—of being torn in opposite directions.

Consider some of the kinds of conflict that assail college students. Some students engage in sexual activity or drinking before they feel ready so that they can earn the approval of other students. They are in conflict because their behavior is inconsistent with their values, or at least with their own timetables for sexual and social experimentation.

Or consider the daily conflict of having to study for a course that you do not like. The course may seem boring or you may believe that you will never use what you are learning, but it is part of the core requirement. So if you want to get that degree, from time to time you may have to work at something that you don't enjoy.

As you draw near the end of your college career, you may wonder whether you should take a job when you graduate or go on for advanced training. If you choose a job, cash will soon line your pockets, but as time goes on, you may question whether you received enough education to reach your potential. By advancing your education, you will delay independence and the satisfaction of making a living, but you may eventually attain a more gratifying position.

Type A Behavior

Some students create or compound their stress through the Type A behavior pattern. College success requires consistent application, but Type A students have an unreasonable sense of time urgency. They feel that things must get done *right now,* even if they are not due for weeks. They tend to hand assignments in early and to be prepared for tests well in advance. They talk, walk, even eat rapidly. They lose patience with students who take things at a more leisurely pace. Type A students are highly driven and competitive; their competitiveness borders on hostility and aggression.[8] They try to control group discussions.[9] Do you recall the song "Accentuate the Positive"? Type A's do the opposite: They accentuate the negative by looking for ways in which they fall short of perfection.[10] They also criticize themselves mercilessly for minor shortcomings.[11]

When they give themselves some time off, Type A students don't just dash out onto the courts and bat the ball back and forth for fun. They scrutinize their form, polish their strokes, and insist on consistent self-improvement.

The payoff is that Type A students earn higher grades than less driven students who are equal in ability.[12] The drawback is found in one word: health. Type A students respond to the challenges of college life with higher blood pressure than other students.[13] Moreover, the Type A behavior pattern does not end with graduation. It tends to follow us throughout our lives. And Type A behavior, especially hostility, has been linked to throbbing migraine headaches[14] and heart disease.[15]

Later we shall consider a number of ways of altering the Type A behavior pattern—and of getting more enjoyment out of life.

EFFECTS OF STRESS

And so college students are assailed by many sources of stress. Stress has many different effects on us, as we see in this section.

Physical Effects

Why can too many hassles and life changes impair our health? What are the effects of frustration and conflict on the body? Why do Type A people run a greater risk of migraine headaches?

Researchers have found that the body under stress is like a clock with an alarm that keeps on ringing until it is dangerously weakened.[16]

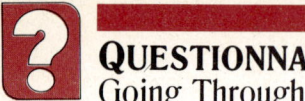

QUESTIONNAIRE
Going Through Changes: The Social Readjustment Rating Scale

Life changes are stressful, even when they're enjoyable. What kinds of life changes have you encountered during the past year? To compare the change-related stress you have experienced with that of other students, complete this questionnaire.

Directions: Indicate the number of times ("frequency") you experienced these events during the past 12 months. Then multiply the frequency (do not enter a number larger than 5) by the number of life-change units ("value") associated with each event. Write the answer in the total column to the right. Then add up all the points and check the key at the end of the chapter.

Event	Value	Frequency	Total
1. Death of a spouse, lover, or child	94		
2. Death of a parent or sibling	88		
3. Beginning formal higher education	84		
4. Death of a close friend	83		
5. Miscarriage or stillbirth of pregnancy of self, spouse, or lover	83		
6. Jail sentence	82		
7. Divorce or marital separation	82		
8. Unwanted pregnancy of self, spouse, or lover	80		
9. Abortion of unwanted pregnancy of self, spouse, or lover	80		
10. Detention in jail or other institution	79		
11. Change in dating activity	79		
12. Death of a close relative	79		
13. Change in marital situation other than divorce or separation	78		
14. Separation from significant other whom you like very much	77		
15. Change in health status or behavior of spouse or lover	77		
16. Academic failure	77		
17. Major violation of the law and subsequent arrest	76		
18. Marrying or living with lover against parents' wishes	75		
19. Change in love relationship or important friendship	74		
20. Change in health status or behavior of a parent or sibling	73		
21. Change in feelings of loneliness, insecurity, anxiety, boredom	73		
22. Change in marital status of parents	73		
23. Acquiring a visible deformity	72		
24. Change in ability to communicate with a significant other whom you like very much	71		
25. Hospitalization of a parent or sibling	70		
26. Reconciliation of marital or love relationship	68		
27. Release from jail or other institution	68		
28. Graduation from college	68		
29. Major personal injury or illness	68		
30. Wanted pregnancy of self, spouse, or lover	67		
31. Change in number or type of arguments with spouse or lover	67		
32. Marrying or living with lover with parents' approval	66		
33. Gaining a new family member through birth or adoption	65		
34. Preparing for an important exam or writing a major paper	65		
35. Major financial difficulties	65		
36. Change in the health status or behavior of a close relative or close friend	65		
37. Change in academic status	64		
38. Change in amount and nature of interpersonal conflicts	63		
39. Change in relationship with members of your immediate family	62		
40. Change in own personality	62		
41. Hospitalization of yourself or a close relative	61		
42. Change in course of study, major field, vocational goals, or work status	60		
43. Change in own financial status	59		
44. Change in status of divorced or widowed parent	59		
45. Change in number or type of arguments between parents	59		
46. Change in acceptance by peers, identification with peers, or social pressure by peers	58		

Event	Value	Frequency	Total
47. Change in general outlook on life	57	___	___
48. Beginning or ceasing service in the armed forces	57	___	___
49. Change in attitudes toward friends	56	___	___
50. Change in living arrangements, conditions, or environment	55	___	___
51. Change in frequency or nature of sexual experiences	55	___	___
52. Change in parents' financial status	55	___	___
53. Change in amount or nature of pressure from parents	55	___	___
54. Change in degree of interest in college or attitudes toward education	55	___	___
55. Change in the number of personal or social relationships you've formed or dissolved	55	___	___
56. Change in relationship with siblings	54	___	___
57. Change in mobility or reliability of transportation	54	___	___
58. Academic success	54	___	___
59. Change to a new college or university	54	___	___
60. Change in feelings of self-reliance, independence, or amount of self-discipline	53	___	___
61. Change in number or type of arguments with roommate	52	___	___
62. Spouse or lover beginning or ceasing work outside the home	52	___	___
63. Change in frequency of use of amounts of drugs other than alcohol, tobacco, or marijuana	51	___	___
64. Change in sexual morality, beliefs, or attitudes	50	___	___
65. Change in responsibility at work	50	___	___
66. Change in amount or nature of social activities	50	___	___
67. Change in dependencies on parents	50	___	___
68. Change from academic work to practical fieldwork experience or internship	50	___	___
69. Change in amount of material possessions and concomitant responsibilities	50	___	___
70. Change in routine at college or work	49	___	___
71. Change in amount of leisure time	49	___	___
72. Change in amount of in-law trouble	49	___	___
73. Outstanding personal achievement	49	___	___
74. Change in family structure other than parental divorce or separation	48	___	___
75. Change in attitude toward drugs	48	___	___
76. Change in amount and nature of competition with same sex	48	___	___
77. Improvement of own health	47	___	___
78. Change in responsibilities at home	47	___	___
79. Change in study habits	46	___	___
80. Change in number or type of arguments or close conflicts with close relatives	46	___	___
81. Change in sleeping habits	46	___	___
82. Change in frequency of use or amounts of alcohol	45	___	___
83. Change in social status	45	___	___
84. Change in frequency of use or amounts of tobacco	45	___	___
85. Change in awareness of activities in external world	45	___	___
86. Change in religious affiliation	44	___	___
87. Change in type of gratifying activities	43	___	___
88. Change in amount or nature of physical activities	43	___	___
89. Change in address or residence	43	___	___
90. Change in amount or nature of recreational activities	43	___	___
91. Change in frequency of use or amounts of marijuana	43	___	___
92. Change in social demands or responsibilities due to your age	43	___	___
93. Court appearance for legal violation	40	___	___
94. Change in weight or eating habits	39	___	___
95. Change in religious activities	37	___	___
96. Change in political views or affiliations	34	___	___
97. Change in driving pattern or conditions	33	___	___
98. Minor violation of the law	31	___	___
99. Vacation or travel	30	___	___
100. Change in number of family get-togethers	30	___	___

Source: Peggy Blake, Robert Fry, & Michael Pesjack, *Self-assessment and behavior change manual* (New York: Random House, 1984), pp. 43–47. Reprinted by permission of Random House, Inc.

For example, our bodies' stores of sugar are released, adding fuel to the fire. Adrenaline stokes the nervous system and increases the heart and respiration rates. The nervous system focuses on spending energy to fight off the outside threat rather than on building reserves of energy. So it shuts down the digestive processes.

TRUTH OR FICTION *Revisited*

Yes, stress can indeed give you indigestion.

The stresses of college may activate these changes in our bodies for hours, days, or months on end. Our capacities for resisting stress vary, but stress can eventually exhaust us. As a result we may develop stress-related physical problems ranging from allergies and hives to headaches and heart problems.

Physical changes are related to changes in our feelings.[17] So stress also has emotional effects.

Emotional Effects

Stress leads to various kinds of emotional reactions, including anxiety, anger, and depression.

Anxiety Anxiety is a normal response to a threat. Stressors such as dangers, loss of someone we care about, and failure in school are clear threats. Anxiety can be triggered by specific stressors such as the approach of a major exam, a job interview, a big date, or a visit to the dentist. But anxiety can also linger throughout the term as students fret about exams, their social lives, financial woes, and whether it will all pay off.

Anxiety tends to arouse us and make us more attentive to the things happening around us and what we need to do to get by. So some anxiety in college may encourage us to plan ahead and study regularly—both of which are positive.

TRUTH OR FICTION *Revisited*

So a little anxiety, like a little stress, can be a good thing. It keeps you alert and occupied.

Anxiety can also impair our ability to function in college in a number of ways. Note the following effects of anxiety:

1. Psychologists have found that high levels of anxiety can make it difficult for us to perform complex tasks. So even while anxiety can encourage you to study for a test, high levels of anxiety during the test may make it more difficult to solve complex math problems or balance equations in chemistry.
2. High levels of anxiety may also trigger habitual and maladaptive ways of coping with problems. Perhaps you have been working to develop social skills for dates or to develop ways of talking to professors so that you can get help from them to do better in difficult courses. High levels of anxiety can make you tongue-tied on dates or lead you to argue with professors—thus turning them off rather than enlisting their cooperation.

QUESTIONNAIRE
Are You a Type A Student?

Are you a Type A student? Are you hard driving? Must you complete assignments early? Are you chronically discontent with your achievements, even though you're doing well?

The following questionnaire will help you discover whether you are a Type A student.[18] For each item, place a checkmark in the Yes column if the item describes you, and in the No column if it does not. Then check the key at the end of the chapter.

	Do you:	Yes	No
1.	Strongly stress important words in your normal speech?	___	___
2.	Walk quickly from class to class, or from your room to class?	___	___
3.	Believe that college is by nature extremely competitive?	___	___
4.	Get restless when you see someone completing an assignment or a test slowly?	___	___
5.	Press other students to finish what they're trying to say?	___	___
6.	Find it extremely annoying to be stuck in lines at the cafeteria or at college offices?	___	___
7.	Think about the things you have to do even when you're listening to a professor or to another student?	___	___
8.	Try to eat while you're getting dressed, or try to jot down notes while you're driving?	___	___
9.	Catch up on school work when you're on vacations?	___	___
10.	Direct class discussions to topics that interest you?	___	___
11.	Feel as if you're letting something important go just because you're spending a few minutes relaxing?	___	___
12.	Find that you're so engrossed in school work that you rush by the attractive points on campus without noticing them?	___	___
13.	Find yourself so wrapped up in grades that you never have the opportunity to express your creativity or get involved in social causes or concerns?	___	___
14.	Schedule as many classes as you're permitted to take?	___	___
15.	Always arrive in class ahead of the scheduled meeting time?	___	___
16.	Clench your jaws or make fists to get across your views?	___	___
17.	Believe that you've accomplished what you have because of your ability to work swiftly?	___	___
18.	Feel that any uncompleted assignments must be done *now* and rapidly?	___	___
19.	Focus on finding more efficient ways to complete assignments?	___	___
20.	Strive always to win at games rather than focus on having a good time?	___	___
21.	Interrupt other students in class discussion?	___	___
22.	Feel annoyed when other students come to class after it has begun or hand in assignments late?	___	___
23.	Leave the cafeteria right after eating?	___	___
24.	Feel as if there's never enough time?	___	___
25.	Feel unhappy about how much you're getting done?	___	___

3. High levels of anxiety can also distract us from the tasks at hand. That is, rather than figuring out what to do to improve our situations, we may focus instead on our physical reactions. Focusing too much on feelings of anxiety can heighten them rather than alleviate them!

Negative emotional reactions like anxiety are signs that something is wrong. They should encourage us to survey our environments to learn where the stresses are coming from, and then to make plans to remove them or react to them in less upsetting ways. But when we keep on focusing on the anxiety, it may mushroom. Then we may get to the point where we feel that we must do anything that will allow us to escape—such as using drugs, putting work out of our minds and socializing hour after hour, or dropping out of college—regardless of the cost.

Anger We tend to feel anxious when we perceive a threat. We are likely to feel angry when we are frustrated—especially if we think that other people are purposefully placing obstacles in our paths—or when other people provoke us. Mentally, anger may involve ideas to the effect that tests are unfairly hard or that a roommate isn't doing his or her part. When we are angry, we may get into arguments and, sometimes, act aggressively. But anger can also be expressed indirectly. For example, students who are frustrated by being crowded into small living quarters with too many roommates are more likely to complain about their roommates and think of them as uncooperative.[19]

Depression Depression is the most common emotional problem we face. Depression can be triggered by loss (as of a friend, lover, or relative) or by failure. Depression can also develop from prolonged exposure to stress. At first, the college whirlwind may cause anxiety and physically activate our bodies. But when stress is prolonged, we may become exhausted. Depression is the emotion we are most likely to feel when we have run out of coping ability.

Mentally, depression is linked to ideas that we are helpless to make things better—or that we are unworthy. If we believe that we're wasting

IN YOUR OWN WRITE

Most of us get depressed now and then. Depression is so common that it has been labeled the "common cold" of psychological problems. How do you know when you are depressed? What types of thoughts do you have? How is your behavior affected?

_____
_____
_____
_____
_____
_____
_____

our hard-earned money (or our family's hard-earned money) on a college experience that's going nowhere, we're likely to feel depressed about it. If we see ourselves in the middle of a hopeless mess, so that there's nothing we can do to pull ourselves out of it, we're likely to feel depressed.

One of the major contributors to depression is unreasonable self-blame. If you flunk a test, it can be helpful to admit that you didn't study enough or that you weren't prepared for the course. Either thought may suggest ways of achieving future success—as by studying harder or by making sure you have the required prerequisites for a course. But believing that you're just not smart enough is usually unreasonable. It makes you feel helpless and offers no solution except, perhaps, dropping out of college. If you foul up a date, it can be helpful to admit that you have trouble making small talk. But believing that you're a social disaster and that nobody could ever be interested in you is unreasonable and offers no solution—unless you would consider taking up residence in a closet a solution.

Depressed students also tend to minimize the things they accomplish in college: Keep in mind that learning to do your own laundry is an accomplishment. So is getting good grades (even if not A's) in most of your courses. So is making a couple of new acquaintances. But depressed students focus so much on the negative that they forget to pat themselves on the back when they should.

Depression and Suicide At Cornell University, there are magnificent gorges, cliffbound miniature paradises through which fresh water courses brightly, slapping against the rocks and pebbles. Unfortunately, now and then a Cornell student is overcome by the stress of college life and "gorges out"—commits suicide by leaping into a chasm.

Despite the fact that college students have much to live for, suicide is more common among students than among nonstudents. Each year, about 10,000 students attempt suicide. In fact, suicide is the second leading cause of death among students.

TRUTH OR FICTION Revisited

Suicide does happen to be more common among college students than among nonstudents.

Why do college students take their own lives? Most suicides are linked to feelings of depression.[20] Suicidal people also feel more anxious, excitable, angry, guilt-ridden, helpless, and inadequate than others.[21] Their problems seem to be beyond solution—hopeless.[22] They are experiencing unendurable psychological pain, and suicide is their way of trying to put an end to the pain.[23] In a Boston University study, college women who had tried to commit suicide often implicated their parents as a source of their pain.[24] And so they could not turn to their parents for help with their feelings of desperation. Nor did they feel comfortable turning to others for help.

Let us make two very important points here. First, it is *not* abnormal to entertain suicidal thoughts when we are under stress. Most people have thought of suicide now and then, when things looked particularly bleak.

TRUTH OR FICTION Revisited

It is *not* abnormal to think about committing suicide when we are under a great deal of stress and feel hopeless to change things.

Some campuses have suicide "hot lines" to help students who don't know where to turn. Many cities also have suicide prevention centers that can be called anonymously, either by suicidal students or those who care about them.

Second, in most cases, these thoughts pass. So when you are feeling especially down, remember that things will probably look better as time passes and you get a better perspective on things. Don't shut yourself off from friends and other sources of social support—unless these people are part of the problem. Do go to the college counseling center—or, if need be, the emergency room of a hospital—to talk to someone about your feelings. The "What Do You Do Now?" exercise below offers some suggestions about what you can do when a friend confides in you that he or she is contemplating suicide.

WHAT DO YOU DO NOW?
Coping with a Suicide Threat: Ten Things to Do When You Fear That Nothing Can Be Done

You're having a heart-to-heart talk with your best friend on campus, Joni. Things have been pretty tough, you know. Joni's grandfather died last month and they were very close. Joni's grades have been sliding, and it's been downhill with her boyfriend, too. Still you're shocked when Joni says, "I've been going over this for days, and the only way out is to end it once and for all—to kill myself."

When a friend confides that he or she is contemplating suicide, you will probably feel horrified and confused, as if a great burden has been put on your shoulders. Yes, one has. Your goal should be to get Joni to see an experienced mental-health worker, or to see one yourself as soon as you can. But if Joni refuses to confide in anyone else and you can't break free to do so, you can temporize by doing the following things:

1. Draw Joni out. Edwin Shneidman, a cofounder of the Los Angeles Suicide Prevention Center, suggests asking, "What's going on?" "Where do you hurt?" "What would you like to see happen?"[25] Such questions encourage people to verbalize frustrated needs and thus offer some relief. And they give you time to estimate the risk and reflect.

2. Be empathetic. Demonstrate that you grasp how troubled Joni is. Don't say things like, "Don't be silly." Saying "Don't be silly" negates the reality and importance of Joni's feelings and may do more harm than good.

WAYS OF MANAGING STRESS

We all react to stress—even when we fail to recognize that we are under stress, even when we try to ignore it. So the question isn't *whether* we react to stress. The question is *how* we react to stress.

POOR WAYS OF REACTING TO STRESS

Many ways of handling stress are basically defensive and not very good. They lessen the shock of the stressor, but there are costs. Relying on drugs or acting aggressively are two poor ways of handling stress. These behavior patterns create more problems than they solve. Another is avoidance of problems—withdrawing from them. Still another is self-deception, as when we deny that they exist. By withdrawing from problems, or by denying that they exist, we lose the chances to get ahead and to feel good about ourselves.

Drugs

Alcohol and some other drugs, such as tranquilizers, dull feelings of stress, anxiety, and frustration by blunting the activity of the nervous system. Alcohol also diminishes self-awareness, stemming the emotional tide that might otherwise reflect recognition that we have fallen short of our goals or values.[26]

Many people—not only college students—use alcohol as a scapegoat. For example, they blame unseemly aggressive or sexual behavior on alcohol. By drinking before they get into fights at bars, or before they go home with strangers, they can say, "It wasn't me—it was the alcohol." College

---

3. Similarly, don't tell Joni she's "crazy." That's the *last* thing she needs to hear.
4. Propose that means other than suicide may solve the predicament, even if they are not apparent at the time. Shneidman finds that self-destructive people often envision only two ways of resolving their problems—either death or some magical solution. Professionals frequently try to widen the mental blinders of despondent people.
5. Tell Joni that you read that most people think of suicide when things are bad, but that as time goes on they usually feel better and find other ways to handle their problems. (It's true and it offers hope.)
6. Ask Joni how she plans to commit suicide. People with definite plans and the means to implement them are in greater danger. Ask Joni if you might keep the weapon (e.g., pills) for a while. She may say yes.
7. Propose that Joni go *with you now* to seek professional help. The campus infirmary or counseling center, the emergency room of a nearby hospital, even campus or local police may be of help. Some campuses have suicide hotlines. Many cities have suicide-prevention centers that can be called anonymously.
8. Extract a pledge that Joni won't kill herself before seeing you again. Make a specific time and location to meet. Seek professional advice as soon as you get away.
9. Don't insist that Joni seek contact with specific people, such as her parents or lover. Conflict with them may have given rise to the suicidal impulses.
10. Above all, keep in mind that your central goal is to confer with a helping professional. Don't go it alone one minute more than you must.

students also use alcohol as a way of handling stress. Students given harder assignments are more likely to turn to alcohol.[27]

Regular use of drugs as a way of handling stress is called psychological dependence on drugs. Students can become dependent on various drugs that blunt perception of stress or distort what has become an unappealing reality.

Aggression

College students sometimes turn to threats, insults, even violence as a way of handling social provocations and feelings of frustration. However, threatening or fighting with a roommate may get one expelled from college housing, and, sometimes, from college itself. Threatening a professor when you receive a poor grade is more likely to anger the professor than earn sympathy. Moreover, it is illegal as well as against college rules to attack a professor, and aggressive students now and then land in jail, wrecking their careers. Students who have problems keeping their tempers can usually find help at the college counseling center or at a community mental-health center.

Withdrawal

When students are highly stressed or feel that there is nothing they can do to help themselves, they may withdraw. There are different kinds of withdrawal. Depression is a kind of emotional withdrawal in which students may lose interest in their classes or in fellow students. Withdrawal can also mean quitting school. Students in packed dormitories sometimes withdraw from the stress of crowding by avoiding optional mingling.[28] Students who move to big-city campuses may withdraw from social contacts with strangers as a way of protecting themselves from social overload and the threat of crime.[29]

Temporary withdrawal can help us manage stress. It can give us the chance to find preferable ways of handling things. And withdrawal is sometimes justified when there really is no way to handle a tough situation. But prolonged retreat from responsibilities and relationships deprives us of the opportunity to develop solutions and damages our belief in our ability to cope.

Denial

Some students deny—or refuse to face the fact—that they are reeling from stress. If things are not going your way, but you have the attitude "I can't flunk out—it can't happen to me," you may be using denial. Your first author was an expert at using denial as an undergraduate. Not only did he deny that he was facing academic problems, but he used to run off with friends on long rides or play bridge all night long rather than study for courses he didn't like.*

We also tend to use denial in health-related problems. For example, many college students tell themselves that they will give up smoking long before they have to worry about the risks of cancer or that they will cut down on their drinking once they have graduated from the pressure cooker. And women who discover lumps in their breasts sometimes delay consulting a doctor for fear of what the lumps might mean.†

Denial may lower the immediate impact of stressors, but it also denies us the opportunity of taking action to ward off authentic threats.

---

* Your second author is happy she didn't know him then.
† Lumps are usually benign, but early detection is of paramount importance when they are not. College women are therefore encouraged to have regular checkups and to learn how to examine their own breasts. It is never too early to begin to take charge of one's own health.

BETTER WAYS OF REACTING TO STRESS

Now that you've seen some ways of handling stress that can make things worse, let's consider some ways that can be of real help.

Making Decisions

Sometimes the best way to handle stress is to decide whether or not we are doing what is right for us and, if necessary, to make major changes (or even change our majors). If we're having trouble with a roommate, we need to decide whether or not to move out—and when. If we always dreamed about majoring in physics but find that we hate college physics, we need to decide whether or not we should try another major. (How about talking to your advisor or to someone at the counseling and testing center?) Or the part-time job may be killing too much study time. So we may have to decide whether or not to cut our course load, give up the job, or transfer to a less expensive college.

Making decisions can be painful. Decisions may mean losing money or swimming in uncharted waters—as in trying out a new major. But when we try to make decisions, at least we face the fact that problems exist. We weigh the pluses and minuses of anticipated courses of action, rather than allowing stress to mount until we snap.

In Chapter 12 we discuss sexual decision making, and students who feel sexual pressures and conflicts are advised to look ahead. In Chapter 14 we discuss career decisions. Choosing a major is similar to a career decision, and students who are unsure about their fields may want to look ahead.

> When you have a choice to make and don't make it, that is in itself a choice.
>
> WILLIAM JAMES

IN YOUR OWN WRITE

Have you been putting off making major decisions in your own life? What are the dangers of continuing to put them off? How can you go about making an informed decision?

_____
_____
_____
_____
_____
_____
_____
_____

Finding the Humor in Things

Reflect upon the biblical adage, "A merry heart doeth good like a medicine."[30] Throughout the history of civilization, it has been common knowledge that humor lightens the burdens of the day and helps us handle stress.[31] Sigmund Freud, the originator of psychoanalytic theory, considered humor a great defense against distress. Through humor, Freud wrote, we spare ourselves stress or anxiety by creating more enjoyable emotions.[32] Research has also shown that college students with a good sense of humor are less affected than other students by hassles and negative life events.[33]

TRUTH OR FICTION *Revisited*

Laughter actually can make stress more bearable.

So don't be afraid to laugh at yourself, even when you are encountering academic and social problems. But *use the emotional relief afforded by humor to face your problems and make needed decisions as to what to do.*

Knowing What to Expect

Knowing what to expect moderates the impact of stress. Predictability permits us to brace ourselves and, often, to plan ways of handling stressors. For example, we cope better with being crowded into small spaces, such as dormitory rooms, when we are forewarned as to how we are likely to react.[34]

So we can better handle the stresses of college by getting as much information about them as we can. For example, we should ask professors for information about the types of tests they give. We should ask other students about courses and professors and study course syllabi at the beginnings of courses. If we don't understand something, we should ask questions. Sexually active students need to learn what they can about sexually transmitted diseases so that they can take effective preventive action. By filling in the information about college and community resources in the exercise in Chapter 2, we can determine what to do in case of emergency.

Using Social Support

Social support—that is, a network of friends, family, and, when necessary, professional resources—also helps us handle stress.[35] There are five kinds of social support:[36]

1. *Emotional support.* Emotional support is offered by friends, professionals in the counseling center, and, sometimes, by resident advisors, academic advisors, and professors. It includes listening to our problems and expressing feelings of caring, understanding, and reassurance. Letters and phone calls to and from home are also emotional supports.

Consider the biblical adage, "A merry heart doeth good like a medicine." Through humor, wrote Sigmund Freud, we spare ourselves stress by creating more enjoyable emotions. College students with a sense of humor are less affected than others by hassles and negative life events.

Socializing—doing things with other students—helps students handle stress unless, of course, excessive socializing is a major source of their stress!

2. *Instrumental support.* Instrumental support consists of the material aids that help us get by from day to day. Money, clothing, food packages ("CARE packages"), help in setting up an apartment, a typewriter or microcomputer, a car—all these are instrumental supports.
3. *Information.* This kind of support consists of helpful guidance and advice. Classmates, friends, and tutors can offer insights as to how to prepare for exams. Coaches and teammates can provide advice on training for athletic competition.
4. *Appraisal.* Appraisal is feedback as to how well we're doing. Classmates and friends (and this book!) can help students make sense of what they're feeling and experiencing.
5. *Socializing.* Socializing—doing things with other students—is helpful in and of itself. Simple conversation, sharing recreational activities, studying with a friend, going shopping with someone—all offer the benefits of social support.

It is helpful for stressed students to get together and talk about their ideas and feelings so that they can give one another various kinds of support. This is most often done informally, among groups of classmates and friends. But it can also be done at the college counseling center.

IN YOUR OWN WRITE

What is the difference between using socializing to withdraw from academic stress and using social support as a way of managing stress? When do you think that social support becomes part of the problem rather than part of the solution?

_____
_____
_____
_____
_____
_____

Keeping Things in Perspective

We need to recognize and think about the hassles and frustrations that are affecting us, but we shouldn't blow them out of proportion. Consider these examples:

1. If you have trouble with the first question on a test and then assume you're going to flunk the test, you're blowing things out of proportion. You make yourself more anxious about the test and find it more difficult to focus on the questions.
2. If you want to ask your roommate (or, if you're a returning student, your teenager) to turn down the stereo but fear that you won't be able to tolerate a hostile response, you're blowing things out of proportion.
3. If you haven't been able to get to sleep for 15 minutes and assume that you're going to lie awake all night and be a wreck in the morning, you're blowing things out of proportion.

Sure, a tough test question can be upsetting. Yes, standing up to your roommate or child can be stressful. And true, lying awake at night can be annoying. But as suggested in the quote from *Hamlet*, the way we *think* about these things can make them more stressful than they have to be. We can make aggravating mountains out of annoying molehills. We

> There is nothing either good or bad, but thinking makes it so.
>
> SHAKESPEARE, *Hamlet*, II, ii

TABLE 8.1. Thoughts That Blow Stressors Out of Proportion and Alternatives That Help Keep Things in Perspective.

THOUGHTS THAT BLOW STRESSORS OUT OF PROPORTION	ALTERNATIVE THOUGHTS THAT HELP KEEP THINGS IN PERSPECTIVE
"Oh my God, it's going to be a mess! I'm losing all control!"	"This is annoying and upsetting, but I haven't lost all control yet, and I don't have to."
"This is awful. It'll never end."	"It's bad, but it doesn't have to get the best of me. And upsetting things do come to an end, even if it's sort of hard to believe right now."
"I just can't stand it when Mom (Dad/my roommate/my date) gives me that look."	"Life is more pleasant when everyone is happy with me, but I have to be myself, and that means that other people are going to disagree with me from time to time."
"There's no way I can get up there and perform/give that speech! I'll look like an idiot."	"So I'm not perfect; that doesn't mean I'm going to look like an idiot. And so what if someone thinks I look bad? It doesn't mean I *am* bad. And if I am bad, so what? I can live with that, too. I don't have to be perfect every time. So stop being such a worrywart and get up and have some fun."
"My heart's beating a mile a minute! It's going to leap out of my chest! How much of this can I take?"	"Take it easy! Hearts don't jump out of chests. Just slow down a minute—stop and think. I'll find a way out. And if I don't for the time being, I'll survive. Some day I'll look back on this and laugh at how upset I got myself."
"What can I do? I'm helpless! It's just going to get worse and worse."	"Take it easy. Just stop and think for a minute. Just because there's no obvious solution doesn't mean that I won't be able to do anything about it. There's no point to getting so upset. Why don't I just take it from minute to minute for the time being. If I can't think of anything to do, I can always talk to other people about it."

Do you tend to blow things out of proportion and compound the stress you encounter? We can chop stressors down to size by keeping things in perspective.

can turn hassles into catastrophes—because of what we tell ourselves about them.

Psychologists suggest that we monitor our thoughts when we are upset and consider whether or not we are keeping things in perspective.[37] If we are blowing things out of proportion, psychologists challenge us to look at things more logically. We can't predict the types of thoughts that you may use if and when you blow things out of proportion, but we offer examples of such thoughts in Table 8.1. If they apply to you, you may recognize them readily enough. You may also want to ask yourself if you'd be doing yourself a favor by using one of the suggested alternatives instead.

Relaxing

Stress and tension tighten our muscles, raise our blood pressure, and set our hearts to pounding. There's a silver lining in this cloud: These feelings are a sign that something is wrong and prompt us to examine our situations and do something about them. But once we know that we are under stress and are working on ways of handling it, it no longer helps to have blood coursing so fiercely through our veins. Psychologists and other researchers have developed many ways of helping us relax the physical features of stress. Let us consider two of them—meditation and muscle relaxation.

Meditation Meditation is one way of relaxing the body when it is under stress. There are many kinds of meditation, but each narrows awareness so that the pressures of the world outside ebb away. Each method suspends worry and the concerns of the day.

Many students regularly engage in transcendental meditation (TM), a form of meditation brought to the United States from India. TM is practiced by repeating *mantras*—that is, relaxing words or sounds like *om* (rhymes with *home*) and *ieng* (pronounced *ee-eng*). TM produces a relaxation response in many people.[38] That is, it reduces the heart and respiration rates, the metabolic rate (the rate at which we convert food to energy), and muscle tension.

If you'd like to try meditation, the following instructions may help:

1. Try meditation once or twice a day for 10 to 20 minutes at a time.
2. Embrace an accepting attitude: Tell yourself, "What happens, happens." In meditation, you take what you get. You don't *strive* for more. Striving of any kind hinders meditation.

Meditation is one way of relaxing the body when it is under stress. Meditation also suspends worry and the concerns of the day.

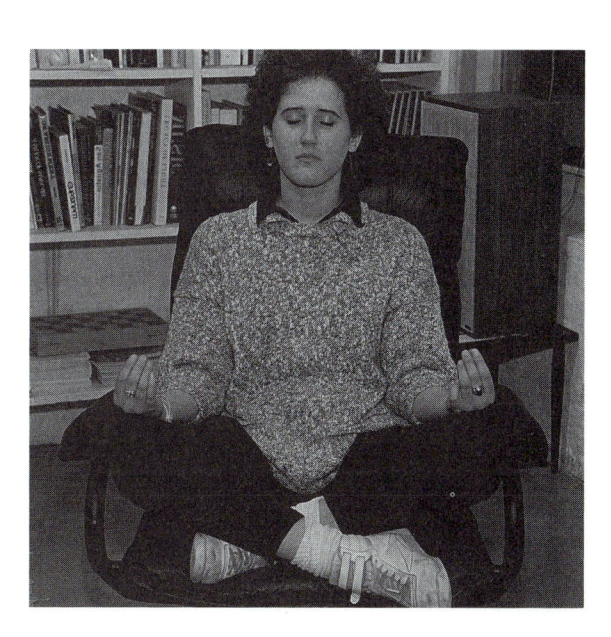

3. Devise a hushed, calming environment. For example, don't face a light directly.
4. Avoid eating for an hour before you meditate. Avoid caffeine (found in coffee, tea, many soft drinks, and chocolate) for at least two hours.
5. Get into a relaxed position. Modify it as needed. You can scratch or yawn if you want to.
6. For a focusing device, concentrate on your breathing, sit in front of a serene object like a plant or incense, or think the word *one* each time you breathe out. Or think the word *in* as you breathe in and *out,* or *ah-h-h,* as you breathe out.[39] Or try mantras like *ah-nam, rah-mah,* and *shi-rim.*
7. When preparing for meditation, repeat your mantra aloud many times—if you're using a mantra. Enjoy it. Then say it more softly. Close your eyes. Focus on the mantra. Allow thinking the mantra to become more and more "passive" so that you "perceive" rather than think it. Again, embrace your "What happens, happens" attitude. Keep on focusing on the mantra. It may become softer or louder, or fade and then reappear.
8. If unsettling thoughts drift in, allow them to pass through. Don't worry about squelching them, or you may tense up.
9. Take what you get. Meditation and relaxation cannot be forced. You cannot coerce the relaxing effects of meditation. Like sleep, you can only set the stage for them and then permit them to happen.
10. Let yourself drift. (You won't get lost.) What happens, happens.

Muscle Relaxation One physical sign of stress is muscle tension. As with anxiety, methods that relax the muscles counter the effects of stress on the body and calm you down as well. There are many methods of muscle relaxation, but one suggested by many psychologists is progressive relaxation, as described on pages 179–183.[40]

As in handling test anxiety, first practice progressive relaxation through alternate tensing and relaxing of muscle groups. Then practice relaxing fully by letting go of muscle tensions only. After you have become relaxed, enjoy the sensations for 10 to 20 minutes, once or twice a day. This approach is similar to meditation. But you can also call on relaxation skills as needed. When you feel assaulted by stress, breathe easily, tell yourself to relax, and allow feelings of relaxation to flow in. Remember: You can practice relaxing regularly—as with meditation—or when you are under stress.

Decreasing Type A Behavior

Type A people show time urgency and hostility. Most college students need not yet fear heart disease, but Type A behavior is linked to heart attacks among older people. So it is never too soon to recognize Type A behavior and to consider changing one's lifestyle. In this section, we report a number of methods that have been successful in helping Type A heart-attack victims change their behavior to avert future attacks.[41] They aim to alleviate the sense of time urgency and hostility.

Alleviating the Sense of Time Urgency How often do we bounce out of bed to a harsh alarm, jump into the shower, arrive at class with no time to spare, and then first become enmeshed in our frantic day. For Type A students, the day starts urgently and doesn't let up.

The following exercises ease the sense of time urgency:

1. Get involved in more social activities with friends. This advice is in-

tended for Type A students who go through life with social blinders on—not for students who already socialize too much!

2. Read popular books; visit museums; go to films, concerts, the ballet, the theater.
3. Take time to write letters to family and friends.
4. Find time for a course in art, or start up piano lessons.
5. Remind yourself each day that assignments and projects do *not* have to be handed in early.
6. Ask a roommate or classmate what he or she did that day, and actually listen to the answer.
7. Get a congenial alarm clock!
8. Move about in a leisurely way when you awaken. Stretch.
9. Drive at a more leisurely pace. It's safer, uses less gas, and is less likely to arouse the ire of traffic police.
10. Leave home earlier so you can take the scenic route to school. Avoid rush-hour bottlenecks.
11. Don't wolf lunch. Find a pleasant spot on or off campus to eat. Make lunch an occasion.
12. Don't tumble out words. Speak at a more leisurely pace. Interrupt others less often.
13. Wake up earlier so you can sit and relax, read the paper, have a leisurely cup of tea, or meditate before going to class or work. It may help to go to bed earlier.
14. Don't do too many things at once. Don't schedule too many classes or study sessions back to back.
15. Use breaks between classes to relax, read, or exercise. Limit use of stimulants like caffeine. Try decaffeinated coffee (which is pretty tasty when brewed).
16. When rushed, allow unessential chores to go until the next day. Schedule some time for yourself—for music, socializing, exercising, a hot bath, relaxing—or for looking at the mountains, the shore, or the stars.

Alleviating Hostility   The following methods will help alleviate your hostility:

1. Tell someone close that you appreciate or love him or her (if it's true!).
2. Make a new friend.
3. Go out of your way to help a classmate or friend.
4. Don't talk to classmates or roommates about disputed subjects that get you into arguments.
5. When classmates and roommates say or do stupid things, don't assume that they're out to annoy you.
6. Look for the joy and beauty in things, or think about things you enjoy when you are losing your temper.
7. Don't curse so much! Are you just expressing feelings, or are you actually compounding your aggravations?
8. When others encourage you or try to help you, tell them you appreciate the effort (even if you could have done it by yourself!).
9. Play to lose, at least occasionally. (Ouch?)
10. Say "Hi!" cheerfully to classmates and friends.
11. Check out your face in the mirror now and then as the day wears on. Search for signs of anger and aggravation. Ask yourself if you really want to look like such a grump.

IN YOUR OWN WRITE

Before moving on to the next section, explain whether you feel that people generally get what they work for in life, or whether reaping the rewards of life is pretty much a matter of luck.

Increasing Resistance to Stress

Some of us are more resistant to stress than others. Some of us are physically hardier, but others of us have attitudes and behavior patterns that appear to promote resistance to stress. These attitudes and behavior patterns are referred to as *psychological hardiness.* Our knowledge of psychological hardiness is based largely on studies of business executives who successfully resist illness despite heavy loads of stress.[42] Hardy executives seem to differ from their less sturdy peers in three ways:

1. Hardy people are *committed* to what they're doing, even if their endeavors are stressful. They don't feel alienated, or like reluctant participants. Committed college students *want* to be in college and in their programs—despite the sacrifices and the work load.

2. Hardy people seek *challenge.* They see change as normal, as the spice of life. They see change as a challenge to personal development, not as a threat to their security. Similarly, hardy students view the life changes of college as a stimulating challenge, not as a price they must pay for an education.

3. Hardy people feel in *control* of their lives. They believe that they can determine whether or not they obtain the rewards of life. Nonhardy individuals see their fates as being out of their hands. Similarly, hardy college students believe that their grades reflect the effort they put into their work. They believe that they can cope with adversity. (Did your response to the preceding "In Your Own Write" exercise suggest that you see yourself as being in control of the rewards you obtain in life?)

TRUTH OR FICTION *Revisited*

Some people do turn out to be psychologically hardier than others.

Psychologist Salvatore Maddi believes that we can enhance our psychological hardiness—our resistance to stress—by using three strategies: situational reconstruction, focusing, and compensatory self-improvement.[43]

These strategies enhance our senses of commitment and control and render our challenges meaningful.

Situational Reconstruction: "It's Not Awful, But Can You Make It Better?"

In situational reconstruction, we imagine ways in which our situations could be worse and ways in which they could be better. This method puts stressful situations into a broader perspective. It alerts us to our assumptions about things, which are sometimes off-base, and encourages us to use our problem-solving skills.

Michael, a first-year student, was upset by a C+ midterm average that resulted in a warning that he could lose his financial aid unless he pulled up his grades to a B. Michael imagined outcomes that would have been worse, such as getting D's or not having financial aid to begin with. He also imagined outcomes that would have been better, such as getting a B average for the same amount of work. Since the term wasn't over and Michael hadn't lost the aid, he realized that his work wasn't all that bad; thus, he raised his senses of control and self-esteem. Also, his grades were not likely to improve unless he worked harder and made his professors aware of it. Michael realized that he could make professors aware of him by seeking their advice on how to improve his grades. So Michael exercised control and gave himself concrete challenges by initiating conferences with his professors to explore ways of making a greater commitment to his courses and elevating his performance.

And think of those frustrating registration lines. Things could be worse, much worse: After all, you wouldn't have to cope with those lines if you weren't in college. In other words, they're a part of college life. Being committed to college may mean committing yourself to handling registration lines. And things would be better if you found entertainment in the lines. So bring an enjoyable book—or friends.

Focusing: "What's Really Eating at You?"

Sometimes students feel unhappy or distressed but are unable to locate the sources of their feelings. Focusing enhances insight into the origins of negative feelings. In this method, students concentrate on their negative body sensations, like tightness in the chest, and think about when the sensations usually occur. By focusing on the tightness in her chest and the churning in her stomach, Nan realized that these sensations had originated in elementary school when she hadn't done her homework and feared teacher disapproval. Now she had similar sensations when she feared that there would not be enough time to write papers and study for exams.

Nan's recognition of the sources of her problem challenged her to work on something specific—not a nameless feeling. As a result, her sense of control was restored and she committed herself to developing more efficient study and writing schedules.

Compensatory Self-Improvement: "If Love Eludes You, Take Up Aerobics"?

Ron was up against a roadblock in his love life—his girlfriend insisted on ending the relationship. Nothing he could do would change her mind, and so he saw himself as powerless and became depressed. Also, his failure to win her back seemed symbolic, to him, of a general inability to take charge of his life.

After discussion back and forth at the counseling center, a counselor suggested that Ron take up aerobics. Aerobics may seem irrelevant when one's love life is in a shambles, but Ron was also sporting a few pounds too many and tended to lead a solitary, sedentary life.

So Ron signed up for a college aerobics class. At first, he huffed and puffed, had some soreness in the legs, and messed up some of the routines. But gradually he worked himself into condition. The workouts became more fun and less work. The soreness left his legs and he followed the routines easily. Moreover, he made new acquaintances in the class and had something to share with them. He availed himself of social supports and created new possibilities for dating. He also felt that now he was taking charge of his life; he wasn't just allowing things to happen to him.

TRUTH OR FICTION *Revisited*

So joining an aerobics class can be a fine way of handling stress.

And isn't taking charge the way you want to go through college and the rest of your life—not just allowing things to happen to you?

SUMMING UP

1. What daily hassles are you encountering as your college career gets underway?
2. What kinds of life changes does college entail for you? What different kinds of life changes tend to affect residential students, commuters, and returning students?
3. Do you notice any Type A tendencies in yourself? Do you think that you need to do anything about them?
4. Are you experiencing any of the physical or emotional effects of stress? Which ones?
5. Have you fallen into any of the ineffective ways of managing stress that are discussed in the chapter? For example, do you snap at people when you're frustrated?
6. Do you have any decisions to make about your college career? Are you facing them or putting them off?
7. What is the advantage in knowing what to expect in college? What can you do to make the stresses you face more predictable?
8. Do you tend to keep things in perspective or blow them out of proportion? If you tend to magnify your problems, what can you do about it?
9. What are the methods for relaxing described in the chapter? Would they be of help to you?
10. Do you think that you are a psychologically hardy student? What can you do to enhance your resistance to stress?

Answer Key for the "Social Readjustment Rating Scale"

Add the scores in the "Total" column to arrive at your final score.

Interpretation Your final score suggests the amount of stress you have experienced during the past 12 months:

>   From 0 to 1,500 = Minor stress
>   1,501–3,500 = Mild stress
>   3,501–5,500 = Moderate stress
>   5,501 and above = Major stress

Research shows that the chances of becoming physically ill within the *following* year is linked to the amount of stress experienced during the *past* year. College students who experience minor stress have a 28 percent chance of becoming ill; mild stress, a 45 percent chance; moderate stress, a 70 percent chance; and major stress, an 82 percent chance. The seriousness of the illness also increases with the amount of stress.

These percentages reflect previous research with college students. So you're not necessarily doomed to illness if you have encountered a great deal of stress. Also keep in mind that psychologically hardy students may be able to withstand amounts of stress that harm less sturdy students.

Answer Key for "Are You a Type A Student?" Questionnaire

In this questionnaire, Yes answers suggest the Type A behavior pattern, which is marked by a sense of time urgency and hostility. In appraising whether you are Type A, don't be overly concerned with the precise number of Yes answers. But you should have little trouble spotting Type A tendencies in yourself if you are being honest with yourself.

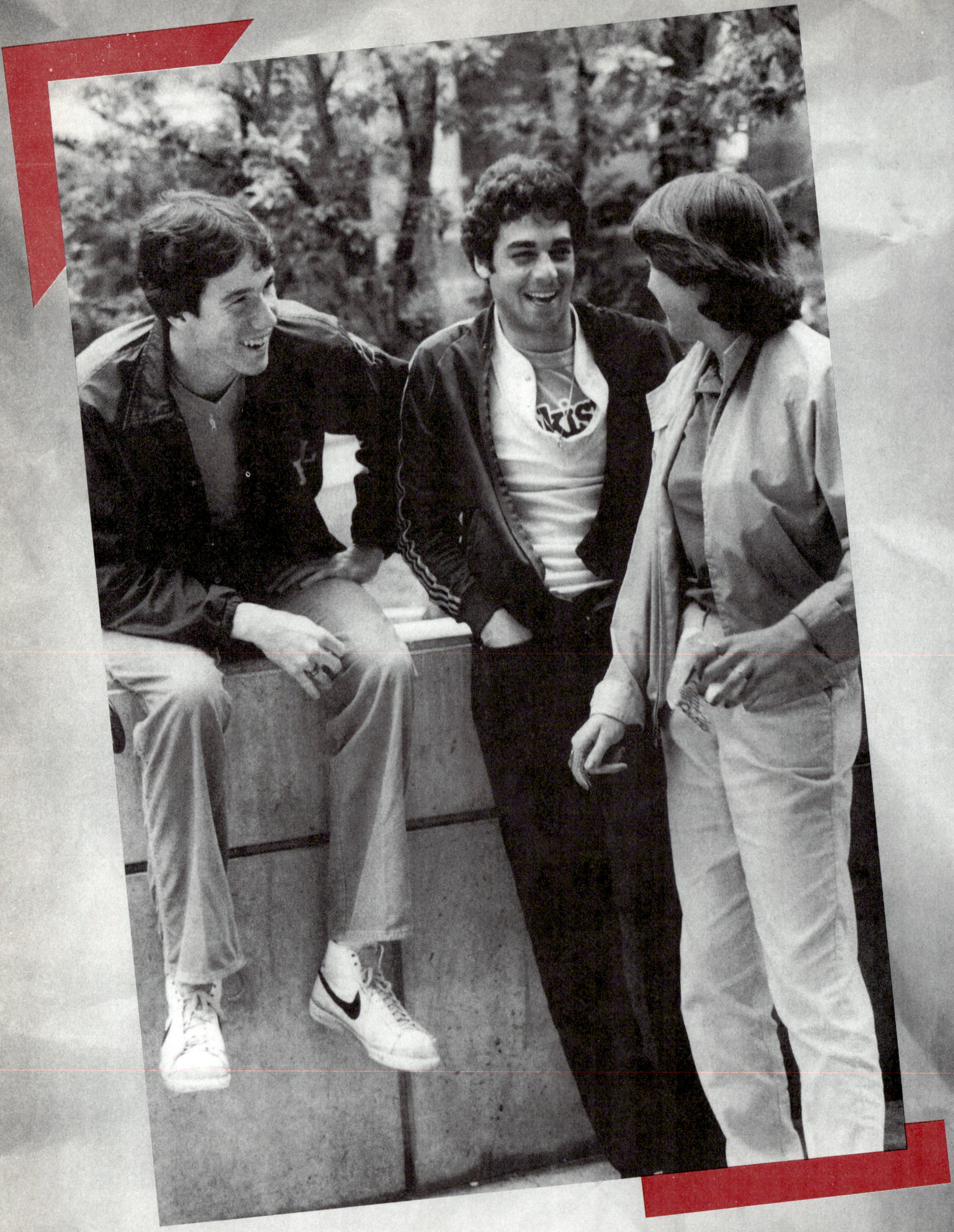

9

Developing Relationships and Dealing with Loneliness

TRUTH OR FICTION?

____ Warmth is the most strongly desired trait in a friend.

____ According to college students, selflessness is one of the qualities of love.

____ College men favor college women who are more slender than the women assume.

____ Physical appeal is the chief characteristic we seek in partners for enduring, meaningful relationships.

____ When you're smiling, when you're smiling, the whole world . . . thinks you're better looking.

____ Opposites attract.

____ Small talk is an awkward way to launch a relationship.

____ Prompt self-disclosure of intimate information is the best method for building a relationship.

____ Once a relationship begins to deteriorate, there's nothing you can do about it.

____ Many students are lonely for fear of social rejection.

No man is an island, entire of it self.

JOHN DONNE

How well we remember Donne's line from high school English. At one time, we interpreted the line largely in terms of the social nature of human beings. Today, no doubt, we would also comment on the sexist language and chide the poet for not writing "No man or woman is an island, entire of it self."

All right, we'll get on with our point: College men and women are not islands "entire of" themselves. We are also social creatures. Our relationships with other people are important to us. We share our feelings and experiences with friends. Our families often provide us with an abiding love and a sense of security. Our love relationships enhance our feelings of self-esteem and, perhaps, help us meet our sensual needs. Social support, as noted in Chapter 8, helps us manage stress.

But when we enter college, especially a residential college, our social worlds may meet with upheaval. We may leave friends and family behind—including boyfriends and girlfriends. Relationships and sources of support that we had taken for granted may be many miles—and expensive telephone calls—away. Rapid answers to letters may address problems that we were thinking about last week. Residential students need to form new friendships and dating relationships at college.

> Will you, won't you, will you, won't you, will you join the dance?
>
> LEWIS CARROLL,
> *Alice in Wonderland*

Commuting students, too, face social challenges. For them, as for residential students, college is made less stressful by congenial relationships with classmates and professors. Commuters usually want to develop closer relationships with students in elective courses and major fields because they share common interests. Commuters, like residential students, are likely to develop romantic relationships with other students. Even returning students find it valuable to develop relationships with other returning students; other returning students, after all, are best able to understand what they are going through.

> It takes an enemy and a friend, working together, to hurt you to the heart. The one to slander you, and the other to get the news to you.
>
> MARK TWAIN

In this chapter, we first discuss friendship—what it is and what we want from it. We consider the Greek-letter organizations—fraternities and sororities—and see what kinds of roles they play in helping us meet our social needs. Then we turn our attention to love, sweet love. And we take on the task that has eluded the poets all these centuries—defining what love is. Friendships and love both develop from feelings of attraction—the force that draws people together—and so our next task will be to explore the factors that contribute to attraction. Then we'll see how relationships develop, and, of course, offer advice on helping them along. Finally, we'll talk about a social problem that affects thousands of students all over the country, even on populous campuses—loneliness. We'll see why students are lonely and, if you're one of them, what you can do about it.

FRIENDSHIP

> Friendship, friendship, What a perfect blendship . . .
>
> COLE PORTER,
> "Friendship"

From childhood, friends play essential roles in our lives.[1] During our teenage years, it is important to be able to share our feelings with our friends.[2] We want to tell friends "everything," without having to worry whether they will spread stories about us.[3] This kind of intimacy is especially important to girls.[4] Our college friendships, as in the song, are often "perfect blendships." Our friends tend to be like us in race, values, and social class.

Chapter 9

What do we tend to look for in friends? Knowing what friends want and need can help us be good friends.

In high school and college, we often become parts of cliques and crowds. A clique is a small group of intimate friends who share their innermost feelings. A crowd is a relatively large, loosely knit bunch of friends who share activities. The crowd may party or go to game together. But we share our private feelings about the people at the party with members of the clique.

Qualities of Good Friends

Keep smiling, keep shining,
Knowing you can always count on me, for sure,
That's what friends are for,
That's what friends are for.

"That's What Friends Are For," a popular song

What do we tend to look for in friends? Knowing what friends want and need from others can help *you* be a good friend. Consider the results of a *Psychology Today* survey of its readers, most of whom were college graduates.[5] They reported that keeping confidences and loyalty were the most important qualities in a friend (Table 9.1).

TRUTH OR FICTION Revisited

Among college-educated adults, loyalty (keeping confidences is one facet of loyalty), not warmth, is the leading requirement for friendship.

However, the social-supportive features of the affiliation—warmth, humor, and willingness to make time for one's friend—are also important. Traits like honesty, independence, and intelligence also count.

Unfortunately, many physically intimate love relationships lack the essential kind of intimacy demanded of friendships—ability to keep confidences and general loyalty. Let us now consider the pluses and minuses of fraternities and sororities, where many college students find groups of "built-in" friends.

> Friendship is a common belief in the same fallacies, mountebanks and hobgoblins.
>
> H. L. MENCKEN

Developing Relationships and Dealing with Loneliness

TABLE 9.1 Sought-After Qualities in Friends.

QUALITY	PERCENTAGE OF RESPONDENTS ENDORSING THE QUALITY
1. Ability to keep confidences	89
2. Loyalty	88
3. Warmth and affection	82
4. Supportiveness	75
5. Honesty and frankness	73
6. Humor	72
7. Willingness to set aside time for me	62
8. Independence	61
9. Conversational skills	59
10. Intelligence	58
11. Social conscience	49

FRATERNITIES AND SORORITIES: "THE GREEKS VERSUS THE GEEKS?"

> I don't care to belong to a club that accepts people like me as members.
> — GROUCHO MARX

> May God defend me from my friends: I can defend myself from my enemies.
> — VOLTAIRE

> The worst solitude is to be destitute of sincere friendship.
> — FRANCIS BACON

"The Greeks versus the Geeks" is an advertising slogan from a *Revenge of the Nerds* sequel. Sad to say, on some campuses, there is so much pressure to join fraternities and sororities that nonjoiners are looked upon with scorn or suspicion. The assumption is that everyone who can become a brother or a sister does, and those who do not are perceived as rejects. Fraternities and sororities have a lower profile on many campuses, and some colleges do not allow them at all. These societies tend to take on somewhat more prominence on campuses where most students live away from home. On these campuses, fraternities and sororities may provide housing and surrogate parents as well as social diversion.

Let us consider some of the advantages and disadvantages of Greek-letter societies. With this knowledge, you may be able to make a more informed decision about whether they are for you.

Advantages and Disadvantages of Fraternities and Sororities

Fraternities and sororities confer advantages such as the following:

1. They offer handy sources of social support.
2. They offer a crowd of people with whom to do and share things.
3. They confer prestige upon brothers and sisters. On many campuses, members of Greek organizations feel superior to nonmembers. Also, there is frequently a pecking order of such organizations on campuses, with some houses having a reputation, for example, for pledging fine athletes. We think it's more important for our self-esteem to be based on our personal qualities rather than our group memberships. We realize, however, that most of us identify with one group or another, and that our self-esteem is often tied up in the reputation of the group.
4. They offer the beginnings of a lifelong network that may be of use in obtaining jobs and climbing the corporate ladder.
5. They channel social life into house and college occasions. Rather than wondering what you're going to be doing on a weekend, especially a "big" weekend, you're welcome at the house's parties and functions.

Are fraternities and sororities for you? What are some of their advantages and drawbacks?

If you don't have a date, a brother or sister may fix you up with someone from a brother fraternity or sister sorority, where the members tend to share interests and values. Houses also arrange mixers with brother fraternities or sister sororities. In other words, they do much social screening for members.

6. Joiners become part of a tradition. Fraternities and sororities have histories and aims that affect members in the same way the nation, one's religious group, and the college at large affect the individual.

7. Fraternities and sororities frequently provide high-quality living arrangements. They are often housed in splendid buildings, sometimes in converted mansions.

8. They provide social inducement to play on university and intramural athletic teams. Athletics are valued by many houses, and as a member of a fraternity or sorority, you may also be on the society's intramural teams.

9. They offer social inducement to participate in the planning of social occasions and in the management of house business. These chores provide the opportunity to develop administrative and interpersonal skills that can be of help later on.

10. Many houses encourage studying. Although some value academics more than others do, most recognize that the primary goal of college is to receive an education, and they inspire their members to do so.

11. Upperclass members often provide valuable information about the strengths and weaknesses of various courses and professors.

12. Although this is certainly not a sufficient reason for joining a fraternity or sorority, it should also be noted that many of them have superb, legitimately compiled test files. Members who have taken courses place copies of their exams in the file, and old exams often contain reused questions. Some professors, in fact, reuse examinations in their entirety from time to time.

So fraternities and sororities offer many benefits. But there are drawbacks, and what is of value to one person may be a hindrance to another. It really depends on who you are and who you really want to be.

Fraternities and sororities have these disadvantages:

1. One of the drawbacks is that fraternities and sororities have expectations for behavior, called norms, that pressure members to conform. Students may try to join societies that reflect their own values, but there is never a perfect fit. When "rushing"—that is, visiting fraternities

Developing Relationships and Dealing with Loneliness

and sororities so that the houses and students can decide who and where to pledge—*be yourself*. Express your own ideas and values—not what you think the brothers or sisters of the house want to hear. It is a mistake to join a house whose members are very different from you. A moment of glory—being invited to pledge for a prestigious society—may give way to years of mutual discomfort.

2. Another disadvantage is that members who seek friends among nonmembers may face disapproval. This is the flip side of the advantage of finding an instant cadre of "friends." As we grow, we often reappraise our values and seek different qualities in friends. The society that meant so much to us as first-year students may hold us back as juniors or seniors.

3. Similarly, there may be pressure to date the "right kind" of people. This is the flip side of the advantage that fraternities and sororities often provide "built-in" pools of potential dates. A member of a Christian fraternity, Carlos, was dating a Jewish girl, Fran, and he heard a number of comments about it.

4. Exclusivity is also reflected in pressure to socialize with members of your own house and a number of similar "acceptable" houses. Peer pressure may thus prevent you from socializing with groups of people you will find in the "real world" once you graduate—people from diverse racial, ethnic, and socioeconomic groups. You may enter college with an open mind and pledge a house with blinders on.

5. For some, the living arrangements offered by the fraternity or sorority are not satisfactory. Some students prefer an apartment with one or two roommates to the hustle and bustle of the fraternity or sorority house. In many cases, however, members are required to live in the fraternity or sorority house, at least for a year.

6. The opportunity to play on intramural teams may provide pressure that you really don't want. Are you athletic? If not, do you really want to join a group that prizes athletics? And if you are only somewhat athletic, do you prefer to compete against others, which is the "Greek" way, or do you prefer self-developing solitary jogs, bicycle rides, and swims?

7. The opportunity to help plan and manage house functions can also translate into pressure to take on administrative burdens. Many would prefer to spend their spare time in other ways—and for some, such duties kill their spare time.

8. Although fraternities and sororities may promote academics on certain levels, there may also be subtle—and, in some cases, spoken—pressures not to study. At athletically oriented houses, being overly cerebral may be seen as nerdish. Then, of course, the profusion of social activities, house responsibilities, and demands of pledging may eat into valuable study time. We have seen many students flunk out of college because they could not limit their involvements with their societies. It does little good to pledge a prestigious house if the demands of pledging mean that you will not last long enough at college to reap the benefits of membership. It is one thing to wear silly clothes to class; it is another to be so busy memorizing the names and addresses of the grandparents of house members that there's no time to study!

9. Then there are the perils of hazing. Over the years, hazing practices have ranged from the silly and annoying to the painful and dangerous. There have been times and places when pledges have been required to eat live goldfish. This may seem yucky (to use a sophisticated term), but goldfish are usually nutritious. However, hazing can also involve running naked in winter or overdosing on alcohol. Now and then, a pledge dies from an alcohol overdose. Now and then, fraternity members go to jail because of it. Hazing practices are usually not so noxious, but they are intended to be demanding hurdles—both to test pledges' sincerity and build their loyalty to the house. (The thinking goes like this: If pledges tell themselves they went through hell to join, they'll

believe that their fraternities and sororities must be very, very special.) You have to decide for yourself just what you'll go through—just where you'll draw the line.

Should *you* pledge a fraternity or a sorority? We wish we could answer this for you, but we can't. We hope that we have given you a number of factors to weigh in making your decision. We will say this: If you're into athletics and a social whirl and don't particularly value solitary, contemplative hours, a fraternity or sorority may be right for you. But if you're the type of person who would rather socialize with one or two intimate friends, and you're not "into" belonging to prestigious groups, a fraternity or sorority could be a senseless diversion for you. On many campuses, fraternity or sorority membership is synonymous with social acceptance and success. Students on such campuses may not be certain that these societies are for them, yet they may still be motivated to pledge by fear of social rejection.

We noted that many fraternity and sorority members find their love relationships among the members of sister and brother organizations. Let's now consider the topic of love, which makes the world go round on campus for many students. We'll see that lovers, sad to say, are not always friends. Enduring love relationships, however, combine friendship and love.

LOVE

From the dawn of civilization, philosophers and poets have sought to capture love in words. Our poets have portrayed love as ethereal and heavenly. But passionate love—romantic love—is also lusty, brimming with sexual desire. For many students, love rules campus life. And for many, love is indeed "blind." That is, we tend not to perceive the flaws in our lovers and, now and then, we do rather silly things for love.

Social scientists as well as poets speak of love. Romantic love consists of feelings of passion and caring[6] (Figure 9.1). Passion embraces fascination with the loved one; sexual desire; and a longing for exclusiveness—that is, an exclusive relationship with the loved one. Caring means desire to champion the interests of the loved one and to give one's all for the loved one, to sacrifice one's own interests, if need be. College undergraduates view the wish to help lovers as central to the idea of love.[7]

> Love is the triumph of imagination over intelligence.
> H. L. MENCKEN

> Love: a grave mental disease.
> PLATO

> But love is blind, and lovers cannot see
> The pretty follies that themselves commit.
> SHAKESPEARE, *The Merchant of Venice*

Plato branded love as "a grave mental disease." Just what is love and what role does it play in our lives?

Developing Relationships and Dealing with Loneliness 219

> Love rules the camp, the court, the grove—for love is heaven, and heaven is love.
>
> LORD BYRON,
> *Don Juan*

> I'm tired of all this nonsense about beauty being only skin deep. That's deep enough. What do you want, an adorable pancreas?
>
> JEAN KERR

Romantic Love

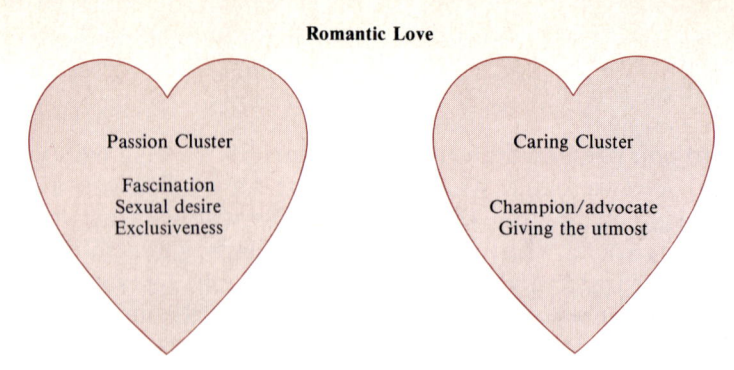

Passion Cluster
Fascination
Sexual desire
Exclusiveness

Caring Cluster
Champion/advocate
Giving the utmost

Just What Is Romantic Love? College students characterize romantic love as consisting of two clusters of feelings: passion and caring. Passion includes sexual desire, idealization, and the desire for an exclusive relationship. Caring includes trying to help the loved one and putting the loved one's interests ahead of one's own.

TRUTH OR FICTION *Revisited*

And so college students do think of selflessness—of sacrifice—as one of the attributes of romantic love.

Romantic lovers idealize one another.[8] They amplify each other's positive attributes and overlook their defects.

The questionnaire on page 221 may afford you some insight into your own feelings toward people you are seeing.

ATTRACTION

Now that you're an expert on friendship and love, let's look at the factors that encourage feelings of attraction.

Physical Appearance: How Vital Is Looking Good?

You might think college students are so bright and sophisticated that they find physical attractiveness less important than warmth and sensitivity in the traits that they look for in their dates. Social scientists have found, however, that physical attractiveness is the major force behind feelings of attraction and considering others as candidates for dates, sexual involvements, even marriage.[9]

Are our standards for beauty subjective? Is beauty, as Margaret Wolfe Hungerford wrote in 1878, "in the eye of the beholder"? Or is there a consensus as to what is alluring? There may be no universal criteria for beauty,[10] but there are pervasive standards in our society.

Tallness is a general plus for college men, although college women prefer men who are medium-tall in height—not the centers on the basketball squad.[11] Tall women are viewed less positively. Undergraduate women favor dates who are about 6 inches taller than they are. College men typically fancy their dates to be about 4 1/2 inches shorter.[12]

Chubbiness is valued in some foreign cultures, which may be one reason that these cultures are "foreign" to us. College men and women, however, both find reasonable slenderness alluring.[13] Most college women prefer men with a V-taper, with medium-wide shoulders and backs, and with waists, buttocks, and legs that taper from medium-thin to thin.[14]

> Love is only a dirty trick played on us to achieve the continuation of the species.
>
> W. SOMERSET MAUGHAM

QUESTIONNAIRE
The Love Scale

Are you in love?

Your first author developed this scale to measure love when he was teaching at Northeastern University in Boston. To see whether your love relationship (or relationships, if you have been active) are as passionate as those of the Northeastern University students, think about your dating partner (or partners) and circle the numbers with each of them in mind. Then total your score(s) and turn to the key at the end of the chapter.

Directions: Circle the number that best shows how true or false the items are for you according to this code:

7 = definitely true
6 = rather true
5 = somewhat true
4 = not sure, or equally true and false
3 = somewhat false
2 = rather false
1 = definitely false

1. I look forward to being with _____ a great deal.   1 2 3 4 5 6 7
2. I find _____ to be sexually exciting.   1 2 3 4 5 6 7
3. _____ has fewer faults than most people.   1 2 3 4 5 6 7
4. I would do anything I could for _____ .   1 2 3 4 5 6 7
5. _____ is very attractive to me.   1 2 3 4 5 6 7
6. I like to share my feelings with _____ .   1 2 3 4 5 6 7
7. Doing things is more fun when _____ and I do them together. 1 2 3 4 5 6 7
8. I like to have _____ all to myself.   1 2 3 4 5 6 7
9. I would feel horrible if anything bad happened to _____ .   1 2 3 4 5 6 7
10. I think about _____ very often.   1 2 3 4 5 6 7
11. It is very important that _____ cares for me.   1 2 3 4 5 6 7
12. I am most content when I am with _____ .   1 2 3 4 5 6 7
13. It is difficult for me to stay away from _____ for very long. 1 2 3 4 5 6 7
14. I care about _____ a great deal.   1 2 3 4 5 6 7

Total Score for Love Scale: _____

There are interesting sex differences in perceptions of the most appealing body shape. College men, by and large, think that their physiques approximate the ideal and the physique that women find most alluring.[15] But college women generally view themselves as noticeably heavier than the figure that men find most appealing, and heavier yet than the ideal female figure (Figure 9.2). Ironically, college men and women both err in their guesses as to the desires of their opposites. College men fancy women who are heavier than women assume—about halfway between the width of the average woman and the figure that the woman believes is most pleasing. And college women favor men who are slimmer than the men imagine.

> Love is the only sane and satisfactory answer to the problem of human existence.
>
> ERICH FROMM

Developing Relationships and Dealing with Loneliness

> A woman without a man is like a fish without a bicycle.
> GLORIA STEINEM

> Love is the word used to label the sexual excitement of the young, the habituation of the middle-aged, and the mutual dependence of the old.
> JOHN CIARDI

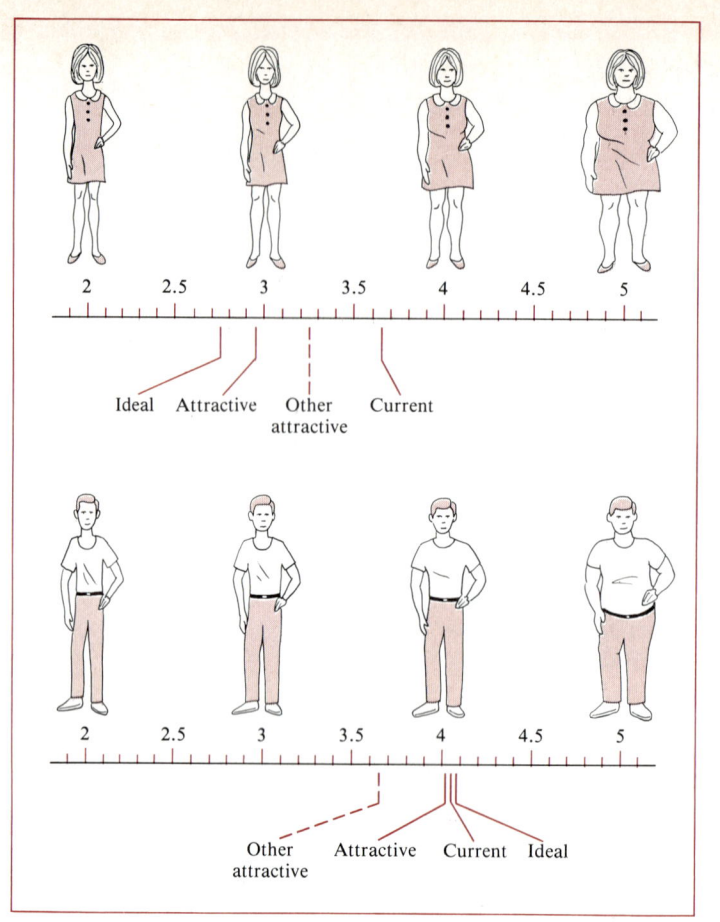

How Thin Is Thin Enough? Researchers have found that most college women believe they are heavier than they ought to be, whereas college men, on the average, see their current weights as being close to ideal. However, college men like their women somewhat heavier than the women imagine, and college women would like their men to be a bit thinner than the men assume. In any event, contemporary pressures on women to be thin may be contributing to eating disorders such as anorexia and bulimia.

TRUTH OR FICTION Revisited

College men actually favor women who are a bit heavier than the women imagine.

The importance of physical attractiveness is related to the type of relationship. Among college students, physical appeal is the chief consideration mostly in sexual relationships.[16] Personal qualities like honesty, loyalty, warmth, and sensitivity are more consequential in long-term, meaningful relationships.

TRUTH OR FICTION Revisited

Personal traits such as honesty take on relatively more prominence when we are thinking about long-term, meaningful relationships.

But college men are relatively more influenced by the physical attributes of their partners. Women are relatively more likely to focus on qualities like warmth, need for achievement, assertiveness, and wit.

QUESTIONNAIRE
What Do You Look at First?

What do you notice first when you meet a member of the opposite sex or a person of the same sex? Use the following code to indicate how important each of the listed items is to you:

    4 = Extremely important
    3 = Moderately important
    2 = Slightly important
    1 = Not at all important

PERSON OF OPPOSITE SEX	PERSON OF SAME SEX
____ 1. Ankles	____ 1. Ankles
____ 2. Clothing	____ 2. Clothing
____ 3. Eyes	____ 3. Eyes
____ 4. Face as a whole	____ 4. Face as a whole
____ 5. Figure as a whole	____ 5. Figure as a whole
____ 6. Hair	____ 6. Hair
____ 7. Hands	____ 7. Hands
____ 8. Height	____ 8. Height
____ 9. Knees	____ 9. Knees
____ 10. Legs as a whole	____ 10. Legs as a whole
____ 11. Smile	____ 11. Smile
____ 12. Teeth	____ 12. Teeth

So, are you knocked off balance by an even-featured face? Do you look for sensitive eyes? Do brilliant teeth bite into your attention? Or, for you, do clothes make the man or the woman?

A Roper poll found that the largest number of women (35 percent) first note a man's clothing, and 29 percent of men are first influenced by the way in which a woman is dressed.[17] The biggest group of men (45 percent) first notes a woman's figure, whereas 29 percent of women are initially concerned with a man's physique. Men and women also tend to pay attention to the eyes (22 percent of men; 30 percent of women), face (34 percent of men; 27 percent of women), smile (24 percent of men; 27 percent of women), and hair (16 percent for both sexes). Hands, height, legs, and teeth all earn less than immediate attention, if they're noticed at all.

When meeting someone of their own sex, men (39 percent) and women (41 percent) are both most likely to attend to the person's clothing. Men and women are similarly impressed by the person's face (28 percent of men; 26 percent of women) and figure (16 percent of men; 20 percent of women). Women (27 percent) are more concerned than men (13 percent) about the new person's hair, but men (15 percent) are more likely than women (2 percent) to be influenced by the person's height.

So even though we're reared not to judge books by their covers, we are apparently influenced by other people's clothing. Also, our figures or physiques seem to have somewhat more prominence than our facial features. There's a message in all this, of course. Perhaps we can't do all that much about our facial features, but we can maximize our overall attractiveness by means of diet, exercise, even strategic dressing. That's two out of three— figure and clothing, and that's not bad.

Developing Relationships and Dealing with Loneliness

Also, we are considered more appealing when we're are smiling.[18] And so there is very good reason, as the song says, to "put on a happy face" when you meet new people or seek a date.

TRUTH OR FICTION Revisited

So we are considered more physically appealing when we're smiling.

College women also seem to favor men who are sociable and assertive.[19] Social dominance in men is also viewed favorably by many college women.[20] However, college men do not necessarily reciprocate these attitudes. College men often respond negatively to assertive, socially dominant women.[21] Despite the emancipating trends of recent times, many men still seek women who are willing to take a back seat. We would not advise assertive women to throttle themselves in order to appeal to men who value demureness. After all, what could be more frustrating than establishing a long-term relationship with a domineering man and then encountering years of conflict?

Similarity in Attitudes

Do opposites attract, or do birds of a feather flock together? It turns out that similarity in attitudes and interests enhances the formation of friend-

IN YOUR OWN WRITE

> What's in a name? that which we call a rose
> By any other name would smell as sweet.
>
> Shakespeare, *Romeo and Juliet*

What's in a name? Perhaps a great deal.

This exercise differs from other "In Your Own Write" exercises. Rather than writing a few sentences, we're simply going to ask you to sign your name. Go ahead. Sign your name here:

_____

Now sign again, this time as if you were president of the United States:

_____

How did the two signatures differ, if at all? Psychologist Richard Zweigenhaft had students at Wesleyan University engage in this exercise, and three out of four students signed their names larger in the role of president.[22] Moreover, the presidential signatures were harder to read. Prestige is apparently associated with bigger signatures and less need to make them legible. Wesleyan University professors also signed their names larger than people lower in status, including the Wesleyan students and blue-collar university employees.

Now try this. Imagine that your name is Edward Michael Smith or Elizabeth Melissa Smith. Now sign your imaginary name in full or abbreviated form (e.g., E. M. Smith, Ed or Liz Smith) as seems fit for the following purposes:

1. On a job application: _____
2. On a letter to your teacher: _____
3. On a petition: _____
4. On a personal letter to a friend: _____

ships and romantic relationships.[23] College students are most attracted to dates who are physically alluring and see the world in much the same way.[24] A meeting of the minds on religious and political matters is apparently a powerful aphrodisiac.

But be warned. We tend to assume that people who attract us also think as we do.[25] Perhaps when we're turned on, we deceive ourselves that the hitches in a relationship will be trivial—that all the kinks can be ironed out. But they can't. Later we'll see that they can sow the seeds of destruction in relationships.

All attitudes are not equal. For example, a University of Nevada study found that college men were more affected by sexual than religious attitudes.[26] But university women were more drawn to men whose religious views mirrored their own. College women may be relatively less interested in a physical relationship and more attentive to creating a family with cohesive values. Attitudes toward religion and having and rearing children are more critical in selecting mates than attributes like kindness and professional standing.[27]

TRUTH OR FICTION *Revisited*

So opposites are unlikely to attract in the formation of relationships. We are most strongly drawn to people who are physically appealing and share our attitudes. That is, birds of a feather tend to flock together.

---

5. On a check:_____
6. On a final examination:_____
7. On a love letter:_____
8. On a letter to your senator:_____
9. On a complaint to your municipality about the collection of refuse:_____
10. On a letter-to-the-editor of the local newspaper:_____

How did you sign for each situation? What forms did you prefer? E. M. Smith? Edward (Elizabeth) Smith? E. Smith? E. Michael (Melissa) Smith? Just Ed or Liz? It seems that E. and E. M. Smith tend to be more formal and conservative than Edward M. and Elizabeth M. Smith. Students at California Community Colleges tend to prefer Ed or Edward (or Liz or Elizabeth) Smith on the formal occasions, rather than E. M. Smith.[28] College men and older people were more likely to use their middle names than women and younger people. What about you?

Our names also affect the ways in which other people think of us. Social scientists have run experiments in which they assigned various names to the same photographs of women and then had the photos rated for attractiveness by different groups of men. When photos were assigned the names Kathy, Jennifer, and Christine, they were rated as more alluring than when they were assigned the names Ethel, Gertrude, and Harriet.[29] Does it seem unfair? After all, we are given our names. True enough, but if you're unhappy with your name—whether you're a woman or a man—why not try out a more appealing nickname? Starting off in college or at a new job is a strategic time for doing so. Another name might better fit the "real you" or the real you that you are creating. But if you are content with an unappealing or unusual name, keep it! If you're happy with yourself, people tend to take you as you are.

Now let us consider the stages in relationships. Naturally we shall be suggesting ways of advancing the development of your relationships.

STAGES IN RELATIONSHIPS

Some social scientists believe that relationships undergo five stages of development.[30]

Initial Attraction

The first stage of a relationship, *initial attraction*, begins when people grow aware of one another. Recurrent meetings, positive emotional reactions, and the desire to get involved all feed into initial attraction.

During the stage of initial attraction, our impressions are largely visual. We may encounter initial attraction during a mixer, when we spot a new student in the cafeteria, or when we enter a new class. Most of the time, we meet other people by chance. Students who live near one another, attend the same classes, or have mutual acquaintances are most likely to form initial attractions.

Building a Relationship

Second is the stage of building a relationship. We are most likely to strive to develop relationships with people who are similar to us in attractiveness and attitudes, and who seem to return our initial interest in them. We may hesitate to approach people who are much more attractive than we, for fear of rejection.[31]

Small Talk: Is It Really "Small"? When we try to build a relationship, we frequently test the waters by looking for common ground (e.g., shared attitudes and overlapping interests). We also check out our feelings of attraction. The decision to pursue the relationship is often made because of successful small talk. Small talk is a shallow kind of dialogue in which superficial information is exchanged. Small talk focuses on breadth of topic coverage, not on profound discussion.

TRUTH OR FICTION *Revisited*

So even though it's superficial, small talk is a significant step in building a relationship.

Students may flit about at mixers as they exchange small talk. Now and then, you can see that common ground has been found as they begin to pair off.[32]

The "Opening Line": How to Get Things Started One special type of small talk is very superficial, but it can be crucial: It is the opening line.

Opening lines are usually prefaced by eye contact. If the person to whom you are attracted is willing to be approached, he or she will usually return your eye contact. People who do not want to be approached—and shy people—may avoid your eye contact. When you decide to try to go beyond initial attraction, venture a smile (it's friendly and it also makes you more attractive) and some eye contact. If the eye contact is returned, use an opening line.

What role does similarity play in interpersonal attraction? Do birds of a feather flock together?

IN YOUR OWN WRITE

In the following spaces, write down three of the opening lines you have used, or think would be effective. Then check the discussion that follows.
Opening lines:

1. _____
   _____

2. _____
   _____

3. _____
   _____

Scholars of communication have recorded opening lines such as these:[33]

Spoken salutes, like "Good morning."

Personal probes, like "How are you doing?" (often pronounced, "How yuh doin'?")

Compliments, for example, "I love that sweatshirt!" or "You have a great voice."

References to mutual environs, such as "Nice day, huh?" "That wind really goes through you," "With all the money they spent on this campus, you'd think they could have put some windows into these classrooms," or "This is a great dorm."

Reference to events or people outside your current setting, such as "What did you think of that class?" or "Did you catch that speech last night?"

References to the other person's behavior, such as "You really look like you know what you're doing on the track," "I saw you sitting all by yourself and hoped it would be okay if I sat down," or "It seems that I see you in this part of the library almost every evening."

References to yourself, or to your own behavior, like "I've been trying to figure out how to use this index—any ideas?" or "Hi, my name is Ed Smith." (Feel free to use your own name, if you prefer.)

The elementary salute "Hi" or "Hello" is very serviceable. A congenial glance and a chipper hello should provide you with an indication as to whether your feelings of attraction are reciprocated. If your hello is returned with a cordial smile and engaging eye contact, proceed with another line, perhaps your name, an allusion to the other person's behavior, or to your surroundings.

Initial conversations are likely to exchange name, major field, and home town—or, as communications experts put it, "name, rank, and serial number."[34] Students are seeking sociological profiles of one another in hope that common ground will allow them to pursue a conversation. There seems to be an unspoken rule for such discussions: If I give you information about me, you reciprocate by providing me with an equivalent amount of data about you. That is: "I'll tell you my home town if you tell me yours."[35] If a person you select does not play by this rule, he or she may not be

Developing Relationships and Dealing with Loneliness

interested. But he or she may also not know the rules. Also, you could be clumsy or be revealing too much too soon, which can turn off the other person.

Small talk may have a "phony" ring to it, but it serves a purpose. Giving another person too much information too soon can be repellent.[36] After all, how would you react if a stranger began talking to you about his or her hemorrhoids?

Self-Disclosure: How Much? How Soon? Self-disclosure, or opening up, is necessary in building relationships. But how much can you safely disclose when you've just met someone? If you say nothing about yourself, you may look detached or as if you're concealing things. But if you tell a new acquaintance that your underwear is cutting into your flesh, you're being too familiar too soon. People who offer too much too soon are seen as phonier, less secure, less mature, and less well adjusted than people who reveal personal information when a relationship has begun to ripen.[37] Well-adjusted people reveal a lot but keep a lid on things that would be self-damaging or prematurely revealing.[38]

TRUTH OR FICTION *Revisited*

We actually need to be careful not to disclose too much too soon. We may seem phony, insecure, and poorly adjusted if we reveal intimate information prematurely.

WHAT DO YOU DO NOW?
How to Improve Date-Seeking Skills

Let's take a break. We're talking about ways of advancing relationships once you experience an initial attraction. Now you have reason to believe that Mr. or Ms. Right may be right in your class or in the dorm across the quad. So what do you do now? How do you make a date?

Some people may seem "naturally" better at starting relationships and making dates than others, but, fortunately, date-seeking skills can be acquired. We can improve social skills, like date-seeking skills, in a step-by-step fashion. (Psychologists refer to this method as "successive approximations."[39]) You can practice a series of tasks that are graded in difficulty. At each level, you fine-tune your skills and gather self-confidence. You can practice some skills with friends who take the role of the person you want to ask out. Friends can give you candid feedback about your effectiveness.

The following suggestions are adapted from *Behavior Therapy*.[40] They include a sequence of graded activities that students can practice to hone their date-seeking talents:

Easy Practice Level Select a person with whom you are friendly, but one whom you have no desire to date. Practice making small talk about the weather, about new films that have come to campus, television shows, concerts, museum shows, political events, and personal hobbies.

Select a student you might have some interest in dating. Smile when you meet him or her in class, in the library, in the cafeteria, or elsewhere, and say "Hi." Engage in this activity with students and others of both sexes to increase your skills at greeting others.

Practice with your mirror. Pretend that you are sitting next to the person you would like to date. Say "Hello" with a broad smile and introduce yourself. Work on the smile until it looks inviting and genuine. Make some comment about the setting—the library, the cafeteria, the laundry room, whatever. Use a friend to obtain feedback about the effectiveness of the smile, your tone of voice, posture, and choice of words.

Despite the dangers of premature disclosure, college students tend to reveal personal information early.[41] A study of college couples who had been together for an average of eight months found that more than half had informed their partners of former sexual relationships.[42]

Our own opinion is that it is important to be open about most of your ideas and feelings in your current relationships, but your past is precisely that—*your* past. An exception is the area of sexually transmitted diseases, as we'll see in Chapter 12. Your partner has a right to know about threats to health.

Reciprocity Reciprocity of feelings fosters development of relationships. When we feel cherished and praised, we are inclined to return these feelings. Relationships may blossom when one person tells the other "I really like you a lot," or "I love you." The recipient is likely to bask in the statement's glow. At the very least, such declarations prompt recipients to consider the depth of their own feelings and to decide how far the relationship should go.

Mutuality When feelings of attraction are reciprocated, couples may experience powerful feelings of liking or love. If they then begin to think of themselves as "we"—no longer two "I's" meeting superficially—they reach a state of mutuality. They view their needs and interests as coinciding; they face the world as a couple, not as disconnected individuals.

Medium Practice Level Sit next to the person you'd like to date and get engaged in small talk. If you are in a classroom, talk about a homework assignment, the seating arrangement, or the instructor (be kind). If you are at a part-time job, talk about the building or some recent event in the neighborhood. Ask your intended date how he or she feels about the event. If you are at a mixer or in an aerobics group, tell the other person that you are there for the first time and ask for advice on how to relate to the group.

Engage in small talk about the weather and campus events. Channel the conversation into an exchange of personal information. Give your "name, rank, and serial number"—who you are, your major field, where you're from, why you're attending this college. The other person is likely to return equivalent information. Ask how he or she feels about the class, the college, the town or city the college is in, and so forth.

Practice asking the person out before your mirror or a friend. You may ask the person to go with you for "a cup of coffee" or to a film being shown at the library. "A cup of coffee" is easier because it doesn't sound like a real date. After all, you were headed in that direction and are just being friendly. It is also less threatening to ask someone out to a gathering at which "some of us will be getting together." Or you may rehearse asking the person to accompany you to a cultural event, such as an exhibition at a museum in town or a concert—like the invitation to coffee, it's sort of a date, but less anxiety inducing.

Target Behavior Level Ask the person out on a date. If the person says he or she has a previous engagement or can't make it, you may want to say something like, "That's too bad," or "I'm sorry you can't make it," and add something like, "Perhaps another time." You should be able to get a feeling for whether the person you asked out was just seeking an excuse or has a genuine interest in you and, as claimed, could not, in fact, accept the invitation.

Before asking the person out again, pay attention to his or her apparent comfort level when you return to small talk on a couple of occasions. If there is still a chance, the person should smile and return your eye contact. The other person may also offer you an invitation. In any event, if you are turned down twice, it would probably be pointless to ask a third time. But don't catastrophize the refusal. Look up. Note that the roof hasn't fallen in. The birds are still chirping in the trees. You still have to get that paper written. Then give someone else a chance to appreciate your fine qualities.

In Your Own Write

If you have a relationship that you'd like to continue, what are three things that you can do to enhance variety and maintain interest? (Hint: Perhaps you can try some new cultural activities together or go on trips together.)

1. _____
_____

2. _____
_____

3. _____
_____

What are three things you can do to indicate your enduring positive feelings and esteem?

1. _____
_____

2. _____
_____

3. _____
_____

What are three things that you (and your partner!) can do to enhance the fairness in your relationship, so that you both feel that you are getting as much out of the relationship as you are putting into it?

1. _____
_____

2. _____
_____

3. _____
_____

Continuation

Once a relationship is established, it enters the stage of continuation. The following factors foster continuation of relationships:

1. Seeking ways of enhancing variety and maintaining interest (e.g., willingness to try new social activities and—in sexual relationships— new ways of making love). Boredom, or falling into a rut, is a key problem in relationships.
2. Indicating enduring positive feelings and esteem (e.g., remembering birthdays and anniversaries and sending Valentine's Day cards). Evidence of low esteem, as shown by bickering and forgetting anniversaries and other occasions, damages relationships.

3. Lack of jealousy. Unfortunately, about 54 percent of adults report themselves to be jealous.[43] Feelings of jealousy render relationships less rewarding and lower the jealous party's self-esteem.[44]
4. Perceived fairness (e.g., in marriages, an equitable distribution of breadwinning, homemaking, and child-rearing chores). If, for example, the man insists that the woman has the sole responsibility for keeping the house and rearing the children, women who believe in dual-career families or sharing household tasks will be dissatisfied. Relationships are also more secure when both partners perceive them to be equitable—when they feel that they are getting out of them what they are putting into them.[45]
5. Mutual general satisfaction.

Jealousy   Jealous people are often dependent. They may have feelings of inadequacy and worry about sexual exclusivity.[46] Now that AIDS is upon the scene, of course, concerns about sexual exclusiveness can also extend to health.

Sad to say, many college students play jealousy "games." They flirt openly. They let their partners know about their interest in others. They may even manufacture tales to stir their partners to give them greater attention or to verify the depth of their partners' feelings.[47] And sometimes partners play jealousy games as revenge for infidelity.

Deterioration

The fourth stage in the evolution of relationships is deterioration. Deterioration, of course, is not necessarily desirable. Nor is it inevitable. Relationships are less likely to deteriorate when we are patient and put time and effort into improving them. On the other hand, relationships deteriorate when we decide to end them, when we allow deterioration to proceed unchecked, or when we fail to work at maintaining them. Deterioration usually begins when one or both partners view the relationship as less worthwhile than it had been.[48]

Partners respond to a relationship's deterioration in active or passive ways.[49] An active response means taking charge by doing things that may

IN YOUR OWN WRITE

Do you or your partner play jealousy games? What are they? Do they threaten your relationship? How?

_____
_____
_____
_____
_____
_____
_____

save the relationship (e.g., trying to work out differences, improving communication skills, or getting professional help) or making the decision to terminate the relationship. A passive response usually means waiting or doing nothing—either sitting back and letting problems resolve themselves or worsen until the relationship dies.

We encourage students to respond actively when relationships are deteriorating—not to permit things to happen to them. Rather than letting misery drag on, talk things over and decide to work together to iron out the wrinkles or to dissolve the relationship. It is irrational and destructive to believe that ideal relationships do not require work. We are never perfectly matched. Unless one of the couple is a doormat, there will be conflict. It is more useful to try to resolve conflicts than to close our eyes to them and have them linger.

TRUTH OR FICTION *Revisited*

There's a great deal that we can do if we want to forestall the deterioration of a relationship. But to do so, we need to talk about problems and make decisions.

Ending

The fifth and final stage of a relationship is its ending. Ending, like deterioration, is not inescapable. Factors that help prevent deteriorating relationships from ending include a commitment to persevere, persistence of some satisfaction in the relationship, and belief that it will work out in the end. We are also more likely to maintain relationships when we have made heavy investments in them and when other partners are not waiting in the wings.[50] It is easy to see why student relationships are less likely to endure than marriages. We are more likely to make investments in a marriage (bearing children and arranging for joint ownership of a home are heavy investments). Also, in college there are usually other attractive people all around us. But once we are in the world beyond college, there may be fewer obvious alternatives, especially if one partner remains at home during the day.

Why Do Relationships End? Researchers followed 200 college couples for two years, during which more than half broke up. Why? Boredom was the most commonly cited reason, followed by differences in interests and attitudes. Apparently, as the fires of passion waned, similarity became a more powerful determinant of continuation. If relationships are to last, "companionate love"—which is based on respect and unidealized knowledge of one's partner—is apparently at least as important as passion.

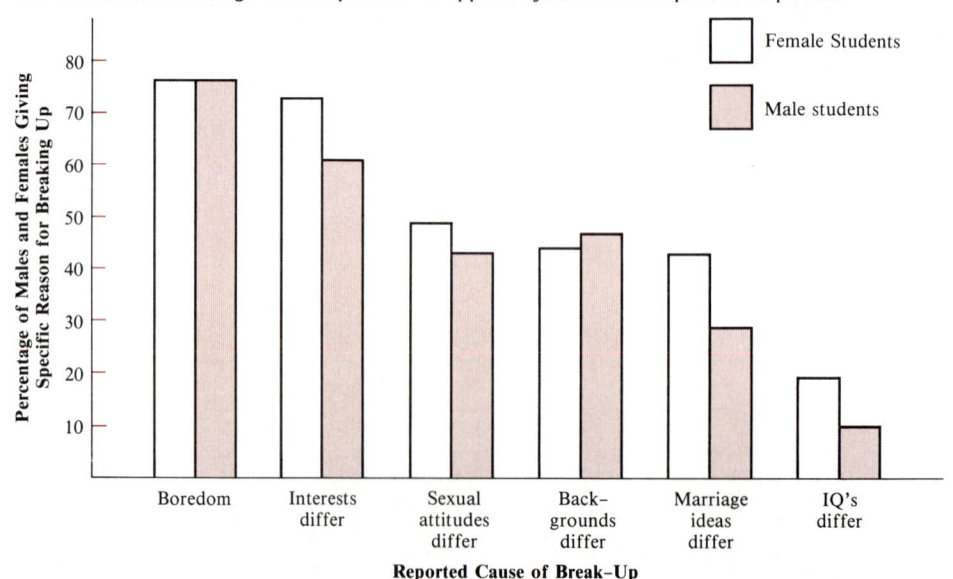

Of course, terminating relationships is not necessarily a bad thing, even if it is painful. When partners are incompatible and attempts to maintain the relationship have fallen through, termination allows both partners the chance of developing better relationships with others. A good reason for taking an active approach to handling deteriorating relationships is that they are more likely to be terminated prior to marriage, while the partners are young and there are no children who will get hurt. Partners are also more likely to attract new, more harmonious partners when they are young.

Why do college couples end their relationships? One group of researchers[51] followed 200 college couples for two years. During this period, more than half of them broke up. Figure 9.3 shows the reasons offered for the breaks. They can be condensed into a combination of boredom and recognition of dissimilarities in attitudes and interests. When the early passion fades, boredom and differences also give rise to a third factor—lessened mutual esteem.[52]

Once passion and idealization have begun to fade, couples have a better chance of maintaining relationships if they have developed "companionate love."[53] Companionate love is based on mutual respect, appreciation, loyalty, trust, and sharing of feelings. It includes some willingness to sacrifice. Companionate love is built on accurate knowledge of your partner's strengths and weaknesses, not idealization. It sounds a little like friendship.

LONELINESS

Being lonely differs from being alone. Being alone can mean pleasurable solitude—a chance to study, to listen to one's favorite music, or to reflect on the world and one's place in the world. But loneliness is a painful feeling in which we feel cut off or isolated. Many college students are lonely, even when they live on swarming campuses.

Students who are lonely are more likely than others to spend time by themselves, including weekends, and to eat dinner alone. They participate

> All the lonely people, Where do they all come from?
>
> "Eleanor Rigby," a Beatles song

Loneliness is a painful feeling in which people feel cut off or isolated from one another. Many college students are lonely, even though they live on swarming campuses. What can students do to overcome loneliness?

in fewer social activities and are unlikely to date.[54] Lonely people may know as many people as those who are not lonely, but their relationships are relatively superficial. They are unlikely to share confidences with their acquaintances.[55] Loneliness usually peaks in adolescence, when most of us are supplanting close ties to parents with peer relationships.

Causes of Loneliness

What are the causes of loneliness? Apparently they are many and complex, but lonely students have many of these earmarks:

1. They lack social skills. They are unresponsive to the feelings of others. They do not know how to make friends or how to handle conflicts.[56]
2. They fear social rejection.

TRUTH OR FICTION *Revisited*

So many students do turn out to be lonely because of fear of rejection.

3. They lack interest in other people.[57]
4. They lack empathy and understanding.[58]
5. They criticize themselves sharply because of their social difficulties and expect to fail in their dealings with others.[59]

QUESTIONNAIRE
The UCLA Loneliness Scale

How about you? Are you socially active or lonely most of the time? Below is a brief form of the UCLA Loneliness Scale. The scale is used extensively in research on loneliness. Answer items by using this code:

1 = Never
2 = Rarely
3 = Sometimes
4 = Often

When you have finished, you will find the answer key at the conclusion of the chapter.

_____ 1. How often do you feel unhappy doing so many things alone?
_____ 2. How often do you feel you have nobody to talk to?
_____ 3. How often do you feel you cannot tolerate being so alone?
_____ 4. How often do you feel as if nobody really understands you?
_____ 5. How often do you find yourself waiting for people to call or write?
_____ 6. How often do you feel completely alone?
_____ 7. How often do you feel you are unable to reach out and communicate with those around you?
_____ 8. How often do you feel starved for company?
_____ 9. How often do you feel it is difficult for you to make friends?
_____ 10. How often do you feel shut out and excluded by others?

6. They fail to engage in self-disclosure with possible friends.[60]
7. They are cynical about human nature. They expect the worst from people.
8. They expect too much too soon. For example, they misconstrue other people as aloof and antagonistic rather than naturally cautious in the early stages of relationships.[61]
9. They are generally pessimistic.
10. By and large, they assume that what happens to them is out of their own hands.[62]

How to Handle Loneliness

Psychologists have learned that we can do many things to develop social relationships and combat loneliness. Let's go through a list of them, and, as we do so, we'll review a few of the suggestions made in this chapter:

1. Challenge your feelings of pessimism. Adopt the attitude that things happen when you make them happen. This is as true of social relationships as it is of getting good grades.
2. Challenge your cynicism about human nature. Yes, lots of people are selfish and not worth knowing, but if you assume that all people are like that, you can doom yourself to a lifetime of loneliness. Your task is to find people who possess the qualities that you value.
3. Challenge the idea that failure in social relationships is awful and a valid reason for giving up on them. Sure, social rejection can be painful, but unless you happen to be Harrison Ford or Kim Basinger, you're not going to appeal to the majority of people. We must all learn to live with some rejection. But keep looking for the people who possess the qualities you value and who will find things of equal value in you.
4. Follow the suggestions for date-seeking spelled out in the chapter. Sit down at a table with people in the cafeteria, not off in a corner by yourself. Smile and say "Hi" to people who intrigue you. Practice opening lines for different occasions—and a few follow-up lines. Try them out in the mirror. (Stop being so hard on yourself!)
5. Make numerous social contacts. Join committees for student activities. Try intramural sports. Join social-action groups like the environmental group Greenpeace. Join clubs like the photography club or the ski club. Get on the school yearbook or newspaper staff.
6. Be assertive. Express your genuine opinions. (We'll talk more about becoming assertive in Chapter 10.)
7. Become a good listener. Ask people how they're "doing." Ask them for their opinions about classes, politics, the campus events of the day. Then actually *listen* to what they have to say. Tolerate diverse opinions; remember that no two of us are just alike. Maintain eye contact. Keep your face friendly. (No, you don't have to remain neutral and friendly if someone becomes insulting toward a religious or ethnic group.)
8. Give people the chance to get to know you. Exchange opinions and talk about your interests. Yes, you'll turn some people off—who doesn't?—but how else will you learn whether you and others share common ground?
9. Fight fair. Friends will inevitably disappoint you and you'll want to tell them about it. Do so—but fairly. You can start by asking if it's okay to be open about something. Then say, "I feel upset because you . . . " You can ask your friend if he or she realized that his or her behavior upset you. Try to work together to find a way to avoid recurrences. Finish by thanking your friend for helping you resolve the problem. (We'll learn more about resolving conflicts in Chapter 10.)

10. Remember that you're worthy of friends. It's true—warts and all. None of us is perfect. We're all unique, but you may connect with more people than you imagine. Give people a chance.
11. Go to the counseling center. Many thousands of students are lonely but don't know what to do about it. Others just haven't got the courage to approach other people. College counseling centers are very familiar with this problem of loneliness, and you should consider them a valuable resource. You might even ask if there's a group at the center for lonely students. What could be more perfect than that?

So how about you: "Will you, won't you, will you, won't you, will you join the dance?"

SUMMING UP

1. What qualities do you look for in friends? Are you a good friend?
2. Are fraternities and sororities important on your campus? Are there any on your campus that seem consistent with your values and interests?
3. How do you know when you're in love? What did Shakespeare mean when he wrote "love is blind"?
4. What do you find attractive in people? What do you look at first when you meet someone?
5. What qualities do you seek in a partner for a long-term, meaningful relationship?
6. Do you feel comfortable asking people out on dates? What can you do to improve your date-seeking skills?
7. What kinds of small talk do you use when you meet someone?
8. What kinds of things can you do to prevent a relationship from deteriorating?
9. Have you been lonely? Do you have any attitudes that contribute to loneliness?
10. What can you do to overcome loneliness?

Scoring Key for the "Love Scale"

The key for the Love Scale was developed with a sample of 220 undergraduates aged 19–24 from Northeastern University. Students signified whether they were "absolutely in love," "probably in love," "not sure," "probably not in love," or "definitely not in love" with a person they were seeing. Then they filled out the Love Scale items with that person in mind.

Table 9.2 displays the average score for each category. Mean scores for college men and women did not differ, so they were combined. If, for example, your Love Scale score for your partner is 78, your feelings may lie somewhere in between those of Northeastern University students who indicated that they were "probably in love" and "not sure."

TABLE 9.2. Love Scale Scores of Northeastern University Students.

CONDITION	N[a]	MEAN SCORES
Absolutely in love	56	89
Probably in love	45	80
Not sure	36	77
Probably not in love	40	68
Definitely not in love	43	59

[a] N = Number of students.

Be warned: Some students broke into arguments because their Love Scale scores differed by a few points! Don't take the scale too much to heart. Discrepant scores will not hold up in court as grounds for divorce.

Key for the "Brief Version of the UCLA Loneliness Scale"

Add your responses to attain your total score. In a *New York Times* article, Lear[63] suggested that respondents who attain a score of 30 or above might have significant pangs of loneliness. Students who are concerned about their feelings may want to discuss them at the college counseling center.

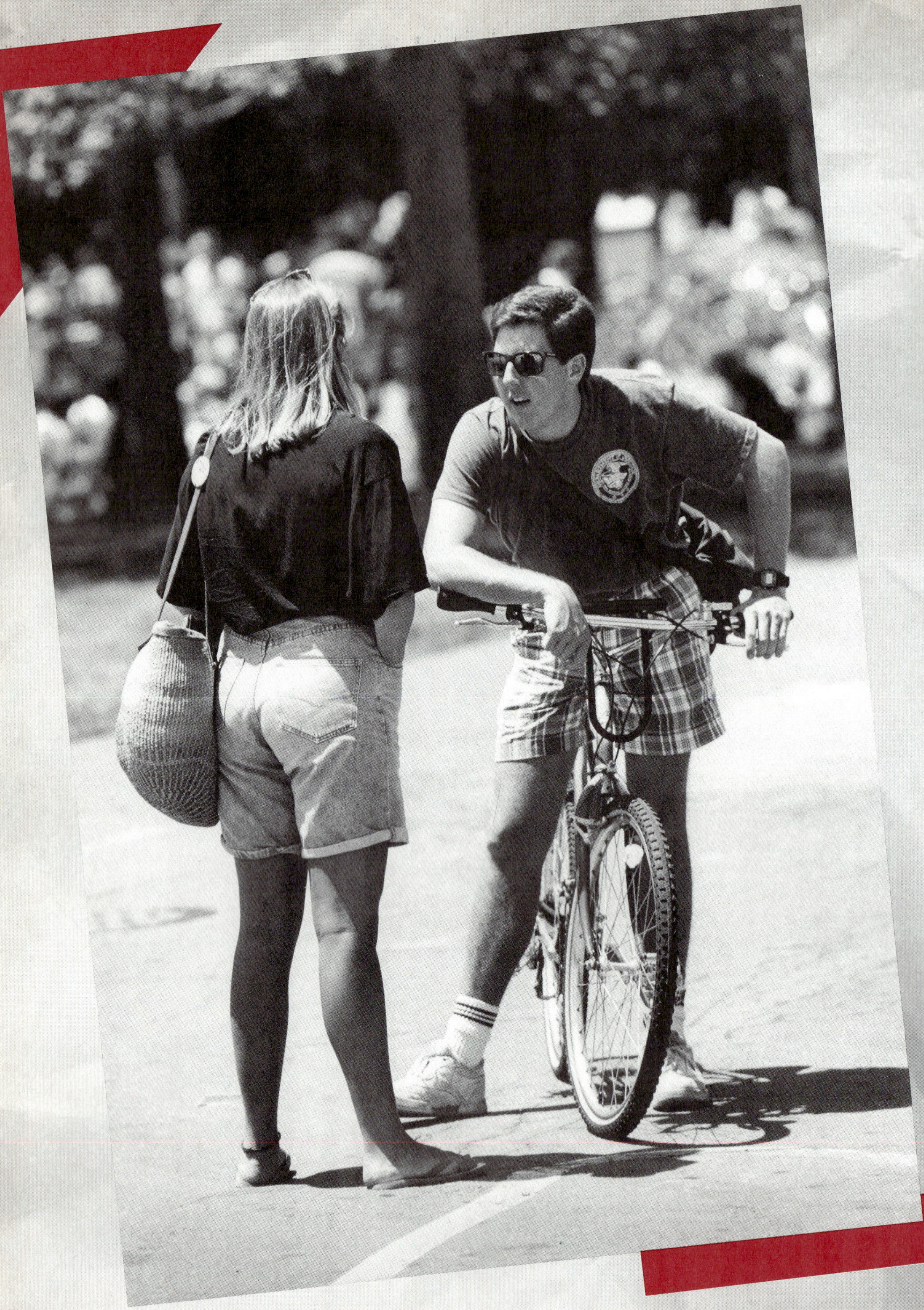

10

Resolving Social Conflicts

TRUTH OR FICTION?

___ Disagreement is destructive to a relationship.

___ It's best to get something off your chest immediately.

___ The most effective way to handle criticism from a friend or lover is to retaliate.

___ Relationships cannot prosper unless conflicts are resolved.

___ Skill in business is inconsistent with the traditional female sex-role stereotype.

___ In past centuries, girls were deemed unsuited to education.

___ Women are more talkative than men.

Only part of your college education is academic. College also prepares you for the larger world by introducing you to people with different value systems and social expectations. The diversity found among faculty and the student body provides a good deal of the stimulation found in the college experience—and also some of the conflict.

Conflict is part of the social fabric in the world at large, and conflict occurs on campus as well. Students encounter conflict with professors, other students, and their families. Unless students are doormats, it is practically impossible to evade at least an occasional conflict with a professor or a fellow student. Lack of skill in handling conflicts can transform social interactions into unbearable chores.

College is a laboratory not only for the development of general knowledge and occupational skills, but also for the formation of social skills. In this chapter, we focus on the social skills that are involved in handling social conflicts that are likely to arise with professors, other students—including roommates—family members, and lovers. We shall see that part of the job is clarifying our motives to ourselves when we get into conflicts. Part involves knowing what to say, and part lies in becoming a generally more assertive (not aggressive!) individual. Then we consider those conflicts that are bred by prejudice. We shall focus on two kinds of prejudice that are especially germane to college students: sexism and racism.

> The most immutable barrier in nature is between one man's thoughts and another's.
>
> WILLIAM JAMES

HOW TO HANDLE CONFLICTS IN RELATIONSHIPS

Conflict is inevitable—even with the most understanding roommate or spouse, even with the most supportive boyfriend or girlfriend. No two people agree on everything. No two roommates share the same expectations as to who should handle which chore.

Conflicts arise over things like money—for example, over how much should be spent for food, or over a roommate's leaving the lights on when he or she leaves the apartment. Conflicts arise from difficulties in communication (for example, not complaining until one explodes), personal interests (one partner in a relationship likes horror films and the other is turned off by them), sex (what kind? how much?), in-laws (is any example needed?), friends (for example, going out drinking with the boys or with the girls), and children (when to have them, how many, how to rear them).

When roommates and couples take up housekeeping, they are faced with the task of deciding who does what. When men and women live together, responsibilities are often delegated according to sex-role stereotypes. Women often get stuck with cleaning the floors and the bathrooms. Men may be more likely to make repairs and take out the garbage. When men take on an apartment, they usually have the bathrooms cleaned every few months, whether they need to be cleaned or not.*

When conflict arises, means such as the following may be of help.

Challenging Irrational Expectations

All college students (and nonstudents) disagree from time to time. We are more likely to accept this idea when it concerns friends and roommates. But when it comes to love relationships, some students expect that their

---

* All right, it's a pretty lame joke.

relationships should be flawless and erroneously believe that well-matched couples do not disagree.[1]

TRUTH OR FICTION *Revisited*

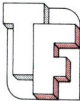

Disagreement is practically inevitable in a relationship. However, disagreements can be destructive when they are handled poorly.

They presume that conflict about sex, distribution of chores, or their partner's family signifies lack of love or that the relationship is on the rocks. Moreover, students with troubled relationships may irrationally believe that friends and lovers should somehow *know* what's disturbing them or that their friends and lovers are the way they are and can't (or won't) change.[2]

Negotiating Differences

In social relationships, one person frequently exercises power over others—deciding, for example, what they'll do in their spare time and who will do what around the apartment. But to constructively negotiate differences

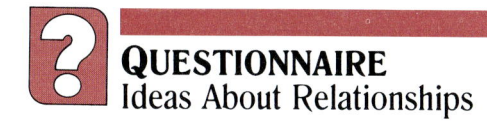

QUESTIONNAIRE
Ideas About Relationships

Here are some ideas about relationships. Write a checkmark next to any that have ever crossed your mind. Then see below.

1. "My parents (or friend, roommate, or lover) don't love me if they don't support me in everything I want or do." ____
2. "When people have a solid relationship, they don't raise their voices to one another." ____
3. "It's terrible if a conflict or a disagreement isn't resolved right away." ____
4. "If my roommate (or lover) really cared about the paper I have to get done, he (or she) would treat me more nicely." ____
5. "If my parents (or friend, roommate, or lover) really gave a damn about my anxiety (or feelings of depression, or pain in the stomach), they wouldn't be acting this way." ____
6. "My roommate leaves the radio that loud just to bug me." ____
7. "My roommate leaves the cap off the toothpaste just to get to me." ____
8. "When people really care about one another, they can tell if something's on their friends' (or lovers') minds." ____
9. "If my lover really cared about me, he (or she) would know what I need and I wouldn't have to try to explain it." ____
10. "You don't have to work at a good relationship. Things just fall into place." ____

Actually each of these ideas is irrational and harmful to relationships. They all enlarge conflicts and heighten the stress in relationships. The belief that people who care about us should know what pleases and displeases us, even though we don't tell them, is especially destructive. Our friends and lovers may know that there's something on our minds if we wear perpetually crabby faces, but they still can't read our minds. So we should be frank and clear about our wants and our feelings.[3]

about household chores, the volume on the stereo, and so on, it is helpful for students to share the power in the relationship.[4] When relationships get off on the wrong foot, so that one person dominates another, differences in bargaining power may impair negotiations. Disadvantaged students often are not heard, resentments can mount, and relationships may consequently be dissolved.

The following method helps spouses and roommates handle discrepancies in bargaining power in the distribution of chores. First, three columns are drawn on a sheet of paper (Table 10.1). The title *Chores* and each spouse or roommate's name head a column. Then the chores are listed. We have written in five chores. What other things have to be taken care of in your room, apartment, or house? List those that you can think of in the blank spaces.

TABLE 10.1. Chores That Can Be Used in Negotiating Differences.

CHORES	LESLIE'S PREFERENCES	RONNIE'S PREFERENCES
Washing dishes	_____	_____
Cooking	_____	_____
Scrubbing the floors	_____	_____
Shopping for food	_____	_____
Shopping for toiletries	_____	_____
Doing the laundry	_____	_____
Cleaning shower, toilet, etc.	_____	_____
Vacuuming	_____	_____
_____	_____	_____
_____	_____	_____
_____	_____	_____
_____	_____	_____

Once the list is drawn up, roommates can rank them according to their desirability. Ronnie and Leslie ranked the least "yucky" task as a 1, and, since there were 12 items on the list, the most yucky task was ranked as 12. Ronnie wound up doing the laundry and washing the dishes because Ronnie had ranked them as not too yucky (5 and 6) and Leslie thought they were quite a bit yuckier. Leslie wound up vacuuming (3) and paying the bills (a chore that was added to the list) in a similar manner. The roommates agreed to alternate washing the floors and cleaning the bathroom, chores that both had ranked as relatively yucky. They specified a schedule for the yuckiest chores so that they wouldn't put them off and eventually get into an argument over them.

Exchanging New Behavior

Another method for resolving conflicts is to make a contract to exchange new behavior patterns. We all do things that irk the people we socialize and live with (yes, even you). So students can list the behavior patterns that disturb each other and modify their own obnoxious behavior patterns in exchange for their roommates', lovers', or families' modifying theirs. Consider the following sample contract:

> RONNIE: I agree to keep the stereo off after 8:00 P.M. every weekday evening if you agree not to allow your friends to smoke in the apartment.

LESLIE: I agree to replace the toilet paper when we run out if you, in return, clean your hair out of the bathroom sink.

Increasing Positive Interactions

When relationships are disturbed, we tend to focus on the negative. But it is also possible to accentuate the positive. Students who get along with one another tend to behave positively toward one another. And happy dating and married couples tend to show each other more pleasurable behavior than do discontented couples.[5] Think for a minute. If your roommate or the person you have been seeing has been trying to bring more pleasure into your life, have you been appreciative or have you worn a grumpy face? If your own efforts to be nice have gone unnoticed, why not try saying something like, "Hey! Notice what's going on! I'm admitting that you're right. I respect your point of view and I'm even smiling!"

Types of positive interactions that enhance relationships are shown in Table 10.2. Most of them apply to friendships and roommates, although a couple apply more directly to dating couples. There are a few blank spaces at the end. Can you think of additional positive interactions?

Now let us consider one of the most basic ways of resolving conflicts in social relationships: enhancing communication skills.

TABLE 10.2. Types of Positive Interactions.

TYPE OF INTERACTION	EXAMPLES
Paying attention, listening	Actually turning off the TV or putting down the book when your roommate is trying to tell you something; encouraging your friend to tell you about a disappointing grade
Agreeing with the person (that is, when you actually agree)	Saying "Yes, you're right," rather than saying nothing or changing the subject
Showing approval when you are pleased by the other person	Telling your instructor, "I really enjoyed that discussion"; telling your roommate, "Wow, that bathroom looks like we had Mr. Clean in here"
Positive physical interactions such as hugging and touching	Giving a friend a warm handshake and patting him on the back when you haven't seen him for a few days; hugging a friend who looks depressed
Showing concern	Asking your roommate how a term paper is coming along; asking a friend how his or her family is getting along when you return from a vacation
Showing humor	Laughing and smiling; sharing a funny story with a friend
Compromising on disagreements	You always want the stereo off and your roommate wants it on, so you try to find days of the week and times of the day when it is least likely to disturb you and can be left on
Complying with reasonable requests	Picking up a book at the library for your roommate; not leaving your blow dryer dangling from the outlet above the bathroom mirror
_____	_____
_____	_____
_____	_____

ENHANCING COMMUNICATION SKILLS

We tend to take communication for granted. After all, most of us communicate with other students, our instructors, our friends, and our families on a regular basis. But do your methods of communication help you learn about other people's needs? Do they communicate your own needs effectively? Are you capable of criticizing someone you love? Of disagreeing with a professor without hurting feelings or jeopardizing the relationship? Can you accept criticism and keep your self-respect? What do you do when you and your roommate or your lover are at an impasse?

Some students communicate more effectively than others, perhaps because they are more sensitive to other people's needs or perhaps because their parents provided good models as communicators. But communication skills can be learned at any time. Learning requires time and work, but the following guidelines should prove helpful if you want to communicate more effectively.[6]

IN YOUR OWN WRITE

One of the most complicated aspects of communication is getting started. Let's assume that you are upset with your roommate or spouse because he or she leaves the bathroom in bad shape. How do you go about bringing the issue up?

Write down some of your ideas in the spaces provided, and then compare them with the suggestions that follow. Perhaps we'll be on the same wavelength. Perhaps you'll have a better idea.

1. _____
   _____

2. _____
   _____

3. _____
   _____

Getting Started

So, how do you get started on tough topics? Here are a couple of possibilities.

Talking About Talking   You can start by talking about talking. For example, you can explain to your roommate that it is difficult for you to talk about problems and conflicts: "You know, I've always found it awkward to find a way of bringing things up," or, "You know, I think other people have an easier time than I do when it comes to talking about some things." You can allude to troublesome things that happened in the past when you attempted to resolve conflicts. This approach encourages your roommate to invite you to proceed.

Requesting Permission to Bring Up a Topic   Another possibility is to request permission to raise an issue. For example, you can tell your roommate, "There's something on my mind. Do you have a few minutes? Is now a good time to tell you about it?" Or you can say, "There's something that we need to talk about, but I'm not sure how to bring it up. Can you help me with it?"

Getting started talking is one of the most difficult aspects of communicating. Try "talking about talking" or requesting permission to raise a troubling topic.

Listening to the Other Side

Hearing the other person out is an essential aspect of resolving conflict. Listening not only gives you information; it also serves as a model for the other person, demonstrating how he or she can better listen to you.

IN YOUR OWN WRITE

Imagine that you and your instructor have been going back and forth about a disputed grade on an essay question. Your instructor is trying to explain why your essay doesn't say quite what you thought it said. What are some things you can do or say to listen better? Write your ideas in the spaces provided and then check below.

1. _____
   _____
2. _____
   _____
3. _____
   _____

Listening Actively First, adopt the attitude that you might actually learn something—or perceive things from another vantage point—by listening. Second, recognize that even though the other person is doing the talking, you need not sit back passively. In other words, it is not helpful to stare off into space while your instructor is talking, or to offer a begrudging "mm-hmm" now and then to be "polite." Instead, you can listen actively by maintaining eye contact with your instructor. You can also modify your facial expression to show that you understand his or her feelings and ideas. For example, nod your head when it is appropriate.

Listening actively also involves asking helpful questions, such as, "Would you please give me an example?" or, "Could you tell me what this sentence said to you?"

Paraphrasing You can use paraphrasing to show that you understand what your instructor is trying to express. In paraphrasing, you recast or

Resolving Social Conflicts

restate what the other person is saying to confirm your comprehension. For example, if your instructor says, "This part about Thoreau describes his life at Walden Pond accurately, but the question asked you to interpret his aphorism that you should avoid doing things that require new clothing," you can paraphrase by saying something like, "So it seems that I strayed from the question."

Reinforcing the Other Person for Communicating Even when you disagree with what the other person is saying, you can maintain generally good relations and keep the channels of communication open by saying something like, "I appreciate your spending this much time with me," or, "I hope you'll think it's okay if I continue to see that point differently, but I'm glad that we had a chance to talk about it."

Using Unconditional Positive Regard Psychologists use the concept of unconditional positive regard to describe feelings of warmth and acceptance that are not contingent on another person's behavior from minute to minute.[7] In other words, many parents continue to have unconditional positive regard for their children even if their children disappoint them in their behavior from time to time. In the same way, positive student relationships with friends, lovers, and instructors can be maintained when other people do something that is upsetting. For example, even when one disagrees with a lover, it is possible to show that the lover is still valued as a person. One can say something like, "I care for you very much, but it annoys me when you . . ." rather than, "You're really contemptible for doing . . ."

Learning About the Other Person's Needs

Listening is basic to learning about another person's needs, but sometimes it helps to go a few steps further.

Asking Questions to Draw the Other Person Out You can phrase questions that will help you learn more. In Chapter 7, we noted that test questions tend to be short-answer and focused, or else essay-type questions, which are more open-ended. Similarly, the questions you ask to draw other people out can suggest a focused or limited range of answers, or they can be open-ended.

IN YOUR OWN WRITE

Things seem tense between you and your roommate, but you're not sure what's going on. In fact, you're not even sure that your relationship is the problem. What are some things you can do or say to learn about your roommate's needs? Write some of your ideas in the spaces provided and then see below.

1. _____
   _____

2. _____
   _____

3. _____
   _____

These yes-or-no questions request a concrete, focused response:

"Do you think I leave the toothpaste on the sink just to bug you?"

"Does it bother you that I go to bed later than you do?"

"Do you think that I do things that are inconsiderate when you're studying for a test?"

Yes-or-no questions afford specific information. Open-ended questions, however, allow you to explore broader issues. Here are some examples of open-ended questions that can be used with roommates, instructors, and lovers:

To a roommate: "What do you think of us as roommates?" "Are there any things I should know about?" "How do you feel about this apartment?"

To an instructor: "How do you think I'm doing in this course?" "What do you think of me as a business major?" "Is there anything you think I should be doing that I'm not?"

To a lover: "What things do you like best about our relationship?" or, "Does anything disappoint you about our relationship?" "Is there anything that you think we need to change?"

If the other person finds open-ended questions too general, you can provide examples. Consider the questions to your instructor. If your instructor asks you, "What do you mean?" you can follow up with something like the questions on the next page.

IN YOUR OWN WRITE

Write down some open-ended questions that you think might help you learn more about the needs of your friends and family:

Open-ended questions to a friend:

1. _____
2. _____
3. _____

Open-ended questions to your family:

1. _____
2. _____
3. _____

Resolving Social Conflicts

Open-ended question	Follow-up question
"How do you think I'm doing in this course?"	"Do you think I grasp the subject matter?" "Are my assignments good enough in quality?"
"What do you think of me as a business major?"	"Do you think I'm in the right field for me?" ("Why?" or "Why not?") "Am I doing as well as other business majors?" "Do I seem to have the attributes of people who are successful in the field?"
"Is there anything you think I should be doing that I'm not?"	"Are there any ways in which I'm falling short of your expectations?" "Do you think there are some things I could be working on to improve myself?" "Does it seem to you that I'm living up to my potential?"

Open-ended questions can provide you with information that you could not have anticipated. So if the other person has trouble with the broadness of the question, you can follow up by narrowing it a bit, but try not to make it so specific that you forego the chance of learning anything important.

Using Self-Disclosure Remember that self-disclosure is an important aspect of developing relationships. You can also use self-disclosure as a way of learning about other people's needs, because by communicating your own feelings and ideas, you invite reciprocation. If you want to find out if your roommate is concerned about your relationship with a friend, you can try something like, "You know, I have to confess that sometimes I worry that you feel much closer to your sorority sisters than to me. I get the feeling that I serve a certain role in your life, but that there are some things that you would consider doing only with them . . ."

Granting Permission for the Other Person to Say Something That Might Upset You You can ask your roommate, instructor, or friend to level with you about an irksome issue. You can say that you recognize that it might be awkward to discuss it, but that you will try your best to listen conscientiously and not get too disturbed. You can also limit communication to one such difficult issue per conversation. If the whole emotional dam were to burst, the task of mopping up could be overpowering.

IN YOUR OWN WRITE

Imagine that you are having some difficulties with an instructor. You have the feeling that your instructor does not like you because the two of you have disagreed heatedly in class on certain issues. You also wonder whether the instructor's feelings (presuming they are negative) have translated into poor grades on some of your assignments. Write some ways that you can request your instructor to reexamine his or her evaluation of you and then check below.

1. _____

2. _____

3. _____

Making Requests

A basic part of resolving social conflicts is asking other people to change their behavior—to do something in a different way, or to stop doing something that is painful or harmful to you. So the skill of making requests now comes to the fore.

The first step in making requests is attitudinal—being willing to take charge of what happens to you.

Taking Responsibility for What Happens to You The initial step in making requests is internal or psychological—taking responsibility for the events in your life. If you want other people to change their behavior, you must be amenable to requesting the change. Then, if others refuse to change, you must take responsibility for the way in which you will deal with the standoff.

Being Specific It helps to be specific in requesting changes. For example, it will probably accomplish little to say to your instructor, "Be nicer to me." Your instructor may not realize that his or her behavior is *not* nice and may not understand your request. It is probably more useful to say something like, "I would appreciate it if you would have another look at this assignment. I feel that I was right on target in answering your questions." Or, "I am concerned about your tone of voice with me in class. It seems very harsh and I would appreciate it if you would be more receptive to my expressing my points of view, even if you disagree with them."

Of course, you can precede your specific requests with openers such as, "There's something on my mind. Is this a good time for me to bring it up with you?" or, "You know, it's hard bringing up certain things with professors, because sometimes professors think you're challenging their power when you're only asking for a fair hearing." These ways of getting started may encourage the professor to try to see things from your point of view.

Using "I-Talk" Notice that the above examples make liberal use of the word *I*. Using the word *I* serves many purposes. For one thing, it is self-assertive. In fact, psychologists who help students and other people become more assertive often encourage them to use the words *I, me,* and *my* in their speech.[8] For example, saying "I would appreciate it if you would reevaluate my assignment" will probably attain better results than "Do you reevaluate assignments when students ask about them?" Saying "I find it very painful when you use a harsh voice with me in class" is probably more effective than, "Sometimes students' feelings get hurt when professors speak to them harshly in front of the class."

It can be helpful to practice *I*-talk in front of a mirror or with a friend before using it with other people. In this way, you can see whether your facial expression and tone of voice are consistent with what you are saying, and friends might also give you pointers on the content of what you are saying.

Delivering Criticism

Delivering criticism effectively is a skill. It requires focusing other people's attention on the problem and changing their behavior without inducing resentment or reducing them to trembling masses of guilt or fear.

Evaluating Your Motives First try to evaluate your goals forthrightly. Is it your primary intention to punish the other person, or are you more interested in gaining cooperation? If your goal is punishment, you may as well be coarse and disparaging, but if your goal is to resolve conflicts, a tactful approach may be in order.

IN YOUR OWN WRITE

Put yourself in this situation. You've been waiting for a phone call about a part-time job, and it came. There's just one problem: Your roommate was in the apartment at the time and didn't get the name or number. It's happened before and this time you can't let the problem go. You need to say something—in fact, something fairly critical. But what?

Write down some of the things that you might do or say in the spaces provided. Then check the text discussion of delivering criticism.

1. _____

2. _____

3. _____

Picking the Right Time and Place Deliver criticism privately—not in front of other students or faculty members. Other people have a right to be upset when you express criticism in public. Making private matters public induces indignation and cuts off communication. But if you're not certain whether the time and place are right, you can try asking permission. You can ask, "There's something on my mind. Is it okay if we talk about it here and now?"

TRUTH OR FICTION *Revisited*

It is *not* necessarily best to get things off your chest at once. It may be more effective to find the proper time and place.

Being Specific It is even more important to be specific in delivering criticism than in making requests. By being specific about the *behavior* that disturbs you, you bypass the trap of disparaging the other person's personality or motives. In other words, it is more effective to tell your roommate, "I could lose this job because you didn't write down the message," than "You're completely irresponsible" or "You're a flake." Similarly, it is more effective to say, "The bathroom looks and smells dirty when you throw your underwear on the floor" than "You're a filthy pig." It is more to the point (and less intimidating) to complain about specific, modifiable behavior than to try to overhaul another person's personality.

Expressing Displeasure in Terms of Your Own Feelings It is less threatening to express displeasure in terms of your own feelings than to attack the other person.[9] Attacks often arouse defensive behavior and, sometimes, retaliation, rather than resolve conflict. For example, say, "You know, it's really bad news for me when an important message doesn't get through." Don't say, "You're so self-absorbed that you never think about anyone else." In the example of confronting the professor who has been speaking to you harshly in front of the class, it can be more effective to say, "You know, it really *upsets me* and, frankly, it frightens me when you speak to me so harshly in front of the class" than "You're a totally inconsiderate person."

250   Chapter 10

IN YOUR OWN WRITE

Here are three situations in which it is appropriate to express displeasure. We've written in some (very bad!) examples of expressing displeasure by attacking the other person. For each example, write in a way of expressing displeasure in terms of your own feelings so that there is some chance of resolving the situation rather than making it worse.

Situation	Expressing displeasure by attacking the other person	Expressing displeasure in terms of your own feelings
Your instructor asks you if you have been looking at another student's paper during a test. (You haven't been.)	You say, "You've got some nerve accusing me of cheating! Who the hell do you think you are?"	
It was your roommate's turn to bring in food for dinner, but he forgot.	You say, "What's the matter with you, space brain? Do I look like the maid or something?"	
You're trying to study in the library, and the student in the next carrel keeps on banging his foot nervously against the wall.	You say, "Look, this is a library. If you've got bugs up your leg, why don't you check yourself into the infirmary?"	

Keeping Criticism and Complaints to the Present How many times have you been in an argument and heard things like, "You never appreciated me!" or "Last summer you did the same thing!" Bringing up the past during conflicts muddles current issues and heightens resentments. When your roommate forgets to jot down the details of the message, it is more useful to note that "This was a vital phone call" than "Three weeks ago you didn't tell me about the phone call from Chris and as a result I missed out on seeing *Rambo Meets Crocodile Dundee.*" It's better to leave who did what to whom last year alone. It may also be unprofitable to say to your lover, "Whenever I call my mother you always manage to find something to fight about afterwards!" Try to resolve current issues rather than connect them to every imaginable conflict that separates you from the other person.

Attempting to Express Criticism Positively Just as your second author was about to write this section, she had a look at built-in bookcases that were being painted in her office. Things generally looked good, but she was concerned that there were dark spaces between the edges of some of the shelves and the wall, both of which were being painted white. Rather than say, "Could you caulk the spaces between the shelves and the wall?" she said, "This is some good job you're doing," and she pointed in the general direction of some of the edges. The painter replied, "It's comin'

Resolving Social Conflicts

good, but I gotta caulk those shelves again." Maybe she was lucky, but the story points out that you can sometimes call attention to problems in positive ways. In so doing, you avoid inducing resentments and negativism.

When possible, express criticism positively and combine it with a concrete request. For example, when your roommate forgets to jot down the details of the message, you can say something like, "You know, you're normally very thoughtful. Whenever I need help, I feel that I can ask you for it. Now I need help from you when somebody calls me and I'm out. Would you please write down the messages for me?" Or you can say, "You know, you're really a much better cook than I am. I really look forward to the

QUESTIONNAIRE
The Rathus Assertiveness Schedule

Being assertive is not simply a matter of speaking up. It includes expressing your authentic feelings—positive as well as negative—standing up for your legitimate rights, and refusing requests that impress you as unreasonable.[10] Being assertive also means withstanding improper social pressures (for example, refusing to participate in repulsive hazing activities), disobeying authority figures who you believe are making immoral demands, and refusing to conform to group standards that run counter to your own beliefs (for example, declining to use drugs even when it seems that "everyone's doing it"). Assertive behavior also means expressing positive feelings like love and admiration. It's as assertive to tell a professor that you enjoyed a class as to suggest ways to improve a class.

Similarly, assertive behavior involves initiating new relationships—friendships and romances. Assertive students also try to persuade others to join them in worthwhile social and political enterprises. They often take leadership roles in political campaigns, conservationist groups, and other activities.

Assertive behavior is to be distinguished from aggressive behavior. Aggressive behavior includes attacks—both verbal and physical—threats, and insults.

How assertive are you? Do you demand your rights, or do you permit others to treat you like a doormat? Do you vocalize your genuine feelings or what you think others want to hear? Do you launch relationships with alluring people, or do you shy away from them?

You can gain insight into how assertive you are by taking the following questionnaire.[11] When you have finished, turn to the scoring key at the end of the chapter to see how to compute your score. (The asterisks are explained there.) You can also use the key to compare your assertiveness to that of students from campuses across the United States.

Directions: Indicate how well each item describes you by using this code:

    3 = very much like me
    2 = rather like me
    1 = slightly like me
  −1 = slightly unlike me
  −2 = rather unlike me
  −3 = very unlike me

_____ 1. Most people seem to be more aggressive and assertive than I am.*

_____ 2. I have hesitated to make or accept dates because of shyness.*

_____ 3. When the food served at a restaurant is not done to my satisfaction, I complain about it to the waiter or waitress.

_____ 4. I am careful to avoid hurting other people's feelings, even when I feel that I have been injured.*

next thing you're whipping up," rather than, "You rarely offer to do your share of the cooking, and I'm sick of it." Or you can tell your roommate, "You do such a good job on the bathroom that it really makes a difference when you haven't gotten to it for a while," rather than, "Would it really kill you to stick to the schedule we agreed on and clean the bathroom?"

Making requests and delivering criticism are examples of assertive behavior. Before moving on to the next topic, ways of receiving criticism, why not take the questionnaire below to see how assertive you are in comparison to other college students.

_____ 5. If a salesperson has gone to considerable trouble to show me merchandise that is not quite suitable, I have a difficult time saying "No."*

_____ 6. When I am asked to do something, I insist upon knowing why.

_____ 7. There are times when I look for a good, vigorous argument.

_____ 8. I strive to get ahead as well as most people in my position.

_____ 9. To be honest, people often take advantage of me.*

_____ 10. I enjoy starting conversations with new acquaintances and strangers.

_____ 11. I often don't know what to say to attractive persons of the opposite sex.*

_____ 12. I hesitate to make phone calls to business establishments and institutions.*

_____ 13. I would rather apply for a job or for admission to a college by writing letters than by going through with personal interviews.*

_____ 14. I find it embarrassing to return merchandise.*

_____ 15. If a close and respected relative were annoying me, I would smother my feelings rather than express my annoyance.*

_____ 16. I have avoided asking questions for fear of sounding stupid.*

_____ 17. During an argument I am sometimes afraid that I will get so upset that I will shake all over.*

_____ 18. If a famed and respected lecturer makes a comment that I think is incorrect, I have the audience hear my point of view as well.

_____ 19. I avoid arguing over prices with clerks and salespeople.*

_____ 20. When I have done something important or worthwhile, I manage to let others know about it.

_____ 21. I am open and frank about my feelings.

_____ 22. If someone has been spreading false and bad stories about me, I see him or her as soon as possible and have a talk about it.

_____ 23. I often have a hard time saying "No."*

_____ 24. I tend to bottle up my emotions rather than make a scene.*

_____ 25. I complain about poor service in a restaurant and elsewhere.

_____ 26. When I am given a compliment, I sometimes just don't know what to say.*

_____ 27. If a couple near me in a theater or at a lecture were conversing rather loudly, I would ask them to be quiet or to take their conversation elsewhere.

_____ 28. Anyone attempting to push ahead of me in a line is in for a good battle.

_____ 29. I am quick to express an opinion.

_____ 30. There are times when I just can't say anything.*

IN YOUR OWN WRITE

Put yourself in this situation. You're getting started on an assignment, and your roommate surprises you with, "It's about time you did something about the bathroom." You feel threatened and irritated, but you manage to stop and think before saying anything.

So what do you do or say? Write some possible answers in the spaces provided, and then compare your ideas with those presented below.

1. _____

2. _____

3. _____

Receiving Criticism

> Honest criticism is hard to take, particularly from a relative, a friend, an acquaintance, or a stranger.
>
> FRANKLIN P. JONES

Delivering criticism can be tricky, especially when you want to inspire cooperation. But receiving criticism can be even trickier. Nevertheless, the following suggestions offer some help.

Clarifying Your Goals When you hear "It's time you did something about . . . ," it would be understandable if the hairs on the backs of your arms did a headstand; after all, it's a rather blunt challenge. And when we are confronted harshly, we are likely to become defensive and think of retaliating. But if your objective is to resolve rather than intensify conflict, take a few moments to stop and think. To resolve conflicts, we need to learn about the other person's concerns, keep lines of communication open, and find ways of changing problem behavior.

So when your roommate says, "It's about time you did something about the bathroom," stop and think before you summon up your most menacing voice and say "Just what the hell is that supposed to mean?" Ask yourself what you want to find out.

Asking Clarifying Questions When you are delivering criticism, it helps to be specific. Similarly, when you are receiving criticism, encourage the other person to be specific. Rather than contributing to a shouting match, it might be helpful to learn whether the criticism is intended as the opening salvo of a war that's about to erupt or is limited to a problem with the bathroom. You can help your roommate be specific and, perhaps, avert the worst, by asking clarifying questions such as "Can you tell me exactly what you mean?" or, "The bathroom?"

Consider a situation in which a friend or lover says something like, "You know, you're one of the most irritating people I know." Again, rather than retaliating and hurting the relationship further, you can say something like, "How about foregoing the character assassination and telling me what I did that's bothering you?" This response assertively requests an end to insults and requests that the other person be specific.

Acknowledging the Criticism Even when you disagree with criticism, you can keep lines of communication open by saying something like "I hear you," or—in the case of the battle of the bathroom—"I understand that the tub and toilet don't meet with your standards. I only had time to give them a once-over."

On the other hand, if you are at fault, you can acknowledge that forthrightly. For example, you can say, "You're right. It was my day to clean the bathroom and it totally slipped my mind" or "I was so busy, I just couldn't get to it." Now the two of you should look for a way to work out the problem. When you acknowledge criticism, it is the other person's social obligation to back off a bit and look for ways in which to improve the situation. But what if your roommate then becomes abusive and says something like, "So you admit you blew it?" You might then try a little education in conflict resolution. You could say, "I admitted that I was at fault. If you're willing to work with me to find a way to handle it, great; but I'm not going to let you pound me into the ground over it."

Rejecting the Criticism Now, if you think that you were not at fault—for example, that your understanding with your roommate was different—express your feelings. Use "*I*-talk" and be specific. Don't seize the opportunity to angrily point out your roommate's shortcomings. By doing so, you may shut down lines of communication.

Negotiating Differences Remember that when the other person has a point, it can be helpful to negotiate your differences. You may want to say something like, "Would it help if I . . . ?" And if there's something about your obligation to clean the bathroom that seems totally out of place, perhaps you and your roommate can work out an exchange—that is, you are relieved of cleaning the bathroom in exchange for taking on a chore that your roommate finds odious.

If none of these approaches helps resolve the conflict, it could be because the other person has a hidden agenda and is using the comment about the bathroom as a way of getting you both worked up. You may find out by saying something like, "I've been trying to find a way to resolve this thing, but nothing I say seems to be helping. Is this really about the bathroom, or are there other things on your mind?"

And notice that we haven't suggested that you seize the opportunity to strike back by saying, "Who're you to complain about the bathroom? What about your breath and that pig sty you call your bedroom?" Retaliation is tempting, but you can more profitably use the college years to find ways of resolving conflicts without becoming aggressive.

TRUTH OR FICTION *Revisited*

Retaliation is an inferior way to handle criticism—that is, if your goal is to resolve conflict.

Taking criticism isn't easy, whether it's as a student, a worker, or a marriage partner. But it's a bit easier when you remember that you're not perfect and that some criticism is bound to be headed your way from time to time. Learn to handle it now. Also remember that your goals in receiving criticism ought to be to find out about the other person's concerns, to keep lines of communication open, and to discover or negotiate ways of resolving problems. But of course you need not accept verbal abuse and should speak up loudly and clearly when criticism overshoots acceptable limits.

Handling Impasses

At one point when he was an undergraduate, your first author had the idealistic notion that all of the world's problems, including his own, could be resolved if people were willing to communicate with each other. Perhaps

Resolving Social Conflicts

IN YOUR OWN WRITE

Let's return to an issue that was raised in Chapter 1. Assume that you and your philosophy professor have irreconcilable differences over whether women should have the right to have an abortion. The two of you have been back and forth over it in class a few times. Your professor seems to be getting heated up about the issue, and you suspect that you are beginning to sound a bit shrill. What kinds of things can you say or do to handle the standoff? Write your ideas in the spaces provided and then consider the text suggestions on handling impasses.

1. _____
   _____

2. _____
   _____

3. _____
   _____

not. Communication does help, but people sometimes have profound, substantial disagreements. Even when their communication skills are excellent, now and then they reach an impasse.

Looking at the Situation from the Other Person's Perspective It may be possible to resolve some of the conflict by (honestly!) saying something like, "I still disagree with you, but given your premises, I can understand why you take your position." If that sounds stuffy to you, try, "I don't see it that way, but I can see where you're coming from." In this way, you confirm your opponent's honesty and good will. So you may lessen tensions.

Seeking Validating Information On the other hand, if you do not follow the other person's logic, you can say something like, "Please believe me: I'm trying very hard to look at this from your point of view, but I can't follow your reasoning. Would you try to help me understand your point of view?"

Taking a Break Sometimes when we reach a stalemate, it helps to allow the problem to "incubate" for a while.[12] If you and the person with whom you are in conflict allow each other's viewpoints to incubate, perhaps a resolution will dawn on one of you later on. If you wish, schedule a follow-up discussion so that the issue won't be swept under the rug.

Tolerating Differentness Remember that college is a broadening experience. Many of us had backgrounds in which we were exposed to limited points of view on social, political, and religious matters. However, the United States is a pluralistic society, and part of our endurance and our ability to form a consensus in time of crisis depends on our ability to tolerate discrepant points of view. Even if we maintain our major allegiances with people similar in background in our choice of college, fraternity or sorority, and personal friends, we must eventually swim in broader social seas if we are to find our places in the business world. Moreover, we are all unique and cannot agree across the board even with people who share our backgrounds. So the ability to respect or at least tolerate each other's differentness helps us cope from day to day. When we have a solid sense of who we are as individuals and what we stand for, we are more apt to be able to tolerate differentness in others.[13]

TRUTH OR FICTION *Revisited*

Relationships can continue and improve even when we reach impasses. But it is important for us to tolerate differentness in other people if relationships are to do so.

Agreeing to Disagree When all else fails, we can agree to disagree on various issues. You can remain a solid, respected student, and your professor can remain a well-informed, effective teacher even when the two of you disagree on issues. You can get along generally with your roommates even if they come from different backgrounds and are at the other end of the political spectrum. You can handle an impasse by focusing on things that you and other people have in common, such as the desire to participate in an interesting, fairly run class.

PREJUDICE

College is a microcosm of society at large, and prejudice is found on campus as well as off campus. Social scientists define prejudice as an attitude toward a group. Prejudices influence people to evaluate group members in negative ways and stir up feelings of dislike or hatred. Prejudices may influence us to expect that target group members will be poor students or workers, or that they will stick together and ostracize outsiders. At worst, we may assume that the objects of our prejudices are basically criminals or subhuman.

Vartan Gregorian, president of Brown University, notes that at college

> . . . many students confront their own attitudes about race for the first time. Because there is still de facto segregation in our country, some of our freshmen are unprepared for the diverse population they encounter in our colleges and universities.[14]

Prejudices are sometimes expressed straightforwardly in terms of verbal and written slurs and insults, and sometimes more subtly through discrimination. In April, 1989, for example, graffiti was scrawled on a dormitory and leaflets were distributed that said things like "Keep white supremacy alive" and "Kill homos."[15] Expressions such as these have been found on some campuses, like Brown and Tufts, to violate college codes that prohibit harassment of students. Melissa Russo, a political science major at Tufts University, notes that Tufts has responded to harassment of minority students by creating three levels of "allowable speech." She also notes that these prohibitions conflict with Constitutional guarantees of free expression:

> Varying degrees of expression are permissible on campus, depending upon the ability of others to avoid "offensive" speech.
> In public areas and campus publications, freedom of speech is protected; even controversial T-shirts [such as those listing 15 reasons why beer is better than women at Tufts] can be sold or quoted. In other spaces, such as classrooms, dining halls and libraries, derogatory or demeaning speech can be restricted. The prohibition does not cover material relevant to class discussions.
> In dormitories, Tufts has deemed the right of free speech to be subordinate to that of privacy. It argues that students should be free from [offensive speech] in their own homes.[16]

College is a microcosm of society at large, and prejudice is found on as well as off campus. Prejudices influence people to evaluate group members in negative ways and stir feelings of dislike or hatred.

> I imagine one of the reasons people cling to their hates so stubbornly is because they sense, once hate is gone, they will be forced to deal with pain.
> JAMES BALDWIN

> Indifference, to me, is the epitome of evil.
> ELIE WIESEL

> Silence is the virtue of fools.
> FRANCIS BACON

> I am free of all prejudices. I hate everyone equally.
> W. C. FIELDS

Resolving Social Conflicts

Discrimination is the denial of privileges on the basis of group membership. In the world at large, discrimination usually takes the form of denial of access to jobs, housing, and club membership. On campus, discrimination may take the form of exclusion from fraternities and sororities, or the handing out of poor grades. Our prejudices may also affect whom we sit next to in the cafeteria and the library, and whom we confide in or ask out.

Two common forms of prejudice are sexism and racism.

Sexism

> Whatever women do they must do twice as well as men to be thought half as good. Luckily, this is not difficult.
>
> CHARLOTTE WHITTON
> (Mayor of Ottowa)

Sexism is the belief that people possess negative traits or perform badly because they are male or female. Historically, sexism has been directed against women. Women in modern society tend to be viewed as gentle, helpful, kind, and patient, which are positive traits, but also as dependent and submissive, which are not.[17] Men are more likely to be seen as independent, competitive, and tough—traits that aid them in the business world—but also as protective and gentlemanly toward their families. Women are more often seen as warm but emotional, and as fit to take care of the kids and cook the meals.[18] Men are traditionally expected to head the family and put bread on the table. Some people still believe that women are unsuited to the business world and that they should be educated in traditional areas such as homemaking and child-rearing.

TRUTH OR FICTION *Revisited*

Skill in business *is* inconsistent with the traditional female sex-role stereotype. However, that does not mean that women are actually poor in business ability. A stereotype is a widely held belief, not a fact.

These perceptions of the sexes generally reflect the traditional distribution of men into breadwinning roles and women into homemaking roles.[19] When women work, they are less likely to be seen as fitting in the traditional role—so long as they work because of choice, and not necessity.[20]

Does sexism influence your expectations of the opposite sex—or your self-expectations? Today men and women are perceived as about equal in overall intellectual ability. Women are generally expected to surpass men in verbal skills, however, whereas men are usually expected to outperform women in math, science, and spatially related tasks. These female engineers do not fit the stereotype.

QUESTIONNAIRE
Sex Differences: Vive la Différence or Vive la Similarité?

The French have a saying, "Vive la différence," which reflects their (and our?) delight that men and women are anatomically different. But how different are the sexes in terms of intellectual abilities and personality traits?

Below are a number of statements that reflect cultural sex-role stereotypes. That is, most Americans tend to believe that all of them are accurate. However, not all of them have been supported by psychological research. Check True for each item that you believe is accurate, and False for each item that you believe is inaccurate or unproven. The answers are at the end of the chapter.

		True	False
1.	Men are more socially dominant.	___	___
2.	Men have greater mathematics ability.	___	___
3.	Men are more competitive than women.	___	___
4.	Women are more suggestible.	___	___
5.	Men are more logical and analytical.	___	___
6.	Women have greater verbal ability.	___	___
7.	Women lack achievement motivation.	___	___
8.	Men are more active than women.	___	___
9.	Men are more aggressive than women.	___	___
10.	Men have higher self-esteem.	___	___
11.	Men have greater visual-spatial ability.	___	___
12.	Women are more sociable than men.	___	___
13.	Women are more timid and anxious than men.	___	___
14.	Women are more talkative.	___	___

These sex-role stereotypes have exacted an enormous price, especially on women. For example, it is only in the twentieth century that girls have been considered suitable for education.

TRUTH OR FICTION Revisited

Girls were deemed unsuited to education in past centuries. How much skill and talent has prejudice led us to waste over the centuries?

Even the Swiss-French philosopher Jean-Jacques Rousseau, who spearheaded an open approach to education, considered girls irrational and disposed to child-rearing and homemaking—not to business and technology.

Today men and women are perceived as about equal in overall intellectual ability, but boys are still expected to outperform girls in math, science, and spatially related tasks. Because of these expectations, boys are more apt to take math courses in high school and college.[21] By junior high school, boys see themselves as more proficient in math than girls do, even when their grades are the same.[22] Girls are more likely to have "math anxiety," and it becomes progressively harder to persuade high school and college women to take math courses, even when their ability is superior.[23]

Resolving Social Conflicts 259

Stereotyping also impairs our psychological well-being and our interpersonal relationships. For example, women who accept the traditional feminine sex role are also apt to think that women should be seen but not heard. And so they are unlikely to make known their needs and wants. As a result, they are apt to experience frustration. And men who believe in the traditional masculine sex role are not apt to feel comfortable in bathing, dressing, and feeding children, which impairs their participation in child-rearing.[24] Traditional men are less likely to ask for help—including medical help—when they need it.[25] And they are less apt to be compassionate and to express feelings of love—frustrating the women who care for them.[26]

We have been discussing the costs of sex-role stereotypes. Before we move on, you may want to take the questionnaire on page 259 on actual sex differences.

Racism

> I have a dream that one day on the red hills of Georgia, the sons of former slaves and the sons of former slave owners will be able to sit together at the table of brotherhood.
>
> MARTIN LUTHUR KING, JR.

In racism, one race or ethnic group holds negative attitudes toward another. Racism colors our perceptions. Social scientists have shown people photographs of people of different races in which one individual is holding a knife. Interestingly, many white viewers erroneously report that a black was holding the knife when the aggressor was actually white.[27] On the other hand, many blacks are more likely to assume that whites are aggressors.[28]

Blacks and hispanics frequently encounter racism on campus. Fraternities and sororities frequently exclude them—not necessary because they are black or hispanic, but because the Greek-letter organizations look for people similar in attitudes and behavior. When people look different, we may assume that their beliefs and behavior patterns are different as well—even when they are not. These minorities also complain that many white students assume that they are equal-opportunity students—that they were admitted to fill minority quotas despite academic deficiencies. We have even seen cases in which white professors told us they felt "threatened" by minority students requesting that grades be raised. However, when they described the behavior of the minority students, it was identical to that of whites requesting higher grades—but the whites were not perceived as menacing.

Let's briefly consider some of the origins of prejudice and then consider some ideas as to how to handle prejudice. But first write down some of your own ideas about the origins of prejudice.

IN YOUR OWN WRITE

What do you think are some of the reasons for prejudice?

1. _____

2. _____

3. _____

Sources of Prejudice

Prejudice has many sources. Let us contemplate some of them, and then we shall see what we can do to cope with them.

1. *Attitudinal differences.* As noted in Chapter 9, we tend to like people whose attitudes coincide with ours. Our opinions about other people are affected by their attitudes as well as by their race.[29] People from other religious and racial groups have frequently been reared in environments that differ from our own and are likely to harbor different values and attitudes. But we may tend to assume that people of different religions and races do not share our attitudes, even when they do.

2. *Social conflict and economic competition.* Many religious and racial groups have been at odds for centuries, even thousands of years. Social and economic conflict tend to breed negative attitudes.[30] For example, many students in the white majority, whose families are going into debt to finance their education, resent minority students who have received equal-opportunity scholarships and grants. From their perspective, tax money that their parents can ill afford is being used to finance the competition. Minority students, on the other hand, perceive majority resistance as part of a continuing effort to oppress them.

3. *Scapegoating.* Some social scientists argue that religious and racial minorities serve as convenient scapegoats when things go wrong. That is, there is a tendency to blame the troubles of the country on blacks, hispanics, Jews, and other minorities.

4. *Learning from parents.* We tend to acquire many attitudes and opinions from other people, especially our parents. Social scientists note that children like to imitate their parents and that parents often reward children for doing so. And so prejudices are apt to be transmitted from generation to generation.

5. *Stereotyping.* Even when we do not think of ourselves as being prejudiced, we may be susceptible to stereotypes. And stereotypes can lead to discrimination, sometimes in unexpected ways. Blacks, for example, are frequently stereotyped as athletic and aggressive. For this reason, a football coach might assume that a black student will do a better

Many campuses conduct workshops and discussion groups concerning gender, race, and diversity as ways of combating stereotyping and prejudice.

Resolving Social Conflicts

WHAT DO YOU DO NOW?
How to Handle Prejudice

Prejudice has been with us throughout history, and it is unlikely that a miracle cure is at hand. Yet there is much that we can do. It is easier to change discriminatory behavior than people's feelings. Laws prohibit denial of access to an education and jobs on the basis of religion, race, and handicaps, but inner feelings cannot be legislated.

1. *Intergroup contact.* Stereotypes are fixed, conventional ideas about *groups*. Negative stereotypes encourage us to avoid other groups, which is especially unfortunate because intergroup contact is one way of breaking down stereotypes. Contact shows that religious and racial groups are composed of individuals who are anything but homogeneous in their values, abilities, interests, and personalities.[31] Intergroup contact is especially effective when the following conditions are met.[32] First, because competition stirs feelings of antagonism, individuals should strive to meet common goals. Playing together on the same team, working on a joint educational project, or working on the yearbook together are examples. Second, it helps if the individuals come from comparable socioeconomic circumstances. Then they are more likely to have some things in common. Third, informal contacts—such as sitting next to one another in the cafeteria—are more helpful than formal ones. Structured contacts—as in a class debate—can allow participants to maintain a distance from one another. Last, contact is more effective when it is prolonged. Brief contacts are less likely to produce lasting changes of opinion.

2. *Obtaining compliance with the law.* It is appropriate to seek legal remedies when we have been discriminated against on the basis of gender, religion, race, or other ethnic factors. When students feel that they have been denied access to living accommodations or jobs

job than a white on defense. But because of the stereotype that whites are more intelligent and make better leaders, the same coach might look for a white quarterback. The coach might say and believe that he has nothing against blacks, but his stereotyping may prevent a black from being considered for the position of quarterback on his team. Similarly, stereotypes concerning male logic and superiority in math and spatial-relations skills, may prevent college women from attaining leadership roles in legal and technological societies.

SUMMING UP

1. How do you react when you run into conflict with friends, roommates, family members, or professors? Do your reactions tend to make things better or worse?
2. Have you ever tried to handle conflicts by negotiating differences or agreeing to exchange new behavior? Have you stuck to your agreements?

because of prejudice, they are advised to consult with their academic advisors, the college equal-opportunity office, or the office of the dean of students.

3. Maria Russo, the Tufts University student, suggests conducting workshops and discussion groups concerning gender, race, and diversity.[33]

4. *Self-examination.*

> I'm starting with the man in the mirror,
> I'm asking him to change his ways,
> And no message could have been any clearer,
> If you want to make the world a better place,
> Take a look at yourself and make that change.*

Prejudice isn't just "out there." Prejudice resides in people, and we are people. It is easy for us to focus on the prejudices of others, but what of our own? Even if we do not harbor feelings of racial or religious enmity, are we doing anything to counter these feelings in others? Do we confront people who express stereotypical beliefs? Do we belong to organizations that deny access to people of other racial and religious groups? Do we strike up conversations with people from other groups? College is meant to be a broadening experience, and we deny ourselves much of the education we could be receiving when we refuse to stray from groups formed by people who share our backgrounds.

* "Man in the Mirror." Words and music by Glen Ballard and Siedah Garrett. © Copyright 1987 by MCA Music Publishing, a division of MCA Inc., Aerostation Corporation and Yellowbrick Road Music. Rights of Aerostation Corporation administered by MCA Music Publishing, a division of MCA Inc., 1755 Broadway, New York, NY 10019. International copyright secured. All rights reserved.

---

3. How can you get started when you have some unpleasant business to bring up with another person?
4. What is meant by "active listening"? Are you a good listener? Do you want to be one?
5. How can you learn about another person's needs?
6. Are you good at delivering and receiving criticism? Do you manage to keep lines of communication open when doing so? How?
7. Are you an assertive person? Do you express your genuine feelings, make requests, and demand your rights? Do you sometimes feel like a doormat? Do you sometimes explode when you're upset and threaten or belittle the other person?
8. What happens when you arrive at an impasse with another person? Do you "toss the person into the wastebasket" or find ways of living with disagreements?
9. Do you harbor any prejudices based on gender, race, or religion? (Are you sure?) What are they? Where do they come from?
10. How can we combat prejudices in ourselves and others?

Resolving Social Conflicts   263

Scoring Key for the Rathus Assertiveness Schedule

Tabulate your score as follows: For those items followed by an asterisk (*), change the signs (plus to minus; minus to plus). For example, if the response to an asterisked item was 2, place a minus sign (−) before the two. If the response to an asterisked item was −3, change the minus sign to a plus sign (+) by adding a vertical stroke. Then add up the scores of the 30 items.

Scores on the assertiveness schedule can vary from +90 to −90. Table 10.3 shows how your score compares to those of 764 college women and 637 men from 35 campuses across the United States.[34] For example, if you are a woman and your score was 26, it exceeded that of 80 percent of the women in the sample. A score of 15 for a male exceeds that of 55–60 percent of the men in the sample.

TABLE 10.3 Norms for the Rathus Assertiveness Schedule.

WOMEN'S SCORES	PERCENTILE	MEN'S SCORES
55	99	65
48	97	54
45	95	48
37	90	40
31	85	33
26	80	30
23	75	26
19	70	24
17	65	19
14	60	17
11	55	15
8	50	11
6	45	8
2	40	6
−1	35	3
−4	30	1
−8	25	−3
−13	20	−7
−17	15	−11
−24	10	−15
−34	5	−24
−39	3	−30
−48	1	−41

Key to Questionnaire on Sex Differences

Psychological research has supported some assumed sex differences, disproved others, and thrown still others into question. The following key indicates which items have been supported by research (T), disproved (F), or placed in doubt (?):[35]

?	1.	Men are more socially dominant.
T	2.	Men have greater mathematics ability.
?	3.	Men are more competitive than women.
F	4.	Women are more suggestible.
F	5.	Men are more logical and analytical.
T	6.	Women have greater verbal ability.
F	7.	Women lack achievement motivation.
?	8.	Men are more active than women.
T	9.	Men are more aggressive than women.
F	10.	Men have higher self-esteem.
T	11.	Men have greater visual-spatial ability.
?	12.	Women are more sociable than men.
?	13.	Women are more timid and anxious than men.
F	14.	Women are more talkative.

TRUTH OR FICTION *Revisited*

Despite the stereotype, men are actually more talkative than women.

The current state of the research suggests that women excel in verbal abilities, men in math and spatial-relations abilities, and that men are more aggressive than women. However, a number of factors suggest that caution is in order concerning these sex differences:

1. In most cases, the differences in verbal, math, and spatial-relations abilities are very small.[36]
2. The differences in verbal, math, and spatial-relations skills are *group* differences. For example, the difference between women who have good verbal skills and those who have poor verbal skills is greater than the difference between the average woman and the average man. Millions of men exceed the "average" woman in verbal skills, such as writing and spelling. Millions of women outperform the "average" man in math and spatial abilities. Men have produced great authors, and women, noted scientists.
3. The small differences that exist may reflect cultural expectations and environmental influences rather than native tendencies.[37] Verbal skills are stereotyped as feminine in our society, but math and spatial abilities are stereotyped as masculine. Female introductory psychology students given just a few hours of training in visual-spatial skills, like rotating geometric figures in space, do as well as men on these tasks.[38] And when women are angered, when they believe that the social environment will tolerate aggression from them, and when they have the means to behave aggressively, they can be as aggressive as men.[39]

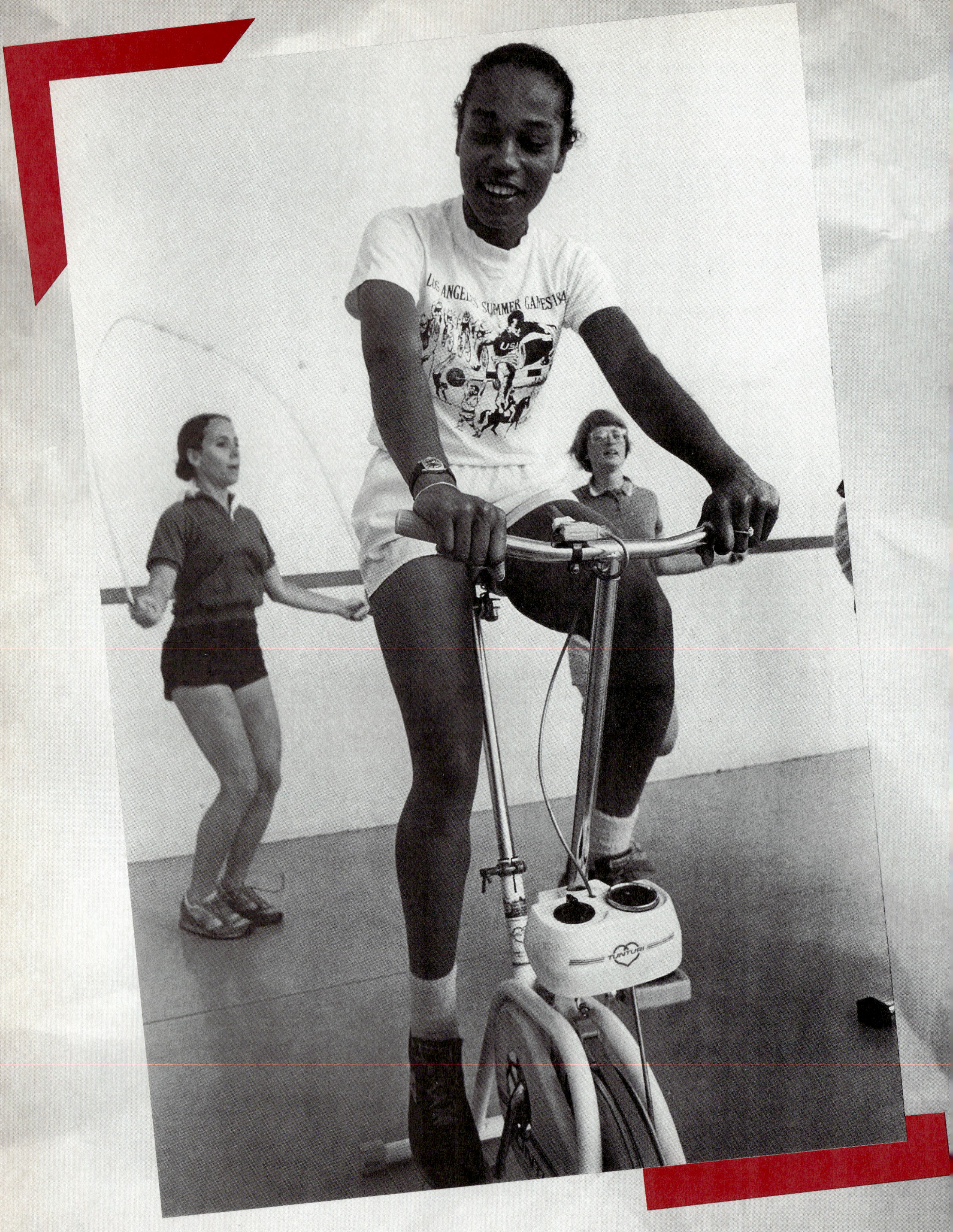
TUNTURI

11

Staying (and Becoming) Physically Fit

TRUTH OR FICTION?

_____ Most college-age people are concerned about what they eat.

_____ You can never be too rich or too thin.

_____ Many college women control their weight by binging and then throwing up what they have eaten.

_____ Harvard University alumni who exercise regularly live longer than alumni who are couch potatoes.

_____ If you're going to start jogging, it really doesn't matter what running shoes you buy.

_____ You need to average about eight hours of sleep a night to get through the semester in good health.

_____ If you try too hard to get to sleep, sleep will probably elude you.

_____ When you're sick, you should try to continue to attend classes and keep up with your assignments.

_____ When you visit the doctor, it's best to follow instructions and not to ask too many questions.

Students who begin college at 18 or so usually do not spend too much time thinking about their health. They will have generally gotten past what health professionals refer to as the usual childhood diseases, and they have many years to go before they encounter the health concerns of middle age and late adulthood. Then, too, many students say that with all they have to do, they are too busy to think about their health. They plan to catch up on health matters (e.g., stop smoking or start exercising) after they graduate or later, perhaps when they're established in careers. When it comes to matters like diet, the most frightening potential consequences of poor eating habits—for example, heart disorders and cancers—may be 30 to 50 years away. But classes, tests, studying, papers, the need to catch a quick (and filling) snack, and a few social obligations are *now*.

Diet is one of the topics we'll discuss in this chapter. We'll also talk about exercise and sleep. (Most students feel that they don't get enough of either.) And even though most college students are young and reasonably healthy, they also get sick. So we'll talk about how to tell when you're sick (which isn't always as simple as it seems) and what to do about it.

> Be careful about reading health books. You may die of a misprint.
>
> MARK TWAIN

> The only way to keep your health is to eat what you don't want, drink what you don't like, and do what you'd rather not.
>
> MARK TWAIN

> There is no sincerer love than the love of food.
>
> GEORGE BERNARD SHAW

NUTRITION

For some busy college students, out of sight is out of mind. They skip meals, especially breakfast, and eat on the run. Others are slaves to the colorful trays of food that line the glass cases at the cafeteria. Their food cards allow them to take at least one of everything, and they do so with a vengeance. Still others chomp mindlessly through bags of potato chips and jars of peanuts while they are studying. Others heed the call when someone suggests going out for pizza—even if they are not hungry.

If you are like many other college students, you may not give very much thought to nutrition at all. A *New York Times* poll[1] of 2,000 people found that those aged 30 and above described more nutritious diets than 18-to-29-year-olds. So returning students may pay more attention to their diets than younger students. And women paid more attention to what they ate than men (Table 11.1).

IN YOUR OWN WRITE

How much thought do you give to what you eat? Do you just eat what's there, or do you consider the effects of various foods on your health?

_____
_____
_____
_____
_____
_____
_____
_____

TABLE 11.1 Percentage of *New York Times* Respondents Who Attend to the Listed Dietary Components at Every Meal[2]

DIETARY COMPONENT	GENDER MEN	GENDER WOMEN	AGES COLLEGE AGE (18–29)	AGES 30 AND ABOVE
Cholesterol	19	31	13	30
Salt	43	60	39	57
Fats	31	46	26	44
Additives and preservatives	20	25	16	25
Sugar and sweets	34	42	30	42
Calories	16	36	21	29
Fiber	12	21	10	19
Caffeine	21	30	20	28

> Value [health] next to a good conscience; for health is the second blessing that we mortals are capable of; a blessing that money cannot buy.
>
> IZAAK WALTON, *Compleat Angler*

TRUTH OR FICTION *Revisited*

Most college-age people really do *not* pay attention to the nutritional value of what they eat.

> One should eat to live, not live to eat.
>
> MOLIÈRE, *L'Avare*

Why do young adults pay less attention to their diets than do their elders? Bonnie Liebman, director of nutrition at the Washington Center for Science in the Public Interest, notes that "Instead of teaching good nutrition in schools, we subject our kids to television commercials that push fast foods, soft drinks, candy bars, and sugary cereals. And then we wonder why kids don't ask for fruits and vegetables."[3] Fabian Linden, executive director of the consumer research center of the Conference Board, a marketing information service, adds that "Youth has a magic feeling that they are invulnerable. They don't pay attention to the medical wisdom we have accumulated."[4]

Most students prefer french fries, which are high in fats, to baked potatoes, which have none unless you smear them with butter. Most prefer red meats—again, high in fats—to fish and poultry; and soft drinks, which are high in sugar and lacking in vitamins, to fruit juices. Many students also fool themselves that they are eating healthful fish or chicken, but they eat fish fried or baked in butter (pure animal fat) or have Southern fried chicken (chicken deep fried in fat). Or if they have roast chicken, they eat the fatty skin.

How much thought do you give to what you eat? Do you just eat what's there, or do you consider the effects of various foods on your health?

Nutrition and Health

We now know a great deal about the impact of nutrition on health. For example, nearly 60 percent of the cases of cancer in men and 40 percent in women are connected with dietary habits.[5] Food preservatives, fats, and vitamin deficiencies all pose risks. High levels of cholesterol intensify risks of cardiovascular disorders such as arteriosclerosis (hardening of the arteries) and heart attacks.[6] Vitamins, calcium, fruits and vegetables, and nonfatty fish[7] appear to lower the probability of developing cancer.

Calories are a basic component of the diet. Ingesting too many calories often causes our most common nutrition-related problem—obesity.

Obesity

Many of those snacks we get from vending machines between classes are loaded in "food energy," or calories. Chocolate bars, cookies, potato chips, soft drinks, even granola bars are brimming with calories. Pizzas, butter and margarine, hamburgers (and especially cheeseburgers), and beer are all loaded with calories. And most of the special meals for the holidays—our favorite cookies and pies, or the ethnic dishes (e.g., kielbasa and knishes) that we missed on campus—are stuffed with calories.

During our late teens and into our early twenties, our metabolic rates tend to be in overdrive, so we burn off a good deal of what we consume. But our metabolic rates inevitably slow down so that patterns of overeating catch up with us. Moreover, many college students are overweight—or obese. Obesity is defined as being at least 20 percent over your ideal body weight. How widespread is being overweight or obese in the United States? Consider these figures:

> Forty percent of Americans judge themselves overweight.[8]
> Thirty-five percent would like to take off at least 15 pounds.[9]
> Twenty percent of American adults are obese—that is, that is, they weigh at least 20 percent more than their recommended weight.
> Eleven million Americans are severely obese—that is, they exceed their recommended weight by at least 40 percent.
> Twenty-one percent of us are on diets.[10]
> Women dieters exceed the number of male dieters significantly.[11]
> Within a few years, about two-thirds of "successful" dieters have regained every ounce they've lost—and then some.[12]

Slender people are viewed as more attractive, but there are also health-related reasons for maintaining a reasonably lean profile. Obese people incur more than their share of illnesses, including diabetes, heart disease and high blood pressure, gout, even some kinds of cancer.[13] The configuration of fat also matters. People who put on fat at the waistline (called "apples" by some researchers) are more likely to incur heart disease, high blood pressure, diabetes, and gall bladder problems than those who put on fat in the hips and thighs (who are referred to as "pears").[14] But big gains and losses of weight over the years also intensify the risk of heart disease. As a result, some professionals suggest that a few extra pounds may be less harmful than "yo-yo dieting" in the long run.[15]

Why are so many of us overweight? Do we just eat too much? Actually, the origins of obesity are not so simple.

Origins of Obesity Obesity runs in families. It was once the conventional wisdom that heavy parents fostered obesity in children by setting bad examples and stuffing the pantry with fattening foods. But studies of adopted children suggest that heredity also plays a role.[16]

Apparently we can inherit different numbers of fat cells—cells that store fats, which are also referred to as adipose tissue. As time elapses after a meal, the blood sugar level drops. Fat is then drawn from fat cells to supply nourishment. At a point called the *set point*, the brain is signaled of the fat shortage in these cells, and the hunger drive is triggered.

Heavy people feel hungry sooner after meals, apparently because the large numbers of fat cells barrage the brain with signals. Formerly heavy people also feel hungry rapidly because dieting doesn't eliminate fat cells—it shrivels them so that they signal the brain in distress. So many people who lose weight gripe that they are perpetually famished when they try to keep it off.

Also, our metabolic rates (the rates at which we burn food) tend to slow down when we are dieting or trying to maintain lower weight levels.[17] If you think about it, this would help us survive during a famine. Sad to say, however, most of the time the metabolic slowdown just makes it harder to lose weight.

Repeated cycles of dieting and regaining lost weight—"yo-yo dieting"—knock the set point off balance. These cycles teach the body to expect intermittent food deprivation and to curb the metabolic rate the next time you diet.[18] So formerly heavy people must eat less than people of the same weight who were always slim, if they expect to maintain a slender profile.

Another problem is that fat tissue metabolizes food more slowly than muscle tissue, which is one reason why athletic students can afford to eat more than sedentary students. (The exercise itself burns calories too, of course). But yo-yo dieters tend to take off more muscle than they put back on. Psychologist Kelly Brownell offers an example with a college student named Christine:

> Christine . . . drops from 140 pounds down to 120 pounds. She might lose 15 pounds of fat and 5 pounds of muscle. If she regains the 20 pounds, will she replace all 5 pounds of muscle? [Animal studies] suggest that she won't, so Christine may replace 18 pounds of fat and only 2 pounds of muscle. She may be the same weight before and after this cycle, but her metabolic rate would be lower after the cycle because she has more fat, which is less metabolically active than muscle.[19]

The second time around, it is harder for Christine to just maintain a weight of 140 pounds. If she consumes as many calories as when she had been 140 pounds before, she is likely to add more weight. Now that her body, with its higher ratio of fat to muscle is less metabolically active, it will be more difficult for her to take off another 20 pounds.

So there are a number of biological, or internal, reasons for putting on weight—and for feeling as though we hit a wall when we try to take it off. But there are also external reasons, like the aroma or sight of food. Sitting at a table in the cafeteria where everyone else goes for second desserts is a murderous temptation. Being home for the holidays when all your relatives conspire to concoct your favorite dishes and desserts is another:

> Have just one bite, please! Just a nibble! I made it just for you. How can just a little taste hurt? Come on! I know they don't feed you right in that college cafeteria. . . .

Palling around with a crowd that descends on the pizza parlor nightly is another problem. All these situations may provide you with more temptation than you can handle.

Now that we have listed some of the factors that can sabotage efforts to take off a few pounds—from microscopic cells within the body to large people who cook up fabulous desserts—let us offer some encouraging news: It has been shown that self-help manuals can help take the pounds off and keep them off.[20] Where will you find a trustworthy manual? Why we just happen to have one—right here.

Taking It Off and Keeping It Off! The first rule of scientific dieting is this: Forget fads! Ignore the promises on book jackets in the bookstores. Forget extended fasting (unless you have close medical supervision), eliminating carbohydrates, or limiting your diet to one food such as grapefruit or rice. Successful, safe diets consist of changes in lifestyle that involve four elements:[21]

> Americans can eat garbage, provided you sprinkle it liberally with ketchup, mustard, chili sauce, tabasco sauce, cayenne pepper, and any other condiment which destroys the original flavor of the dish.
>
> HENRY MILLER

> A cucumber should be well-sliced, dressed with pepper and vinegar, and then thrown out.
>
> SAMUEL JOHNSON

Enhancement of nutritional knowledge
Lowering of calorie intake
Exercise
Behavior modification

Enhancement of Nutritional Knowledge Eating fewer calories is the primary means of taking off pounds. Therefore, we need to be sure that we will consume key food elements and avoid feeling too deprived when we reduce calories. Consuming fewer calories means eating smaller portions and switching to some foods that are lower in calories. Depend more on fresh fruits and vegetables (such as apples in the place of apple pie); fish and poultry; lean meats; and skim milk and cheese products. Reduce or eliminate the oils, butter, margarine, and sugar in your diet. In the cafeteria, select salad without dressing rather than predressed salad; use vinegar but little or no oil. If you do use oil, make it olive oil, which appears to lower blood levels of harmful cholesterol. (Diet dressings usually have oil substitutes; read the labels.)

Foods that help us take off weight are also usually healthful for other reasons: They tend to be high in fiber and vitamins and low in fats. For this reason, they also reduce our risk of cardiovascular disorders, cancer, and other diseases.

Lowering Calorie Intake The relationship between the number of calories you take in and the number you expend ("burn") largely determines whether you'll gain weight, lose weight, or remain the same. You can use a calorie book to estimate how many calories you take in.* You may need a scale to weigh portions of food you cook. You also need to consider "hidden calories." When you have eggs, make sure to include calories for the butter or other kind of fat in which they were cooked. (Spray the pan with Pam or another noncaloric shortening if you must eat eggs.)

We also recommend that you stop by the college health center or check with your personal physician about going on a diet. Various medical conditions make dieting dangerous unless it is carried out under careful guidelines. You will also find that fasting or sudden large decreases in calorie intake may be harmful. Successful dieting requires lifelong changes in eating habits. It is usually better to cut down gradually than to suddenly discontinue all fats or to halve calorie intake.

How many calories do you burn in a typical day? Table 11.2 offers approximations of the calories you burn in various activities. You can use these estimates to fill out Table 11.3, which helps you approximate the number of calories you burn in a day. If we were to try to be perfectly accurate, we might use a series of tables based on your sex and age. Men usually burn a few more calories than women equal in weight, because women usually have a higher fat-to-muscle ratio. Younger people have somewhat faster metabolisms. However, we are dealing with estimates, and you will find out for yourself whether your approximations are helpful.

Remember that your day consists of 24 hours, so make sure you've put in enough activities to fill up your typical day. To double-check your addition, see if your totals are consistent with these broad guidelines: A 150-pound college man probably burns between 2,400 and 4,000 calories a day, depending on his level of activity. A 125-pound college woman probably burns somewhere between 1,750 and 2,500 calories a day.

Exercise Exercise also promotes weight loss. Exercise consumes calories,[22] so dieting and exercise together is more productive than dieting

---

*Many are on the market and will usually be found in your campus bookstore. Select a calorie book that includes brand names to make your addition easier.

TABLE 11.2 Calories Expended in One Hour According to Activity and Body Weight.

	BODY WEIGHT (in pounds)				
ACTIVITY	100	125	150	175	200
Sleeping	40	50	60	70	80
Sitting quietly	60	75	90	105	120
Standing quietly	70	88	105	123	140
Eating	80	100	120	140	160
Driving, housework	95	119	143	166	190
Desk work	100	125	150	175	200
Walking slowly	133	167	200	233	267
Walking rapidly	200	250	300	350	400
Swimming	320	400	480	560	640
Running	400	500	600	700	800

TABLE 11.3 Approximate Number of Calories You Burn on a Typical Weekday.

ACTIVITY	HOURS/DAY		CALORIES/HOUR		SUBTOTAL
Sleeping	_____	×	_____	=	_____
Desk work	_____	×	_____	=	_____
Driving	_____	×	_____	=	_____
Eating	_____	×	_____	=	_____
Sitting in class	_____	×	_____	=	_____
Hobbies	_____	×	_____	=	_____
Other activities	_____	×	_____	=	_____
Exercise activity 1	_____	×	_____	=	_____
Exercise activity 2	_____	×	_____	=	_____
Exercise activity 3	_____	×	_____	=	_____
TOTALS	24				_____

alone.[23] But recall that when we diet, our metabolic rates slow down to compensate for the loss of food.[24] Because of compensation, some dieters protest of "plateaus" from which they cannot drop further weight without starving.[25] But exercise helps maintain the higher, predieting metabolic rate.[26]

Behavior Modification Helping professionals have also found many ways in which behavior modification helps heavy people take pounds off and keep them off.[27] We recommend reading through the following procedures and picking those that sound as if they will work for you:

1. Determine your calorie baseline. Before starting to diet, keep a record of the calories you take in. Also note the kinds of situations that tempt you most. Many students keep a notebook in which they enter what they've eaten, the number of calories, the time of day, where they are, and what they're doing at the time (e.g., snacking on candy bars

> . . . try the Andy Warhol New York City diet: when I order in a restaurant, I order everything that I don't want, so I have a lot to play around with while everyone else eats. Then, no matter how chic the restaurant, I insist that the waiter wrap the entire plate up like a to-go order, and after we leave the restaurant I find a little corner outside in the street to leave the plate in, because there are so many people in New York who live in the streets, with everything they own in shopping bags.
>
> ANDY WARHOL

Staying (and Becoming) Physically Fit

from a vending machine before freshman composition). This kind of record suggests foods that you may want to cut down on or eliminate; places to avoid; and times of the day when you are most likely to snack.

2. Establish daily calorie goals. Create a concrete plan for losing weight with calorie intake goals.[28] If the goal seems formidable, like taking in 500 calories fewer than your baseline, why not approach the goal progressively? For example, reduce daily intake 100 calories a week for five weeks.

3. Track calories. Behavior-modification programs usually apply tracking or self-monitoring. In dieting, it is better to track calories than weight. Transient fluctuations as caused by water retention can make tracking your weight a discouraging experience. Self-monitoring also stimulates awareness of the problem behavior (eating) and helps motivate you to stick to your diet.

4. Eat in the cafeteria or in the dining area of your apartment only. Break the habit of eating while studying or writing or watching TV.

5. Bypass trouble spots you discovered in your baseline record. Don't while away time in the lounge with the vending machines before class. Avoid dessert by leaving the cafeteria right after the main course. Shop at the mall with the health-food restaurant, not the McDonald's and the ice cream shop.

6. Leave a little food on your plate—even a bite—so that you overcome the feeling that you are obliged to finish everything on your plate.

7. When possible, use smaller plates so that your portions look bigger. Remove or throw out leftovers quickly.

8. Don't starve yourself. If you let yourself get too hungry, that vending machine may look more tempting. Preplan a low-calorie snack or two to tide you over between meals, if necessary. (Count the calories in them!)

9. Don't check out every dish in the cafeteria. Pick up your salad or other light dish and get out of the line. Pay attention to your plate only—not what your skinny friend is gorging on. (Get social support and avoid temptation by sitting with a couple of friends who are also dieting.)

10. If you keep your own apartment or home and go shopping, shop from a list. Walk quickly through the grocery store, preferably after you've eaten and are no longer hungry. If you browse, appetizing packages may get the best of you.

11. Avoid the kitchen and the lounge with the vending machines. Study and write letters elsewhere.

12. Keep fattening foods and snacks out of the room, apartment, or house.

13. Don't cook for (slender) roommates or for family members—or, if you do, cook only the foods you can eat. The "middleman" often reaps more than his fair share of the "profits."

14. Stuff your mouth with carrots, not potato chips and candy.

15. Go jogging or for a brisk walk when you're tempted to eat an unplanned snack.

16. Break down the mindless aspects of habitual gorging by making a place setting before you eat, even if it's only a snack. Take small bites and chew thoroughly. Put your utensils down on the table between bites. (Take your hands off them!)

17. Take a five-minute break during a meal to allow your blood sugar level to rise and reduce feelings of hunger. Consider whether you really need to finish the entire portion before you go back to eating.

18. Schedule frequent, low-cal snacks when you start dieting. But space them farther apart and abolish one or two as you progress.

19. Build your exercise routine by a few minutes each week.
20. Remove fattening foods from your menu one by one.
21. Make rewards contingent on desired behavior. For example, do not go to that movie unless you meet your weekly calorie goal.
22. When you meet your weekly calorie goal, sock away cash toward your vacation or that camera you've been wanting.
23. Punish falling short. Dock your vacation fund $5 when the nachos win.
24. Use positive visualization. Imagine that you reach for something fattening. Stop! Congratulate yourself for showing self-control. Envision your pride; picture friends applauding you. Remind yourself how fantastic you'll look on the beach next summer.
25. If you're a residential student, mentally rehearse your next visit home. Plan ways to courteously but firmly say no to seconds. Envision how proud you will feel.
26. Tempted by the potato chips in the vending machine? Fantasize that they're rotten, that you are nauseated by the taste. You feel sick all day.
27. Feel like bingeing? Strip down in front of the mirror. Touch a bloated part of your body. Think: Do you *really* want to enlarge it or do you prefer to show self-control? Or consider the load the extra weight places on your heart. Envision your arteries clogging with alarming material (pretty much on target!).

Again, not every measure is for every reader. Try them out. If they work, keep them. If they don't, try others. But be suspicious of yourself. If nothing helps, question your motivation to lose weight—not the list.

Before leaving the section on dieting, place yourself in an all-too-familiar situation and see how you can handle it.

IN YOUR OWN WRITE

Not only do dieters have to contend with the lure of food; they must also handle people (often, well-meaning people) who sabotage their efforts to remain in control. If you're a residential student, it's one thing to keep fattening snacks out of the dorm or apartment. But what can you do at your relatives' over the holidays when the dessert "made just for you" is brought out?

"Look at this!" says Uncle Harry. "I remembered. I made it just for you. It's the same recipe you've loved since you were this high."

How would you handle this situation? Write the possibilities in the spaces provided. Then check the suggestions that follow.

_____
_____
_____
_____
_____
_____
_____
_____

WHAT DO YOU DO NOW?
How to Handle an Invitation to Eat

What a predicament! You have been sticking to your diet at school, but it's hard to disappoint a relative. The trick is to assert yourself in a way that expresses your appreciation and also enlists your relative's cooperation—if possible. Here are some ideas:

1. You could say: "It looks wonderful, Uncle Harry. I truly appreciate your going all out for me. But the thing is I've been dieting for the whole semester, and sticking to it means a lot to me. So I'll just have to make do with that terrific roast you made!"

2. Or, "It really looks great, but I've been skipping desserts for the whole semester and really been feeling good about myself. I'd enjoy it while eating it, but afterwards I would be sick about it for days. I hope you'll let me pass it up so I can keep on feeling good about things."

3. "You know I'd love to have a piece, but I'm bent on fitting into a normal-size swimming suit this July."

And what if you give in and eat the dessert? The lapse is lethal to your diet *only if you believe it's lethal.* Many successful dieters include exceptional circumstances as part of their initial plan. But even if you hadn't planned for exceptions, there is no reason that you cannot return to your diet the following day. Really, there isn't.

Anorexia Nervosa and Bulimia Nervosa

Have you heard the saying "You can never be too rich or too thin"? At most, it's half right. People can be too thin, and many college students, especially women, fit this description with a disorder known as *anorexia nervosa.* Students with anorexia have an intense fear of being overweight. Others tell them they look "like skin and bones," but they deny it. As a result of a distorted body image, they refuse to eat enough to preserve a healthful body weight.

There is a saying, "You can never be too rich or too thin." At most, it's half right. People can be too thin, and many college students, especially women, starve themselves to meet—and surpass—cultural ideals of slenderness.

Anorexia may affect as many as one in 200 college women.[29] Anorexia is not just a problem in appearance; it is life-threatening. Anorexic women may shed 25 percent of their weight in one year, triggering amenorrhea (discontinuation of menstruation).[30] Their health declines, and nearly 5 percent die.[31]

TRUTH OR FICTION *Revisited*

Perhaps you can never be too rich, but you can definitely be too thin. Extreme weight loss, as in anorexia nervosa, is life-threatening.

Bulimia nervosa is a related problem. To gain insight into bulimia, consider the case of Nicole:

> Nicole awakens in her cold dark room and already wishes it was time to go back to bed. She dreads the thought of going through this day, which will be like so many others in her recent past. She asks herself the question every morning, "Will I be able to make it through the day without being totally obsessed by thoughts of food, or will I blow it again and spend the day bingeing?" She tells herself that today she will begin a new life, today she will start to live like a normal human being. However, she is not at all convinced that the choice is hers.[32]

Nicole starts the day with eggs and toast. Then, within 45 minutes, she binges on cookies; bagels smeared with cream cheese, butter, and jelly; doughnuts; bowls of cereal with milk; granola; and candy bars. When she can cram food no longer, the purging begins. In the bathroom she ties her hair back, turns on the shower so nobody will overhear, downs a glass of water, and makes herself throw up. Afterward she pledges, "Tomorrow, I'll change." But she suspects that tomorrow will bring a repetition.

Bulimia is defined as repeated cycles of binge eating and dramatic purging. Purging methods include self-caused throwing up, fasting, using laxatives, and spirited exercise. Bulimic people are also highly concerned about their weight. Bulimia afflicts more women than men by nearly a 10:1 ratio.[33]

Bulimia is more common than anorexia, and on college campuses, many women students confess to at least a sporadic cycle of bingeing and purging.[34]

TRUTH OR FICTION *Revisited*

Many college women do control their weight by cycles of binge eating and throwing up. They are considered bulimic.

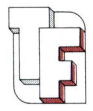

We will not go into the theoretical causes of anorexia and bulimia in depth. Let us just note that some psychologists point to a role for the cultural pressure on women to be thin. As noted in Chapter 9, college women generally view themselves as heavier than the physique that is most appealing to men, and stouter, still, than the "ideal" female figure.[35] Our culture idealizes slender women so much that the normal eating pattern for today's women is dieting.[36]

Whatever the origins of anorexia, you can find some recommendations in the following "What Do You Do Now?" feature.

WHAT DO YOU DO NOW?
How to Handle Anorexia Nervosa

When Stephanie returned from her summer vacation, you thought that she looked thinner, but you weren't sure—and soon you got used to her slimmer profile. But now, with the spring term getting under way, she impresses you as being skin and bones. She always goes to the cafeteria with you and loads her plate with food, but lately you've noticed that she only picks a little here and there. Hardly anything gets eaten.

You care about Stephanie and think that it's time to do something, but what? Write some of your ideas down in the spaces provided. Then check some of the thoughts below.

1. _____
   _____

2. _____
   _____

3. _____
   _____

Let us begin with a suggestion as to what *not* to do. Don't play doctor. Don't offer Stephanie your diagnosis of her condition. You may be correct, but you are not trained to follow up.

Yet there are some things you can do and ought to do. You can tell Stephanie that you've noticed a severe weight loss and that you're concerned. You can ask her if she's aware of it and, if so, whether she's purposefully dieting. There may be a good explanation.

If you don't buy the explanation, you can suggest that Stephanie go with you to the college counseling center or health center for an evaluation. Anorexic people tend to deny that they have problems, however. Stephanie may also say that she's under the supervision of her physician at home (perhaps she is).

If Stephanie refuses to go with you to the counseling or health center, go yourself and ask for advice. It is probably *not* a good idea to call Stephanie's parents or talk to a friend or sorority sister of hers—at least not without getting professional advice first. If Stephanie's weight loss reflects conflicts she's having, these people may be part of the problem. Get help. Don't play doctor.

And what if you've been taking off weight and your friends express their concern to you? Don't you think you might profit from visiting the counseling center or the health center for a chat?

EXERCISE: NOT FOR ATHLETES ONLY

Why should busy college students find time for exercise? For lots of reasons, as we'll see. In this section we'll talk about two types of exercise—aerobic and anaerobic. We'll discuss the benefits and hazards of exercise. We'll also share some tips for getting started.

TYPES OF EXERCISE

There are many different types of exercise, but the important distinction we'll make is between aerobic exercise and anaerobic exercise. Aerobic exercise requires sustained elevation in the use of oxygen. Fast walking, running

Exercise fosters *fitness*—strength, stamina, suppleness, an increase in the body's muscle:fat ratio, and cardiorespiratory fitness. Cardiorespiratory fitness allows the body to use more oxygen during robust activity and to pump more blood with each heartbeat.

in place, jogging and running, aerobic dancing, jumping rope, swimming, basketball, racquetball, bicycling, and cross-country skiing are all aerobic. At least five minutes of sustained effort is required to achieve the training effects of aerobic exercise—that is, to enhance cardiovascular fitness.[37]

Anaerobic exercises involve brief bursts of activity and not sustained elevation in oxygen consumption. Examples include weight training, use of Nautilus-type equipment, sports like baseball in which you mostly stand around, and calisthenics, which generally permit rest periods between exertions.

Anaerobic exercises can strengthen muscles and enhance flexibility, but aerobic exercise can also confer cardiovascular benefits.

Physical Benefits of Exercise

Exercise fosters *fitness*. Fitness has several aspects: muscle strength; muscle endurance; flexibility or suppleness; in the case of aerobic exercise, cardiorespiratory fitness; and an increase in the body's muscle-to-fat ratio. Weight training and calisthenics like chin-ups and push-ups foster muscle strength. Flexibility is enhanced by slow stretching. Flexibility helps prevent injuries during other exercises and is desirable in and of itself. Many runners stretch first to help avoid injuries. Stretching is often a part of the warm-up and cool-down stages of an aerobic exercise regimen.[38]

Cardiovascular condition or fitness allows the body to use more oxygen during robust activity and to pump more blood with each heartbeat.[39] Since conditioned athletes pump more blood with each beat, their pulse rates are slower in the resting state. But during exercise, they can safely sustain double or triple their resting heart rates for several minutes.

Exercise elevates the metabolism, burning more calories than in the resting state. Aerobic exercise of at least 30 minutes four times weekly fosters weight loss by raising the metabolic rate of dieters through the day.[40] Exercise also raises the muscle-to-fat ratio and muscle burns more calories pound for pound than fat.

Sustained activity also reduces the incidence of cardiovascular illnesses, as measured by heart attacks and mortality rates.[41] One research group has been following 17,000 Harvard University alumni through univer-

> I like long walks, especially when they are taken by people who annoy me.
>
> FRED ALLEN

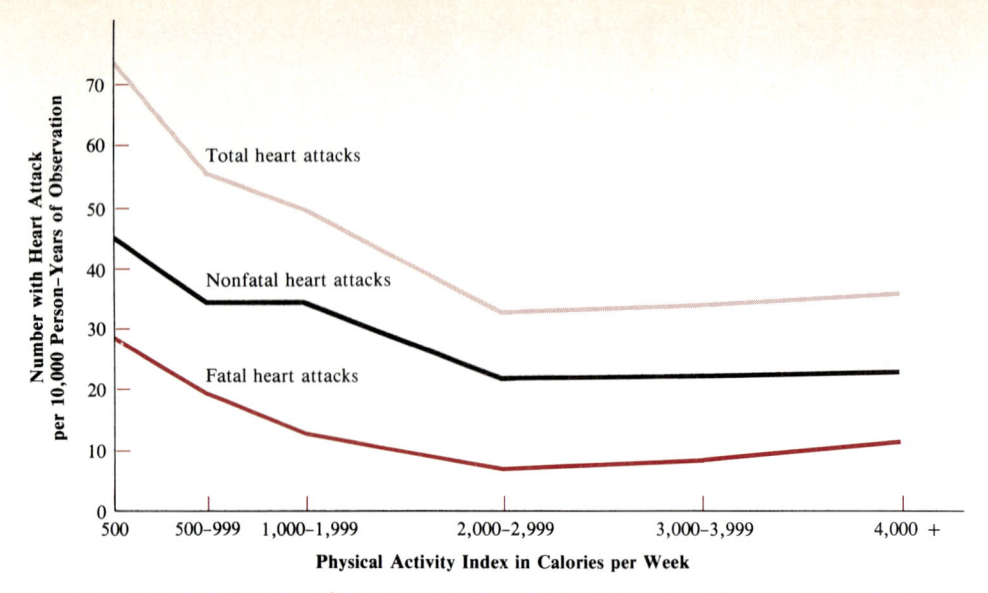

Level of Physical Activity and Incidence of Heart Attacks. Researchers have been using questionnaires and university records to follow the behavior and health of 17,000 Harvard University graduates. They have found that the incidence of fatal and nonfatal heart attacks decreases as their activity levels rise to burning about 2,000 calories per week. The incidence of heart attacks begins to climb once more for alumni who expend more than 2,000 calories per week, but not steeply.

sity records and questionnaires. The incidence of heart attacks declines as the alumni's activity level rises to "burning" 2,000 calories weekly—the exercise equivalent of jogging about 20 miles a week (Figure 11.1). Above 2,000 calories a week, the incidence of heart attacks climbs once more, but slowly. Inactive alumni run the highest risk of heart attacks, and alumni who burn 2,000 calories or more a week live an average of two years longer than their inactive counterparts.[42]

TRUTH OR FICTION *Revisited*

Harvard University alumni who exercise regularly live two years longer, on the average, than their couch-potato peers.

Hazards of Exercise

Exercise also has its hazards. Injuries are an obvious example, especially for students who overdo it. For example, running pressures joints severely, so most enthusiasts accept soreness and minor injuries as part of the price they pay. Good-quality equipment sometimes helps avert injuries, so it sometimes makes sense to spend a bit more for better running shoes. Still, recent issues of *Consumer Reports* point out that the most expensive shoes may not be worth the difference, except in snob appeal. (Check out the magazine in the library.)

TRUTH OR FICTION *Revisited*

The running shoes you buy can make a major difference.

Injuries are one thing, but now and then an enthusiast collapses and dies while exercising, as did runner James Fixx. Does exercise increase the likelihood of heart attacks? Yes and no. People *with cardiovascular illness* are more apt to die from them when exercising vigorously,[43] but other exercisers are likely to find that exercise does more good than harm. Students can learn whether or not they are at cardiovascular risk through stress tests. We recommend clearing your exercise plans with a doctor at the college health center if you fall into one of these categories:

You've never exercised vigorously, or haven't for several years.

You smoke.

You're overweight.

There is a history of cardiovascular disorders in your family.

You are over 40.

You're not sure whether you fall into one of these categories.

But keep things in perspective: People with preexisting medical conditions are at risk when they engage in strenuous exercise without medical guidance. For most others, regular exercise confers more health benefits than hazards.[44]

Psychological Benefits of Exercise

In recent years, it has also become clear that exercise has psychological benefits. For example, aerobic exercise can make dramatic inroads into alleviating feelings of depression in college students.[45] Sustained exercise also alleviates feelings of anxiety and boosts feelings of self-esteem.[46] How does exercise help? Probably in several ways:

Exercise enhances our feelings of physical well-being.

Exercise improves our physical health.

Exercise permits us to successfully achieve (exercise) goals.

Exercise enhances our sense of control over our bodies.

Exercise lends us the social support of fellow exercisers.

We've alerted you to some of the benefits and hazards of exercising. Our presentation has been biased in favor of exercising, we'll admit. There are other negatives, however, like expenditure of time and money. You may jog half an hour four times a week, for example, but have to get dressed for it, wash up and change afterwards, and take care of the extra laundry. If you swim, figure in the time for trips to the pool and back. Then there's the expense of, say, good running shoes and some running outfits. (Good runners dress efficiently; they're not fashion plates.) Aerobics classes cost money, and so on and so forth.

Below are some spaces to help you add up the pluses and the minuses in making your own decisions about exercise. We've pointed you in certain directions but have also given you some room. If you decide that exercising may be for you, check out the "What Do You Do Now?" feature on getting started.

Reasons for exercising   Reasons for not exercising

A. Physical benefits (specify):   Time considerations (specify):

    _____   _____

    _____   _____

    _____   _____

    _____   _____

B. Psychological benefits (specify):
_____
_____
_____
_____

Financial considerations (specify):
_____
_____
_____
_____

C. Social benefits (specify):
_____
_____
_____
_____

Other:
_____
_____
_____
_____

D. Starting lifelong healthful exercise habits:
_____
_____
_____
_____

Other:
_____
_____
_____
_____

E. Other:
_____
_____
_____
_____

Other:
_____
_____
_____
_____

WHAT DO YOU DO NOW?
How to Get Started Exercising

And now, what about you? Have you decided that exercise might be of benefit? If so, the following suggestions may be of help:

1. If you haven't recently exercised, check with the college health center or your personal physician. If you smoke, are overweight, or have a family history of cardiovascular problems, consider a stress test.

2. Why not join an aerobics class for beginners? Class leaders may not be medical experts, but they usually know the right steps. You'll also be one of many beginners (you won't stand out with your klutziness), and you'll derive the benefits of social support. (And lots of romances start in these classes.)

3. Most colleges offer many physical education classes, but students tend to take only the required minimum. Take some elective courses to try out and get some skill in various potential lifetime activities.

4. Get the right equipment. It may mean spending a few dollars more, but proper equipment facilitates performance and can help prevent injury.

5. Read up on the kind of exercise you're thinking about. There are lots of good books on the market, like Kenneth Cooper's books on aerobic exercise.*

6. Consider activities that you can engage in for a lifetime. Tennis is preferable to football as a lifelong activity, for example, even if it's less glamorous on campus. Swimming's good. So is fast walking.

7. Don't try to improve your performance too rapidly. Overdoing can cause injury and fatigue. Have the attitude that you've got a lifetime to improve. (You do, you know.) Have fun, and strength and endurance will come on their own. If you're not having fun, you're unlikely to stick to exercise.

8. Keep a diary to make note of your progress and your thoughts while exercising. If you're jogging, make note of the paths you follow, the distance, weather conditions, and any interesting details. (When your first author was teaching at New Mexico State University, he now and then hopped over snakes as he ran, flushed quail from their shelters, and was once kept company by a coyote who paralleled his course 50 yards away.) Your diary will make exercise an adventure.

9. If you have harsh pain, it is usually better to stop than to try to exercise through it. Soreness is normal for beginners (and, now and then, for old-timers). But sharp pain is usually a sign that something is wrong. If pain persists, go to the college health center.

10. Enjoy yourself. If you're exercising for health and hating every minute of it, you've probably selected the wrong activity. Think it through and perhaps start again.

*Cooper, K. H. (1982). *The aerobics program for total well-being.* New York: Evans; Cooper, K. H. (1985). *Running without fear: How to reduce the risks of heart attack and sudden death during aerobic exercise.* New York: Evans.

SLEEP

One of the chronic complaints of college students is that they don't get enough sleep. After all, the day has only 24 hours. Some days are filled with classes, extracurricular activities, studying, socializing and, of course, some time devoted to eating. When bedtime comes along, many students still have hours of work.

Also, many students complain of insomnia— problems in falling asleep and staying asleep. Feelings of anxiety and depression tend to give rise to insomnia.[47] Insomnia also comes and goes with many students; it is harder for susceptible students to get to sleep when they are overwhelmed by work or have a big exam coming up. Students can also intensify insomnia when they try desperately to get themselves to sleep.[48] How many students have lain awake counting off the hours that remain before they have to get up for a big test, only to find that sleep has eluded them entirely? Their worry heightens the nervous system activity and muscle tension, making it harder to fall asleep.

IN YOUR OWN WRITE

Do you feel that you get enough sleep? Why or why not?

_____
_____
_____
_____
_____
_____
_____

How Much Sleep Do We Need?

Most students gripe when they have slept less than five or six hours. Sleep seems to help us rejuvenate a fatigued body and to recuperate from stress.[49] Many students have remained awake all night and felt "wrecked" the next day. They often go to bed earlier the next night to "get their sleep back."

So how much sleep do we really need? Research with students suggests that we may get by with few serious problems when we pull an all-nighter. Participants in such experiments usually show temporary deficits in attention, and some confusion.[50] But they don't necessarily get sick. (Perhaps their mental lapses are fleeting episodes of light sleep.)

And what of students who switch from a preferred 8 to 10 hours to, say, 5 1/2 hours a night so that they can complete their assignments? To find out, sleep researcher Wilse Webb studied 15 college men who limited sleeping to 5 1/2 hours a night for two months. Throughout the experiment, they displayed little fall-off in intellectual functioning, as assessed, for example, by the capacity to recall and compute numbers.[51] The men felt drowsy during the day or fell asleep in class during the first week of the study only. Beginning with the second week, they were more alert than before the study began!

So most students can probably get by with 5 1/2 hours or so of sleep. If you pull an all-nighter now and then, you will probably survive that, too. But we would not recommend driving if you've been up all night—especially as the following day wears on. And we also would not recommend getting into the habit of using stimulants like amphetamines to stay up. As you'll see in Chapter 13, substance use can have a way of sliding into substance abuse.

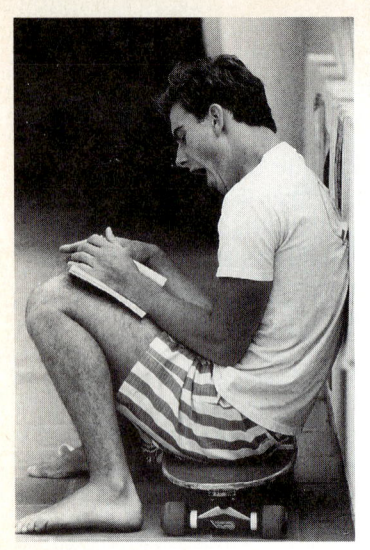

How much sleep do students need? Research suggests that we may get by with few serious problems when we pull an "all-nighter." Participants in such studies usually show temporary deficits in attention and some confusion, but they don't necessarily get sick.

TRUTH OR FICTION *Revisited*

You probably only need five to six hours of sleep a night, though you might prefer to have more.

How to Handle Insomnia

In most endeavors, hard work pays off—but not in trying to get to sleep. Students with insomnia frequently intensify their sleep woes by working at forcing themselves to fall asleep. You cannot force sleep. You can only set the stage for it by relaxing when you are fatigued. Dread of insomnia intensifies, rather than lowers, the nervous system activity and muscle tension that keeps you awake.

TRUTH OR FICTION *Revisited*

Sleep probably will elude you if you try too hard to force yourself to get to sleep. Striving to get to sleep increases your level of tension, and tension is a major cause of insomnia.

Americans most often tackle insomnia with sleeping pills. Popping pills often helps—for a while. Sleeping pills reduce tension and nervous system activity, which can, in turn, ease us into sleep. Expectations of success are also probably a factor.

But sleeping pills have their problems. For one thing, you credit the pills for success, not yourself. And so you risk becoming dependent on the pills. For another, you rapidly develop tolerance for sleeping pills. That means that if you continue using them, you must progressively raise the dose for them to remain effective. Finally, large doses of sleeping pills are dangerous, particularly when combined with an alcoholic drink or two.

There are safer ways of handling insomnia, such as using relaxation to lessen nervous system activity and muscle tension, rethinking anxiety-provoking ideas that can heighten tension, distracting yourself from trying to get to sleep, and creating conditions that are conducive to sleep.

Relaxing

The progressive-relaxation instructions described in Chapter 7 have been shown to reduce tension and the time it takes to fall asleep.[52] By using relaxation instructions, we sleep longer and feel more rested when we awaken in the morning.[53] A good way to go about this is to practice the full-length instructions in Chapter 7 for several days, then to switch over to letting go of muscle tensions only. When you're lying in bed, just let the tensions go in various muscle groups—don't tense up first. Practice the full-length tensing and relaxing instructions during the day every month or so to keep your relaxation skills sharp.

Rethinking Anxiety-Provoking Ideas

Relaxing helps you get to sleep. So you can see why believing that unless you get to sleep *right now*, you'll flunk the final, is likely to keep you up. Ideas like this are usually exaggerated and they also heighten tension.

Below is a sample of the anxiety-evoking ideas that keep many students up at night. In the column to their right are more accurate tension-reducing ideas. If any of the anxiety-evoking ideas mirror your own, why not challenge them with the alternatives? At the end, there are some spaces in which you can record some of the ideas that tend to keep you awake. Why not rethink them, using the information provided in this section, and write down some helpful alternatives?

Anxiety-evoking idea	Alternative, more accurate idea
1. "If I can't get to sleep right now, I'll be wrecked in the morning."	1. "I may be somewhat tired as the day wears on, but I won't necessarily be wrecked. And if I'm tired, I'll just turn in early tomorrow night."
2. "It's harmful to my health if I don't get more sleep."	2. "It may not be. There's no proof that I'll get sick if I miss a night or even two. And people can get by on an average of five and a half hours or so. It would be nice to get eight hours, but there's no reason to think I need that much sleep."
3. "I'll ruin my schedule for the entire week if I'm not asleep within a half hour."	3. "Stop torturing yourself! Stop worrying about the whole week. You'll get up in the morning and do what you have to do tomorrow— that's all. And if you want to, you can get to bed earlier tomorrow night."

4. "If I can't get to sleep now, I won't be able to concentrate on my midterm/final."

4. "Stop exaggerating and making yourself miserable! You may not be 100 percent tomorrow, but you'll be close enough. Why lie here and get all worked up? You might as well get up for a while and have a glass of milk or listen to some relaxing music. When you're tired, you'll get to sleep. And if you don't, you'll also survive."

5. _____

5. _____

6. _____

6. _____

Using Fantasy: Taking Relaxing Mind Trips

Fantasies or "mind trips" can help distract you from your nightly chore of confronting insomnia and compelling yourself somehow to get to sleep. Many students ease themselves into sleep by concentrating on pleasant, relaxing images, like lying on sun-drenched sands as waves lap up against the shore, or like ambling through a summer meadow high in the hills. It's helpful to incorporate your own soothing experiences. These can be firsthand experiences (things you did yourself) or secondhand experiences (such as picking up on a restful theme you saw at the movies). Some students use fantasies with plots—although they usually fall asleep before they get to the end. Others just allow their thoughts to sort of wander on their own.

Creating Conditions Conducive to Sleep

What does your bed mean to you? Is it an arena for a nightly contest with sleep, or is it a relaxing place where you recover from the tensions of the day? Psychologists have discovered that we can make our beds more condu-

IN YOUR OWN WRITE

Use the following lines to sketch some fantasies that might help you get to sleep. Try recounting some soothing experiences.

_____
_____
_____
_____
_____
_____
_____

cive to sleep by contemplating the chores of the morrow elsewhere. When you get into bed, give yourself some time to organize your thoughts about the day and the next. But then permit yourself to rest and, perhaps, to go on a mind trip. You needn't ignore and forget important thoughts that pop in—jot them down on a nearby pad. But get out of bed if you decide to work them through. Let bed become a place for relaxing, not a study or a testing room where you go over exam questions.[54] It can also help to abstain from snacking or studying in bed. These activities also color your bed with meanings that may be inconsistent with sleep.

It can also help to establish a routine, at least on weeknights. Get up at the same time each morning regardless of how long you have slept. If you sleep late in the morning because of trouble getting to sleep the night before, you may have trouble falling asleep at the "normal" hour next evening. Also consider avoiding naps. Naps also push back the hour at which you will be ready for sleep.

Perhaps the overriding principle for handling insomnia is this: Embrace the idea that you'll survive if you don't get to sleep by a magic hour—that you'll probably be okay even if you miss a night or so of sleep. Millions of college students have gotten by with less sleep than they would have liked. If necessary, so can you.

IF YOU GET SICK . . .

Even when we eat well, exercise, and get enough sleep, from time to time we are going to get ill. And sometimes when we are sick, we need to see the doctor.

Students differ concerning decisions about seeing the doctor. Some students refuse to see the doctor unless they're totally immobilized. Others rush off to the doctor with the appearance of any symptom. Some students deny or minimize aches and pains and other symptoms. Others have little tolerance for discomfort and want it relieved immediately. Some students make good use of visits to the doctor, whereas others do not. Some students follow doctor's orders carefully; others ignore them. Let's begin our discussion of what to do if you get ill by reviewing the factors that determine whether we seek medical advice when we feel sick.

When it comes to going to the doctor, we often do not practice what we preach. By and large, we're more willing to advise our friends and families to see the doctor than we are to go ourselves, perhaps because we are afraid of what the doctor will find. But many other factors—such as gender and the impact of symptoms on our daily routines—affect the decision to see the doctor.

IN YOUR OWN WRITE

Are you reluctant to go to the doctor when you feel sick? Why or why not?

Factors That Affect Willingness to Go to the Doctor

When it comes to going to the doctor, we often do not practice what we preach. By and large, we're more willing to advise our friends and families to see the doctor than we are to go ourselves.[55] Why are we reluctant to go to the doctor? For one thing, we are often afraid of what the doctor will find. (For the same reason, most of us try not to think about our symptoms until they force themselves on our attention!) But many other factors affect willingness to see the doctor.

Women students, for example, are more apt to go for medical help than men.[56] This sex difference may reflect the stereotype of the rugged, independent male. Men, that is, are assumed to be self-reliant. It also turns out that students from higher socioeconomic backgrounds are more likely than those of lower socioeconomic status to go for medical advice, even though indigent people are more likely to get sick. *Even if it isn't customary for your family to see the doctor when they get sick, you should go to the health center when you're in doubt as to what you have and how bad it is.*

Various symptom characteristics also influence whether or not students go for medical advice.[57] One is visibility of the symptom. Students with rashes or cuts on the face are more likely to go for help than students with similar problems on the torso or legs. A second is the apparent severity of the symptom. More serious symptoms cause greater anxiety and are more likely to prompt a visit to the doctor. A third is the degree to which symptoms interfere with students' lives. Students are more likely to visit the doctor when symptoms interfere with getting around, eating, sleeping, sex, or elimination. Finally, persistent symptoms are more apt than sporadic symptoms to induce students to go for help.

Pitfalls in Thinking About Illness

Now let's note some pitfalls in ways that students tend to think about illness. These pitfalls can prevent them from getting help when they need it and sticking to medical advice when they should.

Attributing Symptoms to Minor, Common Illnesses Identifying what is wrong with us is basic to getting help and following advice.[58] Chest pains, for example, can mean anything from a heart attack to minor indigestion. Many people assume that symptoms are not serious, because they do not want to find out the worst. Minor, common illnesses are also more apt to be within our experiences, especially because most college students are relatively young. *When symptoms persist, are unusual for you, or interfere with your daily activities, have them checked out.*

Failing to Follow Through on Treatment Many illnesses, such as bacterial infections, require us to follow through on treatment (for example, antibiotic pills) for a certain amount of time, even if symptoms abate. *When the doctor advises you to take* all *the pills, do so. If you're not sure why you should, ask; don't just ignore the advice.*

Assuming That There's Nothing We Can Do When We Get Sick True: Sickness is a part of life. True: Most of the time when we get sick, we do not require medical treatment. True: In the case of many minor illnesses, we just have to let them run their course. All these things are true, but they do not apply to all illnesses. Again, when symptoms persist, interfere with your life, or are not easy for you to identify, go for medical advice.

Trying to Struggle Through Many students moralistically try to struggle through their illnesses by attending classes and keeping up with assignments, no matter how weak they feel. (Others, of course, are only too glad to seize the opportunity to have a respite from the grind.) *You need medical advice to determine whether you would be better off in the long run by taking some time off now.* Sometimes we prolong our illnesses when we fail to rest.

TRUTH OR FICTION *Revisited*

When you're sick, it may be better to take some time off and rest. But you need medical advice to make this decision. *Go get it.*

Being Afraid of the Doctor Many students are reluctant to take the doctor's time. They may have deep-seated questions about their self-worth or think that other students may have more serious disorders and really need the doctor's time. Nonsense! *You are as important as anyone else, and the reason for seeing the doctor is that you have some reason to believe you need his or her expertise.*

Not Asking the Doctor Questions This pitfall is related to fear of the doctor. It is essential to ask questions! Patients who ask questions get more out of their visits.[59] You need to know what is wrong with you, what the course (outcome) of your illness is, and the rationale behind the treatment. Many patients do not comply with medical instructions.[60] *People comply better with medical advice when they believe that it will work.*[61] They are more likely to believe that a certain treatment will work if they know why *it is being prescribed.* Ask *why.* You also want to know about side effects of the treatment so that you can be prepared for them. So,

- Ask for the diagnosis.
- Ask about the course of the illness (what happens, how long it takes to get better, etc.).
- Ask why the treatment is being prescribed (how it works). If you don't understand the explanation, ask the doctor to try to phrase it in such a way that you will understand.
- Ask about the side effects of treatments so that you can brace yourself for unpleasant effects and know that what you're experiencing is not unusual.
- Ask how you know when it's okay to discontinue treatment.

WHAT DO YOU DO NOW?
Encouraging a Student to Go for Medical Advice

Leslie, your roommate, has had abdominal pains for several days. Leslie has missed a couple of classes and has been awakened in the night with the pains. But Leslie has not gone to the college health center or been in touch with the physician back home. True, it could be nothing. The pains could go away and never return. But it could be something serious, and you do care about what happens to Leslie. What do you do now?

Write down what you might do in the spaces provided. Then check the following discussion.

_____
_____
_____
_____

We would recommend saying something along these lines: "Leslie, these pains have been bothering you for several days. What do you think they are?" This approach can help draw Leslie out so you can see if Leslie is falling into any of the pitfalls noted earlier. You can find out this way if Leslie is minimizing the symptoms or, at the other extreme, assuming that they mean something life-threatening.

What if you find out that Leslie has been minimizing the symptoms because Leslie declares "Oh, I'm sure they're nothing at all." What might you say then? Write down your thoughts and then see below:

_____
_____
_____
_____

We would say something like, "True, they could be nothing, but you can't be sure. I'm concerned about you and I'd feel much better if you saw the doctor." Offer to accompany Leslie to the doctor. Now you've done two helpful things: helped correct possible minimizing of the symptoms and offered social support. (Does this ring a bell? It's similar to what we suggested for helping out Stephanie, whom you suspect of having anorexia nervosa.)

And what if it turns out that Leslie has been assuming the worst—that Leslie is avoiding the doctor for fear of a death sentence? What would you say? Write down some thoughts and then check the following text:

_____
_____
_____
_____

We recommend saying something like, "I appreciate your apprehension. I'm not a doctor, but I read that most of the time even severe pain doesn't mean that we're in serious danger. But this is what I think: Rather than worrying about what's going on, why don't you let the doctor take a look at you. It could be nothing, like you say, and the doctor can put your mind at ease. And if there is something wrong, the doctor can probably do something to help you. Come on, let's go. You shouldn't have to put up with this thing."

> **TRUTH OR FICTION** *Revisited*
>
> When you visit the doctor, you should ask all the questions you need to ask to understand what's wrong with you and how your illness should be treated. If you don't ask these questions, you are less likely to comply with medical advice.

Now and then we all get sick—even those of us with those fabled "iron constitutions." When in doubt, get medical advice. You're a good person and you owe it to yourself.

SUMMING UP

1. How much attention do you pay to your health? Do you find reasons for putting off health decisions and healthful behavior patterns?
2. How much do you know about nutrition? Does college life make it easy or difficult for you to eat in accord with your nutritional knowledge?
3. Are you satisfied with your weight? Why or why not?
4. Have you tried to diet? Have you been successful? Are your dieting practices harmful or healthful? How do you know?
5. What role does exercise play in your life? Are you doing too little? Too much?
6. What kinds of issues should you consider in deciding what kinds of exercise are right for you?
7. Do you generally feel that you get enough sleep? How does college life affect your sleep patterns?
8. Do you suffer from insomnia? What are some healthful ways in which you can handle insomnia?
9. Are you reluctant to get medical advice when you are not feeling well? Why or why not?
10. Do you follow medical advice? Why or why not?

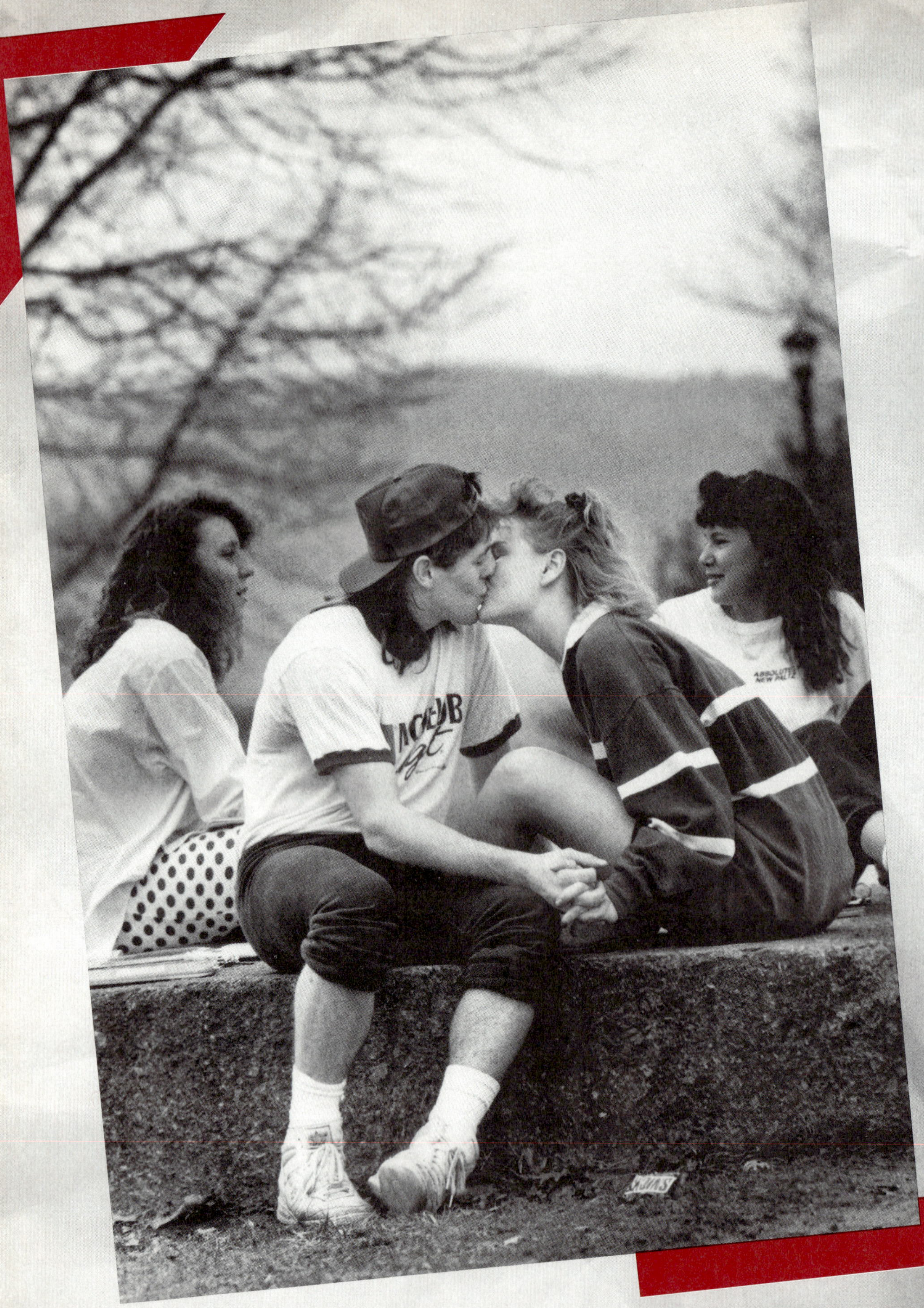

12

Living with Sex

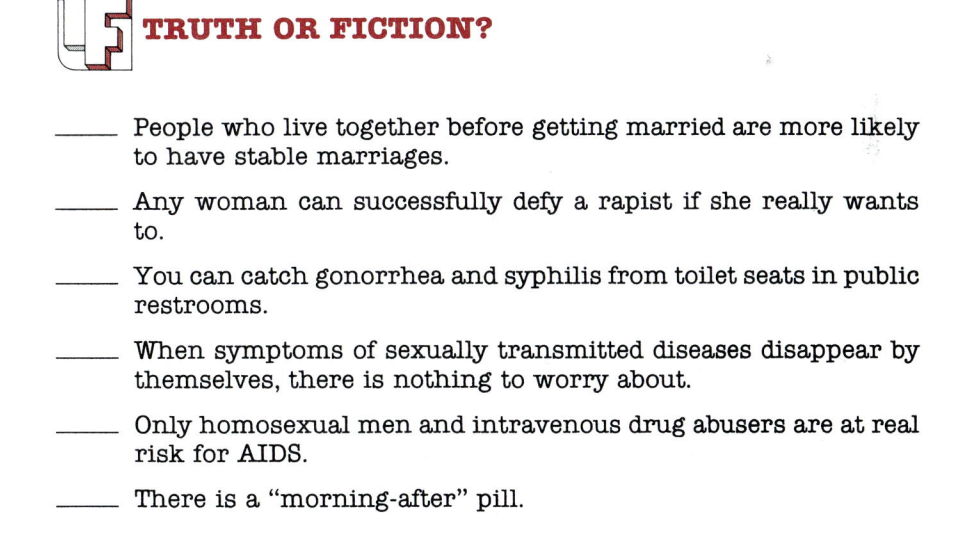

TRUTH OR FICTION?

_____ People who live together before getting married are more likely to have stable marriages.

_____ Any woman can successfully defy a rapist if she really wants to.

_____ You can catch gonorrhea and syphilis from toilet seats in public restrooms.

_____ When symptoms of sexually transmitted diseases disappear by themselves, there is nothing to worry about.

_____ Only homosexual men and intravenous drug abusers are at real risk for AIDS.

_____ There is a "morning-after" pill.

Collegiate Sexual Behavior in Perspective: A Tale of Three Generations

When your first author went off to college, men were usually not allowed into women's dormitory rooms. When a woman and he went out, she had to sign out of her dormitory, and she had to sign back in—before curfew. On more than one campus, she also had to write the name of her escort into the signout book and their destination. (No, he didn't have to take a blood test.)

Years later, when he went off to graduate school, dormitories had become coeducational, and men and women often shared bathrooms.* American sexual values and behavior remain in flux. Not only do college students' sexual practices vary widely from generation to generation, but also from person to person. Today's students are affected by many forces, including the so-called sexual revolution and more conservative trends.

The Three R's of Sex: Repression, Revolution, and Reaction

Before World War II, and for the decade after it, American sexual practices were repressed, by today's standards. Women were expected to be virgins when they married, although there was a sexual double standard that was more permissive toward men. That is, men were allowed to sow their wild oats—although the standards for women raised a question as to whom young men could sow their oats with.

Sex was assumed to be more pleasurable for men than for women. This conjecture became a self-fulfilling prophecy for many couples. That is, they usually didn't try to find ways of intensifying sexual pleasure. On the other hand, Alfred Kinsey's surveys on sexual practices suggested that college-educated women were more willing to experiment and enjoy sex.[1]

A Pendulum Swing . . . The so-called sexual revolution occurred during the 1960s and 1970s. People became more willing to talk about their sexual ideas and needs. William Masters and Virginia Johnson[2] published research that disclosed that women could reach and enjoy orgasm just as men could. They found, in fact, that with adequate stimulation, women could have multiple orgasms. During the revolution, the incidence of premarital sex increased dramatically.

Some people took up "recreational sex"—they detached sex from commitment and romance. The motto of the sexual revolution, for some, was expressed tongue-in-cheek by Bob Newhart, who played a psychologist in television's "Bob Newhart Show" of the 1970s: "If it feels right, go with it." But even during the height of the sexual revolution, most college students disapproved of sex without affection. And most college women limited premarital sex to very few partners, much of the time to an individual whom they hoped to marry.[3]

According to Kinsey's research reported in 1953, by the age of 19, 20 percent of unmarried women had engaged in sexual intercourse.[4] Twenty years later, at the height of the revolution, this figure had risen to 57 percent.[5] Interestingly, the same surveys did not show an increase in the statistics for men; 72 percent of the unmarried men in each sample had engaged in premarital intercourse by the age of 19. The sexual revolution may have been more revolutionary for women than for men.

> Is sex dirty? Only if it's done right.
> — Woody Allen

> If your sexual fantasies were truly of interest to others, they would no longer be fantasies.
> — Fran Lebowitz

> I consider promiscuity immoral. Not because sex is evil, but because sex is too good and too important.
> — Ayn Rand

---

*Your second author doubts that readers are interested in the first author's sad "exploits."

IN YOUR OWN WRITE

Do students on your campus seem generally liberal or conservative when it comes to sexual matters? What kinds of sexual pressures have you experienced at college?

___

. . . And Back? Today it seems that political and religious conservatism, in combination with fears of sexually transmitted diseases—particularly herpes and AIDS, has reversed some of the revolutionary trends.[6] The incidence of premarital sex on campus appears to have declined over the 1980s. Sex is also more likely to take place within a committed relationship.[7] One survey found that less than 40 percent of female college undergraduates were sexually active during the 1980s, as compared to about 50 percent during the latter part of the 1970s.[8]

Today's college students are exposed to many influences—parental and religious attitudes, community standards, the behavior and attitudes of their peers, R- and X-rated films, and a patchwork of recent historic trends. When they make sexual decisions, they integrate information from many sources.

Today's college students tend to be more conservative than their counterparts of the 1960s. They generally give more thought to their choice of partners and their sexual behavior.

Living with Sex

PATTERNS OF SEXUAL BEHAVIOR

Let us now consider a number of sexual practices. We shall provide information that you can use in arriving at your own decisions.

Masturbation

> In solitude he pollutes himself, and with his own hand blights all his prospects for both this world and the next. Even after being solemnly warned, he will often continue this worse than beastly practice, deliberately forfeiting his right to health and happiness for a moment's mad sensuality.
>
> J. W. Kellogg, M.D., *Plain Facts for Old and Young*, 1882. 1882.

> Don't knock masturbation—it's sex with someone I love.
> Woody Allen

> The good thing about masturbation is that you don't have to dress up for it.
> Truman Capote

The Kellogg account of masturbation by one of the founders of breakfast cereals was standard for its day. Cancer, epilepsy, heart attacks, insanity, sterility, warts, and itching—all were deemed the fate of the masturbator, despite a lack of evidence. By the way, Kellogg also warned that foods such as alcohol and coffee could stir the sex organs. He advocated "unstimulating" grains instead. In case it comes up at a mixer, you are now an authority on the genesis of corn flakes.

Ignorance was not restricted to the days of yore. The majority of a mid-1970s sample of college students believed that masturbation could be harmful.[9] Each of more than 300 men interviewed by Masters and Johnson thought that "excessive" masturbation could cause psychological problems.[10] But in one of the more self-serving details of survey history, not one thought that his frequency of masturbation posed a threat. *Is masturbation harmful?* The consensus among contemporary medical researchers and psychologists is that it is *not*.[11]

Most people—including most college students—masturbate. Men are more likely to masturbate than women. Surveys of college students report that from 89 to 97 percent of males and from 61 to 78 percent of females have masturbated.[12] Religious orthodoxy seems to suppress masturbation. But one survey found that even among regular churchgoers, 92 percent of the men and 51 percent of the women have masturbated.[13]

IN YOUR OWN WRITE

Have you been told that masturbation is harmful? What types of problems were attributed to masturbation?

_____
_____
_____
_____
_____
_____
_____
_____

None of this information means that you *should* masturbate. In addition to information about medical and psychological findings, we also consider our moral values and beliefs in our decisions. People who believe that masturbation is morally wrong or sinful are more likely to encounter anxiety when they masturbate.

Petting

Petting is touch or massage of another person's breasts or genitals. Some writers include oral–genital sex as forms of petting. Fellatio (pronounced *fell-LAY-she-oh*) is oral stimulation of the male genitals. Cunnilingus (*cun-nil-LING-us*) is oral stimulation of the female genitals. Petting is used to produce pleasure and to reach orgasm. When it is used to intensify one's partner's sexual arousal as a prelude to sexual intercourse, petting is referred to as *foreplay*.

Many students use petting as a compromise between sexual abstinence and intercourse. It allows them to express affection and encounter sexual excitement but avoid pregnancy and maintain virginity. Surveys have found touch or massage of one's partner's breasts and genitals to be almost universal among college men and women.

Premarital Intercourse

The incidence of premarital intercourse right after World War II reflected the sexual double standard that made sex more permissible for men than for women. By the age of 20, 77 percent of the single men in Kinsey's sample, but only 20 percent of single women, had participated in premarital intercourse. By age 25, 83 percent of the single men and 33 percent of single women had done so.[14]

As noted earlier, during the 1970s the incidence of premarital intercourse expanded for young singles, especially women.[15] The percentage of sexually active, unmarried, female college undergraduates probably peaked during the 1970s.[16]

People abstain from premarital intercourse for a variety of reasons: moral or religious; fear of being caught; fear of pregnancy; and fear of disease.[17] The advent of AIDS has apparently convinced many single people to be more vigilant in their choice of partners.[18] One male college student says, "Today you have to think twice. If sex looks too easy, you just don't take it." The majority of single women responding to a survey by *Glamour Magazine* reported that they had become more cautious because of AIDS.[19]

But conservatism and fear of AIDS have not killed all aspects of the sexual revolution. For one thing, college students remain more willing to talk openly about their sexual needs and feelings. Also, many collegians continue to engage in premarital intercourse. But they seem to be giving the issue more thought. They seem more discerning in their choice of partners and more apt to use safeguards against disease.

Cohabitation: "There's Nothing That I Wouldn't Do If You Would Be My POSSLQ"

There's Nothing That I Wouldn't Do If You Would Be My POSSLQ is the name of a book by CBS newsperson Charles Osgood.[20] POSSLQ? That's the dispassionate abbreviation for "Person of Opposite Sex Sharing Living Quarters"—the bureaucratic term used for cohabiters by the U.S. Bureau of the Census. Cohabitation refers to people who live together and share a sexual relationship without being married.

Cohabitation once was moralistically dubbed "living in sin." In the early 1960s, a female Columbia University student was discovered to be

IN YOUR OWN WRITE

Do many students at your college cohabit? What attitudes are expressed toward cohabitation?

cohabiting with her boyfriend off campus. There was so much adverse publicity that she was forced to withdraw from the university.

Today cohabitation is more often referred to as "living together"—period. Since the early 1960s, cohabitation has become a fairly common lifestyle for college students. As many as one student in three will cohabit at some time during his or her college career.[21] The availability of birth control methods, decreased emphasis on virginity, relaxed housing regulations, and, probably, the sense that "everyone's doing it" have all swelled the ranks of cohabiters.

So who are the cohabiters? Do they differ from students who wait until they tie the knot to set up housekeeping?

By and large, cohabiters sound like typical students. Most come from stable homes.[22] Their grades equal those of students who maintain separate lodgings. The great majority (96 percent of cohabiters surveyed at 14 state universities) look forward to eventual marriage.[23] Cohabiters often, but not always, intend to marry their POSSLQ's.[24] Many students see cohabitation as part of the courtship process.[25] Ninety percent of the cohabiters in one study of students see their lifestyle as normal and enabling them to share a close, affectionate relationship.[26]

Most cohabiters believe that their parents would disapprove, but only 7 percent regard cohabitation as morally wrong.[27] And of those students who do not cohabit, only half cite moral reasons. Most noncohabiters report, instead, that they haven't yet found Mr. or Ms. Right, or that their partners live too far away to make it sensible.

Still, most cohabiters try to hide their living arrangements from their parents. One study[28] found that:

> 57 percent were jealous of their partners' interests in other people or activities
>
> 62 percent felt "overinvolved" with their partners and partially isolated from others
>
> 49 percent felt trapped now and then
>
> 62 percent had encountered fear of pregnancy
>
> 71 percent had experienced conflicting desires for frequency of sex
>
> 62 percent of women students had intermittent difficulty reaching orgasm

All in all, the list sounds like the adjustment problems of newlyweds.

298   Chapter 12

About one-third of college students cohabit for some part of their college careers.

Since cohabiters have an opportunity to adjust to one another, do they stay together if they decide to get married? *Actually, cohabiters are more likely to get divorced than couples who did not live together before getting married.*[29] But do not conclude that cohabitation *causes* divorce. Cohabiters are less traditional than couples who choose not to cohabit, and nontraditional people are also more likely to seek divorce as a remedy to marital unhappiness.

TRUTH OR FICTION *Revisited*

People who cohabit before getting married are *not* more likely to have stable marriages.

IN YOUR OWN WRITE

If a woman is petting with a man and then asks him to stop, does he have the right to try to force her to have intercourse with him? Why or why not?

_____
_____
_____
_____
_____
_____
_____
_____

Living with Sex

Rape

Why include a discussion of rape in a book for college students? For a number of reasons. First, college women, like other women, are susceptible to rape, and as many as 450,000 rapes may take place in the United States each year.[30]

Second, the incidence of rape on campus is a pressing concern. Nine percent of a national sample of 6,159 college and university women reported that they had assented to sexual intercourse because of threats or force.[31] If we include cases of forced kissing and petting, the numbers swell. Forty-four percent of these women admitted that they had "given in to sex play" because of a "man's continual arguments and pressure." Almost 70 percent of 282 women surveyed at one college had been assaulted (mostly by dates and friends) at least once since starting college.[32] In a survey of college men, 40 percent acknowledged using force to unfasten a woman's clothing, and 13 percent admitted that they had coerced a woman into sexual intercourse.[33]

College women may be particularly vulnerable to date rape when they are away from home—perhaps for the first time—and unaware of how to handle themselves in novel situations. They may assume that a fellow student would not want to take advantage of them, and they may be overly trusting of their dates. They may not realize that some men interpret a date's willingness to go to their room or apartment as assent to sexual activity.

Why do college men commit date rapes? Usually they value sexual "scoring" over the feelings of their dates. They also frequently see themselves in a game or "sex war" with women in which men are expected to take what they can get. This adversarial view of male–female relationships may encourage them to misinterpret their dates' behavior, even when women tell them that they do not want to have sex. That is, they view the woman's

QUESTIONNAIRE
Attitudes That Contribute to Rape

Many men—and some women—share attitudes that increase the likelihood of rape. These include the ideas that "Only bad girls get raped" and that "Girls can resist rapists if they really want to."[38] Attitudes like these deny the impact of the assault and transfer the blame from the rapist to the victim. Men who believe them are more likely to view male–female relationships in terms of game playing and to misinterpret their dates' protests as just part of the game. Such men focus on "winning," not on the feelings of their dates.

Below are a number of attitudes toward rape and toward victims of rape.* Indicate whether you think each is true or false by circling the T (for True) or the F (for False).

T F 1. A girl who goes to a date's room or apartment on their first date implies that she is willing to engage in sexual activity.
T F 2. Only girls who are looking for it get raped.
T F 3. Girls often claim that they've been raped just to call attention to themselves.
T F 4. Any woman can successfully defy a rapist if she really wants to.
T F 5. When girls go around campus without bras or with short skirts and tight tops, they are asking for trouble.
T F 6. Most rape victims are "easy" or have bad reputations.
T F 7. If a girl necks or pets, she can't expect her partner then to stop just because she says to.
T F 8. Girls who hitchhike can't blame men who pick them up if they try to have sex with them.

protests as part of the "game."[34] Consider the remarks of a 20-year-old college man who was turned in to the campus police:

> I guess that I probably forced five or six women into having sex with me on dates. While I was doing it, I never saw it as rape. It was just the game that males and females play, and I was the winner. When Sara reported me to the campus cops, I laughed about it at first. After all, how could she say that I raped her after the way she'd been flirting with me in the library? How could she prove anything, you know? But now I realize that what I did was wrong, even though it didn't feel wrong to me then. It just made me feel strong and powerful. I never really thought about how the girls felt, though. I guess I sort of thought it was a game for them, too.[35]

A third reason for discussing rape is that forewarned is forearmed. When women are alerted to the nature of the problem, they are more likely to take preventive measures.

Prevention Rape prevention takes two paths. One concerns rape by strangers who may attack women who find themselves in hazardous situations. The second concerns date rapes, which comprise the great majority of campus incidents, and which call for somewhat different tactics.

The following procedures can be used to lower the likelihood of rape by strangers:

Have the campus security phone number or the local police number handy.

Arrange signals with other women in the dormitory or the neighborhood.

List first initials only in the telephone directory or on the mailbox.

T F 9. Girls who think that they're too good for men need to be taught a lesson.

T F 10. Many girls have unconscious wishes to be raped, and so they may unconsciously set up a situation in which they are vulnerable to attack.

T F 11. If a girl gets drunk at a party and has intercourse with a man she's just met there, she should be considered fair game to other men at the party who want her, whether she wants to or not.

T F 12. Many girls claim that they've been raped as a way of punishing a man for something.

T F 13. Many rapes are fabricated by pregnant women who are trying to protect their reputation.

Each of these items shows a callous attitude toward women and increases the likelihood of rape. Readers who agree with one or more of them are encouraged to carefully examine their beliefs about women and about male–female relationships.

TRUTH OR FICTION *Revisited*

It is *not* true that any woman can successfully defy a rapist if she really wants to. This is one of the attitudes that supports rape in our culture.

Living with Sex   301

Rape is a pressing concern on many campuses. College women find themselves vulnerable to rape by members of the community and—more often!—by their dates.

Use dead-bolt locks. In a dormitory, get the housing office's permission to install one.

Keep windows locked, and get iron grids for first-floor windows.

Keep doorways and entrances well lit.

Have keys ready for the car or the front door.

Do not walk by yourself in the dark. Campus security will usually accompany you from one point on campus to another after dark. Give them a call.

Stay away from deserted areas.

Don't allow strange men into your room or apartment without checking their credentials. Ask them to wait outside while you call their dispatcher. They should freely give you the phone number through the door.

Drive with the door locked and the windows up.

Check the back seat of the car before getting in.

Don't live in a risky building. Live a bit farther off campus, if necessary.

Do not pick up hitchhikers (including women hitchhikers, who occasionally flag down victims for male companions).

Do not converse with strange men. Be a bit suspicious. Not everyone you meet in the library or the cafeteria is a registered student. But the person who has sat next to you for several classes most likely is.

Shout "Fire!" not "Rape!" if you're attacked.[36] People crowd around fires but avoid scenes of violence.

The following tactics may help prevent date rapes:

Avoid getting into secluded situations until you know your date very well. (As noted in the questionnaire on pages 300–301, some men interpret a date's willingness to accompany them to their room as an agreement to engage in sexual activity.) But be aware that victims of date rapes have sometimes gotten to know their assailants.

Be very assertive and clear concerning your sexual intentions. Some rapists, particularly date rapists, tend to misinterpret women's wishes.

302   Chapter 12

If their dates begin to implore them to stop during kissing or petting, they construe pleading as "female game playing." So if kissing or petting is leading where you don't want it to go, speak up. Sad to say, some studies have found that rape victims are less self-assertive than nonvictims—and less likely to express their feelings.[37]

Talk to your date about his attitudes toward women. If you get the feeling that he believes that men are in a war with women, or that women try to "play games" with men, you may be better off dating someone else.

You can find out about attitudes by discussing items from the questionnaire on pages 300–301 with a man you are considering dating. You can say something like, "You know, my friend's date said that . . . What do you think about it?" It's a good way to find out if he has attitudes that can lead to trouble.

SEXUALLY TRANSMITTED DISEASES

Sexually transmitted diseases (STDs)—also referred to as venereal diseases—are widespread on campus, but, as shown by the comments of one woman, protecting oneself can be awkward:

> It's one thing to talk about "being responsible about STD" and a much harder thing to do it at the very moment. It's just plain hard to say to someone I am feeling very erotic with, "Oh, yes, before we go any further, can we have a conversation about STD?" It's hard to imagine murmuring into someone's ear at a time of passion, "Would you mind slipping on this condom or using this cream just in case one of us has STD?" Yet it seems awkward to bring it up beforehand, if it's not yet clear between us that we want to make love with one another.[39]

Because of difficulty talking over STDs with sex partners, some students confess that they "wing it."[40] They may also be aware that homosexuals and drug abusers have been at the greatest risk for AIDS and assume that "It can't happen to me"—especially in a nice, protected campus environment. Even though many students have become more cautious about sex because of AIDS, others have not. And so the incidence of several STDs has risen on the campuses. AIDS is far from the only source of concern.

Other diseases to think about include gonorrhea, syphilis, chlamydia, and herpes. Let's have a frank talk about the kinds of diseases that are around today, how they are contracted, what they do, and what we can

IN YOUR OWN WRITE

What are some of the problems students encounter in trying to protect themselves from sexually transmitted diseases?

> You're not just sleeping with one person, you're sleeping with everyone *they* ever slept with.
>
> Dr. Theresa Crenshaw, President, American Association of Sex Educators, Counselors and Therapists

do about them. Some of them are frightening, but it's more frightening to pretend that they don't exist.

In the case of AIDS, which has thus far eluded efforts to produce a vaccine or a cure, prevention is the primary weapon.[41] So we shall be talking about "safer" sex—rather than "safe" sex—because there are few guarantees.

Bacterial Infections

Several STDs, including gonorrhea, syphilis, and chlamydia, are caused by bacterial infections.

Gonorrhea Gonorrhea is the second most frequently occurring STD on campus, and 1.8 million new cases per year are reported in the United States.[42] The *Neisseria gonorrhoeae* bacterium causes gonorrhea, and it can be transmitted by vaginal, oral, or anal intercourse.

Infected men have a penile discharge that begins within three to five days. The discharge is clear at first. Within a day it turns yellow to yellow-green, thickens, and becomes puslike. The urethra (urinary passage) becomes inflamed and it burns when he urinates.

Ironically, gonorrhea can be more troublesome to women because most women do *not* have symptoms during the early stages of infection. And so they are apt to go untreated. But when left untreated, gonorrhea spreads through the genital and urinary tracts, where it can cause infertility and other problems. One problem is pelvic inflammatory disease (PID), which makes periods painful and irregular and causes lower abdominal pain, fever, headaches, and nausea. *Given the potentially tragic outcomes of gonorrhea and other infections, it is morally imperative for people who learn that they have STDs to inform their partners.*

Gonorrhea is detected from samples of discharges. Doctors treat it (and nearly always cure it) with antibiotics like penicillin. New, penicillin-resistant strains have appeared, but they are usually cured by other antibiotics or larger doses of penicillin.

Syphilis Syphilis infects nearly 85,000 Americans annually. The *Treponema pallidum* bacterium, which causes syphilis, can be transmitted by genital, oral, or anal sex.

TRUTH OR FICTION *Revisited*

Gonorrhea and syphilis are *not* communicated by toilet seats in public restrooms.

Syphilis has four stages of development. In the primary stage, a painless chancre (a round, hard, ulcerlike lesion that has raised edges) develops at the site of infection two to four weeks after contact. The chancre disappears in a few weeks. If left untreated, however, syphilis continues to develop beneath the skin. In the secondary stage, which begins a few weeks to a few months later, a skin rash develops. It consists of painless, reddish bumps that darken and then burst, emitting a discharge. There may be sores in the mouth, a sore throat, painful and swollen joints, and headaches and fever, so that a victim may think he or she has the flu. These symptoms disappear, too; syphilis then enters the latent stage, in which it may lie dormant for as many as 40 years. Some people eventually experience final, or tertiary, syphilis, which may generate large ulcers and destroy the central-nervous and cardiovascular systems. Tertiary syphilis killed the painter Paul Gauguin.

Because the primary and secondary symptoms of syphilis always disappear, sufferers may be tempted to delude themselves that they are no longer in danger and not see the doctor. This is unfortunate. Syphilis can be diagnosed by a simple blood test (called a "VDRL"), and it can be eradicated by penicillin. If you had suspicious symptoms and they went away, go to the health center, a hospital, or a private physician. You can treat, and eradicate, syphilis at any stage.

TRUTH OR FICTION *Revisited*

There can still be a great deal to worry about after the symptoms of sexually transmitted diseases subside. See your doctor.

Chlamydia   Chlamydial infections have been mushrooming, and there are now 4 million new infections each year.[43] The incidence is particularly high among college students. Moreover, about 45 percent of those who contract gonorrhea also have chlamydia.[44]

Chlamydia is caused by the *Chlamydia trachomatis* bacterium. Symptoms are similar to but usually milder than those of gonorrhea. Men have burning urination and a discharge. Chlamydia causes frequent and painful urination in women, disrupts the menstrual cycle, and can give rise to PID. Antibiotics like tetracycline and erythromycin are more effective than penicillin in treating chlamydia. *Students who find that they have one STD should ask to be diagnosed for others, and they may need more than one type of treatment.*

Less Common Bacterial Infections   The incidence of rarer sexually transmitted bacterial infections—e.g., chancroid, lymphogranuloma, and granuloma inguinale—has also risen in recent years.[45] They are all characterized by genital or rectal ulcers, or by enlarged lymph nodes in the groin. They are all treated with antibiotics. Because of their relative rareness, these diseases are often misdiagnosed. If the first doctor you see doesn't find anything, or tries a treatment but symptoms persist, get another opinion. (It is a good idea *and standard patient procedure* to get a second opinion when in doubt!)

Viral Infections

Viruses also cause STDs. Diseases include genital herpes, AIDS, and genital warts.

Herpes   There are different kinds of herpes. Each is caused by a variety of the *Herpes simplex* virus. Most common is the HSV-1 virus. HSV-1 usually causes cold sores or fever blisters on nongenital areas like the lips or in the mouth. The HSV-2 virus gives rise to genital herpes, which is symptomized by painful sores and blisters in the genital region.

Nearly 100 million Americans have been infected by the HSV-1 virus, and another 10 million have genital herpes.[46] The HSV-1 virus is spread readily by kissing, by sharing a drinking cup or towels, and so on. The HSV-2 virus is usually transmitted by vaginal, oral, and anal sex, and there are half a million new cases a year.[47]

People with genital herpes have reddish, painful bumps ("papules") in the genital region. The bumps develop into small, painful blisters that contain infectious fluid. The blisters fill with pus, then rupture. Sufferers may also have headaches, muscle aches, fever, swollen lymph nodes, burning urination, and, in women, a vaginal discharge. The blisters crust over and heal in about two weeks, but about half of victims have recurrent episodes. Genital herpes is most infectious when symptoms are out in the open, but it can also be communicated between flare-ups.[48]

Women are in greater danger from genital herpes. Men typically must contend with discomfort only, but some infected women have developed cervical cancer. Women can also pass genital herpes on to babies during childbirth, and the disease can be fatal to newborns.[49]

Doctors diagnose genital herpes by visual examination during a flare-up or from fluid samples taken from the base of sores. We do not yet have a cure for herpes, but the medication *acyclovir* and more recently developed drugs provide some symptom relief. Aspirin, warm baths, and loose clothing also help.

IN YOUR OWN WRITE

What do you think are your chances of contracting AIDS? Why?

___

Acquired Immune Deficiency Syndrome (AIDS) AIDS is caused by human immunodeficiency virus, which is more commonly called "the AIDS virus." The AIDS virus is communicated by vaginal and anal intercourse, and in ways that permit the transmission of contaminated blood—for example, sharing hypodermic needles (as when a group of people shoot up a drug), blood transfusions, and childbirth.[50] The virus is found in large amounts in blood, semen, and vaginal secretions. Contaminated semen can infect cells of the cervix and the rectum and may also enter the body through tiny rips in the vaginal or rectal lining. There is no evidence that the AIDS virus has been spread by kissing, but small quantities of it are found in the saliva of victims. So deep or "French" kissing in which saliva is passed from mouth to mouth can theoretically pose a threat.

Helen Singer Kaplan,[51] director of Cornell University's Human Sexuality Program, suggests that the AIDS virus can be transmitted any time it comes into contact with a mucus membrane, such as the areolas (the dark rings that surround the nipples of the breasts) or the inner lining of the mouth, and whenever it breaches a crevice in the skin, such as a tiny wound or scrape. Some might consider Kaplan's position extremist, but by 1989, more than 2,000 women had contracted AIDS from heterosexual activity.[52] There is no evidence that AIDS can be contracted by using public toilets, hugging or holding infected people, or sharing living quarters or classrooms with infected people. Table 12.1 describes the risks associated with various sexual behavior patterns.

The AIDS virus does its damage by killing white blood cells (T-helper lymphocytes) of the immune system. T-helper lymphocytes recognize disease

Campuses have become inundated by literature on the fatal sexually transmitted disease, AIDS. Since no vaccine or cure for AIDS has been discovered, prevention is the wisest strategy for coping with AIDS.

agents and "instruct" other white blood cells (B lymphocytes) to manufacture antibodies that combat these agents. Because of loss of T-helper lymphocytes, the body becomes prey to opportunistic disease organisms that wouldn't stand much of a chance of maturing in people with intact immune systems.

TABLE 12.1 Sexual Transmission of AIDS: Degrees of Risk

KIND OF RISK	DEGREE OF SAFETY	KIND OF ACTIVITY
1. No-Risk Sex. No touching each other.	100 percent safe.	Celibacy, no sex at all. Talking sexy; sharing your sexual fantasies, sharing erotica; telephone sex.
2. Safe Sex: Dry Sex: No exchanged body fluids.	Probably 100 percent safe.	Caressing the dry parts of each other's bodies; masturbating in each other's presence but without physical contact.
3. Low-Risk Sex: No mingling of infected body fluids.	Probably not 100 percent safe, but close to it.	Stimulation of each other's genitalia to orgasm without mingling of body fluids; vaginal, anal, or oral sex using a latex condom with a partner you have reason to believe is not infected but whose AIDS status you are not certain of. (But watch out: Exciting sexual experiences can sweep you away into an unsafe sexual act.)
4. High-Risk Sex.	A significant possibility of infection if your partner is a carrier of the AIDS virus.	Vaginal or anal intercourse using condoms, with a high-risk person, or with a person who might have been exposed, or with a stranger whose exposure history you do not know.
5. Suicidal Sex.	A strong probability that you will become infected with the AIDS virus with repeated sex, but you can catch AIDS on a single exposure.	Unprotected vaginal, anal, or oral sexual relations with a high-risk person or with a stranger, or with a known carrier of the AIDS virus.

Living with Sex

The AIDS virus has affected fewer people than the bacterial infections and the virus that causes genital herpes. But the nation has been preoccupied with AIDS because AIDS appears fatal to everyone who develops a full-blown case. Not everyone who is infected develops a full-blown case, however, and the medical community has not agreed on the percentage of infected people who will do so.

People who develop AIDS often come down with an illness resembling mononucleosis from a week to many months following infection. Symptoms include fatigue, fever, and swollen glands. A rash, headaches, and nausea may also be present. These symptoms normally fade within a few weeks. Within a few months, the person may develop AIDS-related complex (ARC), which is mainly known by swollen lymph glands. Weeks or months later, the sufferer may develop a full-blown case with fatigue, fever, swollen glands, diarrhea, and weight loss. Opportunistic diseases may take hold, including cancers (many gay males with AIDS have contracted Kaposi's sarcoma, a cancer of the blood cells) and a type of pneumonia (PCP) that is symptomized by coughing and shortness of breath.

You belong to the group "college students." The following groups have been at greatest risk for contracting AIDS:[53]

1. Homosexual men: The gay communities of San Francisco and New York were particularly hard hit.[54] About 62 percent of cases of AIDS are among homosexual and bisexual males. Gays and bisexuals have accounted for *decreasing* percentages of the incidence of new cases over the past few years.[55]
2. Intravenous (IV) drug abusers: nearly 27 percent of cases.[56] The incidence among drug abusers has been increasing.
3. Sex partners of IV drug abusers.
4. Babies born to sex partners of IV drug abusers.
5. Prostitutes.
6. Men who frequent prostitutes.
7. Sex partners of men who frequent prostitutes.
8. People receiving blood transfusions—mostly surgery patients and hemophiliacs. (This avenue of infection is unlikely today because of precautions taken by the medical community.)

Although persons on this list may be at greatest risk, others cannot assume that they have nothing to worry about. A few short years ago, homosexual males accounted for three of four AIDS victims. But the gay community has responded to education about AIDS, and they are accounting for smaller percentages of new cases each year. IV drug abusers and their sex partners are accounting for increasing numbers of new cases. Although gay males and IV drug abusers from major metropolitan areas have been at the highest risk, it is foolhardy to assume that students at the University of Iowa, Creighton University, Skidmore, and Los Angeles Pierce College can afford to ignore the threat of AIDS.

TRUTH OR FICTION *Revisited*

It is *not* true that only homosexual men and intravenous drug abusers are at real risk for AIDS. One's behavior and not the group to which one belongs places one at risk for AIDS.

Infection by the AIDS virus is diagnosed by blood tests. It can take several months after infection for signs of the disease to develop, so repeated blood tests may be necessary.

Unfortunately, we have no vaccine or cure for AIDS, and the prospect of a breakthrough remains uncertain.[57] Antiviral drugs like AZT apparently slow the progress of the disease, especially when they are used in combination with drugs that combat the opportunistic illnesses that afflict AIDS victims.[58] AZT has negative side effects, however, and the eventual outcome—as of today—continues to look bleak. So the only rational way to respond to AIDS is through *prevention*, as described in the discussion of "safe(r)" sex.

For the latest information on AIDS, call the National AIDS Hotline at 1-800-342-2437. If you prefer your information in Spanish, call 1-800-344-7432.

Genital Warts A less virulent virus produces genital warts (also called venereal warts). There are 1 million new cases of genital warts each year.[59] On moist areas, warts are pink and soft. On dry skin they are yellow-gray and hard. Warts may be vaporized, frozen off, surgically removed, treated with podophyllin, or burned off—by a doctor!

Other STDs

There are many other STDs, but we can only mention a few of them here. We advise readers who want more information to consult human-sexuality or health textbooks, their doctors, or their college counseling and health centers.

Moniliasis is a yeast infection that affects women. Yeast is a fungus—that is, a form of microscopic plant life. Moniliasis irritates the vagina and causes a white, cheesy discharge. It can be cured by vaginal suppositories or creams.

Trichomoniasis ("trich") affects both sexes and is caused by a protozoan—that is, a one-celled animal. Trich irritates the genital region and causes a white or yellow discharge with a disagreeable odor. It is treated in men and women with metronidazole (brand name, Flagyl).

Pubic lice ("crabs") are lice that can be seen with the naked eye and are spread by bringing together pubic hair or sharing infested clothing or bedding. Lice mainly cause itching. They can be eradicated by gamma benzene hexachloride (brand name, Kwell) or by A-200 pyrinate.

Now that we know of the things that can happen when we are infected by STDs, we may agree that the most sensible way to cope with them is to avoid them.

Safe(r) Sex in the Age of AIDS

Preventing STDs is not a pleasant topic, but it is crucial to consider precautions that lower the danger of contracting them. So here are some things that sexually active readers can do. Some are rather easy to do. Others require some courage. Some are more important than others. Some have a moralistic ring, perhaps, but the goal is to remain healthy—and alive. These measures will make sex safer, but no one can guarantee absolute safety.

1. *Be discerning.* Undertake sexual activity only with people whom you know well and who are not members of the high-risk groups for AIDS. Consider the levels of sexual safety described in Table 12.1.
2. *Inspect your partner's sex organs.* It may be feasible to visually inspect your partner's sex organs for rashes, chancres, blisters, discharges, warts, and lice during foreplay. A disagreeable odor is a warning sign.
3. *Wash your sex organs before and after.* Washing before protects your partner; washing right after with soap and water can remove some

WHAT DO YOU DO NOW?
Making Sex Safe(r) in the Age of AIDS

You've seen Jamie several times and things are going well. Jamie is clever, seems to see many things as you do, and is altogether very appealing. Now the day is drawing to a close. The two of you have been nuzzling and you can sense where things are leading.

The warning bulb lights up! As fantastic as Jamie is, you realize that you don't know all the places Jamie has "been." Jamie seems healthy enough, but you can't see what's swimming in Jamie's bloodstream either.

What do you do now? How do you guard yourself without alienating Jamie?

Consider the few possibilities and write some down in the following spaces. Then see below to compare your ideas with ours.

1. _____

2. _____

3. _____

What an awkward situation! If you inquire about STDs, it is implying that you want to engage in sexual relations. Maybe you're not sure Jamie is thinking along those lines. And even if you're sure that Jamie is, will you seem too direct? Will talking about it dampen passions and kill spontaneity?

Yes, talking about it might do all these things. Life has its risks. But which is more hazardous: a clumsy moment or infection with a lethal illness? Or look at it this way: Are you truly prepared to die for sex?

---

     disease agents. Urinating afterwards may be of help, especially to men, because urine's acid content can kill some disease organisms in the urethra.

4. *Use spermicides.* Spermicides are touted as means of birth control, but many jellies, creams, and foams kill disease organisms along with sperm.[60] Ask a pharmacist.

5. *Use condoms.* Latex condoms help prevent transmission of the microbes that cause gonorrhea, syphilis, and AIDS.[61] It is more effective to combine condoms with spermicides (which also kill many disease organisms).

6. *See a physician about medicines.* Antibiotics following unprotected sex may guard against bacterial infections, but they are of no use against herpes or AIDS. Also, routine use of antibiotics renders them less effective when you need them.

7. *Get regular medical checkups.* Checkups include blood tests. Checkups enable you to learn about and treat many disorders that might have gone unnoticed. Although there is no cure for AIDS, early detection permits treatment by drugs that retard growth of the virus[62] and deter some of the opportunistic diseases that assail infected individuals.

8. *When you have reservations, stop.* If you're in doubt as to whether what you're contemplating is safe, don't do it. First get advice from a source you trust.

We grant that there may be no perfect answer, but here are some things you can do:

1. Ask pleasantly, "Is there anything I should know about?" The question is open-ended. If Jamie is as clever as you assume, Jamie should take the hint and give you the information you need.

2. If Jamie responds "I love you," be pleased. It's good to hear. You can answer with something like, "I'm mad about you, too." But then you add, "Is there anything *else* to tell me?"

3. If Jamie asks, "Like what?" you can be indirect again and say, "Well, you weren't locked in a closet all your life just waiting for me, were you? I don't know about everywhere you've been . . ."

4. If you find that too awkward, or if you prefer to be more direct, you can say, "I'm in perfect health as far as I know. Have you had any problems I ought to know about?" By stating that you are healthy, you invite Jamie to reciprocate by offering similar information.

5. If Jamie denies infection with STDs, you can then bring up the issue of prevention. For example, you can say, "I've brought something that I'd like to use . . . " (that is, a condom).

6. Or, "I realize this is clumsy . . . ," (you are expressing a genuine feeling and requesting permission to pursue an awkward topic; Jamie ought to help out by saying something like "I know" or "Don't worry about it— what're you thinking about?") "but things aren't as safe as they used to be. Can we talk about what we're thinking of doing?"

Yes, preventing STDs can be difficult to talk about, but by becoming knowledgeable about STDs and by self-assertion, you can markedly reduce the risk of contracting AIDS and other STDs.[63] Moreover, your partner doesn't dwell in an isolated cave. Your partner knows of the perils of STDs—or ought to—and should work with you so that sex is unpressured and safe. You are willing to trade some spontaneity for health, some passion for security. If your partner doesn't value your feelings and urges unsafe sex, you may want to reconsider the value of the relationship. We have confidence in you. We know you can do better.

BIRTH CONTROL

Sexually active college students also need to face the question of birth control. Assuming that you'll be okay most of the time is like playing Russian roulette—but you're playing with the well-being of your partner and also, potentially, with the welfare of a child who may be unwanted or be reared by parents who are not ready. Let us consider a number of methods.

> Familiarity breeds contempt—and children.
>
> MARK TWAIN

The "Pill"

The most widely used birth-control method by unmarried women between the ages of 15 and 44 is the "pill."[64] There are various kinds of pills, but they all contain hormones called estrogens and progestins, singly or in combination. Women cannot conceive children when they are already pregnant, and combination pills (that contain estrogens and progestins) fool the brain into acting as though women are pregnant. So-called minipills contain progestins only. Minipills act in two ways. They thicken the cervical mucus and prevent many sperm from passing into the uterus and fallopian tubes where they normally fertilize egg cells (ova). Minipills also make the inner lining of the uterus unreceptive to the egg; and so if the woman does conceive, the fertilized egg is passed from the body. *For these reasons, many users look upon the combination pill as a contraceptive—that is, an agent that prevents conception—but they see the minipill as an early way of aborting an embryo.* Birth-control pills are available only by a doctor's prescription.

Birth control pills are about 96 percent effective, which means that 4 percent of sexually active users will become pregnant within a year. However, the great majority of pregnancies that occur while on the pill reflect failure to follow directions (mostly skipping pills). Pills are taken from 20 to 28 days each month. Users are advised to take them at the same time each day and in sequence to prompt memory.[65]

The great advantage to the pill is that it makes sex spontaneous and usually doesn't interfere with sexual sensations. *But the pill does not prevent STDs, so its proper use, biologically speaking, is within a monogamous sexual relationship with a partner who is known to be free of STDs.*

The main drawbacks of pills concern side effects. Minor side effects from estrogen include nausea and vomiting (usually during the first day or two of usage), fluid retention (feeling "bloated"), weight gain, headaches, tenderness in the breasts, and dizziness.[66] More serious—but uncommon—problems include benign tumors, jaundice, gall bladder problems, migraine headaches, and elevated blood pressure. Blood clots, strokes, and hemorrhages are also reported. There are intermittent reports of connections between the pill and cancer, so some authorities suggest using low-dose pills for the shortest time possible.[67] College students may find comfort in the fact that users are not considered at high risk for most disorders until they turn 35. Even then, many women continue to use the pill—under closer medical supervision.

Progestins actually foster male characteristics, so women who take the minipill are likely to encounter side effects such as acne, increase in facial hair, thinning of scalp hair, reduction in breast size, vaginal dryness, and missed or shorter periods. *When on either kind of pill, women should discuss any physical changes with their physicians.*

The "Morning-After Pill" So-called morning-after pills also consist of estrogens or progestins. Women ovulate (release an egg cell from an ovary) during the middle of the month, and morning-after pills can prevent implantation of the egg after it has been fertilized. So usage of this pill is actually an early abortion technique. Morning-after pills are most effective when administered within 72 hours (three days) after ovulation.[68] They are higher in hormone content than most birth-control pills and are sometimes taken two or more times per day. Because of the high doses, morning-after pills cause nausea in about 70 percent of users and vomiting in one-third.[69]

TRUTH OR FICTION *Revisited*

There really is a morning-after pill. But most users encounter nausea.

The morning-after pill usually does the job—it terminates pregnancy. However, it is controversial because it is an abortion technique—not a contraceptive technique—and because of the side effects. *The morning-after pill must be begun within 72 hours after ovulation. Women who wait to see whether they have missed a period are no longer candidates for usage.*

Intrauterine Devices (IUDs)

IUDs are used by about 3 percent of unmarried women.[70] The IUD is fixed in the uterus by a physician and can be left in place for a year or more.

(Some IUDs made of copper have remained effective for eight years.[71]) No one knows exactly how IUDs work. The main theory is that they produce uterine inflammation that (1) can destroy sperm as they travel through to meet eggs in the fallopian tubes and (2) prevent fertilized eggs from becoming implanted after they enter the uterus from a fallopian tube. In the latter case, the IUD would, in effect, be effecting an early abortion.

Fewer than 1 percent of women become pregnant with an IUD in place. The IUD, like the pill, allows for spontaneous sex, and it does not diminish sexual sensations. Also like the pill, it offers no protection against STDs.

Why, then, are IUDs relatively unpopular? For one thing, they can be painful to insert. For another, about 10,000 American users per year are hospitalized with fallopian tube infections and pelvic inflammatory disease (PID) that can be attributed to the devices.[72] These infections can cause infertility. Also, a number of devices are expelled by the user. Finally, the uterine wall is sometimes perforated (torn) by the IUD—a potentially lethal problem that afflicts 900 American users each year.

Diaphragms

Diaphragms are preferred by about 4 percent of unmarried American women. Diaphragms are shallow cups with flexible rims that are made of thin rubber. A physician fits them to the contours of the vagina. A cream or jelly that kills sperm (i.e., a spermicide) is spread on the inside of the cup and it is placed against the cervix. The diaphragm is normally inserted within six hours before intercourse. (Some suggest that the spermicide remains effective for only two hours.[73]) When placed properly, it fits snugly over the cervix, denying sperm passage into the uterus. But as a barrier device, the diaphragm is not reliable. Its main function is to hold the spermicide in place. The diaphragm with a spermicide is nearly as reliable as the pill—so long as the spermicide is applied carefully and the diaphragm is inserted properly. Perhaps because of carelessness, about 17 percent of users become pregnant within a year.[74]

A great advantage of the diaphragm is the nearly complete lack of side effects. The occasional woman who is allergic to rubber can switch to a plastic model. About 1 man or woman in 20 encounters irritation from the spermicide, a problem that is often alleviated by switching brands. Another plus is the fact that spermicides offer some protection against gonorrhea and PID.

Given all these pluses, why is the diaphragm relatively unpopular? One reason is the inconvenience of having to insert it prior to intercourse. It kills the spontaneity. And if it is inserted an hour or so before the date, the woman may wind up watching the clock.

By the way, spermicides can be used without diaphragms, but diaphragms help keep them in place.

Contraceptive Sponges

The contraceptive sponge (brand name, Today) came into use in the 1980s. The sponge is a soft, disposable device that is inserted into the vagina and is available without prescription. Unlike the diaphragm, it need not be fitted. Like the diaphragm, it provides a barrier that holds a spermicide. But the sponge can be inserted up to 18 hours before intercourse and may have the additional effect of absorbing sperm. It is odorless and tasteless, and users find it less drippy than the diaphragm. All in all, the contraceptive sponge appears to have the benefits of the diaphragm without the mess. And since the spermicide is longer-lasting, users are not as likely to get involved in clock-watching. Another advantage is that the sponge provides flexibility. A woman who is sexually active on an intermittent basis can keep a sponge on hand or pick one up. She is not making the commitment to regular sexual activity that is implied by going on the pill or by using the IUD. Nor need she see the doctor to use the sponge—more convenient, again, than the diaphragm.

Now the negative. Chances of failure are comparable to those of the diaphragm. About 1 user in 20 (male and female) encounters mild irritation from the spermicide. There is a very remote chance of toxic shock syndrome (TSS): One case arises for every 4 *million* days of use. (The chances of problems due to pregnancy are much greater, and the spermicide in the sponge also helps prevent gonorrhea and PID.) The chances of TSS are made still more remote by leaving the sponge in place for less than the maximum effective time.

Four percent of unmarried women use contraceptive sponges, but this figure will probably rise.

Cervical Caps

Cervical caps are made of rubber or plastic and fitted over the cervix. Unlike the diaphragm, they can be kept in place by suction for up to several weeks at a time. They function as a barrier that prevents sperm from reaching the uterus and fallopian tubes, where fertilization normally occurs. An important advantage to the cap is the apparent lack of side effects, although some women report that it is uncomfortable. Use of the cervical cap can be combined with spermicide, and the combination is apparently about as reliable as that of the diaphragm and spermicide.

Disadvantages are that women must be fitted for the cap and that many women are contoured so that the caps do not remain in place. Also, caps sometimes become dislodged during intercourse. For these reasons, and because caps can be hard to get, they are not used by many American women.

Condoms

Condoms are used by about 16 percent of unmarried women (and a similar percentage of married women).[75] All condoms can be used to prevent pregnancy. Latex condoms ("rubbers," "safes") also provide protection from STDs, including the AIDS virus. This is why they are also referred to as *prophylactics* (meaning "agents that protect against disease"). Condoms are readily available in pharmacies without prescription, from family-planning clinics, and, in many locales—including some college dormitories—from vending machines. They are the only device that is worn by the man rather than the woman. They serve as barriers that prevent sperm (and microscopic disease organisms) from entering the woman. Conversely, they protect the man from infected vaginal fluids.

Condoms are highly reliable when they are put on (and removed!) carefully. Use of a spermicide with a condom is even more reliable.

Use of condoms changes the psychology of sexual relations. First, it shifts much of the responsibility for contraception to the man. Other methods we described focus on the woman. In each case, the woman suffers the side effects and the inconvenience and is perceived as responsible for avoiding pregnancy. *Avoiding unwanted pregnancy is a shared obligation, of course.*

Second, use of condoms makes sex less spontaneous, a concern reported by nearly 70 percent of the respondents to a recent survey.[76] Third, condoms decrease sexual sensations somewhat, predominantly for the man. For these reasons, many men refuse to use them. But because condoms are free of side effects (an advantage reported by 70 percent of the female respondents to the same survey[77]) and are reliable (when used properly), many women are assertive about using them.

Coitus Interruptus

Coitus (pronounced co-EET-us) interruptus, or the "withdrawal method"—is removal of the penis from the vagina prior to ejaculation. Let us tell you a joke: "What do you call couples who use coitus interruptus?" "Parents."

We include coitus interruptus as a birth-control method because you may hear about it from other sources. As implied in the joke, it is unreliable. Even if the man does manage to withdraw before ejaculating, sperm is present in fluids that are typically discharged prior to ejaculation. Still, 6 percent of unmarried women rely on withdrawal! Enough said?

Rhythm Methods

There are a number of rhythm methods—also referred to as natural birth control. Each is based on awareness of the phase of the woman's menstrual cycle. Women can conceive only for about 48 hours after they ovulate. After that, an egg cell (ovum) can no longer be fertilized. Sperm can live for about 72 hours in the female reproductive tract. So if the woman knows exactly when she is ovulating, she can avert pregnancy by avoiding intercourse for three days prior to ovulation and two days afterward.

Most women who have regular 28-day cycles can use the calendar method reliably. Women ovulate 14 days before their periods begin. So regular women can track their cycles on calendars and place sex off limits for a few days before and after ovulation—perhaps four days before and three days after, just to be safe.

For women with irregular cycles, the math becomes complicated, and the period of abstention becomes protracted. Other rhythm methods involve tracking the woman's basal body temperature or the viscosity (stickiness) of her cervical mucus. These methods are explained in detail in Howard Shapiro's *The New Birth-Control Book** and in human-sexuality textbooks. You may also find helpful advice at the college health or counseling center, at a local family-planning clinic, or from a private gynecologist. Ovulation-predicting kits are available without prescription from pharmacies, but they're very expensive and can be complicated to use. (They are normally used by people with fertility problems who want to optimize their chances of becoming pregnant.)

There are a number of advantages to the rhythm method. Since they do not use artificial devices, they are acceptable to the Catholic church. (Premarital sex, of course, is not.) Second, there are no side effects. Third, sexual spontaneity and sexual sensations are kept intact—at least on "safe" days. Combining the rhythm method with, say, a contraceptive sponge or a condom, renders conception all but impossible. On the other hand, the rhythm method provides no protection from STDs.

Other Methods

There are a number of other methods, including douching and sterilization. Douching is flushing the vagina with a stream of water or another liquid following intercourse. The function of the water is to wash sperm out, although some commercial douches also kill sperm. However, Shapiro[78] characterizes douching as "totally ineffective," essentially because large numbers of sperm manage to reach beyond the range of the douche within seconds after ejaculation.

Sterilization is nearly 100 percent effective and is actually the most commonly used birth-control method by married people. Sterilization involves surgery, and the major methods in use today are the tubal ligation

---

* Shapiro, H. I. (1988). *The New Birth-Control Book*. Englewood Cliffs, NJ: Prentice-Hall.

in women and the vasectomy in men. The tubal ligation cuts and ties back the fallopian tubes, which carry egg cells (ova) from the ovary to the uterus. The vasectomy severs the vas deferens, which transport semen from the testes to the penis in men. Although these operations are sometimes reversible—especially when doctors strive to carry them out in a way that enhances the chances of reversibility—they are still considered "permanent." If you want to have children someday, sterilization is not for you. By the way, many college-age people who believe that they will never want to have children change their minds in their late twenties and their thirties.[79]

So there is a good deal to think about concerning birth control. If you are sexually active and want to avoid pregnancy, there are decisions to be made—which brings us to our final topic: sexual decision making.

SEXUAL DECISION MAKING

We are all faced with sexual decisions. We decide whether or not we will be sexually active—and with whom. We decide whether we will masturbate, whether we will confine sexual activity to meaningful relationships, how we will handle sexual problems, and what we will do about the possibilities of contracting STDs and becoming pregnant. Even when we think that we are not making our own decisions but are following the teachings of our parents or our religions, we are still deciding to follow these teachings. *Deciding not to decide is a way of making a decision.* Whether we want to be or not, we are responsible for our own sexual behavior. We are responsible for the people who place trust in us and for ourselves.

In the first author's human-sexuality text, he first suggested using a balance sheet like the one in Figure 12.1 to help college students make decisions.[80] Hundreds of students have found that the balance sheet helps them make up their minds on various matters.

The balance sheet helps you weigh the pluses and minuses of possible courses of action. Let's consider the case of Steffi, a student at a California State College who had been involved in a sexual relationship for several weeks and was contemplating going on the pill. Steffi used the balance sheet to list the projected gains and losses for herself and her partner according to five criteria:

Experiential: How will it feel? What is its effect on sexual relations? How does it affect sexual sensations and spontaneity?

Biological: For example, what are the side effects of birth-control methods? What are the effects on STDs?

Financial: Can you afford it—literally? For example, how much do pills cost? How much do babies cost?

Ethical: Is what you are considering consistent with your religious and parental teachings? Is that important to you? Will you experience guilt, anxiety, or shame? Is the course of behavior consistent with your ideas concerning sex roles and who takes the responsibility for the decision? (For example, if you are a woman, do you think that responsibility for birth control should be placed on your shoulders only?)

Legal: Are you contemplating something that is against the law? What could happen to your partner and to you?

As shown in Figure 12.1, Steffi filled in some of the spaces on the sheet to indicate the following pieces of information:

Sex can be spontaneous.

For all practical purposes, the pill can be considered 100 percent effective (I'm assuming I'll take them as directed).

I'm 20 years old (young enough not to be too worried about the pill's potential effect on my health).

The pill is kind of expensive—about $20 per month.

I am a Catholic.

The pill is legal.

The remaining blank spaces prompted Steffi to consider other issues. For example, she realized that she forgot to think about the side effects of the pill and the fact that it is useless against STDs. The information prompted by using the balance sheet is placed in parentheses.

Steffi decided not to go on the pill for several reasons: (1) She was concerned about side effects; (2) she didn't want to spend the money; and (3) she felt that by taking the pill, she was assuming all responsibility for birth control and that she would rather share it with her partner. Her periods were regular and she decided (1) to use the rhythm method (to abstain from intercourse for a week in the middle of her cycle), and (2) to have her partner use condoms every time they made love. Other college women in similar situations have gone on the pill.

Research shows that people who use the balance sheet to carefully weigh their alternatives usually have fewer regrets and are more likely to

FIGURE 12.1. Steffi's Balance Sheet for Deciding Whether or Not to Use Birth-Control Pills

		POSITIVE ANTICIPATIONS	NEGATIVE ANTICIPATIONS
Experiential gains and losses	For self	Sex would be spontaneous	(Possible side effects: nausea, bloating, etc.)
	For partner	Sex would be spontaneous	None
Biological gains and losses	For self	High effectiveness	Probably no negative impact on health; (useless against STDs)
	For partner	High effectiveness	None
Financial gains and losses	For self	Needn't worry about the cost of a child—Expensive!	
	For partner	Needn't worry about the cost of a child	None!
Ethical gains and losses	For self	Would not risk bearing unwanted child or having to decide whether to have an abortion if became pregnant	Moderate concern about using artificial means of birth control; responsibility for birth control would be all mine
	For partner	Would not have to worry about causing pregnancy	None!
Legal factors	For self		None
	For partner		None

Living with Sex

stick to their decisions.[81] Steffi was reasonably content with her decision. We hope that you will be content with yours. The balance sheet in Figure 12.2 is blank. It's meant for you to use. What decisions have you been putting off? By carefully weighing the pluses and the minuses of your anticipated choices, your decisions may be wiser—for you.

FIGURE 12.2. The Balance Sheet for Sexual Decision Making

		POSITIVE ANTICIPATIONS	NEGATIVE ANTICIPATIONS
Experiential gains and losses	For self		
	For partner		
Biological gains and losses	For self		
	For partner		
Financial gains and losses	For self		
	For partner		
Ethical gains and losses	For self		
	For partner		
Legal factors	For self		
	For partner		

SUMMING UP

1. Do students on your campus openly discuss sex? What kinds of sexual pressures do students encounter on your campus?
2. What beliefs do you have about masturbation? Where do these beliefs come from?
3. What attitudes do your fellow students express toward petting and premarital intercourse? Would you classify these attitudes as liberal or conservative?
4. Do many students at your college cohabit? Do the cohabiting students you know seem to differ from students who choose not to cohabit? How or how not?
5. Do you know of female students who complain that their dates have coerced them into sexual activity? How do the victims respond to their assaults? What can be done to decrease the probability of so-called date rape?
6. Do students on your campus show concern about sexually transmitted diseases (STDs), or do they seem to assume that they are safe from them?
7. What can you do to protect yourself from STDs? Can any college or community resources be of help?
8. Do students on your campus seem to show concern about birth control?
9. What kinds of birth control are used by your sexually active friends? Can any college or community resources be of help?
10. Do you have any sexual decisions to make? Can the balance sheet be of use to you?

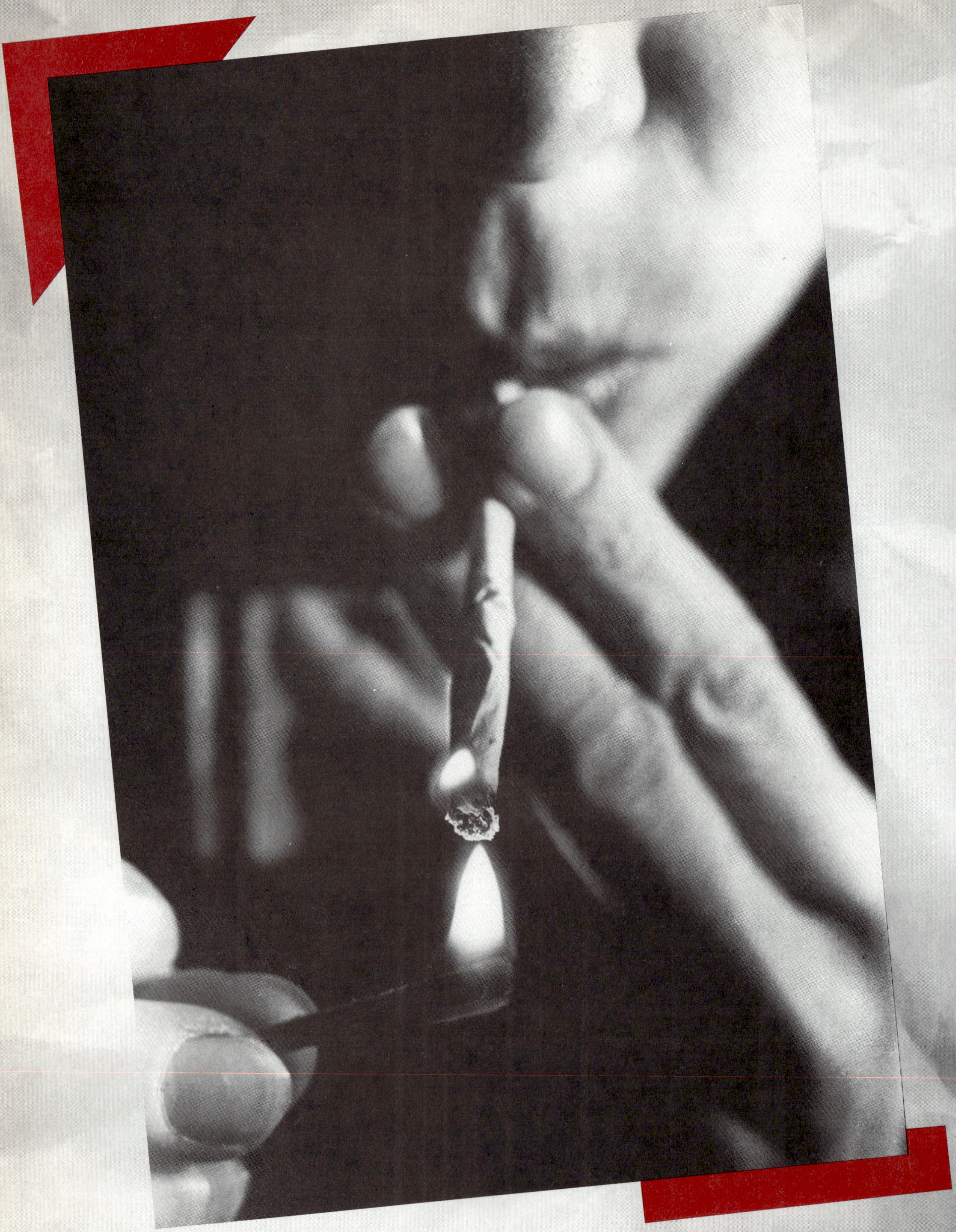

13

Handling Drugs

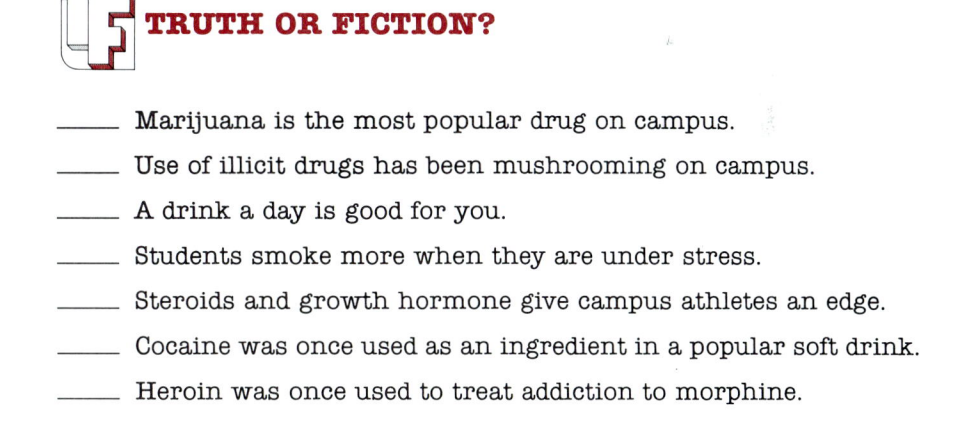

TRUTH OR FICTION?

_____ Marijuana is the most popular drug on campus.

_____ Use of illicit drugs has been mushrooming on campus.

_____ A drink a day is good for you.

_____ Students smoke more when they are under stress.

_____ Steroids and growth hormone give campus athletes an edge.

_____ Cocaine was once used as an ingredient in a popular soft drink.

_____ Heroin was once used to treat addiction to morphine.

Whether we like it or not, our campuses, like our streets, are a supermarket of drugs. Campuses across the nation are inundated with drugs that get students going in the morning, relax them in the evening, transform their perceptions, and give them an edge in athletic competition. Many students use drugs because their friends do. Some students become involved with drugs because their parents and authority figures warn them not to. Some students are seeking pleasure, others are looking for inner truth.

The most popular drug in the high schools and the colleges is that old standby—alcohol.[1]

TRUTH OR FICTION *Revisited*

Alcohol, not marijuana, is actually the most popular drug on campus.

The majority of college students have used marijuana at least once, and approximately one in five students smokes it frequently. Cocaine was until recent years a toy for the well-to-do, but price breaks have brought it into the lockers of students. Given medical warnings, strong laws, moral pronouncements, and—from time to time—a horror story, the use of most proscribed drugs has declined somewhat in recent years.[2] But all things considered, drugs remain a significant feature of the campus scene.

TRUTH OR FICTION *Revisited*

Use of illicit drugs on campus has actually been in a mild decline in recent years.

This chapter is about drugs and how to handle them. We'll share with you the scientific knowledge that has been accumulated over the years. We promise that we won't give you any phony horror stories, but we're not going to paint a rosy picture either. We'll spend most of the time talking about alcohol and nicotine, which is the stimulant found in cigarettes, because these drugs are most readily available and most widely used. But we'll also discuss steroids and growth hormone, which are used by many college (and professional) athletes to get an edge on opponents, and a number of other substances.

WHAT IS SUBSTANCE ABUSE?

From a legal point of view, any use of an illegal drug constitutes abuse. But people in the helping professions usually define abuse in terms of what the drug means to the individual. For example, the American Psychiatric Association defines substance abuse as persistent use despite the fact that the substance is causing or complicating problems in functioning.[3] In other words, if you are missing school because of the effects of drugs, or if your grades have been suffering because of them, you are abusing drugs. The amount that you use is not the critical factor. What's crucial is whether your usage impairs other areas of functioning.

Another concept is that of physical addiction. Regular use of addictive drugs changes the body so that users feel normal only when the drug is in them. Addiction is known by tolerance and by withdrawal symptoms. Tolerance means that users' bodies get acclimated to the drug so that they have to take more to achieve the same effects.

Let us give you an example of tolerance. One student couldn't lift his head from the pillow for two hours the first time he tried the commonly prescribed tranquilizer Valium. He had taken 2 milligrams of the drug. But he liked its "mellowing" effects and started using it regularly to help him get to sleep. Within a few months, he was taking 40 milligrams at a time and it no longer fatigued him at all.

But tolerance alone does not define addiction. When people are addicted to a drug, a cluster of withdrawal symptoms (also referred to as an abstinence syndrome) occur when usage is suddenly curtailed.[4] The abstinence syndrome for alcohol includes shakiness, restlessness, anxiety, rapid pulse, high blood pressure, and weakness.

It is possible for people to come to rely on drugs without being addicted to them. Another student got into the habit of using small amounts of Librium, another tranquilizer, before taking tests. It got to the point where she believed that she couldn't face a test without Librium. This kind of reliance on drugs is referred to as psychological dependence. To depend on something is to rely on it, to need it, to be anxious about trying to do without it.

HOW DO STUDENTS GET INVOLVED WITH DRUGS?

Students get involved with drugs for many reasons. A handful of reasons include curiosity, rebelliousness, a desire to escape from pressure or boredom, and conformity to peer pressure.[5] Folklore to the effect that we are influenced by "the company we keep" applies perfectly. If your fraternity has beer parties, it may be hard to avoid being sucked in. If your roommates use marijuana and hallucinogens, you may feel pressured to try them. Anytime you are in an environment in which you get the idea that "everyone does it," you can feel enormous social pressure at least to try drugs.

Some social scientists suggest that initial use of drugs like alcohol, marijuana, nicotine (in cigarettes), and tranquilizers like Valium comes from watching others use them or from a recommendation by someone.[6] Subsequent usage may be bolstered by the substance's positive impact on

IN YOUR OWN WRITE

Are drugs widely used on your campus? Have you encountered any pressure to try or use drugs? Which drugs? What kinds of pressure?

mood and its abatement of anxieties, fears, and feelings of stress. (But later we'll see that cigarettes probably only help us handle the stress of trying to do without cigarettes.) Students who get addicted are also motivated to avoid withdrawal symptoms. Carrying the substance around is comforting because one then need not fear having to get by without it. Some students, for example, will not leave the dormitory or the house without Valium.

Students whose parents use drugs like alcohol, tranquilizers, and stimulants are even more likely to turn to them. Parental usage increases a student's knowledge of drugs and provides examples of when to use them—for example, under stress or when they are anxious or depressed.

There is also evidence that we can be genetically predisposed toward becoming addicted to certain drugs.[7] Numerous studies have been done on children of alcoholics, children reared by their natural parents and by adoptive parents. It turns out that the biological children of alcoholics who are reared by adoptive parents are more likely to develop alcohol problems than the natural children of the adoptive parents.[8] Moreover, alcoholics and their children tend to share a greater-than-average tolerance of alcohol. For example, the college-age offspring of alcoholics display better balance and coordination when they drink than do the children of nonalcoholics given the same amount of alcohol.[9] They also appear less intoxicated when they drink large amounts of alcohol, and so they are likely to drink more.

Let us now turn to the effects of various drugs.

ALCOHOL

> An old saying and a true, "much drinking, little thinking."
>
> JONATHAN SWIFT, *Journal to Stella*

The most widely used drug on campus (and elsewhere) is perfectly legal if you are of age: alcohol. No other drug has become so firmly embedded in our culture. We use alcohol to accompany dinner, to help us get to sleep at night, and as a prop to help us mix at parties. We use alcohol to celebrate holy days, extol our achievements, and declare cheerful wishes. Adolescents use alcohol as a means of asserting their maturity. Alcohol is imbibed at least once in a while by about 90 percent of college students.

Whereas tranquilizers like Valium and Librium are available by prescription only, alcohol is a tranquilizer that can be bought if you have

The most widely used drug on campus is alcohol. No other drug has become so firmly embedded in our culture. Alcohol is imbibed at least once in a while by about 90 percent of college students.

cash and identification to show that you are of age.* Alcohol provides temporary relief from anxiety, and it can be used publicly without censure or stigma. That is, college men who pop Valium tablets might appear weak, but men who down beer are consistent with the macho stereotype.

Since alcohol is the most widely used drug, it is also the most widely abused. Ten to 20 million Americans abuse alcohol. Alcohol abuse is linked to lower grades, loss of productivity on the job, loss of jobs, and downward drift in social standing.[10]

College students generally report beliefs to the effect that alcohol reduces tension, diverts them from worrying, intensifies pleasure, enhances social skills, and changes experiences for the better.[11] What *does* alcohol do? Alcohol's effects vary with the amount that is imbibed and the span of use. Low amounts of alcohol tend to have stimulating effects, but higher amounts have a sedative effect,[12] which is why alcohol is classified as a depressant. Depressants act in part by slowing the activity of the nervous system. Other depressants we'll talk about include opiates and opioids, barbiturates and methaqualone.

Many students use alcohol to combat feelings of depression. Short-term use of alcohol may alleviate feelings of depression, because alcohol can induce feelings of elation and euphoria that are powerful enough to wash away self-doubts and self-criticism. But regular use for a year or so can heighten depression.[13] Many college athletes have discovered that alcohol can blunt aches and pains. But alcohol also intoxicates. That is, alcohol impairs mental functioning: It is more difficult to learn and remember course material when you have been drinking. Alcohol slurs the speech. Alcohol also slows down reaction time and impairs motor coordination—

> Man, being reasonable, must get drunk.
>
> LORD BYRON,
> "Don Juan"

IN YOUR OWN WRITE

What are the effects of alcohol? Write down some of the effects (mental and physical) that alcohol has on you, or that you believe it has. Then check the following discussion.

1. _____

2. _____

3. _____

4. _____

5. _____

6. _____

---

*Sad to say, in the towns that abut many campuses, the "counter test" takes the place of an I.D. card. That is, if you're big enough to put your money on the counter, you're old enough to buy alcohol.

Handling Drugs 325

which are additional discoveries of many athletes. Alcohol is connected with nearly half of all automobile fatalities.

Alcohol is addictive. When addicted people abstain, they can experience a gnawing craving, shakiness, weakness, high blood pressure, and—at its most dangerous—convulsions and death. One well-known withdrawal problem is delirium tremens, or "the DT's," which afflicts some chronic alcoholics when they suspend drinking. The DT's are characterized by heavy sweating, restlessness, general disorientation (for example, not knowing the time or place), and terrifying hallucinations. Hallucinations include "seeing things," "hearing things," even "feeling things" that are not actually there. People with the DT's sometimes hallucinate creepy, crawling animals on their skin.

Alcohol impairs our ability to make decisions and inhibit impulses. So some students may do things while under the influence that they would not do ordinarily.[14] When drunk, we may be less able to foresee the injurious consequences of our behavior and even less apt to summon up our moral standards. When we drink, we grow less cognizant of our personal standards and less aware of straying from them.[15] So we are less apt to have feelings of guilt and shame about behavior we would not tolerate when sober. Alcohol can also afford an excuse for unacceptable behavior.[16] We can tell others or delude ourselves, "It wasn't me. It was the alcohol."

Drinking among students has been strongly linked to bad grades and other problems.[17] Alcohol blunts the immediate impact of academic stresses and failures, although, of course, it does nothing to help us take charge of our lives. Some researchers believe that students who drink as a means of coping with stress are at very high risk for developing alcoholism.[18]

And remember: Regardless of why we start drinking, once addicted, we are motivated to avoid withdrawal symptoms. But even when alcoholics have successfully "dried out," or withdrawn from alcohol, many start drinking again because they still want alcohol to blunt the stress of unfulfilling lifestyles and to provide an excuse for their failures.

Now let us discuss the effects of alcohol on sex. Consider the following exchange between Macduff and a minor character in Shakespeare's play, *Macbeth*:

PORTER: Drink, sir, is a great provoker of three things.
MACDUFF: What three things does drink especially provoke?
PORTER: Marry,* sir, nose-painting,† sleep, and urine. Lechery, sir, it provokes and unprovokes; it provokes the desire, but it takes away the performance.

> Wine makes a man better pleased with himself; I do not say that it makes him more pleasing to others.
> SAMUEL JOHNSON

> I envy people who drink—at least they know what to blame everything on.
> OSCAR LEVANT

What of it? *Does* alcohol "provoke lechery"?—that is, arouse sexual desire? *Does* alcohol curb sexual response ("take away the performance")?

Most people seem to think that alcohol enhances their sexual pleasure, women even more so than men. And many people think that alcohol enhances or does not at all affect their sexual performance.[19] It is possible that alcohol enhances the pleasure many of us derive from sex, but scientific studies have shown that alcohol actually *decreases* sexual response, as measured by size of erection and vaginal blood pressure.[20] So the porter in *Macbeth* may have been right. If we believe that alcohol enhances sexual pleasure, we may be more likely to focus on pleasure when we have been drinking—regardless of alcohol's true physical effects. But drinking, especially moderate to heavy drinking, can also "take away the performance."

So students' beliefs about alcohol may differ from its true effects. But our responses to drugs reflect the physical changes induced by the drugs and our expectations. If we feel sexier when we are drinking, it may be

---
*"By Mary," referring to the mother of Jesus.
†Referring to the rupture of the small blood vessels in the nose which is caused by chronic drinking and provides a ruddy, bulbous appearance.

because of a combination of general feelings of euphoria, lowered awareness of personal standards that might otherwise have inhibited sexual activity, and our expectations about drinking. So you may be more likely to experiment with sex when you have been drinking, but probably not because alcohol directly stimulates sexual responsiveness. Forewarned is forearmed.*

Now let us consider some of the health consequences of drinking. There is general agreement that heavy drinking is unhealthful, but research on light to moderate drinking has been somewhat surprising.

Alcohol and Health

Alcohol is high in calories but void of nutrients like vitamins and protein. So alcohol is fattening, yet chronic drinkers may be malnourished. Alcohol also interferes with the absorption of some vitamins, including thiamine—an important B vitamin. Chronic drinking therefore leads to illnesses like cirrhosis of the liver, which is linked to protein deficiency, and Korsakoff's syndrome, which is connected with vitamin B deficiency.[21] In cirrhosis of the liver, fiber replaces working liver cells, obstructing circulation of the blood. Korsakoff's syndrome is a brain disease that is characterized by memory loss, confusion, and disorientation. Chronic drinking is also connected with gout, coronary heart disease, and high blood pressure.[22]

Heavy drinking is connected with cancers of the pancreas and stomach.[23] One study reported that women who have one or two alcoholic drinks a day markedly raise the risk of developing breast cancer,[24] but other studies have not confirmed this finding.[25] Still, women are advised to check with the college health service or their personal physicians. Drinking by a pregnant woman may damage the embryo.[26]

These findings, with the exception of those concerning breast cancer, are widely accepted by the medical establishment. Most college men, of course, will conclude that they needn't worry about their own drinking. After all, with few exceptions, they will not have been drinking for very long. Also, most college students are light to moderate drinkers. While many students are justified in feeling this way—we promised you no phony horror stories—some are falling into traps of regular and progressively heavier drinking.

Is a Drink a Day Good for You? Having given you the negative, we should also report some positive findings on the relationships between alcohol and health. A number of studies suggest that light to moderate drinking can be beneficial.

Most studies have observed the incidence of coronary heart disease and mortality rates among men. Thousands of men have been followed for decades in locations such as Hayward, California; Alameda County, California; Framingham, Massachusetts; and Albany County, New York. The studies concur that light drinkers (men who have up to 60 ounces of alcohol per month) have lower mortality rates and fewer heart attacks and strokes than heavy drinkers and—surprisingly—nondrinkers.[27] A national study of more than 80,000 nurses similarly found that women who had 3 to 15 drinks per week had fewer strokes† and heart attacks than nondrinkers and heavier drinkers.[28]

> Once, during Prohibition, I was forced to live for days on nothing but food and water.
>
> W. C. FIELDS

---

*By the way, we are not prudishly advising against alcohol and sex. But we think that we are happier with ourselves when we act on the basis of conscious decisions, and not on the basis of clouded consciousness and social pressures. Do things—or don't do things—on the basis of your active choice—not by placing yourself in situations in which you allow other people and drugs to make your decisions for you. Failure to make your own decisions is degrading and, as we saw in Chapter 12, potentially dangerous.

†Here we are talking about strokes that are caused by blocked blood vessels in the brain, which are the most common type of strokes. But these women had more strokes that were caused by bleeding in the brain. Students who are at risk for the second kind of stroke do not share the described benefits of alcohol. You can ask your college health service or personal physician about which category you might fall in.

Why may light drinking be beneficial? Some researchers believe that light drinking increases the quantity of high-density lipoproteins (HDL), or "good cholesterol," in the blood. Good cholesterol, in turn, helps clear blood vessels of obstruction by "bad cholesterol"—that is, low-density lipoproteins (LDL).[29]

However, the researchers who ran these studies do not recommend that nondrinkers take up light drinking to reap its possible benefits. William Castelli, who participated in the Framingham study, points out that we "can get the benefit [of light to moderate drinking] in other ways, such as by stopping smoking, lowering [our] cholesterol or . . . blood pressure, and [not] run the risk of becoming an alcoholic."[30]

QUESTIONNAIRE
Reasons for Drinking

Do you drink? If so, what are your reasons for drinking? For pleasure? As a way of handling problems? To help you get by at mixers? Americans drink for many reasons. And about 18 million Americans are alcoholics. College students who believe that alcohol will assist them in reducing tensions are apparently at higher risk than other students for developing alcoholism.[31]

To foster understanding or your own reasons for drinking, take the following questionnaire.[32] Check *True* if an item is true or mostly true for you, and *False* if it is false or mostly false for you. Then check the key at the end of the chapter.

		True	False
1.	I find it painful to go without alcohol for any period of time.	____	____
2.	It's easier for me to relate to other people when I have been drinking.	____	____
3.	I drink so that I will look more mature and sophisticated.	____	____
4.	My future prospects seem brighter when I have been drinking.	____	____
5.	I enjoy the taste of beer, wine, or hard liquor.	____	____
6.	I don't feel disturbed or uncomfortable in any way if I go for a long time without having a drink.	____	____
7.	When I drink, I feel calmer and less edgy about things.	____	____
8.	I drink in order to fit in better with the crowd.	____	____
9.	When I am drinking, I worry less about things.	____	____
10.	I have a drink when I'm with my family.	____	____
11.	Drinking is a part of my religious ceremonies.	____	____
12.	I'll have a drink to help deaden the pain of a toothache or some other physical problem.	____	____
13.	I feel that I can do almost anything when I'm drinking.	____	____
14.	You really can't blame people for the things they do when they have been drinking.	____	____
15.	I'll have a drink before a big exam or a big date so that I feel less concerned about how things will go.	____	____
16.	I like to drink for the taste of it.	____	____
17.	There have been times when I've found a drink in my hand even though I can't remember placing it there.	____	____
18.	I tend to drink when I feel down or when I want to take my mind off my troubles.	____	____
19.	I find that I do better both socially and sexually after I've had a drink or two.	____	____

TRUTH OR FICTION *Revisited*

So there is evidence that a drink a day flushes harmful cholesterol from the body. However, researchers note that even one drink a day by a pregnant woman can harm the embryo, and the possibility remains that light drinking contributes to breast cancer in women. Moreover, a drink a day can potentially lead to alcoholism with many individuals.

Now that we have surveyed some of the behavioral and physical consequences of drinking, the questionnaire below may offer some insight into your own reasons for drinking—if you drink at all.

20. I have to admit that drinking sometimes makes me do reckless and asinine things.
21. I have missed classes or work because of having a few too many.
22. I feel that I am more generous and sympathetic when I have been drinking.
23. One of the reasons I drink is that I like the look of a drinker.
24. I like to have a drink or two on festive occasions and special days.
25. My friends and I are likely to go drinking when one of us has done something well, like aced a tough exam or made some great plays on the team.
26. I'll have a drink or two when some predicament is gnawing at me.
27. Drinking gives me pleasure.
28. Frankly, one of the lures of drinking is getting "high."
29. Sometimes I'm surprised to find that I've poured a drink when another one is still unfinished.
30. I find that I'm better at getting other people to do what I want them to do when I've been drinking.
31. Having a drink keeps my mind off problems at home, at school, or at work.
32. I get a real, gnawing hunger for a drink when I haven't had one for a while.
33. One or two drinks relax me.
34. Things tend to look better when I've been drinking.
35. I find that my mood is much improved when I've had a drink or two.
36. I can usually see things more clearly when I've had a drink or two.
37. One or two drinks heightens the pleasure of food and sex.
38. When I run out of alcohol, I buy more right away.
39. I think that I would have done better on some things if it hadn't been for the alcohol.
40. When I'm out of alcohol, things are practically unbearable until I can obtain some more.
41. I drink at fraternity or sorority parties.
42. When I think about the future and what I'm going to do, I often go and have a drink.
43. I like to go out for a drink when I've gotten a good grade.
44. I usually have a drink or two with dinner.
45. There have been times when it's been rough to get through a class or through practice because I wanted a drink.

WHAT DO YOU DO NOW?
How to Cope with the Urge to Drink

Helping professionals suggest many ways of cutting down drinking that you may be able to apply on your own.[37] However, if you suspect that you are addicted to alcohol, we recommend that you explore your concerns at the college counseling center or at an off-campus health facility. If you are addicted, you may be advised to enter a hospital for a couple of weeks to become detoxified. You may be able to arrange admission over a vacation.

But if you are not addicted and are seeking ways of cutting down, here are some methods that may be of help:

1. Stay away from situations that incite heavy drinking. If you drink heavily at fraternity or sorority parties, consider attending fewer such parties. Befriend people who drink less.
2. Switch to beverages with lower alcohol content. For example, switch from hard liquor to beer or wine. Switch from regular beer to a light (that is, low-calorie, low-alcohol-content) beer.
3. Pause between sips. Put the alcoholic beverage down. Ask yourself if you really want more before taking another sip.
4. Keep very little alcohol in your room or house. For example, buy two cans of beer instead of two six-packs. If your roommates stock up heavily, get new roommates.
5. Interpret feelings of stress and tension as a sign that a problem needs to be solved, not as a cue to have a drink. Then go about solving that problem, seeking advice at the college counseling center, if necessary.
6. Acquire relaxation skills, as described in Chapters 7 and 8. When you feel tense, take a deep breath, tell yourself to relax, and let the breath out.
7. Check out the list of turn-ons discussed in Chapter 4. Reward yourself for keeping your drinking within your desired limits by engaging in a couple of pleasant events every day you are successful.
8. Every day that you keep your drinking within your desired limits, put some money away toward a vacation or some desired object, like a camera. On days when you drink more than desired, take an equivalent amount out of the fund.
9. Think of the potential consequences of many years of moderate to heavy drinking—cirrhosis of the liver, confusion and disorientation, heart problems, and cancer. Remind yourself that you are forming lifelong behavioral patterns *now*. So you're *not* too young to have to think of the consequences of your drinking.
10. Buy a copy of the latest edition of *How to Control Your Drinking*, by William Miller and R. Muñoz. It's published by the University of New Mexico Press. (Read it.)
11. If you're having trouble controlling your drinking on your own, go to the college counseling center or a local health agency. If you are religious, AA may provide help. If you're not, AA may not be for you.

Treatment of Problem Drinking

Treatment of alcohol abuse has two aspects: helping addicted individuals safely through the abstinence syndrome and helping people find better ways of handling stress. The process of helping people through the abstinence syndrome is referred to as detoxification. Detoxification is a straightforward medical procedure that takes about a week and is usually carried out in a hospital.[33] Helping problem drinkers learn to handle stress in other ways is the more difficult task.

Most professionals and nonprofessionals alike consider Alcoholics Anonymous (AA), a nonprofessional organization, the most effective means of treating alcoholics. AA members who abstain are referred to as "recovering alcoholics"—they are never considered to have "recovered" fully. In fact, AA supports the view that just one drink is disastrous for members (this is not always true). There is also a pervasive religious ambience to AA. Members dedicate themselves to God, publicly confess their drinking "sins," and publicly commit themselves never to touch another drop. AA members also support each other during times of temptation.

It would be safe to drop the issue here, but we can't recommend AA for everyone. The group reports a success rate of about 75 percent,[34] but skeptics note that this figure refers only to people who stay in treatment over the long haul. Most people who try AA drop out after a few meetings.[35]

AA claims that professionals have failed in their efforts to help alcoholics. But the facts of the matter suggest that psychologists and other helping professionals have been at least as successful as AA—and perhaps more so.[36] We describe a number of the methods that professionals have found to be of help in the "What Do You Do Now?" feature on the previous page.

CIGARETTES

All right—you purists have us: Cigarettes are not drugs. However, they contain nicotine, a potent stimulant. Stimulants act in part by increasing the activity of the nervous system.

Nicotine causes a discharge of the hormone adrenaline. Adrenaline, as noted in Chapter 8, incites activity in parts of the nervous system. The heart rate accelerates and sugar is poured into the blood, upping energy levels. Adrenaline also provides a mental kick. Despite cigarette smoke's stimulating properties, most smokers report that they find smoking relaxing.

The stimulating properties of nicotine are short-lived. In the long run, nicotine can cause fatigue. Nicotine can also make the skin feel clammy and cold, cause faintness and dizziness, nausea and vomiting, and diarrhea. These symptoms are frequently part of the initiation rites into smoking.

In addition to nicotine, tobacco smoke contains carbon monoxide. Carbon monoxide combines with hemoglobin, the chemical in red blood cells that transports oxygen. Thus it locks out some oxygen. One outcome is shortness of breath. Cigarette smoke also contains hydrocarbons, or "tars." Hydrocarbons are the irritating substances that are assumed to cause cancer.

> Neither do thou lust after that tawney weed tobacco.
>
> BEN JONSON,
> *Bartholomew Fair*

IN YOUR OWN WRITE

Do you smoke? How did you get started? Would you like to quit? Can you?

Many students smoke cigarettes in the belief that cigarettes help them cope with stress. Actually, smoking may only be helping them cope with withdrawal symptoms from nicotine.

Nicotine is the agent that causes addiction to cigarettes.[38] Experiments have shown that regular smokers calibrate their rate of smoking so that they maintain reasonably even levels of nicotine in the bloodstream.[39] When we are addicted to a substance, curtailed intake causes withdrawal symptoms. Symptoms of nicotine withdrawal include nervousness, energy loss, drowsiness and fatigue, headaches, irregular bowels, lightheadedness and dizziness, insomnia, cramps, heart palpitations, tremors, and heavy sweating. Many of these symptoms—such as lightheadedness, insomnia, shakiness, and sweating—mimic feelings of anxiety, so for many years they were not interpreted as binding evidence that cigarettes are addictive.

Nicotine is excreted more quickly when we are under stress. Stress increases the level of acid in the urine, and acid speeds the removal of nicotine from the body. So regular smokers may smoke more when they are under stress just to maintain the same level of nicotine in the blood. But since smoking keeps withdrawal symptoms at bay, stressed smokers may ironically think that their increased smoking is helping them keep a lid on their stress.

> To cease smoking is the easiest thing I ever did; I ought to know because I've done it a thousand times.
> MARK TWAIN

> It has always been my rule never to smoke when asleep, and never to refrain when awake.
> MARK TWAIN

TRUTH OR FICTION *Revisited*

Students do appear to smoke more when they are under stress.

Cigarettes and Health

Here we do have some horror stories, but they are well documented. For example, cigarette smoking can cause cancers of the lungs, larynx, esophagus, and oral cavity. It may contribute to cancers of the bladder, kidneys, and pancreas. Cigarette smoking is also connected with death from heart disease and chronic lung and respiratory disorders.[40] Women who smoke while pregnant risk miscarriage, premature birth, and birth defects.

Because of these risks, the percentage of Americans who smoke dropped from about 42 percent in 1966 to 25 percent in the late 1980s.[41] However, one-third of a million Americans continue to die from smoking-related diseases each year—seven times the number who die from auto accidents.[42] On average, smokers die five to eight years earlier than nonsmokers.[43]

Knowledge of the dangers of smoking is now so widespread that peer pressures seem to be favoring *not* smoking. In fact, many people now consider smoking a form of "deviant behavior," despite the fact that cigarettes are legal for people who are of age.[44] Some smokers even find it difficult to attain jobs because many employers wonder about the judgment of those who continue to smoke despite mounting evidence of its self-destructive qualities.

> Many people find smoking objectionable. I myself find many—even more—things objectionable. I do not like aftershave lotion, adults who roller-skate, children who speak French, or anyone who is unduly tan.
> FRAN LEBOWITZ

WHAT DO YOU DO NOW?
Methods for Quitting and Cutting Down on Smoking

How about you? You are as aware of the hazards of smoking as anyone. What are you going to do about it?

College students, of course, tend to think, "The consequences of smoking are years away. College is stressful and I need cigarettes to handle college now, today. After I graduate and get things on an even keel, I'll quit." Guess what, students? Your life today is as real as and probably no more stressful than your life after college. Careers and family life also hold their fair share of stresses, so don't indulge in the fantasy that there's a day of liberation ahead—a magic moment beyond which all the waters are calm and the sails swell magnificently with the winds. The day of reckoning for your smoking is now, today. You are forming habitual ways of handling the challenges of life as you read these words. If you delay indefinitely, you'll always find some excuse why you should give up smoking next year, and not now.

On the other hand, there is something to be said for finding a strategic time to quit smoking. But such a time is at hand within the next few weeks or months, not a year from now.

Evidence is mixed as to whether it is more useful to cut down gradually or to quit "cold turkey" (all at once). Some smokers find it more effective to go cold turkey.[45] Others find it more effective to cut down gradually.[46] Cutting down is better than doing nothing at all. And some smokers have been able to cut cigarette consumption in half and have maintained lower smoking levels for two years or more.[47] So cutting down now with the goal of quitting later can also work.

Quitting Cold Turkey Psychologists and health professionals have assembled recommendations like the following to help people quit cold turkey:

1. Make a public commitment to quit by informing other students and your family of your intentions.

2. Challenge your excuses for not quitting smoking. A couple of examples of common excuses follow, along with the facts. In the spaces provided, write down some of your own reasons for not quitting. Then reconsider them—be skeptical!—and write down what you think is the real story.

Reasons why I can't quit smoking now	The facts
A. I just don't have the willpower.	That's true only if you believe it's true. Millions of people have managed to quit, and so can you.
B. I'm too busy to quit now.	You can pick a strategic time in the near future. You'll probably feel that you're "too busy to quit now" for the rest of your life.
C. _____	_____
D. _____	_____
E. _____	_____

(continues on next page)

(continued)

3. Make a list of things to tell yourself when you feel the urge to have a cigarette. Write some of them down in the spaces provided. Hints: You won't have to think about lung cancer, and you'll have more wind for athletic competition.

    A. _____

    B. _____

    C. _____

4. Remind yourself that the first days of withdrawal are the most difficult. Withdrawal symptoms wane dramatically after that.

5. Think of yourself as more in control of your own destiny than nonquitters.

6. Quit when you awaken in the morning, not during the day. When you get up, you've already gotten through several hours without nicotine.

7. Time quitting to coincide with a vacation like Christmas or the January or spring breaks. In that way, you'll be away from the places and circumstances in which you usually smoke.

8. Get rid of ashtrays and don't let other students smoke when they're in your room or apartment. If your roommates smoke, it may be worthwhile to make new living arrangements and time quitting to coincide with moving.

9. Study in sections of the library where smoking is not permitted. Sit in sections of the cafeteria where smoking is not allowed.

10. Keep busy. True, college students are usually busy enough, but if there are slack periods when you were used to smoking, fill them with novel activities. This is another opportunity to pick from the list of turn-ons in Chapter 4.

11. If you want to have something in your mouth, you may want to stock a temporary supply of sugar-free mints or gum. (Try not to light them up.)

12. Consider switching to a nicotine gum. Nicotine gum reduces withdrawal symptoms and does not contain harmful hydrocarbons or carbon monoxide. It provides a useful "halfway house" for many smokers, weaning them from cigarettes and allowing them to decrease usage of the gum afterward.[48]

13. Rather than dreading withdrawal symptoms, look upon them as signs that you're winning the battle and growing healthier. Withdrawal symptoms mean that your body is readjusting and that freedom from cigarettes will soon be yours.

14. Sock away the cash that you would have been spending on cigarettes and buy yourself presents with it.

Cutting Down Gradually The following suggestions may be of help to students who would rather try to cut down than quit completely. Some students do well at cutting down first and quitting at a later date. Of course, it is best not to smoke at all, but smoking less is less harmful than smoking more. Also, by cutting down, you are acclimating your body to a lower level of nicotine, which may make it easier for you to quit later on.

1. Count the cigarettes you smoke for a number of days to arrive at a baseline figure of how much smoking you do. Also determine approximately how long you go between cigarettes.

2. Set yourself a concrete goal for controlled smoking. We recommend that you plan to decrease your smoking to 50 percent of your baseline. (Once you have successfully remained at the lower level for a couple of months, you can repeat the procedure.)

3. Stop smoking in a couple of settings. On many campuses, smoking is not permitted in classrooms, but even if it is, you can make a rule not to smoke there. Many students find it helpful to begin with a simple rule to quit smoking during meals.

4. Become involved in activities that are incompatible with smoking. Perhaps you're not on the varsity track team, but if you take up jogging, you'll find that you do better when you smoke less. This discovery may add to your incentives for cutting down—especially if you take to jogging.

5. Switch to a brand of cigarettes that you don't particularly like. You'll be meeting your cravings for nicotine, but you'll be enjoying smoking less—making it a bit easier to cut down.

6. Hold cigarettes in your nondominant hand only. That is, if you are a "rightie," hold cigarettes in your left hand, and vice versa. When you break habitual ways of doing things, you become more aware of them. So holding cigarettes in the nondominant hand makes you more cognizant of each cigarette, intensifying your motivation to cut down.

7. Keep only enough cigarettes around to meet your reduced daily goals. Buy packs one at a time. It's more expensive, but it'll encourage you to smoke less. And why shouldn't you feel a financial pinch as a reminder that you're hurting your body whenever you smoke?

8. Use sugar-free gum or candies as substitutes for some cigarettes each day.

9. Check the list of pleasant events in Chapter 4. Go for a brief walk instead of lighting up. Or call a friend or write a letter.

10. Pause before you light up. Ask yourself if you really want *this* cigarette. If you do, wait a minute and then light up. In this way, you learn that you needn't respond immediately to the urge to smoke, and now and then you will decide to forego the cigarette.

11. Put the cigarette down in an ashtray between puffs. (Take your hand off it!) Before inhaling, ask yourself if you really want another puff or if you're finishing the cigarette simply because it's there. If you smoke half of each of 20 cigarettes, you've smoked only 10 cigarettes.

12. Put out the cigarette before reaching the end. (Stop eating the filters.)

13. Gradually increase the amount of time that elapses between cigarettes.

14. Picture living a prolonged, healthy life. Ah, the freedom of not having to be concerned about lung cancer!

15. When you are smoking, picture blackened lungs. Think of the coughing fits you have had. (Your first author quit smoking one day when he woke up and couldn't catch his breath from coughing for nearly two hours.) Focus on the potential of cancer and other lung diseases.

Many students have cut down their cigarette intake and quit by using these strategies. Be warned: There's a high relapse rate for quitters. We are most likely to be tempted to light up when we're nervous, irate, or depressed.[49] But when you feel the urge, you can enhance the likelihood of fighting the urge by using just about any of these strategies.[50] For example, have a mint, remind yourself of your reasons for quitting, or go for a walk—breathe some fresh air.

Remember: The time to cut down or quit is now—not next year, not when you graduate.

IN YOUR OWN WRITE

Are steroids widely used on your campus? By whom? What are your feelings about them?

___

STEROIDS AND GROWTH HORMONE

Many college students (and professional athletes) take steroids and growth hormone not for their mental effects but to gain an edge in athletic competition. Steroids are hormones that are normally produced by the adrenal glands and the testes. They help us handle stress and stoke development of male characteristics like the muscle mass. So-called anabolic steroids are synthetic versions of the male sex hormone, testosterone. Anabolic steroids increase the sex drive (some male athletes complain about frequent or persistent erections) and seem to have some mild psychoactive effects: They apparently boost self-confidence.[51] Steroids also help make energy available for peak performances.

Growth hormone is produced by the pituitary gland in the brain. It regulates gains in size and, like steroids, forms muscle. Many top bodybuilders of both sexes use steroids and growth hormone, which can be prescribed by physicians, to acquire the muscle mass and definition that judges focus on in competitive meets.

Many college students (and professional athletes) take steroids to gain an "edge" in athletic competition. Steroids help us handle stress and stoke the muscle mass. They also increase the sex drive and apparently boost self-confidence. Unfortunately, steroids also have negative side effects, including liver damage and the lowering of "good cholesterol" (HDL) levels.

336   Chapter 13

Unfortunately, these drugs have some negative side effects, including liver damage (steroids are metabolized in the liver) and the lowering of "good cholesterol" (HDL) levels. HDL checks the action of "bad cholesterol" (LDL). So by lowering HDL levels, steroids boost the activity of LDL, increasing the likelihood of cardiovascular damage. If athletes take steroids for only a few weeks each year to prepare for the heights of their seasons, they probably do themselves less harm than by using steroids constantly. A number of athletes who have used them, like nine-time world-champion weight lifter Larry Pacifico, have developed cardiovascular problems, like blocked arteries, which have caused heart attacks. Moreover, when we discontinue anabolic steroids, we are likely to encounter sleep disturbances and feelings of depression and apathy—sort of the mirror image of the heightened energy and self-confidence we may feel when we are on steroids.

TRUTH OR FICTION *Revisited*

Steroids and growth hormone can give athletes an edge by boosting self-confidence and stoking development of the muscle mass. On the other hand, a number of health costs appear to accompany use of these drugs.

MARIJUANA

Marijuana is classified as a hallucinogenic or psychedelic drug because it sometimes produces mild hallucinations, particularly distortions of perceptions. A common perceptual distortion is a slowing down of the sense of passage of time. Marijuana is produced from the *Cannabis sativa* plant, which grows wild in many parts of the world and has been cultivated, from time to time, on window sills in dormitories. In addition to producing mild hallucinations, marijuana may foster feelings of relaxation and lift the mood.

The main psychoactive chemical in marijuana is *delta-9-tetrahydrocannabinol*, which is mercifully abbreviated THC. THC is found in Cannabis branches and leaves and is concentrated in the sap of the female plant. Hashish ("hash") is derived from the sap. It is more powerful than marijuana, but its effects are similar. Parts of the Cannabis plant are occasionally eaten (for example, used as an ingredient in cookies), but they are usually rolled and smoked like cigarettes.

IN YOUR OWN WRITE

Is marijuana popular on your campus? What have you heard about it?

Handling Drugs

In the last century, marijuana was bought without prescription and could be found in almost any drugstore. It was used as aspirin is now used for headaches and other aches and pains. Today marijuana is illegal in most states, but scientists are exploring other medical uses for the drug. For example, marijuana decreases nausea and vomiting among cancer patients who are receiving chemotherapy, helps glaucoma victims by lowering fluid pressure in the eye, and may be helpful in relieving asthma.[52] But there is also cause for concern, as noted in the 1982 report of the Institute of Medicine of the National Academy of Sciences. For example, marijuana

> Impairs coordination and the perceptual functions used in operating machinery, such as automobiles. (Don't smoke and then drive!)
>
> Impairs memory and retards learning. (Don't smoke and then study.)
>
> Causes feelings of anxiety and gross confusion in some users.
>
> Increases the heart rate up to 140–150 beats per minute from the normal 70 or so beats per minute.
>
> Raises the blood pressure. (This increase in workload threatens users with hypertension [high blood pressure] and heart problems.)
>
> Irritates the lungs, oral cavity, larynx, and esophagus. (Marijuana cigarettes contain about 50 percent more hydrocarbon than tobacco smoke.)*

The psychological effects of marijuana are related to the level of intoxication. Early phases of intoxication are often characterized by agitation, which usually gives way to feelings of serenity. Fair to strong intoxication is connected with intensified perceptions, a sense of self-insight, creative thought, and empathy with other people. Strongly intoxicated users perceive time to pass more slowly (a song may seem to last an hour, not a few minutes) and report heightened awareness of bodily sensations like the heartbeat. Many report that strong intoxication also intensifies sexual pleasure. Some report seeing things that are not there (that is, visual hallucinations). Strong intoxication can also cause disorientation. If the user also has feelings of euphoria, disorientation may be perceived as a sort of unity with the ebb and flow of things.

Some users find strong intoxication disturbing. The rapid heart rate and intensified awareness of body reactions causes some users to worry that their hearts are "running away" with them. Disorientation is very threatening to some users who struggle to retain their sense of who and where they are. Occasionally, strong intoxication induces nausea and vomiting. Students who encounter experiences like these smoke marijuana infrequently—or just once.

Some students claim that marijuana helps them socialize at parties. But the congeniality that characterizes early intoxication frequently gives way to self-absorption with stronger intoxication.[53]

Marijuana is not addictive. People can become psychologically dependent on marijuana, but regular users do not appear to develop tolerance. In fact, "reverse tolerance" has been reported: Regular users frequently require less, not more, marijuana to attain similar effects. Perhaps THC and other psychoactive substances in marijuana require a long time to be metabolized by the body. So the effects of new doses would be amplified by those of the chemicals remaining in the body. But frequent users also anticipate particular effects. Their expectations may augment mild bodily sensations to yield results previously attained only by means of higher doses.

---

*Marijuana users often argue that they only smoke a few "joints" a day, whereas cigarette smokers may smoke 20 to 40 or more cigarettes a day.

The effects of marijuana are related to the level of intoxication. Many smokers report feelings of serenity, intensified perceptions and hallucinations, creative thought, empathy with other people, and feelings of euphoria. Other smokers have negative experiences, such as extreme anxiety.

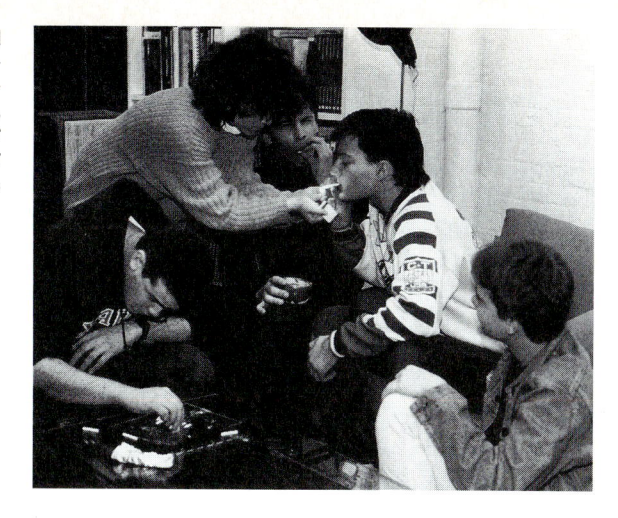

It was once argued that marijuana causes "amotivational syndrome." The Greek prefix *a-* means "not" or "without," and amotivational syndrome describes a condition in which the desire to achieve is hampered, ambition melts away, and students have difficulty concentrating on school work. Some studies report no connection between heavy marijuana use and intellectual deficiencies,[54] but the concern about amotivational syndrome has been fueled by findings that heavy college smokers do not work as hard to achieve good grades as nonsmokers and occasional smokers do. It may simply be, however, that students who choose to smoke heavily already differ from other students.[55] Perhaps heavy smokers are more interested in emotional experiences and fantasy than in intellectual achievement. Their overall approach to life may account both for their related lack of ambition and their heavy use of marijuana.

COCAINE

Have you seen the TV commercials that claim "Coke adds life"? Given its high sugar and caffeine content, Coke (that is, the soft drink, Coca-Cola) can get quite a rise out of drinkers. But, to paraphrase another commercial, not since 1906 has Coca-Cola been "the real thing." That is when the manufacturer ceased including cocaine in the formula.

IN YOUR OWN WRITE

Is cocaine used widely on your campus? What questions do you have about cocaine?

_____
_____
_____
_____
_____
_____
_____
_____

Handling Drugs

TRUTH OR FICTION *Revisited*

Cocaine was once used as an ingredient in Coca-Cola.

Cocaine is a stimulant that is derived from coca leaves—the plant from which both Coca-Cola and the drug derive their names. Cocaine creates feelings of euphoria (a powerful "high"), reduces feelings of hunger, deadens pain, and boosts self-confidence. As a stimulant, cocaine sometimes facilitates performance. Because of these effects and price breaks, cocaine has mushroomed in popularity, both on and off campus. Many athletes believe that cocaine, like steroids and growth hormone, give them the edge they need. A survey of young adults (averaging 25 years of age) found that 24 percent of women and 37 percent of men had tried cocaine.[56] Perhaps 5 million Americans use it regularly.[57]

Cocaine is ingested in various ways. It can be brewed from coca leaves like tea, snorted (breathed in as a powder), and shot up (injected as a liquid). The powerful, unrefined derivative "crack" is smoked.

Until recent years, many people, including some research scientists, believed that the worst effects of cocaine were cosmetic. That is, snorting of cocaine constricts blood vessels in the nose. With repeated usage, the skin is dried, cartilage may be exposed, and the nasal septum (the tissue dividing the nostrils) may be perforated. But now we know that cocaine offers other sources of danger.

One danger is the possible contamination of cocaine by foreign substances. People who inject cocaine and share needles risk contracting the AIDS virus.[58] Unrefined and inexpensive derivatives like crack and "bazooka" are frequently contaminated with toxic heavy metals, which can cause brain damage.

Even when well refined, cocaine sparks abrupt rises in blood pressure; constriction of blood vessels, which decreases the oxygen supply to the heart; and acceleration of the heart rate.[59] As a result, even strong college

Cocaine is a powerful stimulant that has recently attracted much press, because price breaks have made derivatives like crack available to more people and because of its effects on the cardiovascular system.

students and young athletes occasionally encounter respiratory and cardiovascular collapse, as in the deaths of the athletes Len Bias, Don Rogers, and David Croudip. Cocaine overdoses cause agitation and sleeplessness, tremors, headaches, nausea, convulsions, hallucinations, and, sometimes, paranoid beliefs (as, for example, that some group is "out to get" the user). Cocaine gradually lowers the brain's threshold for seizures in laboratory animals; even when moderate doses of cocaine have no immediate effects, there is a cumulative tendency for brain seizures and sudden death.[60]

Although it is widely believed that cocaine is addictive, some researchers consider the question unsettled. Users do not necessarily develop tolerance for cocaine, and no specific abstinence syndrome has been defined.[61] But users rapidly come to crave cocaine.

By the way, cocaine is used medically as an anesthetic and is still preferred for surgery on the nose and throat.

AMPHETAMINES

Amphetamines, or "uppers," are a class of stimulants that were first used during World War II to help soldiers remain alert through the night. Truck drivers also use them to remain awake. When your first author was an undergraduate, doctors were willing to prescribe amphetamines to help students remain awake for all-night cram sessions. Amphetamines also reduce the appetite and increase the metabolic rate, so an overweight roommate of his was prescribed heavy doses of amphetamines to, well, help him lighten up.

Also referred to as speed, bennies (for Benzedrine), and dexies (for Dexedrine), amphetamines are frequently abused for the euphoric rush they can provide, especially in high doses. Most students take amphetamines in pill form, but hardened drug abusers inject, or shoot up, the most potent variety, liquid Methedrine. Users can remain awake and high day after day, but such highs eventually end. Students who have been on extended highs occasionally "crash." That is, they fall into a deep sleep or a sudden, powerful depression. How painful is this depression? Some users commit suicide when they are crashing.

Amphetamines boost self-confidence and allow students to remain awake to study and during exams. They also combat feelings of depression that can attend prolonged stressful periods. Tolerance develops quickly, so that students may find themselves taking what formerly seemed like massive doses when they use them regularly, but amphetamines are not considered addictive. Overdoses can cause agitation, hallucinations, paranoid delusions, sleeplessness, and loss of appetite. In a so-called amphetamine psychosis (pronounced *sigh-CO-sis*), hallucinations and delusions mimic the symptoms of the mental disorder called paranoid schizophrenia.

Opiates

Opiates are a class of narcotics (derived from the Greek *narke*, meaning "sleep") that are derived from the opium poppy. Morphine, heroin, codeine, and meperidine (Demerol) are some of the better known opiates, whose major medical application is analgesia—deadening of pain. Morphine (from *Morpheus*, the mythical Greek god of sleep) was introduced during the Civil War and used to blunt the pain of wounds. Morphine addiction was dubbed the "soldier's disease." Heroin—so named because it made people feel "heroic"—was once used to "cure" morphine addiction. Opioids like methadone, which is now used to treat heroin addiction, are chemically similar to opiates, but they are synthesized in the laboratory.

TRUTH OR FICTION Revisited

Heroin was once used to treat addiction to morphine. This method of "swapping addictions" is still used: Today many heroin addicts are placed on the synthetic narcotic methadone.

Opiates are depressants that can provide a euphoric rush. Use of some of them, especially heroin, is so pleasurable to some users that they prefer it to food or sex. Before heroin became legally restricted, it was used liberally in patent medicines that were ordered by catalogue from establishments like Sears. At one point, it was referred to as G.O.M.—"God's own medicine." Heroin and similar drugs seem to act by stimulating brain centers that arouse pleasure and lead to addiction.[62]

Having said all this, it should be noted that opiates are used only rarely on campus. Although we may have half a million addicts in the United States, only about one half of one percent of college students have tried heroin.[63] Many fewer use it and related drugs with any regularity—although we have known some students who have urged their physicians to renew their prescriptions for codeine cold preparations when they have long recovered from their illnesses.

Opiates and opioids can have disquieting abstinence syndromes. They may begin with flulike symptoms and develop into cramps, tremors, alternating chills and sweating, rapid pulse, high blood pressure, sleeplessness, vomiting, and diarrhea. But abstinence varies from person to person. Some Vietnam veterans who used heroin regularly overseas apparently halted usage with few withdrawal symptoms when they were allowed to come home.

Although frequent users develop tolerance for opiates, overdoses can cause drowsiness and stupor, alter time perception, impair judgment—and, in extreme cases, cause coma and death.

TRANQUILIZERS

Tranquilizers include several classes of depressants that reduce the anxieties and tensions of everyday life. Tranquilizers are popular as illicit campus drugs because they relax the muscles and produce a mild state of euphoria.

IN YOUR OWN WRITE

Do you know people who use tranquilizers? What are your feelings about the people and the drugs?

_____
_____
_____
_____
_____
_____
_____

342 Chapter 13

They include so-called minor tranquilizers like Valium, Librium, and Atarax; barbiturates like amobarbital, phenobarbital, pentobarbital, and secobarbital; and methaqualone, sold under the brand names Quaalude and Sopor.

Minor tranquilizers are generally prescribed when patients ask their doctors for something to help them cope with tension. Unfortunately, popping pills does nothing to help people learn how to handle tension or remove the sources of tension in their lives. Moreover, we rapidly develop tolerance for them, so we need higher and higher doses to relax.

Barbiturates have a number of medical uses, including the deadening of pain, and treatment of epilepsy and high blood pressure. But barbiturates are abused because of the mellow feelings they can induce and because they help users get to sleep at night. Overdoses of tranquilizers result in drowsiness, poor coordination, slurred speech, irritability, poor judgment—and, in extreme cases, coma or death. Tranquilizers should never be mixed with alcohol, because both substances are depressants, and their effects are additive.

Barbiturates and methaqualone rapidly cause addiction, and their abstinence syndromes can be dangerous. Addicted people who are withdrawn abruptly may have convulsions and die. Overdoses of methaqualone can also cause internal bleeding. If you *must* use tranquilizers, at least stick to the minor tranquilizers (Valium, Librium, Atarax, etc.).

You will find that most professionals at the counseling center oppose use of tranquilizers for the run-of-the-mill anxieties and tensions that accompany college life. As we have suggested, students become dependent on them rapidly and they do nothing to teach students how to change their environments or alter disturbing patterns of behavior.

LSD: "LUCY IN THE SKY WITH DIAMONDS"

Back in the 1960s, Timothy Leary, a former professor at Harvard University, popularized the phrase, "Tune in, turn on, drop out." The expression voices the wave of social protest that struck campuses during that decade, when so many young people were deciding that climbing the corporate ladder—and the education that made it possible—were not for them. And one of Leary's major methods for "tuning in" and "turning on" was the use of hallucinogenic drugs such as marijuana and LSD.

LSD stands for lysergic diethylamide acid, a hallucinogenic drug that is synthesized in the laboratory. If you remember your 1960s popular music, the Beatles had a song entitled "Lucy in the Sky with Diamonds," which many observers believe was a reference to LSD and the type of hallucinations it engenders. "Acid" users assert that LSD opens new worlds and "expands consciousness." Users sometimes think that they have achieved great insights while "tripping," but when the drug wears off users usually cannot recall or effectively apply their discoveries.

LSD is a potent drug that produces vivid and colorful hallucinations, also called "trips." But LSD trips can be erratic. Some users have "good trips" only. Some have one "bad trip" and swear off acid use. Occasionally someone "flips out" while under the influence and has difficulty regaining touch with reality after the drug has worn off. LSD supporters argue that people who flip out were probably psychologically unstable to begin with. In all fairness, it may be that people who experience the worst reactions have a history of psychological problems.[64] But this does not guarantee that psychologically healthy students will have good trips!

One of the supposed effects of LSD and other hallucinogenic drugs is "flashbacks." Flashbacks are distorted perceptions or hallucinations that occur days or weeks after the drug has worn off but which mimic the

LSD trip. Some observers have assumed that flashbacks reflect chemical changes in the brain that are induced by LSD. Others offer psychological explanations for flashbacks.[65]

For example, "trippers" who have flashbacks are more likely to allow their thoughts to wander; they are more oriented toward fantasy than those without flashbacks. They are also more introverted—more likely to focus on internal sensations. If they experience sensations that remind them of a trip, they may label them flashbacks and permit themselves to concentrate on them, encouraging the replay of a drug-related experience.

Some other hallucinogenic drugs are mescaline, which is derived from the peyote cactus, and phencyclidine, or PCP. Frequent use of hallucinogenics can lead to tolerance, but they are not known to lead to abstinence syndromes and hence are not considered addictive. High doses can impair coordination and judgment, alter one's mood dramatically, and produce frightening hallucinations and paranoid delusions.

In this chapter we have tried to alert you to the effects of several drugs. If you are involved with one of them, we hope that we have given you some helpful information. If you are not involved, we hope that we have given you enough information so that you can decide what role, if any, these substances will play in your life. We cannot make your decisions for you.

SUMMING UP

1. Do you know students who abuse drugs or are addicted to drugs? How did they become involved with drugs?

2. What are your reasons for using alcohol, if you do? How does alcohol affect your behavior? How would you know if you had an alcohol problem?

3. Do you smoke cigarettes? If you do, are you happy about it? If not, what can you do about it?

4. Do you know students who use steroids or growth hormone? What are their motives? What are the dangers involved?

5. Is marijuana popular on your campus? Do users believe that it is harmless? What are its dangers?

6. Is cocaine popular on your campus? What are its dangers?

7. Are amphetamines used by students on your campus? What are their motives?

8. Have you ever used opiates or opioids? (Think about cold syrups you may have taken and injections you may have been given to deaden pain.) What were their effects?

9. Do you know people who use tranquilizers? How do you feel about tranquilizers and people who rely on them? Can you see yourself coming to depend on tranquilizers? Why or why not?

10. Do you know of students who use hallucinogens like LSD? What do you hear about these drugs?

Scoring Key for "Reasons for Drinking" Questionnaire

What are your reasons for drinking? Score your questionnaire by seeing the number of items you answered for each of the following reasons for drinking. Regard the key as suggestive only. In other words, if several of your answers agreed with those listed on the *addiction* factor, we advise you to examine what your drinking means to you. But a few test items do not offer conclusive proof of addiction.

Addiction (Items answered in the following manner suggest physiological dependence)

1. T
6. F
32. T
38. T
40. T
45. T

Anxiety/Tension Reduction

7. T
9. T
12. T
15. T
18. T
26. T
31. T
33. T
42. T

Pleasure/Taste

2. T
5. T
16. T
27. T
28. T
35. T
37. T

Transforming Agent (Items answered in the following direction suggest that you use alcohol to change your experiences for the better)

2. T
4. T
19. T
22. T
28. T
30. T
34. T
36. T

Social Reward

3. T
8. T
23. T
41. T

Celebration

10. T
24. T
25. T
43. T

Religion

11. T

Social Power

2. T
13. T
19. T
30. T

Scapegoating (Items answered in the following direction suggest that you may use alcohol as an excuse for failure or social misconduct)

14. T
15. T
20. T
21. T
39. T

Habit

17. T
29. T
44. T

Handling Drugs 345

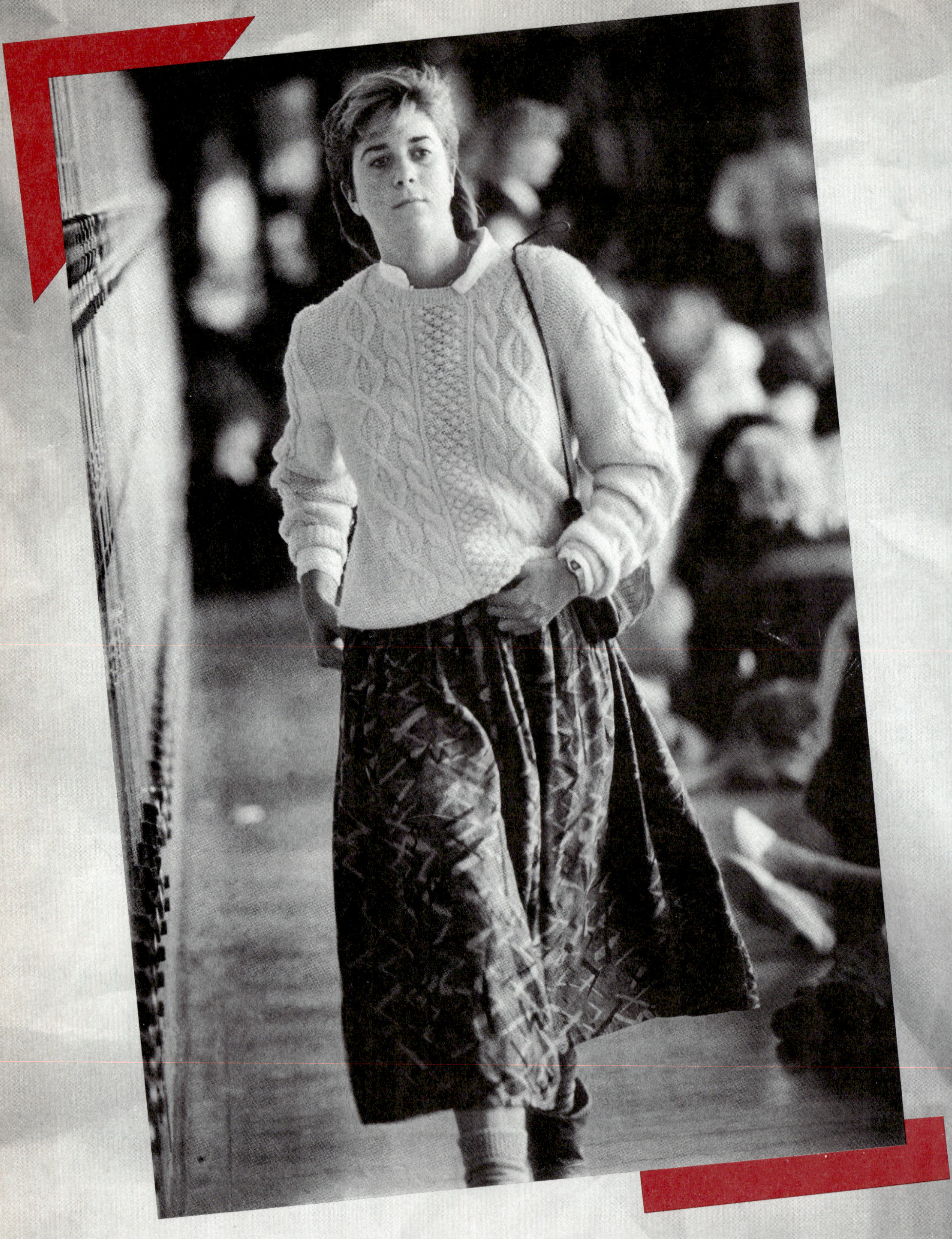

14

Making the Transition from College to the Career World

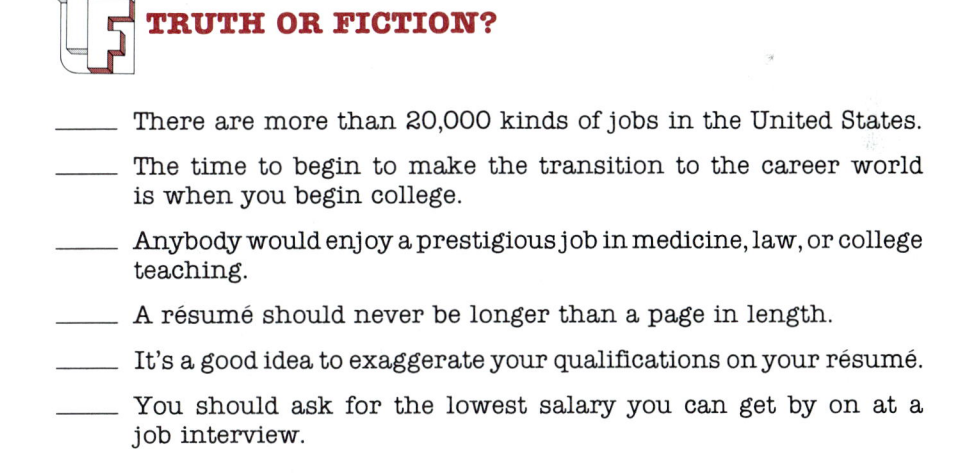

TRUTH OR FICTION?

____ There are more than 20,000 kinds of jobs in the United States.

____ The time to begin to make the transition to the career world is when you begin college.

____ Anybody would enjoy a prestigious job in medicine, law, or college teaching.

____ A résumé should never be longer than a page in length.

____ It's a good idea to exaggerate your qualifications on your résumé.

____ You should ask for the lowest salary you can get by on at a job interview.

America is the land of golden opportunity. America is also the land of decision anxiety. One of the things you have to decide is what you are going to *do*. You will find that *"What* do you do?" is a more momentous question at social gatherings than *"How* do you do?" "What do you do?" is usually the first question raised in small talk. The prestige attached to what we do—and what we don't do—is fundamental to our social standing.

In societies with caste systems, such as old England or India, people usually did what their parents did. Throughout their formative years, they assumed that they would follow in their parents' footsteps. Caste systems save people the necessity of deciding what they're going to do with themselves. Caste systems also squander unique talents and make a mockery of personal freedom.

In the United States, some young people aspire to their parents' occupations, but usually when their parents are well rewarded and proud of their work. A study of occupational choice among 76,000 first-year college students found that the offspring of teachers, physicians, and scientists leaned toward their parents' specialties.[1] If, however, you are the first member of your family to go to college, your parents are less likely to have become professionals.

> . . . if one advances confidently in the direction of his dreams, and endeavors to live the life which he has imagined, he will meet with a success unexpected in common hours.
>
> HENRY DAVID THOREAU,
> *Walden*

HOW TO MAKE CAREER DECISIONS

There is a baffling array of occupational prospects. The *Dictionary of Occupational Titles*, published by the U.S. Department of Labor, lists more than 20,000 occupations.

TRUTH OR FICTION *Revisited*

Yes, there are more than 20,000 kinds of jobs in the United States.

There is a baffling array of occupational prospects in the United States. The U.S. Department of Labor's Dictionary of Occupational Titles *lists more than 20,000 occupations.*

Most of us do not choose careers by leafing through the dictionary, of course. Our sense of what is available to us tends to be much, much narrower.[2] And one college student in three postpones making a career decision until after graduation.[3] Many graduates fall into careers not because of special skills and interests, but because of what is open at the time, family pressures, the lure of high pay or of a particular style of life.[4] Some graduates take the first job that happens along after graduation. For them, whether or not things work out is a matter of chance.

Our consistent message to you has been not to leave things to chance. Managing time and money, doing well in your courses, making friends—you can exert control over all of these. Similarly, there are things that you can do to determine where you fit in in terms of a career—where you will be able to express your talents and find satisfaction.

We'll get to some of those things in a minute. First, however, let us note when you begin to make your transition to the career world. For many of you, it's right at the beginning. Right at the beginning of college, that is—when you select a major field. For example, if you want to become an engineer, an architect, a mathematician, a natural scientist, a physician, or a business person, it's usually best to schedule courses in these or related fields as early as your first year. That's because the required courses must be taken in certain sequences. If you don't start early, you run out of time. On the other hand, if you're not sure what you want to do, or if you want to major in the liberal arts, you've got more time.

> People who work sitting down get paid more than people who work standing up.
>
> OGDEN NASH

TRUTH OR FICTION *Revisited*

For many of you, the time to begin to make the transition to the career world *is* when you begin college. This is especially so for students who are thinking about entering technical fields.

Children are ruled by fantasy. When they think about careers, young children focus on the glamour professions—things like acting, sports, medicine, and law enforcement. They give little thought to practical concerns, such as whether or not these occupations suit their abilities. By the time

IN YOUR OWN WRITE

As a first-year student, how vital does career selection seem to you right now? Are your thoughts about careers influencing your choice of courses? Are your career aspirations affecting your motivation to study? Are you concerned or confused about careers?

_____
_____
_____
_____
_____
_____
_____

Making the Transition from College to the Career World

we reach high school, reality begins to creep in. We begin to gravitate toward jobs that seem to bear some connection with our interests, abilities, and limitations. When we enter college, our choices tend to narrow and become still more realistic.[5] Many of us weigh job requirements, rewards, even the futures of occupations. We appraise ourselves more accurately and try to mesh our personal traits and values with a job. Many of us also direct our educations toward supplying the knowledge and skills we'll need to land the chosen field and do well in it. On the other hand, some of us never make realistic choices, but sort of fall into jobs.

Whatever major you select, whatever field you go into, think about it early. If you're not sure what you want to do, talk to someone about that. People on your campus have been specially trained to go over these things with you. You'll find them at the counseling and testing center or at the placement office.* Give them a call. You wouldn't want them to lose their jobs for lack of work, would you?

Let's Party! (Let's Attend the Job-Hunting Party, That Is)

We'll get back to career selection in a minute, but now that school's out—or almost out—let's take some time out to party. Figure 14.1 shows an aerial view of a room in which a party is going on. What happened is this: When the party got underway, people started chatting with one another. As time went on, they discovered mutual interests and collected into various parts of the room according to those interests.

All right, now imagine that you enter the room. Although groups have already formed, you decide not to hang around by yourself. You catch snatches of conversation in an effort to decide which group to join. Now read the following questions† and place the name of the proper group (R, I, A, S, E, or C) in the "Group" column. Then read on.

> An unlearned carpenter of my acquaintance once said in my hearing: "There is very little difference between one man and another; but what little there is, is very important." This distinction seems to me to go to the heart of the matter.
>
> WILLIAM JAMES

Questions	Group
1. Which group would you join? If you had to choose just one group of people with whom to hang out, to which group would you be drawn?	_____
2. A half hour passes. The members of the group you have joined must leave to attend another party. You decide not to remain alone. Of the remaining groups, which holds most interest for you? Which group do you join now?	_____
3. Another half hour goes by. The second group you joined also departs. Four groups remain—along with you. Which group do you join now?	_____

> Hard work never killed anybody, but why take a chance?
>
> CHARLIE MCCARTHY
> (Edgar Bergen)

The "job party" is an exercise that can help you decide where you may fit in. A proper "fit," in terms of our abilities, interests, and personal traits, enhances our satisfaction on the job from day to day.

Put another way: What does it matter that you're bringing home the bacon if you feel trapped in your job and hate getting up to face it? Also, if you don't like your job, you'll find it more stressful and will be very unlikely to give it your best.[6] When you do a poor or mediocre job, you're unlikely to get ahead. You could even get fired.

Predicting whether or not we will adjust to an occupation involves matching our traits to the job. Psychologist John Holland has had success

---

* The services offered in these offices were described in Chapter 2.

† The party idea and the questions are based on the work of Richard N. Bolles, author of *the 1989 What Color Is Your Parachute?* (Berkeley, CA: Ten Speed Press) and the National Career Development Project. Bolles' work is based on the typology of John Holland.

FIGURE 14.1. The Party. Where would you have the most fun?

These people have clerical or numerical skills. They like to work with data, to carry out other people's directions, or to carry things out in detail.

These people have mechanical or athletic abilities. They like to work with machines and tools, to be outdoors, or to work with animals or plants.

These people like to work with people. They like to lead and influence others for economic or organizational gains.

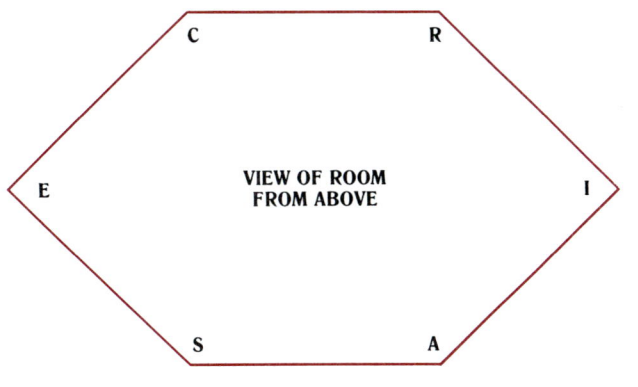

VIEW OF ROOM FROM ABOVE

These people like to learn new things. They enjoy investigating and solving problems and advancing knowledge.

This group enjoys working with people. They like to help others, including the sick. They enjoy informing and enlightening people.

This group is highly imaginative and creative. They enjoy working in unstructured situations. They are artistic and innovative.

in predicting how well we will enjoy a certain kind of work by matching six personal traits to the job: realistic, investigative, artistic, social, enterprising, and conventional.[7] Each of the six groups in Figure 14.1 represented a particular trait:

1. *Realistic (R).* "Realistic" people tend to be concrete in their thinking, mechanically oriented, and interested in jobs that involve physical activity. They're often rugged and practical and like outdoor work. Examples include barber; coach; electrical contractor; equipment operator; farmer; jeweler; physical education instructor; tailor; unskilled laborer, such as gas station attendant; and skilled trades, such as construction and electrical work.

2. *Investigative (I).* "Investigative" people tend to be scientifically oriented. They are abstract and creative in their thinking. Often they are "loners." They tend to enjoy positions such as college or university professor, computer programmer, engineer, laboratory researcher, physician, and technical writer.

3. *Artistic (A).* "Artistic" individuals tend to be creative, emotional, unconventional, and independent. They tend to gravitate toward the visual arts and the performing arts. They enjoy positions in architecture, art, editing, music, reporting, cinema and photography, public relations, and interior design.

4. *Social (S).* "Social" people tend to be outgoing, socially concerned, and popular with others. They frequently show strong verbal ability and strong needs for associating with others. They usually enjoy jobs in social work, counseling, nursing, religion, career planning, and teaching children.

5. *Enterprising (E).* "Enterprising" individuals tend to be adventurous and impulsive, socially dominant, and outgoing. They gravitate toward leadership and planning roles in industry, government, and social organizations. The successful real-estate developer or tycoon is usually enterprising. Positions in sales, law, politics, industrial relations, and television production often suit them.

> Work is the refuge of people who have nothing better to do.
>
> OSCAR WILDE

Are you artistic? According to one occupational theory, there are various vocational "types," including realistic, investigative, social, enterprising, conventional, and—yes—artistic. By knowing what types we are, perhaps we can make more effective career choices.

6. *Conventional (C).* "Conventional" people tend to enjoy routines and positions with firm structure. They are usually conscientious and efficient. Jobs that suit them include bank teller, accountant, statistician, data processor, hospital administrator, insurance administrator, office manager, and clerk.

In going through these traits, it may have occurred to you that two or three seem to describe you quite well. Sure—few people are a "pure" type. That is also why the questions as to which groups you would join gave you second and third preferences.

Here are some examples of mixed types: A copywriter in an advertising agency might be both artistic and enterprising. Clinical and counseling psychologists tend to be investigative, artistic, and socially oriented. Military people and beauticians tend to be realistic and conventional. Military leaders who plan major operations and form governments are also enterprising, however, and people who create new hair styles and fashions are also artistic.

TRUTH OR FICTION *Revisited*

Not everybody would enjoy a prestigious job in medicine, law, or college teaching. Different types of people are happy in different kinds of work. What type or types are you?

> I like work; it fascinates me; I can sit and look at it for hours.
>
> JEROME K. JEROME

You can get a clearer idea of where you belong at the "party" by visiting the college counseling and testing center. There you can take the Vocational Preference Inventory written by John Holland in order to assess these traits, or the Strong/Campbell Interest Inventory, which measures these traits and a lot more.

Let's see how these and other tests can be used to help you pinpoint your career objectives. In doing so, we'll also explore using the balance sheet to make career decisions.

How to Use the Balance Sheet to Make Career Decisions

In Chapter 12, we discussed the balance sheet in the context of making sexual decisions. We saw that Steffi used it to help her decide whether or not to go on the pill. Balance sheets can also be used in making career decisions. For example, wise decision making is based on weighing adequate information. Sometimes, however, we are not sure about whether or not we know enough to make a decision. A study at Yale found that the balance sheet helped seniors heighten awareness of gaps in information they needed.[8] The balance sheet can also be of help to you.

Consuela, a Mexican-American first-year liberal arts major at the University of Texas at El Paso, wondered whether to pursue premedical studies. There were no physicians in her family with whom to talk it over. A counselor in her university counseling center advised her to fill out the balance sheet shown in Table 14.1 to help weigh the pluses and minuses of medicine.

TABLE 14.1. Consuela's Balance Sheet for the Possibility of Taking Premedical Studies

AREAS OF CONSIDERATION	POSITIVE ANTICIPATIONS	NEGATIVE ANTICIPATIONS
Tangible gains and losses for Consuela	1. Solid income	1. Long hours of studying 2. Worry about acceptance by medical school 3. High financial debt
Tangible gains and losses for others	1. Solid income for benefit of family	1. Little time for family life
Self-approval or self-disapproval	1. Pride in being a physician	
Social approval or disapproval	1. Other people admire doctors	1. Some people frown on women and Mexican-American doctors

Consuela's balance sheet showed that she knew that other people admired physicians, but she had not pondered how she would feel about herself as a physician. The balance sheet encouraged her to seek further information about her personal needs.

Consuela's balance sheet suggested the kinds of pieces of information she needed to make a decision. How, for example, would she cope with intense, sustained studying and intense, sustained work hours? What was the likelihood of being accepted by a medical school? How did the day-to-day nitty-gritty of medical work fit with her personal needs?

Consuela's need for information is not specific to students considering medicine. Regardless of the career you are contemplating, finding answers to the kinds of questions shown in Table 14.2 will help you make an informed decision.

How to Use Psychological Tests to Make Career Decisions

Consuela's career counselor used a number of psychological tests. Most career counselors combine testing with information from personal interviews and knowledge of their clients' personal histories. All this information helps provide a rounded picture of their clients' interests, abilities, personalities, and motivation.[9] Whereas basic skills and academic placement tests

> I do not like work even when another person does it.
>
> MARK TWAIN

TABLE 14.2. Kinds of Questions That Need to Be Answered in Making an Informed Career Decision

AREAS OF CONCERN	QUESTIONS TO BE ANSWERED	INFORMATION RESOURCES
Intellectual and Educational Appropriateness: Is your intended career compatible with your own intellectual and educational abilities and background?	Have you taken any ("preprofessional") courses that lead to the career? Have you done well in them? How intelligent are people who function well in the career? Is your own level of intelligence comparable? What kinds of special talents and intellectual skills are required for this career? Are there any psychological or educational tests that can identify where you stand in your possession of these talents, or in the development of these skills? If you do not have these skills, can they be developed? How are they developed? Is there any way of predicting how well you can do at developing them? Would you find this field intellectually demanding and challenging? Would you find the field intellectually sterile and boring?	College or university counseling or testing center, college placement center, private psychologist or vocational counselor, people working in the field, professors in or allied to the field.
Intrinsic Factors: Is your intended career compatible with your coping style, your psychological needs, and your interests?	In Holland's terms, does the job require realistic, investigative, artistic, social, enterprising, or conventional traits? Which of these traits describe your own personality? Is there a good "fit"? Is the work repetitious, or is it varied? Do you have a marked need for change (perpetual novel stimulation), or do you have a greater need for order and consistency? Would you be working primarily with machinery, with papers, or with other people? Do you prefer manipulating objects, doing paper work, or interacting with other people? Is the work indoors or outdoors? Are you an "indoor" or an "outdoor person"? Do you have strong needs for autonomy and dominance, or do you prefer to defer to others? Does the field allow you to make your own decisions, permit you to direct others, or require that you closely take direction from others? Do you have strong aesthetic needs? Is the work artistic? Are you Type A, Type B, or somewhere in between? Is this field strongly competitive or more relaxed?	Successful people in the field. (Do you feel similar to people in the field? Do you have common interests? Do you like them and enjoy their company?) Written job descriptions. Psychological tests of personality (e.g., coping style and psychological needs) and interests.
Extrinsic Factors: What is the balance between the investment you would have to make in the career and the probable payoff?	How much time, work, and money would you have to invest in your educational and professional development to enter this career? Do you have the financial resources? If not, can you get them? (Do the sacrifices you would have to make to get them—such as long-term debt—seem worthwhile?) Do you have the endurance? The patience? What will the market for your skills be like when you are ready to enter the career? In 20 years?	College financial aid office, college placement office, college counseling center, family, people in the field.

are given to many first-year students as a routine administrative procedure, the tests discussed in this section are usually administered only on the basis of student request.

Intelligence Tests Consuela had wondered whether or not she was intelligent enough to become a physician. Her counselor administered a Wechsler Adult Intelligence Scale (WAIS) to answer this question. The WAIS and the Stanford-Binet Intelligence Scales are the most widely used intelligence tests, and the WAIS is the most widely used with adults. The WAIS consists of verbal subtests and performance subtests (see Table 14.3). Verbal subtests require knowledge of verbal concepts, such as the meanings of words or ways in which concepts are alike, and performance subtests require familiarity with spatial-relations concepts.

Consuela's WAIS performance was on a par with that of people who did well in medical studies. Any academic problems would probably reflect

> Work is of two kinds: first, altering the position of matter at or near the earth's surface relatively to other matter; second, telling other people to do so. The first kind is unpleasant and ill-paid; the second is pleasant and highly paid.
>
> BERTRAND RUSSELL

TABLE 14.3. Subtests from the Wechsler Adult Intelligence Scale (WAIS)

VERBAL SUBTESTS	PERFORMANCE SUBTESTS
1. *Information*: "What is the capital of the United States?" "Who was Shakespeare?"	7. *Digit symbol*: Learning and drawing meaningless figures that are associated with numbers.
2. *Comprehension*: "Why do we have zip codes?" "What does the saying *A stitch in time saves nine* mean?"	8. *Picture completion*: Pointing to the missing parts in a series of pictures.
3. *Arithmetic*: "If 3 candy bars cost 25 cents, how much will 18 candy bars cost?"	9. *Block design*: Copying pictures of geometric designs using multicolored blocks.
4. *Similarities*: "How are *good* and *bad* alike?"	10. *Picture arrangement*. Arranging cartoon pictures in sequence so that they tell a meaningful story.
5. *Digit span*: Repeating series of numbers backwards and forwards.	11. *Object assembly*: Putting pieces of a puzzle together so that they make up a meaningful object.
6. *Vocabulary*: "What does *duct* mean?"	

Note: Reprinted from S. A. Rathus & J. S. Nevid. (1989). *Psychology and the challenges of life*, 4th ed. New York: Holt, Rinehart and Winston, p. 434.

---

lack of motivation or of specific prerequisites, not general inability. Her counselor also told Consuela that sometimes "The best predictor of future behavior is past behavior." In other words, if you have excelled in an academic area in the past, you are likely to do so in the future.* Because premedical programs are dominated by chemistry, Consuela's excellent performance in high school chemistry was reassuring.

In surveying her balance sheet, Consuela realized that she hadn't really explored how she would enjoy the day-to-day work of a physician. She had recognized that physicians are admired in the United States. So she had assumed that she would feel pride in herself. But would the work of a physician meet her personal needs? The counselor furnished helpful information through the Strong/Campbell Interest Inventory (SCII) and the Edwards Personal Preference Schedule (EPPS).

The Strong/Campbell Interest Inventory (SCII) is the most widely used test in college counseling and testing centers.[10] With the SCII, students compare their interests to those of people who have chosen various occupations. They also learn which groups (R, I, A, S, E, or C) they fit in with at "the party."

The Edwards Personal Preference Schedule (EPPS) gives students insight into their strongest personal needs. They can learn, for example, whether they have a stronger need for dominance than for deference (taking direction from others), or strong needs for order or to be helped by others.

The SCII suggested that Consuela was *investigative*. She would enjoy scientific work—including medical science—and mathematics. But she was not particularly *social*. Well-adjusted physicians are usually investigative and social.

The EPPS showed strong needs for achievement, order, dominance, and endurance. These factors meshed well with premedical studies—the long hours and the desire to learn—to make things fit together and work properly. The EPPS report dovetailed with the SCII report. Neither showed Consuela as particularly socially oriented. The EPPS also showed that Consuela was not particularly interested in caring for others or promoting their well-being.

---

*The converse is not always true, however. We may improve our performance in areas in which we have struggled by increasing our motivation and filling in missing academic background.

With this information in hand, Consuela realized that she didn't sense a strong desire to help others through medicine. Her medical interests were more academic. Nevertheless, Consuela chose to pursue premedical studies, to take courses that would lay the groundwork for various careers in medically related sciences. The courses were of interest even if she chose to become a pure scientist and not a physician. Contingency plans such as these are useful for all of us. If we can keep alternatives in mind as we head down the paths toward our goals, we are better equipped to deal with unanticipated forks in the road.

In one way or another, college careers lead to jobs. Let's now consider ways of finding a job.

HOW TO FIND A JOB

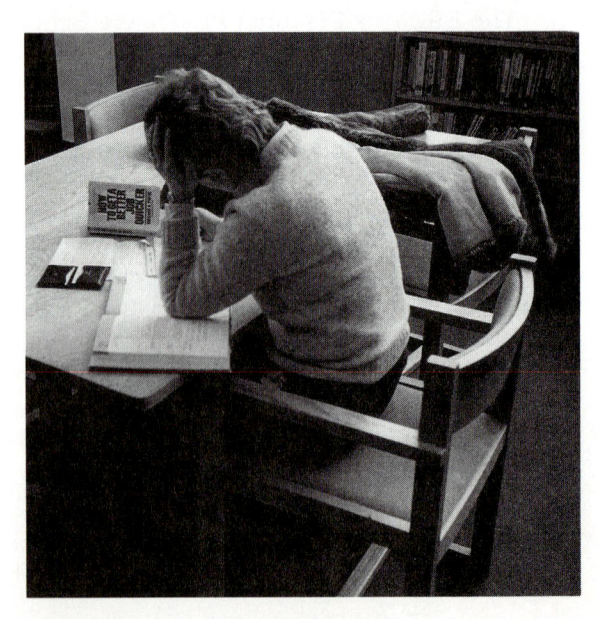

> I love work. Why, sir, when I have a piece of work to perform, I go away to myself, sit down in the shade, and muse over the coming enjoyment. Sometimes I am so industrious that I muse too long.
>
> MARK TWAIN

If you're concerned about what you'll do after college, you're not alone. Eighty percent of the students in the Carnegie Foundation's National Survey of Undergraduates reported being at least "somewhat" worried about the job prospects after leaving college.[11] Thirty-five percent were worried "quite a lot" or "a great deal." Only 20 percent were "not at all worried."

Despite their concerns, the great majority of graduates will land jobs. Engineering graduates are highly desirable in the job market, with 83 percent of them employed at time of graduation.[12] Only 24 percent of education majors and 38 percent of liberal arts majors have jobs when they graduate. However, after nine months, 97 percent of the education majors and 94 percent of the liberal arts majors have landed positions. Although it may take a while to get placed, liberal arts majors are not unhappy with their educations. One noted, "College didn't fit me for any certain career, but it taught me how to learn."[13]

An initial step in finding a job is to visit your college's placement or career services office. The placement office, as noted in Chapter 2, receives job listings, and they offer invaluable advice about salaries, letters of application, résumés, and interviews. The placement office also assembles your credentials (including your letters of reference, a duplicate of your transcript, and a record of your work experience), keeps them on file, and makes them available on request.

We are going to give you some specific advice on how to put together your best foot forward—your résumé—because you can make use of a résumé in hunting for part-time and summer jobs as well as upon graduation.

If you're concerned about what you'll do after college, you're not alone. Eighty percent of the students in the Carnegie Foundation's National Survey of Undergraduates reported being at least "somewhat" worried about the job prospects after leaving college.

Your résumé is your "best foot forward." How do you go about writing an effective résumé?

HOW TO WRITE A RÉSUMÉ

When you apply for a job, you usually send a résumé with a cover letter. The primary purpose of a résumé is to convince a hiring manager that you are well qualified for a position and that interviewing you will be a worthwhile investment.[14] But until you are called in for an interview, your résumé *is* you. So give it the same attention you would give your grooming.

Before getting into the mechanics of the résumé, it helps to know who will be looking at it and deciding whether to toss it into the "circular file"—that is, the wastepaper basket. Résumés are usually first screened by a secretary or administrative assistant, who may chuck it if it's sloppy, illegible, incomplete, and incompatible with the job requirements. Then it is usually seen by an employment or personnel manager, who may screen it out if it is incompatible with job requirements or does not show the specifications required of candidates. Employment managers also discard résumés that show inadequate experience or educational credentials, incompatible salary requirements, and lack of U.S. citizenship or lack of permanent resident status.[15] They also eliminate résumés that are too long. A résumé is a *summary* of your qualifications, not a diary or a book. On the other hand, it is acceptable for a résumé to run to a couple of pages if you really can't condense your qualifications to one page.[16]

TRUTH OR FICTION *Revisited*

A résumé can exceed one page in length, but if you must run to two pages, be certain that your qualifications cannot be condensed. Why not get advice at the placement office?

Finally, the hiring officer—often this is the same person who would be supervising you if you got the job—may screen out your résumé if it shows that you lack the right qualifications. You may also be eliminated if you're *over*qualified. Why? If you're too highly skilled or too well educated for the job, you probably won't be happy in it. And if you're not happy, you won't give it your best and you may quit early.

The bottom line is this: Be neat and show that you are precisely right for the job. Rather than send out the same résumé to all hiring officers through the placement office, keep a general résumé on file in a word processor and fine-tune it for the specific position. However, don't be dishonest. After all, if you lie about your qualifications, two bad things can happen. First, you can be eliminated if your dishonesty is found out from references or through the interview. Second, you may get the job, but if you're not qualified, you'll probably be miserable in it. The point is that you should use the particular job description to decide which of your qualifications to highlight.

TRUTH OR FICTION *Revisited*

It's not a good idea to exaggerate your qualifications on your résumé.

Parts of the Résumé

Résumés consist of

1. A heading
2. A statement of your job objective
3. A summary of your educational background
4. A summary of your work experience
5. Personal information
6. A list of references

The Heading The heading contains your name, address, and telephone number. If you are living at home, center the heading as follows:

MARK P. KNIGHT
12 Hazleton Road
Newton Centre, Massachusetts 02159
Telephone: (617) 735-2495

But if you are living at school, you might want to provide both a temporary and a permanent address, as follows:

ALISON HARTFORD

Temporary Address:	Permanent Address (After 5/26/91):
Brubacher Hall—Room 135 1435 Washington Avenue Albany, New York 12115 Telephone: (518) 573-1295	156 Franklin Avenue Cedarhurst, New York 11735 Telephone: (516) 429-1945

The Job Objective Try to tailor the job objective to the opening. Don't be too general or too blatantly specific. Say the job advertised is for a computer salesperson trainee in Phoenix, Arizona. A job objective of "Marketing or Sales" might be too general and suggests that you do not know what you're after. A job objective of "Computer sales trainee in the southwestern

United States" is too obvious and just plain silly. Also avoid saying things that will screen you out, like "Sales trainee with rapid advancement opportunities to management." You're being considered for the sales trainee position, not president of the company!

A reasonable objective would be "Sales, computer equipment," or "Sales of technical merchandise."

Educational Background   For each school attended, you need to include the following:

1. The degree awarded (or expected)
2. Name of school (and address, if school is not well known)
3. Year graduated (or expected to graduate)
4. Major field or specialties
5. Grade point average (when 3.0 or better)
6. Honors and awards
7. Professional certificates (e.g., teaching, interior design)
8. Extracurricular activities

List schools attended in reverse chronological order. That is, put the most recent school first. For example:

Education	B.A.:	Arizona State University, Tempe, 1991
	Major:	Psychology
	G.P.A.:	3.8/4.0
	Honors:	Magna Cum Laude
	Activities:	President, Psychology Club, 1990–1991
	A.A.:	Mesa Community College, Phoenix, 1989
	Major:	Psychology
	Diploma:	Scottsdale High School, Scottsdale, Arizona, 1987

In the preceding example, the solid G.P.A., the honors earned at Arizona State, and the presidency of the Psychology Club are all listed. The less impressive performances in high school and at Mesa are not detailed.

As an exercise, use the format in Figure 14.2 to outline your educational experiences in college or in high school. List the most important extracurricular activities, and be sure to indicate that you played a leadership role, wherever possible. Most students approaching graduation do not have extensive work experience, so having been editor of the yearbook, president of a club, or captain of a team is a notable achievement.

At the end of the chapter, you'll find additional worksheets that will help you organize information about your educational background.

Work Experience   Don't list the normal childhood jobs of babysitting and lawn mowing, unless you organized and ran a babysitting or lawn-mowing business in your home town. Pay particular attention to the jobs that are related to the position you are seeking. If you can show that you have been pursuing the same field for a number of years, you will be seen as more organized, purposeful, and motivated—desirable job qualities. Of particular importance are internships and full-time positions. Also of interest are summer and part-time positions that show that you handled some responsibility. Don't pad your résumé with irrelevant, unimportant positions. Remember that you're applying for a job as a fresh college graduate, not as a mature professional on the move from one executive position to another.

FIGURE 14.2. Worksheet for Outlining Educational Background

Degree: _____

School: _____

Graduation date: _____
(Enter date
expected if
not received)

Major Field: _____

Specialties: _____
_____

Honors: _____
_____

Scholarships: _____
_____

Professional _____
Certificates: _____

Extracurricular 1. _____
Activities:
 2. _____
 3. _____
 4. _____
 5. _____

For each position, include information such as the following:

1. Title of position held
2. Dates of employment
3. Whether job was full- or part-time; number of hours per week
4. Name of employer
5. Division of employer, or location of employment
6. Brief statement of job responsibilities, using action verbs (see sample below)
7. Brief statement of chief achievements

Don't list the names of your supervisors, unless you are willing to have all of them called by your prospective employer. As with your educational background, list positions in reverse chronological order—most recent position first. Consider this example:

<u>Work</u> 1. February 1990-May 1991
<u>Experience:</u>   San Diego State University
    <u>Assistant to the Director, University Art Gallery</u>

    Responsibilities: Catalogued art works in permanent collection; arranged shipping of works for exhibitions; assisted in the hanging of exhibitions; arranged printing of exhibition catalogues and mailers

    Major Achievements: Curated Christo exhibition; co-authored exhibition catalogue <u>Conceptual Art.</u>

 2. June 1980–September 1989
    Etc.

360   Chapter 14

FIGURE 14.3. Worksheet for Outlining Work Experience

Dates: _____

Status _____
(part-time, hours
per week, full-time)

Employer: _____

Division/location: _____

Responsibilities: 1. _____

2. _____

3. _____

4. _____

5. _____

Chief achievements: 1. _____

2. _____

3. _____

4. _____

5. _____

As an exercise, use the format in Figure 14.3 to outline information concerning a former or current job. Additional work-experience worksheets are found at the end of the chapter.

Personal Information This is a section in which you may indicate your age, marital status, number of children, citizenship, health, and so on. Go along with the suggestion of Richard M. Beatty,[17] vice-president of an executive search firm, that you leave this section out entirely, if possible. Beatty notes many pitfalls. For example, some employers hold the prejudice that women with children are only interested in a second income and would be absent whenever a minor crisis or an illness hit the household. Other employers are prejudiced against married women when a job calls for travel. Discrimination based on gender is illegal, of course, but a hiring manager can screen you out without an explanation. Also, lack of U.S. citizenship or of permanent resident status can knock you out of contention.

When you are graduating from college, employers expect you to be youthful. Why tell them that you went back to school once your kids entered their teens and that you're 43 years old? We know you're great, but prospective employers may be prejudiced against people starting their professional lives at later ages. If that's you, consider not listing your high school education (why give away the graduation date?) or years of preprofessional work—unless, of course, you had notable achievements. They'll see that you're older than 21 in the job interview, but then you can also overwhelm the interviewer with your mature judgment, strong motivation, and clear sense of direction. So you've got to get to that interview first.

References References would be placed last on the résumé, but Beatty[18] recommends not using them, unless specifically requested, for fear that the prospective employer may check them out before inviting you to an interview. If the slightest negative bit of information turns up, you may be knocked out of contention. Say "References will be furnished upon request" in your cover letter, which is the next subject.

The Cover Letter

The cover letter accompanies your résumé and has the following parts:

1. Explanation of the purpose of the letter
2. Explanation of how you learned about the opening
3. Comparison of your qualifications and the job requirements
4. Statements of desired salary and geographic limitations (optional)
5. Request for an interview or other response to the letter
6. Statement that references will be sent upon request
7. Thanks for the prospective employer's consideration

Consider the cover letter and remarks shown in Table 14.4.

TABLE 14.4. A Cover Letter to Accompany a Résumé

SECTION OF LETTER	REMARKS
I enclose my résumé in application for the position of computer sales trainee, as described in the job notice sent to my college's placement office.	Refers to enclosed résumé States writer is applying for position Indicates how writer learned of position
My education and work experience appear to fit well indeed with your job requirements. My major field is business, with a specialty in marketing. I have four courses in computer science. I hold a part-time position in the college computer center, where I advise students how to use our mainframe and microcomputers. Moreover, I have held part-time and summer sales positions, as outlined in the résumé.	Good! The writer shows extensive experience (for a fresh college graduate) both in sales and in computers.
Salary is relatively unimportant to me. However, my wife is employed in town here, so I would not be able to relocate.	Mistakes! Salary is always important—to the employer if not to you. Say nothing about salary unless a statement of "salary requirements" is specifically required in the job listing. Also, don't go into marital status and possible relocation problems. You can deal with them after you get to the interview. Here you've knocked yourself out of contention by stating that family commitments may well prevent you from doing your job.
I look forward to the prospect of an interview. I can get off from work or miss a class or two if I have to.	Yes, no. Yes to desiring an interview; no to the preoccupation with the mechanics of breaking free for the interview.
References will be furnished upon request.	Fine—keep it short.
Thanks for your consideration.	Spell out "Thank you"; otherwise, fine.

Congratulations! The résumé and cover letter were very good. In fact, you've been invited to an interview. Now what?

HOW TO HANDLE A JOB INTERVIEW

The job interview is a special social interaction that presents many opportunities and pitfalls. Indicate some of your concerns about interviewing "In Your Own Write," and then see the suggestions for handling an interview given below.

IN YOUR OWN WRITE

The interview is both a social occasion and a test. Jot down some of your concerns about being interviewed. Might it be worthwhile to discuss your concerns with someone at the counseling center or placement office?

___

First impressions and neatness count at interviews, so dress well and look your best. When other things are held equal, people who look their best usually get the job.[19] Maintain direct eye contact with your interviewer, but look alert, cooperative, and friendly—don't stare.

One way to prepare for an academic test is to try to anticipate your instructor's questions. Similarly, anticipating your interviewer's questions will help prepare you for the interview. Once you have arrived at a list of likely questions, rehearse answers to them. It helps to recruit a friend to role-play the interviewer and practice them aloud.

Despite your enthusiasm (or your "nerves"!), don't try to do all the talking in the interview. Be patient. Let the interviewer tell you about the position and the organization without trying to jump in. Be attentive. Nod now and then. Don't champ at the bit.

Some interview questions will test your knowledge of your field, and we can't help you forecast those. But others are likely to be a part of any interview, and some of them are found in the following "What Do You Do Now?" exercise.

The interview. It may seem that the interviewer is fully in charge and that the prospective employee is the "victim." Not so. There are many, many things that job candidates can do to prepare for interviews.

Making the Transition from College to the Career World

WHAT DO YOU DO NOW?
Coping with a Job Interview

In this exercise, we ask questions and then give you room for one answer. Then we offer our thoughts on the subject and try to alert you as to what your interviewer is looking for. We don't necessarily furnish a precise answer. The exact words need to be consistent with the nature of your field, the organization to which you have applied, your geographical setting, and so on.

All right, the applicant ahead of you is finished, and it's your turn for an interview! Here are the questions. What do you do now?

1. *How are you today?*

   _____
   _____

   Our recommendation: *Don't* get cute or fancy. Say something like, "Fine, thank you. How're you?"

2. *How did you learn about the opening?*

   _____
   _____
   _____

   Don't say, "I indicated that in my application." Yes, you probably did specify this on your application or in the cover letter for your résumé, but your interviewer may not be familiar with the letter or may want to follow standard procedure anyhow. So answer concisely.

3. *What do you know about our organization?*

   _____
   _____

   Your interviewer wants to learn whether you actually know something about the organization or applied everywhere with equal disinterest. Do your homework and show that you know quite a bit about the organization. Suggest how the organization is an ideal setting for you to reach your vocational goals.

4. *What are you looking for in this job?*

   _____
   _____

   This is another opportunity to relate your background and goals to the job description and duties. Show that you have concrete goals; that's what interviewers are looking for. Mention things like the opportunity to work with noted professionals in your field, the organizational personality (organizations, like people, can be conceptualized as having personalities), the organization's leadership in its field, and so on. *Don't* say "It's close to home." You can say that you know that salaries are good, but also refer to opportunities for personal growth and self-fulfillment.

5. *What do you plan to be doing 10 years from now?*

   _____
   _____

   Your interviewer wants to hear that you have a clear understanding of the corporate ladder and that your career goals are consistent with company needs. Preplan a coherent answer, but also show flexibility—perhaps that you're interested in exploring a couple of branches of the career ladder. This will show your interviewer that you're not rigid and that you recognize that the organization will affect your concept of your future.

6. *Are you willing to relocate after a year or two if we need you in another office/plant?*

_____

_____

Your interviewer wants to hear that you would be willing—that your ties to the company would be more important than your geographic ties. *Don't* say that your fiancé or spouse is flexible; it implies that he or she really is not, and you just don't want to get into this.

7. *What are your salary needs?*

_____

_____

Entry-level salaries in many positions are fixed, especially in large organizations. But if this question is asked, *don't* fall into the trap of thinking you're more likely to get the job if you ask for less. It's a good idea to research typical entry salaries for the field in the placement office before the interview. Then mention a reasonably high—not ridiculously high—figure. You can also mention the figure "with an explanation"—reemphasizing your experience and training. Good things don't come cheap, and organizations know this. And why should they think more of you than you think of yourself?)

TRUTH OR FICTION *Revisited*

It's not a good idea to ask for the lowest salary you can get by on. If you don't value yourself, why should your prospective employer value you?

8. *What is the first thing you would do if you were to take the job?*

_____

_____

Your interviewer probably wants to know (a) if you're an active, take-charge type of person and (b) whether you do have an understanding of what is required. *Don't* say you'd be shocked or surprised. Say something like, "I'd get to know my supervisors and co-workers to learn the details of the organization's goals and expectations for the position." Or it might be appropriate to talk about organizing your workspace, or evaluating and ordering equipment, depending on the nature of the occupation.

9. *Do you realize that this is a very difficult (or time-consuming) job?*

_____

_____

It is or it isn't, but the interviewer doesn't want to hear that you think the job's a snap. Say something to the effect that you will dedicate yourself to your work and that you have boundless energy. You can also ask your interviewer to amplify on the question so that you can fine-tune your eventual answer.

10. *What do you see as your weaknesses?*

_____

_____

Trap time! *Don't* make a joke and say that you can't get along with anyone or know nothing about the job! Your interviewer is giving you a chance to show that you are arrogant by denying weaknesses or to drop some kind of bombshell—that is, admit to a self-disqualifying problem. Don't do either. Turn the question into an opportunity for emphasizing strengths. Say something like, "I think my weakness is that I have not already done this job (or worked for your organization), and so we cannot predict with certainty what will happen. But I'm a fast learner and I'm pretty flexible, so I'm confident that I'll do a good job."

(continues on next page)

(continued)

11. *Do you have any questions?*

Having intelligent questions is a sign that you are interested and can handle the job. Prepare a few good questions before the interview. In the unlikely event that the interviewer manages to cover them all during his or her presentation, you can say something like, "I was going to ask such and such, but then you said that such and such. Could you amplify on that a bit?"

12. Finally, what do you say when the interview is over?

Say something like, "Thank you for the interview. I look forward to hearing from you."

> These, then, are my last words to you: Be not afraid of life. Believe that life is worth living and your belief will help create the fact.
>
> WILLIAM JAMES

In a minute, we will say, "Thank you for reading our book. We look forward to hearing from you." First, however, let us express the hope that the skills you have acquired from this book will work for you for a lifetime. Life is not a matter of chance. To make the most of life, try to get a sense of what lies ahead and be prepared to make decisions—tough decisions. You may not always make the right decision, but by making decisions it will always be your life.

You will continue to develop in the coming years. People tend to reevaluate their lives and sometimes make major changes in their late twenties, in their thirties, even in their forties. Many people choose new careers, for example, into their forties and beyond.

But right after college it's not usually easy to recognize that we might be better off doing something else. As journalist Gail Sheehy noted in her book *Passages*, at that time we often feel "buoyed by powerful illusions and belief in the power of the will [so that] we commonly insist . . . that what we have chosen to do is the one true course in life."[20] This "one true course" usually turns out to have many swerves and bends. As we go on in life, what seemed meaningful one year may lose its allure in the next. That which we had hardly noticed can leap into prominence. Keep an open mind. If you think you may be better off doing something else, follow through—at least to the point of talking to someone about it. Even 10 or 15 years later, you will be welcome at your old college counseling and testing center. Go ahead: Give them a try. It's not too late. Trust us. Trust yourself.

In Chapter 1, we noted that this book was about beginning: beginning college, beginning adulthood, beginning again. Entering the career world is another beginning. Getting married, having children, changing careers, entering new stages of life—these, too, are beginnings.

Since this book is about beginnings, we suppose that we could go on interminably. On the other hand, we can also follow Lewis Carroll's suggestion, which we first noted in Chapter 6:

> "Begin at the beginning," the King said, gravely, "and go on till you come to the end: then stop."

SUMMING UP

1. How close are you to making a career decision? What aspects of various careers are alluring to you?
2. Do you know people who have "fallen into" their lines of work? How happy do they seem in them?
3. How are your own career aspirations affecting your choice of courses?
4. Are you a realistic person? Investigative? Artistic? Social? Enterprising? Conventional? What lines of work seem to fit your personality traits?
5. Are there any psychological tests that might help you make a career decision?
6. Which office on your campus can provide career counseling and, if deemed helpful, administer these tests?
7. How can you use the balance sheet to help you make a career decision?
8. What are the kinds of strengths you think you should highlight in your résumé?
9. What are some of the traps to avoid during a job interview?
10. What office on your campus can help you put together a résumé and prepare for a job interview?

Education and Work Experience Worksheets follow on the next pages.

Education and Work Experience Worksheets

Educational Background Worksheet List schools in reverse chronological order, most recent first:

1. Degree: _____

   School: _____

   Graduation date: _____
   (Enter date
   expected if
   not received)

   Major Field: _____

   Specialties: _____
   _____

   Honors: _____
   _____

   Scholarships: _____
   _____

   Professional _____
   Certificates: _____

   Extracurricular 1. _____
   Activities:
                   2. _____

                   3. _____

                   4. _____

                   5. _____

2. Degree: _____

   School: _____

   Graduation date: _____

   Major Field: _____

   Specialties: _____
   _____

   Honors: _____
   _____

   Scholarships: _____
   _____

   Professional _____
   Certificates: _____

   Extracurricular 1. _____
   Activities:
                   2. _____

                   3. _____

                   4. _____

Work Experience Worksheet List your jobs in reverse chronological order— most recent position first.

1. Dates: _____

   Status _____
   (part-time, hours
   per week, full-time)

   Employer: _____

   Division/location: _____

   Responsibilities: 1. _____

   2. _____

   3. _____

   4. _____

   5. _____

   Chief Achievements: 1. _____

   2. _____

   3. _____

   4. _____

   5. _____

2. Dates: _____

   Status _____
   (part-time, hours
   per week, full-time)

   Employer: _____

   Division/location: _____

   Responsibilities: 1. _____

   2. _____

   3. _____

   4. _____

   5. _____

   Chief Achievements: 1. _____

   2. _____

   3. _____

   4. _____

Making the Transition from College to the Career World

Notes

CHAPTER 1

[1] "College age" means almost any age. (1989, October 25). *The New York Times*, B7.
[2] Boyer, E. L. (1987). *College: The undergraduate experience in America.* New York: Perennial Library, 198.
[3] Boyer (1987). *College*, 44.
[4] Ibid.
[5] Cantrell, R. P., Stenner, A. J., & Katzenmeyer, W. G. (1977). Teacher knowledge, attitudes, and classroom teaching correlates of student achievement. *Journal of Educational Psychology, 69*, 180–190; Hines, C. V., Cruickshank, D. R., & Kennedy, J. (1985). Teacher clarity and its relation to student achievement and satisfaction. *American Educational Research Journal, 22*, 87–99.
[6] Boyer. (1987). *College*, 88.
[7] Cousins, N. (1978, December). How to make people smaller than they are. *Saturday Review*, 15.
[8] Bandura, A. (1982). Self-efficacy mechanism in human agency. *American Psychologist, 37*, 122–147; Bandura, A. (1986). *Social foundations of thought and action: A social-cognitive theory.* Englewood Cliffs, NJ: Prentice-Hall; Bandura, A., Taylor, C. B., Williams, S. L., Medford, I. N., & Barchas, J. D. (1985). Catecholamine secretion as a function of perceived coping self-efficacy. *Journal of Consulting and Clinical Psychology, 53*, 406–414; Betz, N. E., & Hackett, G. (1981). The relationships of career-related self-efficacy expectations to perceived career options in college women and men. *Journal of Counseling Psychology, 28*, 399–410; Schifter, D. E., & Ajzen, I. (1985). Intention, perceived control, and weight loss: An application of the theory of planned behavior. *Journal of Personality and Social Psychology, 49*, 843–851.
[9] Fibel, B., & Hale, W. D. (1978). The generalized expectancy for success scale—A new measure. *Journal of Consulting and Clinical Psychology, 46*, 924–931.

CHAPTER 2

[1] Boyer, E. L. (1987). *College: The undergraduate experience in America.* New York: Perennial Library, 210.
[2] Boyer. (1987). *College*, 170–171.
[3] Ibid., p 181.
[4] Trost, C. (1987, February 12). Child-care center at Virginia firm boosts worker morale and loyalty. *Wall Street Journal*, 27.
[5] Saddler, J. (1987, February 12). Low pay, high turnover plague day-care industry. *Wall Street Journal*, 27.
[6] Ruopp, R. (1979). *Children at the center.* Cambridge, MA: Abt Associates.
[7] Boyer. (1987). *College*, 190.
[8] Ibid.

CHAPTER 3

[1] Johnson, S. M., & White, G. (1971). Self-observation as an agent of behavioral change. *Behavior Therapy, 2*, 488–497.
[2] Atkinson, R. L., Atkinson, R. C., Smith, E. E., & Hilgard, E. R. (1987). *Introduction to psychology*, 9th. ed. San Diego: Harcourt Brace Jovanovich, p. 114.
[3] Rathus, S. A. (1990). *Psychology*, 4th ed. New York: Holt, Rinehart and Winston.
[4] Abramis, D. J. (1989, March). Finding the fun at work. *Psychology Today*, pp. 36–38.
[5] Ellis, A. (1977). The basic clinical theory or rational-emotive therapy. In A. Ellis & R.

Grieger (Eds.), *Handbook of rational-emotive therapy.* New York: Springer; Ellis, A. (1985). Cognition and affect in emotional disturbance. *American Psychologist, 40,* 471–472; Ellis, A. (1987). The impossibility of achieving consistently good mental health. *American Psychologist, 42,* 364–375.

CHAPTER 4

[1] Boyer, E. L. (1987). *College: The undergraduate experience in America.* Perennial Library: New York.
[2] The College Board. (1988). *The college cost book.* New York: College Entrance Examination Board, p. 30.
[3] Many of these items were inspired by items from D. J. MacPhillamy & P. M. Lewinsohn, *Pleasant Events Schedule, Form III-S,* University of Oregon, Mimeograph, 1971.

CHAPTER 5

[1] Meyer, B. J. F., Brandt, D. M., & Bluth, G. J. (1980). Use of top-level structure in text: Key for reading comprehension of ninth-graders. *Reading Research Quarterly, 15,* 72–103.
[2] Knowlton, W. A., Jr., & Mitchell, T. R. (1980). Effects of causal attributions on a supervisor's evaluation of subordinate performance. *Journal of Applied Psychology, 65,* 459–466; Williams, K. (1986, February 7). The role of appraisal salience in the performance evaluation process. Paper presented at a colloquium, State University of New York at Albany; Woolfolk, A. E. (1987). *Educational psychology,* 3d ed. Englewood Cliffs, NJ: Prentice-Hall.
[3] Doctorow, M., Wittrock, M. C., & Marks, C. (1978). Generative processes in reading comprehension. *Journal of Educational Psychology, 70,* 109–118; Hamilton, R. J. (1985). A framework for the evaluation of the effectiveness of adjunct questions and objectives. *Review of Educational Research, 55,* 47–86.
[4] Robinson, F. P. (1970). *Effective study,* 4th ed. New York: Harper & Row.
[5] Adams, A., Carnine, D., & Gersten, R. (1982). Instructional strategies for studying context area texts in the intermediate grades. *Reading Research Quarterly, 18,* 27–53; Anderson, J. R. (1985). *Cognitive psychology and its implications,* 2d ed. San Francisco: W. H. Freeman; Benecke, W. M., & Harris, M. B. (1972). Teaching self-control of study behavior. *Behaviour Research and Therapy, 10,* 48–54.
[6] Rathus, S. A. (1990). *Psychology,* 4th ed. New York: Holt, Rinehart and Winston.
[7] Atkinson, R. C. (1975). Mnemotechnics in second-language learning. *American Psychologist, 30,* 821–828.
[8] Brown, R., & Kulik, J. (1977). Flashbulb memories. *Cognition, 5,* 73–99; Thompson, C. P., & Cowan, T. (1986). The neurobiology of learning and memory. *Science, 233,* 941–947.
[9] For example, Devine, T. G., & Meagher, L. D. (1989). *Mastering study skills.* Englewood Cliffs, NJ: Prentice Hall.

CHAPTER 6

[1] Matlin, M. W. (1987). *The psychology of women.* New York: Holt, Rinehart and Winston.
[2] Boyer, E. L. (1987). *College: The undergraduate experience in America.* New York: Perennial Library, p. 88.
[3] Rathus, S. A. (1988). *Understanding child development.* New York: Holt, Rinehart and Winston.
[4] Rathus, S. A. (1990). *Psychology.* New York: Holt, Rinehart and Winston.
[5] Boyer. (1987). *College,* 171–172.

CHAPTER 7

[1] Brown, R., & McNeill, D. (1966). The tip-of-the-tongue phenomenon. *Journal of Verbal Learning and Verbal Behavior, 5,* 325–337.
[2] Galassi, J. P., Frierson, H. T., & Sharer, R. (1981). Behavior of high, moderate, and low test anxious students during an actual test situation. *Journal of Consulting and Clinical Psychology, 49,* 51–62.
[3] Galassi, J. P., Frierson, H. T., Jr., & Siegel, R. G. (1984). Cognitions, test anxiety, and test performance: A closer look. *Journal of Consulting and Clinical Psychology, 52,* 319–320; Holroyd, K. A., Westbrook, T., Wolf, M., & Badhorn, E. (1978). Performance, cognition, and physiological responding in test anxiety. *Journal of Abnormal Psychology, 87,* 442–451; Meichenbaum, D. H., & Butler, L. (1980). Toward a conceptual model for the treatment of test anxiety: Implications for research and treatment. In I. G. Sarason (Ed.), *Test anxiety: Theory, research, and application.* Hillsdale, NJ: Erlbaum.
[4] Arkin, R. M., Detchon, C. S., & Maruyama, G. M. (1982). Roles of attribution, affect, and cognitive interference in test anxiety. *Journal of Personality and Social Psychology, 43,* 1111–1124; Bandura, A. (1977). *Social learning theory.* Englewood Cliffs, NJ: Prentice

Hall; Sarason, I. G. (1984). Stress, anxiety, and cognitive interference: Reactions to tests. *Journal of Personality and Social Psychology, 46,* 929–938.

[5] Goldfried, M. R. (1988). Application of rational restructuring to anxiety disorders. *The Counseling Psychologist, 16* (1), 50–68; Goldfried, M. R., Linehan, M. M., & Smith, J. L. (1978). Reduction of test anxiety through cognitive restructuring. *Journal of Consulting and Clinical Psychology, 46,* 32–39.

[6] Goldfried et al. (1978).

[7] Ibid., 34.

[8] Jacobson, E. (1938). *Progressive relaxation.* Chicago: University of Chicago Press; Paul, G. L. (1969). Physiological effects of relaxation training and hypnotic suggestion. *Journal of Abnormal Psychology, 74,* 425–437; Rathus, S. A., & Nevid, J. S. (1977). *Behavior therapy.* New York: Doubleday; Wolpe, J. (1958). *Psychotherapy by reciprocal inhibition.* Stanford, CA: Stanford University Press; Wolpe, J. (1973). *The practice of behavior therapy.* New York: Pergamon Press.

[9] Suinn, R. M., & Deffenbacher, J. L. (1988). Anxiety management training. *The Counseling Psychologist, 16*(1), 31–49.

[10] Harvey, J. R. (1978). Diaphragmatic breathing: A practical technique for breath control. *The Behavior Therapist, 1*(2), 13–14.

CHAPTER 8

[1] Selye, H. (1980). The stress concept today. In I. L. Kutash, L. B. Schlesinger, et al. (Eds.), *Handbook on stress and anxiety.* San Francisco: Jossey-Bass.

[2] Eckenrode, J. (1984). Impact of chronic and acute stressors on daily reports of mood. *Journal of Personality and Social Psychology, 46,* 907–918; Stone, A. A., & Neale, J. M. (1984). Effects of severe daily events on mood. *Journal of Personality and Social Psychology, 46,* 137–144.

[3] Lazarus, R. S. (1984). Puzzles in the study of daily hassles. *Journal of Behavioral Medicine, 7,* 375–389.

[4] Kanner, A. D., Coyne, J. C., Schaefer, C., & Lazarus, R. S. (1981). Comparison of two modes of stress measurement: Daily hassles and uplifts versus major life events. *Journal of Behavioral Medicine, 4,* 1–39.

[5] Most hassles are based on findings by Lazarus, R. S., DeLongis, A., Folkman, S., & Gruen, R. (1985). Stress and adaptational outcomes: The problem of confounded measures. *American Psychologist, 40,* 770–779.

[6] Cohen, S., Evans, G. W., Krantz, D. S., Stokols, D., & Kelly, S. (1981). Aircraft noise and children: Longitudinal and cross-sectional evidence on adaptation to noise and the effectiveness of noise abatement. *Journal of Personality and Social Psychology, 40,* 331–345; Cohen, S., Evans, G. W., Stokols, D., & Krantz, D. S. (1986). *Behavior, health, and environmental stress.* New York: Plenum Publishing Co.

[7] Holmes, T. H., & Rahe, R. H. (1967). The social readjustment rating scale. *Journal of Psychosomatic Research, 11,* 213–218; Lloyd, C., Alexander, A. A., Rice, D. G., & Greenfield, N. S. (1980). Life events as predictors of academic performance. *Journal of Human Stress, 6,* 15–25; Thoits, P. A. (1983). Dimensions of life events as influences upon the genesis of psychological distress and associated conditions: An evaluation and synthesis of the literature. In H. B. Kaplan (Ed.), *Psychosocial stress: Trends in theory and research.* New York: Academic Press.

[8] Holmes, D. S., & Will, M. J. (1985). Expression of interpersonal aggression by angered and nonangered persons with the Type A and Type B behavior patterns. *Journal of Personality and Social Psychology, 48,* 723–727; Matthews, K. A., Krantz, D. S., Dembroski, T. M., & MacDougall, J. M. (1982). Unique and common variance in structured interview and Jenkins Activity Survey measures of the Type A behavior pattern. *Journal of Personality and Social Psychology, 42,* 303–313.

[9] Yarnold, P. R., Mueser, K. T., & Grimm, L. G. (1985). Interpersonal dominance of Type A's in group discussion. *Journal of Abnormal Psychology, 94,* 233–236.

[10] Cooney, J. L., & Zeichner, A. (1985). Selective attention to negative feedback in Type A and Type B individuals. *Journal of Abnormal Psychology, 94,* 110–112.

[11] Brunson, B. I., & Matthews, K. A. (1981). The Type-A coronary-prone behavior pattern and reactions to uncontrollable stress. *Journal of Personality and Social Psychology, 40,* 906–918.

[12] Glass, D. C. (1977). *Stress and coronary-prone behavior.* Hillsdale, NJ: Erlbaum.

[13] Holmes, D. S., McGilley, B. M., & Houston, B. K. (1984). Task-related arousal of Type A and Type B persons: Level of challenge and response specificity. *Journal of Personality and Social Psychology, 46,* 1322–1327.

[14] Rappaport, N. B., McAnulty, D. P., & Brantley, P. J. (1988). Exploration of the Type A behavior pattern in chronic headache sufferers. *Journal of Consulting and Clinical Psychology, 56,* 621–623.

[15] Barefoot, J. C., Dahlstrom, W. G., & Williams, R. B., Jr. (1983). Rapid communication, hostility, CHD incidence, and total mortality: A 25-year follow-up study of 225 physicians. *Psychosomatic Medicine, 45,* 59–63; Bernardo, M., DeFlores, T., Valdes, M., Mestre, L., & Fernandez, G. (1985, May). Type A and personality in a coronary disease sample. Paper presented at the Fourth World Congress of Biological Psychiatry, Philadelphia; DeBacker, G. et al. (1983). Behavior, stress, and psychosocial traits as risk factors. *Preventative Medicine, 12,* 32–36; French-Belgian Collaborative Group (1982). Ischemic heart disease and psychological patterns: Prevalence and incidence in Belgium and France. *Advances in Cardiology, 29,* 25–31; Shekelle, R. B., et al. (1983). Hostility, risk of coronary heart disease, and mortality.

Psychosomatic Medicine, 45, 109–114; Shekelle, R. B., et al. (1985). The MRFIT behavior pattern study: II. Type A behavior and incidence of coronary heart disease. *American Journal of Epidemiology, 122,* 559–570; Weiss, M., & Richter-Heinrich, E. (1985). Type A behavior in a population of Berlin: GDR. Its relation to personality and sociological variables, and association to coronary heart disease. *Activitas Nervosa Superior (Prague), 27,* 7–9; Wright, L. (1988). The Type A behavior pattern and coronary artery disease: Quest for the active ingredients and the elusive mechanism. *American Psychologist, 43,* 2–14. For a review of the possible causal connections between Type A behavior and coronary heart disease, see Chapter 11 ("Health Psychology") in Rathus, S. A. (1990). *Psychology.* Fort Worth: Holt, Rinehart and Winston.

[16] Selye, H. (1976). *The stress of life,* Rev. ed. New York: McGraw-Hill.

[17] Rathus, S. A. (1990). *Psychology,* 4th ed. New York: Holt, Rinehart and Winston.

[18] Questionnaire items based on descriptions of Type A people found in books and articles such as Friedman, M., & Ulmer, D. (1984). *Treating Type A behavior and your heart.* New York: Fawcett Crest; Matthews, K. A., Krantz, D. S., Dembroski, T. M., & MacDougall, J. M. (1982). Unique and common variance in structured interview and Jenkins Activity Survey measures of the Type A behavior pattern. *Journal of Personality and Social Psychology, 42,* 303–313; Musante, L., MacDougall, J. M., Dembroski, T. M., & Van Horn, A. E. (1983). Component analysis of the Type A coronary-prone behavior pattern in male and female college students. *Journal of Personality and Social Psychology, 45,* 1104–1117.

[19] Baron, R. A., Mandel, D. R., Adams, C. A., & Griffen, L. M. (1976). Effects of social density in university residential requirements. *Journal of Personality and Social Psychology, 34,* 434–446.

[20] Leonard, C. V. (1974). Depression and suicidality. *Journal of Consulting and Clinical Psychology, 42,* 98–104; Schotte, D. E., & Clum, G. A. (1982). Suicide ideation in a college population: A test of a model. *Journal of Consulting and Clinical Psychology, 50,* 690–696.

[21] Mehrabian, A., & Weinstein, L. (1985). Temperament characteristics of suicide attempters. *Journal of Consulting and Clinical Psychology, 53,* 544–546.

[22] Cole, D. A. (1988). Hopelessness, social desirability, depression, and parasuicide in two college student samples. *Journal of Consulting and Clinical Psychology, 56,* 131–136; Petrie, K., & Chamberlain, K. (1983). Hopelessness and social desirability as moderator variables in predicting suicidal behavior. *Journal of Consulting and Clinical Psychology, 51,* 485–487; Schotte, D. E., & Clum, G. A. (1987). Problem-solving skills in suicidal psychiatric patients. *Journal of Consulting and Clinical Psychology, 55,* 49–54.

[23] Shneidman, E. S. (1985). *Definition of suicide.* New York: Wiley; Shneidman, E. S. (1987). A psychological approach to suicide. In G. R. VanderBos & B. K. Bryant (Eds.), *Cataclysms, cries, and catastrophes: Psychology in action* (Master Lecture Series, Vol. 6, pp. 151–183). Washington, DC: American Psychological Association.

[24] Cantor, P. C. (1976). Personality characteristics found among youthful female suicide attempters. *Journal of Abnormal Psychology, 85,* 324–329.

[25] Shneidman. (1985). *Definition of suicide.*

[26] Hull, J. G. (1981). A self-awareness model of the causes and effects of alcohol consumption. *Journal of Abnormal Psychology, 90,* 586–600; Hull, J. G., Levenson, R. W., Young, R. D., & Sher, K. J. (1983). Self-awareness-reducing effects of alcohol consumption. *Journal of Personality and Social Psychology, 44,* 461–473.

[27] Tucker, J. A., Vuchinich, R. E., & Sobell, M. B. (1981). Alcohol consumption as a self-handicapping strategy. *Journal of Abnormal Psychology, 90,* 220–230.

[28] Baum, A., & Valins, S. (1977). *Architecture and social behavior.* Hillsdale, NJ: Erlbaum; Paulus, P. B. (1979). Crowding. In P. B. Paulus (Ed.), *Psychology of group influence.* Hillsdale, NJ: Erlbaum.

[29] Lavrakas, P. J. (1982). Fear of crime and behavior restriction in urban and suburban neighborhoods. *Population and Environment, 5,* 242–264; Milgram, S. (1977). *The individual in a social world.* Reading, MA: Addison-Wesley.

[30] Proverbs 17:22.

[31] Lefcourt, H. M., & Martin, R. A. (1986). *Humor and life stress: Antidote to adversity.* New York: Springer-Verlag.

[32] Freud, S. (1959). Humour. In J. Strachey (Ed.), *Collected papers of Sigmund Freud,* Vol. 5. New York: Basic Books.

[33] Martin, R. A., & Lefcourt, H. M. (1983). Sense of humor as a moderator of the relation between stressors and moods. *Journal of Personality and Social Psychology, 45,* 1313–1324.

[34] Baum, A., Fisher, J. D., & Solomon, S. (1981). Type of information, familiarity, and the reduction of crowding stress. *Journal of Personality and Social Psychology, 40,* 11–23; Fisher, J. D., & Baum, A. (1980). Situational and arousal-based messages and the reduction of crowding stress. *Journal of Applied Social Psychology, 10,* 191–201; Paulus, P. B., & Matthews, R. (1980). Crowding, attribution, and task performance. *Basic and Applied Social Psychology, 1,* 3–13.

[35] Cohen, S., & Wills, T. A. (1985). Stress, social supports and the buffering hypothesis. *Psychological Bulletin, 98,* 310–357; Pagel, M., & Becker, J. (1987). Depressive thinking and depression: Relations with personality and social resources. *Journal of Personality and Social Psychology, 52,* 1043–1052; Rook, K. S., & Dooley, D. (1985). Applying social support research: Theoretical problems and future directions. *Journal of Social Issues, 41,* 5–28.

[36] Fiore, J. (1980). *Global satisfaction scale.* Unpublished manuscript, University of Washington, Department of Psychiatry and Behavioral Sciences, Seattle; House, J. S. (1981). *Work stress and social support.* Reading, MA: Addison-Wesley; House, J. S. (1984). Barriers to work stress: I. Social support. In W. D. Gentry, H. Benson, & C. deWolff (Eds.), *Behavioral medicine: Work, stress, and health.* The Hague: Nijhoff.

[37] Carrington, P. (1977). *Freedom in meditation.* New York: Doubleday.

[38] Jacobson, E. (1938). *Progressive relaxation.* Chicago: University of Chicago Press;

Paul, G. L. (1969). Physiological effects of relaxation training and hypnotic suggestion. *Journal of Abnormal Psychology, 74,* 425–437; Rathus, S. A., & Nevid, J. S. (1977). *Behavior therapy.* New York: Doubleday; Wolpe, J. (1958). *Psychotherapy by reciprocal inhibition.* Stanford, CA: Stanford University Press; Wolpe, J. (1973). *The practice of behavior therapy.* New York: Pergamon Press.

[39] Ellis; Meichenbaum, D., & Jaremko, M. E. (Eds.) (1983). *Stress reduction and prevention.* New York: Plenum Publishing Co.

[40] Benson, H. (1975). *The relaxation response.* New York: Morrow.

[41] Friedman & Ulmer; Suinn, R. A. (1982). Intervention with Type A behaviors. *Journal of Consulting and Clinical Psychology, 50,* 933–949.

[42] Kobasa, S. C. (1979). Stressful life events, personality, and health: An inquiry into hardiness. *Journal of Personality and Social Psychology, 37,* 1–11; Kobasa, S. C. (1985). Personality and health: Specifying and strengthening the conceptual links. In P. Shaver (Ed.), *Self, situations, and social behavior.* Beverly Hills: Sage Press; Kobasa, S. C., Maddi, S. R., & Kahn, S. (1982). Hardiness and health: A prospective study. *Journal of Personality and Social Psychology, 42,* 168–177; Kobasa, S. C., Maddi, S. R., & Zola, M. A. (1983). Type A and hardiness. *Journal of Behavioral Medicine, 6,* 41–51; Kobasa, S. C., & Puccetti, M. C. (1983). Personality and social resources in stress resistance. *Journal of Personality and Social Psychology, 45,* 839–850.

[43] Fischman, J. (1987). Getting tough. *Psychology Today, 21*(12), 26–28. In a pilot study at Illinois Bell, executives who received hardiness training reported greater job satisfaction, had fewer headaches, and slept better. Even their blood pressure dropped.

CHAPTER 9

[1] Berndt, T. J., & Perry, T. B. (1986). Children's perceptions of friendships as supportive relationships. *Developmental Psychology, 22,* 640–648; Damon, W. (1977). *The social world of the child.* San Francisco: Jossey-Bass; Rathus, S. A. (1988). *Understanding child development.* New York: Holt, Rinehart and Winston.

[2] Berndt & Perry. (1986). "Children's perceptions."

[3] Ibid.

[4] Berndt, T. J. (1982). The features and effects of friendships in early adolescence. *Child Development, 53,* 1447–1460.

[5] Parlee, M. B. (1979). The friendship bond: *Psychology Today's* survey report on friendship in America. *Psychology Today, 13*(4), 43–54, 113.

[6] Davis, K. E. (1985). Near and dear: Friendship and love compared. *Psychology Today, 19*(2), 22–30.

[7] Steck, L., Levitan, D., McLane, D., & Kelley, H. H. (1982). Care, need, and conceptions of love. *Journal of Personality and Social Psychology, 43,* 481–491.

[8] Driscoll, R., Davis, K. E., & Lipetz, M. E. (1972). Parental interference and romantic love. *Journal of Personality and Social Psychology, 24,* 1–10.

[9] Byrne, D. (1971). *The attraction paradigm.* New York: Academic Press; Green, S. K., Buchanan, D. R., & Heuer, S. K. (1984). Winners, losers, and choosers: A field investigation of dating initiation. *Personality and Social Psychology Bulletin, 10,* 502–511; Hatfield, E., & Sprecher, S. (1986). *Mirror, mirror . . . The importance of looks in everyday life.* Albany, NY: State University of New York at Albany Press.

[10] Ford, C. S., & Beach, F. A. (1951). *Patterns of sexual behavior.* New York: Harper & Row.

[11] Graziano, W., Brothen, T., & Berscheid, E. (1978). Height and attraction: Do men and women see eye-to-eye? *Journal of Personality, 46,* 128–145.

[12] Gillis, J. S., & Avis, W. E. (1980). The male-taller norm in mate selection. *Personality and Social Psychology Bulletin, 6,* 396–401.

[13] Harris, M. B., Harris, R. J., & Bochner, S. (1982). Fat, four-eyed, and female: Stereotypes of obesity, glasses, and gender. *Journal of Applied Social Psychology, 12,* 503–516.

[14] Horvath, T. (1981). Physical attractiveness: The influence of selected torso parameters. *Archives of Sexual Behavior, 10,* 21–24; Lavrakas, P. J. (1975, May). Female preferences for male physiques. Paper presented at the Midwestern Psychological Association, Chicago.

[15] Fallon, A. E., & Rozin, P. (1985). Sex differences in perceptions of desirable body shape. *Journal of Abnormal Psychology, 94,* 102–105; Rozin, P., & Fallon, A. (1988). Body image, attitudes to weight, and misperceptions of figure preferences of the opposite sex: A comparison of men and women in two generations. *Journal of Abnormal Psychology, 97,* 342–345.

[16] Nevid, J. S. (1984). Sex differences in factors of romantic attraction. *Sex Roles, 11*(5/6), 401–411.

[17] Roper Poll (1984). *Psychology Today, 18*(1), 17.

[18] Mueser, K. T., Grau, B. W., Sussman, S., & Rosen, A. J. (1984). You're only as pretty as you feel: Facial expression as a determinant of physical attractiveness. *Journal of Personality and Social Psychology, 46,* 469–478.

[19] Riggio, R. E., & Woll, S. B. (1984). The role of nonverbal cues and physical attractiveness in the selection of dating partners. *Journal of Social and Personal Relationships, 1,* 347–357.

[20] Sadalla, E. K., Kenrick, D. T., & Vershure, B. (1987). Dominance and heterosexual attraction. *Journal of Personality and Social Psychology, 52,* 730–738.

[21] Riggio & Woll. (1984). Role of nonverbal cues; Sadalla et al., (1987). Dominance.

[22] Zweigenhaft, R. L. (1970). Signature size: A key to status awareness. *Journal of Social Psychology, 81,* 49–54.

[23] Jellison, J. M., & Oliver, D. F. (1983). Attitude similarity and attraction: An impression management approach. *Personality and Social Psychology Bulletin, 9,* 111–115.

[24] Byrne, D., Ervin, C. R., & Lamberth, J. (1970). Continuity between the experimental study of attraction and real-life computer dating. *Journal of Personality and Social Psychology, 16,* 157–165.

[25] Marks, G., Miller, N., & Maruyama, G. (1981). Effect of targets' physical attractiveness on assumption of similarity. *Journal of Personality and Social Psychology, 41,* 198–206.

[26] Touhey, J. C. (1972). Comparison of two dimensions of attitude similarity on heterosexual attraction. *Journal of Personality and Social Psychology, 23,* 8–10.

[27] Buss, D. M., & Barnes, M. (1986). Preferences in human mate selection. *Journal of Personality and Social Psychology, 50,* 559–570; Howard, J. A., Blumstein, P., & Schwartz, P. (1987). Social or evolutionary theories: Some observations on preferences in mate selection. *Journal of Personality and Social Psychology, 53,* 194–200.

[28] Zweigenhaft, R. L. (1975). Name styles in America and name styles in New Zealand. *Journal of Social Psychology, 97,* 289–290.

[29] Garwood, S. G., Cox, L., Kaplan, V., Wasserman, N., & Sulzer, J. L. (1980). Beauty is only "name deep": The effect of first-name in ratings of physical attraction. *Journal of Applied Social Psychology, 10,* 431–435.

[30] Levinger, G. (1980). Toward the analysis of close relationships. *Journal of Experimental Social Psychology, 16,* 510–544.

[31] Shanteau, J., & Nagy, G. (1979). Probability of acceptance in dating choice. *Journal of Personality and Social Psychology, 37,* 522–533.

[32] Knapp, M. L. (1978). *Social intercourse: From greeting to goodbye.* Boston: Allyn & Bacon, p. 112.

[33] Ibid., 108–109.

[34] Berger, C. R., & Calabrese, R. J. (1975). Some explorations in initial interaction and beyond: Toward a developmental theory of interpersonal communication. *Human Communication Research, 1,* 99–112.

[35] Knapp, (1978). *Social intercourse,* 114.

[36] Rubin, Z. (1975). Disclosing oneself to a stranger: Reciprocity and its limits. *Journal of Experimental Social Psychology, 11,* 233–260.

[37] Rathus, S. A. (1990). *Psychology,* 4th ed. New York: Holt, Rinehart and Winston.

[38] Rathus, S. A., & Nevid, J. S. (1977). *Behavior Therapy.* New York: Doubleday, pp. 114–115.

[39] Wortman, C. B., Adesman, P., Herman, E., & Greenberg, P. (1976). Self-disclosure: An attributional perspective. *Journal of Personality and Social Psychology, 33,* 184–191.

[40] Cozby, P. C. (1973). Self-disclosure: A literature review. *Psychological Bulletin, 79,* 73–91.

[41] Altman, I., & Taylor, D. A. (1973). *Social penetration: The development of interpersonal relationships.* New York: Holt, Rinehart and Winston.

[42] Rubin, Z., Hill, C. T., Peplau, L. A., & Dunkel-Schetter, C. (1980). Self-disclosure in dating couples: Sex role and ethic of openness. *Journal of Marriage and the Family, 42,* 305–317.

[43] Pines, A., & Aronson, E. (1983). Antecedents, correlates, and consequences of sexual jealousy. *Journal of Personality, 51,* 108–136.

[44] Mathes, E. W., Adams, H. E., & Davies, R. M. (1985). Jealousy: Loss of relationship rewards, loss of self-esteem, depression, anxiety, and anger. *Journal of Personality and Social Psychology, 48,* 1552–1561.

[45] Utne, M. K., Hatfield, E., Traupmann, J., & Greenberger, D. (1984). Equity, marital satisfaction, and stability. *Journal of Social and Personal Relationships, 1,* 323–332.

[46] White, G. L. (1981). Some correlates of romantic jealousy. *Journal of Personality, 49,* 129–146.

[47] White, G. L. (1980). Inducing jealousy: A power perspective. *Personality and Social Psychology Bulletin, 6,* 222–227.

[48] Levinger (1980). "Toward analysis."

[49] Rusbult, C. E., Johnson, D. J., & Morrow, G. D. (1986). Impact of couple patterns of problem solving on distress and nondistress in dating relationships. *Journal of Personality and Social Psychology, 50,* 744–753; Rusbult, C. E., & Zembrodt, I. M. (1983). Responses to dissatisfaction in romantic involvements: A multi-dimensional scaling analysis. *Journal of Experimental Social Psychology, 19,* 274–293.

[50] Rusbult, C. E. (1980). Commitment and satisfaction in romantic associations: A test of the investment model. *Journal of Experimental Social Psychology, 16,* 172–186; Rusbult, C. E. (1983). A longitudinal test of the investment model. *Journal of Personality and Social Psychology, 45,* 101–117; Rusbult, C. E., Musante, L., & Soloman, M. (1982). The effects of clarity of decision rule and favorability of verdict on satisfaction with resolution of conflicts. *Journal of Applied Social Psychology, 12,* 304–317.

[51] Hill, C., Rubin, Z., & Peplau, L. A. (1976). Breakups before marriage: The end of 103 affairs. *Journal of Social Issues, 32,* 147–168.

[52] Byrne, D., & Murnen, S. (1987). Maintaining love relationships. In R. J. Sternberg & M. L. Barnes (Eds.), *The anatomy of love.* New Haven: Yale University Press.

[53] Berscheid, E., & Walster, E. (1978). *Interpersonal attraction.* Reading, MA: Addison-Wesley.

[54] Russell, D. (1982). The measurement of loneliness. In L. A. Peplau & D. Perlman (Eds.), *Loneliness: A sourcebook of current theory, research, and therapy.* New York: Wiley; Russell, D., Peplau, L. A., & Cutrona, C. E. (1980). The revised UCLA Loneliness Scale: Concurrent and discriminant validity evidence. *Journal of Personality and Social Psychology, 39,* 472–480.

[55] Williams J. G., & Solano, C. H. (1983). The social reality of feeling lonely: Friendship and reciprocation. *Personality and Social Psychology Bulletin, 9,* 237–242.

[56] Baron, R. A., & Byrne, D. (1987). *Social psychology: Understanding human interaction,* 5th ed. Boston: Allyn and Bacon; Rubin, Z. (1982). Children without friends. In L. A. Peplau & D. Perlman (Eds.), *Loneliness: A sourcebook of current theory, research, and therapy.* New York: Wiley.

[57] Cutrona, C. E. (1982). Transition to college: Loneliness and the process of social adjustment. In L. A. Peplau & D. Perlman (Eds.), *Loneliness: A sourcebook of current theory, research, and therapy.*

[58] Lear, M. (1987, December 20). The pain of loneliness. *The New York Times Magazine,* pp. 47–48.

[59] Jones, W. H., Freeman, J. A., & Goswick, R. A. (1981). The persistence of loneliness: Self and other determinants. *Journal of Personality, 49,* 27–48; Lear; Schultz, N. R., Jr., & Moore, D. W. (1984). Loneliness: Correlates, attributions, and coping among older adults. *Personality and Social Psychology Bulletin, 10,* 67–77.

[60] Berg, J. H., & Peplau, L. A. (1982). Loneliness: The relationship of self-disclosure and androgyny. *Personality and Social Psychology Bulletin, 8,* 624–630; Solano, C. H., Batten, P. G., & Parish, E. A. (1982). Loneliness and patterns of self-disclosure. *Journal of Personality and Social Psychology, 43,* 524–531.

[61] Lear (1987). Pain of loneliness.

[62] Jones, W. H. (1982). Loneliness and social behavior. In L. A. Peplau & D. Perlman (Eds.), *Loneliness: A sourcebook of current theory, research, and therapy.* New York: Wiley.

[63] Lear. (1987). Pain of loneliness.

CHAPTER 10

[1] Epstein, N., Finnegan, D., & Bythell, D. (1979). Irrational beliefs and perceptions of marital conflict. *Journal of Consulting and Clinical Psychology, 47,* 608–610; Overturf, J. (1976). Marital therapy: Toleration of differentness: *Journal of Marriage and the Family, 2,* 235–241.

[2] Eidelson, R. J., & Epstein, N. (1982). Cognition and relationship maladjustment: Development of a measure of dysfunctional relationship beliefs. *Journal of Consulting and Clinical Psychology, 50,* 715–720.

[3] Jacobson, N. S. (1984). A component analysis of behavioral marital therapy: The relative effectiveness of behavior exchange and communication/problem-solving training. *Journal of Consulting and Clinical Psychology, 52,* 295–305.

[4] See, for example, Scanzoni, J., & Polonko, K. (1980). A conceptual approach to explicit marital negotiation. *Journal of Marriage and the Family, 42,* 31–44.

[5] Robinson, E. A., & Price, M. G. (1980). Pleasurable behavior in marital interaction: An observational study. *Journal of Consulting and Clinical Psychology, 48,* 117–118.

[6] Crooks, R., & Baur, K. (1987). *Our sexuality,* 3d ed. Menlo Park, CA: Benjamin/Cummings; Gottman, J., Notarius, C., Gonso, J., & Markman, H. (1976). *A couple's guide to communication.* Champaign, IL: Research Press; McKay, M., Davis, M., & Fanning, P. (1983). *Messages: The communication book.* Oakland, CA: New Harbinger.

[7] The concept of unconditional positive regard is attributed mainly to Carl Rogers. See, for example, Rogers, C. R. (1951). *Client-centered therapy.* Boston: Houghton Mifflin; Rogers, C. R. (1959). A theory of therapy, personality and interpersonal relationships, as developed in the client-centered framework. In S. Koch (Ed.), *Psychology: A study of science,* Vol. 3. New York: McGraw-Hill; Rogers, C. R. (1972). *Becoming partners: Marriage and its alternatives.* New York: Delacorte Press; Rogers, C. R. (1974). In retrospect: 46 years. *American Psychologist, 29,* 115–123.

[8] Rathus, S. A. (1978). Assertiveness training: Rationales, procedures, and controversies. In J. M. Whiteley & J. V. Flowers (Eds.), *Approaches to assertion training.* Monterey, CA: Brooks/Cole.

[9] Rogers. (1972). *Client-centered therapy.*

[10] Rathus. (1978). Assertiveness training.

[11] Reprinted from Rathus, S. A. (1973). A 30-item schedule for assessing assertive behavior. *Behavior Therapy, 4,* 398–406.

[12] Rathus, S. A. (1990). *Psychology,* 4th ed. New York: Holt, Rinehart and Winston.

[13] Rogers (1951, 1972); Satir, V. (1967). *Conjoint family therapy.* Palo Alto, CA: Science and Behavior Books.

[14] *The New York Times.* (1989, September 27). Brown U. to strengthen rules against racism. *The New York Times,* p. B8.

[15] Ibid.

[16] Russo, M. (1989, September 27). Free speech at Tufts: Zoned out. *The New York Times,* p. A29.

[17] Cartwright, R. D., Lloyd, S., Nelson, J. B., & Bass, S. (1983). The traditional-liberated woman dimension: Social stereotype and self-concept. *Journal of Personality and Social Psychology, 44,* 581–588.

[18] Deaux, K. (1984). From individual differences to social categories: Analysis of a decade's research on gender. *American Psychologist, 39,* 105–116; Myers, A. M., & Gonda, G. (1982). Utility of the masculinity–femininity construct: Comparison of traditional and androgyny approaches. *Journal of Personality and Social Psychology, 43,* 514–523.

[19] Eagly, A. H., & Steffen, V. J. (1984). Gender stereotypes stem from the distribution

of men and women into social roles. *Journal of Personality and Social Psychology, 46,* 735–754.

[20] Atkinson, J., & Huston, T. L. (1984). Sex role orientation and division of labor early in marriage. *Journal of Personality and Social Psychology, 46,* 330–345.

[21] Meece, J. L., Parsons, J. E., Kaczala, C. M., Goff, S. B., & Futterman, R. (1982). Sex differences in math achievement: Toward a model of academic choice. *Psychological Bulletin, 91,* 324–348.

[22] Ibid.

[23] Eccles, J. S. (1985). Sex differences in achievement patterns. In T. Sonderegger (Ed.), *Nebraska symposium on motivation.* Lincoln: University of Nebraska Press; Eccles, J. S., & Hoffman, L. W. (1984). Sex roles, socialization, and occupational behavior, In H. W. Stevenson & A. E. Siegel (Eds.), *Research in child development and social policy,* Vol. 1. Chicago: University of Chicago Press; Fox, L. H., Brody, L., & Tobin, D. (1985). The impact of early intervention programs upon course-taking and attitudes in high school. In S. F. Chipman, L. R. Brush, & D. M. Wilson (Eds.), *Women and mathematics: Balancing the equation.* London: Erlbaum; Tobias, S., & Weissbrod, C. (1980). Anxiety and mathematics: An update. *Harvard Educational Review, 50,* 63–70.

[24] Bem, S. L. (1975). Sex role adaptability: One consequence of psychological androgyny. *Journal of Personality and Social Psychology, 31,* 634–643; Bem, S. L. (1983). Gender schema theory and its implications for child development: Raising gender-aschematic children in a gender-schematic society. *Signs: Journal of Women in Culture and Society, 8,* 598–616; Bem, S. L., & Lenney, E. (1976). Sex typing and the avoidance of cross-sexed behaviors. *Journal of Personality and Social Psychology, 33,* 48–54; Helmreich, R. L., Spence, J. T., & Holahan, C. J. (1979). Psychological androgyny and sex-role flexibility: A test of two hypotheses. *Journal of Personality and Social Psychology, 37,* 1631–1644.

[25] Rosenstock, I. M., & Kirscht, J. P. (1979). Why people seek health care. In G. C. Stone, F. Cohen, & N. E. Adler (Eds.), *Health psychology: A handbook.* San Francisco: Jossey-Bass.

[26] Coleman, M., & Ganong, L. H. (1985). Love and sex roles stereotypes: Do macho men and feminine women make better lovers? *Journal of Personality and Social Psychology, 49,* 170–176.

[27] Loftus, E. F. (1979). *Eyewitness testimony.* Cambridge, MA: Harvard University Press; Ugwuegbu, D. C. E. (1979). Racial and evidential factors in juror attribution of legal responsibility. *Journal of Experimental Social Psychology, 15,* 133–146.

[28] Ugwuegbu. (1979). Racial and evidential factors.

[29] Goldstein, M., & Davis, E. E. (1972). Race and belief: A further analysis of the social determinants of behavioral intentions. *Journal of Personality and Social Psychology, 22,* 345–355.

[30] Sherif, M. (1966). *In common predicament: Social psychology of intergroup conflict and cooperation.* Boston: Houghton Mifflin.

[31] Amir, Y. (1976). The role of intergroup contact in change of prejudice and ethnic relations. In P. A. Katz (Ed.), *Towards the elimination of racism.* New York: Pergamon Press; Stephan, W. G. (1978). School desegregation: An evaluation of predictions made in *Brown v. Board of Education. Psychological Bulletin, 85,* 217–238.

[32] Clore, G. L., Bray, R. M., Itkin, S. N., & Murphy, P. (1978). Interracial attitudes and behavior at a summer camp. *Journal of Personality and Social Psychology, 36,* 107–116; Kennedy, D. T., & Stephen, W. G. (1977). The effects of cooperation and competition on ingroup–outgroup bias. *Journal of Applied Social Psychology, 7,* 115–130; Wilder, D. A., & Thompson, J. E. (1980). Intergroup contact with independent manipulations of in-group and out-group interaction. *Journal of Personality and Social Psychology, 38,* 589–603; Worchel, S., Andreoli, V. A., & Folger, R. (1977). Intergroup cooperation and intergroup attraction: The effect of previous interaction and outcome of combined effort. *Journal of Experimental Social Psychology, 13,* 131–140.

[33] Russo. (1989). Free speech at Tufts.

[34] Reprinted from Nevid, J. S., & Rathus, S. A. (1978). Multivariate and normative data pertaining to the RAS with the college population. *Behavior Therapy, 9,* 675.

[35] Sources for information about sex differences include Benbow, C. P., & Stanley, J. C. (1980). Sex differences in mathematical ability: Fact or artifact? *Science, 210,* 1029–1031; Benbow, C. P., & Stanley, J. C. (1983). Sex differences in mathematical reasoning ability: More facts. *Science, 210,* 1029–1030; Frodi, A. M., Macauley, J., & Thome, P. R. (1977). Are women always less aggressive than men? A review of the experimental literature. *Psychological Bulletin, 84,* 634–660; Hyde, J. S. (1981). How large are cognitive gender differences? *American Psychologist, 36,* 892–901; Maccoby, E. E., & Jacklin, C. N. (1974). *The psychology of sex differences.* Stanford, CA: Stanford University Press; Maccoby, E. E., & Jacklin, C. N. (1980). Sex differences in aggression: A rejoinder and reprise. *Child Development, 51,* 964–980; Sadker, M., & Sadker, D. (1985). Sexism in the schoolroom of the 1980s. *Psychology Today, 19*(3), 54–57.

[36] Deaux, K. (1984). From individual differences to social categories: Analysis of a decade's research on gender. *American Psychologist, 39,* 105–116; Hyde.

[37] Frodi et al., Are women always less aggressive? Matlin, M. (1987). *The psychology of women.* New York: Holt, Rinehart and Winston; Tobias, S. (1982). Sexist equations. *Psychology Today, 16*(1), 14–17.

[38] Stericker, A., & LeVesconte, S. (1982). Effect of brief training on sex-related differences in visual-spatial skill. *Journal of Personality and Social Psychology, 43,* 1018–1029.

[39] Richardson, D. C., Bernstein, S., & Taylor, S. P. (1979). The effect of situational contingencies on female retaliative behavior. *Journal of Personality and Social Psychology, 37,* 2044–2048.

CHAPTER 11

[1] Burros, M. (1988, January 6). What Americans really eat: Nutrition can wait. *The New York Times*, C1, C6.

[2] Ibid, C6.

[3] Ibid, C1, C6.

[4] Ibid, C6.

[5] Simone, C. B. (1983). *Cancer and nutrition*. New York: McGraw-Hill.

[6] Stamler, J. (1985a). Coronary heart disease: Doing the "right things." *New England Journal of Medicine, 312*, 1053–1055; Stamler, J. (1985b). The marked decline in coronary heart disease mortality rates in the United States, 1968–1981: Summary of findings and possible explanations. *Cardiology, 72*, 11–12; Stamler, J., Wentworth, D., & Neaton, J. D. (1986). Is the relationship between serum cholesterol and risk of premature death from coronary heart disease continuous and graded? Findings in 356,222 primary screenees of the Multiple Risk Factor Intervention Trial (MRFIT). *Journal of the American Medical Association, 256*, 2823–2828.

[7] Kromhout, D., Bosschieter, E. B., & de Lezenne Coulander, C. (1985). The inverse relation between fish consumption and 20-year mortality from coronary heart disease. *New England Journal of Medicine, 312*, 1205–1209.

[8] Burros. (1988). What Americans really eat.

[9] Toufexis, A., Garcia, C., & Kalb, B. (1986, January 20). Dieting: The losing game. *Time magazine*, pp. 54–60.

[10] Burros. (1988). What Americans really eat.

[11] Toufexis et al. (1986). Dieting.

[12] Toufexis et al. (1986). Dieting.

[13] Feist, J., & Brannon, L. (1988). *Health psychology*. Belmont, CA: Wadsworth Publishing Co.; Sorlie, P., Gordon, T., & Kannel, W. B. (1980). Body build and mortality—The Framingham Study. *Journal of the American Medical Association, 243*, 1828–1831.

[14] Hartz, A. J., Rupley, D. C., & Rimm, A. A. (1984). The association of girth measurements with disease in 32,856 women. *American Journal of Epidemiology, 119*, 71–80; Smith, U. (1985, January). American Heart Association Science Writers Forum presentation. Monterey, CA.

[15] Borkan, G. A., Sparrow, D., Wisniewski, C., & Vokonas, P. S. (1986). Body weight and coronary heart disease risk: Patterns of risk factor change associated with long-term weight change. The Normative Aging Study. *American Journal of Epidemiology, 124*, 410–419.

[16] Stunkard, A. J., Sorensen, T. I. A., Hanis, C., Teasdale, T. W., Chakraborty, R., Schull, W. J., & Schulsinger, F. (1986). An adoption study of human obesity. *New England Journal of Medicine, 314*, 193, 198.

[17] Keesey, R. E. (1980). A set-point analysis of the regulation of body weight. In A. J. Stunkard (Ed.), *Obesity*. Philadelphia: W. B. Saunders Co.; Keesey, R. E., & Powley, T. L. (1986). The regulation of body weight. *Annual Review of Psychology, 37*, 109–133.

[18] Brownell, K. D. (1982). Obesity: Understanding and treating a serious, prevalent, and refractory disorder: *Journal of Consulting and Clinical Psychology, 50*, 820–840; Brownell, K. D. (1988). Yo-yo dieting. *Psychology Today, 22*, 20–23.

[19] Brownell. (1988). Yo-yo dieting, 22.

[20] Wing, R. R., Epstein, L. H., & Shapira, B. (1982). The effect of increasing initial weight loss with the Scarsdale diet on subsequent weight loss in a behavioral treatment program. *Journal of Consulting and Clinical Psychology, 50*, 446–447.

[21] Brownell (1988); Epstein, L. H., Wing, R. R., Woodall, K., Penner, B. C., Kress, M. J., & Koeske, R. (1985). Effects of family-based behavioral treatment on obese 5- to 8-year-old children. *Behavior Therapy, 16*, 205–212; Israel, A. C., Stolmaker, L., & Andrian, C. A. G. (1985). The effects of training parents in general child management skills on a behavioral weight loss program for children. *Behavior Therapy, 16*, 169–180; Stalonas, P. M., & Kirschenbaum, D. S. (1985). Behavioral treatments for obesity: Eating habits revisited. *Behavior Therapy, 16*, 1–14.

[22] Epstein, L. H., Woodall, K., Goreczny, A. J., Wing, R. R., & Robertson, R. J. (1984). The modification of activity patterns and energy expenditure in obese young girls. *Behavior Therapy, 15*, 101–108.

[23] Epstein, L. H., Wing, R. R., Koeske, R., & Valoski, A. (1984a). Effects of diet plus exercise on weight change in parents and children. *Journal of Consulting and Clinical Psychology, 52*, 429–437.

[24] Apfelbaum, M. (1978). Adaptation to changes in caloric intake. *Progress in Food and Nutritional Science, 2*, 543–559; Polivy, J., & Herman, C. P. (1985). Dieting and binging: A causal analysis. *American Psychologist, 40*, 193–201.

[25] Brownell. (1988). Yo-yo dieting.

[26] Donahoe, C. P., Jr., Lin, D. H., Kirschenbaum, D. S., & Keesey, R. E. (1984). Metabolic consequences of dieting and exercise in the treatment of obesity. *Journal of Consulting and Clinical Psychology, 52*, 827–836.

[27] Rathus (1990); Rathus, S. A., & Nevid, J. S. (1989). *Psychology and the challenges of life: Adjustment and growth*. New York: Holt, Rinehart and Winston.

[28] Stuart, R. B. (1978). *Act thin, stay thin*. New York: Norton.

[29] Boskind-White, M., & White, W. C. (1983). *Bulimarexia: The binge/purge cycle*. New York: W. W. Norton; Boskind-White, M., & White, W. C. (1986). Bulimarexia: A historical-sociocultural perspective. In K. D. Brownell & J. P. Foreyt (Eds.), *Handbook of eating disorders*. New York: Basic Books; Strober, M. (1986). Anorexia nervosa: History and psychological con-

cepts. In K. D. Brownell & J. P. Foreyt (Eds.), *Handbook of eating disorders*. New York: Basic Books.

[30] Sullivan, W. (1988, February 16). New studies link exercise to delays in menstruation—and less cancer. *The New York Times*, p. C3.

[31] Szmukler, G. I., & Russell, G. F. M. (1986). Outcome and prognosis of anorexia nervosa. In K. D. Brownell & J. P. Foreyt (Eds.), *Handbook of eating disorders*. New York: Basic Books.

[32] Boskind-White & White. (1983). *Bulimarexia*, 29.

[33] American Psychiatric Association (1987). *Diagnostic and statistical manual of the mental disorders–Third Edition–Revised*. Washington, DC: American Psychiatric Press, Inc.

[34] Foreyt, J. P. (1986). Treating the diseases of the 1980s: Eating disorders. *Contemporary Psychology, 31*, 658–660.

[35] Fallon, A. E., & Rozin, P. (1985). Sex differences in perceptions of desirable body shape. *Journal of Abnormal Psychology, 94*, 102–105.

[36] Polivy, J., & Herman, C. P. (1987). Diagnosis and treatment of normal eating. *Journal of Consulting and Clinical Psychology, 55*, 635–644.

[37] Cooper, K. H. (1982). *The aerobics program for total well-being*. New York: Evans; Cooper, K. H. (1985). *Running without fear: How to reduce the risks of heart attack and sudden death during aerobic exercise*. New York: Evans.

[38] Kuntzleman, C. T. (1978). *Rating the exercises*. New York: Morrow.

[39] Pollock, M. L., Wilmore, J. H., & Fox, S. M., III. (1978). *Health and fitness through physical activity*. New York: Wiley.

[40] Donahoe et al., 1984; Epstein, L. H., & Wing, R. R. (1980). Aerobic exercise and weight. *Addictive Behaviors, 5*, 371–388.

[41] Morris, J. N., et al. (1953). Coronary heart disease and physical activity of work. *Lancet, 2*, 1053–1057, 1111–1120; Paffenbarger, R. S., Jr. (1972). Factors predisposing to fatal stroke in longshoremen. *Preventive Medicine, 1*, 522–527.

[42] Paffenbarger, R. S., Jr., et al. (1978). Physical activity as an index of heart attack risk in college alumni. *American Journal of Epidemiology, 108*, 161–175; Paffenbarger, R. S., Jr., et al. (1984). A natural history of athleticism and cardiovascular health. *Journal of the American Medical Association, 252*, 491–495; Paffenbarger, R. S., Jr., et al. (1986). Physical activity, all-cause mortality, and longevity of college alumni. *New England Journal of Medicine, 314*, 605–613.

[43] Siscovick, D. S., et al. (1982). Physical activity and primary cardiac arrest. *Journal of the American Medical Association, 248*, 3113–3117; Siscovick, D. S., et al. (1984). The incidence of primary cardiac arrest during vigorous exercise. *New England Journal of Medicine, 311*, 874–877.

[44] Siscovick et al. (1982, 1984). Physical activity.

[45] Buffone, G. W. (1984). Running and depression. In M. L. Sachs & G. W. Buffone (Eds.), *Running as therapy: An integrated approach*. Lincoln, NE: University of Nebraska Press; Greist, J. H. (1984). *Exercise in the treatment of depression. Coping with mental stress: The potential and limits of exercise intervention*. Washington, DC: National Institute of Mental Health; McCann, I. L., & Holmes, D. S. (1984). Influence of aerobic exercise on depression. *Journal of Personality and Social Psychology, 46*, 1142–1147.

[46] Long, B. C. (1984). Aerobic conditioning and stress inoculation: A comparison of stress-management interventions. *Cognitive Therapy and Research, 8*, 517–542; Sonstroem, R. J. (1984). Exercise and self-esteem. *Exercise and Sport Sciences Reviews, 12*, 123–155.

[47] Freedman, R. R., & Sattler, H. L. (1982). Physiological and psychological factors in sleep-onset insomnia. *Journal of Abnormal Psychology, 91*, 380–389; Haynes, S. N., Adams, A., & Franzen, M. (1981). The effects of presleep stress on sleep-onset insomnia. *Journal of Abnormal Psychology, 90*, 601–606; Marks, P. A., & Monroe, L. J. (1976). Correlates of adolescent poor sleepers. *Journal of Abnormal Psychology, 85*, 243–246; Monroe, L. J., & Marks, P. A. (1977). MMPI differences between adolescent poor and good sleepers. *Journal of Consulting and Clinical Psychology, 45*, 151–152.

[48] Kamens, L. (1980). Cognitive and attribution factors in sleep-onset insomnia. Unpublished doctoral dissertation, Southern Illinois University at Carbondale; Youkilis, H. D., & Bootzin, R. R. (1981). A psychophysiological perspective on the etiology and treatment of insomnia. In S. N. Haynes & L. R. Gannon (Eds.), *Psychosomatic disorders*. New York: Praeger.

[49] Hartmann, E. L. (1973). *The functions of sleep*. New Haven, CT: Yale University Press; Kimble, D. P. (1988). *Biological psychology*. New York: Holt, Rinehart and Winston.

[50] Goleman, D. J. (1982). Staying up. *Psychology Today, 16* (3), 24–35.

[51] Ibid.

[52] Lick, J. R., & Heffler, D. (1977). Relaxation training and attention placebo in the treatment of severe insomnia. *Journal of Consulting and Clinical Psychology, 45*, 153–161; Woolfolk, R. L., & McNulty, T. F. (1983). Relaxation treatment for insomnia: A component analysis. *Journal of Consulting and Clinical Psychology, 51*, 495–503.

[53] Haynes, S. N. Follingstad, D. R., & McGowan, W. T. (1974). Insomnia: Sleep patterns and anxiety level. *Journal of Psychosomatic Research, 18*, 69–74; Weil, G., & Goldfried, M. R. (1973). Treatment of insomnia in an eleven-year-old child through self-relaxation. *Behavior Therapy, 4*, 282–294.

[54] Morin, C. M., & Azrin, N. H. (1987). Stimulus control and imagery training in treating sleep-maintenance insomnia. *Journal of Consulting and Clinical Psychology, 55*, 260–262.

[55] Feldman, J. (1966). *The dissemination of health information*. Chicago: Aldine.

[56] Rosenstock, I. M., & Kirscht, J. P. (1979). Why people seek health care. In G. C. Stone, F. Cohen, & N. E. Adler (Eds.), *Health psychology: A handbook*. San Francisco: Jossey-Bass.

[57] Mechanic, D. (1978). *Medical sociology*. New York: Free Press.

[58] Leventhal, H., Nerenz, D. R., & Steele, D. J. (1984). Illness representations and coping with health threats. In A. Baum, S. E. Taylor, & J. E. Singer (Eds.), *Handbook of psychology and health: Vol. 4. Social psychological aspects of health*. Hillsdale, NJ: Erlbaum; Meyer, D., Leventhal, H., & Gutman, M. (1985). Common-sense models of illness: The example of hypertension. *Health Psychology*, 4, 115–135.

[59] Thompson, S. (1988, August). An intervention to increase physician–patient communication. Paper presented to the American Psychological Association, Atlanta.

[60] Sackett, D. L., & Snow, J. C. (1979). The magnitude of compliance and noncompliance. In R. B. Haynes, D. W. Taylor, & D. L. Sackett (Eds.), *Compliance in health care*. Baltimore: Johns Hopkins University Press.

[61] Brownlee-Duffeck, M., Peterson, L., Simonds, J. F., Goldstein, D., Kilo, C., & Hoette, S. (1987). The role of health beliefs in the regimen adherence and metabolic control of adolescents and adults with diabetes mellitus. *Journal of Consulting and Clinical Psychology*, 55, 139–144.

CHAPTER 12

[1] Kinsey, A. C., Pomeroy, W. B., & Martin, C. E. (1948). *Sexual behavior in the human male*. Philadelphia: W. B. Saunders; Kinsey, A. C., Pomeroy, W. B., Martin, C. E., & Gebhard, P. H. (1953). *Sexual behavior in the human female*. Philadelphia: W. B. Saunders.

[2] Masters, W. H., & Johnson, V. E. *Human sexual response*. Boston: Little, Brown, 1966.

[3] Rathus, S. A. (1983). *Human sexuality*. New York: Holt, Rinehart and Winston, pp. 240–242.

[4] Kinsey et al. (1953). *Sexual behavior*.

[5] Sorensen, R. C. (1973). *Adolescent sexuality in contemporary America*. New York: World.

[6] Baron, R. A., & Byrne, D. (1990). *Social psychology: Understanding human interaction*, 6th ed. Boston: Allyn & Bacon.

[7] Psychology Today. (1989, March). Sex cools on campus. *Psychology Today*, p. 14.

[8] Gerrard, G. (1986). Are men and women really different? In K. Kelley (Ed.), *Females, males, and sexuality*. Albany, NY: State University of New York at Albany Press.

[9] Abramson, P. R., & Mosher, D. L. (1975). Development of a measure of negative attitudes toward masturbation. *Journal of Consulting and Clinical Psychology*, 43, 485–490.

[10] Masters & Johnson. (1966.) *Human sexual response*.

[11] Crooks, R., & Baur, K. (1990). *Our sexuality*, 4th ed. Menlo Park, CA: Benjamin/Cummings; Masters, W. H., Johnson, V. E., & Kolodny, R. C. (1988). *Human sexuality*, 3d ed. Glenview, IL: Scott, Foresman.

[12] Arafat, I., & Cotton, W. L. (1974). Masturbation practices of males and females. *Journal of Sex Research*, 10, 293–307; Miller, W. R., & Lief, H. I. (1976). Masturbatory attitudes, knowledge, and experience: Data from the Sex Knowledge and Attitude Test. *Archives of Sexual Behavior*, 5, 447–468.

[13] Hunt, M. (1974). *Sexual behavior in the 1970s*. New York: Dell Books.

[14] Kinsey et al. (1948, 1953). *Sexual behavior*.

[15] Hunt. (1974). *Sexual behavior*.

[16] Baron & Byrne. (1990). *Sexual psychology*; Gerrard. (1986). *Men and women*.

[17] Hunt. (1974). *Sexual behavior*. Rathus, S. A. (1990). *Psychology*. New York: Holt, Rinehart and Winston.

[18] Cochran, S. D., & Mays, V. M. (1989). Women and AIDS-related concerns. *American Psychologist*, 44, 529–535; Schulte, L. (1986). The new dating game. *New York*, 19(9), 92–94, 98, 103–104, 106; Wallis, C. (1987, February 16). The big chill: Fear of AIDS. *Time Magazine*, pp. 50–56.

[19] *Glamour Magazine*. (1988, January). Women's views survey: Sex, money, work, family. *Glamour Magazine*, pp. 142–145, 202–208.

[20] Osgood, C. (1981). *There's nothing that I wouldn't do if you would be my POSSLQ*. New York: Holt, Rinehart and Winston.

[21] Henslin, J. M. (1980). *Marriage and family in a changing society*. New York: Free Press.

[22] Macklin, E. D. (1976). Unmarried heterosexual cohabitation on the university campus. In J. P. Wiseman (Ed.), *The social psychology of sex*. New York: Harper & Row.

[23] Bower, D. W., & Christopherson, V. A. (1977). University student cohabitation: A regional comparison of selected attitudes and behaviors. *Journal of Marriage and the Family*, 39, 447–453.

[24] Macklin, E. D. (1980). Nontraditional family forms: A decade of research. *Journal of Marriage and the Family*, 42, 905–922.

[25] Henslin, J. M. (1980). *Marriage and family in a changing society*. New York: Free Press.

[26] Macklin. (1976). Unmarried heterosexual cohabitation.

[27] Ibid.

[28] Ibid.

[29] Barringer, F. (1989, June 9). Divorce data stir doubt on trial marriage. *The New York Times*, pp. A1, A28.

[30] Allgeier, E. R., & Allgeier, A. A. (1984). *Sexual interactions*. Lexington, MA: Heath.

[31] Koss, M. P., Gidycz, C. A., & Wisniewski, N. (1987). The scope of rape: Incidence and prevalence of sexual aggression and victimization in a national sample of higher education students. *Journal of Consulting and Clinical Psychology*, 55, 162–170.

[32] Kanin, E. J., & Parcell, S. R. (1977). Sexual aggression: A second look at the offended female. *Archives of Sexual Behavior, 6,* 67–76.

[33] Rapoport, K., & Burkhart, B. R. (1984). Personality and attitudinal characteristics of sexually coercive college males. *Journal of Abnormal Psychology, 93,* 216–221.

[34] Lipton, D. N., McDonel, E. C., & McFall, R. M. (1987). Heterosocial perception in rapists. *Journal of Consulting and Clinical Psychology, 55,* 17–21.

[35] Masters, Johnson, & Kolodny. (1988). *Human sexuality.*

[36] Boston Women's Health Book Collective. (1984). *Our Bodies, Ourselves.* New York: Touchstone Books.

[37] Myers, M. B., Templer, D. I., & Brown, R. (1984). Coping ability of women who become victims of rape. *Journal of Consulting and Clinical Psychology, 52,* 73–78.

[38] Burt, M. R. (1980). Cultural myths and supports for rape. *Journal of Personality and Social Psychology, 38,* 217–230.

[39] Boston Women's Health Book Collective. (1984), 267.

[40] Wallis. (1987). The big chill.

[41] Cochran & Mays (1989); Kaplan, H. S. (1987). *The real truth about women and AIDS.* New York: Simon & Schuster/Fireside; Reinisch, J. M. (1988, August 14). Sexual behavior in the age of AIDS. Paper presented to the annual meeting of the American Psychological Association, Atlanta, GA.

[42] Centers for Disease Control. (1988). 1988 STD treatment guidelines. *Morbidity and mortality report.*

[43] Leary, W. E. (1988, July 14). Rare venereal diseases increase sharply. *The New York Times,* p. B6.

[44] Masters, Johnson, & Kolodny (1988). *Human sexuality.*

[45] Leary. (1988). Rare venereal diseases.

[46] Centers for Disease Control. (1986). 1986 STD treatment guidelines.

[47] Leary. (1988). Rare venereal diseases.

[48] Centers for Disease Control. (1985). Self-reported behavioral change among gay and bisexual men—San Francisco. *Morbidity and mortality weekly report, 34,* 613–615; Mertz, G., et al. (1985). Frequency of acquisition of first-episode genital infection with herpes simplex virus from symptomatic and asymptomatic source contacts. *Sexually transmitted diseases, 12,* 33–39.

[49] Sweet, R. (1985). Chlamydia, group B streptococcus, and herpes in pregnancy. *Birth, 12,* 17–24.

[50] Baum, A., & Nesselhof, S. E. A. (1988). Psychological research and the prevention, etiology, and treatment of AIDS. *American Psychologist, 43,* 900–906; Hall, N. R. S. (1988). The virology of AIDS. *American Psychologist, 43,* 907–913. Kaplan; Kolata, G. (1988, February 16). Recent setbacks stirring doubts about search for AIDS vaccine. *The New York Times,* pp. 1, C13; Peterson, J. L., & Marin, G. (1988). Issues in the prevention of AIDS among Black and Hispanic men. *American Psychologist, 43,* 871–877.

[51] Kaplan, H. S. (1987). *The Real truth about women and AIDS.* New York: Simon & Schuster/Fireside.

[52] Centers for Disease Control. (1989, January 2). [AIDS information] Public Access AIDS data tape. (These tapes are available from the Centers of Disease Control, 1600 Clifford Road, Office of AIDS, AIDS Program, Public Health Service, Atlanta, GA 30333.)

[53] Mays, V. M., & Cochran, S. D. (1988). Issues in the perception of AIDS risk and risk reduction activities by Black and Hispanic/Latina women. *American Psychologist, 43,* 949–957; Reinisch, J. M., Sanders, S. A., & Ziemba-Davis, M. (1988). The study of sexual behavior in relation to the transmission of human immunodeficiency virus: Caveats and recommendations. *American Psychologist, 43,* 921–927; Stall, R. D., Coates, T. J., & Hoff, C. (1988). Behavioral risk reduction for HIV infection among gay and bisexual men: A review of results from the United States. *American Psychologist, 43,* 878–885.

[54] Boffey, P. M. (1988, February 14). Spread of AIDS abating, but deaths will still soar. *The New York Times,* pp. 1, 36.

[55] U.S. Centers for Disease Control; *New York Times, The* (1988, February 20). AIDS risk articles criticized. *The New York Times,* p. 9.

[56] Consumer Reports. (1989, March). Can you rely on condoms? *Consumer Reports,* pp. 135–142.

[57] Altman, L. K. (1989, June 9). Salk says tests of vaccine show halt of AIDS infection in chimps. *The New York Times,* p. A8; Kolata. (1988). Recent setbacks.

[58] Altman, L. K. (1989, April 24). Experts on AIDS, citing new data, push for testing. *The New York Times,* pp. 1, B8; Kolata, G. (1989, August 4). Strong evidence discovered that AZT holds off AIDS. *The New York Times,* pp. 1, B6.

[59] Leary. (1988). Rare venereal diseases.

[60] Centers for Disease Control. (1985, September). 1985 STD treatment guidelines. *Morbidity and mortality weekly report supplement;* Lourea, D., Rila, M., & Taylor, C. (1986). Sex in the age of AIDS. Paper presented to the Western Region Conference of the Society for the Scientific Study of Sex, Scottsdale, AZ.

[61] Conant, M., et al. (1986). Condoms prevent transmission of the AIDS-associated retrovirus. *Journal of the American Medical Association, 255,* 1706; Heilman & LoPiccolo; Koop, C. E. (1988). *Understanding AIDS.* HHS Publication No. (CDC) HHS-88-8404. U.S. Government Printing Office, Washington, DC.

[62] For example, AZT (azidothymidine) delays the onset of AIDS in about half of those who have been infected by the AIDS virus but are still symptom-free. AZT also slows the progress of the disease in people with mild symptoms (Hilts, P. J. [1989, August 18]. Drug said to help AIDS cases with virus but no symptoms. *The New York Times,* pp. A1, A13.)

[63] Kelly, J. A., St. Lawrence, J. S., Hood, H. V., & Brasfield, T. L. (1989). Behavioral

intervention to reduce AIDS risk activities. *Journal of Consulting and Clinical Psychology, 57*, 60–67.

[64] Kolata, G. (1988, July 28.) Use of condoms lags, survey of women finds. *The New York Times*, p. B7.

[65] Ibid.

[66] Shapiro, H. I. (1988). *The new birth-control book.* Englewood Cliffs, NJ: Prentice Hall.

[67] For example, Clair Chilvers of the Institute of Cancer Research in London, in reporting results of a 1989 study on links between pill usage and breast cancer. New link between pill and cancer reported, *The New York Times*, May 6, 1989, p. 28.

[68] Ibid.

[69] Ibid.

[70] Kolata. (1988). Use of condoms.

[71] Shapiro. (1988). *The new birth-control book.*

[72] Ibid.

[73] Crooks & Baur. (1990). *Our sexuality.*

[74] Rathus, 1983.

[75] Kolata. (1988). Use of condoms.

[76] Consumer Reports. (1989). Can you rely on condoms?

[77] Ibid.

[78] Shapiro. (1988). *The new birth-control book*, 154.

[79] Sheehy, G. (1976). *Passages: Predictable crises of adult life.* New York: Dutton.

[80] Rathus. (1983). *Human sexuality.*

[81] Janis, I. L., & Mann, L. (1977). *Decision-making.* New York: Free Press.

CHAPTER 13

[1] DeAngelis, T. (1989). Colleges target drug awareness. *APA Monitor, 20*(4), 31.

[2] Kerr, P. (1988, July 10). The American drug problem takes on two faces. *The New York Times*, Section 4, p. 5.

[3] American Psychiatric Association (1987). *Diagnostic and statistical manual of the mental disorders–Third Edition–Revised.* Washington, DC: American Psychiatric Press, Inc., p. 169.

[4] American Psychiatric Association. (1987). pp. 166–168.

[5] Brook, J. S. Lukoff, J. F., & Whiteman, M. (1980). Initiation into marijuana use. *Journal of Genetic Psychology, 137*, 133–142; Conger, J. J., & Petersen, A. (1984). *Adolescence and youth: Psychological development in a changing world.* New York: Harper and Row; Kandel, D. B. (1980). Drug and drinking behavior among youth. *Annual Review of Sociology, 6*, 235–285; Mittelmark, M. B., et al. (1987). Predicting experimentation with cigarettes: The Childhood Antecedents of Smoking Study. *American Journal of Public Health, 77*, 206–208.

[6] Wilson, G. T. (1987). Cognitive studies in alcoholism. *Journal of Consulting and Clinical Psychology, 55*, 325–331.

[7] Goodwin, D. W. (1985). Alcoholism and genetics. *Archives of General Psychiatry, 42*, 171–174; Schuckit, M. A. (1987). Biological vulnerability to alcoholism. *Journal of Consulting and Clinical Psychology, 55*, 301–309; Vaillant, G. E., & Milofsky, E. S. (1982). The etiology of alcoholism. *American Psychologist, 37*, 494–503.

[8] Goodwin. (1985). Alcoholism and genetics.

[9] Kolata, G. (1987, November 10). Alcoholism: Genetic links grow clearer. *The New York Times*, pp. C1, C2.

[10] Baum-Baicker, C. (1984). Treating and preventing alcohol abuse in the workplace. *American Psychologist, 39*, 454; Mider, P. A. (1984). Failures in alcoholism and drug dependence prevention and learning from the past. *American Psychologist, 39*, 183; Vaillant & Milofsky.

[11] Brown, S. A. (1985). Expectancies versus background in the prediction of college drinking patterns. *Journal of Consulting and Clinical Psychology, 53*, 123–130; Brown, S. A., Goldman, M. S., & Christiansen, B. A. (1985). Do alcohol expectancies mediate drinking patterns of adults? *Journal of Consulting and Clinical Psychology, 53*, 512–519; Brown, S. A., Goldman, M. S., Inn, A., & Anderson, L. R. (1980). Expectations of reinforcement from alcohol. *Journal of Consulting and Clinical Psychology, 48*, 419–426; Christiansen, B. A., Goldman, M. S., & Inn, A. (1982). Development of alcohol-related expectancies in adolescence. *Journal of Consulting and Clinical Psychology, 50*, 336–344; Rohsenow, D. J. (1983). Drinking habits and expectancies about alcohol's effects for self versus others. *Journal of Consulting and Clinical Psychology, 51*, 752–756.

[12] Niaura, R. S., Rohsenow, D. J., Binkoff, J. A., Monti, P. M., Pedraza, M., & Abrams, D. B. (1988). Relevance of cue reactivity to understanding alcohol and smoking relapse. *Journal of Abnormal Psychology, 97*, 133–152.

[13] Aneshensel, C. S., & Huba, G. J. (1983). Depression, alcohol use, and smoking over one year: A four-wave longitudinal causal model. *Journal of Abnormal Psychology, 92*, 134–150.

[14] Hull, J. G., Levenson, R. W., Young, R. D., & Sher, K. J. (1983). Self-awareness-reducing effects of alcohol consumption. *Journal of Personality and Social Psychology, 44*, 461–473; Steele, C. M., & Southwick, L. L. (1985). Alcohol and social behavior I: The psychology of drunken excess. *Journal of Personality and Social Psychology, 48*, 18–34.

[15] Steele, C. M., & Josephs, R. A. (1988). Drinking your troubles away. II: An attention-allocation model of alcohol's effect of psychological stress. *Journal of Abnormal Psychology, 97*, 196–205.

[16] Abrams, D. B., & Wilson, G. T. (1983). Alcohol, sexual arousal, and self-control. *Journal of Personality and Social Psychology, 45,* 188–198.

[17] Chassin, L., Mann, L. M., & Sher, K. J. (1988). Self-awareness theory, family history of alcoholism, and adolescent alcohol involvement. *Journal of Abnormal Psychology, 97,* 206–217; Mann, L. M., Chassin, L., & Sher, K. J. (1987). Alcohol expectancies and risk for alcoholism. *Journal of Consulting and Clinical Psychology, 55,* 411–417; Wills, T. A. (1986). Stress and coping in adolescence: Relationships to substance use in urban school samples. *Health Psychology, 5,* 503–530.

[18] Cooper, M. L., Russell, M., & George, W. H. (1988). Coping, expectancies, and alcohol abuse: A test of social learning formulations. *Journal of Abnormal Psychology, 97,* 218–230.

[19] Wilson, G. T., & Lawson, D. M. (1978). Expectancies, alcohol, and sexual arousal in women. *Journal of Abnormal Psychology, 87,* 609–616; Wilson, G. T., Lawson, D. M., & Abrams, D. B. (1978). Effects of alcohol on sexual arousal in male alcoholics. *Journal of Abnormal Psychology, 87,* 609–616.

[20] Briddell, D. W., & Wilson, G. T. (1976). Effects of alcohol and expectancy set on male sexual arousal. *Journal of Abnormal Psychology, 85,* 225–234; Wilson & Lawson.

[21] Eckhardt, M. J., Harford, T. C., Kaelber, C. T., Parker, E. S., Rosenthal, L. S., Ryback, R. S., Salmoiraghi, G. C., Vanderveen, E., & Warren, K. R. (1981). Health hazards associated with alcohol consumption. *Journal of the American Medical Association, 246,* 648–666.

[22] Ibid.

[23] Heuch, I., Kvale, G., Jacobsen, B. K., & Bjelke, E. (1983). Use of alcohol, tobacco and coffee, and risk of pancreatic cancer. *British Journal of Cancer, 48,* 637–643; Popham, R. E., Schmidt, W., & Israelstam, S. (1984). Heavy alcohol consumption and physical health problems: A review of the epidemiologic evidence. In R. G. Smart et al. (Eds.), *Research advances in alcohol and drug problems,* Vol. 8. New York: Plenum Publishing Co.

[24] Stipp, D. (1987, May 7). Breast-cancer risk may increase 40% with moderate alcohol use, studies say. *The Wall Street Journal,* p. 34.

[25] Kolata, G. (1988, March 21). Latest study disputes link of breast cancer to alcohol. *The New York Times,* p. A14.

[26] Rathus, S. A. (1988). *Understanding Child Development.* New York: Holt, Rinehart and Winston.

[27] Berkman, L. F., & Breslow, L. (1983). *Health and ways of living: The Alameda County Study.* New York: Oxford University Press; Klatsky, A. L., Freidman, G. D., & Siegelaub, A. B. (1981). Alcohol and mortality: A ten-year Kaiser-Permanente experience. *Annals of Internal Medicine, 95,* 139–145; Gill, J. S., Zezulka, A. V., Shipley, M. J., Gill, S. K., & Beevers, D. G. (1986). Stroke and alcohol consumption. *New England Journal of Medicine, 315,* 1041–1046; Gordon, T., & Doyle, J. T. (1987). Drinking and mortality: The Albany Study. *American Journal of Epidemiology, 125,* 263–270.

[28] Stampfer, M., & Hennekens, C. (1988, August 4). *The New England Journal of Medicine, 319.*

[29] Ibid.

[30] Castelli, W. (1988). Cited in Kolata, G. (1988, August 3). Study backs heart benefit in light drinking. *The New York Times,* p. A24.

[31] Brown. (1985). Expectancies.

[32] Items adapted from (1) general discussion of expectancies about alcohol in Christiansen et al. (1982) and (2) smokers' self-testing items analyzed by Leventhal and Avis (1976).

[33] Rada, R. T., & Kellner, R. (1979). Drug treatment in alcoholism. In J., Davis & D. J. Greenblatt (Eds.), *Recent developments in psychopharmacology.* New York: Grune & Stratton.

[34] Wallace, J. (1985). The alcoholism controversy. *American Psychologist, 40,* 372–373.

[35] Miller, W. R., & Muñoz, R. F. (1983). *How to control your drinking,* 2d ed. Albuquerque: University of New Mexico Press.

[36] Elkins, R. L. (1980). Covert sensitization treatment of alcoholism. *Addictive Behaviors, 5,* 67–89; Miller (1982); Olson, R. P., Ganley, R., Devine, D. T., & Dorsey, G. (1981). Long-term effects of behavior versus insight-oriented therapy with inpatient alcoholics. *Journal of Consulting and Clinical Psychology, 49,* 866–877.

[37] Miller & Muñoz. (1983). *How to control your drinking.*

[38] Koop, C. E. (1988, May 17). Excerpts from Koop report on smoking. *The New York Times,* p. C4.

[39] Schachter, S. (1977). Nicotine regulation in heavy and light smokers. *Journal of Experimental Psychology: General, 106,* 5–12.

[40] Epstein, L. H., & Perkins, K. A. (1988). Smoking, stress, and coronary heart disease. *Journal of Consulting and Clinical Psychology, 56,* 342–349.

[41] Mansnerus, L. (1988, April 24). Smoking becomes "deviant behavior." *The New York Times,* Section 4, pp. 1, 6.

[42] Cowley, G. (1988, April 11). Science and the cigarette. *Newsweek,* pp. 66–67.

[43] Fielding, J. E. (1985). Smoking: Health effects and control. *New England Journal of Medicine, 313,* 491–498, 555–561.

[44] Mansnerus. (1988). Smoking.

[45] Flaxman, J. (1978). Quitting smoking now or later: Gradual, abrupt, immediate, and delayed quitting. *Behavior Therapy, 9,* 260–270.

[46] Glasgow, R. E., Klesges, R. C., Godding, P. R., & Vasey, M. W., & O'Neill, H. K. (1984). Evaluation of a worksite-controlled smoking program. *Journal of Consulting and Clinical Psychology, 52,* 137–138.

[47] Glasgow, R. E., Klesges, R. C., Godding, P. R., & Gegelman, R. (1983). Controlled smoking, with or without carbon monoxide feedback, as an alternative for chronic smokers. *Behavior Therapy, 14,* 396–397; Glasgow, R. E., Klesges, R. C., Klesges, L. M., Vasey,

M. W., & Gunnarson, D. F. (1985). Long-term effects of a controlled smoking program: A two and one-half year follow-up. *Behavior Therapy, 16,* 303–307.

[48] Hall, S. M., Tunstall, C. Rugg, D., Jones, R. T., & Benowitz, N. (1985). Nicotine gum and behavioral treatment in smoking cessation. *Journal of Consulting and Clinical Psychology, 53,* 256–258.

[49] Shiffman, S. (1982). Relapse following smoking cessation: A situational analysis. *Journal of Consulting and Clinical Psychology, 50,* 71–86.

[50] Hall et al. (1984); Shiffman (1982); Shiffman, S. (1984). Coping with temptations to smoke. *Journal of Consulting and Clinical Psychology, 52,* 261–267.

[51] Taylor, W. N. (1985). Super athletes made to order. *Psychology Today, 19*(5), 62–66.

[52] Grinspoon, L. (1987, July 28). Cancer patients should get marijuana. *The New York Times,* p. A23.

[53] Fabian, W. D., Jr., & Fishkin, S. M. (1981). A replicated study of self-reported changes in psychological absorption with marijuana intoxication. *Journal of Abnormal Psychology, 90,* 546–553.

[54] Schaeffer, J., Andrysiak, T., & Ungerleider, J. T. (1981). Cognition and long-term use of ganja (cannabis). *Science, 213,* 465–466.

[55] Maugh, T. H. (1982). Marijuana "justifies serious concern." *Science, 215,* 1488–1489.

[56] Kandel, D. B., Davies, M., Kraus, D., & Yamaguchi, K. (1986). The consequences in young adulthood of adolescent drug involvement. *Archives of General Psychiatry, 43,* 746–754.

[57] Altman, L. K. (1988, January 26). Cocaine's many dangers: The evidence mounts. *The New York Times,* p. C3.

[58] Lambert, B. (1987, December 13). New York City maps deadly patterns of AIDS. *The New York Times,* pp. 1, 58.

[59] Altman. (1988). Cocaine's dangers.

[60] Bales, J. (1986, November). New studies cite drug use dangers. *APA Monitor,* p. 26.

[61] Van Dyke, C., & Byck, R. (1982). Cocaine. *Scientific American, 44*(3), 128–141.

[62] Ling, G. S. F., MacLeod, J. M., Lee, S., Lockhart, S. H., & Pasternak, G. W. (1984). Separation of morphine analgesia from physical dependence. *Science, 226,* 462–464.

[63] Kerr. (1988). American drug problem.

[64] Barber, T. X. (1970). *LSD, marihuana, yoga, and hypnosis.* Chicago: Aldine.

[65] Heaton, R. K., & Victor, R. G. (1976). Personality characteristics associated with psychedelic flashbacks in natural and experimental settings. *Journal of Abnormal Psychology, 85,* 83–90; Matefy, R. (1980). Role-playing theory of psychedelic flashbacks. *Journal of Consulting and Clinical Psychology, 48,* 551–553.

CHAPTER 14

[1] Werts, C. E. (1968). Parental influence on career choice. *Journal of Counseling Psychology, 15,* 48–52.

[2] Shertzer, B. (1985). *Career planning,* 3d ed. Boston: Houghton Mifflin.

[3] Ibid.

[4] Rice, B. (1985). Why am I in this job? *Psychology Today, 19*(1), 54–59.

[5] Ginzberg, E. (1972). Toward a theory of occupational choice: A restatement. *Vocational Guidance Quarterly, 20,* 169–176; Super, D. E. (1957). *The psychology of careers.* New York: Harper & Row; Super, D. E., & Hall, D. T. (1978). Career development: Exploration and planning. In M. R. Rosenzweig & L. W. Porter (Eds.), *Annual Review of Psychology, 29.* Palo Alto, CA: Annual Reviews.

[6] Chemers, M. M., Hays, R. B., Rhodewalt, F., & Wysocki, J. (1985). A person–environment analysis of job stress: A contingency model explanation. *Journal of Personality and Social Psychology, 49,* 628–635.

[7] Holland, J. L. (1975). *Vocational preference inventory.* Palo Alto, CA: Consulting Psychologists Press.

[8] Janis, I. L., & Wheeler, D. (1978). Thinking clearly about career choiced. *Psychology Today, 12*(12), 66–76, 121–122.

[9] Rice. (1985). Why am I in this job?

[10] Lubin, B., Larsen, R. M., Matarazzo, J. D., & Seever, M. (1985). Psychological test usage patterns in five professional settings. *American Psychologist, 40,* 857–861.

[11] Boyer, E. L. (1987). *College: The undergraduate experience in America.* New York: Perennial Library, pp. 267–268.

[12] Barnard, C. L., & Bechtel, D. S. (1983). Influences and considerations: Issues guiding placement and recruitment today. *Journal of College Placement, 44,* p. 35.

[13] Calvert, R., Jr. (1969). *Career patterns of liberal arts graduates.* Cranston, RI: The Carroll Press, p. 122.

[14] Beatty, R. H. (1984). *The resume kit.* New York: Wiley, p. 51.

[15] Ibid. 12.

[16] Ibid. 18.

[17] Ibid. 62.

[18] Ibid. 63.

[19] Cash, T. F., & Kilcullen, R. N. (1985). The age of the beholder: Susceptibility to sexism and beautyism in the evaluation of managerial applicants. *Journal of Applied Social Psychology, 15,* 591–605.

[20] Sheehy, G. (1976). *Passages: Predictable crises of adult life.* New York: Dutton, p. 33.

Acknowledgments

Figures, Tables
Page 16 Fibel, B. and Hale, W. D. "The generalized expectancy for success scale—A new measure." *Journal of Consulting and Clinical Psychology*, Vol. 46, pp. 924–31. © 1978 by the American Psychological Association. Reprinted by permission of the APA and the author. 95 MacPhillamy, D. J. and Lewinsohn, P. M., "The pleasant events schedule: studies on reliability, validity, and scale intercorrelations." *Journal of Consulting and Clinical Psychology*, 1982, 50, 363–80. Used by permission. 176 Galassi et al. "A table on percent of positive and negative thoughts for university students." *Journal of Consulting and Clinical Psychology*, Vol. 49, pp. 51–62. © 1981 by the American Psychological Association. Reprinted by permission of the APA and the author. 177 © 1971 by Richard M. Suinn. The complete "Suinn Test Anxiety Behavior Scale" is available from Rocky Mountain Behavioral Science Institute, Inc., P. O. Box 1066, Fort Collins, CO 80522. 180 Rathus, S. and Nevid, J. "Rational alternatives to irrational cognitions concerning test taking," *Psychology and the Challenges of Life*, 4th ed. Orlando: Holt, Rinehart and Winston, p. 378. © 1989 by Holt, Rinehart and Winston, Inc. Reprinted by permission of the publisher. 181 Wolpe, J. and Lazarus, A. A. "Progressive Relaxation Techniques," *Behavior Therapy Techniques*. New York: Pergamon Press, pp. 177–80. © 1966 Pergamon Press PLC. Reprinted with permission. 192 Peggy Blake, Robert Fry, and Michael Pesjack (1984). *Self-assessment and behavior change manual*. New York: Random House, pp. 43–47. 214 Lyrics from "Friendship." © 1939, 1966 Chappell & Co., Inc. All rights reserved. Used by permission. 215 Lyrics from "That's What Friends Are For." © 1985 WB Music Corp. Warner-Tamerlane Publishing Corp. All rights reserved. 221 Rathus, S. "The love scale," *Psychology*, 4th ed. Orlando: Holt, Rinehart and Winston, p. 335. © 1990 by Holt, Rinehart and Winston, Inc. Reprinted by permission of the publisher. 233 Lyrics from "Eleanor Rigby." © 1966 Northern Songs Ltd. Rights for U.S., Canada, and Mexico controlled and administered by EMI Blackwood Music Inc. Under license from ATV Music (Maclen). All rights reserved. International copyright secured. Used by permission. 234 Items from the "UCLA Loneliness Scale" from "The Pain of Loneliness," *The New York Times Magazine*, December 20, 1987, pp. 47–48. © 1987 by The New York Times Company. Reprinted by permission. 301 Burt, M. R. "Material attitudes that contribute to rape." *Journal of Personality and Social Psychology*, Vol. 38, pp. 217–30. © 1980 by the American Psychological Association. Revised items based on a scale reprinted by permission of the APA and the author. 307 Kaplan, H. S. "A table on sexual transmission of AIDS: Degrees of risk," *The Real Truth about Women and AIDS*, New York: Simon & Schuster/Fireside, pp. 77. Used by permission. 353 Rathus, S. and Nevid, J. "Table on the possibility of taking premedical studies," *Psychology and the Challenges of Life*, 4th ed. Orlando: Holt, Rinehart and Winston, p. 432. © 1989 by Holt, Rinehart and Winston, Inc. Adapted by permission of the publisher. 354 Rathus, S. and Nevid, J. "Table on questions for making an informed career decision," *Psychology and the Challenges of Life*, 4th ed. Orlando: Holt, Rinehart and Winston, Inc., p. 433. © 1989 by Holt, Rinehart and Winston, Inc. Adapted by permission of the publisher. Rathus, S. and Nevid, J. "Coping with a job interview," *Psychology and the Challenges of Life*, 4th ed. Orlando: Holt, Rinehart and Winston, Inc., pp. 436–37. © 1989 by Holt, Rinehart and Winston, Inc. Reprinted by permission of the publisher. 232 Figure 13.3 from *Psychology and the Challenges of Life: Adjustment and Growth*, Fourth Edition by Spencer A. Rathus and Jeffrey S. Nevid, copyright © 1989 by Holt, Rinehart and Winston, Inc., reprinted by permission of the publisher. 364 Figure 8.13 from *Psychology*, Fourth Edition by Spencer A. Rathus. Copyright © 1990 by Holt, Rinehart and Winston, Inc., reprinted by permission of the publisher. 280 Figure 11.5 from *Psychology*, Fourth Edition by Spencer A. Rathus, copyright © 1990 by Holt, Rinehart and Winston, Inc., reprinted by permission of the publisher. 222 Figure 15.2 from *Psychology*, Fourth Edition by Spencer A. Rathus, copyright © 1990 by Holt, Rinehart and Winston, Inc., reprinted by permission of the publisher.

Photographs
2 Arthur Tress/Photo Researchers 4 Mimi Forsyth/Monkmeyer Press 9 Michael Weisbrot/Stock, Boston 13 Howard Dratch/The Image Works 15 Frank Siteman/Jeroboam 18 Frank D. Smith/Jeroboam 24 Jane Scherr/Jeroboam 29 Hugh Rogers/Monkmeyer Press 31 Jane Scherr/Jeroboam 36 Teri Leigh Stratford 37 Paul Fortin/Stock, Boston 39 Patricia Beringer/The Image Works 44 Barbara Rios/Photo Researchers 50 Randy Matusow 56 Hugh Rogers/Monkmeyer Press 58 Gale Zucker/Stock, Boston 64 Jim Fossett/The Image Works 60 Hewlett-Packard 70 Bob Daemmrich/The Image Works 73 Laimute E. Druskis/Stock, Boston 80 Marc Anderson 81 Jim Fossett/The Image Works 83 Mimi Forsyth/Monkmeyer Press 87 Shmuel Thaler/Jeroboam 102 Laimute E. Druskis 105 Kent Reno/Jeroboam 107 Alexander Lowry/Photo Researchers, Inc. 111 Jean-Claude Lejeune/Stock, Boston 117 Joseph Schuler/Stock, Boston 123 Mike Kagan/Monkmeyer Press Photo 126 Jerry Howard/Stock, Boston 131 Jay Seeley 134 Hugh Rogers/Monkmeyer Press 135 Univ. of Texas at Austin 141 Russell Abraham/Stock, Boston 146 Bohdan Hrynewych/Stock, Boston 147 Lionel J-M Delevigne/Stock, Boston 147 Richard Wood/Taurus Photos 156 David Burnett/Contact Press Images 159 Richard Wood/Jeroboam 161 Randy Matusow 166 D. Krathwohl/Stock, Boston 172 Frank Siteman/Taurus Photos 186 Laimute E. Druskis/Jeroboam 189 Barbara Alper/Stock, Boston 198 Paul Fortin/Stock, Boston 202 Harriet Gans/The Image Works 203 Harriet Gans/The Image Works 205 Arlene Collins/Monkmeyer Press 212 Peter Vandermark/Stock, Boston 215 Elizabeth Crews/The Image Works 217 Bob Daemmrich/The Image Works 219 Barbara Alper/Stock, Boston 226 Robert Kalman/The Image Works 233 Laimute E. Druskis/Stock, Boston 238 Kent Reno/Jeroboam 245 Harriet Gans/The Image Works 257 Gale Zucker/Stock, Boston 258 Spencer Grant/Monkmeyer Press Photo 261 Howard Dratch/The Image Works 266 J. Berndt/Stock, Boston 269 Stock, Boston 276 Bob Daemmrich/The Image Works 279 Jane Scherr/Jeroboam, Inc. 284 Spencer Grant/Photo Researchers, Inc. 287 Mimi Forsyth/Monkmeyer Press 292 Jim Fossett/The Image Works 295 Arvind Garg/Photo Researchers 299 Spencer Grant/Stock, Boston 302 Spencer Grant/Monkmeyer Press Photo 307 Robert Kalman/The Image Works 320 Charles Gatewood/Stock, Boston 324 Alan Carey/The Image Works 332 Laimute E. Druskis 336 Hugh Rogers/Monkmeyer Press Photo 339 Arlene Collins/Monkmeyer Press Photo 340 Arlene Collins/Monkmeyer Press Photo 346 Ron Delany/Jeroboam 348 Spencer Grant/Photo Researchers, Inc. 352 Robert Footnorap/Jeroboam, Inc. 356 Jack Spratt/The Image Works 357 Richard Sobol/Stock, Boston 363 Michael Kagan/Monkmeyer Press Photo

Index

A

Absences, 35
Abstinence syndrome, 323, 342, 343, 344
Abstracts, 32, 148
Academic freedom, 12
Academic placement tests, 353
Academic services, 26–33
   copying services, 26
   computer center, 27–28
   libraries, 28–32
   registrar, 32
   tutoring, 32–33
Access: The Supplementary Index to Periodicals, 32
Acid rain, 43, 138
Acknowledging criticism, 254–55
Acquired immune deficiency syndrome, 9, 231, 295, 297, 303, 304, 306–10, 314, 340
Acronyms, 118, 121
Active listening, 245
ACT Student Assistance Program, 88
Acyclovir, 306
Addiction, 322–23, 324, 325, 332, 338, 342, 343, 344
Adding courses, 32
Adipose tissue, 270
Adjustment and life changes, 190
Adrenaline, 194
   nicotine and, 331
Advance organizers, 109
Advice to a Young Tradesman, 52
Aerobic exercise, 278–79
   classes, 39, 209, 281
   psychological benefits of, 281
"Age cannot wither her . . . ," 22, 31
Aggression, 196, 200, 252
   alcohol and, 199
   type A behavior and, 191
Agreeing to disagree, 257
AIDS (*see* Acquired immune deficiency syndrome)
   _____-related complex, 308
Air Force ROTC Four–Year Scholarship Branch, 91
Airline reservations, 80
Alcohol, 189, 191, 285, 296, 322, 324–331
   health and, 327–28
   peer pressure and, 323
   stress and, 199–200
   treatment of problem drinking, 330–31
Alcoholics Anonymous, 330–31
Allen, Woody, 148, 294, 296
All-nighters, 284, 341
Allowable speech, 257
Almanacs, 31
Alumni placement services, 38
Ambulances, 40
Amenorrhea, 277
American Express, 80
American Heritage Dictionary, 18
"A merry heart doeth good . . . ," 201
Amis, Kingsley, 142
Amotivational syndrome, 339
Amphetamines, 284, 341
Anabolic steroids, 336 (*See also* Steroids)
Anaerobic exercise, 278, 279
Anecdotes in papers, 142
Anger
   stress and, 196
Animal Farm, 35
Anorexia nervosa, 222, 276–78, 290
Annual Register of Grant Support, 94
Answering machines, 65
Antibiotics, 289, 304, 305, 310
Antony and Cleopatra, 22, 31
Antonyms, 21
Anxiety, 36, 323
   cognitive aspects of, 175, 176, 178, 204–5
   drugs and, 324, 325, 332, 338, 342
   exercise and, 281
   humor and, 201
   insomnia and, 285–86
   physical aspects of, 175
   stress and, 194, 196, 204
   test _____, 37, 174–84, 204, 206

Apartments, 34, 82, 83
Apple computers, 20
Applied Science and Technology Index, 32
Appraisal as a form of social support, 203
Aptitudes, assessment of, 37
"Are You a Type A Student?" questionnaire, 195, 211
Argumentative themes, 129, 132, 138, 143
Army ROTC Scholarship Program, 91
Art galleries, 39, 43
Art history, 122
Art Index, 32
Arts and sciences, 16, 30
Asking questions in communication, 246–48
ASPCA, 43
Assertiveness, 252–53, 264, 302, 303
   attractiveness and, 224
   loneliness and, 235
   _____ training, 37
Atarax, 343
Athletics, 11
   alcohol and, 325–26
   equipment, cost of, 75, 86, 87
   facilities, 38–39
   fraternities, sororities, and, 217, 218
   intercollegiate, 38–39, 217
   intramural, 39, 217, 235
   steroids and, 322, 336–37
   time management and, 53, 60
Atlases, 31
Attendance policies, 104
Attending classes, 104–10
   attitudes and, 107, 108
   focusing your attention, 105–9
   getting there, 104–5
   participating, 110
Attention span, 57
Attitudes
   differences in _____ and prejudice, 261
   problems in _____ and attending class, 106, 107, 108
   similarity in _____ and attraction, 224–25, 226
   toward students, 110
"Attitudes That Contribute to Rape" questionnaire, 300–301
Attraction, 220–26
   physical appearance and, 220–24
   similarity in attitudes and, 224–26
Austen, Jane, 29
Automobiles, 81–82
   insurance, 76
   maintenance and repairs, 76, 77
   rental, 80
AZT, 309

B

Babysitting, 43 (*see also* Child care)
Bacon, Francis, 5, 15, 104, 117, 216, 257
Bacterial infections, 304–5, 308
Balance sheet, 316, 317, 318
   career decisions and, 353, 355
Baldwin, James, 257
Banks, 79, 86, 89
Barbiturates, 343
Bartholomew, Cecilia, 144
Bartholomew Fair, 331
Baseline, recording
   in cutting down on smoking, 335
   in time management, 53, 55
Basic equipment for college, 18–22
Basic-skills
   _____ courses, 11, 131
   _____ tests, 353
Basinger, Kim, 235
Beatles, 343
Beatty, Richard M., 361
Behavioral and social sciences, 16
Behavior modification, 272, 273–75
Being specific, 255
   in delivering criticism, 250
   in making requests, 249
Benzedrine, 341
Bergen, Edgar, 350
Berke, Jacqueline, 147

Bias, Len, 341
Bibliographic sources of financial aid, 94
Bibliographies of papers, 136, 150
Billings, Josh, 75
Binders for papers, 153
Binge eating, 276, 277
Biographical reference materials, 31
Biological rhythms, 54, 56
Birth control, 37, 41, 189, 298, 311–16
   cervical caps, 314
   coitus interruptus, 315
   condoms, 314
   contraceptive sponges, 313–14
   decision making and, 316–17
   diaphragms, 313
   intrauterine devices, 312–13
   morning–after pill, 312
   the "pill," 311–12
   rhythm methods, 315
   sterilization, 315–16
Blocks of text, moving, 20
Blocks to studying, 65–67
Blood pressure, 189, 204, 270, 312, 323, 338, 342, 343
   alcohol and 327
   cocaine and, 340
   type A behavior and, 191
B lymphocytes, 307
Bodies of papers, 56, 67, 141, 143
Bok, Derek, 72
Bolles, Richard N., 350
Bonaparte, Napoleon, 148
Books, cost of, 72, 75, 77, 91
Bookstores, 19, 39
Boredom in relationships, 230, 232, 233
Boston University, 197
Boyer, E. L., 54
Brainstorming, 145
Breaks
   _____ in communicating, 256
   studying and, 57, 124
   writing papers and, 145
Brown, Joe E., 134
Brown, Rita Mae, 85
Brownell, Kelly, 271
Brown University, 257
Budgeting, 74–79
   expense record, 78–79
   monthly budget, 76–78
   yearly budget, 75–76
Bulimia nervosa, 222, 276, 277
Bulletin boards, 39
Bureau of Indian Affairs Higher Education Grants, 94
Burns, Robert, 62
Byron, Lord, 220, 325

C

Caffeine, 207
Calculator, 18, 19, 161, 162
Calendar, 59
California State University at Los Angeles, 29
Call number, 30, 31
Calorie(s), 269, 270, 271, 272, 273, 274, 279, 327
   _____ baseline, 273
   _____ goals, 274
   tracking _____, 274
Campus centers, 39
Campus Crusade, 40
Campus life office, 38
Campus maps, 34
Campus police, 40, 42, 45, 302
Campus resources, 25–40, 202
   academic services, 26–33
   college information resources, 33–36
   professional services, 36–38
   recreational and cultural services, 38–39
   religious services, 40
   security, 40
Campus security (*see* Campus police)
Cancer, 268, 269, 272, 296
   alcohol and, 327, 330
   cervical _____, 306
   cigarettes and, 331, 332

marijuana in treatment of, 338
the pill and, 312
Cannabis sativa, 337
"Canst thou not minister to a mind diseas'd . . . ," 44, 174
Capote, Truman, 296
Card catalogue, 30, 56
Cardiovascular disorders (*see* Heart disease)
Career decisions, 201, 348–56, 366
Career testing and counseling, 37, 38, 350, 352, 353–56
Carnegie Foundation for the Advancement of Teaching, 10, 12, 54, 356
Carrels, 28
Carroll, Lewis, 10, 60, 139, 214, 366
Cars, 45, 81–82, 189
   insurance, 76
   maintenance and repairs, 76, 77
   rental, 80
Cash card, 80
Caste systems, 348
Catalogue (college), 34, 92, 154
Catastrophizing, 67, 204–5
   tests and, 174–75, 176, 178–79, 180, 204
Categorization, 121
Catholic Church, 315, 317
Cervical caps, 314
Chambers of commerce, 43
Chancroid, 305
Changing answers on tests, 164–65
Chapels, 40
Chapter outlines, 109
Chapter summaries, 109
Checking accounts, 79–80, 85
Cheever, John, 133
Chemical Index, 32
Child–abuse hotlines, 42
Child care, 36, 41, 42
Child Development Abstracts and Bibliography, 32
Chlamydia, 303, 305
   _____ trachomatis, 305
Cholesterol, 269
   alcohol and, 328–29
   steroids and, 337
Chores
   negotiating differences and, 242
   time management and, 56, 60
Churches, 45, 93
Ciardi, John, 222
Cigarettes, 189, 200, 268, 322, 323, 331–35
   cutting down and quitting, 333–35
   health and, 332
Cirrhosis of the liver, 327, 330
Clarifying goals in receiving criticism, 254
Clarifying questions, 254
Class participation, 110, 116
Cliques, 215
Closed stack systems, 31
Clothing, cost of, 75, 77, 83, 84, 85–86
Coca, 340
Coca–Cola, 339
Cocaine, 322, 339–41
   athletics and, 340
Codeine, 341, 342
Cognitive restructuring of test anxiety, 178–79, 180
Cohabitation, 297–99
Coitus interruptus, 315
Cold turkey, 333
College Blue Book, 94
College catalogue, 34, 154
College English, 130
College health center, 272, 278, 281, 327, 330
College information resources, 33–36
   campus life office, 33
   college catalogue, 34
   college newspaper, 34
   course list, 34
   housing office, 34–35
   preprofessional advisors, 35
   professors, 35
   student handbook, 35–36
College newspaper, 34
College Scholarship Service, 88

College sources of financial aid, 92–93
Color monitor, 20
Columbia University, 297
Combination pills, 311–12
Communication, 240, 244–57
    enhancing communication skills, 244–57
Community mental–health centers, 44, 200
Community resources, 41–48, 202
    community service agencies, 41–43
    community information resources, 35, 43
    environmental organizations, 43–44
    health facilities, 44–45, 330
    public transportation, 45
    social and religious organizations, 45
Community service agencies, 41–43
    day–care centers, 41, 42
    family agencies and guidance centers, 41
    family–planning clinics, 41–42, 314, 315
    fire stations, 42
    hotlines, 42
    humane societies, 43
    Legal Aid Society, 43
    police, 43
Commuting, 6, 9, 26, 37, 190
    cars and, 81–82
    relationships and, 214
    time management and, 53
    time pressure and, 189
Companionate love, 233
Compaq computers, 20
Compensatory self–improvement, 208, 209–10
Competition in college, 11, 107
    type A behavior and, 191
Compleat Angler, 269
Compliance with medical advice, 289
Compound interest, 80
Computer, 18, 19–21, 83, 203
    computer centers, 27–28
    computer literacy, 28
    computer searches, 28
    use during tests, 161, 162
Concise Columbia Encyclopedia, 19
Conclusions
    of essay questions, 172
    of papers, 140, 141, 143–44
Condoms, 310, 311, 314, 315, 317
Conflict, 135, 188
    _____ resolution, 36, 64, 239–65
    types of, 190–191
    (see also Social conflict)
Consonant shifts, 120–21
Consumer's Index to Product Evaluation and Information Sources, 32
Contraceptive sponges, 313–14, 315
Controlling spending, 76, 83–87
Cooper, Kenneth, 282, 283
Cooperative education, 38, 92–93
Copying (see Photocopying)
Core curriculum, 15–16, 67, 191
Cornell University, 197
Coronary heart disease (see Heart disease)
Cosby, Bill, 11
Costs of college, 72 (see also Money management)
Counseling and testing centers, 36–37, 198, 200, 201, 202, 203, 209, 236, 278, 330, 350, 352, 353, 366
Course lists, 34
Course–related hassles, 189
Cousins, Norman, 16
Cover letter for a résumé, 357, 362
Cowper, William, 57
Crack, 340
Cramming, 122, 177, 341
Creativity, 129
    writing papers and, 131, 149
Credit cards, 80, 85
Credit profile, 79
Creighton University, 308
Crenshaw, Theresa, 304
Crisis intervention, 37
Critical thinking, 11–13, 129
    writing papers and, 131, 132
Criticism, 244
    delivering _____, 244, 249–53
    receiving _____, 244, 253, 254–55
Croudip, David, 341
Crowds, 215
Cultural facilities, on campus, 39
Curfew, 8, 10

D

Daily hassles, 188–90, 191, 204
    humor and, 202
Date rape, 300, 302–3
Dating, 189, 194, 214
    attraction and, 220, 224–25
    cost of, 76, 78
    date–seeking skills, improving, 228–29
    fraternities, sororities, and, 217
    loneliness and, 234
    (see also Stages in relationships)
Day care, 36, 41, 42
Dean of student affairs, 33
Decision making, 201, 281, 366
    alcohol and, 326
    (see also Career decisions; Sexual decision making)
Deficits, budget, 76
Delay of gratification, 190, 191
Delimitation of topics for papers, 56
Delirium tremens, 326
Delivering criticism, 244, 249–53
Delta–9–tetrahydrocannabinol, 337
Demerol, 341
Denial, 199, 200
Dentists, 45
Dependence on drugs, 285, 322–23
Depressants, 325, 342 (see also Alcohol; Opiates; Tranquilizers)
Depression, 36, 200
    drugs and, 324, 325, 341
    exercise and, 281
    steroids and, 337
    stress and, 196–98
    suicide and, 197–99
Descriptive themes, 129–30
Detoxification, 330
De Vries, Peter, 129
Dewey Decimal System, 30
Dexedrine, 341
Diabetes, 270
Diaphragmatic breathing, 179, 183–84
Diaphragms, 313, 314
Dictionaries, 18, 28, 31, 116, 150, 161, 162
Dictionary of Occupational Titles, 348
Diderot, Denis, 13
Directories, 31
Directory of Financial Aids for Minorities, 94
Directory of Financial Aids for Women, 94
Dirksen, Everett, 73
Discrimination, 258
Discussion sections, 110
Disk drive, 20, 148
Display copy, 148
Distractions
    anxiety as a source of, 176, 179, 180, 196
    fraternities and sororities as _____, 218, 219
    studying and, 62–65, 123–24
Distractors in multiple–choice test items, 160, 163, 164, 165
Distributed learning, 122
Division of Student Life, 33
Doctoral dissertations, 34
Doctorow, E. L., 129
Donne, John, 214
Do not disturb! signs, 64, 65
Do's and don'ts of class participation, 111
Dot–matrix printer, 154
Drafts of papers, 138, 142, 146, 148
    final _____, 153–54
Drew University, 147
Drexel University, 19
Drill, 122
Drinking (see Alcohol)
Dropping courses, 32
Drugs, 321–45
    alcohol, 324–31
    amphetamines, 341
    cigarettes, 331–35
    cocaine, 339–41
    drug abuse and AIDS, 308
    growth hormone, 336–37
    hotlines, 42
    LSD, 343–44
    marijuana, 337–39
    opiates, 341–42
    overdoses, 37
    steroids, 336–37
    stress and, 196, 199–200
    tranquilizers, 342–43
DT's, 326
Duke University, 29

E

East Carolina State University, 41
Ecumenical Campus Ministries, 40
Editing papers, 144, 147, 148 (see also Revision of papers)
Education Abstracts, 32
Educational background, 358, 359
    _____ worksheets, 360, 368
Educational loans (see Loans)
Educational Opportunity funds, 37
Education Index, 32
Edwards Personal Preference Schedule, 355
"Eleanor Rigby," 223
Elements of Style, 19
Eliot, Charles W., 104
Ellis, Albert, 64
Emergency funds, 76, 80, 87
Emergency rooms, 45, 198
Emerson, Ralph Waldo, 29
Emotional effects of stress, 194–99
    anger, 196
    anxiety, 194–96
    depression, 196–98
Emotional support, 202
Encyclopedia, 19, 28, 31
Endowments, 92
English 101, 130
English usage, 132, 135, 154
    common errors in, 150–53
    handbooks of, 19, 131
    proofreading and, 149
Entertainment, cost of, 76, 77
Entomology, 120
Entrance examinations, 35
Environmental hassles, 189
Environmental organizations, 33, 43–44
EPPS, 355
Epson, 20
Equipment for taking tests, 161–62
Errors in English usage, 131, 150–53
Essay test questions, 18, 121, 129, 132, 159
    guiding words and, 160, 170–71
    introductory statements, 172
    length of, 173
    outlines and, 140, 160, 171
    summarizing statements, 172
    ways of handling, 170–74
Etymology, 120, 121
Evaluating motives in delivering criticism, 249
Evaluations of professors, 34
Exchanging new behavior, 242–43
Exercise, 268, 278–83
    facilities, 45
    hazards of, 280–81
    physical benefits of, 279–80
    psychological benefits of, 281–82
    time management and, 53
    types of, 278–79
    weight control and, 271, 272–73, 275
    (see also Athletics)
Expectancy for Success scale, 16–17, 23
Expense record, 75, 78–79
Expository themes, 129–30
Expressing displeasure, 250–52

F

Faculty information, 34
Family agencies and guidance centers, 41
Family Financial Statement, 88
Family–planning clinics, 41–42, 314, 315
Fantasy
    as a means for handling insomnia, 286
    career selection and, 349
Fat, 269, 270, 272
    _____ cells, 270
    _____–to–muscle ratio, 272, 279
Faulkner, William, 144
Fear of rejection, 226
    loneliness and, 234
Federally Insured Student Loans, 89
Federal sources of financial aid, 89–91
Fiber, 272
Fiction, writing of, 129
Fields, W. C., 257, 327
Fill–in–the–blanks questions, 167–68
Final draft of papers, 15, 56
Financial aid, 36, 72, 73, 76, 87–94
    showing need, 88
    sources of aid, 88–94
Financial Aid Form, 88
Financial Aids for Higher Education, 94
Financial Aid to Education, 94
Financial resources of college students, 72–74

Financial responsibility hassles, 189
Firefighters, 40, 42
First draft (of papers), 15
Fitness, 267–291
    cardiovascular, 39, 279
    centers, 38
Fixed disks, 148
Fixx, James, 280
Flagyl, 309
Flashbacks, 343–44
Flashbulb memories, 120
Flash cards, 122
Flexibility, exercise and, 279
Flexibility in scheduling, 58
Floaters, 83
Floppy disks, 20, 148
Focusing, 208, 209
    _____ attention (see Paying attention in class)
Footnotes, 20, 136, 137
    automatic renumbering of, 20, 147, 148
    format of, 150
Ford, Harrison, 235
Foundation Grants to Individuals, 94
Franklin, Benjamin, 52, 79, 86
Fraternities, 33, 76, 214, 323
    advantages and disadvantages, 216–19
    discrimination and, 258, 260
    test files and, 160
Freedom
    cars and, 81
    class attendance and, 104
    college life and, 6–10, 52
Free speech, 257
Free turn–ons, list of, 95–97, 124, 184
Freshman composition, 14, 19, 129, 130–32 (see also Writing papers)
Freud, Sigmund, 29, 201
Friendship, 214–16
Fromm, Erich, 221
Frustration, 188, 190, 191, 196, 204
Future–security hassles, 190

G

Garman, Steve, 130
Gauguin, Paul, 304
Gay student groups, 33
Genital herpes, 295, 303, 305–6, 308
Genital warts, 306
Getting Yours: The Complete Guide to Government Money, 94
GI Bill, 91
Gilbert, Sir William, 54
Gone with the Wind, 76
Gonorrhea, 303, 304, 310, 313
Grade changes, 32
Graduate Record Examination, 35, 162
Grammar, 11, 32
    keeping a journal and, 135
    test items and, 164, 168, 169
    writing papers and, 131
Granting permission in communication, 248
Grants, 88
Granuloma inguinale, 305
Graphics, 28
Great books, 16
Gregorian, Vartan, 257
Greenhouse effect, 31, 43, 129, 138
Greenpeace, 44, 235
Group therapy, 44
Growth hormone, 322, 336–37, 340
Guaranteed Student Loan Program, 72, 73, 75, 89
Guessing on tests, 165, 166
Guidelines for writing papers, 132–54
Guiding words of essay questions, 160, 170–71, 174 (see also Essay test questions)

H

Hallucinogens, 323, 337, 343–44 (see also Marijuana; LSD)
Hamlet, 89, 204
Handbooks, 31
    of English usage, 19, 131
Handwriting, 19
Hard copy, 148
Hardiness, psychological, 208–10
Hardware, computer, 19–21
Harvard University, 104, 343
Hashish, 337
Hassles (see Daily hassles)
Hazing, 219–20
Headaches, 191, 304, 305, 332, 338, 341
    (see also Migraine headaches)
Heading of résumé, 358

Index   **387**

Health, 229, 267–91
　alcohol and, 327–28
　nutrition and, 269
　stress and, 191, 194
Health center, college, 272, 278, 281, 327
Health facilities in the community, 44–45, 330
　community mental health center, 44–45
　dentists, 45
　emergency rooms, 45
Health hassles, 189
Health insurance, 75, 82–83
Health services on campus, 37, 272
Heart disease, 191, 206, 268, 269, 272, 288, 296
　alcohol and, 327, 330
　cigarettes and, 332
　cocaine and, 341
　exercise and, 279–80, 281
　steroids and, 337
Help-wanted ads, 34, 43
Hemingway, Ernest, 144
Heroin, 341–42
Herpes, 295, 303, 305–6, 308
　_____ simplex, 305
Herrick, Robert, 54
Higher Education Opportunities for Minorities and Women, 94
High school versus college, 11
　earnings of graduates, 72
　high school teachers versus college professors, 13–15
High school, writing in, 129
Highlighters, 112
Hillel House, 33, 40
Holland, Harry, 27
Holland, John, 350, 352
Holy Cross, College of the, 29
Home–equity loans, 90
Homesickness, 80
Hospitals, 82, 83
Hostility, 191, 206, 207
Hotlines, 37, 42
　National AIDS _____, 309
Household hassles, 189
Housing office, 34–35
How the Military Will Help You Pay for College, 94
How to Control Your Drinking, 330
HSV–1, 305
HSV–2, 305
Humane societies, 43
Humanities Index, 32
Hubbard, Elbert, 78
Humor and stress, 201–2
Hungerford, Margaret Wolfe, 220
Hutchins, Robert M., 11
Huxley, Aldous, 117
Hydrocarbons, 331, 334

I

IBM, 20, 21
　IBM–compatible clones, 20
　IBM–DOS, 20, 27–28
"Ideas About Relationships" questionnaire, 241
Identification cards, 45
Illness, 45, 189, 190, 268, 269, 270, 272, 287–91 (see also Cancer; Heart disease; Sexually transmitted diseases; etc.)
Impasses in communication, 255–56
Immune system, 306–7
Incompletes, 35–36
Increasing positive interactions, 243
Independence, 189, 191
Indexes to periodicals, 32
Individual therapy, 44
Injury, 45
　exercise and, 280
In loco parentis, 8
Inner-concern hassles, 189
Inpatient care, 37
Insomnia, 283, 284–87
　drugs and, 332, 337, 341, 342, 343
Instrumental support, 203
Insurance, 77, 82, 83, 90
Intelligence, assessment of, 37, 354–55
Interference with studying, 66
Interlibrary loan, 28
Internships, 359
Interviews, job, 38, 194, 356, 362–66
Intrauterine devices, 312–13, 314
Introductions
　_____ of essay questions, 172
　_____ of papers, 56, 141, 142–43
Introduction to College Writing, 130

Irony in writing, 142, 144
Irrational cognitions about test taking, 176, 178–79, 180
Irrational expectations and social conflict, 240–41
I-talk, 249, 255

J

James, Henry, 133
James, William, 12, 201, 240, 350, 366
Jealousy, 231
Jefferson, Thomas, 136
Jerome, Jerome K., 352
Jewish Family Services, 41
Job–hunting party, 350–51
Job interviewing, 38, 194, 356, 362–66
Job objective, 358–59
Job placement, 36, 356 (see also Placement)
Jobs, 348–50
Jogging, 38, 274, 279, 280, 281 (see also Running)
Johnson, Samuel, 11, 19, 29, 57, 83, 117, 129, 136, 146, 271, 326
Johnson, Virginia, 294, 296
Jones, Franklin P., 254
Jonson, Ben, 331
Journal of Consulting and Clinical Psychology, 29
Journals of students, 135–36, 147
Journal to Stella, 324
Julius Caesar, 6
"Just Say No," 64

K

K, 20
Kafka, Franz, 9
Kaplan, Helen Singer, 306, 307
Kaposi's sarcoma, 308
Kellogg, J. W., 296
Kerr, Jean, 174, 220
Key words and concepts, 109, 111, 112, 113, 116, 121
　tests and, 160
Kilobytes, 20
King, Martin Luthur, Jr., 260
Kinsey, Alfred, 294, 297
Korsakoff's syndrome, 327
Kuder scales, 37
Kwell, 309

L

Laboratory assistants, 92
Laboratory fees, 75
Laboratory reports, 129
Lady Macbeth, 129, 174
Lady Windermere's Fan, 84
Laertes, 89
L'Avare, 270
Law School Aptitude Test, 35
Learning center, 131, 145, 150
Leary, Timothy, 343
Leases, 34
Lebowitz, Fran, 294, 332
Lecture notes (see Note taking)
Legal Aid Society, 43
Legal services, on campus, 38
Length
　_____ of essay questions, 173
　_____ of papers, 130, 136
Lesbian student groups, 33
Letter–quality printer, 20, 154
Letters of reference, 38
Levant, Oscar, 326
Librarians, 29–30, 33
Library, 28–32, 56, 84, 136, 280
　card catalogue, 30, 56
　Dewey Decimal System, 30
　indexes to periodicals, 32
　librarians, 29–30, 33
　Library of Congress system, 30
　open and closed stack systems, 31
　periodicals, 31–32
　reference materials, 31
　reserve materials, 32
　work–study in, 89
Librium, 323, 324, 343
Liebman, Bonnie, 269
Life changes, 188, 190, 191, 192–93
Linden, Fabian, 269
Listening actively, 245
Loans, 72–73, 75, 86, 88, 89, 90, 91, 92, 190
　questions to consider before taking out a _____, 90
　(see also Financial aid)

Loneliness, 13, 188, 233–36
　causes, 234–235
　how to handle _____, 235–36
Long–term assignments, 59, 60
Loose–leaf paper, 112, 113, 140, 161
Los Angeles Pierce College, 308
Louis, Joe, 76
Love, 214, 219–20
　"_____ is blind . . . ," 219
　"_____ rules the camp . . . ," 220
"Love Scale," 221, 237
Loyola University, 29
LSAT, 35
LSD, 343–44
"Lucy in the Sky with Diamonds," 343
Lymphogranuloma, 305
Lysergic diethylamide acid, 343

M

Macbeth, 44, 174, 326 (see also Lady Macbeth)
Macduff, 326
Maddi, Salvatore, 208
Mainframe computers, 27
Main points of lectures, 111
Maintenance rehearsal, 122
Making decisions, 201, 281, 366
　alcohol and, 326
　(see also Career decisions; Sexual decision making)
Making requests in communicating, 249
Malamud, Bernard, 140
Managing money (see Money management)
Managing stress, 187–211 (see also Stress)
Managing time (see Time management)
Manchester Community College, 29
"Man in the Mirror," 263
Mantras in meditation, 205, 206
Manual for Writers of Term Papers, Theses and Dissertations, 19
Manuals, 31
Maranathas, 33, 40
Margins of papers, 153, 154
Marijuana, 322, 323, 337–39, 343
Marvell, Andrew, 56
Marx, Groucho, 216
Mason, Perry, 128
Mastercard, 80
Masters, William, 294, 296
Masturbation, 296–97
Matching questions on tests, 168–70
Math anxiety, 259
Mathematics and sex roles, 259, 262, 265
Maugham, W. Somerset, 220
MCAT, 35
Mead, Margaret, 8
Meal tickets, 75, 77
Measure for Measure, 84
Mediation, 120, 121
Medical College Admissions Test, 35
Medical insurance, 45, 75, 82–83
Medicine, 75
Meditation, 205–6
Megabyte, 20, 31
Memory and memorization, 56
　mnemonic devices and, 118–22
　PQ4R study method and, 117–23
　random access memory, 20
Memory traces, 122
Mencken, H. L., 12, 29, 138, 215, 219
Merchant of Venice, 219
Merging programs, 20
Metabolic rates, 271, 273, 279, 341
Methadone, 341
Methaqualone, 343
Methedrine, 341
Miami–Dade Junior College, 29
Microcomputers, 27
Microfiche, 28
Microsoft Word, 28
Migraine headaches, 191, 312
Mikado, 52
Miller, Arthur, 8
Miller, Henry, 271
Miller, William, 330
Milton, John, 30
Minipills, 311, 312
Minor tranquilizers, 343
Mixers, 217, 226
Mizner, Wilson, 12
Mnemonic devices, 118–22
Mnemosyne, 121
Molière, 269
Money Management, 71–101, 188, 189, 349
　budgeting, 74–78

cars, 81–82
checking accounts, 79–80
controlling spending, 83–87
credit cards, 80
exercise and, 281
expense record, 78–79
financial aid, 87–94
health insurance, 82–83
renter's insurance, 83
saving money, 86–87
telephones, 80–81
Moniliasis, 309
Monochromatic monitor, 20
Mononucleosis, 308
Montclair State College, 29
Monthly budget, 75, 76–78
Monthly calendar, 59
Monthly Index (of U. S. Government Printing Office), 32
Morgan, J. P., 79
Morning–after pill, 312
Morphine, 341
Mozart, Wolfgang Amadeus, 144
MS–DOS, 20, 27
Multiple–choice questions on tests, 159, 160
　ways of handling, 162–65
Muñoz, R., 330
Muscle relaxation, 206
　test anxiety and, 179–83
Muscle–to–fat ratio, 279
Museums, 39, 43
Music practice rooms, 39
Mutuality, 229

N

Nabokov, Vladimir, 139
Nash, Ogden, 349
National Commission for Cooperative Education, 93
Natural birth control, 315
Navigators, 40
Navy–Marine Corps NROTC Scholarship Program, 91
Near–letter–quality printer, 20, 154
Neatness on essay questions, 173, 174
NEC, 20
Need a Lift?, 94
Negotiating differences, 241–42, 255
Neisseria gonorrhoeae, 304
New Birth–Control Book, The, 315
Newhart, Bob, 294
Newman Club, 33, 40
New Mexico State University, 29
Newspaper, college, 34
New York Times, 29, 142, 268, 269
New York Times Index, 32
Nicotine, 322, 323, 331, 332
　_____ gum, 334
　stress and, 332
"No man is an island . . . ," 214
Nonfiction, writing of, 129
　(see also Writing papers)
Northeastern University, 92, 221
North Lake College, 6
Notebook, keeping a, 135–36
Notes for book, 370–85
Note taking, 56, 59, 104, 100–116, 159
　equipment for, 112–13
　jotting down key words and phrases, 113, 116
　phrasing questions about subject matter, 113
　reasons for, 110–12
　summaries, 121
　ways of, 112–16
　writing papers and, 130
Nutrition, 268–78
　anorexia nervosa, 276–78
　bulimia nervosa, 276, 277
　health and, 269
　obesity, 270–275

O

Obesity, 270–75, 341
　attraction and, 220, 221, 222, 223
　origins of, 270–71
　weight control, 271–76
Occupations, 37
Offensive speech, 257
Office hours, 14
O'Hara, Scarlet, 76
Ohio State University, 29
Oil spills, 43
Open–ended questions, 246, 247, 248
Opening lines, 226–27
Open stack systems, 31

388　Index

Operating system of computer, 20, 27–28
Opiates, 341–42
Opioids, 341, 342
Orwell, George, 35
Osgood, Charles, 297
Othello, 84
Outlines
 essay questions and, 160, 171–72, 174
 papers and, 15, 56, 138, 140–42, 146
 taking notes and, 113–16
Overcoming writing blocks, 145
Overlearning, 122
 test anxiety and, 178
Oxford Dictionary of Quotations, 31
Ozone layer, 43

P

Pacifico, Larry, 337
Paper, quality of, 154
Papers, 15, 20, 32, 34, 56, 58, 81, 268
 final drafts, 153–54
 kinds of, 129–30
 length of, 130, 136
 outlines and, 15, 56, 138, 140–42
 plagiarism and, 136–38, 148, 150
 proofreading of, 148–53
 revision of, 56, 144, 146–48
 time pressure and, 189
 topic selection, 138–39
 writing _____, 127–56
Paramedics, 40
Paraphrasing in communication, 245–46
Parent Loans for Undergraduate Students, 89–90
Parker, Dorothy, 80, 144
Part–time work, 38, 58, 73–74, 75, 76, 82, 88, 189, 190, 201
 résumés and, 356
 time pressure and, 189
Passages, 366
Pastoral counseling, 40
Paying attention in class, 104, 105–110
 heading off attitude problems, 107
 participating in class, 110, 116
 picking out key terms and concepts, 109
 previewing lecture material, 109, 110
 "Reasons for Not Paying Attention in Class" questionnaire, 106
 reviewing notes from the previous lecture, 109
 sitting front and center, 107
PCP, 308, 344
Peace Corps, 89
Peer counseling, 37, 89
Pell Grant Program, 73, 75, 89
Pelvic inflammatory disease, 304, 305, 313
Perfectionism, 190, 191
Performance anxiety, 175
Performance subtests, 354–55
Periodicals, 31–32
Perkins Loan Program, 75, 89
Permanent address, 358
Personal ads, 34
Personal computers, 19–21, 27, 83 (*see also* Computer)
Personal confession of first author, 4
Personal counseling (*see* Counseling and testing centers)
Personal expenses, 72, 75, 77
Personal information on résumé, 358, 361
Personal values (*see* Values)
Petting, 297
Phencyclidine, 344
Philippians, 72
Photocopying, 26, 84, 112
Phrasing questions
 about subject matter, 113–16, 117, 122
 in communication, 246–48
Physical addiction, 322–23
Physical appearance and attraction, 220–24
Picking the time and place for delivering criticism, 250
PID (*see* Pelvic inflammatory disease)
"Pill," the, 311–12, 313, 314, 316, 317
Pituitary gland, 336
Placement offices, 38, 350, 356
Placement tests, 11
Plagiarism, 136–38, 148, 150
Planned Parenthood, 41
Planning ahead (in exam preparation), 56
Plato, 219
Pleasant Events List, 58
Pledging, 219, 220
Pliny the Younger, 138

PLUS loans (*see* Parent Loans for Undergraduate Students)
Pocket computer, 162
Pocket dictionary, 18, 161, 162
Podophyllin, 309
Police, 43 (*see also* Campus police)
Polonius, 31, 89
Poor Richard's Almanac, 52
Porter, Cole, 214
Positive interactions, 243
Positive visualization, 275
POSSLQ, 297, 298
PQ4R study method, 116–23
 previewing and questioning, 117
 reading, 117
 reciting, 121
 reflecting, 117–21
 reviewing, 121–23
Practice tests, 160
Predictability of stressors, 202
Prejudice, 240, 257–63
 fraternities, sororities, and, 218, 260
 racism, 260
 sexism, 258–59, 260
 sources of, 261–62
 ways of handling _____, 262–63
Premarital sex, 294, 297, 315
Prerequisites, importance of, 34
Previewing lecture material, 109, 110
Priorities in scheduling, 59
Private sources of financial aid, 93–94
Pro Write, 28
Professional services on campus, 36–38
 child care, 36
 counseling and testing center, 36–37
 financial aid office, 37
 health services, 37–38
 legal services, 38
 placement office, 38
Progressive relaxation, 179–83
 insomnia and, 285
 stress and, 206
Proofreading, 32, 56
 of papers, 148–53
"Psyching out" test questions, 112, 160
Psychological Abstracts, 32
Psychological dependence on drugs, 200, 323, 338
Psychological hardiness, 208–10
Psychological services, 36–37 (*see also* Counseling and testing centers)
Psychological tests and career decisions, 353–56
Psychology Today, 215
Public Affairs Information Service Bulletin, 32
Public speaking, 110
Public transportation, 43, 45
Punctuation, 11, 32
 writing papers and, 128, 129, 149
Purging (in bulimia nervosa), 277
"Put money in thy purse. . . ," 87

Q

Qualifying terms in test items, 164, 166
Queensborough Community College, 50
Questions and answers in notes, 113–15, 122
Quizzes (*see* Tests)
Quotation marks, 137
Quotations in papers, 142

R

Racism, 240, 260, 262–63
Raft, George, 83
RAM, 20, 31
Rambler, 19
Random access memory, 20, 31
Random House College Dictionary, 18
Rand, Ayn, 294
Rape, 300–303
 hotlines, 42
Rathus Assertiveness Schedule, 252–53, 264
Reaction paper, 133
Reader's Guide to Periodical Literature, 32
Reading (in PQ4R method), 117
"Reasons for Drinking" questionnaire, 328–29, 345
"Reasons for Not Paying Attention in Class" questionnaire, 106
Receiving criticism, 244, 253, 254–55
Reciprocity in developing relationships, 229
Recitation sections, 14, 110
Reciting (in PQ4R method), 121, 122

Recreational and cultural services on campus, 38–39
 athletic facilities, 38–39
 campus center, 39
 cultural facilities, 39
 music practice rooms, 39
Recreation and studying, 58
Reference
 letters of, 356
 list of, 358, 361
Reference materials, 31
References in papers, 130
Reflecting (in PQ4R method), 117–21
 mnemonic devices and, 118–22
Registrar, 32
Registration fees, 75, 77, 82
Reinforcing a communicator, 246
Rejecting criticism, 255
Relating information to what is known already, 107
 PQ4R method and, 117–20
 (*see also* Reflecting)
Relationships, 13, 36, 200, 213–37
 attraction, 220–26
 conflict in _____, 239–57
 fraternities and sororities, 216–19
 friendship, 214–16
 loneliness, 233–36
 love, 219–20
 stages in _____, 226–33
Relaxation, 205–6, 330
 insomnia and, 285
 _____ response, 205
 test anxiety and, 179–84
Relearning, 122
Religious affiliation
 financial aid and, 93
 fraternities, sororities, and, 217
 prejudice and, 261
Religious attitudes
 attraction and, 225
 sexual decisions and, 316
Religious organizations in the community, 45
Religious services on campus, 33, 40
 chapels, 40
 religious organizations, 40
Rent, 76
Renumbering footnotes, 147, 148
Repetition in learning, 121, 122
Requests
 making _____, 249
 requesting permission to bring up a topic, 244
Reserve materials, 32
Reserve Officers' Training Corps, 91
Residency requirements, 92
Resident advisers, 92, 202
Resistance to stress, 208–10 (*see also* Stress)
Resolving social conflicts, 239–65 (*see also* Social conflict)
Résumés, 38, 356, 362
 writing _____, 357–61
Returning students, 6, 26, 189, 190
Revenge of the Nerds, 216
Reviewing subject matter, 109, 116, 121–23
 as a way of reducing test anxiety, 177
 (*see also* PQ4R)
Revision of papers, 56, 144, 146–48
Rhetorical questions, 142, 144
Rhythm methods, 315, 317
Rides available and wanted, 34
Robinson, Francis P., 116
Rogers, Don, 341
Roget's International Thesaurus, 21
Romantic love, 219–20
Romeo and Juliet, 224
Room and board, 72, 75, 77, 189
ROTC (*see* Reserve Officers' Training Corps)
Rote repetition, 122
Rousseau, Jean–Jacques, 259
"Rules for Good Writing" questionnaire, 130, 155
Running, 38, 279, 280
Russell, Bertrand, 132, 354
Russo, Maria, 257, 263

S

Salutes as opening lines, 227
Sandburg, Carl, 131
Saturday Review, 16
Save the Whales, 33
Savings, 72, 73, 75, 77, 80, 86–87
Scapegoating, 261

Scheduling, 34, 52, 54–62, 189
 trial schedule, 61
 (*see also* Time management)
Scholarships, 37, 73, 75, 88–94, 104, 189
Scholastic Aptitude Tests, 162
Science and sex roles, 259
SCII, 37, 352, 355
Security (campus police), 40
Self–blame and depression, 197
Self–defeating thoughts and test anxiety, 175, 176, 178–180
Self–disclosure
 building a relationship and, 228–29
 communication and, 248
 loneliness and, 235
Self–reward, 58
 money management and, 86
 studying and, 124
Sentence–completion questions on tests, 167–68
Service clubs, 33
Set point, 270, 271
Sex, 293–319
 alcohol and, 326–27
 birth control, 311–16
 illness and, 288
 marijuana and, 338
 sexism, 214, 240, 258–60
 sexual behavior, 188, 189, 191, 294–303
 sexual decision making, 201, 295, 316–18
 sexually transmitted diseases, 9, 37, 189, 202, 229, 295, 303–11, 312, 313, 314, 315, 316, 317
"Sex Differences" questionnaire, 259, 265
Sex–role stereotypes, 240, 258–60, 288
 alcohol and, 325
Shakespeare, 6, 20, 22, 31, 44, 84, 87, 89, 133, 204, 219, 224, 326
Shapiro, Howard, 315
Shaw, George Bernard, 9, 72, 86, 268
Sheehy, Gail, 366
Shenstone, William, 73
Shneidman, Edwin, 198
Short–answer questions on tests, 129, 167–68
Shuttle buses, 82
Shyness, 37, 188 (*see also* Assertiveness; Loneliness)
Sickness, 45, 189, 190, 268, 269, 270, 272, 287–91, 303–311 (*see also* Cancer; Heart disease; Sexually transmitted diseases; etc.)
Sierra Club, 44
Situational reconstruction, 208, 209
Skidmore, 308
Sleep, 188, 189, 204, 283–87, 288
 insomnia, 283, 284–87
 time management and, 53, 60
Sleeping pills, 284–85
SLS (*see* Supplemental Loans for Students)
Small talk, 226
Smiling and attractiveness, 224
Smoking (*see* Cigarettes)
Snacks, 75, 77, 78, 124
Social and religious organizations in the community, 45
Social conflict, 13, 239–65
 prejudice, 257–63
 (*see also* Conflict)
Social Readjustment Rating Scale, 190, 192–93, 211
Social–relationship hassles, 189
Social skills
 alcohol and, 325
 conflict resolution and, 239–57
Social support, 202–3, 210, 214
 dieting and, 274
 exercise and, 281
 fraternities, sororities, and, 216
 socializing, 203
Software, 20 (*see also* Spreadsheets; Word-processing; etc.)
Soldier's disease, 341
Some Like It Hot, 134
Sororities, 33, 76, 214
 advantages and disadvantages, 216–19
 discrimination and, 258, 260
 test files and, 160
Sources of financial aid, 88–94
 bibliographic sources, 94
 college sources, 92–93
 federal sources, 89–91
 private sources, 93–94
 state sources, 91–92
Sources of money, 72–74
Spaced learning, 122

Index 389

Spatial–relations ability
  sex roles and, 259, 262, 265
  Wechsler Adult Intelligence Scale and, 354
Spell–checking software, 20
  word–processing and, 147, 148
Spelling, 18, 20, 32
  essay questions and, 173
  writing papers and, 128, 131
Spermicides, 310, 313, 314
"Spoon–feeding," 15
Sports clubs, 33
Spreadsheets, 20
Stafford Student Loan (see Guaranteed Student Loan Program)
Stages in relationships, 226–33
  building a relationship, 226–30
  continuation, 230–31
  deterioration, 231–32
  ending, 232–33
  initial attraction, 226
Stanford–Binet Intelligence Scale, 354
State sources of financial aid, 91–92
STDs (See Sexually transmitted diseases)
Steinem, Gloria, 130, 222
Stereotypes, 261–62
  sex-role _____, 240, 258–60, 288
  writing and, 128
Sterilization, 315–16
Steroids, 322, 336–37, 340
Stimulants, 207, 284, 324, 331, 340 (see also Amphetamines; Cigarettes; Cocaine)
Stress, 187–211
  alcohol and, 326
  athletic facilities and, 39
  drugs and, 324
  effects of, 191, 194, 196–98
  health and, 191, 194
  nicotine and, 332
  sleep and, 194
  sources of, 188–91
  steroids and, 336
  suicide and, 197–99
  ways of managing, 199–210
Stretching, 279
Strong/Campbell Interest Inventory, 37, 352, 355
Strunk, William, 19
Student Aid Annual, 94
Student centers, 39
Student government, 33
Student Guide: Five Federal Aid Programs, 94
Student handbook, 35–36
Student loans (see Loans)
Study diskettes, 19
Study groups, 160
Study guides, 159
  practice tests in, 160
Studying, 53, 104, 116–24, 158, 190, 191, 268, 287
  anxiety and, 194
  distractions from, 62–65
  finding a place for, 123–24
  fraternities, sororities, and, 217, 218
  notes and, 112
  PQ4R method, 116–23
  recreation and, 58
  scheduling time for, 56, 60
  self-reward and, 124
  test anxiety and, 175, 176–78
  tests and, 160
  time pressure and, 189
  variety and, 57
Study lounges, 39
Style sheet, 15
Substance abuse, 322–23 (see also Alcohol; Drugs; etc.)
Successive approximations, 228
Suicide, 40
  depression and, 197–99
  hotlines, 42
  prevention, 37, 42, 198–99
Suinn Test Anxiety Behavior Scale, 177, 178, 185
Summer employment, 72, 73, 75, 76, 190
  résumés and, 356

Supplemental Educational Opportunity Grant Program, 89
Supplemental Loans for Students, 91
Survey of Political and Social Attitudes, 33, 49
Sutton, Willie, 94
Swift, Jonathan, 324
Syllabi, 59, 109, 154, 159, 202
Symptoms of sickness, 287, 288, 289, 290
Synagogues, 45, 93
Synonyms, 21
Synthesizers, 27
Syphilis, 303, 304–5, 310

T

Tables of contents of term papers, 154
Taking notes, 104, 100–116
  equipment for, 112–13
  jotting down key words and phrases, 113, 116
  phrasing questions about subject matter, 113
  reasons for, 110–12
  summaries, 121
  ways of, 112–16
  writing papers and, 130
Taking tests, 129, 157–85 (see also Tests)
Talking about talking, 244
Tallness and attraction, 220
Tars, 331
TA's (see Teaching assistants)
Task, The, 57
Teaching assistants, 14, 15, 110, 116
Technical writing, 128
Telephones, 80–81
  cost of, 76, 77, 78
  studying and, 65
Temporary address, 358
Temptations, coping with, 83–84
Term papers, 129, 130, 136, 138, 143, 154
  outlines and, 140–42
Test anxiety, 37, 159, 174–84, 194, 204, 206
  definition, 175
  origins, 175–76
  Suinn _____ Behavior Scale, 177, 185
  ways of handling _____, 176–84
Test files, 159–60
  fraternities, sororities, and, 217
Test–preparation books and courses, 35
Tests, 129, 157–85, 202, 268, 341
  depression and, 197
  equipment for, 161–62
  essay questions, 170–74
  general advice on, 159–60
  matching questions, 168–70
  multiple–choice questions, 162–65
  sentence–completion questions, 167–68
  Short–answer questions, 167–68
  test anxiety, 159, 174–84
  time pressure and, 189
  true–false questions, 165–67
Test–wiseness, 35, 160
  attending classes and, 105
  "psyching out" test questions, 112, 160
  (see also Tests)
"That's what friends are for . . . ," 215
THC, 337, 338
"The best laid schemes . . . ," 62
T–helper lymphocytes, 306–7
Theme papers, 129, 130, 132, 138, 143
  outlines and, 141
"There is nothing either good or bad . . . ," 204
Thesaurus, 20, 21–22, 31
  word-processing and, 147, 148
Thesis statements, 139, 142, 147 (see also Writing papers)
Thoreau, Henry David, 138, 246, 348
Through the Looking-Glass, 10, 53
Time management, 50–69, 349
  exercise and, 281
  handling distractions, 62–65
  setting up a schedule, 54–62
  time chart for baseline recording, 55

Time–pressure hassles, 189
Time urgency, 191, 206–7
"To His Coy Mistress," 56
Tolerance
  for drugs, 285, 323, 324, 341, 343, 344
  for frustration, 190
Tolerating differentness, 256
Toothache, 45
Tomlin, Lily, 189
Topic delimitation, 139
Topic selection (for papers), 15, 56, 138–39
"To Virgins, to Make Much of Time," 54
Toxic shock syndrome, 314
Tracking calories, 274
Tranquilizers, 323, 324, 342–43
Transcendental meditation, 205–6
Transcripts, 32, 356
Transferring credits, 32, 35
Transportation, 34, 80
  cost of, 72, 76, 77, 78
  public, 43, 45
  (see also Automobiles; Cars)
Treasury Bills, 89
Treponema pallidum, 304
Trial schedule, 61
Trichomoniasis, 309
True–false questions on tests, 165–67
Tubal ligation, 315–16
Tuchman, Barbara, 129
Tufts University, 257, 263
Tuition, 72, 75, 77, 82, 83, 86, 91, 92, 189
  remission, 92
Turabian, Kate L., 19
"Turn–ons," list of, 95–97, 124, 184, 330
Tutoring, 15, 26, 31–32, 75, 203
  writing papers and, 131, 145, 149
TV, 64
Twain, Mark, 65, 74, 138, 214, 268, 311, 353, 356
Type A behavior, 188, 191, 195
  decreasing _____, 206–7
  questionnaire, 195, 211
Typing, 19, 21, 34, 43, 136, 145, 154

U

"UCLA Loneliness Scale," 234, 237
Unconditional positive regard, 246
University of Iowa, 308
University of Michigan, 6
University of Nebraska, 29
University of Nevada, 225
University of Texas at El Paso, 353
Unix, 20, 27
Unusual associations as an aid to memory, 120–21
Updike, John, 146
Uppers, 341
Usage (see English usage)
U.S. Constitution, 12
U.S. Department of Labor, 348
Utilities, cost of, 75, 76, 77, 78

V

Vacation
  spring _____, 87
  travel packages and, 34
Valium, 323, 324, 325, 343
Values, 189, 191, 240, 297
  attraction and, 225
  sexual decisions and, 316
Variety in scheduling, 57
Vasectomy, 316
VDRL, 305
Venereal disease (see Sexually Transmitted Diseases under Sex)
Verbal ability and sex roles, 265
Verbal subtests, 354, 355
Veteran's organizations, 33
Viral infections, 305–311
Visa card, 80
Vitamins, 269, 272, 327
Vocabulary learning (foreign language), 120, 121, 122, 162
Vocational Preference Inventory, 352
Vocational types, 351–52

Voltaire, 74, 136, 216
Vorse, Mary Heaton, 140
Vowel shifts, 120

W

WAIS, 354–55
Walden, 348
Walton, Izaak, 269
Warhol, Andy, 6, 43, 54, 86, 88, 189, 273
Watch, 161
Webb, Wilse, 284
Webster's Biographical Dictionary, 31
Webster's New Collegiate Dictionary, 18
Webster's New World Dictionary, 18, 116
Wechsler Adult Intelligence Scale, 354–55
Weight and attraction, 220, 221, 222, 223
Weight control, 39
Weight training, 38, 45
Wesleyan University, 224
West, Mae, 135
What Color Is Your Parachute?, 350
"What Do You Look at First?" questionnaire, 223
"What's in a name?", 224
White, E. B., 19
Whitehead, Mary Beth, 143
Whitton, Charlotte, 258
"Who's in Charge Here?" questionnaire, 7–8, 23
"Who steals my purse steals trash . . . ," 84
Who's Who, 31
Wiesel, Elie, 257
Wilde, Oscar, 76, 84, 351
Wilderness Society, 44
Withdrawal, 199, 200
  _____ method, 315
  _____ symptoms, 323, 324, 326, 332, 334, 342
Wodehouse, P. G., 140
WordPerfect, 20, 28
Word processing, 19, 20, 27, 28, 140, 145
  papers and, 147–48, 154
Wordstar, 28
Work experience, 356, 358, 359, 360
  _____ worksheets, 361, 369
Work hassles, 190
Worksheets
  educational background _____, 368
  expense records, 100, 101
  time chart, 55
  trial schedule, 61
  what Do You Do When . . . , 46–48
  work experience _____, 369
  yearly budget, 75–76, 98–99
Work–study programs, 36, 37, 73, 75, 88, 89, 92
Writing blocks, 145
Writing papers, 127–56
  final drafts, 153–54
  freshman composition, 130–32
  guidelines for, 132–54
  kinds of writing, 129–30
  making mistakes and, 134–35
  outlines and, 15, 56, 138, 140–42
  plagiarism and, 136–38
  proofreading and, 148–53
  revision, 56, 144, 146–48
  topic selection, 138–39
  writing clearly and simply, 133–34
  writing for one's audience, 133

Y

Yale University, 353
Yardley University, 27
Yearbooks, 31
Yearly budget, 75–76
YMCA, 45
YMHA, 45
Young Americans for Freedom, 33
Yo-yo dieting, 270, 271
YWCA, 45

Z

Zip code directories, 28
Zweigenhaft, Richard, 224

390   Index